ORGANIZING WORDS

T 09

Society

Organizing Words

A CRITICAL THESAURUS FOR SOCIAL AND ORGANIZATION STUDIES

Yiannis Gabriel

OXFORD

UNIVERSITY PRESS

OXFORD

UNIVERSITY PRESS

Great Clarendon Street, Oxford OX2 6DP

Oxford University Press is a department of the University of Oxford.
It furthers the University's objective of excellence in research, scholarship,
and education by publishing worldwide in

Oxford New York

Auckland Cape Town Dar es Salaam Hong Kong Karachi
Kuala Lumpur Madrid Melbourne Mexico City Nairobi
New Delhi Shanghai Taipei Toronto

With offices in

Argentina Austria Brazil Chile Czech Republic France Greece
Guatemala Hungary Italy Japan Poland Portugal Singapore
South Korea Switzerland Thailand Turkey Ukraine Vietnam

Oxford is a registered trade mark of Oxford University Press
in the UK and in certain other countries

Published in the United States
by Oxford University Press Inc., New York

British Library Cataloguing in Publication Data

Data available

Library of Congress Cataloging in Publication Data

Gabriel, Yiannis, 1952–
Organizing words : a critical thesaurus for social and organization studies / Yiannis Gabriel.
    p. cm.
ISBN 978–0–19–921321–4 – ISBN 978–0–19–921322–1
1. Organizational sociology—Terminology. 2. Organization—Terminology. I. Title.
HM786.G33 2008
302.3′503—dc22   2008022384

Typeset by SPI Publisher Services, Pondicherry, India
Printed in Great Britain
on acid-free paper by
CPI Antony Rowe, Chippenham, Wiltshire

ISBN 978–0–19–921322–1 (hbk.)
ISBN 978–0–19–921321–4 (pbk.)

1 3 5 7 9 10 8 6 4 2

For George Gabriel (1916–2004)

CONTENTS

R

T

S

U

WITH CONTRIBUTIONS FROM THE
FOLLOWING AUTHORS

David Boje, New Mexico State University — Postmodernism
Andrew Brown, University of Bath — Identity
Emma Carmel, University of Bath — Policy
Adrian N. Carr, University of Western Sydney — Psychological contract
Peter Case, University of West of England — Strategy
Barbara Czarniawska, Göteborg University — Fashion
Michaela Driver, University of Aarhus — Spirituality
Gail T. Fairhurst, University of Cincinnati — Communication
Ewan Ferlie, King's College, University of London — New Public Management
Peter Fleming, Queen Mary College, London University — Resistance
Marianna Fotaki, University of Manchester — Public-sector organizations
David Gann, Imperial College London — Innovation
Chris Grey, University of Warwick — Career
Keith Grint, Cranfield University — Leadership
Chris Hackley, Royal Holloway University of London — Advertising
Loizos Heracleous, University of Warwick — Globalization
Jannis Kallinikos, The London School of Economics — Information
Alice Lam, Royal Holloway University of London — Human Resource Management
Tim Lang, City University — Sustainable development
David P. Levine, University of Denver — Creativity
Frank Longstreth, University of Bath — Economy
Slawek Magala, Erasmus University, Rotterdam — Management of meaning
Rita Mano, University of Haifa — Voluntary organizations
Glenn Morgan, University of Warwick — Governance
Tim Morris, University of Oxford — Professions and professionals
Anders Örtenblat, Halmstad University — (The) learning organization
Theodore Papadopoulos, University of Bath — Market
Dana Rosenfeld, University of Keele — (The) body
Howard S. Schwartz, University of Oakland — Diversity
Jonathan Seglow, Royal Holloway University of London — Multiculturalism
Ruth Simpson, Brunel University — Gender
Neil J. Smelser, University of California, Berkeley — Terrorism
Vangelis Souitaris, Cass Business School, City University — Entrepreneurship
Andre Spicer, University of Warwick — Post-structuralism
Howard F. Stein, University of Oklahoma — Downsizing
Mark Stein, Imperial College London — Risk
Peter Stokes, University of Central Lancashire — Genocide
Andrew Sturdy, University of Warwick — Consultants and clients
Russ Vince, University of Bath — Learning
Tony J. Watson, University of Nottingham — Social construction of reality

INTRODUCTION

WORDS. Words are important. We have always known this. They help us think, communicate, analyse, and create. Words have an existence of their own. Since the 1970s, when Raymond Williams published his great little book *Keywords*, we have known that words have stories and that their stories are an inevitable part of the meanings they carry. Williams's book was a splendid compendium of essays on some 140 *key*words in the English language, words that perform a useful binding function linking ideas together and indicating certain pervasive ways of thinking.

The great asset of Williams's book was to show how ways of thinking and speaking (what we would today call 'discourses') change historically; words bring ideas together and, fifty or a hundred years later, they draw them apart.

Thus the word 'culture', one of Williams's fortes and favourites, originated in the Latin *colere*, meaning inhabit, cultivate, protect and honour. It was imported into **the** English **language** in the seventeenth century to indicate the tending of crops and animals and evolved to signify sophisticated minds and tastes. It did not assume its widespread contemporary sense that we encounter in words like multi-cultural, cross-cultural, and so forth until the late 19th century. Another off-shoot of 'colere' travelled a different way, yielding the words colony and colonialism.

Words, Williams taught us, travel and through their travels, they metamorphose, merge, atrophy and at times disappear. Thus Williams included 'sensibility' as one of his keywords, even though by the mid-20th century it had lost its ability to unlock many doors or bind many ideas together. By contrast, the word 'identity', ever-present and ever-dominant today makes no appearance in his work—its spectacular rise has occurred in the last twenty years or so. 'Race' and 'sex', absent from Williams's first edition, made an appearance in the second edition of *Keywords*, in 1983.

Williams's interest in the careers of words was characteristic of the time he wrote and of the character of his scholarship. The value of his work is undiminished today, when globalization, the internet, and the increasing dominance of the English language have generated an unprecedented fluidity and complexity in the meanings and uses of words. New words, often spawned by new forms of technology, enter the vocabulary (e.g. 'blogging' and 'podcasting') and have meteoric rises, and sometimes disappear almost as quickly. More importantly, however, our preoccupation with language has grown very considerably since the 1970s.

Today, most social scientists recognize that the words we use do not merely describe social realities but constitute them. A 'linguistic turn' has been taking place in philosophy, sociology, psychology, cultural studies, and many of the human sciences—a recognition that the way we talk about things creates these things as discernible entities. It is not as if families, crowds, organizations, and groups exist and then we start talking about them; by describing something as a family, a crowd, an organization, or a group, we ascribe to it certain qualities constructing it as a recognizable entity. In the many languages that do not have the word 'management', it becomes impossible to think of a non-political form of running an organization, a group, or indeed a family without importing the English word.

This book takes an approach that departs from that of Williams. It stems from a contemporary view, a view that emphasizes not that words have evolving meanings, but that words *work for us*—they work in helping us express ourselves, in helping us make sense of our experiences and our actions. Some words work better than others. Consider how poorly the word 'man' is working today in describing a species which includes both women and men. And consider how well the word 'culture' is working today, when all kinds of differences, difficulties, and disagreements can be put down to it. One wonders how cultures prior to ours (even those of fifty years ago) could ever manage without the word 'culture' in their vocabulary, in the same way that one wonders how the ancient Greeks managed without a word for 'society'. The title of this book, *Organizing Words*, refers to the words' ability to help us organize our experiences, our thoughts, and even our feelings. Discovering the right word for a particular situation is a vital step towards making sense of it, placing it in the company of or in opposition to other situations that we have experienced, and triggering off an appropriate emotional response. Describing a situation as a 'difficulty' prompts a different emotion from describing it as a crisis, an opportunity, a challenge, a disaster, or a fiasco.

This book is neither an encyclopedia nor a dictionary but a *thesaurus*. It does not aim to be canonical or all inclusive. Some of the entries may strike readers as too long and some too short; some words that some readers regard as important are missing and others that they may view as idiosyncratic feature entries of their own. This is in the nature of a thesaurus, a word that originally meant treasure or treasure trove. A treasure trove does not contain every important gem in the world, not even a specimen of every important type of gem, but it does contain a variety of fascinating, valuable, original gems (and maybe some fakes too). In the same way, I hope that every reader of this book will discover something interesting, something original, and something helpful in every page.

Some readers may be puzzled at the absence of certain terms—'empowerment' and 'burn-out' do not have entries of their own, nor do Total Quality Management and Business Process Re-engineering, though they get covered under 'fads and fashions in management'. Some of the words may appear idiosyncratic ('death') or uncommon ('othering'). In selecting the words for inclusion, I tended to concentrate on words that seem to me to be full of possibilities and tensions (culture, identity), words that become battlefields for heated debates (diversity), words that are currently unleashing their potential (information, spectacle), or words that have become too 'comfortable' and seem to call for some probing (motivation). Inevitably, the words I chose reflect my own interests. As I was working on the book, however, it occurred to me that it would be interesting to broaden the horizon by inviting some of my scholarly friends to make a contribution. I therefore invited some forty colleagues to contribute a single entry each to the project, a gift plant to my garden so to speak. I have been delighted with their contributions, which give the work greater variety and depth than I could have managed on my own.

Identifying some important words, describing them as 'organizing words', and offering an essay to help readers make use of them is the major reason for writing this book. There are, however, two additional, parallel reasons—the surfeit of information available to all of us and the tendency of words today to disintegrate in the hands of politicians, consultants, and spin doctors. When Diderot and d'Alembert wrote their great *Encyclopedia* as part of the Enlightenment project of the eighteenth century, most people had too little information. Entries on Canada, chocolate, clitoris, commerce, Constantinople, cosmology, and cutting a suit could find themselves in the same neighbourhood of the encyclopedia by virtue of nothing more that the accidental sequence of letters that made them up. Today, the ready availability of information on any term on the internet creates different difficulties. Although it is undoubtedly a source of reassurance, it creates insecurities of its own—which sources can we trust and how should we combine and frame information in the different sources? This book aims to offer a reliable and original resource without setting out to be exhaustive, reducing what is a mass of literature into something meaningful, accessible, and useful.

Words work for us. But words deceive us too. This is especially so at a time dominated by spin, advertising, and public relations, a time when innumerable people are involved in the production of vacuous linguistic drivel, seeking and often succeeding in passing it off as meaningful text. 'I know those little phrases that seem so innocuous and, once you let them in, pollute the whole of speech. Nothing is more real than nothing. They rise up out of the pit and know no rest until they drag you down into its dark' (Samuel Beckett). These little phrases have a tendency to proliferate in those areas of government, management, and journalism where they become black holes into which meaning drains. Quality, excellence, targets, transparency, best practice, cutting edge, impactful, deliverables, engage, solutions, vision, bottom line—the list of words that risk losing their bearings is nearly endless. Clichés, jargon, and, more disturbingly, euphemisms can poison language, deceiving and obfuscating. Consider, for example, the management euphemism of 'downsizing' meaning 'dismissing people', the military euphemism of 'collateral damage' meaning dead civilians, or the politicians' euphemism of 'economically deprived people' for 'poor people'. Such euphemisms insult our intelligence and yet they rapidly become assimilated and naturalized in the language.

Words then are not only useful. They are also dangerous, something that our era with its concern for politically correct expression is acutely sensitive about. The use of a particular word can come to be viewed as more insulting to a particular individual or group than acts of injustice and oppression. Politicians, corporate leaders, and even football managers have been forced to resign for using unaccept-able language; sheer incompetence rarely creates the same opprobrium as the use of an insulting term. Words perform tasks for us—their uses and abuses can create deep misunderstandings and conflicts, every bit as concretely as deeds.

A preoccupation with the ways words are used and especially abused has long been the characteristic of dogmatists and bigots; they have tried in vain to police language and stop words being incorrectly or inappropriately used. Infinitives should not be split, nouns like stress, conflict, and gender should not be turned into verbs and the word 'hopefully' should be restricted to individuals engaging in particular activities with cheerful optimism. Such Canute-like attempts to stop particular ways of using words, grammar, or syntax can easily be parodied and it is far from the intention of this book to establish 'correct' uses and incorrect abuses of language. Experimenting with new words (including ones 'borrowed' from foreign languages), new ways of using old words, and new combinations of old words is something that will go on, regardless of the efforts of the language police. What this book seeks to achieve is to give students, scholars, and researchers wishing to familiarize themselves with the key ideas surrounding specific concepts a first port of call. It seeks to clarify concepts and theories presented in textbooks and establish connections between core theories and applications. It seeks to become a resource for essay writing and a useful tool in planning and carrying out projects and dissertations. Above all, it will offer its users the security of understanding the usages of concepts and ideas in an appropriate and well-informed manner before they can experiment with novel and unusual uses themselves.

The book is primarily aimed at those interested in social and organizational studies, though I hope that it will appeal to all those interested in the human sciences. Each entry seeks to enlighten and help, without patronizing or obscuring disagreements and difficulties. The book seeks to be reassuring without being complacent or 'comfortable', to be authoritative without being doctrinaire, to be reliable without being canonical, to be critical without being destructive. Above all, however, it seeks to stimulate its users to broaden their linguistic resources in the firm belief that a better understanding of these organizing words will help us handle our affairs better in this potentially chaotic and confusing world we inhabit.

HOW TO USE THIS BOOK

You should use this book in any way that fits your purpose and your style. You may look up particular entries that you encounter in your reading elsewhere or prior to a writing assignment if you are interested in gaining a deeper insight into their meaning and uses. You may dip in and out of the entire book as a way of generating ideas for essays and projects. You may visit families of related terms as a way of creating the platform for a literature review in your dissertation.

Within each entry, significant references to terms that have entries of their own are signalled with **bold** print. Some of the matches are not perfect—the word **bureaucratic** may be in bold, leading you to the entry on **bureaucracy**. *Italics* are used for emphasis throughout. At the end of many entries, suggestions are given for visiting related terms whose reading will enrich your understanding. If you are looking for a term that does not have an entry of its own, you should visit the *Index* which is likely to direct you to the relevant pages.

Throughout the book there are references to authors whose ideas and arguments have been used. If you want to develop your understanding of a particular term or area of knowledge, your next port of call may be to visit the original works of these authors.

ACKNOWLEDGEMENTS AND DEDICATION

There are many people I would like to thank. In planning this project, David Musson of Oxford University Press proved once again both a shrewd and an inspiring interlocutor. Numerous people helped with suggestions, criticisms, and ideas, none more than Steve Fineman and David Sims with whom I have collaborated over many years. The very word 'Thesaurus' is one that we jointly came up with and used in describing the extended glossary that formed a part of our textbook *Organizing and Organizations*. Several ideas co-created in the course of writing and revising that book over several editions have found their way into this project.

Many thanks are also owed to my forty academic friends who contributed entries of their own, greatly enriching the book. It is deeply gratifying to have contributions from colleagues whose work I have respected and admired over the years, including Neil Smelser, my Ph.D. supervisor, as well as from several of my own students. Thanks are also due to the nine reviewers who diligently read through all the entries of the book and came up with corrections and suggestions for improvements—Stewart Clegg, Barbara Czarniawska, Keith Grint, Mary Jo Hatch, Marek Korczynski, Ray Loveridge, Judi Marshall, Burkard Sievers, and Tony Watson. Remaining infelicities are, of course, entirely down to me.

Finally, thanks are due to my late father, whose library, a true thesaurus of encyclopedias and dictionaries, novels, chemistry manuals, and a rich scattering of the great books, first aroused my passion for words. He would have liked this book. He loved words and used them well. To his memory, I dedicate this book.

August 2007

Achievement

Achievement signifies the successful completion of a task or an activity—an achievement means creating something of value, an object, an event, or a legacy. Achievement is celebrated in many **stories** and **narratives** in which the protagonist prevails against the odds to achieve his or her mission. Thus achievement represents a wider set of cultural values that we encounter in families, organizations, or entire societies. An achievement '**ethic**' (i.e. set of values, norms, and recipes) has its roots in religious and cultural practices which encourage and reward individual accomplishments, such as creating a fortune, becoming famous, moving up a career ladder, or generally being successful in sport, politics, business, the media, etc. These are seen as 'good things'. Societies that emphasize and reward achievement tend to reinforce the view that **success** is all that matters in life. The non-achiever, the failed achiever, or the 'has been' can easily become an outsider in such a society.

Achievement is a concept of considerable use to both psychologists and sociologists. Thus, psychologist Douglas McClelland argued that human **motivation** derives from three fundamental **needs**.[1] One of these is need for achievement, referred to as nAch. The others are the need for power and the need for affiliation. High nAch people, or people with a strong need for achievement, he argued, are products of an upbringing that encourages independence and the taking of risks where there is a moderate (rather than very low or high) probability of success. High nAch people are not gamblers. They will take calculated risks where the outcome depends more on their own efforts than on chance. They also appreciate constructive feedback on the results of their endeavours so they can learn from their failures. McClelland, and other researchers, have argued that managerial performance, entrepreneurial success, as well as the economic development of entire countries, like England or the USA during their rapid industrialization phases, or countries like South Korea, Hong Kong, and China more recently, can all be linked to levels of nAch.

A different approach to achievement and to human motivation in general is taken by Freud. Freud did not regard achievement as a primary drive (a drive that cannot be attributed to something more fundamental than itself).[2] Instead, he argued that achievement emerges in early life as the child strives to gain parental approval and admiration. The motive to achieve is thus fuelled by parental exhortation and becomes linked to a person's **narcissism** or self-love: *if* you achieve, be it in your studies, art, science, politics, business, or sport, *then* you will be loved and admired. Freud believed that many successful people suffered the loss of a parent in early life—their attempt to impress such an absent parent led them to ever higher achievements.

While psychologists have tried to account for why some people are more driven by achievement than others, sociologists have discussed why entire societies and cultures come under the grip of achievement. In his pioneering work *The Protestant Ethic and the Spirit of Capitalism*,[3] Max Weber argued that the rise of Protestantism entailed the dominance of certain **values**, like hard work, frugality, entrepreneurship, cleanliness, and community-mindedness, that

[1] McClelland, 1961.   [2] Freud, 1914/1984.   [3] Weber, 1958.

coincided with the growth of capital accumulation and the capitalist system of production. Weber referred to these values as the *Protestant ethic* and sociologists, like Adrian Furnham,[1] have argued that the achievement motive derives from this **ethic**. More recently, the achievement motivation has been linked to the *Confucian ethic* and the rapid economic growth of numerous countries in the Asia Pacific region. Several features set the Confucian ethic apart from the Protestant ethic—these include a strong emphasis on collaboration as against competition, as well as on benevolence, righteousness, loyalty, and propriety. Unlike the Protestant ethic that emphasizes the equality of all people in front of God, the Confucian ethic recognizes differences in social *status*. All the same, like the Protestant ethic, the Confucian ethic emphasizes hard work, frugality, and personal responsibility.

Achievement is an important, though not exclusive, motive of **leaders**. Achievement-driven leaders seek to inspire others with their **visions** and dreams, inviting them to turn them into realities. The desire to achieve their mission and leave a legacy is particularly acute in such leaders; in pursuit of this, they are willing to submit themselves and their followers to many privations and adversities. By contrast, leaders who are motivated predominantly by the need for power (in McClelland's typology) are more likely to seek to dominate their followers irrespective of any common task, while leaders motivated predominantly by the need for affiliation are liable to seek to maintain warm relations within their groups or organizations, even at the expense of delivering their task.

• See also *narcissism, success and failure*

Action

Action is a fundamental category of all human sciences. Action represents what people do,

individually or in groups. Playing, working, travelling, shopping, reading, and virtually any other active voice verb all indicate actions. Sometimes actions are juxtaposed to 'words'. A person may then be accused of saying one thing and doing another. Yet, *some* statements can also be viewed as actions in the right context. A judge's statements 'I pronounce you guilty' or 'I pronounce you man and wife' can be viewed as actions.

There are many different ways of theorizing action. Some sociologists tend to regard all action as social, stemming from relatively fixed norms and values within any particular society. **Symbolic interactionists**, on the other hand, view the **meanings** behind action as precarious and unstable, constantly being negotiated among the interacting parties. Behaviourist psychologists disregard the meanings that people attribute to their actions altogether and focus on behaviour itself. Yet another school, known as depth psychologists, question some of the meanings people claim for their actions, suspecting that these are **rationalizations** or excuses; they argue that the **motives** of many actions are **unconscious**— in other words, we may have very strong motives for our actions (e.g. ambition, rivalry, imitation) but, for much of the time, we are not consciously aware of them.

How is action to be studied? Weber advocated that in order to understand action, the researcher must try to enter into the way of thinking of the actor.[2] This creates a type of understanding based on empathy, sometimes referred to as *verstehen*, a knowledge from within rather than from without. Thus to understand the *actions* of a grieving father or an anorexic girl we must try to understand the meanings of their action, something that does not apply to understanding the *behaviour* of a molecule, a magnet, or a mouse. In Weber's writings, we also find a distinction that has since been widely debated between action that is instrumental, driven by **rational** calculation of

[1] Furnham, 1992.   [2] Weber, 1947.

consequences and a choice among alternatives, and action that is affective, driven by emotional and often irrational **desires** and wishes.[1] This distinction is now questioned by some theorists who believe that **emotion** itself can be seen as a rational basis for certain types of action.[2] Weber also identified another important distinction between routine or traditional action which is based on unthinking repetition and non-routine action which is triggered off by unusual circumstances.

One way of studying action that has become increasingly prevalent in the social sciences is through the use of **narratives**. By turning themselves into story characters and placing their actions within plots, individuals seek to 'make sense' of their past actions or discover plausible reasons for them. Equally, however, narratives can actively define those events that qualify as actions, as against others which are seen as accidental or random. Labov has argued that narratives do not only describe actions but also evaluate them—they judge whether they were right or wrong, sensible or foolish, intended or unintended.[3] In this way, they offer **interpretations** for action.

One especially important aspect of action is the **learning** that it generates. 'Action learning' is an approach to education and training which emphasizes a 'hands-on' approach, where active participation by the learner is indispensable in generating and disseminating knowledge. Kolb's learning cycle is one variant of action learning theory, which seeks to bring together knowledge and action, theory and practice.[4] The relationship between theory and practice is one that has long preoccupied organizational and management scholars, and in Kolb's view it is a cyclical relationship where **experience** and action continuously act as triggers for reflection, which in turn generates theoretical and conceptual schemes, which in turn are tested through further action. Action learning has been described

as a way of dealing with situations that do not have straight right and wrong answers and entail a considerable amount of **risk**. It generally involves a partnership between different actors (often **consultants** and their clients) which may be formalized in what are known as 'action sets'.

Action research

Action research is a form of enquiry in which the researcher makes small or large interventions in a situation or a **system** he or she is studying and then observes the outcomes of these actions and adjusts them. These interventions can be seen as quasi-experiments or imperfect experiments, where all external conditions cannot be controlled but convincing links can be made between causes and effects. The term action research was coined by social psychologist Kurt Lewin in the 1940s, who defined it as 'a spiral of steps, each of which is composed of a circle of planning, action, and fact-finding about the result of the action'.[5] Lewin was very keen to develop theories that could have practical applications in improving the lot of people and claimed famously that 'there is nothing so practical as a good theory'.[6] Action research has become an important way of studying situations that are too complex, fluid, and troublesome to be studied through other research methods. It has been used extensively in studying and dealing with different types of crises, as different attempts to address a crisis are carefully monitored and evaluated. It is a form of research favoured by consultants and other practitioners, such as managers, teachers, therapists, and policy makers.

Actor network theory (ANT)

Actor network theory (ANT) is an approach in social and organizational studies developed by two French theorists, Michel Callon and Bruno

---

[1] See Smelser, 1998b; 1998c.   [2] Fineman, 2000c.   [3] Labov and Waletzky, 1967.   [4] Kolb, 1985.   [5] Lewin and Lewin, 1948, p. 206. [6] Lewin, 1951, p. 159.

Latour, in their examination of science and technology, currently finding an increasing range of applications in organization studies. Its inspiration comes from the **narrative** theory of French-Lithuanian semiologist Algirdas Greimas, who suggested that the main unit in the analysis of narratives should be 'actants', that is, units that act or are acted upon. Actants have action programmes, and they may succeed or fail. The actants that succeed are usually those who convince other actants to join their programme (or to combat anti-programmes). Only by the end of the narrative do we learn which actants succeeded in becoming actors and acquiring a proper **voice**.

Callon and Latour,[1] following Greimas's insights, argued that it is only at the end of the story (that is, the study) that we can know who is a real actor and who has remained an actant; actants acquire 'character' (or **identity**) as they go through their programmes. Social scientists make a mistake in assuming that they know the characteristics of the actors they study at the outset. Furthermore, what the observers see as macro-actors are usually **networks** of actants, successfully pretending to be one actor and to speak with one voice. This is possible because they managed to translate their interests so that they are not in conflict, stabilize their connections, and mobilize jointly when needed.

Actor network theory is actually a research design, not a theory. The word 'theory' was added because a 'T' was needed to denote the main metaphor, that of an ant. In place of a 'bird's-eye view' of macro-sociologists, ANT researchers follow systematically connections between actants as they develop. ANT is especially suitable for studies of science and technology, as actants do not have to be human: they can be plants, animals, machines, and any other object that can act or be acted upon. According to some versions of this theory, a physical object (for example a weapon or a piece of physical equipment, a tank or a wooden cross) can,

under some circumstances, assume the position of **leader** and act as one.[2]

(WITH SPECIAL THANKS TO BARBARA CZARNIAWSKA)

Advertising

Advertising is a familiar word which seems to organize **meaning** quite neatly and expressively. But although everyone has an opinion on it, there is a striking lack of consensus on what it is, what it does, and how it does it. A hundred years ago advertising was defined as 'salesmanship in print' by Albert Lasker and John E. Kennedy,[3] and this axiom still retains considerable currency in many advertising agencies. Also known as the 'reason why' approach, this motif characterizes advertising that has a strongly persuasive rational appeal. It sells stuff. Following the same line of thought Strong devised a simple linear model of advertising persuasion known as AIDA (Attention-Interest-Desire-Action) which is, even today, repeated solemnly as a model of how advertising 'works' in practically every marketing management textbook.[4] AIDA is the best known of the 'hierarchy-of-effects' family of theories which purport that each exposure to an advertisement moves the recalcitrant consumer incrementally along a continuum of attitudinal and behavioural modification. One may argue that the question of how advertising 'works' is no more reducible to mechanistic explanations than the question of how literature or art 'work'. Nevertheless, there is a vast and earnestly pursued industry of academic **cognitive** research based on this **information**-processing analogy.[5]

Alternatively, advertising can be seen to have a uniquely **ideological** character. As such, it achieves its force in an **unconscious** way without us fully realizing what is happening. It is a **discourse** which, paradoxically, is regarded as both trivial yet profoundly influential. Advertising is widely regarded as a venal and degraded cultural form, and its practitioners are held in similarly low regard.[6] Many ordinary people insist that

[1] Callon and Latour, 1981. [2] Grint, 2005b. [3] Fox, 1984. [4] Strong, 1925. [5] See e.g. Wells, 1997. [6] Hackley and Kover, 2007.

they are not influenced by advertising's sinister wiles at all, and there is plenty of research evidence that we pay little conscious attention to advertisements. Yet advertising is a persistent site of controversy and public debate. Most usually, this controversy surrounds its supposed ill effects. Advertising allegedly makes us smoke and drink too much, drive too fast, have sex too young (and too often). While we're out having sex and drinking, advertising is busy exploiting our children with images of fast food consumption, premature sexualization, and unattainable **body** sizes.[1] The outbreaks of moral panic that are articulated through complaints about advertising give some idea of its ideological power. Our deep suspicion of the psychology behind advertising is still expressed well by Packard's notion of the 'Hidden Persuaders',[2] but beyond a popular but mistaken idea that advertising somehow reaches us in 'subliminal' ways we still don't really understand why it makes us uneasy.

Advertising's power to act on a wider cultural level is expressed well by Marchand,[3] who showed that, collectively, it can be seen as an ideological screen selling the American Dream. Through advertising and its sub-disciplines of public relations, merchandizing, direct mail, and so on the big business machine in America painted itself a human face and gained a legitimacy which, in the early part of the century, was fiercely contested.[4] Advertising has been central to the evolution of the **consumer** society—at a cultural level it is a kind of social **communication** based on the symbolism of brands.[5] As such it is central to modern notions of social and self-**identity**.

Contemporary practice and changes in the **mass media** infrastructure have blurred the distinctions between sub-categories of promotional communication such as advertising and public relations, sales promotion, merchandising, and so on, resulting in a hybrid promotional culture predicted by left-wing scholars.[6] The merging of advertising with editorial is epitomized by the burgeoning practice of placing brands within mediated entertainment vehicles like movies, TV shows, magazines, stage plays, and mobile phone games.[7] Product placement in art and entertainment was used 200 years ago by entrepreneurs such as Josiah Wedgwood and Thomas Holloway, but under the influence of new media the worlds of advertising and entertainment have become closer than ever.

● See also *aesthetics, consumerism, consumers and consumption, mass media*

CHRIS HACKLEY, ROYAL HOLLOWAY UNIVERSITY
OF LONDON

Aesthetics

The fact that aesthetics does not have a clear and agreed meaning has not stopped it becoming a widely used term in social and organizational theories. Traditionally aesthetics was juxtaposed to **ethics**—the former concerning judgements of beauty and ugliness, the latter concerning judgements of good and bad. But while aesthetics refers to beauty, it also refers to the senses through which we perceive beauty and, more importantly, to the social conventions through which we come to regard different things as beautiful. Some aesthetic judgements concern artistic representation—thus it is perfectly possible to have a beautiful representation of an ugly person and an ugly representation of a beautiful person. Many aesthetic judgements today, however, have little to do with representation or indeed beauty itself and concern style, fashion, and design. We have become increasingly mistrustful of beauty and often attracted to the unusual, the subversive, and the provocative as a way of satisfying our senses. Thus, ugliness can acquire an aesthetic currency all of its own.

In his widely read book *Distinction: A Social Critique of the Judgement of Taste*, French

---

[1] Hackley, 2005.   [2] Packard, 1957.   [3] Marchand, 1985.   [4] Marchand, 1998.   [5] Leiss et al. 2005.   [6] Horkheimer and Adorno, 1947/1997; Wernick, 1991.   [7] Hackley and Tiwsakul, 2006.

sociologist Pierre Bourdieu argued that aesthetic judgements are linked to people's positions in the **class** system.[1] He viewed working-class tastes as directly linked to physical, sensuous pleasures—hefty fillet steaks, images of tropical sunsets, and music with strong rhythmic and melodic qualities. By contrast, he argued that middle and upper classes aspire to 'higher and finer' pleasures linked to abstract, non-representational qualities. He argued that criticizing someone's tastes can become an instrument of **power** and even terror, establishing social distinctions of superiority and inferiority. In a curious reversal of Bourdieu's theory, a new stream of conceptual artists and fashion designers mostly from working-class backgrounds dramatically altered the dominant aesthetics, with their attempt to shock, subvert, and provoke. In another reversal of Bourdieu's theory, ever-increasing sections of society resort to stylish home furnishing stores in order to turn their houses into objects of aesthetic pleasure, not just material comfort. In this way, ever-increasing areas of **consumer society** come to be 'aestheticized'—they become objects of aesthetic judgements. Clothes, food, drink, cars, home furnishings, and even holiday destinations are judged in terms of the aesthetic value that they add to or subtract from an individual's image.

Image becomes as important for organizations as it is for consumers, since the image of an organization, its products, its buildings, its logos, and its employees, becomes appropriated by consumers in creating their own images. In this way, the premises of an organization, the stylishness of its products, the elegance of its logo, the smartness of its employees become a vital part of what it sells to its customers, whether the company is Starbucks, IKEA, or BMW. It is now argued that part of the service that many companies offer their customers is aesthetic—fee-paying students, for example,

want to be taught in stylish classrooms and fancy buildings, not the old functional building of welfare state architecture. Spending large amounts of money on spectacular buildings by famous architects or new corporate logos may once have been regarded as wasteful or profligate; given the power of the image in today's society, however, such spending can be seen as an investment.

By the same token, some scholars have argued that part of the service that employees offer is aesthetic. This is referred to as aesthetic labour, by analogy to **emotional labour**.[2] Looking smart is part of the job and may require long hours of grooming, shopping, and caring for one's appearance and image. Employees must look right, just as buildings, logos, and products must. Any of these ingredients can tarnish a company's image as surely as a work of art can be tarnished by an unsightly frame or inappropriate lighting. Aesthetic labour places employees in something of an ambiguous position. On the one hand, they enjoy being on display as part of a winning brand and a glamorous image; on the other hand, they feel constantly exposed to the critical stare of the customers and often judged against highly idealized standards.

In the last twenty years or so, a movement of organizational aesthetics has started to emerge which brings the study of organizing, leadership, and management under the focus of aesthetics.[3] The organizational aesthetics point of view examines the beauty or ugliness of organizing and its outcomes (joy, exploitation, etc.) and asks questions like what would happen if we brought aesthetic judgements to bear on economically driven decisions or if we valued the dramatic gifts of a CEO as highly as his or her ability to cut costs?

Aggression

Humans are not the only species to inflict violence on each other. The males of many

---

[1] Bourdieu, 1984.   [2] Hancock and Tyler, 2000; Tyler and Taylor, 1998; Warhurst et al., 2000; Witz, Warhurst, and Nickson, 2003.
[3] See e.g. Gagliardi, 1990; Strati, 1999.

species are known to compete or fight to secure resources like **status**, territory, or access to females. The females of many species too are known to fight in order to protect their young. What sets people apart is the frequency and savagery of aggression against their own. Aggression takes many forms from shouting, insulting, and humiliating others to threats to their lives and well-being, blackmail, physical violence, torture, rape, and murder. A particularly human aspect of aggression is that it is not always tied to material or symbolic gain. Acts of gratuitous violence, aggression just for the fun of it, are every bit as common as aggression calculated to bring about actual benefits to the perpetrator or acts sparked by panic, fear, and frustration. Another specifically human aspect of aggression is its relation to moral codes which may simultaneously seek to control it but also authorize its use.

Aggression is studied from many points of view. Biologists have identified the parts of the brain that trigger off and control violence; animal ethologists and evolutionary psychologists have studied the evolutionary advantages conferred by intra-species aggression, such as balancing the distribution of the species, selection of the strongest, and defending the young;[1] cultural anthropologists have noted the differing preponderance of violence in different human cultures. Questions on whether actual violence is caused or boosted by watching violent movies or playing violent video games are liable to cause occasional moral panics in contemporary societies as are the relation between violence and alcohol consumption and violence perpetrated by or against children.

There is considerable evidence that aggression is a gendered phenomenon. Males are more aggressive than females, perpetrating a substantial majority of the crimes and acts of violence often with women as their victims. There are many explanations for this discrepancy, from biological to psychological and social. One interesting argument put forward by Gilligan is that men are more likely to perpetrate violence in the confident belief that they are doing the right thing;[2] they are able to detach themselves from the actual pain and suffering they inflict believing that they act in the name of a superior principle, such as justice, rationality, or social progress. Thus, male **morality** may oppose cruelty and violence but is quite content to deploy them in pursuit of its aim. Female morality, on the other hand, is less likely to feature violence because it is built around an 'ethic of care', more concerned with compassion and maintaining supporting relations than maintaining absolute standards of justice or rationality.

Aggression in organizations takes many forms. Some are 'hot'—**bullying**, harassment, insults, and humiliations. Physical violence and even homicide are also part of life in some organizations. But some forms of aggression are 'cold'—laying off employees, redeploying them in different places or different jobs with no consultation or concern for their well-being, the imposition of long hours of work and unhealthy working conditions, and so forth. Just as human cultures vary in the extent and prevalence of aggression, so too do organizations. Macho, **authoritarian** cultures are liable to encourage the display of aggression in different forms as a principle for establishing social status distinctions ('pecking orders') as well as for maintaining discipline and control.

Given the nature and extent of human aggression one may wonder at the ability of humans as a species to survive thus far. One of the helpful characteristics of human aggression is that it is highly malleable; it can be contained, controlled, unleashed, modified, and sublimated. When channelled into **competition**, it can fuel **achievement**; when sublimated into artistic pursuits, it can stimulate creativity; when turned into fantasy, it can defuse itself; and when turned against itself, it can neutralize itself. It was these two features of aggression, its apparent independence

---

[1] Lorenz, 1966.   [2] Gilligan, 1982.

from other human impulses and its endless ability to mutate, that led Freud to view it as an independent drive. Inspired by the ancient philosophy of Empedocles of Acraga (c.490–430 BC) that postulated an eternal opposition between Love (*philia*) bringing life together and Discord (*neikos*) that brought about disintegration, Freud argued that the human life was the unfolding of two great motivational principles, Eros (see **sexuality)** and the **death** instinct.[1] Aggression is one of the forms adopted by the death instinct, when it turns into violence, physical or symbolic, against other people. But the death instinct can also be sublimated into competition, where the desire to destroy an opponent turns into a wish to excel him or her. It can also turn into a compulsive repetition seeking to achieve a state of inertia through routine—this is of considerable importance for the functioning of organizations and also for religious and social **rituals**. Finally, the death instinct can turn into aggression against the individual's ego in the form of guilt and **conscience**. The individual may then suffer for crimes he or she never committed. Freud's theory of the death instinct has not received widespread recognition (even among psychoanalysts), though it can contribute to our understanding of some of the most puzzling and unsettling vicissitudes of human aggression.[2]

• See also *violence*

Alienation

Alienation is an important concept in sociology, following the central position of the concept in the works of the great German philosopher and revolutionary Karl Marx. In his early writings, Marx used the concept of alienation to describe the condition of humanity under **capitalism**,[3] a condition which is summed up in Brecht's phrase 'man can only live by forgetting that he is a human being'. The root cause of alienation for Marx is capitalist production,

which separates workers from the products of their **labour**, from the activity of labour, from their fellow humans, and from what Marx called man's 'species being', i.e. those features that make humans a unique species. Through the sale of their labour and through the production of commodities, workers surrender their productive capacities (which is what Marx believed make them distinctly human) to alien domination. A part of themselves is separated from them, it becomes estranged from them and confronts them as an oppressor. The alienated beings can be thought of as animals separated from their essential nature, animals which have spent their entire lives in captivity. They are unhappy, oppressed, and unfulfilled, but more importantly they are not aware of the causes of their condition, their consciousness is systematically distorted. False consciousness which may include belief in the inevitability of capitalism, in male or white supremacy, religious and nationalist beliefs, and so forth is an integral part of human alienation.

Marx envisaged everyone under capitalism (including the owners of capital and the managers) as alienated; yet he also conceived of the possibility of human emancipation and freedom in a society in which the **control** of the productive process is restored to the direct producers. As the concept of alienation has passed into everyday use, its meaning has shifted and has come to mean frustration and separation. The sociologist Robert Blauner argued that alienation in the workplace comprises four emotional states: powerlessness, meaninglessness, isolation, and self-estrangement.[4] He found that increasing automation leads to increasing alienation, though very highly automated chemical plants were seen as having low alienation. His theory was that as industries move from craft to mass production alienation increases, but as they move further to fully automated process production, alienation declines. His optimistic conclusion that in the long run alienation will

---

[1] Freud, 1923/1984; 1930.　[2] See, for example, Carr and Lapp, 2006; Gabriel, 1984.　[3] Marx, 1844/1972.　[4] Blauner, 1964.

be resolved by the very factors which fuel it, technology and automation, has been criticized as reflecting the optimism of the 1950s; his arguments, however, that link technology to the individual's experiences in the workplace and the degree of job satisfaction have proven influential.

Alienation became a very fashionable concept in the 1960s and early 1970s when it captured the frustrations and discontents of young people, academics, women, and minority groups in industrialized countries. In the works of Herbert Marcuse it came to occupy a central position.[1] Alienation, in his view, was caused not only by oppressive conditions of work, but equally by the false consolations offered by **consumer culture**. Capitalism, argued Marcuse, generates false **needs** that it then purports to satisfy through different material goods, automobiles, clothes, jewellery, and so forth. These, however, only intensify the discontents that feed them, creating a spiral of alienation, frustration, and discontent. Marcuse believed that human liberation needed to go far beyond the overthrow of the capitalist mode of production; it required a total refashioning of human beings and their relations, a liberation of **sexuality**, imagination, and **creativity** far beyond what Marx envisaged.

Since the late 1980s, interest in alienation along with concepts like 'false needs' and 'false consciousness' has ebbed among academics. While newspapers commonly refer to alienated youths, minorities, and groups, scholars have set out to **deconstruct** consumer culture rather than criticize it as alienating and oppressive. Thus interest has shifted towards looking at how individuals may, with the help of commodities, construct their **identities** and selfhoods, rather than how such identities and selfhoods supplant their essential humanity. More generally, the idea of an authentic human nature that becomes alienated under capitalism has come under much criticism. Human nature, it is argued, is itself a construct that different cultures create after their own concerns and priorities, not an invariant essence common to all humans.

Anomie

Anomie is a state of collapse of social **norms** and social **controls**. This concept is often linked to **alienation** as a form of social pathology, although its origin is different. It was developed by Emile Durkheim, one of the founders of sociology, who used it to account for certain social phenomena, like suicide. Durkheim argued that the cohesion of social **groups** and **societies** is achieved through two social mechanisms, which exist over and above the individuals making up the groups and societies.[2] (i) Social integration, the product of strong social bonds, unites groups like families, clans, military, and religious groups together; (ii) social regulation controls the individuals' needs and desires, bringing them into line with the means available for their satisfaction. In Durkheim's view social regulation is accomplished through the internalization of norms. Anomie occurs when such norms are weakened, especially during periods of rapid economic **change** or social transformation when aspirations and desires grow disproportionately. Their inevitable frustration leads to feelings of injustice, unfairness, and disorientation.

Durkheim argued that anomic societies display an increase in suicide rates and all kinds of manifestations of social deviance. Like alienation, anomie has had a long career in academic discourse and its meaning has lost some of the sharpness which Durkheim bestowed on it. Like alienation, anomie has assumed an increasingly psychological quality, indicating a state of being rather than a social phenomenon coming to signify a generalized condition of **meaninglessness**, normlessness, and disintegration which affects numerous social groups and individuals. For example, sections of the industrial working class as well as the 'yuppies' may be seen as

---

[1] Marcuse, 1955; 1964.   [2] Durkheim, 1951.

experiencing anomic tendencies, for very different reasons. The former have seen their expectations of a 'job for life', something they had come to regard as a right, undermined by technological developments and the arrival of downsizing and retrenchment since the 1980s. By contrast, the young whizz-kids commanding vast salaries for speculating in the world markets saw their expectations soar out of all control in the 'culture of greed' of the United Kingdom and the United States in the 1980s. Both groups could then be seen as experiencing anomic tendencies whose results may range from fatalism and deviance to **stress** disorders.

Does anomie afflict organizations? If organizations are viewed through the prism of Max Weber's ideal-type **bureaucracy**, they run no risk of anomie. Written rules control behaviour and there is no need for social norms or social cohesion. Such a view, however, seems highly unhelpful. Real organizations are full of cohesive groups and they themselves can vary in the degree of cohesion and unity among their members. We have now come to view organizations increasingly as **cultures** rather than as machines; as cultures, they may have more or less integration and more or less regulation. Those organizations that have 'strong cultures' run no risk of anomie (unless for those who feel excluded and marginalized from them), though those whose culture is highly fragmented may be more at risk. An anomic organization is one where there is little sense of collective purpose and belonging and where people's behaviour shows little sense of acknowledging the needs and aspirations of others. Organizations that have gone through a protracted trauma due to **downsizing**, where their members feel that they may be the next ones in line to be sacked, may well lapse into anomic states.[1] Likewise, organizations with very weak **leadership** and no sense of direction or collective purpose may lapse into anomie. In such organizations, one would expect individuals to be easily corruptible (since there are no norms or

values against corruption), mobile (they would readily move elsewhere if offered better terms since they have no sense of belonging or allegiance to their employer), uncooperative, and detached.

Anxiety

It is frequently argued that we live in an Age of Anxiety, brought about by continuous change, conflict, and uncertainty. People in Western societies are meant to be anxious about terrorism and crime, about holding on to their jobs and property, about growing old and dying, about their physical image and bodies, about the activities of big business and big government, about the discoveries of scientists and technologists, and so forth. Anxiety is undoubtedly an unpleasant **emotion**, associated with uncertainty and exposure. It is also a very important emotion, acting as the trigger of different social and psychological processes. As the psychologist William McDougall pointed out, anxiety alerts the individual to the possible existence of threats and focuses our attention on how to deal with them.[2]

There is no integrated theory of anxiety in the human sciences, although there is general agreement that it is a feature of many core psychological processes. Psychoanalysis distinguishes between fear (which is associated with a frightening object), fright (which is the result of a lack of preparedness), and anxiety (which is relatively unfocused, yet can be prolonged and highly incapacitating). A number of different types of anxiety have been identified, including separation anxiety, moral anxiety, realistic anxiety, depressive anxiety, paranoid anxiety, and neurotic anxiety. Anxiety can act as a signal for **defensive mechanisms**, although it can equally be a signal that defence processes have failed or backfired. Neurotic anxiety, in contrast to realistic anxiety, involves feelings disproportionate to the magnitude of threat facing an individual

---

[1] Stein, 2001; Uchitelle, 2006.   [2] McDougall, 1908/1932.

and may result in inhibitions (avoidance of particular people, areas, or types of behaviour) or symptom formation.

Many organizational processes generate anxiety. **Leadership** is a process which awakens many primitive anxieties. Is the leader worthy of faith and obedience? Will he or she take advantage of his or her followers? Is he or she sincere? Are his or her claims to legitimacy genuine?[1] Teams and **groups** also awaken numerous anxieties. Will the group accept us? Will it respect our individuality? Will we be able to live up to our partners' expectations? Keeping anxieties in check is a fundamental requirement if groups, organizations, and even societies are to function effectively. Excessive anxieties may induce paralysis or alternatively aggression and destructiveness. Effective leaders are said to 'contain' anxiety, in other words temper it, allay it, and channel it towards effective action.

Anxiety is also an important emotion associated with **learning**. Learning is an anxiety-laden process; the learner is anxious about understanding what he or she has to learn, anxious about failing, and anxious about making a fool of themselves in the process of learning. It is, therefore, important that learning institutions and teachers control such anxieties. Excessive anxiety is likely to incapacitate learning; like a person who is drowning, an excessively anxious learner is likely to cling on to whatever relieves the anxiety rather than assimilate and appreciate new material. On the other hand, the total absence of anxiety is also likely to inhibit learning, since it encourages one to remain within a comfort zone of already acquired learning.[2]

Undoubtedly, anxiety becomes exacerbated in periods of extreme organizational change taking place within highly unpredictable, complex, or even chaotic environments. Stacey has argued that in such environments, organizations succeed and survive if they can operate in a state of 'bounded instability' or near chaos.[3] To do so, their members must be able to accept a degree

of anxiety, channelling this anxiety into learning, creativity, and inventiveness. More generally, the fundamental changes in the structure of capitalist organizations, including outsourcing, downsizing, constant restructuring, and re-engineering, generate chronic feelings of anxiety among employees. So too does the endless **consumerism** which stimulates a wide range of insecurities (Am I attractive enough? Am I growing old? Does my breath smell? Is my hair falling out? Am I getting enough fun out of life? etc.) in order to offer solutions in the form of different goods and services. Previous generations of people also worried about many things—what is perhaps different in our times is the general belief that we have **choices** and that our fate rests in our own hands. Instead of relieving our anxiety, however, the availability of choices often exacerbates them. When you have a profusion of things to choose from, you inevitably start worrying whether you made the right choice and whether in the long term you will come to regret it.

Authoritarianism

Authoritarianism is a concept that was originally developed to measure and account for individuals' susceptibility to anti-democratic **ideology**. The original measure was generally referred to as the F scale (F for Fascism), and it was believed by the theorists who developed it to be a general **personality** characteristic of certain people, rather than something specific to a situation, or to attitudes towards one group of people.[4] After the Second World War, questions were asked about how it could be that so many people could have obeyed orders to carry out so many atrocious crimes against their fellow human beings. How could people obey orders which led them into imprisoning, torturing, and killing other people on the grounds of ethnic difference? The shock was all the greater because this happened in Germany, a country that was widely

[1] Gabriel, 1999.   [2] Antonacopoulou and Gabriel, 2001.   [3] Stacey, 1992; 1995.   [4] Adorno et al., 1950.

considered to have one of the most advanced and 'civilized' cultures in the world at the time, and because so many sectors of society were implicated.

Adorno's argument was that 'authoritarian personalities' are individuals who possess certain unique traits, usually all of them together. These include

- a mechanical surrender to conventional values (e.g. pro-family, hard work, etc.);
- blind submission to authority together with blind hatred of all opponents and outsiders;
- anti-introspectiveness (i.e. a dislike for people who look inwards, such as poets, psychologists, and artists);
- rigid stereotyped thinking (i.e. 'women are not cut out to be leaders', 'the young today show no respect for authority');
- superstition (i.e. the belief that they are under the influence of forces far greater than themselves and when these forces work against them, there is nothing they can do);
- vilification, half-moralistic and half-cynical, of human nature (i.e. the belief that ordinary people are lazy, stupid, deceitful, and cheating and that they need a strong man to control them);
- projectivity (i.e. anything unpleasant about themselves they 'project' onto others—'It is not I who am afraid, it is the others' 'It is not I who am deceitful, it is others').

Authoritarianism is generally associated with people who, during their childhood, were the subjects of excessive discipline and insufficient love; they grew up (sometimes in boarding schools) admiring those who were strong and contemptuous of those who were weak and 'sensitive'. **Love** is seen by many of these people as weakness and, therefore, denigrated.

Authoritarianism is a concept of considerable interest in connection with **leadership**. Authoritarian leaders are liable to demand unqualified loyalty, are extremely harsh in their treatment of others, and are very reluctant to change their mind, even when their decisions work against them. They view changing one's mind as a sign of weakness and, like Margaret Thatcher, pour scorn on 'U-turns'. This is why, according to military psychologist Norman Dixon,[1] they are responsible for some major military and other leadership disasters.

Authoritarianism thrives under certain social conditions, such as times of widespread anxiety and confusion, when there may be an attraction to anyone who offers 'strong leadership'. This has been observable at national level several times since the Second World War. For example, in the UK, a time of economic and industrial uncertainty produced the conditions in which voters enthusiastically accepted repeated doses of authoritarian leadership from Margaret Thatcher.

Authoritarianism often operates through a group of people who accept each other as being 'one of us' while mistrusting and excluding any outsider. So in the twenty-first century, with its emphasis on networking, we are seeing a particular form of authoritarianism operating through cronyism; **authority** is maintained through a **network** of people who see each other as 'one of us' and who are under threat of losing their 'crony, insider status' if they step too far out of line with the authority figure. All the same, social conditions today do not favour the emergence of authoritarian leaders. Such leaders tend to lack the feel-good, photogenic, warm qualities that followers expect of their leaders. They also lack the creative imagination, the **emotional intelligence**, and the visionary qualities that many organizations require. Instead of authoritarian leaders, many of today's organizations seem to attract people who are almost the diametrical opposite of authoritarian, namely, **narcissistic** leaders.

Another approach to the study of authoritarianism was taken by experimental psychologists like Milgram and Zimbardo,[2] who carried

---

[1] Dixon, 1976.   [2] Milgram, 1974; Zimbardo, Maslach, and Haney, 1999.

out famous experiments trying to understand why people give and why they obey orders, even when they lead to cruelty and abuse. In their different ways, both of these authors emphasize that brutality may have more to do with the situations in which people find themselves rather than their own characters as authoritarian personalities. They showed that perfectly ordinary people are capable of acts of extraordinary savagery when placed in certain conditions where they are detached from the civilizing constraints of society, friends, and everyday realities. Their studies indicate that most of us have authoritarian tendencies that, under everyday circumstances, we hold in check. It is when authoritarianism cannot be contained, in conditions of acute stress, that it leads to the terrifying consequences with which we are familiar.

• See also *organizational pathologies*

Authority

Authority is traditionally identified with legitimate **power**, or an unequal relationship in which the right of the superior party to order others is recognized by the subordinates as legitimate. Max Weber, one of the founders of sociology, elaborated on Machiavelli's view that people obey orders either for fear or for love; he distinguished coercion, when the superior's orders are obeyed unwillingly by the subordinate, out of fear, from authority (or domination), under which the orders are obeyed willingly. He then identified three sources of authority: charisma, tradition, and a rational system of rules. **Charismatic** authority is based on the extraordinary qualities of the leader which command unconditional respect and loyalty. Traditional authority is based on the sanction of custom and practice; the leader is seen as the rightful heir of old lines of authority. In both of these, personal and emotional commitment to the leader are central to the legitimization process. Weber's third type of

authority is rational-legal authority based on a system of rules which command respect because of their **rationality**.[1]

Orders are obeyed in as much as they are consistent with these rules. Unlike the previous two types, rational-legal authority is based on calculation rather than **emotion**, and is impersonal, i.e. it does not stem from the person but from the position which the person occupies. Weber saw charismatic leadership as essentially unpredictable and turbulent and argued that there is a gradual shift towards the rational-legal type; he referred to this process as rationalization and identified its principal institution as **bureaucracy**. Most contemporary organizations involve combinations of all three types of authority as well as a variable measure of coercion and force.

Weber's scheme has been refined and revised by numerous commentators. Rational-legal authority, it has been argued, involves two distinct principles which do not always go together—respect for positions and **rules**, on the one hand, respect for expert **knowledge**, on the other. In many **professional** organizations, expert professionals with highly sophisticated knowledge are often supervised by managers with lesser knowledge. Where does authority ultimately reside—in the holder of the higher office or the person with superior knowledge? In a widely quoted article, French and Raven distinguished between 'legitimate power' based on position and 'expert power' based on knowledge.[2] Likewise charisma has been split into respect for those leaders with truly remarkable personal qualities and for those more familiar persons from our environment, like parents, colleagues, and managers, whom we personally respect without according them superhuman qualities. The term 'referent power' (or authority) has been used for this latter form.

Over long periods of time, patterns of authority in society change. In traditional societies, authority associated with long-standing

[1] Weber, 1946.   [2] French and Raven, 1959.

religious, political, and civic **institutions** was dominant. The rise of **modernity** brought with it new forms of authority based on knowledge and on positions. This coincided with the rise of **science** and **rationality**, which were seen as displacing traditional beliefs and practices. More recently, the unquestioned power of science has been contested. **Post-structuralists**, like Michel Foucault,[1] have argued that power and knowledge form an indissoluble entity to which he refers as power/knowledge. It is not as if a set of ideas is scientific and therefore commands authority; rather, various practices and discourses *at the same time* assume scientific standing and command authority. More generally, post-structuralist thinking has refused to acknowledge a difference between authority and power, and has sought to identify the way that power operates through **discourses**, the way that words and phrases are used. For example, if the term 'dyslexic' is accepted as a scientific description of a particular condition, a person previously categorized as dull or unintelligent gets treated differently. He or she is no longer excluded from various activities, like going to university or becoming a physicist. The 'discourse of dyslexia' enables this person to claim authority that they would not have had without it. The opposite happens if a person is classified as 'mad', or, until the 1960s in many countries, as 'homosexual'. These conditions are seen as 'pathological' and a person described by them is excluded from many of the privileges and rights available to others.

Another significant development since the high point of modernity is that the authority of science and experts is itself being increasingly questioned. It is questioned on account of numerous perceived failings of science, including disastrous experiments, accidents, food scares, blunders, and miscalculations. Some of the challenges to science are raised by religion; however, a different challenge to expertise comes from everyday **experience**. While science reigned supreme, it overrode any claims

to genuine insight offered by experience. You may suffer from diabetes, but science will tell you how to deal with it; your child is at risk of contracting rubella, science will offer you the vaccine to immunize her. Increasingly, however, the authority of science is supplanted by the authority of the person who has had a personal experience. Thus, sufferers from asthma or back pain are as likely to consult other sufferers (through the internet or patient support groups) and resort to complementary or alternative medicine, as accept what they perceive as ineffective or toxic medication provided by their doctors. This juxtaposition between the voice of first-hand, personal experience and the voice of scientific expertise is played out today in many fields, including medicine, law, history, therapy, and education.[2]

A result of this trend has been the argument, implicit or explicit, that *only* he or she who has lived through a certain experience can speak with authority about it—thus, only black people can speak authoritatively about race, only gay people about sexual marginalization, and, more contentiously, only people suffering from cancer about cancer. In this way, the ability of such people to tell their **story** is part of a process of discovering a **voice**, through which individuals and groups can describe, communicate, debate, and share their experience with other people. In this way, they build their **identities**, their sense of who they are and how they should be treated. Some scholars are now suggesting that a new **ideology** is emerging, one that aggressively proclaims, 'Thou shalt not deny my experience; thou shalt not silence my voice!', thus challenging the uncontested authority of scientific expertise.[3]

• See also *bureaucracy, experience, power*

Autopoiesis

A concept proposed by biologists Maturana and Varela to account for the difference between

---

[1] Foucault, 1980.   [2] Gabriel, 2004c.   [3] See e.g. Maton, 1998; Moore and Muller, 1999.

living and inorganic systems.[1] Autopoiesis is a Greek neologism meaning self-production or self-construction and provides the basis for understanding the behaviour of living systems, by explaining mechanisms of **cognition** and **language** as self-producing processes of the nervous system. Contrary to behaviourist and other models seeking to explain the relation between a **system** and its **environment** as one of adaptation, Maturana and Varela made a strong case that interactions between system and environment are determined solely by the biology of the individual. Their approach treats the nervous system as an operationally closed, self-referential system, already programmed to carry out certain actions. In this sense, a system can be said to be autopoietic if the interactions and transformations of its components generate more components and interactions of the same type. Of course, the environment can introduce perturbations which act as triggers for **change**, but it is the nervous system itself which determines which environmental factors act as perturbations.

Maturana and Varela rejected the view that social systems themselves can be considered autopoietic or that social behaviour and social learning are autopoietic, although such arguments have been put forward and have acquired some currency.[2] Increasingly, the concept of autopoiesis is used in a metaphorical way to indicate a system which is dynamic and can regulate itself through a process akin to thought. Several authors have pointed out the similarity between autopoiesis and Bateson's idea of co-evolution as well as Weick's idea of the enacted environment. Both of these approaches dismiss the notion that environments are 'given' and highlight systems' ability to define their environments.

---

[1] Maturana and Varela, 1980.   [2] Luhmann, 1990; Mingers, 1995.

B

(The) body

Long the self-declared remit of the natural sciences, the human body has only recently become an explicit topic in organizational studies. Turner was the first to call for a sociology of the body and triggered off a recent 'embodied turn' in social studies that places the body at the core of most social phenomena.[1] Turner attributed the body's earlier neglect to sociology's early rejection of biologically based explanations for social **action**; we can see the consequences of this in the discipline's continued emphasis on human consciousness and social structure. Durkheim's *Suicide* was pivotal in distancing the sociological opus from biological and psychological explanations for social action.[2] The Weberian emphasis upon **rationality** and the **symbolic interactionists**' emphasis on meaning creation deepened this gulf. This led to the recent charge that sociology naively replicates the Cartesian mind/body dualism. Turner uncovered a tacit concern with the body in classical sociological theory, from Weber's sexually constrained Protestant to the Marxian concern with the reproduction of social life. Among symbolic interactionists, Goffman assumed a communicative body that becomes a source of claims about the **self**.[3] Despite such acknowledgements, classical sociological theory remains overly cognitive; the mind drives social action, the body is its unwitting and often unremarked recipient.

The body has featured in the sociology of organizations, but only as the focus of the organization. Medical sociology, for instance, explores living bodies as targets of medical intervention, and cadavers as targets of medical investigation and training. Medical sociology thus shares an almost incidental concern with the body with disciplines like the sociology of death, sport, fashion, and care giving (for example, nursing homes and rehabilitation centres). Similarly, the sociology of health and illness treats the concrete body as the container of good or bad health rather than an object of reflection and an interactive tool. Thus embodiment, the lived experience of the body, has been notably absent in traditional organization studies.

In the midst of this barren landscape, however, two sociological thinkers working before the recent 'embodied turn' stand out for having topicalized the body, albeit in an exclusively macro-historical form. The first is Elias,[4] whose *Civilizing Process* documented the pacification of civil life and the increasing suppression and **control** of bodily impulses, grounded in an ever-higher threshold of disgust over corporeal processes, itself inspired by the centralization of state **power** which demanded a calculating, political actor rather than a violent and impulsive one. The second is Foucault,[5] who documented the emergence of biopower during the transition from feudalism to the modern state. Biopower disciplined a newly urbanized and potentially problematic population by managing its daily life. This it did by developing **knowledge** about the individual and the collective body, and constructing both standards for '**normal**' bodies and disciplinary regimes designed to fashion productive citizens who embraced these regimes to become self-regulating. Governmentality, or 'the conduct of conduct', essential to

---

[1] Turner, 1984; 1996.　[2] Durkheim, 1951.　[3] Goffman, 1959; 1963.　[4] Elias, 1994.　[5] Foucault, 1978.

this discipline, is empirically observable within such people-processing institutions as the hospital, the school, the asylum, and the military. It can also can be observed in any organizational setting, as people reproduce regimes of truth and build distinct **subjectivities** through disciplined, if not wholly 'involuntary', action. Moreover, since power is not the exclusive possession of a select few but a web of relations in which all actors are enmeshed, any organization can be scrutinized for the disciplining of bodies, just as it can be explored for the construction and deployment of Elias's restrained, civilized, embodied self.

More recently, a Foucauldian concern with regulation and surveillance informs many studies of the **gendered** body, whether of the feminist or more current 'masculinities studies' persuasion (early feminist writings on the regulation of women's bodies, particularly by medicine, predated Foucault, and should not be conflated with his work). Work on the rise of the postmodern, consuming body by such scholars as Giddens and Shilling shares Foucault's interest in the production of disciplined embodiments and **subjectivities**.[1] They argue that the demise of modernity's **grand narratives** providing personal value has caused the body to serve as a new symbol of moral status, even spiritual perfection; the appearance of health comes to signify virtuous self-control exercised through regimes of bodily practice. This new **identity** is nested within the rise of mass **consumption** and the conspicuous display of possessions, which the body advertises. Here, too, organizations are implicated, as settings for the construction and deployment of the moral embodied self, although this strain of research tends to focus on leisure and consumption.

Given the co-presence of hundreds of bodies within the same organization, it was perhaps inevitable that the new 'embodied' turn within sociology would set its sights on organizational practices, even those that appear 'purely'

cognitive. Partly inspired by Hochschild's early work on flight attendants,[2] which uncovered the emotional character of organizational practice and took the embodiment of emotions, emotion work, and emotional labour as one of its central premises, scholars began to examine emotional and other practices as *embodied* across a range of organizational contexts. Just as social interaction, relations, experience, identities, and order are interactive achievements, so are they embodied ones. People interact through bodies as well as minds, organize themselves physically as well as mentally, and take each other's embodied and verbal claims into account during interaction and subsequent reflection and evaluation. So we have studies of, *inter alia*, embodiment in bureaucratic and service settings, often with a particular interest in gender; the regulation of bodies in schools; media representations of sexualized and racialized bodies; the role of social movement organizations in shaping discourses about the body and actual bodily practices (as in the case of breast cancer); the experience of ill, disabled, and 'different' bodies at work; 'body work' in which care givers, sex workers, and medical personnel engage, and the impact that organizational context has on it; and such organizations as medical, laboratory, and statutory settings that construct and regulate bodies.

These studies approach the body as the focus of particular settings, ranging from hospitals to beauty parlours, seeking to uncover and document the embodied nature of work in such settings. Different settings may construct and present, for example, a female body as submissive, controlled, respectful, flirtatious, or strong as an intrinsic part of the work performed. This is what distinguishes the new 'embodied' turn in sociology and organizational studies from its predecessors. Whereas the earlier approaches examined the body only insofar as a particular organization addresses it as a core task, recent studies look at the lived experience of the body in any organization, even those which do not

---

[1] Giddens, 1991; Shilling, 1993; 2007.   [2] Hochschild, 1983.

focus on the body *per se*, such as insurance agencies and secretarial pools.

• See also **self and selfhood**

DANA ROSENFELD, UNIVERSITY OF KEELE

Boundaries

While boundaries have always been seen as crucial qualities of human societies, groups, and organizations, especially when studied as social **systems**, they have recently come to be seen both as highly problematic and as highly significant features in the changing nature of organizations. Instead of having firm and well-defined boundaries, organizations are increasingly viewed as having permeable, fuzzy, or virtual boundaries, often blending with other organizations or with their wider environment which, at times, makes any distinctions between organizations and their environments meaningless.[1]

The concept of a boundary is fundamental in systems theory of organizations.[2] One of the fundamental qualities of systems is a boundary which separates them from their **environments**. Some organizational boundaries are physical (such as perimeter fences, patrolled by guards and security cameras, walls of a buildings, or areas requiring security passes and keys to enter), but there are also legal, social, psychological, informational, and moral ones. In this sense, organizations have throughputs, such as people, resources, knowledge and information, products and services, waste and by-products, which continuously cross their boundaries. Some of these crossings are legitimate and controlled, others may be clandestine or illegal, for instance, when employees pilfer resources from the organization for their own private use or when intruders make their way into an organization's centre and get away with its secrets or resources. In all these respects, organizations may be thought of as walled cities,

at times transacting openly with their neighbours, at others closing their gates under siege. Boundaries are patrolled, controlled, surveyed, opened carefully at times, violated at times, redrawn, and renegotiated.

One of the foremost boundaries that individuals encounter in organizations is denoted by the idea of a position or **role**. This is both the way an organization defines a person's obligations and rights, and also the way a person experiences them. When using the expression 'my job', we usually refer to those things that we feel obliged to do as part of our **psychological contract** with our employer. In this way, we draw a boundary beyond which we are unwilling to act. Different people draw such boundaries differently. Working late without extra pay may be how some people see their job; for others, 5 o'clock is the precise moment when their time becomes their own and their employer can make no claim on it whatever. Moral boundaries too can be drawn differently. Some people may be willing to tell an innocuous lie for their employer (some of them are called 'marketers' or 'PR specialists'). Others may entertain more serious transgressions of moral codes, such as defamation through slander, incrimination, entrapment, framing, lying, stealing, or even killing. **Feelings** (such as anger, remorse, shame, and embarrassment) are especially important in defining where different boundaries are drawn.[3] If working late makes us feel resentful and angry, we become aware that our employer is expecting us to draw a work/leisure boundary which we find unacceptable.

All of the above conceptualizations of boundaries approach them essentially as defensive phenomena—boundaries protect individuals, groups, and organizations from intruders and are vital in maintaining order and regularity. While at times they may be wrongly drawn, they are viewed as essential for the effective functioning of organizations. Recently, these views have come under some criticism from a number of

---

[1] Hernes, 2004; Lamont and Molnar, 2002.   [2] Katz and Kahn, 1978; Miller and Rice, 1967.   [3] Sandelands and Boudens, 2000.

quarters. **Social constructionism** has challenged the view that separates a system from its environment for accepting unproblematically the existence of objective boundaries. Instead, social constructionist theorists argue that boundaries along with many other social phenomena are negotiated, maintained, dissolved, and redrawn through social interaction. According to this view, boundaries are not given, much less objective. Individuals have a degree of choice on how they place them or whether they place them at all. Weick's concept of the 'enacted environment' suggests that organizations continuously redraw their boundaries by redefining themselves as existing for different ends.[1]

Another criticism of conventional views of boundaries comes from **complexity and chaos theory**. This approach has challenged the view of organizations as linear equilibrium systems, where small changes in the environment produce small changes in the organization and large changes in the environment produce correspondingly large changes in the organization. Instead, it proposes that most organizations operate in states of non-linear equilibrium, where small changes in a complex and unpredictable environment can have far-reaching and potentially catastrophic effects on organizations. In such an environment, organizations that fix their boundaries firmly and seek to defend them are liable to fail. Instead organizations must seek to continuously reinvent themselves by maintaining open, porous, and changeable boundaries.[2] In this manner, it is argued that organizations 'co-evolve' with their environments, neither of them determining the other. Coevolution suggests continuous flux— organizations that were once adversaries or competitors suddenly come to be partners; at times, all boundaries are removed through mergers and acquisitions. Information may flow freely across boundaries and people may be required to work at all places and all times as if work

and leisure boundaries did not exist. Developments in **information technology** accentuate these trends, enabling people to work from home (tele-working) or from their vacation destinations, allowing them to carry the organization wherever they go by means of a simple wireless link. Whether this erosion of boundaries is real or imagined and whether it has positive or negative psychological and social consequences is not yet determined with certainty. However, it is almost certain that the old view of boundary as a fixed perimeter wall that has to be defended and patrolled may be near the limit of its usefulness.

• See also *anxiety, buildings and architecture, system*

Bricolage

Bricolage is a French word meaning 'makeshift', 'handiwork', or 'DIY' ('Do-it-yourself') tinkering. It is a term that has found some interesting applications in describing the work of managers and also the relation between **knowledge** and **action**. Unlike an engineer, a bricoleur does not start with a plan of what it is that he or she wishes, only then proceeding to finding the resources, tools, and raw materials to realize it. Instead, bricolage makes do with whatever resources are at hand, deploying them with imagination to achieve something useful, even if it is not exactly what would have been chosen.[3] Bricolage often makes unorthodox uses of things—a log may double up as a stool, a doorstop, or a goal post. Its results are never 'perfect', but they are often good enough. Unlike the engineer who relies on scientific laws and formulas to carry out his or her tasks, a bricoleur relies on improvisation, rule of thumb, and ad hoc judgement to produce reasonable results.[4]

How is bricolage relevant to the practice of managers? Some authors have argued that bricolage describes the work of most managers;[5]

[1] Weick, 1979; 1995.   [2] Cilliers, 1998; Stacey, 1992; 1995; Tsoukas, 2005.   [3] Knorr Cetina, 1981; Lévi-Strauss, 1966.   [4] Ciborra, 2002.   [5] Gabriel, 2002; Linstead and Grafton-Small, 1990; Weick, 2001a; 2001c.

that is ad hoc, improvisatory, and makeshift. Managers survey their domains to assess what resources are available—tools, space, time, humanpower, skills, information, goodwill, raw materials, etc. They then deploy them in imaginative ways to achieve results that are good enough and make the most of the opportunities and constraints present. Such a view of management is quite different from that of **Scientific Management**, which sees managers proceeding with the cool and scientific efficiency of engineers, and much of **strategic** management, which views managers as making careful plans and deploying resources with the detached certainty of battlefield generals.

If managers' work is approached as bricolage, the education and training of managers is seen in a different light from the way it is seen if management is approached as an art or a science. Instead of seeing **management** learning as a specialist type of scientific or artistic education, management learning requires making the best uses of available resources, cutting corners, constantly redefining objectives, and, above all, taking advantage of unforeseen opportunities. Far from seeking to repeat successful formulas and implementing textbook theories, managers should seek unusual, imaginative, risky, and non-routine solutions to the problems they encounter.

And what of management **knowledge**? If management is seen as bricolage, management theory is akin to a series of *recipes* that skilled practitioners use in a free and improvisatory way rather than in a passive and imitative one. Just as skilled cooks may consider alternative recipes, identify the most useful one for the situation at hand, and then proceed to improvise around it, effective managers can identify the theories that are most likely to be helpful in specific situations and then apply them in loose, creative, and imaginative ways, given the resources available. The creativity of the manager is sometimes like that of the Third World engineer—producing ingenious fixes to problems that no one should have had to face.

Buildings and architecture

When talking of organizations, most of us think of the buildings, towns, and cities that house them. The 'dreaming spires' are a core feature of Oxford University as is the Pentagon of the US Defense Department. Yet organization theory was rather late taking an interest in the physical premises of organizations. Buildings, quite apart from facilitating or inhibiting organizational functioning, are also vital **symbols** of what organizations stand for, what their chief corporate **values** are. Like the old cathedrals, buildings are statements about an organization's **identity**. An open-plan, glass building gives quite a different impression from a concrete tower pyramid or a Kafkaesque castle of dark corridors and oak-panelled boardrooms. In addition to such overall symbolic effects, organizational buildings create symbolic divisions and classifications. The size and siting of each office, its accessories and furnishings, act as significant **status** and **power** symbols of its occupants.[1]

At the functional level, organizational buildings allow and discourage different types of interaction among organizational members. Conflict, collaboration, and control within organizations are all shaped by spatial arrangements. A department split between two sites is liable to develop dual identities and cultures, unless measures are taken to draw the two parts together. Two departments in adjoining parts of a building, sharing some of the social spaces, may work well together, or, alternatively, each may eye the other with suspicion, lest they seek to infringe on their territory.

Buildings define **boundaries**—they therefore both defend and control those inside. In the nineteenth century, the philosopher Jeremy Bentham designed a special type of prison, the Panopticon, in such a way that a single guard,

[1] Hatch, 1990.

located in the centre of a cylindrical structure, could survey every single one of the prisoners. This minimized costs and disobedience since prisoners could never be sure whether the guard's gaze was trained on them. In the twentieth century, the philosopher Michel Foucault viewed the Panopticon as the model upon which many organizational **controls** are based.[1] Organizations constantly and invisibly monitor their employees' every movement, controlling, disciplining, and punishing with a minimum of intrusion and fuss.

Architecture is an integral part of this 'Panoptic society'. Guillen,[2] for instance, has argued that the great modernist architects, like Le Corbusier and Walter Gropius, designed and built spaces of work and leisure that expressed the power dynamics of **Taylorism**—the architect as an omnipotent super-manager of space becomes a designer of cages where people live and work according to his wishes and plans. Space is divided, compartmentalized, standardized, and depersonalized and those using it become deskilled, fragmented, and controlled. Notwithstanding some famous masterpieces, modernist architecture with its buildings of concrete and steel led to some disastrous experiments in urban living and working.

In more recent years, a more 'open', transparent, ornamental, and playful style in architecture has emerged. It is not accidental that **postmodernism**, as a concept, has emerged from the work of architects since the 1960s who reacted against the brutalizing aesthetic and monumental functionalism of modernist architecture. They sought to create effects through sometimes unexpected uses of materials and violent clashes of styles. Glass emerged as the material of choice for building business premises. Postmodern architecture also pioneered unorthodox uses of space through conversions of old buildings (such as factories, warehouses, and department stores) for new uses (offices, museums, and shopping centres). We are thus not surprised

to find that the Judge Business School in Cambridge is housed in what used to be a hospital.

It would be wrong to suggest that postmodern architecture has transferred **control** from managers and architects to the users of space. On the contrary, architects have developed ever more subtle forms of control, seeking to 'engineer' deviance and recalcitrance out of social spaces.[3] New graffiti-proof materials make defilement impossible and new forms of surveillance have proliferated: security cameras everywhere, electronic monitoring and recording of most transactions. Modernist cellular office blocks have been replaced by open-plan offices where, in effect, employees and customers monitor and control each other.

One of the most interesting features of today's organizational buildings concerns the use of glass, as the signature material. Glass has come to represent the dominant **aesthetic** of the twenty-first century. It stands for transparency, openness, and beauty, but also fragility and vulnerability. Glass is a framing material, indicating that what it contains is valuable and precious. But it is also a material that entraps in a subtle way, like those Perspex boxes of magician David Blaine and artist Damien Hirst. The glass building suggests that the modern employee is part of a cast exposed to the admiring gaze of the customer but also a prisoner to be liberated. The glass building can be seen as a glass palace and a glass cage, a fully controlled and air-conditioned environment which prevents its inhabitants from opening and shutting windows and doors, rearranging furniture, or personalizing their work space. It is not so surprising then that it becomes associated with 'sick building syndrome'.[4]

Given the deep-rooted importance of buildings, it is not surprising that physical relocation or even modest spatial restructuring are frequently keenly contested political processes. Individuals and groups about to be relocated are liable to compare their new territory, its size,

---

[1] Foucault, 1977.   [2] Guillen, 1998.   [3] Marx, 1995; 1999.   [4] Gabriel, 2005.

location, and provisions, with their previous one and with the territories of other reference groups. They may then fight for more or different resources or may seek to resist relocation altogether. Physical relocation is then a major dimension of organizational **change**, unleashing political forces of alliance building, conflict, and **resistance**.

Bullying

Interest in workplace bullying has increased very considerably in the last ten years, viewed as a pervasive and highly pernicious phenomenon. Bullying can inflict deep emotional injuries on its victims, ranging from insomnia and depression to anxiety attacks and inability to maintain **boundaries** between personal and work lives. Some victims of bullying commit suicide. In spite of a recognition of the seriousness of the issue, bullying is not easy to define. When does a criticism or an exhortation to work harder turn into bullying? When does a joke turn into an insult? When does a compliment turn into harassment?

Reports indicate that bullying is not an infrequent phenomenon. Evidence from various surveys (not always very reliable when dealing with such issues) indicates that anything up to a third of the workforce report having been bullied in the last five years.[1] Most people understand bullying to involve aggressive and intrusive behaviour that occurs persistently and is not purely the result of work pressures. As Aristotle commented apropos of insults, bullying is surplus to requirement, aimed at humiliating the victim, not at achieving a task. Bullying sometimes takes a collective form of 'mobbing', a single individual being picked upon by many or conversely a single bully violating and oppressing many. It also frequently involves a 'third party', an audience, whose tolerance or even respect for the bully becomes a crucial part of bullying dynamics. The bully sometimes persecutes his or her victim in a very public manner, instilling terror in the audience lest they be next in line. Alternatively, the bully's persecution of his or her victim can be intensely personal, almost like conducting a private love–hate affair, in which occasional praise or support is interspersed with insults, threats, **criticisms**, shouting, and abuse. Similar bullying dynamics have been observed in schools and families.

Why does the victim endure such humiliations? Often victims have no choice. They are trapped; their livelihood depends on their job and they find themselves stuck, feeling helpless, unable to retaliate and unable to leave. Bullying is then linked with differences in power and status. Sometimes, however, victims can collude in their entrapment, developing a dependency on and even respect and admiration for their assailants. This is compounded if the victim suffers from low self-esteem and feelings of worthlessness and guilt. In such situations, the bully's aggression and the victim's passivity and desire for punishment get locked in a cycle of destruction. Bullies, for their part, are often **authoritarian** individuals, whose own sense of self-worth depends on dominating others. They may also have **narcissistic** tendencies—wanting attention and admiration and being unable to appreciate other people's feelings.

The importance of **culture** in relation to bullying cannot be overestimated. There are organizations in which bullying is endemic and others in which it is sporadic but persistent. Bullies are more likely to thrive in cultures where superiors and colleagues turn a blind eye, fearful of confrontation or even in admiration of displays of strength. In some work settings, such as the military, police, and fire service, bullying and victimization can be an unofficial way of testing a new recruit, a rite of passage. To survive bullying makes one a worthy member of the work group. A great deal of research on bullying and mobbing has been carried out by Scandinavian researchers, an area of the world where there is

---

[1] Hoel and Beale, 2006; Rayner, 1997; Rayner and Hoel, 1997.

a concerted social effort to eliminate bullying from schools, factories, and offices.[1]

• See also *aggression, violence*

Bureaucracy

The term bureaucracy has been in the English language since the first half of the nineteenth century. Its rise coincides with the rise of the modern state with its armies of appointed officials, its formal structure, written records, procedures, and rules. It also coincides with the rapid growth of cities during industrialization, the increasing impersonality of modern life, and an emphasis on science and rationality as the basis of economic and political **action**.

Bureaucracy is the subject of a foundational theory of organizations developed by the great German sociologist Max Weber. Weber's fundamental concern was to discover the causes behind the phenomenal growth of organizations and their increasing power in society. In particular, Weber was impressed by the rise of the Bismarckian state with its iron discipline borrowed from the army. He was also able to observe at first hand the growth of many organizations in different areas of social activity, most notably in business. His theory of bureaucracy is an example of 'grand theory', a type of theorizing that combines both great depth and breadth and tries to uncover the deeper truth about a social or a natural phenomenon. It is also a theory that makes claims about a wide range of different phenomena. Such grand theories were as much features of **modernity** as large skyscrapers, powerful organizations, and belief in progress driven by knowledge and science.

Weber viewed bureaucracy as the dominant institution of modern society; in its purest form, bureaucracy is that type of stratified collectivity in which all relations between people are exclusively relations of rational-legal **authority**. It is,

in short, a hierarchy in which people give and receive orders purely on the basis of a rational system of rules, rationally administered. In this way charisma, tradition, and every emotional, fantastic, and irrational aspect is written out of bureaucracy by definition. This is why Weber used the term 'ideal type' to describe it. An ideal type is 'formed by the one-sided accentuation of one or more points of view and by the synthesis of a great many diffuse, discrete, more or less present and occasionally absent concrete individual phenomena, which are arranged according to those one-sidedly emphasized viewpoints into a unified analytical construct (*Gedankenbild*). In its conceptual purity this mental construct cannot be found empirically anywhere in reality.'[2] Thus Weber approached bureaucracy as an abstraction, a model against which different real organizations may be measured. In ideal-type bureaucracy, there are no friendships or enmities, no cliques or alliances, no committees or project teams. There are only people giving and receiving instructions on the basis of a rational system of rules.

Weber identified a number of defining characteristics of this type of bureaucracy which include:

☐ A strict hierarchy of offices in which superior offices control lower ones.
☐ The appointment of individuals to offices on the basis of their expertise, certified by written qualifications.
☐ The conduct of each office on the basis of precise rules and regulations.
☐ Divorce of ownership from **control**, with **power** deriving entirely from the occupation of an office.
☐ Free contractual relationship between the organization and its officials.
☐ Written records of all important transactions.
☐ The complete separation of official activity from private, personal, and emotional life of the officials.

---

[1] See, for example, Einarsen, 2000.   [2] Weber, 1949, p. 90.

□ A system of promotion and careers based on a combination of seniority and achievement.

Weber argued that ideal-type bureaucracy is a formidable tool of administration; its attributes including precision, speed, unambiguity, discretion, subordination, no friction, economy, continuity, and unity. This form of organization permits discreet **control** over individual **performance** without excessive interference. Each official is afforded a **career** structure. He or she knows his or her duties for which he or she is adequately qualified; supervision is carried out by better-qualified and higher-placed officials. No respect or deference is owed to the superiors once outside the bureaucracy; each official has all the information required to fulfil his or her duties but no more. He concluded that

> the decisive reason for the advance of bureaucratic organization has always been its purely technical superiority over any other kind of organization. The fully developed bureaucratic mechanism compares with other organizations exactly as does the machine with the nonmechanical modes of organization.[1]

The image of organization as a machine totally dominates Weber's conception; it is a theme to which he returned often:

> Already now, rational calculation is manifested at every stage. By it, the performance of each individual worker is mathematically measured, each man becomes a little cog in the machine and, aware of this, his one preoccupation is whether he can become a bigger cog.... it is horrible to think that the world could one day be filled with these little cogs, little men clinging to little jobs, and striving towards bigger ones... this passion for bureaucracy is enough to drive one to despair.[2]

Weber's ambivalence towards bureaucracy is ever present. While he admired its technical efficiency, he deplored its effects on humanity, which he likened to an 'iron cage'. As the principal institutional consequence of the **rationalization** it brings with it the 'disenchantment of the word', the stripping away of magic, whim, and imagination and their replacement by cold calculation. Weber believed that the march of bureaucracy was unstoppable; moreover, he saw clearly that bureaucracy would grow irrespective of social or political systems, in liberal democracies as well as dictatorships of the left and the right.

Weber's bureaucracy has been criticized from a variety of angles. Many of the criticisms have focused on his apparent disregard for the 'human factor' in organizational life. Weber would dismiss this and related criticisms for failing to appreciate the sheer magnitude of bureaucratic *impersonality* and for exaggerating the importance of the human factor. Another criticism concerns Weber's lack of interest in establishing how an organization's overall goal, strategy, or vision are established. Weber would have argued that that too is immaterial. Bureaucracy will grow *whatever the goals and objectives*. It is a machine that will process its throughput in a consistent, methodical, and rational way, no matter whether its ultimate aim is the health of people, the making of profit, the education of the young, the conduct of war, or even the extermination of people. In Kafka's bleak accounts of bureaucracy in *The Trial* and *The Castle* we find something of an apotheosis of impersonal bureaucracy, moving slowly, methodically and without a trace of humanity towards its objectives, whose ultimate rationale is immaterial.

Impersonality features in another battery of criticisms directed at Weber that often go under the heading 'dysfunctions of bureaucracy'. A *dysfunction* is a negative, frequently unanticipated, consequence of something or somebody. We can talk of dysfunctional organizations, groups, leaders, or even individuals. Dysfunctions of bureaucracy are those negative consequences of bureaucracy that result from those very features that ensure its efficiency.

---

[1] Weber, 1946, p. 214.   [2] Weber cited in Mayer, 1956, p. 126.

Such dysfunctions include impersonality, rigidity, and departmentalization. These dysfunctions are said to be most damaging when an organization operates in a rapidly changing and complex **environment** where bureaucratic rigidity becomes a serious disadvantage. It is thus argued by critics that, in a highly volatile, changing world, where markets, technologies, political climates change rapidly, organizations which approximate the bureaucratic model are too rigid to take advantage of opportunities and repel threats. They fail to make full use of their members' creativity and imagination. They alienate their customers. For these reasons, they are doomed to be overtaken by leaner, more flexible organizations which have a greater ability to learn from experience and change their strategies and tactics accordingly.

Yet another set of criticisms of Weberian bureaucracy was sparked by one of Weber's disciples, Robert Michels, who dismissed Weber's rational model of organization in favour of a political one. In his 'Iron Law of **Oligarchy**' Michels argued that the rules, procedures, and rationality of organizations are but fig-leaves behind which a ruthless **power** game unfolds, a power game through which the few cynically and ruthlessly control the many. Corruption, manipulation, disinformation, favouritism, and blackmail are vital elements of this game. This is a far cry from Weber's clean and clinical bureaucracy that treats everyone impersonally and therefore equally.

In his provocatively titled book *In praise of bureaucracy*, Paul du Gay has sought to defend bureaucracy against its many critics.[1] Although primarily concerned with the state sector rather than private enterprise, du Gay has argued that the Weberian model provided a control against political interference and politicized agendas. This is currently being challenged by a 'new managerialism', which emphasizes targets, cost effectiveness, competition, and customer-focused ethos. This, argues du Gay, undermines the integrity and the dignity of officials which was meant to ensure impartiality and equality. In the name of cutting red tape, new managerialism undermines the system of rules and procedures which provided the strongest guarantee against corruption.

It may well be that while bureaucracy ruled unopposed for nearly a century, it is now challenged by a variety of new organizational forms and models. It may also be that the days of vast organizations, predictably and reliably processing materials, information, and people, are numbered. All the same, it would be far too early to proclaim the end of bureaucracy from the world of organizations.

Business ethics

Business ethics represents the study of **ethics** and of ethical and unethical practices in business activity. In this sense, it can be seen as a specialist field of ethics, the way that international relations, war, and politics are other fields in which ethics and ethical practices may be studied. Thus business ethics examines what is right and wrong, good and bad, in the sphere of economic activity; how firms should conduct their affairs; and how individuals should behave while doing business. This raises immediately the question of whether business calls for a specialist kind of ethics. Is good behaviour in a business context different from good behaviour in every other context? Does business offer amnesty from certain types of conduct that other spheres of human activity do not offer, in the same way that war may allow certain actions that would certainly be unacceptable in peacetime?

One approach to this issue is to argue that business neither calls for special ethics of its own, nor should seek to provide moral instruction to others. 'The business of business is business!' This was the credo of General Motors President Alfred T. Sloan, Jr., in the 1920s; it resurfaced in

---

[1] du Gay, 2000.

the latter part of the twentieth century and is often attributed to Nobel Prize winner economist Milton Friedman.[1] Most commentators have viewed this as expressing an arrogant indifference of business organizations to the natural environment and the moral sensitivities of their customers and stakeholders. Supporters of this position, however, would argue that businesses should conduct their business in a lawful and ethical manner, rather than force their own **values** and beliefs on others. Other organizations, such as political parties, churches, and many **voluntary organizations**, may seek to change the world or make the world a better place by promoting various **ideologies**. This is not, according to Friedman and others, what businesses should do—instead, they should concentrate on running their affairs effectively, thereby making profits for their shareholders. According to this view, business ethics is redundant or worse—it is an attempt to subvert businesses from their proper **goals**.

Defenders of this position would go a step further—they would argue that it is the task of governments to legislate about issues that are in the public good and not the task of business. If, for example, smoking was deemed to represent a social evil that should be stopped, then it should be the task of government to legislate against it rather than of businesses stopping the production of cigarettes or banning smoking on their premises. Likewise, if environmental protection is a social good, then it should be governments that promote it through international agreements and appropriate legislation rather than corporations. Finally, supporters of this view would argue that businesses, by taking it upon themselves to determine for others what is ethical and unethical, distort the operation of **markets**, thereby leading to inefficiencies and waste.

This approach is currently being challenged, most notably by exponents of social corporate responsibility who argue that businesses, like

individuals, have moral obligations over and above following the law laid down by governments. Critics of the Friedmanesque argument also point out that governments often lack the power, the will, or the wisdom to implement important social policies or that many such policies require intergovernmental cooperation that is difficult to achieve. Governments themselves respond to business pressures in the **policies** that they are willing to pursue. Businesses are major players on the global economic and political stages, it is argued, and they have moral responsibilities towards the environment, the workers, the consumers, and each other. Amartya Sen, like Friedman an economics Nobel Prize winner, has argued that markets never function outside an ethical sphere where social considerations are balanced against individual self-interest and, in any event, markets require political and social interventions to ensure that they function in an ethical manner.[2] Businesses, in other words, have social responsibilities.

Maybe more important than the intellectual challenge to Friedman's view has been the actual fact that most large-scale businesses have embraced *Corporate Social Responsibility* (CSR) as good for their public relations, good for business, and, in many instances, good for the bottom line. This takes us from 'normative business ethics' (how businesses *should* behave) to 'descriptive business ethics' (whether and how ethics actually enters business practices and policies). Initially a feature of socially progressive companies like the Bodyshop, embracing policies of Social Corporate Responsibility is now widespread. Most business websites today advertise their companies' ethical credentials and their commitment to promoting broader social values beyond profitability. Virtually every major firm trumpets its commitment to the environment, to **sustainable development**, to equal opportunities, to **diversity**, and many other social values. Many have CSR departments and employ 'business ethicists' to guide them through issues

---

[1] Friedman, 1970. [2] 1987; Sen and Harvard Institute of Economic Research, 1991.

raised by morality and ethics. This is not accidental. Whether a business's business is animal experimentation, oil exploration, car manufacturing, banking services, pharmaceuticals, or cosmetics, it must negotiate a plethora of moral hazards that could engulf it suddenly with potentially catastrophic results. One of the most significant issues facing every company today is consistency between what it preaches and what it is seen to practise.

Corporate Social Responsibility can then be viewed as a social movement that has altered the **discourse** on business ethics, authorizing **consumers** to reward and punish corporations for their ethical records and forcing companies at least to speak as though they have wider social responsibilities. In this way, business has had to acknowledge that it must consider the interests of a variety of stakeholders that include customers, employees, shareholders, communities, ecological organizations, animals, and even future generations of humans. This obligation is widely accepted as going beyond statutory obligations to comply to the letter of the law and calling for a wider commitment to public good. Corporate Social Responsibility has thus become closely aligned with the principles of sustainable development, which calls for firms to make decisions based not only on financial criteria such as profits or growth, but also on social and environmental ones. The technique of the 'balanced scorecard' was developed as a way of assessing the quality of a company's activities not only in terms of financial outcomes but also on a variety of social and human dimensions that determine these outcomes.[1] A company's vulnerability on ethical issues would adversely affect its balanced scorecard rating.

• See also *ethics, morality*

---

[1] Kaplan and Norton, 1992; 1993.

C

Capital

Capital, as the foundation of **capitalism**, is in the first instance an economic category. It refers to material wealth owned by individuals or groups that can act as productive resources increasing this wealth. Thus, machinery and buildings are long-recognized forms of capital. The term, however, has also been used to describe other types of resources that enable groups or individuals to build on and profit from them. A company can build on its 'intellectual capital', i.e. the stock of knowledge that enables it to gain an advantage against its competitors. Likewise, brands, logos, and the loyalty of employees and customers represent different forms of 'symbolic capital' for organizations. The concept of 'cultural capital' was used extensively by French sociologist Pierre Bourdieu to account for persistent social inequalities based on tastes and lifestyles. He argued that people judge each other and create hierarchies of superiority and inferiority based on how sophisticated or 'cool' their tastes are—judging and criticizing people's tastes sustains social **status** distinctions.[1]

Bourdieu was also the originator of the term 'social capital' that is currently at the centre of heated debates and arguments. In contrast to Weber, who saw class, status, and power as relatively independent of each other for prolonged periods, Bourdieu viewed cultural and social capital as complementing economic capital. Social capital can be thought of in the first instance as the trust, cooperation, and shared assumptions that enable organizations, networks, communities, or nations to function effectively as social and economic units. Thus,

a country like Finland may compete in some fields against countries with far lower wage levels or laxer environmental standards because of the high educational standards of its people, their shared cultural assumptions, the effective civic and services infrastructure, and the overall trust among its citizens that enables them to do business with each other without having to spend enormous amounts of resources in ensuring that they will not be cheated. All of these resources, education, health, trust, and material infrastructure, can be viewed as ways in which a country 'invests' in its future, in short social capital.

Over the past twenty years, a parallel use of social capital has emerged, one that views it as a resource used by individuals to advance their interests and **careers**. This resource consists of people's connections and **networks**. Thus there is a tension between the approach that views social capital as a form of *private* capital that exploits an individual's social connections and acquaintances to promote self-interest and the approach that views it as a form of *collective* or shared capital that advances collective interests and well-being. Both of these meanings link social capital to the Chinese concept of 'guanxi' that is usually translated as 'strong personal relationships'.

Leading exponents of social capital theory have been James Coleman,[2] who viewed it as a resource facilitating individual or collective action, Nahapiet and Ghoshal,[3] who examined how it can lead to competitive advantage for organizations, and, maybe most importantly, Robert Putnam,[4] who has viewed it as the central bulwark for maintaining democracy. Whether social capital is a value-neutral term or a normative one describing a desired state of

---

[1] See e.g. 1984; 1993. [2] Coleman, 1988. [3] Nahapiet and Ghoshal, 1998. [4] Putnam, 1995; 2000; 2002.

affairs is strongly contested, but the term's adoption by the World Bank has offered ammunition to those who view it as an ideologically laden and theoretically barren concept that represents an attempt by economics to colonize the discourses of other social sciences.[1]

Capitalism

Capitalism is a system of production dominated by **market** transactions, in which products and services as well as labour are exchanged as commodities for money, and by the profit motive and capital accumulation, whereby people seek to maximize monetary gain from such transactions. State socialism, or communism, challenged capitalism as a viable alternative for a large part of the twentieth century, but the collapse of Soviet economies marked the end of this challenge. Capitalism as an economic system succeeded feudalism, and has been characterized by a calculated, methodical, and carefully accounted-for approach to capital accumulation. According to sociologist Max Weber,[2] the rise of capitalism coincided with the emergence of the Protestant ethic, a set of values, initially religious, which included hard work, self-reliance, devaluation of sensuous pleasure, and a subordination of passions and **emotions** to **rationality**. Capitalism has gradually expanded to colonize every corner of the globe (see **globalization**) and most spheres of economic and social activity. Thus, while looking after your children, cooking for your family, and doing housework are domestic work activities, employing paid child minders and house cleaners and purchasing take-away food brings capitalism into the domestic sphere.

While capitalism is, in the first place, an economic system, it pervades most political, cultural, and social institutions and relations. Karl Marx,[3] one of the most astute analysts and sophisticated critics of capitalism, viewed it as the basis of modern society, a society in which capitalists, the owners of the means of production (capital, land, know-how), dominate the working **class**, who must sell their labour power in order to ensure their survival and that of their families. This domination is not only economic, but also political and cultural, since the predominant political institutions and cultural ideas of capitalism are those aimed at perpetuating and bolstering the power of the capitalist class. Marx argued that the working class would eventually overthrow this domination and that capitalism would be replaced by socialism, a system that abolishes private property and leads to the withering away of the state.

Some organizations (e.g. armies, the Catholic Church) have existed long before capitalism and some capitalist transactions take place outside the world of organizations (e.g. small-scale independent tradespeople and stall keepers). Yet organizations, and especially profit-making ones, are major **institutions** of capitalism. Corporations dominate international economic activity, many of them having turnovers in excess of the gross national products of entire countries. Other types of organizations, including international bodies, government agencies, **trade unions**, charities, and consumer groups, have also grown to great size, in terms of membership and control of resources.

Under capitalism, tremendous economic growth has been achieved, often at the cost of social, psychological, and environmental devastation. Yet, over the centuries, capitalism has proven a remarkably robust and flexible economic system, able to withstand the deep contradictions it creates. These include immense social and economic inequalities, international rivalries, and constant changes in the lifestyles and values of communities and groups. To what extent then can we talk of a unified capitalist system in spite of the changes that it has undergone over its long history? Scholars disagree on this point. Marxist and post-Marxist

---

[1] Fine, 2001.   [2] Weber, 1958.   [3] Marx, 1867/1967.

theorists emphasize the continuity of capitalism, its enduring emphasis on the profit motive and commodity exchange, along with the inequalities, oppression, and exploitation it breeds, in and out of organizations. Others, however, notably **postmodern** scholars, have argued that we have now moved into a new social and economic phase of history. Outstanding features of this, distinguishing it from capitalism proper, include the increasing importance of consumption and **consumerism**, the revolution in communication and **information technologies**, the gradual eclipsing of the manufacturing sector by the new services and information sectors, and the replacement of **bureaucratic** organizations by new types, such as **network** and **virtual organizations**.

• See also *class, consumerism, modernism and modernity*

Career

The word career carries an unexpected complexity. This can be glimpsed in its etymology, which encompasses both a vehicle—the carriage—and the road or carriageway upon which the vehicle travels (Latin *carrus* = road, wheeled vehicle). When applied to human activity this dual meaning appears, in social science terms, as individual **action** and social **structure**. Career may then be viewed as either or both—a set of **choices** which constitute a trajectory or journey; and the structure of positions or activities, the rungs on the ladder, through or up which the individual must travel. In both versions there is a sense of career as an orderly and comprehensible progression. However, a different sense of career is invoked when we speak of something proceeding in an uncontrolled manner: a careering or runaway horse, for example. All of these meanings of career are spatial—a movement between places—whereas all of the social science and everyday meanings of career are temporal—

a movement over time. Therefore we should recognize that in most of its contemporary uses, 'career' is a metaphorical term.

Although careers are normally associated with paid work, within social science one of the most influential usages of the term has been sociologist and criminologist Howard Becker's notion of the 'deviant career'.[1] Here the progression is from relatively minor acts of delinquency through to full-blown criminality, and the connotation is indeed that of an escalation or an uncontrolled journey. A similar meaning is often found in public policy discussions of drug taking, where it is commonly claimed that an early use of soft drugs such as cannabis will lead inexorably to hard drugs such as heroin.

Within the study of work and organizations, the concept of career can be traced to the foundational writings of Max Weber on ideal-type **bureaucracy**. Here, a central aspect of the definition of bureaucratic organization is the existence of a career structure of ascending offices, each with defined responsibilities, through which the bureaucrat may pass on the basis of qualifications and experience over a lifetime of paid employment. This is a version of the structural meaning of career, the carriage-road, which defines the direction of travel an individual may take. To the extent that bureaucracy is conceived of as an impersonal undertaking, occupancy of an office is analogous to occupying a particular space on the road. Something of this is conveyed when career is used, in a now rather archaic sense, to draw a distinction between the professional and the amateur office holder: for example, a 'career soldier' or 'career diplomat' is one who dedicates a life to military or diplomatic service, in contrast to an irregular or conscripted person doing the same job.

The eclipse of bureaucracy in contemporary Western society may in some respects be more rhetorical than real, but the disruption of lifetime careers within a single organization is one of the more empirically defensible claims of the

---

[1] Becker, 1964.

'end of bureaucracy' thesis. It has heralded the notion of the 'portfolio career', a term often associated with the management writer Charles Handy.[1] A portfolio career consists of a series of jobs, perhaps concurrent, within a variety of organizations. Here the accent is much more upon individual action—the carriage, rather than the road, so to speak.

The view of career as an individual **achievement** highlights its relation to **identity** and its ability to infuse people's work experiences with meaning. Of course, it would be naive to think that the structures of a bureaucratic career are not also important to the identity of individual office holders. But the portfolio career places a particular emphasis on the active, self-making individual as responsible for his or her career. The sociologist Richard Sennett is one of those who has discussed the immense insecurity of identity generated by the collapse of traditional employment structures.[2] Clearly employment careers are only an important source of identity and meaning in societies which place a premium on employed work, pointing to the enmeshment of career with the structures of **globalized** capitalism. To tie identity so closely to employment career would be almost unthinkable within other social and cultural contexts, and although no significant published Marxist account of careers exists, presumably such an account would proceed in this way.

By contrast, the individualizing effects of career have been seized on by some **poststructuralist** commentators on organizations, such as Valerie Fournier,[3] to suggest that this is an example of a disciplinary technology through which the **self** is constituted as a project to be managed. Such an analysis is underscored by the commonplace practice of the *curriculum vitae*. Significantly, the word 'curriculum' (Latin: *curriculum* = course, race-chariot) shares an almost identical double etymology with 'career' (both have the same ultimate root in Latin: *currere* = run), whilst the word 'vitae' (= life) draws atten-

tion to the identity possibilities of the CV: the course of one's life. Post-structuralists see this as an instance of Michel Foucault's insight into the way that apparently mundane practices can have great significance in terms of defining and disciplining individuals.

One way to make sense of this insight is to compare it with the more traditional social science conception of the deviant career. The latter is essentially an analytical construct, a concept by social scientists to describe the journey of their research subjects into deviance. It would not be a term used by those subjects in their self-descriptions (it is difficult to envisage 'career criminals' expressing themselves via a CV). Yet within the workplace people readily self-describe in terms of career and textualize this by use of a CV. Thus career in the latter case is self-proclaimed whilst in the former case it is other-ascribed. Perhaps it is no coincidence, then, that the organizational career is represented as an orderly and meaningful progression whilst the deviant career is implied to be an out of control escalation.

Career is a concept which had virtually no resonance for most people in the nineteenth century; today it has become a routine way of describing our lives. It is the kind of word which normally passes unnoticed yet, when examined, is of profound significance for the way we, at least in the West, and increasingly throughout the world, live and make sense of living.

CHRIS GREY, UNIVERSITY OF WARWICK

Case study

A research and teaching approach which investigates in depth a single case (a single organization, a single individual, or even a single incident) or a small number of cases, rather than seeking to make comparisons across a sample or a population of many similar units or cases. Case studies have been widely used in medicine,

---

[1] 1991; 1994.   [2] Sennett, 1998.   [3] 1997; 1998.

psychology, and psychoanalysis where the development of illness and the consequences of therapeutic interventions are carefully scrutinized. More recently, case studies have been used in organizational theory, both for research and for teaching. The study of a single company in great detail as a way of unravelling its internal political, cultural, and other processes is demonstrated by Pettigrew's study of ICI,[1] Leidner's study of a fast food chain,[2] and Kunda's study of a high-tech engineering company.[3] The identity of the case is frequently concealed as part of a confidentiality agreement. The Harvard Business School has pioneered the case study approach as a teaching method, where individual situations facing particular individuals or organizations are analysed as a way of developing the students' ability to understand theory while applying it to concrete situations. These case studies are often based on real organizations but fictional elements are introduced for narrative or pedagogic reasons.

An advantage of the case study approach is the detail in which the case may be observed and the depth in which they can be analysed. They can reveal processes that are only apparent if a very close study is carried out. An obvious drawback of using case studies is generalizability. Observing, for instance, the management of change in one organization or the onset of senility in one person does not necessarily reveal how these phenomena may occur across a population or in other particular cases. All the same, at the level of theory one may be able to generalize from a single case: as Watson has argued,[4] as long as one applies a clear set of analytical principles or theoretical assumptions to different settings, one can generalize about the basic processual factors which are likely to come into play across these settings.[5] Certain cases may be held to be typical or prototypical of a wide range of instances; their analysis may then be very useful. Alternatively, a case study may be 'critical' in the sense that it affords a unique opportunity

to study a phenomenon which would otherwise be difficult or impossible to study. Such 'one-offs' were prompted, for example, by the reunification of Germany or the transition of state socialist economies to capitalist ones. Most organizational researchers tend to focus not on single cases but on a small number, comparing them and contrasting them. In this way they identify different ways in which a particular process or phenomenon may unfold or fail to take place. Alternatively, they use case studies to generate hypotheses which are later tested on a wider population.

A disadvantage of case studies when used for teaching is that they often present an oversimplified account of a complex reality. The messy **complexity** of everyday life can be at odds with the reduction which is necessary even for a detailed case study. Thus students are given the illusion of a realistic form of learning and may only discover later that it was not as realistic as was claimed.

• See also *ethnographic approaches*

Change

We believe we live in times of unparalleled change. Change is a dominant rhetoric of politicians of every political hue, even if our faith in large-scale reshaping of society through political interventions has waned. But we are not the first era to believe that they live in times of dramatic change. We like to think that technological change has never been so rapid but earlier periods may have just as strong a claim. Consider the dramatic technological change that took place around a hundred years ago: the internal combustion engine (1885), the direct-dial telephone (1889), radio (1893–1901), moving film (1891–5), manned flight (1903), television (1923), rocket propulsion (1914–26). By contrast, today most technological change consists

---

[1] Pettigrew, 1985.   [2] Leidner, 1991.   [3] Kunda, 1992.   [4] Watson, 2001.   [5] See also Yin, 2003.

of surface phenomena or incremental **innovations** as turbo-capitalism leads to ever shorter product life cycles.

Interest in change goes back to the ancient Greeks. Heraclitus maintained that all things are in a constant state of flux. But Socrates argued that, if knowledge or thought is to have an object, then some things must persist. 'Nor can we reasonably say, Cratylus, that there is knowledge at all, if everything is in a state of transition and there is nothing abiding; for knowledge too cannot continue to be knowledge unless continuing always to abide and exist. But if the very nature of knowledge changes, at the time when the change occurs there will be no knowledge.'[1] Plato's doctrine of forms sought to provide such stable, knowledgeable standards of value. 'Being' must coexist with 'becoming' for knowledge to be at all possible and **language** is an attempt to use words to 'fix' the flux. So 'organization' is an attempt to fix the flux of the process of 'organizing'. Both organizing and organization are used in ways that suggest the possibility of stability as well as of change.

Theorists of organization have been acutely preoccupied by change. Indeed, the perspective that social change is now unparalleled prompts the view that organizations must constantly change in order to survive and prosper. Thus change is the most pervasive and most written about aspect of organizations. One study counted the number of articles on change and development at over 1 million even ten years ago,[2] and the flood has continued. Yet in spite of the scholarship that has been generated by change, most organizational change attempts end in failure. According to one estimate only a third of all change initiatives lead to any success at all.[3]

Why then do organizational change initiatives fail? One reason is underestimating the extent to which people need some stability and order in their lives. Change, whether advocated by politicians or business leaders, is seen as a 'good'

thing' and those who **resist** it are deemed to be standing in the way of progress. Yet routine, stability, and order are important to most people's lives. Indeed for many political philosophers and sociologists from Thomas Hobbes on, order was seen as an essential prerequisite for the formation of civil society, let alone for organizations. Without order, social practices cannot be reproduced.

To appreciate this, we can reflect on the stress we experience on entering a new organization, as employees, students, or even customers, before 'we learn our way around'. A great deal of learning takes place during this early period—new people, new layouts, new rules, new timetables, and so forth. What we are doing in these early days is learning the **structure** of the organization. As our learning develops, our actions and our interactions with others become regularized, routinized, predictable. They gradually come to appear 'natural'; they become tacit. Now imagine how difficult it would be if every day this structure was recast into something new, with different timetables, different peers, in different settings with a different sets of expectations. Imagine the complete absence of any structure, if this recasting took place every few seconds. So structure and routine are essential. Although there is much talk of 'managing change', a degree of persistence, a stability which leads to routine in human affairs, is also essential. Indeed, sociologist Richard Sennett has argued that constant calls for flexibility and the short-term nature of contemporary **work** leads to a 'corrosion of character'.[4]

There is a second reason why many change initiatives fail. This lies in the hubris of business leaders—and politicians on the wider stage—who believe that it is both possible and desirable to introduce change, and that, once introduced, change can be **controlled**. Debates over the possibility of controlling change go to the heart of different perspectives that scholars of organizational life and work adopt. Those who

---

[1] Plato, 2004.   [2] Van De Ven and Poole, 1995.   [3] Beer and Nohria, 2000, p. 2.   [4] Sennett, 1998.

believe in the possibility of predicting and controlling human **action** largely draw on the positivist tradition and make parallels with the success of the natural sciences in predicting and controlling natural phenomena. Those who embrace **social construction** or interpretativist approaches, on the other hand, argue that human action stems from the meanings given by actors in different contexts; it is impossible to predict accurately how a given situation will be interpreted by different actors. What is intended as a gift may be received as an insult in some instances. Human action often has unpredictable consequences. In this way, change initiatives may be interpreted and acted upon in very different ways from those envisaged by their originators.

We can now map some of the core theories of organizational change, depending on their views of managers' ability to implement and control change. At one extreme lie theories such as Theory E,[1] which believe control is both possible and desirable and change should be directed. At the other extreme lie complexity and chaos theories,[2] which argue that managers are powerless to control the change process. Other approaches fall in between. Theory O advocates that managers build commitment and so change can only be shaped rather than directed.[3] This is also a line taken by authors studying cultural change in organizations.[4] Theorists of transformative **leadership** see managers' role as one of leading through interpreting or reinterpreting the world,[5] while Pettigrew's processual/emergent model approaches change more as a matter of navigating than controlling.[6]

In conclusion, when confronted with the word 'change' it might be helpful to ask the following:

1. Is the change justified in terms of the disruption to stability and order that will result?

2. Is the change likely to succeed given the difficulties intrinsic to predicting and regulating the practices of others?

3. Is this call for change justified? Recall that there is a choice about whether we describe the world in a language of change or stability. Are those who call for change trying to instil in others a bogus meaning and sense of purpose? Do we really live in a time of accelerating change or is the call for change merely making a contribution towards it?

• See also *culture, leadership, structure*

MICHAEL BROCKLEHURST, IMPERIAL COLLEGE LONDON

Charisma

Charisma is a term brought into social theory by German sociologist Max Weber to capture the attraction and personal magnetism exercised by some leaders over their followers. Charismatic leaders command tremendous loyalty and respect and are capable of unleashing powerful forces of social and personal transformation. Weber's theory of charisma belongs to a long-standing tradition sometimes known as the 'great man' theory of **leadership**. Charismatic leaders emerge in moments of crisis and turbulence and establish themselves through the force of their personality. 'The natural leaders in distress have been holders of specific gifts of the body and spirit; and these gifts have been believed to be supernatural, not accessible to everybody.'[7]

Unlike impersonal bureaucratic **authority**, the authority of charismatic leaders is directly linked to their **personality** and demands total faith. 'Charisma knows only inner determination and inner restraint. The holder of charisma seizes the task that is adequate for him and demands obedience and a following by virtue of his

---

[1] Beer and Nohria, 2000.   [2] Stacey, 1992; 1995.   [3] Beer and Nohria, 2000.   [4] Ogbonna and Harris, 2002.   [5] Tichy and Devanna, 1986.   [6] Pettigrew, Woodman, and Cameron, 2001.   [7] Weber, 1946, p. 245.

mission. His success determines whether he finds them. His charismatic claim breaks down if his mission is not recognized by those to whom he feels he has been sent. If they recognize him, he is their master—so long as he knows how to maintain recognition through "proving" himself."[1] Charisma was seen by Weber as a relation, a quality projected by followers onto a leader, rather than objective qualities of the leader.

Charismatic leaders are not necessarily good or virtuous. They can liberate their followers or lead them to ruination. Many of them meet with violent ends, when their followers become disappointed and turn against them. Charisma brings too many upheavals, in Weber's view, to last. It also wears out if followers come into excessive contact with their leaders. It is best preserved if the leader meets a heroic and premature death; it then becomes gradually 'routinized', as the successors of the charismatic leader seek to consolidate their **power** by appealing to his or her legacy and basing their authority on the tradition that he or she is meant to have founded.

Over the years, the concept of charisma has been diluted as it has become more widely used. Initially reserved by Weber for extraordinary figures, like Moses, Joan of Arc, or Hitler, it is now regularly used in connection with any leader who is able to inspire and rouse their followers in any area of life, including business, politics, sport, and showbusiness. Pop stars and even television celebrities are now said to have charisma. Charisma could then be said to have become routinized, but not in the way envisaged by Weber.

A theorist who sought to develop Weber's insight into charismatic leadership was the psychoanalyst Heinz Kohut.[2] Following Freud, Kohut argued that powerful leaders awaken in their followers **feelings** and **fantasies** that they first experienced in early life in relation to their mother and father. To the little and vulnera-

ble child, mother and father appear as towering symbolic figures (sometimes referred to as 'primal mother' and 'primal father'), becoming the objects of powerful fantasies and emotions. Kohut argued that leaders based on a mother figure can be referred to as *charismatic* and those based on the father figure as *messianic*.

The two types of leaders form very different types of relations with their followers. Charismatic are perceived as uniquely kind, smart, and talented. Everything that they do or say appears to be fascinating, inspired, and magnificent. They seem to have an aura around them, a field of energy that all those who enter experience as hugely invigorating. In their presence, their followers feel smarter and more talented, inspired, and appreciated. Caring is an especially important quality of these leaders, since they are seen as setting great store by each and every one of their followers. Christ, in his capacity as good shepherd, is the archetype of such an all-caring, all-loving leader.

Messianic leaders are very demanding, very critical, and very confrontational. They place little store in maintaining a happy atmosphere and are blind to the sensitivities of their followers. And yet, precisely because they can make each person forget their narrow self-interests, they are capable of stirring them into great **achievements.** Followers of messianic leaders feel meek and sometimes even paralysed in the presence of their leaders. Such leaders inspire fear and awe, making their followers feel worthless and insignificant. Even so, such leaders can generate tremendous commitment, unleashing qualities of dedication, sacrifice, and heroism in their followers. Their grip on their followers rests on an unshakeable conviction that, in spite of sacrifices and hardships, they can get them to the promised land and deliver them from their troubles.

• See also *authority, followership, leadership*

---

[1] Ibid. 246.   [2] Kohut, 1971; 1976.

Choice

Choice is a ubiquitous feature of modern life. People make choices the whole time, about what jobs to apply for, about where to go on holidays, about who to side with in an argument, about whether to buy a new machine, about the price to charge for their goods, and so on. Choice appears to be everywhere. Many life issues that, in earlier societies, were predetermined by social factors, such as who to marry, what career to pursue, what sexual identity to adopt, and so forth, have now come under the remit of free choice. Choice is also deemed to be a good thing; it is a **value**. It is the foundation stone of contemporary freedom, summed up in the consumer's freedom to choose what he or she buys without having to offer any explanations.[1] Choices, however, are not always open; nor does the appearance of choice always indicate the existence of serious alternatives. Some choices may look more open from the outside than the inside. Inside the hurly-burly of social and organizational life, many of our **actions** appear not to have the character of choice. An outsider may see choices ('You could leave your job,' 'You could retrain and start a new career,' etc.) where an insider sees none. Alternatively, an outsider may see compulsion where an insider sees choice ('I *choose* to work sixteen hours per day'). Choice is linked with agency. People who are in control of their own destiny are expected to make choices whereas those who have no choices are seen as failures, receiving charity and having others make choices on their behalf. This puts pressure on employees to see themselves as having choices; otherwise they are owning up to powerlessness.

It is well known that people cannot choose from an infinite variety of alternatives. Chinese restaurants realized that huge menus raise the anxiety levels of many of their customers and sensibly offered set menus as a way of short-circuiting some of this. The concept of *bounded*

rationality has been used to explain how most choices are made. An individual narrows the range of alternatives by excluding various possibilities from the start and then chooses the first alternative that appears to be 'good enough', a process that Herbert Simon described as 'satisficing' rather than optimizing.[2] While **rationality** plays an important part in some choices, others appear to be governed by emotional factors, by **desire**. Many people may acknowledge that a particular individual offers great prospects as a marriage partner (handsome, kind, and rich) and yet follow the dictates of their heart and marry someone who appears to promise excitement, passion, and risk.

A great deal of research has focused on consumer choice; how do people come to choose one product rather than another? This is clearly crucial for any competitive business and is particularly relevant for marketing and **advertising**. There is also much discussion of **strategic** choice, how, in other words, the ruling blocs or coalitions in an organization make choices about the direction in which they wish to steer it. How are alternatives formulated and how are they evaluated? There is also much interest in how **group** choices may differ from individual choices and the extent to which the perception of risk shapes group decision. A particularly intriguing account of how people in organizations make decisions is known as the 'garbage can' model of choice. According to this unexpectedly illuminating idea 'an organization is a collection of *choices looking for problems*, issues and feelings looking for decision situations in which they might be aired, solutions looking for issues to which they might be the answer, and decision-makers looking for work'.[3] Choice, in this model, is not the careful and rational process of selection among alternatives but rather part of an anarchic and almost random process whereby ideas or measures assume the character of choices when they collide with socially constructed problems.

---

[1] Bauman, 1988.   [2] Simon, 1957.   [3] Cohen, March, and Olsen, 1972, p. 2, emphasis added.

Choice was not always seen as an unqualified blessing. Existential theorists from Kierkegaard onward viewed choice as generating **anxiety**. Sartre's concept of 'mauvaise foi' (bad faith) is not so much a state of inauthenticity as a deliberate denial of choices in order to avoid the anxiety that accompanies them.[1] Excessive freedom can be overwhelming. But sometimes, simple choices in conditions of unfreedom can be even more oppressive. In the novel and film *Sophie's Choice*,[2] a mother is sadistically forced by a Nazi officer to choose which of her two children will be murdered. The decision haunts the rest of her life. Likewise, in the novel *Roots*,[3] the recaptured slave Kunta Kinte is allowed to choose what form of dreadful mutilation he will suffer. Such choices have more of the character of humiliation. But life is full of choices that call for painful and even tragic **decisions**. In organizations, managers and employees may be faced with two alternatives both of which are unpleasant, but are forced to choose between them. An employee of a pharmaceutical company might be faced with the choice as to whether to blow the whistle on false research results or collude with the wrongdoing. Far from being an unalloyed value, therefore, choice must be approached in a careful and critical manner to identify whether it is free or not, whether it is enjoyable or not, whether it is meaningful or not, and, above all, whether it is real or not.

• See also *consumers, decisions and decision making*

Class

Class is a foundational concept in sociology and, especially, in the theory of social stratification. Classes are large assemblies of people who share economic interests by virtue of their position in the production process and who may or may not be conscious of themselves as belonging together. Traditionally, **capitalism** has been dominated by two large social classes, the capitalists who own the means of production and live off the profits from their investments, and the working class (or proletariat) who sell their labour power in order to earn their living. Other social classes include landowners and landless peasants, independent shopkeepers and tradesmen (the 'petty bourgeoisie'), an 'underclass' or 'lumpenproletariat' (which includes homeless people, the chronically unemployed, the sick, the criminal sections, and people subsisting on the margins of society). Classes may themselves be subdivided into fractions: thus the working class may include both manual and non-manual workers, skilled and unskilled ones; the bourgeoisie may include both 'old money' and the nouveaux riches.

Academic discussions of social classes are extensive and include questions of the changing constitution and consciousness of social classes, the impact of alternative stratification principles (such as **status** and **power, gender, race,** and sexual preference) and the extent to which class is an element of individual and group **identities**. Currently, the most important debates on class focus on whether it continues to be an important factor of social stratification or whether it has been supplanted by other factors, such as consumption and lifestyles, national, professional, organizational, and other allegiances. In the past, class was meant to colour or even determine an individual's beliefs and values, political behaviour, educational achievement, choice of job and partner, and so forth. This is no longer so pronounced as social mobility generates movement across class boundaries and, possibly, as class itself becomes less and less relevant in **postmodernity.** In particular, it is argued that working class is now more a self-perception or even description of a lifestyle, and a fading one at that, rather than a social category of economic position. Class is seen as giving way to numerous groups and communities, sometimes referred to as 'neo-tribes',[4] characterized

---

[1] Sartre, 1956.   [2] Styron, 1979.   [3] Haley, 1976.   [4] Maffesoli, 1995.

by shared lifestyles and tastes, even if their economic positions are different. Anderson has argued influentially that instead of identifying with their social class, people increasingly form identities out of identification with *imagined communities*, groups that only exist in their own minds, such as 'Volvo drivers' or 'Guardian readers'.[1]

One enduring problem concerns the class position of managers. These were traditionally seen as a class fraction adjunct to the bourgeoisie and representing its interests. The emergence of large-scale organizations, however, led to theories of 'divorce of ownership from control',[2] which viewed managers as an independent social class with distinct social and economic interests from those of the capitalists. These theories have received new currency from views of managers as holders of exclusive **professional skills** and expertise which place them above the **controls** that owners are able to exercise. Undoubtedly, in one way managers are employees and, therefore, workers; like workers, they have to endure the vagaries of the labour markets, changes in employment trends, and **downsizing**. On the other hand, however, they enjoy considerable control and autonomy (some more than others) and their position in the process of production is often dominant rather than subordinate.

Class has maintained a persistent, if never dominant, part in organizational studies. It is particularly prominent in **Labour Process Theory** and **Critical Management Studies**, both of which place much emphasis on power relations and **conflict**. Managers are usually seen as agents of control, seeking to maximize profits for the firm. Class is also an important feature of ethnographic studies of particularly vulnerable and exposed groups of employees, who view themselves as victims of their class position in society.[3] All the same, it would be fair to say that currently class is not employed nearly as frequently in analysing social and cultural phenomena as it used to be. It has been supplanted by other concepts which include gender, race, tastes, choice, culture, values, identity, and consumption.

• See also *capitalism, power, status*

Cognition

Cognition is a term used to describe various psychological processes that involve the collection, processing, testing, organization, and use of **knowledge**. These include perception, memory, **learning**, **decision making**, and **sensemaking**. Cognition has long been seen in juxtaposition to processes linked to **emotion** and **desire** and, for a period, its currency had declined. This is in contrast to its current popularity, which is due to two factors—first, and most importantly, the far-reaching impact of computers on simulating the way the human mind may work and, secondly, more recently, strong evidence that cognition and emotion, far from representing opposite tendencies of the mind, are complementary functions residing in the **body**. Since the 1960s, cognitive psychology has emerged as one of the dominant traditions in psychology and cognitive therapy has become one, today's most popular forms of psychotherapy.

A defining early contribution in cognitive psychology was Donald Broadbent's *Perception and Communication*,[4] which put forward an information-processing model of cognition. Mental processes were studied as software running on a computer that is the human brain. According to this model, the brain receives different types of inputs that it processes, converts, and organizes, leading to certain outputs. **Language** is a key feature of cognitive processes, not merely used to represent the world but also to constitute it in particular ways. One particularly influential theory from this perspective is Festinger's theory of *cognitive dissonance*.[5]

---

[1] Anderson, 1983.   [2] Berle and Means, 1933; Burnham, 1945; Galbraith, 1967.   [3] Terkel, 1985.   [4] Broadbent, 1958.   [5] Festinger, 1962.

According to this, people strive to minimize incongruities between their **actions** and their beliefs, more often than not by modifying their beliefs. Thus, a smoker may rationalize his or her habit by discounting medical evidence of its harmful effects. Another important contribution from this perspective has been the theory of *escalation of commitment*, how, in other words, once a certain course of action has been adopted there is a tendency to commit ever-increasing resources to it, even when there is evidence that it is not leading to the desired results.[1] Both of these theories have had many organizational applications and have proved of value in explaining why organizations and their actors may appear to act in highly irrational ways.

A large part of cognitive psychology developed using **methodologies** and techniques broadly consistent with those used in the natural sciences—observations, measurements, experiments, and so forth.[2] It has generally resisted the use of interpretative methods for analysing human thoughts and feelings. More recently, however, a growing trend among some scholars studying cognitive processes has been to move away from the information-processing model towards other models. Humans, unlike computers, it is argued, do not process large amounts of **information** in a highly repetitive manner but have distinct abilities of filtering out irrelevant information as 'noise' and of identifying various patterns or schemata which enable novel situations to be analysed by analogy to previous **experiences**. Interpretation, pattern recognition, filtering, and sensemaking are, according to this view, essential qualities of human cognition, placing it on a very different level from that of 'intelligent machines'. 'From the moment I set my eyes on Joyce, I knew that she was the person who would inject new ideas to our organization' may seem like a wild intuitive statement, yet the person making it may have identified, consciously or unconsciously,

in Joyce the qualities that she or he associates with creative, dynamic, and innovative people. Searching for signs and interpreting them is seen as a fundamental quality of cognition.

Another emerging set of insights on human cognition is that, unlike the processes taking place inside computers, what people know about the world is closely related to how they feel about it and how they act in relation to it. People often get a sense of what a particular situation means or how it may be approached through their **actions**, i.e. by intervening and experimenting with it. It is in this connection that **bricolage**, tinkering, and improvising are vital dimensions of human cognition in ways that could not be meaningfully applied to computers. People also learn from each other—but again, unlike computers, the sharing of knowledge does not mean the passive downloading of a set of ideas (or data) from one mind to another. Rather, in appropriating someone else's knowledge, we recreate it and reformat it, discovering new possibilities and new nuances. Once again, bricolage is a helpful term, describing how we may borrow each other's recipes and ideas in an active, interventionist manner rather than passively copying them onto our mental hard disks.

No single paradigm or model of cognition has emerged to date to challenge the information-processing one, but various authors have made considerable contributions. Outstanding among them are Michael Polanyi's distinction between tacit and explicit knowledge,[3] Mary Douglas's sophisticated account of the pattern-making and pattern-identifying abilities of the mind,[4] Karl Weick's lifetime theorizing on sensemaking,[5] Jerome Bruner's pioneering work on narrative construction of reality,[6] and Antonio Damasio's decisive demonstration of the interconnectedness between cognitive and emotional processes.[7] Numerous authors have developed these lines of argument, from which human cognition emerges as a dynamic, complex,

---

[1] Brockner, 1992; Staw and Ross, 1987.   [2] See Neisser, 1967.   [3] Polanyi, 1964.   [4] Douglas, 1966/2002.   [5] Weick, 1995.
[6] Bruner, 1986; 1991.   [7] Damasio, 1994.

and emotion-rich domain full of magnificent possibilities and, correspondingly, ruinous blinkeredness.[1]

• See also *epistemology, knowledge*

Communication

'Communication' is a protean term that denotes a field of study and a set of empirical phenomena. While communication has been studied since antiquity, its popularity surged in the twentieth century. Academic interest in communication began in the United States after the Second World War when persuasion and group **decision making** became central concerns. Concurrently, organizational communication emerged out of military, industry, and academic interest in training supervisors in human relations skills.[2] As a sub-discipline of the field of communication studies, organizational communication has since evolved from a focus on managerial interests to a multi-perspective field with an interdisciplinary identity that is eclectic in its approach to theories, methods, and research.[3] Research topics include communication networks and roles; information processing and group decision making; leadership; organizational climate and culture; power and politics; organizational discourse; organizational identity and image; complex adaptive systems; and communication technologies, among others. Organizational communication scholars often join with media scholars, rhetoricians, social psychologists, and discourse analysts to form communication studies programmes worldwide.

As a set of empirical phenomena, communication may be viewed as a primary or a secondary process. When viewed as a secondary process, communication is one of different phenomena that take place 'inside' organizations and between organizations and their environment. This is how communication is approached by most commentators outside the field of communication studies itself. It is then viewed as one of many types of processes or an outcome of an inner motor of traits, states, **emotions**, and cognitive processing styles that cause particular messages or behaviours to be produced. Those outside the field of communication are more likely to view communication as a simple act of transmission, much as in the classic Shannon and Weaver 'Sender → Message → Receiver' model,[4] or the conduit metaphor.[5] As such, the cultural currency of a transmissional view of communication may bolster the authority of technical experts, as against meaning-centred views of communication that are often associated with values like freedom, tolerance, and democracy.[6] These latter views approach communication as a primary process, one through which organizations themselves become constituted.

As a primary social process, communication is viewed as a more complex process—more than a simple act of transmission—because **meaning** is one of the most essential components of human communication. Such meaning-centred approaches to communication draw from the 'linguistic turn' in the social sciences in which **language** is the means through which reality is constituted rather than merely reflected. In varying degrees, researchers are committed to: (a) relational rather than individual units of analyses, signalling co-defined and (potentially) contested meaning formations; (b) process rather than static forms of human systems, often emphasizing the organizing potential of language and the sequential and temporal form of messages; (c) a multi-layered and dynamic view of context in which individual, group, organizational, and socio-historical influences are reflexively interrelated at given moments in time; (d) agency amidst constraint, due to the brute facts of a physical world, science's putative objective procedures, and/or macro-social contexts

---

[1] See e.g. Boje, 2001; Chia, 1998; Czarniawska, 2004; Kearney, 2002; Polkinghorne, 1988; Tsoukas, 2005.   [2] Redding, 1985.
[3] Mumby, 2007.   [4] Shannon and Weaver, 1949.   [5] Axley, 1984.   [6] Craig, 1999.

of institutions and **power** relations; and (e) the operation of **discourse** on more than one level, including discourse as language and social interaction and discourse as systems of thought that supply linguistic resources to communicating actors.

The ontological status of organizations as communication phenomena becomes problematized when viewed from this perspective, which represents a historical breakthrough in changing positivist reifications of organizations.[1] However, debate rages over whether organizations are reducible to communicative constructions, over the role of material forces in relation to discourse, and over the processes through which communication constitutes organizations, including membership negotiation, self-structuring, activity coordination, and institutional positioning.[2] Nevertheless, communication perspectives in the twenty-first century are well positioned to explore alternative forms of organizing, especially those made possible by new **technologies**; the continued impact of discourses of difference (for example, **gender**, **race**, **class**, nationality, and so on) on member subjectivities and organizing processes; and the permeability of organizational **boundaries** between work and family and wider local and global communities.

• See also *advertising, conflict, information, mass media, meaning*

GAIL T. FAIRHURST, UNIVERSITY OF CINCINNATI

Community and community of practice

The term community has a long history in the social sciences. Following the work of Ferdinand Tönnies,[3] community (*Gemeinschaft*) is contrasted to society (*Gesellschaft*). The former is a feature of traditional cultures with strong emphasis on intimate and personal group bonds and solidarity; the latter is a feature of industrial and urban civilizations where people live mostly as unknowns amidst unknowns. In spite of the habitual use of the term 'local communities' by the media and the brief rise of 'communitarianism' in the 1990s,[4] it would be fair to say that community has been in decline in the social sciences. One exception is the term 'imagined community', coined by Benedict Anderson to describe today's nations 'because the members of even the smallest nation will never know most of their fellow-members, meet them, or even hear of them, yet in the minds of each lives the image of their communion';[5] the idea of imagined communities powerfully captures the quality of many of today's 'groups' such as BMW drivers, Louis Vuitton consumers, and *Financial Times* readers.[6]

Another increasingly popular use of community is in the term 'community of practice'. This describes different **groups** of people who share similar problems and have complementary skills and outlooks. They are mostly occupational groups, like airline managers, computer analysts, and academics, but they can also refer to people sharing hobbies or interests, like plane spotters or amateur gardeners. Wenger,[7] one of the early adopters of the term, argues that such communities have histories and develop over time; they often work together, but their members do not have a shared task or agenda; they are not accountable to anyone outside themselves; and they develop their own subcultures as their members learn from each other's experiences.

It is in connection to **knowledge** and **learning** that communities of practice has proven a useful concept.[8] Within such communities, the distinction between knowledge and **action** is diminished; knowledge becomes inscribed in **practices** that are not the property of any one individual. Moreover, a great deal of this knowledge is not scientific; it cannot be codified into generalizable

---

[1] Fairhurst and Putnam, 2004.   [2] McPhee and Zaug, 2000.   [3] Tönnies, 1887/1963.   [4] Etzioni, 1998; Heyning, 1999.   [5] Anderson, 1983, p. 6.   [6] Ibid.   [7] Wenger, 1998.   [8] Cook and Yanow, 1993.

laws and formulas. Instead, it assumes the form of narrative knowledge, which includes **stories**, recipes, and direct accounts of experience.[1] A great deal of this knowledge emerges through **bricolage** and is highly contextual.[2] Two further features of this knowledge are worth pointing out. First, because members of these communities share interests and concerns, they communicate on the same wavelength and use a shared **language**; in this way, they are able to screen out irrelevant **information** or noise and can exchange ideas and experiences in a highly efficient, quick and economical manner; thus, *some* communities of practice can be a breeding ground for rapid **innovation**.[3] The other important issue is collocation (being physically close together). While some communities of practice may operate on the internet, there are immense advantages in face-to-face exchanges. In some instances, like the rise of Silicon Valley, collocation proved the crucial factor—people's ability to communicate quickly and effectively in direct informal conversations, cutting out bureaucratic red tape and information overload. Where collocation is unrealistic or impossible, the getting together of communities of practice in conferences, symposia, workshops, and festivals is vitally important in maintaining the solidarity among their members and also in facilitating the exchange of knowledge.

One of the reasons for the widespread adoption of this term is that it appears to capture well the experiences of managers and consultants; both of these groups readily and somewhat uncritically adopt it to describe themselves. It may be that one of the functions of the Masters of Business Administration (MBA) degree is to enhance the formation of these communities. It could equally be, however, that communities of managers and consultants are more 'imagined' than real[4]—in this case, the transfer of knowledge and group learning would be of less importance than the maintenance of a group

solidarity that transcends other differences, such as those between private and public sector, men and women, large and small enterprise, and so forth.

The concept of communities of practice has proven very influential; yet some authors have criticized it on a number of grounds.[5] Maybe its most serious shortcoming, as it is currently used, is its tendency to obscure **power** issues surrounding the control and monopoly of knowledge in and out of organizations, presenting too cosy an image of knowledge as a resource that is amicably traded and shared. This was precisely what Foucault sought to avoid by proposing an indissoluble entity termed power/knowledge (see **knowledge** and **power**).

• See also ***nation and nationalism***

Competences (or competencies)

What does it take to be an effective manager? Or an effective coach? Or an effective teacher? According to Richard Boyatzis competences are fundamental characteristics of people that enable them to do a job effectively or even better.[6] These may include skills (like communicating well, driving cars, or being able to read financial statements) but also different personality traits (such as self-confidence or extroversion), behaviour characteristics (such as accent and tone of voice), and motivations (such as team player or **achievement** orientation). Others have taken a narrower view of competences, approaching them essentially as **skills** necessary for different jobs. In a pioneering work, Henry Mintzberg argued that management competencies fall into three broad categories, interpersonal, informational, and decisional.[7] More importantly, however, Mintzberg observed that much managerial work takes place in short bursts of activity and what we would today call 'multi-tasking'. Many managers must be able to

---

[1] Tsoukas, 1998a.   [2] Brown and Duguid, 1991; Lave and Wenger, 1991.   [3] Swan, Scarbrough, and Robertson, 2002.   [4] Anderson, 1983.   [5] See e.g. Handley et al., 2006; Roberts, 2006.   [6] Boyatzis, 1982.   [7] Mintzberg, 1973.

think on their feet, to keep several balls in the air simultaneously, and to be flexible in their response to different situations.

A great deal of research has gone into identifying managerial competences, in order to create programmes for developing them. Managers are regularly presented with 'research' that shows that *x* is the vital competence necessary for success. *x* may be emotional intelligence, team building, management of meaning, inspirational leadership, or many others that supplant the earlier ones. On the whole, research aimed at identifying a fixed set of management competencies has not been conclusive; unlike doctors or lawyers, it seems that managers require different types of competencies in different situations. Managers who perform competently or better in one organization may find themselves frustrated and ineffectual in a different one. Critics of the competencies approach argue that management is not one set of activities or roles but many different ones. It is also argued that effective managers may rely more on their ability to identify, make use of, and mix other people's competencies rather than their own. Finally, it is increasingly argued that 'mere competence' is not enough for success, which requires continuous learning, innovativeness, and genuine talent.

In addition to individual competencies, organizations are also said to have 'core competences'. A core competence is 'the collective learning in the organization, especially how to coordinate diverse production skills and integrate multiple streams of technologies...Core competence is also about the organization of work and the delivery of value'.[1] Organizations may be engaged in different types of business and activity, but they have a limited number of core competences; frequently, they are unaware of what their core competences actually are. These competences are not located in any one individual or group but they involve different forms of tacit knowledge, including recipes, routines, and assumptions. In the last twenty years, there has been an increasing emphasis on companies eschewing diversification and concentrating on the things that they can do well—in Peters and Waterman's memorable phrase, successful companies 'stick to the knitting'.[2] In contrast to individual competences, the concept of core competences has seen an increased popularity. This may coincide with the rise of the **resource-based theory** of the firm.

• See also *learning, knowledge, skill*

Competition

Competition is a form of contained **conflict**—conflict in which parties acknowledge certain rules and conditions, even if they do not always act in line with them. Competition can then be thought of as rule-bound **aggression**, or, better still, *sublimated aggression*, aggression which aims not to kill or destroy but to match and excel an opponent. This is what Nietzsche saw as the defining quality of ancient Greek culture, referred to as *agon* (which provides the etymological root for both 'antagonism' and 'agony'). It was the principle behind the Olympic Games and other sporting contests, but equally it drove every aspect of Greek life, individual and collective. Cities competed to have the most impressive public buildings, philosophers, orators, politicians, and poets all competed to outdo and outperform each other. To the winner glory, to the loser shame. Nietzsche saw Greek culture as the purest expression of the will to power, the unending struggle among them to surpass and excel each other in everything.[3]

Competition remains an important feature of our culture in many levels, political, sporting, artistic, but above all economic. **Capitalism** is an economic system built on market competition. **Markets** reward the innovative, the efficient, the

---

[1] Prahalad and Hamel, 1990, p. 81.   [2] Peters and Waterman, 1982.   [3] For a good account of Nietzsche's view of contest, see Kaufmann, 1968.

competitive, and discipline the inflexible, inefficient, and uncompetitive. As a principle that spawns creativity, originality, and hard work, competition is much admired by many economists and politicians. Free market enthusiasts argue that competition is a great system for matching supply and demand and for stimulating entrepreneurship and innovation. In recent years, advocates of competition have sought to enhance the performance of public-sector organizations, like hospitals, schools, and government departments, by introducing competition and market disciplines (see **New Public Management**). Critics, however, point out that competition creates a great deal of waste. If three competing designs are developed for a new product and only one is adopted, the effort and resources that went into the losing designs were wasted.

More importantly, however, competition creates winners and losers; some competitions create a lot of losers and very few winners. How do societies cope with all those losers? How do they support the weak, the uncompetitive, the gentle, the neurotic, and the depressed who are left by the wayside? And what about the cost of competition to the winners? The constant worry that their most recent triumph will be the last one, that it will trigger the envy and enmity of others, that it will be forgotten and overtaken by the victories of others? Competition among institutions like universities, banks, government agencies, and other organizations can often undermine social cohesion and solidarity, creating a perpetual principle of dissatisfaction and **anxiety**.

But where does competition come from? Following Darwin, some psychologists view competition as a natural characteristic of all life forms. Life is a continuous struggle for existence; the fit survive and prosper, the less fit lose out, diminish, and disappear. Social Darwinism, a doctrine that approached society as a terrain where people and social groups constantly compete for

survival, spawned many right-wing theories and has generally gone out of fashion. Evolutionary psychology, on the other hand, is currently popular and relies on the argument that many human characteristics, including memory, perception, emotion, sexuality, and language, are the results of natural selection. They are characteristics that over many generations conferred evolutionary advantage on humans, enabling them to compete and prevail against other forms of life. Psychoanalysis looks at most forms of competition as expressions of human aggression, itself a manifestation of a **death** instinct. In competition, as against naked conflict, the death instinct is controlled or sublimated in legitimate activities. Winning a contest, outperforming the competitors, excelling the rivals, all become permissible and even laudable pursuits. For this reason, political psychoanalyst David Levine has described competition as the 'natural playground of greed and envy'. International competitions such as sporting events, film festivals, and even the Nobel Prize awards can then be seen as ways of defusing potentially destructive antagonisms and legitimizing controlled aggression.

A different approach to the origins of competition is taken by other psychologists and sociologists who view it not as a general characteristic of all people or all forms of life but of specific societies. Chief among them was Karl Marx who emphatically denied that all humans are naturally greedy or competitive, arguing that these are features cultivated by **capitalism**. In a well-known passage from the 1844 Paris Manuscripts, Marx criticized political economy regarding competition as natural when it ought to account for it: 'Exchange itself appears to political economy as an accidental fact. The only wheels which political economy sets in motion are *greed*, and the *war of the greedy—competition*.'[1] The same point, that avariciousness and competitiveness are acquired characteristics rather than invariant features of human

---

[1] Marx, 1844/1972, p. 57.

nature, has been made by numerous other traditions in psychology, sociology, and even evolutionary biology centring around the idea of altruism, which Buddhism considered an essential part of human nature.

• See also *conflict*

Complexity and chaos theories

Complexity and chaos theories emerged in the natural sciences in the 1960s, drawing on the study of non-linear dynamic **systems**, such as the weather or the turbulent flow of fluids. These are situations where there is vital randomness and unpredictability; they are situations which defy domestication within linear mathematical equations. Since its beginnings, complexity theory has found applications in natural and biological sciences ranging from the study of volcanoes and earthquakes to the study of the heart and the brain. More recently, it has found some applications in human sciences, in demography, geography, and economics.[1] In the last fifteen years, complexity theory has started to penetrate organizational and management studies beyond the level of the fashionable cliché, generating some promising ideas.

Non-linear dynamic systems can operate in three types of states, stable, explosive, and complex (or chaotic). Non-linearity implies that a small disturbance may quickly escalate to 'runaway' or 'explosive' situations, in the manner of a vicious circle. The extinction or proliferation of species resulting from relatively small changes in their natural environment are examples of explosive collapse. In human affairs, it may be observed where a minor incident escalates to conflict of calamitous proportions, as when a comment made by the Director of the German Bundesbank in 1992 led to a run on sterling in the international money markets and its eventual devaluation.

One major innovation of complexity theory has been the identification of a third state, one which operates between the other two, combining positive and negative feedback, stability and instability. Under this state, described as chaotic, complex, or 'bounded instability', systems display some interesting qualities. First, self-similarity across scales, illustrated by Mandelbrot's work on fractals,[2] implies that as one 'zooms' in or out of a system, one encounters similar patterns. In organizations, one can imagine encountering the same patterns of authoritarian or paranoid leadership at the highest as well as at the lowest levels. A second property of complex systems is the unexpected consequences of small changes—in Lorenz's famous 'Butterfly effect', a butterfly flapping its wings in Peking today may cause a storm in New York in the future. Tiny differences in initial conditions lead to radically different outcomes for complex systems, just as two leaves blown by an autumn breeze may start from virtually the same position and end up miles apart. This accords complex systems two important characteristics: such systems are not time reversible, i.e. they do not return periodically to their original state, and, within them, the same cause results in different effects, i.e. a cause–effect link observed once cannot be repeated.[3] Complex systems are characterized by a vital unpredictability, making long-term prediction impossible, both in theory and in practice. This is one point to which complexity theory invariably returns— the total impossibility of long-term forecasting in spite of the possibility of modest short-term predictions.

A third property of complex systems is self-organization, a chance but not uncommon ability of complex systems to break out of a disorderly pattern into a spontaneous and unexpected order.[4] Self-organization does not mean that the system has lapsed from complex to stable equilibrium, since it is not achieved with the

---

[1] For a historical overview, see Gleick, 1987.   [2] Mandelbrot, 1982.   [3] Thietart and Forgues, 1995.   [4] Griffin, Shaw, and Stacey, 1998; Stacey, 1992; 1995.

help of damping feedback; instead, it generates what have been described as 'islands of order from the sea of chaos'. These islands are subject to the earlier two properties of complex systems: neither their scale nor their duration may be predicted; a butterfly flapping its wings may lead to their disappearance or reappearance.

Applications of complexity theory on organizations have emphasized the limited nature of managerial **control** in the absence of accurate, long-term forecasts, the precarious nature of order, the importance of self-organization (i.e. of control without anyone being in control), and the general hit-and-miss quality of most managerial interventions. Summarizing the implications of complexity theory for organizations, I have proposed that:

1. Most organizations operate in a chaotic environment, for which they are themselves partly responsible.
2. Many, if not the majority of, organizations may be studied as non-linear dynamic systems.
3. Organizations operating in conditions of both explosive or stable states are likely to become extinct, the former sooner, the latter later.
4. Most successful organizations operate in the area of bounded instability.
5. For these organizations, neither long-term planning nor central control is possible. Simple cause–effect chains do not obtain.
6. Instead, such organizations capitalize on virtuous circles generated by one-off, accidental, or serendipitous events.
7. Such virtuous circles operate at different organizational levels, across scales, in a self-similar manner.
8. A measure of stability in such organizations is not the product of control or rational procedures, but rather the result of spontaneous self-organization, across scales.

9. Reverting to rational procedures, routine, cost and waste minimization, control, and linearity undermines creativity and innovation, the very qualities necessary to survive and succeed.[1]

It is still too early to know whether complexity theory will have a lasting impact on the study of organizations or will prove a temporary fad. All the same, it is one of the theories that is forcing scholars to reconsider what is meant by the term organization itself.

Conflict

Conflict is a feature of every human society, every group, and every organization. It is part of everyone's experience. It is the heart of nearly every story, narrative, and myth. It is the main ingredient of most news items and all drama; it is also an essential part of **politics**.

Conflict comes in many different forms— arguments, fights, wars, genocides, strikes, sabotage, blackmail, insults, legal disputes, political rows, and so forth. It happens at the highest level, that of nations and civilizations, and at the lowest, that of two siblings. Some conflict is experienced by a single person, torn between different desires or wishes. At its mildest, conflict is just a difference of opinions. Difference of opinions, however, rapidly turns into personal rancour, a desire to see your own opinion forced on your rival, or even a wish to humiliate and get rid of him or her.

Sociologists and political scientists, for their part, approach conflict as something that exists at a level below the one experienced by conflicting parties, as something that results from deeper economic and other interests. Following Marx, many sociologists view conflict as an essential consequence of the **class** structure of society. It is helpful then to approach conflict at two levels: (a) *Conflict at the level of interests*—which exists where there is a difference

---

[1] Gabriel, 1998a.

between parties (employers and employees, say, or business owners and customers) over desired outcomes, and (b) *Conflict at the level of behaviour*—which comes about when parties seeking different outcomes either express their differences through such gestures as acting destructively or cooperating in a sullen or grudging manner. This is especially important in the world of employee relations—workers and managers often work in an altogether harmonious manner, whilst both being aware of a basic conflict of interest between them; one which comes to the surface from time to time as grievances emerge and disputes occur.

At the level of behaviour, we can think of conflict as a state of disharmony or opposition, where different parties perceive themselves to have interests or views incompatible with those of other parties. The disharmony may lead to open hostilities, where parties to the conflict seek to force their will or their view on others despite opposition and are willing to inflict and sustain damage in pursuit of this end. One paramount feature of conflict is its tendency to escalate. Many conflicts real and fictional start over trifles; but small disputes quickly get out of control, drawing in more parties and leading to an escalation of hostilities and damage. It is for this reason that conflict is often thought of as *entrapping* those involved; the more sacrifices they make and the longer the conflict goes on the harder it is to withdraw or find a solution.

Another paramount feature of conflict is that it is very often acted out for the benefit of third parties, seeking to draw the audience into the conflict. Today, many conflicts are acted out for the benefit of television audiences, as combatants try to gain the sympathy and support of neutrals. Thus a conflict between two organizations, like Shell and Greenpeace or British Airways and Virgin Atlantic, is played out in front of the media, seeking to win the hearts and minds of neutrals. Likewise, many political and military conflicts are acted out in the hope that neutral parties will enter the fray and tip the balance one way or another.

Yet another fundamental feature of conflict is that it can reveal tensions within conflicting blocs, which sometimes unravel, fragment, and collapse. An alliance can come under strain if different partners see themselves as carrying unequal burdens and drawing unequal benefits from the conflict. Thus, while conflict often appears as an opposition of two parties, it may, in reality involve many others and the parties themselves may turn out not to be solid blocks.

How is conflict resolved? Conflict may be resolved through a decisive victory of one party over another; it may equally be resolved through the mediation of third parties or the agreement on a formula that enables all parties to claim some success. More often than not, the resolution of conflict is temporary; conflict is suppressed but remains dormant and liable to return sometime in the future. The dissolution of states like the Soviet Union and Yugoslavia and the removal of Saddam Hussein from power offered salutary lessons in how ethnic and religious conflicts suppressed for decades can resurface more damagingly than ever. It is for this reason that many industrial sociologists and political theorists prefer to talk of containment and **institutionalization** of conflict rather than its resolution. Institutionalization of conflict means the containment of conflict within particular **institutions**. Instead of escalating, conflict unfolds within certain limits. Thus political conflict may be contained by democratic institutions, such as elections and parliaments, property conflicts may be contained by legal institutions, and industrial conflicts may be contained by institutions like collective bargaining. People who violate institutions automatically place themselves in a weak moral position and certainly lose the support of the neutrals. Institutions emerge over time; they cannot be established by sheer force. Over time, some institutions prove themselves, by helping people to deal with their conflicts without inflicting excessive damage on each other.

What are the causes of conflict? This is a difficult question as often the participants attribute the conflict to different factors. One party may claim that the other broke an earlier agreement, another may claim that they were insulted; yet another may claim that its territory was threatened. Historians have long debated the causes of different armed conflicts, seeking to distinguish between deeper cause of a conflict and the pretext or the event that sparks it off (*casus belli*). It would be fair to say, however, the following factors have an influence in bringing about conflicts:

- limited resources, especially vital ones like water, oil, and, above all, land;
- 'positional' resources, like status or owning the tallest house in a street;
- territory, both in the literal and the metaphorical sense; this is a very common cause of departmental or intra-organizational conflict;
- insults, actual, perceived, and 'engineered' (where one party claims to have been deeply offended by the actions or beliefs of another);
- unequal treatment—a very common cause of conflict in postcolonial situations;
- general instability and change—where expectations and rewards get out of sync with each other;
- interpretation of earlier agreements—especially when compounded by general instability and change;
- violation of legal contracts, like contracts of employment, but also of psychological contracts, i.e. implicit agreements that are not committed to paper.

All of those causes are exacerbated by long years of hostility and mistrust between people or groups. In such circumstances negotiating any settlement may be almost impossible. This is when conflict becomes part of the **identity** of groups or individuals, the rival assuming the standing of the **Other** who comes to embody all that is bad and loathsome, against whom our own sense of worth and goodness

is raised. The Other becomes the recipient of our own **aggression**; our own sense of unity and goodness is raised as the Other is dehumanized; as Jessica Benjamin argued, 'the more the other is subjugated, the less he is experienced as a human subject and the more distance or violence the self must employ against him. The ensuing absence of recognition, indeed of an outside world, breeds more of the same.'[1] For theorists like Benjamin, conflict becomes an important identity resource.

Freud sees the matter even more bleakly: aggression is an 'instinctual endowment' of all humans, a manifestation of a death instinct, one that civilization may sublimate, tame, and direct inwards, but not one that it can eradicate:

> Men are not gentle creatures who want to be loved, and who at the most can defend themselves if they are attacked; they are, on the contrary, creatures among whose instinctual endowments is to be reckoned a powerful share of aggressiveness. As a result, their neighbor is for them not only a potential helper or sexual object, but also someone who tempts them to satisfy their aggressiveness on him, to exploit his capacity for work without compensation, to use him sexually without his consent, to seize his possessions, to humiliate him, to cause him pain, to torture and to kill him. *Homo homini lupus* (Man is a wolf to man).[2]

Under the influence of culture, most people think of conflict as a bad thing. It causes much anxiety and suffering, it leads to waste of resources, effort, and even human life. It also threatens to unleash within each one of us forces (like anger, envy, fear, and hate) that we may not be able to control and we may prefer to disavow. But conflict is not necessarily bad. **Competition** represents a form of conflict that can stimulate **creativity**, hard work, and innovation. And conflict itself can stimulate self-sacrifice and social cohesion; let us not forget that some of the greatest scientific inventions were spawned

[1] Benjamin, 1988, p. 220.   [2] Freud, 1930, p. 302.

by war and some of the greatest artistic master-pieces, from Homer's *Iliad* to Benjamin Britten's *War Requiem*, were inspired by the tragedy of conflict.

• See also *aggression, competition, politics, power*

Conscience

Conscience is a psychological function which establishes the ability to distinguish between right and wrong. It is the psychological basis of what Bauman calls the 'moral impulse',[1] not only the ability to distinguish between good and bad, but also the urge to act according to what is experienced as good and to feel guilty if acting in ways felt to be wrong. Freud viewed conscience as the function of the super-ego, the part of the mind which is formed when children internalize external **authority**.[2] At that point, children curtail some of their **desires** not because of fear of external authority (like the father or the mother) but because the authority is within them, dictating what is good and what is not. This internalization of this authority ensures that people often feel remorse even when they have contemplated an evil act, without actually carrying it out. For this reason, Freud argued that conscience turns the **aggression** of the death instinct against the ego. There is a great deal of argument on how moral development differs between genders and across cultures.

What is the effect of organizations on conscience? Numerous writers, including Weber,[3] Jackall,[4] and Bauman,[5] have argued that organizations impede or neutralize conscience and the moral impulse, by offering rationalizations which supersede feeling. As members of organizations, individuals may carry out acts (disconnect the electricity of debtors, fail students, evict poor tenants, deport refugees, and, on occasion, even commit acts of physical brutality

and murder) which would be abhorrent to them as private citizens. Bauman,[6] a major exponent of this view, has argued that modernity has a tendency to shift moral responsibilities away from the moral self either towards organizations (people merely 'obeying orders'), or dissolving responsibility altogether in what he calls a bureaucratic 'rule of nobody'. Bauman criticizes professional codes of **ethics** and **business ethics** as further removing individual responsibility and paralysing the moral impulse. In different ways, crowds and groups may paralyse the individual moral impulse, through the operation of powerful group norms and dilution of individual responsibility.

Other theorists have taken a less bleak view of the effects of modernity and organizations on conscience. Watson,[7] for example, through his detailed study of managers, argues strongly that, while confused, torn, and ambivalent, managers are not indifferent amoral functionaries, but, like the rest of us, moral agents, who assess the moral implications of different actions and are far from insensitive to the pain and suffering of others. Whistle-blowers are often seen as individuals who act under the impulse of their conscience in revealing organizational wrongdoing, no matter what the personal costs may be. More generally, ten Bos and Willmott argue against Bauman's 'unremittingly negative assessment of rational, or rule-governed, ethics' and propose a rapprochement of reason and emotion as the guiding principle of moral behaviour.[8]

• See also *ethics, morality*

Consultants and clients

Management consultants are conventionally known as expert helpers in the field of management. But definitions are notoriously difficult because consultants are viewed from different perspectives. In particular, it can be argued that

---

[1] Bauman, 1989.   [2] Freud, 1923/1984.   [3] Weber, 1946.   [4] Jackall, 1988.   [5] Bauman, 1993.   [6] Bauman, 1989, p. 32.   [7] Watson, 1994.   [8] ten Bos and Willmott, 2001.

their expertise is as much in selling new business as it is management, and that their help is directed rather selectively—at those who commission them—often at the expense of others. More generally, management consultants carry out a wide range of changing activities. For example, 'consulting' currently represents only a fraction of the fee income of most large management consulting firms in comparison to IT and related outsourcing income. But even within the category of 'consulting', designing and implementing organizational reforms outstrips the traditional advisory role. Despite this, there are those who insist on a core and generic set of necessary consulting skills (e.g. analysis, diagnosis, and change/client management) and seek to establish a professional status for consultants. These people are mostly outside the large or global firms whose strong brands have a resilience with clients which is likely to render the **professionalization** project doomed in comparison to, say, accounting.

Until the 1990s, management consultants received little attention in organizational studies except for their early association with the introduction of scientific management and, more directly, in the accounts of organizational development (OD) practitioners. This latter group was typically concerned with process or counselling-type consultancy which largely eschewed the more prescriptive approaches of 'expert consulting',[1] and often drew on **psychoanalytic** theories of organizations. Prescriptive accounts of all kinds continue today and often contain valuable empirical insights. However, as consultancy expanded numerically as an occupation in the USA, UK, and, increasingly, elsewhere, it has became a focus of more analytical research—theories about consulting more than theories in consulting. Much of this work can be located within the broader field of **management knowledge** and **fashion**, where consultants are seen as key mediators in the growing production, commodification, and dissemination of management ideas, if not knowledge *in toto*. Here, two streams of thought dominate—the **institutional**[2] and dramaturgical or constructionist.[3] The former is mostly concerned with more macro-levels of analysis and the notion of mimetic isomorphism (copying the latest idea) while the latter focused on persuasive consultancy (and guru) performances or rhetoric which were seen as central to their expertise given the ambiguous (or unverifiable) nature of management or knowledge in general. In response to these developments, others looked more closely at clients and pointed to the frequently contested, or at least varied, nature of client–consultant relationships in projects, although difficulties of research access continue to plague studies in this area.[4] At the same time, consultancy research emerged as part of a parallel development to that of **knowledge** mediation whereby consultancy was seen as characterizing 'knowledge intensiveness'. Attention was subsequently given to consulting and comparable professional service firms in terms of how they are managed and how they serve clients, especially in the context of globalization and the decline of the traditional partnership structure. Alongside such studies, some work has explored consulting tools or methods and their co-construction with clients.[5]

This research has generated considerable insights into what has become a high-profile occupation and a widespread activity. However, there is a risk if management consultancy, because of its high profile, is seen as warranting a field of study of its own. Rather more interesting and promising developments can be found by locating consultancy in wider organizational and social debates. For example, recent interest has been shown in management consultancy as part of emerging forms of social elites. This draws attention to the need to explore backstage consulting activity and locates the

---

[1] See e.g. Schein, 1969.   [2] See e.g. Suddaby and Greenwood, 2001. Czarniawska, 2001.   [4] Sturdy, 1997.   [5] Werr and Stjernberg, 2003.   [3] See e.g. Czarniawska-Joerges and Joerges, 1990;

occupation within a much broader notion of **politics** and **power relations** than those associated with organizational-level change.[1] In other words, management consultants do not merely persuade, advise, legitimize, and/or act as scapegoats in the context of specific client projects, but operate with even less visibility and accountability at more senior levels. At the same time, not all organizations and nations use management consultancy, although one might be forgiven for thinking this given the available literature and the love–hate relationship the business media has with consulting. This too, opens up new avenues for research into alternative levels of organizing and managing as well as into popular media consulting **discourses**.

ANDREW STURDY, UNIVERSITY OF WARWICK

Consumerism

Consumerism is a term which assumes several different meanings; all of them revolve around the idea that consumption in late **modernity** has displaced other spheres of human activity, including religion, work, politics, and family relations, as a major source of **meaning**, **identity**, and **value**. Gabriel and Lang have identified five ways in which the term is used.[2]

1. Consumerism as a moral doctrine, proclaiming that the good life is to be found in more consumer choice and ever-increasing standards of living.
2. Consumerism as an **ideology** of conspicuous consumption (i.e. consuming for public display) through which social distinctions are made which supplant traditional **class** distinctions.
3. Consumerism as an economic ideology of global development, providing every country and every region with a vehicle out of poverty and underdevelopment.
4. Consumerism as a political ideology proclaiming consumer sovereignty as a supreme political value and seeking to limit the role of the state in providing goods and services for the common welfare.
5. Consumerism as a social movement seeking to promote and protect the rights of consumers through consumer advocacy.

In all its variants, consumerism places individual **choice** above most other human values, including equality, tolerance, and fraternity. It views consumption and the uninhibited operation of markets as an economic, a political, and even a moral imperative. In Lebergott's view,[3] uninhibited consumer choice in an open marketplace is the best guarantee for human happiness. Numerous authors, including some economists, have challenged this view. In *Happiness: Lessons from a New Science*, Richard Layard argues that even though most people believe that more money would make them happier, most empirical studies find this to be untrue.[4] Once above the level of serious material deprivation and poverty, more money does not make people happier. Over a period of fifty years or so, incomes in all the industrialized countries have grown considerably but people do not report higher levels of happiness. On the contrary, there are much higher incidences of depression, alcoholism, and crime. In a similar vein, Juliet Schor pointed out that as Americans spend more money and more time shopping, they go more deeply into debt.[5] This leads to greater unhappiness which may lead to still more spending, in an almost addictive manner. A significant minority, however, are opting out of consumerism by 'downshifting' and seeking simpler, less ostentatious ways of life. This is also a theme in Naomi Klein's bestselling book *No Logo*,[6] which offers a trenchant critique of contemporary consumerism and its discontents.

In spite of the disappointments and discontents that it generates, consumerism has shown few signs of abating, engulfing ever-increasing

---

[1] Sturdy, Schwarz, and Spicer, 2006. [2] Gabriel and Lang, 1995. [3] Lebergott, 1993. [4] Layard, 2005. [5] Schor, 1998. [6] Klein, 2000.

parts of humanity and leaving others feeling excluded and deprived. All the same, it seems inevitable that in the not too distant future, consumerism will face major challenges from three quarters, environmental, demographic, and social. The environmental challenge to consumerism will arrive from shortages of key resources that underpinned the consumerist feast of the last hundred years, including oil, water, land, soil, clean air, and minerals. Pollution, waste, and climate change leading to desertification will compound the difficulties. Climate change also features in the second challenge to consumerism, the demographic one. This is likely to prove as severe and politically unsettling. The world population passed 6 billion at the beginning of the twenty-first century, and is predicted by the UN Population Fund to rise to 9–10 billion by 2050. Feeding, housing, and providing water for such escalating demands will be an awesome task, made still more difficult by the environmental problems noted above and the demographic disequilibria created by ageing populations of most industrialized countries as against the youthfulness of other countries.[1] The combination of environmental and demographic factors has led some pessimistic theorists to speculate that social unrest, disease, and warfare will reach an unprecedented scale in the longer term.[2]

In the last resort, however, even environmental and demographic factors are mediated by social and cultural forces. It is people, after all, who consume, who vote, who migrate, and who can make a difference. In the light of the escalating problems noted above, it may be that the long-standing equation of consumerism with happiness will begin to uncouple—it may then be that people, including economists, politicians, and the wider public, rediscover the truth of a speech made by Robert F. Kennedy, at the University of Kansas, Lawrence, on 18 March 1968, shortly before his assassination:

For too long we seem to have surrendered personal excellence and community value in the mere accumulation of material things. Our gross national product now is over 800 billion dollars a year, but that gross national product, if we judge the United States of America by that, that gross national product counts air pollution, and cigarette advertising, and ambulances to clear our highways of carnage. It counts special locks for our doors and the jails for people who break them. It counts the destruction of the redwoods and the loss of our natural wonder in chaotic squall. It counts Napalm, and it counts nuclear warheads, and armored cars for the police to fight the riots in our city. It counts Whitman's rifle and Speck's knife and the television programs which glorify violence in order to sell toys to our children. Yet, the gross national product does not allow for the health of our children, the quality of their education, or the joy of their play. It does not include the beauty of our poetry or the strength of our marriages; the intelligence of our public debate or the integrity of our public officials. It measures neither our wit nor our courage; neither our wisdom nor our learning; neither our compassion nor our devotion to our country; it measures everything, in short, except that which makes life worthwhile.

• See also *Disney and Disneyization*

Consumers and consumption

The study of consumption has emerged as a major field of study in the social sciences, drawing on many disciplines, including sociology, economics, anthropology, psychology, management studies, marketing, cultural and media studies, and so forth. A substantial part of this literature seeks to analyse and predict 'consumer

---

[1] Millennium Ecosystem Assessment (Program), 2005.   [2] Diamond, 2005; Lang and Heasman, 2004; Lovelock, 2006.

behaviour' in terms of certain underlying variables, like income, age, gender, personality, and so forth. While emotional factors are recognized as capable of influencing consumer **decisions**, a large part of economic theory is dominated by the assumption that consumers generally act as **rational** economic beings. Interest in consumer behaviour is linked to attempts to establish the effects and effectiveness of **advertising** and the likely success of new products; these are of considerable interest to entrepreneurs, business people, managers, and other practitioners. A different part of the literature deals more widely with the phenomenon of consumption, its economic, social, and psychological dimensions and its implications for societies, economies, and even for the future of the planet. Consumption is now widely seen as a defining domain of modern society.

Human beings (in common with other living organisms) consume—air, water, nutrients are all necessary for life. Humans also consume objects, services, and ideas for pleasure, for meaning, and for **spiritual** and **emotional** sustenance. Every society involves distinct types of production (hunting and gathering, agriculture, manufacturing) but also distinct types of consumption (food preparation, clothing, accommodation, artistic artefacts, music, stories and myths, etc.). What was unique to the twentieth century was *mass consumption*, the quest by ever-widening masses of the population for a better life, through consumption of more and better goods and services. During that century, consumption for survival was overtaken by consumption for enjoyment, for **identity**, and for self-growth, at least in large segments of the industrialized countries. Mass consumption emerged as the corollary of mass production— the supply of ever more cheaper and more novel products and services to ever wider groups of people aimed not at physical survival but at social and personal well-being.

Towards the end of the twentieth century, mass consumption underwent a further transformation. New technologies along with enhanced standards of living permitted an increasing proliferation of alternative products and services, which allowed or even required consumers to exercise ever-increasing **choice** on how they spent their money. In such a culture of **consumerism**, individuals and groups seek to enhance their lives with **meaning**, experiment with and develop their identities, and discover a sense of belonging and success not through work, but through their consumption tastes or, more generally, their lifestyles. In this connection, consumers increasingly turn not to material objects but to **images**, **spectacles**, and **experiences.** Even when they buy material objects, like cars, watches, and clothes, it is the brand image of these objects that makes them desirable rather than their functional utility. Fantasy becomes the driving force behind the desires for new and different experiences, services, and objects. In this way, consumption becomes the great and problematic source of meaning in many accounts of postmodernity.[1]

This has had quite a pronounced effect on the way organizations are conceptualized and managed. The consumer is no longer seen as an 'outsider' to the world of organizations, but very much an insider, whose desires, caprices, and **fantasies** provide an organization's lifeline towards profitability and survival. Organizations dedicate ingenuity, innovation, and resources not merely to devising quicker and cheaper ways of producing standardized outputs, but to imagining original, creative, and expensive ways of enticing consumers to diverse outputs. Furthermore, they take the utmost care and attention to ensure that employees who come in direct contact with consumers project the right organizational image to ensure customer satisfaction and loyalty. Customer service becomes as important as providing reliable products at

[1] Baudrillard, 1970/1988; Bauman, 1992; du Gay, 1996; Featherstone, 1991; Gabriel and Lang, 1995.

competitive prices. As a result, the demands on employees have changed. The display of an attractive personality and the right emotional attitude becomes a vital 'front' of the organization, as employees are increasingly required to perform **emotional labour** in addition to physical and intellectual labour. Some organizational theorists have noted the increasing prevalence of internal organizational **markets** and quasi-markets, which encourage organizational participants to relate to members in other departments and units, not as colleagues but as internal consumers and providers.[1]

A somewhat under-researched aspect of consumption concerns all those products and services (travel, hotels, information systems, telecommunications, office space, hospitality, etc.), which people routinely consume *as* members of their organizations. These may be of an altogether superior standard to the ones they consume as private individuals and may affect the nature of **psychological contracts** between people and their employers; for instance, in exchange for working long hours, forfeiting their privacy at home, and telling the odd lie, employees may be allowed to travel club-class, stay in luxury hotels, and charge company platinum cards.

The rise of the consumer as a contemporary modern archetype embodying the values of freedom, autonomy, and the pursuit of happiness has taken place at the expense of another great archetype, that of *the citizen*. Whereas consumers makes choices only in order to please themselves and have no obligation to offer any explanations for their actions, citizens embody a set of rights and responsibilities. The citizen's choices must be made responsibly; they require an active interest in public affairs, public debate, and a recognition that social needs (e.g. for sound education, a good transport system, etc.) cannot be addressed individually but collectively. Whereas consumers will seek the school that offers the best value for money for the education of their children, citizens will debate what kind of education is desirable for all children, including their own. The rise of the consumer at the expense of the citizen has been accompanied by the wide privatization of what used to be public services, the ever-increasing unwillingness among rich classes in most industrialized countries to pay taxes, and the emergence of **New Public Management** in public-sector organizations.

• See also *Disney and Disneyization, Fordism, McDonaldization*

Contingency theories

Two types of theories are referred to as contingency theories: theories of organizational **structure** and theories of **leadership**. Contingency theory grew out of an impatience with classical management approaches which seemed to prescribe universal solutions to all management situations, irrespective of different local circumstances. For example, Burns and Stalker argued that Weber's ideal type of **bureaucracy** does not represent an ideal structure for all types of real organizations.[2] A structure which serves one organization may well fail when applied to another. Burns and Stalker pointed out that organizational **environment** affects the type of organizational **structure** most likely to be adopted by successful organizations. Woodward and others argued that optimal structures were contingent on the production **technologies** employed by different companies.[3] Other researchers have noted that optimal organizational structure is contingent on the size of the company. Contingency theories of **leadership** argue that no single leadership style is effective in all circumstances, but that leadership styles are contingent on the organizational and situational context. Fiedler developed a technique aimed at

---

[1] Ferlie et al., 1996.   [2] Burns and Stalker, 1961.   [3] Woodward, 1965.

assisting leaders in their diagnoses of this context and enabling them to adopt a style which is likely to prove effective.[1]

Contingency theories were very influential in the 1970s but are now less popular, due to the emergence and development of other approaches to organizations like **institutional theory** and **resource-based theory**, **actor network theory** and **path dependency theory**. They have been criticized for adopting a somewhat mechanistic approach to organizations, disregarding the histories and values of different organizations, and underestimating the importance of **strategy**, **culture**, and **choice**.

- See also **environment, technology**

Control

Control has long been seen as one of the central features of organizations and one of the main functions of **management**. In fact, many uses of the word 'management', such as 'anger management' and 'time management', are virtually synonymous with control. Every society deploys mechanisms of social control seeking to curb the antisocial tendencies of its members; these may include legal provisions, social norms, moral strictures, and various institutions of penal justice. Physical force, such as that exercised by armies and police forces, is the naked form of social control. But some controls operate far more subtly and inconspicuously, for example through mechanisms of surveillance and the physical layout of **buildings** and space.

Within organizations, control tends to be systematic, formal, and ubiquitous. Organizations seek to control resources and outputs, processes and machinery, information, technology, and environment. But above all, organizations seek to control individuals and their physical bodies, to ensure reliable, predictable, and consistent performance or organizational **roles**. This involves the monitoring of performance,

its assessment against some stated standards, provision of feedback, rewards, and sanctions. Timetables, procedures, appraisals, and audits are all control mechanisms, aimed at ensuring that certain standards of individual and organizational performance are achieved. Physical violence was the main control mechanism of slave-drivers. In some early capitalist factories, workers were physically chained to their benches, as a way of ensuring that they put in the required number of work hours. Today, it is not entirely extinct (see **bullying**) but it is overtaken by more discreet types of control. **Rules** and regulations gradually became the foundation of **bureaucratic** control, while **Taylorism** sought to incorporate control in the technical process itself—the moving assembly line and the paperwork chain set the pace and control the movements of those who work. More recently, the importance of **culture** is emphasized as a mechanism whereby control is internalized by the individual as self-control. An organization's **values** and **norms** help to ensure that its members will behave in a certain way, not because they are forced to, but because it has become second nature to them. Generally, lack of control, or **powerlessness**, is seen as a major dimension of **alienation**.

In the last twenty years or so, it has been argued that as we move from modernity to postmodernity, we witness a new and more invasive range of organizational controls; these seek to colonize the individual from within rather than from above or from outside. Foucault's reading of the Panopticon (see **buildings and architecture**),[2] a vast mechanism of surveillance in which individuals police themselves since they can never be sure when the disciplinary gaze is focused on them, has had a considerable influence on scholarly understanding of contemporary controls. **Language** is especially important as a discreet controlling mechanism—naming, listing, classifying, labelling can create distinctions and pigeon holes which can be

---

[1] Fiedler, 1967; Fiedler and Chemers, 1974.   [2] Foucault, 1977.

every bit as oppressive and controlling as direct surveillance.

The study of control is complemented by increased interest in different types of employee recalcitrance and **resistance**. Different types of workplace resistance have been identified. These include the formation of **trade unions** to defend the workers' interests and various forms of industrial action undertaken to that end, including strikes, picketing, and restriction of output. Other forms of resistance include whistle-blowing, sabotage, absenteeism, and pilfering (reclaiming what has been unfairly taken away). Resistance can also take symbolic forms, including **cynicism** and disparaging humour and jokes.

Some types of resistance assume rational forms (e.g. tactical strikes where it hurts or damages an organization), but Fineman and Sturdy have argued that **emotion** becomes a mediator between an organization's controlling practices and an individual's or group's resistance.[1] Emotion can drive acts of overt rebellion and recalcitrance, such as whistle-blowing—in such cases, it is a sense of insult to the employee's pride or sense of justice rather than the experience of oppressive controls which precipitates opposition. Alternatively, **emotion** may lead to passive resistance, such as psychological withdrawal, or resistance through distance, such as the improvised departures from organizational scripts. Finally, emotion can drive a form of resistance that has become increasingly common—exit. Exit means leaving the organization when all avenues of finding a **voice** have been exhausted. Just as consumers exit (or abandon) organizations whose products are no longer seen as meeting their needs or whose moral standards are seen as unsatisfactory, employees may leave companies that appear unresponsive to their concerns and interests. The study of control and resistance is a central focus of the theoretical tradition known as **labour process theory**.

Corporate culture

Corporate culture became a popular concept in organizational studies in the 1980s. Around that time, scholars of organizations turned their attention to culture, partly in an effort to understand the success of Japanese companies. It was then argued that they owed their success to the strong normative **controls** they exercised over their staff.[2] Organizations, like nations, it was suggested, have or 'are' **cultures**, composed of shared values, norms, and meanings. Some organizations have cultures which enhance efficiency, productivity, innovation, and service while others have cultures which hamper collective effort, initiative, and innovation. The emergence of the theory of corporate culture was greeted with much enthusiasm by scholars, consultants, and managers themselves. For a while it appeared to be the magic key that opened every door, offering the answer to almost any question. No longer were organizations to be seen as grey Weberian bureaucracies, populated by rule-bound administrators, 'specialists without spirit, sensualists without heart'.[3] Instead, organizations were suddenly seen as brimming with **stories**, **myths**, and folklore, ripe with emotions, and replete with **rituals** and ceremonies. Successful organizations were those whose leaders successfully 'managed culture', to promote teamwork, customer service, and commitment to quality.

In their influential best-seller *In Search of Excellence*, Thomas J. Peters and Robert H. Waterman argued that successful companies are those which have *strong cultures*, i.e. strong commitment to a shared set of values and norms, which both unite and motivate organizational members. The forging of a strong culture, the strengthening of norms and values, the creation of meanings are all major functions of managers: 'Good managers make meanings for people, as well as money.'[4] Similar conclusions

---

[1] Fineman and Sturdy, 1999. [2] Ouchi, 1981; Pascale and Athos, 1981. [3] Weber, 1958, p. 182. [4] Peters and Waterman, 1982, p. 29.

were drawn by Kanter,[1] who argued that most Western organizations developed bureaucratic cultures that thwarted **innovation** and entrepreneurship by emphasizing adherence to rules and procedures.

Such arguments encouraged the view that managers could manipulate organizational culture almost at will, through the use of symbols, stories, metaphors, and material artefacts, like buildings, logos, and products, to produce a winning cocktail of **values** and **norms**. The management of culture became one of the great management **fads and fashions**. Large amounts of money were spent by many companies on cultural audits, cultural consultants, and value management. Like most fads, corporate culture declined almost as precipitously as it rose. Most of Peters and Waterman's excellent companies fell on hard times; Jan Carlzon and many other manager megastars seemed to lose their magic touch.[2] Even the Japanese economic miracle seemed to wilt.

As gurus and consultants moved on to new pastures, researchers were left to quietly reflect on culture, its importance, but also its resistance to manipulation and to planned **change**. A new set of corporate logos, a new building, a new website, and enthusiastic proclamations of new visions, new missions, and new corporate values are likely to spawn cynical dismissal, especially if they are perceived as insincere and manipulative. Subcultures and counter-cultures may spontaneously grow and prosper, complementing or undermining the official values. Even the strongest-looking cultures can hide significant cracks. Corporate culture may be influenced but it is difficult to manage or control. A large part of it, like all culture, is made of dreams and **fantasies**, through which people express **unconscious** desires and wishes. An attempt to build someone up as a hero may be neutralized or subverted by the desire to view him as a villain, a puppet, or a fool. A ritual aimed at reinforcing union and solidarity can easily turn into one

that reinforces divisions. Even the most carefully choreographed cultural ceremonies entail risks. What this suggests is that organizational culture is, up to a point, **unmanaged and unmanageable**, a dreamworld in which desires, anxieties, and **emotions** find expressions in highly irrational constructions. This aspect of organizations has not received the attention that it merits, since the managed, controlling, and resisted organization is generally privileged within organizational **discourses** at the expense of the unmanaged, the uncontrolled, and the unmanageable.

The chief force in the unmanaged organization is *fantasy* and its landmarks include jokes, gossip, nicknames, graffiti, cartoons, and, above all, **stories**. All too often fantasy in organizations is seen as either a form of escapism reinforcing conformity or a primal form of opposition leading to full-scale resistance. Both of these interpretations steer fantasy and its products back to the dialectic of control and resistance, and thus to the privileged domain of the managed organization. Instead, it has been argued that fantasy can offer a third way to the individual, which amounts to neither conformity nor rebellion, but to a symbolic refashioning of official organizational practices in the interest of pleasure, allowing a temporary supremacy of emotion over rationality and of uncontrol over control.[3]

• See also *culture*

Corporate governance see governance

Corruption

Corruption is a widespread phenomenon that lies at the heart of **ethics**, political theory, and organizational studies. Corruption usually involves a web of improper and usually unlawful practices aimed at private gain. It includes

---

[1] Kanter, 1983.   [2] Carlzon, 1989.   [3] Gabriel, 1995.

extortion, bribery, blackmail, nepotism, **power** abuse, misusing insider information, price fixing, pilfering, and the striking of all kinds of deals that lead to profiteering, exploitation, and oppression of third parties for private gain. Many of these practices take place simultaneously, reinforcing each other and constituting a 'web of corruption'. The precise **boundaries** of corruption vary considerably across cultures; this is most notable in the case of gifts, which may range from the totally innocent to the totally corrupt. While the precise definition of an action as corrupt is influenced by cultural differences, most cultures recognize certain behaviours as corrupt and most languages have a word to denote corruption.

Corruption entails an active dimension—to corrupt someone is to undermine his or her integrity and to make them prone to subsequent episodes of corruption. There is something intensely contagious then about corruption—trying to cover up for corruption leads to more corruption. A corrupt person is a person who will corrupt others in order to maintain his or her privileges. Corruption is often institutionalized and almost always rationalized, in other words, it is seen as an acceptable way to conduct certain types of business. If the only way to get a telephone line is to bribe an official, one may come to view it as acceptable, if not necessarily desirable. In such cases, the bribe may be rationalized away as being insignificant. Where, however, a company or a government pay large sums as commissions to private individuals in order to seal a contract, such a **rationalization** may not be possible. Instead, other rationalizations may be offered, such as that many people's jobs depend on it or that this is the only way to do business with that client. The ingenuity of human beings to explain, justify, and rationalize corruption appears to know no bounds.

Corruption in organizations takes many forms, some opportunistic, some systematic and endemic. Some of the most skilful forms of corruption (and corruption is undoubtedly a **skill** and, some would say, an art) play around several ambiguities as to what is corrupt and what is not, what is widespread and what is not, what has been going on for a long time and what has not. Some cynics would argue that most businesses venture beyond the boundaries of what is legal and moral, but only some, like Enron, get caught. But such cynicism may itself feed and reinforce corruption. *Conspiracy theories* are themselves a symptom of the collapse of social trust which feeds corrupt practices; they also act as justification for further corruption. If everyone is tarred with the brush of corruption, then there is no reason why anyone should avoid it.

David Levine has argued that corruption can be viewed as an attack on **norms** of conduct in organizations.[1] It is an attack, however, that far from representing a rejection of **morality** amounts to a regression to a more primitive morality of greed, arrogance, and a sense of personal entitlement. This morality replaces the conventional understanding of virtue as honesty, integrity, and so forth, with the supreme virtue as personal loyalty. Thus, the corrupt are bound together by a tacit oath that prevents them from divulging what is going on and consigns any whistle-blower to the standing of ultimate traitor. Levine observes the paradox of a CEO who pillages his company, swindling its stakeholders, while professing small-town values. He argues that this paradox disappears if the CEO has come to view the company as something indistinguishable from his self, that is to say, as having no reality independent of his subjective experience and fantasies. For a person like Robert Maxwell, defrauding his staff of their pension entitlements would have appeared as no more than transferring money from one pocket of his trousers to another. And for those who benefited from his ill-gained largesse, it must have seemed no more than fair reward for their loyalty.

[1] Levine, 2005.

If morality itself is no guarantee against it, how can corruption be checked or arrested? Certain leaders, including the 'incorruptible' leaders of the French Revolution, sought to stamp out corruption by imposing draconian penalties—exceptionally harsh penalties even for minor offences. This is rarely successful, the leaders triggering off widespread reaction against their rule or being themselves compromised by being shown not to live by their own high standards. Harsh punishments instead of stamping out corruption may actually enhance it, a well-known occurrence in occupied countries and totalitarian regimes. Such states enhance arbitrary use of power which is itself a recipe for corruption.

What can we learn from countries and organizations that appear to limit corruption? One factor is a culture that discourages greed and does not equate **success** with personal gain. Countries such as Finland, Singapore, and Sweden that consistently come low in rankings of corruption emphasize communal values and discourage ostentatious displays of wealth and power. An inquisitive press and media offer some protection against corruption, but where they accumulate excessive **power**, they may actually become parties to a corrupt system. Threatening a public figure to expose photographs of a minor misdemeanour may enable them to corrupt him or her. The American constitution sought to control abuses of power through a system of checks and balances, whereby no single bloc acquires excessive power. Successful in certain respects, it certainly did not stop widespread corruption in many areas of business, political, and social life.

What then of **bureaucracy** as a bulwark against corruption? Weberian bureaucracy, with its formidable discipline, its unquestioned obedience to rules and regulations, and its unbending subjugation of person to **role**, was unquestionably conceived as an organization resistant to corruption, nepotism, and favouritism. And in some instances this is precisely what bureaucracy was—for example, a civil service that treats all citizens equally or a health service that does not differentiate between the deserving and the undeserving. This was the argument put forward by Paul du Gay in his provocatively titled book *In Praise of Bureaucracy*.[1] Although primarily concerned with the state sector rather than private enterprise, du Gay has argued that the Weberian model provided a control against political interference and politicized agendas. This is currently being challenged by a 'new managerialism', which emphasizes targets at all costs, cost effectiveness, competition, and customer-focused ethos. This, argues du Gay, undermines the integrity and the dignity of officials which was meant to ensure impartiality and equality. In the name of cutting red tape, new managerialism undermines the system of rules and procedures which provided the strongest guarantee against corruption.

Others, however, have criticized bureaucracy for being exactly a recipe for corruption, in which procedures and regulations become fig-leaves for corrupt fiefdoms. Robert Michels's theory of **oligarchy** offers an explanation for this.[2] Bureaucracy, argued Michels, concentrates power in the hands of a few people at the top of an organization. These individuals control resources, such as appointments, finances, and **information**, and develop skills and knowledge that create a social and psychological gulf between themselves and the organization's rank-and-file. Increasingly they become preoccupied with their own position and privileges in the organization, which they defend through precisely the nepotistic and corrupt practices that bureaucracy was meant to discourage. Eventually, oligarchy takes root in every organization, with formal rules and procedures but a smokescreen behind which leaders ruthlessly pursue their own interests. Michels's bleak view of organizations is as one-sided as Weber's ideal-type bureaucracy.

---

[1] du Gay, 2000.　　[2] Michels, 1949.

In conclusion, while no one single factor can prevent corruption a number of factors may keep corrupt practices in check. These include free media, strong normative commitment to transparency and openness, an institutional environment that that stresses integrity and honesty, fair procedures, democratic checks and balances, and the vigilance of citizens.

Creativity

The term creativity refers both to an internal **experience** and to a way of living. The two are connected since our ability to have a special kind of internal experience is what fosters creativity in living. Paediatrician and psychoanalyst Donald Winnicott captures this connection when he speaks of creative living as the 'doing that expresses being'.[1] The primary defining characteristic of creativity is the ability to reject predetermination of thought and conduct, since where thought and conduct are predetermined for us what we do is to comply rather than create. The opposite of creativity is adapting how we think and how we live to what already exists for us. Creativity has a special relation to **modernity** since perhaps the most important quality of modernity is its rejection of predetermination of thought and conduct in custom and tradition. Since creativity rejects predetermination, it involves negation and therefore destruction. This connection is well expressed by Picasso who described a picture as a 'sum of destructions'— for him creation is a sum of destructions. The link between creation and destruction does not, of course, mean that nothing is produced. On the contrary, in the final product 'nothing is lost'.[2] Creativity understood as an orientation to the world and a way of being is not the property of a special group of people we judge creative in the usual sense, for example, artists and writers. In considering creativity this way, we follow Winnicott who insists that 'for creative living we need no special talent'.[3]

The *Oxford English Dictionary* defines the verb to create with reference to a divine agent as 'to bring into being, cause to exist' and includes in the definition the idea that to create is 'to produce where nothing was before' (2nd edn., 1989). The link between someone who creates and the divine is well expressed by Winnicott when he notes how creativity involves 'the retention throughout life of something that belongs properly to infant experience: the ability to create the world'.[4] Our ability to create the world is our ability not to take the world for granted, as something given to us without regard to our experience of ourselves as subjects. This ability originates in the infantile **fantasy** of creating its world with which Winnicott is particularly concerned. The loss of this fantasy and of the creative capacity that goes with it destroys the feeling of aliveness (or being) that, for Winnicott, makes life worth living. Yet, to live creatively is not to live according to a delusion about the world: that it is our product and can be made to fit our wishes. The problem is to live creatively in a world we do not create or **control**. Finding this intermediate space, as Winnicott terms it, between the givenness of things for us and the fantasy of omnipotence is the task of creative living.

Consistent with this line of thought, Larry Hirshberg, founding director of Nissan Design Incorporated, finds the locus of creativity in the 'limbo space, that uncommitted, non-biased, and uncomfortable region in between zones of familiar knowledge'.[5] To get into this space involves a specific act: the suspension of conscious control over thought. Put another way, creativity requires access to a part of the mind that operates according to rules different from those with which we are familiar in our conscious experience of thinking. Creativity entails 'the holding of apparently disconnected,

---

[1] Winnicott et al., 1986.   [2] quoted in Bruner, 1962, p. 27.   [3] Winnicott et al., 1986, p. 44.   [4] Ibid. 40.   [5] Hirshberg, 1998, p. 83.

conflicting, overlapping, or even mutually exclusive thoughts in the mind simultaneously'.[1]

Unprecedented thinking expands the limits of what constitutes appropriate, responsible, reliable, and intelligent thought beyond the strictures of the scientific method. It engages the logical with the emotional, the scientific with the aesthetic. It requires reorientation and disorientation. It engages the instinctive creative capacities of the unschooled child and, like the child, uses the fruits of failure and play.... Creative activity ... does not confine itself to inbounds play. It comes to life at the edges, whether by blurring, abrading, overlapping, or breaking through the partitions.[2]

Creative thinking involves the opening of a channel of a special kind between conscious and pre-conscious mental processes, one in which neither process overwhelms the other.[3] These two processes represent thinking as we usually imagine it, and the suspension of thinking, or the process of not thinking. This process of not thinking opens us to the internal experience of creativity referred to above. It is the starting point and foundation for creative living.

• See also *entrepreneurship, innovation*

DAVID P. LEVINE, UNIVERSITY OF DENVER

Crisis management

This is a useful point of differentiating between *organizing* and *managing*. While organizing aims at what is smooth, predictable, and routinized, managing often deals with the unpredictable, the disruptive, and the urgent. It is believed that the first instance in which the expression 'crisis management' was used was by US Secretary of Defense, Robert McNamara, following the Cuban missile crisis in 1962. 'There is no longer any such thing as **strategy**, only crisis management' is what he is meant to have said. Crisis management suggests a highly turbulent or even chaotic environment, where little can be planned in advance; it suggests an ad hoc approach which responds to changing circumstances in an opportunistic way. It is reactive rather than proactive, and treats situations as one-offs. Crisis management is non-strategic since it stems from the belief that no long-term forecast has any value, a belief that it shares with some variants of **complexity and chaos theory**.

If crisis management suggests limits to some of the manager's traditional functions, notably those of planning and controlling, it paradoxically also implies that crises can be 'managed', so a certain measure of influence remains. In this sense, crisis management can be thought of as a comforting notion, since it extends the remit of **management** to every situation—everything, including crises, then is seen as manageable.

How then does one manage crises? Some crises may be handled in a relatively routine manner. The term 'fire-fighting' suggests that such crises demand urgent attention and call for an interruption of anything else that goes on in an organization. The aim is to limit the damage through the skilled deployment of different resources (fire-fighting equipment, human power, information, public relations, etc.). Theorists who have carried out extensive research on crises, like Mitroff and Weick and Sutcliffe,[4] have emphasized that a state of preparedness and mindfulness is important in handling such crises when they occur. Other crises, however, may refuse this type of 'regularization'. They may be unique 'one-offs', demanding improvisation and creative problem solving under conditions of extreme stress. Events such as those that took place on 11 September 2001 in New York and Washington may fall in this latter category. Our ability to make sense of such events *while they are unfolding* is severely limited. Finding ourselves outside the realm of the familiar and the predictable, our judgements of danger, urgency, and **risk** can be wide of the mark. We may experience

---

[1] Ibid. 22.   [2] Ibid. 24.   [3] Kubie and Schlesinger, 1978.   [4] Mitroff, 2004; Weick and Sutcliffe, 2001.

intense fear (including what is referred to as 'annihilation anxiety') and panic; we may also feel guilt for having failed to anticipate the crisis or to listen to those who warned us about it. As a result, our **actions** are often forced and impulsive, liable to make things worse. We often get to regret **decisions** that we make under crisis conditions. The poet John Keats wrote of '**negative capability**' as the ability to endure uncertainty and potential danger, without seeking instant solutions and resorting to spasmodic action; this has been seen as a highly desirable virtue in a leader during moments of crisis.[1]

There is another sense to the term 'crisis management'. This is when a leader or executive 'engineers' a crisis, creating a sense of emergency in order to unfreeze a situation which will allow him or her to implement a process of **change**. Referring to a situation as a 'crisis', as opposed to a difficulty, a problem, an adversity, or a setback, a leader raises levels of **anxiety** and creates an anticipation of serious and potentially painful changes. In such situations, a crisis is '**socially constructed**' by highlighting supposed failures and threats and presenting various options that might have been unacceptable in times of 'business as usual'. Such crises, if they lead neither to major restructuring nor to major disasters, are liable to diminish the credibility of leaders and erode their followers' trust towards them. An organization that marches from one crisis to another is liable to lose the meaning of crisis.

Critical theory and Critical Management Studies

Critical theory is an influential intellectual tradition founded by a group of scholars associated with the Institute of Social Research in Frankfurt, in the 1920s and 1930s. They are sometimes known as the Frankfurt School, and include Herbert Marcuse, Max Horkheimer, Theodor Adorno, Walter Benjamin, and Erich Fromm. More recently, Jürgen Habermas has been seen as the chief exponent of this tradition. Drawing their inspiration predominantly from Marx and Freud, these theorists viewed Western civilization as profoundly **alienating** and alienated. Unlike conventional social theories which reflect the conditions of alienation (and frequently serve the interests of the powerful), the Frankfurt School advocated critical theory as an emancipatory form of **knowledge**, which brings about an elimination of false consciousness and opens up the possibility of new forms of society free from oppression and exploitation. They viewed emancipation not only in material terms (freedom from exploitation at the workplace), but also in other spheres including sexual, aesthetic, and moral. Their theories anticipated many subsequent developments, providing powerful critical accounts of **consumerism**, liberal democracy, and Soviet Marxism. In the sphere of **epistemology**, they offered influential critiques of positivism and empiricism, arguing that these approaches make the pathologies of contemporary societies (crime, suicide, divorce, etc.) appear natural and inevitable, instead of establishing the way that they are socially defined and rooted and how they may eventually be overcome.

Critical Management Studies represents a diverse and heterogeneous group of theoretical approaches which, generally, stand in opposition to conventional positivistic and empiricist research. They draw their inspiration from critical theory, **Labour Process Theory**, but also **poststructuralist** and **postmodernist** theories including those developed by Foucault, Derrida, and Baudrillard. While not all scholars who associate themselves with this approach can be described as anti-management or anti-capitalist, they generally adopt a critical approach towards the theories and ideas which claim to increase managerial efficiency as well as to managers who seek to increase corporate profits through the use of such ideas.[2]

---

[1] Bennis, 1998; Chia and Morgan, 1996; Simpson, French, and Harvey, 2002.   [2] Alvesson and Willmott, 1992; Willmott, 1993.

Fournier and Grey have argued that Critical Management Studies stem from three fundamental and generally shared assumptions.[1] First, they have a non-performative intent, in other words they are not concerned with making the work of managers easier, more effective, or even more humane. Second, they strongly oppose the 'naturalization' of managerial ideas or concepts. Instead, they seek to show that even seemingly cast-iron entities, such as 'a manager', 'stress', 'race', depend on linguistic conventions and are socially constructed (see **social construction of reality** and **discourse**). Third, they emphasize **reflexivity**, a process whereby every act of creating knowledge alters the object of the knowledge. Representation, therefore, is never a neutral process, but depends on a number of choices, implicit or explicit, made in constructing narratives.

Overall, critical management studies theorists investigate how **power** is exercised in subtle and invisible forms, for instance through linguistic categories, labels, and conventions, through spatial arrangements, and through organizational procedures and routines which appear to be fair or, at least, unbiased. Power is exercised not merely by applying coercive or other regulations, by drawing **boundaries**, or by classifying and pigeon-holing different entities, but by defining reality in such a way that all of the above appear natural and sensible. Furthermore, power operates in subtle ways which block or silence alternative conceptualizations or definitions. In these respects, Critical Management Studies have remained loyal to the common theme of both critical theory and post-structuralism (and before them, classical Marxism), namely that power involves a subtle but unshakeable shaping of consciousness.[2]

A significant divergence of opinions in Critical Management Studies concerns the question of 'who has the right to speak for another person', since in doing so one is liable to construct reality in a way that frames that person, for example as a victim, as a hero, or as a villain. More extreme versions would argue that no one should be authorized to speak on behalf of anyone else—the result tends to be that only women can speak on women's issues, only disabled people on disability, and so forth. Others, like Martin Parker,[3] argue that academics have a moral responsibility to speak for those who are silenced or denied a **voice**, even if in doing so, they may inadvertently compound the silencing and denial.

Criticism and critique

Criticism shares an etymology with crisis (see **crisis management**)—'judgement'. Critical reflection has long been seen as vital to learning and knowledge creation. It is also viewed as a principal aim of many programmes of professional education and management education. Generations of students have seen their work marked down for failing to use concepts and theories in a 'critical' manner or for uncritically embracing assumptions that should be challenged. And generations of teachers have bemoaned the absence of critical reflection among their pupils. This raises various questions: What is criticism? Is the critical spirit on the wane in our times? What is so great about criticism?

Criticism can be positive or negative—at its most basic it involves a judgement of quality. Negative criticism entails a dissatisfaction with the status quo and a decision to challenge it in some way. At its simplest, it states 'x is not good', where x can be a work of art, a person, a theory, or virtually anything else. At a more elaborate level, criticism states 'x is not what it seems'; it then seeks to show that what seemed incontestable can be challenged and shown to be contestable or untrue. The rather unattractive use of 'critique' as a verb often serves to distinguish it from 'criticize'. To criticize usually means that

---

[1] Fournier and Grey, 2000.   [2] See e.g. Alvesson and Willmott, 1992; Boje, 2001; Hassard, Hogan, and Rowlinson, 2001; Wallemacq and Sims, 1998.   [3] Parker, 1995.

something is not good or as good as it should be; to critique suggests that something is not what it appears to be or that some of the conditions of its existence have not been adequately understood.

The Western critical tradition goes back to the Greeks who developed a systematic questioning of what appear as incontestable truths. Western philosophy developed out of questioning received wisdom. In particular, it challenged religion, tradition, and common sense. But the Western tradition also involved a systematic criticism of social and political systems, a systematic criticism of leaders and public officials. Criticism was a major force in the Western Enlightenment and became the foundation for many subsequent scientific developments. The criticism of past theories thus becomes the starting point for developing newer, more powerful ones. The criticism of past political institutions became the starting point for developing newer, better ones. Thus, criticism emerged as a systematic challenge to tradition by what claimed to be the forces of reason. In the twentieth century **critical theory** was developed on the premiss that much of the knowledge generated in a capitalist system becomes itself part of exploitative relations between **classes** and nations. Critical theorists and many Critical Management Studies scholars have argued that our critical spirit becomes blunted, as we uncritically adopt opinions and views disseminated by the **mass media** and become victims of **fads and fashions**.

Critical reflection has emerged as the principal value in most management and professional education programmes today in part as an attempt to counter the passive embracement of panaceas and stock recipes. The 'reflective practitioner' is today's equivalent of Plato's philosopher-king.[1] Unlike the mechanic who uses a toolkit to deal with predictable and routine situations, the reflective practitioner approaches situations that are complex, variable, and unexpected. They require vigilance and inquisitiveness rather than routine **competence**. Critical reflection offers a way of reconciling **experience** with theory in the generation and application of knowledge. Managers, professionals, and practitioners of all sorts (such as consultants, therapists, etc.), according to this approach, should seek to question their practices at every stage. Theoretical knowledge from their disciplines as well as narrative knowledge, communicated through stories, anecdotes, and recipes, should be applied with caution and consideration for the particularities of specific situations.

The value of critical reflection and criticism is sometimes accepted uncritically. Is there a downside to criticism? Criticism can be destructive. This is especially so if it is experienced as unfair; but even fair criticism can undermine or destroy a theory, a process, or a person in their early stages of development. Thus many a good idea has been killed by criticism. Many promising organizational members have been discouraged or devastated by harsh criticism from their leaders. Another negative aspect of criticism is revealed when it is undertaken in the name of fashion—criticizing yesterday's ideas and practices may then amount to little more than uncritical embracement of the new and the modish. Some criticisms are aimed at straw men and driven by envy, hate, or resentment. In all these ways, one should mistrust criticism and critique even when they are extolled as the keys to learning and knowledge. It is not so surprising to encounter people from different cultural backgrounds, notably Far Eastern ones, which honour loyalty and tradition who find the Westerner's propensity to criticism deeply problematic. Criticism is a powerful attitude that can generate new ideas and act as a force for emancipation; but it should be itself subject to criticism.

---

[1] Argyris and Schön, 1978; 1996.

Crowds

Crowds have been the object of serious social research for over a century. Conservative theorists have generally abhorred crowds, which appear to instil a herd instinct among their members, suppressing individuality, morality, and good manners. In a famous study, the psychologist Gustave Le Bon argued that the crowd has a mind of its own that takes over the minds of the individuals which compose it and controls their behaviour.[1] The most important crowd phenomenon is the dominance of **emotion** over intellect. Within crowds, argued Le Bon, emotions are wild and untamed, quickly communicated from person to person as if they were contagious. Both intellectual and moral judgements are impaired and irrational forces gain the upper hand. Le Bon's approach influenced Freud, Bion, and subsequent theorists who argued that **groups** may lapse into irrational, crowd-like phenomena (such as panic, suggestibility, and contagiousness of emotion) under certain conditions.

Le Bon's theory has had its critics. In his study of crowds in the French Revolution, George Rudé showed that in most instances crowd behaviour was driven by legitimate, rational social, and moral concerns, such as the price of bread and the display of brutality on the part of the agents of law and order.[2] One aspect of crowd mental functioning that has attracted much attention since it was first singled out by Freud has been **leadership**.[3] Far from responding irrationally under the grip of random primeval forces, it is now recognized that crowds generally submit themselves to the authority of leaders, whose prompts they may follow with little reflection. Crowd control currently relies extensively on identification and isolation of individuals who assume such leadership functions.[4]

What can organizational theory learn from crowd theory? Some organizations, including the police, football clubs, carnival managers, architectural firms designing shopping malls, and so forth, may be directly involved in managing, controlling, or dissolving crowds. Others, such as armies in disorderly retreat, firms, or stock markets seized by sudden panic, may lapse into crowd like behaviours. In the last resort, however, it must be borne in mind that organizations built around routine execution of different tasks are *not* crowds.

Culture

Since Raymond Williams wrote his influential entry on culture in *Keywords*,[5] the term has marched on, conquering and colonizing many **discourses** and establishing itself in countless texts and conversations. So widespread is its use today that it would not be an exaggeration to say that 'culture' could feature in every single entry of this thesaurus. The adjective 'cultural' can precede an innumerable array of terms: revolution, diversity, relativism, studies, change, forum, identity, tourism, imperialism, jamming, profile, and many others come into sharp focus when the word 'cultural' is placed in front of them. The multicultural society and the multicultural organization have emerged as the chief social spaces of our times, where many of us live and work. And who could argue against **multiculturalism** today without appearing at best provincial and at worst a bigot?

But culture has paid a price for its enormous success. It has become rather too comfortable a term, readily recruited to explain virtually everything (differences and conflicts, successes and failures, emotions and thoughts, ideas and practices, imperialism and provincialism, tastes and styles, etc.); in doing so, it risks explaining very little. If everything can be put down to culture, how does culture ultimately enlighten us? And what exactly is culture?

We can think of culture as the material and **spiritual** heritage of a **community**, a group, or

---

[1] Le Bon, 1885/1960.   [2] Rudé, 1959.   [3] Freud, 1921/1985.   [4] Stott and Drury, 2000.   [5] Williams, 1976; 1983.

an organization. It includes the stock of myths and stories, artistic and craft artefacts, buildings, tools, laws, institutions, rituals, and customs. It is frequently argued that culture is the cement which holds communities together by establishing shared **meanings** and **values**, which enable people to communicate with each other, taking many things for granted. It is interesting to note that this definition of culture depends on the term 'community', a term whose decline has been in opposition to the rise of culture. We can also note that the definition is itself culture-bound—if culture is the source of meaning, then the meaning of culture is itself culturally determined. It could then be argued that different cultures may define culture differently or indeed may be unwilling to define it at all.

In the broad sense noted above, culture is a relatively recent term that emerged in the nineteenth century in contrast to 'civilization'. 'Civilization' was always linked with the idea of progress and development, juxtaposing the civilized to the uncivilized, the savage, and the wild. It is a term loaded with assumptions about the supremacy of certain types of human **achievement**. Culture is a more neutral term. It is perfectly possible to talk of pre-literate, primitive, or tribal cultures, but it would hardly make sense to talk of primitive civilizations. Civilization generally stresses the technical, economic, and political achievements of humanity and presupposes a certain minimum advancement in these areas. Culture, on the other hand, stresses artistic, religious, legal, or ideological forms which characterize different communities and societies. Culture may include mundane and everyday, yet significant, objects and practices. Tools and utensils, eating implements, items of clothing, tattoos, jewellery, advertisements, music and musical instruments, religious rituals, slang, and language in general are all accepted as elements of culture.

Etymologically, culture is related to cultivation. It is the result of human work on nature's own resources. Just as agriculture works on the natural landscape, tames it, and humanizes it, culture works on human beings themselves, turning them from physical, animal beings into members of communities. As Peter Worsley said, culture then is 'everything acquired by human beings which is not physically inherited'.[1]

The popularity of culture since the late nineteenth century is not accidental. It coincides with the rise of cultural anthropology as a discipline that was built around the concept of culture and based on systematic ethnographic fieldwork on pre-literate societies. Early anthropologists were impressed by the truly bewildering variety of social **norms**, traditions, beliefs, and practices across such societies. Related to this variety of cultural forms was the realization that the distinction between 'natural' and 'unnatural' behaviours was highly problematic. What appeared to be a universal truth for all human beings was shown by anthropologists to be true only for *some* cultures. Behaviours that appeared to be universal (such as grieving for the loss of a loved relative) turned out to be acquired behaviours, learnt behaviours, which varied extensively from one place to the next.

Scholarly writing on culture comes in many varieties. Whether describing culture as the 'software of the mind',[2] or as 'the way we do things around here' (used by numerous authors, especially in relation to organizational culture), the idea of culture embodies certain assumptions that are difficult to unpack. One of the most important assumptions is that there is something 'shared' about culture, something that generates a sense of unity and coherence. Culture claims quietly, 'We do things in a particular way around here, don't try doing things differently.' In the first instance, then, culture acts as social **control**; it constrains and stops certain actions. Yet we are all familiar with various cultural prohibitions that are routinely disregarded, bent, or broken. Could it then be that

---

[1] Worsley, 1970, p. 24.   [2] Hofstede, 1991.

the violations are as much part of culture as the prohibitions?

Another important function that culture is said to fulfil is 'meaning infusing'—it acts as the code that reveals the significance of different events and different phenomena. But here too there are difficulties. Different people, in spite of sharing a culture, may read different meanings into the same events. Indeed each individual may read his or her own unique meaning in a particular event—how then could we talk of culture as something shared?

Yet another function of culture is said to be that it offers us a heritage of achievement of which we can feel proud; this is sometimes referred to as the **narcissistic** function of culture. But here too we find fragmentation. One person's achievement is another person's shame; think, for instance, of the contrasting evaluations of the 'British empire'. As a construction, then, culture can easily be said to reify unity, to obscure or obfuscate differences and **conflicts**, and to slot into a functionalist way of thinking, where everything can be 'explained away' as being functional to something else.

Some scholars have sought to overcome these difficulties by proposing alternative perspectives on culture. Martin,[1] and Frost and colleagues,[2] have distinguished three such perspectives. The first is the *integration* perspective—it is close to the one described above as the social cement or glue that holds societies together, made up of shared meanings, values, and assumptions. The *differentiation* perspective, on the other hand, acknowledges the existence of different subcultures and even counter-cultures; thus different **voices**, discourses, and values can coexist within the same social space; at times they ignore each other, at others they reinforce each other or they clash against each other. A third perspective, referred to as the *fragmentation* perspective, looks at the tendency of voices and discourses to break down into fragments within a universe of diverse and unstable meanings and values.

This fragmentation perspective holds some promise for the future. It accords with some of the qualities of postmodernity, when the **grand narratives** of the past, such as science and religion, have exhausted themselves or fragmented into numerous partial ones. Thus scientific institutions, political organizations, mass media, businesses, schools, professional bodies, lobbies, fashion leaders, advertisers, as well as religious organizations and many others, are viewed as having a part in the cultural polyphony of modern societies. However, one of the difficulties that this perspective raises is that it dilutes the idea of culture to the point where it becomes questionable whether it can function as culture. If there are endless stories, endless meanings, and endless variations of values and beliefs, could we not end up with every woman and every man being a cultural island unto themselves? How do they communicate with each other? Why do they sometimes join their voices in celebration, protest, or grief? Why do they applaud the same shows and attend the same ceremonies?

Against the fragmenting tendencies of culture we must note the continuing usefulness of the term and its widespread use to indicate something shared, something lasting, something valued, and something that can offer meaningful explanation. At the last count, Google picked up a quarter of a billion web pages with the word 'cultural' in them. Isn't it curious that there are fewer than 200 entries with the word 'anti-culturalist' in them? And yet, this is precisely what Weber's theory of **bureaucracy** represented, a model of organization that functions in a culture-neutral way, irrespective of local customs and traditions. Such an organization appears strangely unrealistic in our current multicultural times. And in a curious way, the triumph of multiculturalism, the side-by-side coexistence of different cultural traditions,

---

[1] Martin, 1992.   [2] Frost et al., 1991.

suggest that there are certain issues on which differences reinforce an underlying sameness.

• See also *corporate culture*

Customer relations

The last ten years or so have seen a far-reaching reconfiguration of the characters that dominate the world of organizations. For much of its life, the study of organizations was dominated by two central characters, the manager and the worker, whose relationship with all its tensions, conflicts, and accommodations unfolded within a broader environment of markets, governments, shareholders, social institutions, technological forces, and so forth. In the last ten years, however, there has been a substantial movement to change the two-actor show into a three-actor show, the organizational dyad into a triad. The newcomer on stage has been the **consumer**, a character whose whims, habits, desires, and practices are no longer seen as 'impacting on' the activities of managers and workers from the outside but increasingly as defining them. At times the referee in the management–labour contest, the consumer is often called upon to take sides, declare winners and losers, but above all define the rules of the game.

'Customer service' is the label that has come to stand for the incorporation of the consumer in the world of organizations. Following early contributions in this area,[1] this has now gathered pace, as increasing numbers of authors in the area of organizations seek to assess how the discourse of customers and consumers is reshaping the world of organizations. One of the reasons why the consumer has been brought into the world of organizations is the increasing proportion of workers who are working directly with customers in service and other occupations. In sectors like education, health, catering, tourism, retail, finance, transport, professional services, computing, and so forth, large armies of employees are involved in 'front-line work'— dealing with customers, servicing them, advising them, keeping them happy. Front-line work makes different demands on individuals (both managers and workers) and groups from manufacturing or back office jobs, safely insulated from the critical gaze of the customer. Instead, front-line jobs emphasize the importance of the employees' **emotional labour**, social and verbal skills, appearance, and demeanour under pressure.[2] One would hardly use the metaphor of a theatrical performance to describe the behaviour of a metal-basher or a pen-pusher—yet this metaphor becomes quite apt in capturing some of the qualities of front-line work, with its thrills, unpredictability, and audience scrutiny.

In a major study, Frenkel and colleagues studied some 1,000 employees in front-line occupations, in fourteen organizations across three continents.[3] Occupations included sales, service, and knowledge-intensive ones. Frenkel and colleagues reject the pessimistic scenario of increasingly regimented, surveyed, and controlled workers (the 'panoptic nightmare') where employees virtually prostitute themselves and their emotions in the presence of customers. They also reject the optimistic scenario whereby front-line employees are empowered to use learning and knowledge to control and enjoy interactions with the customers. Instead, they found that the routinizing logic in customer relations was not incompatible with service workers claiming to enjoy displays of **emotion** toward the customers. Nor is performance monitoring and evaluation used in a heavy-handed, disciplinarian mode by management, but more often is seen as a means towards enhancing employee **learning** and improving service quality. Service workers, in particular, emerge as quite content from their interactions with customers, in spite of the routine quality of most such interactions. Overall, the authors argue on

---

[1] du Gay, 1996; du Gay and Salaman, 1992; Knights and Morgan, 1993; Leidner, 1993.   [2] Sturdy, Grugulis, and Willmott, 2001.
[3] Frenkel et al., 1999.

the basis of their evidence that the customer is not always the adjudicator in the management–worker relationship. Instead, there are times when managers and workers unite in the face of rude or devious customers; controlling the customer then takes precedence over **control** and **resistance** within the employment relationship. More generally, these authors forcefully argue that neither the increasing complexity of workflows nor the hybridization of organizations with network, entrepreneurial, and knowledge-intensive features marks the demise of **bureaucracy**.

The complexities and ambiguities of service work have been well described by Korczynski, who notes that the service workers' experience with their customers is one of rapidly alternating intense pleasure and pain and their feelings toward them are highly ambivalent.[1] Caught between the customer and management, frontline workers turn to each other for support, sustenance, and escape—they form *communities of coping* (by analogy to **communities of practice**), where emotional labour is not oriented only towards the customer but also towards each other. Communities of coping create informal, dense **cultures** among the service workforce, which cannot be easily controlled or tamed by managers.

• See also *emotional labour*

Cynicism

Cynicism is frequently viewed as a psychological attitude of detachment, disparagement, and suspicion. It takes its name from a philosophical school (whose most famous exponent was Diogenes of Sinope, *c.*399–323 BC) which emphasized the closeness of people to animals (cynicism comes from 'cyon', Greek for 'dog'),

defied all state **authority**, and ridiculed all idealistic and humanist doctrines. Cynic philosophers were well known for their contempt of all comfort, material or **spiritual**, and for their constant questioning of appearances, seeking to discover not just the truth but 'the naked truth'.[2] They refused to write down their philosophical ideas, opting instead to live out their philosophy in their daily lives—Diogenes gained public admiration but also notoriety for living in a barrel, having no earthly possessions, and scandalizing public morality by performing all his bodily functions in public. The fact that they left no written legacy made cynic philosophers easy targets for slander and calumniation by their opponents.

Cynicism is now used mostly in a negative way to denote an embittered suspiciousness and pessimism which stands in the way of **change**, **learning**, and progress. Yet cynicism may be a healthy mechanism of psychological survival in the face of lies, deceptions, and broken promises. Within the context of organizations, cynicism marks a thorough alienation from the organization's vision or moral purpose,[3] which however does not amount to full-scale **resistance** to organizational practices.[4] Fleming and Spicer have argued that cynicism can be viewed as a type of dis-**identification** with dominant power structures within an organization which, however, ensures that employees still practise their parts and, therefore, reinforce these structures.[5]

In a rare attempt to reclaim the original non-pejorative meaning of cynicism, Cutler proposed the image of the cynical manager as one who does away with artificial status distinctions, rejects fads and fashions, submits him- or herself to the same disciplines as those endured by followers, and keeps a flexible and open mind in the face of adversity, instead of seeking to apportion blame and claim credit.[6]

---

[1] Korczynski, 2003.   [2] Sloterdijk, 1988.   [3] Dean, Brandes, and Dharwadkar, 1998.   [4] Kunda, 1992; Watson, 2001.   [5] Fleming and Spicer, 2003.   [6] Cutler, 2000; 2005.

Death

Death is not often discussed in connection with organizations. But it should be. Many organizations are directly or indirectly in the business of death; they include hospitals, abattoirs, funeral directors, legal firms, coroners, police forces, emergency services, armies, and churches. Many other organizations are involved in documenting, representing, and glamorizing death—film, photography, news journalism among them. But death is something that we all carry with us, wherever we go. Rarely are we separated from a death, that of a friend, a relative, an acquaintance, or our own, by more than a thread. And yet, death sometimes seems to be far from our thoughts for long periods. It is often said that death is the one certain thing about every human life and many of our actions are consciously or **unconsciously** linked to it.

The neglect of death by organizational and (to a lesser extent) social sciences was noted by Willmott,[1] who attributed it to the privatization and medicalization of death in modern societies. Willmott argued that the social sciences are guilty of essentializing a morbid and negative construction of death, as something to be managed and coped with, thus stripping away various richer nuances of meaning that different cultures and individuals read into it. In line with his **post-structuralist** orientation, Willmott insisted that the morbid representation of death should be 'recognised as a social product, not reproduced in sociological studies as something that is seemingly innate to the human condition'.[2] A fair point and one that is worth repeating. All the same, our own culture's ambivalent attitude towards death is also significant—on the one hand, one can scarcely see a film without a catalogue of deaths (and increasingly torture); on the other hand, powerful mechanisms operate to screen death out of everyday life and everyday **discourses**. 'Death. How to avoid it, delay it, and, as a last resort, how to cope with it' rather than Willmott's 'Death. So what?' defines our dominant discourse on the subject; Tibetan and other alternative engagements with death and dying are but footnotes in the margins of the dominant discourse.

In coping with death, human beings have turned to different institutions—religion, **spirituality**, therapy, medicine, etc. A long line of thinking has also pointed out that human beings seek to attain a modicum of immortality through the legacy that survives them. This may include various accomplishments, individual and collective, such as works of engineering, art, or science, or business empires and fortunes that outlast their creators. Some people seek to leave a legacy through philanthropic donations or bestowing their name on an institution. For many, their legacy is their children, who will carry their genetic material into the future. Burkard Sievers has noted that organizations too serve their members' desire for immortality.[3] Individuals may indeed be mortal, but being part of a powerful, glamorous, and seemingly immortal organization offers the consolation to those inside that they share something of this immortality just as they share in the power and glamour. It is maybe for this reason that psychotic anxieties of organizational annihilation can be so powerful—the death, actual or fantasized, of an organization is

[1] Willmott, 2000.   [2] Ibid. 649.   [3] Sievers, 1994.

experienced as nothing short of apocalyptic. An author who has developed Sievers's insight on the basis of his extensive research into organizational **downsizing** is Howard F. Stein: in a series of provocative publications,[1] Stein has argued that organizational downsizing, so widespread in corporate America since the 1980s, amounts to an experience of slow death that evokes images of the Nazi **genocide**.

Stein argues that under the regime of short-term profitability, what he calls the religion of the bottom line, American businesses have sought to eradicate the 'dead wood' from the body of the organization in ways that recreate some of the experiences of Nazi extermination camps. 'Organizational darkness is not the fact of the "symbolic" equation of the American workplace and the Holocaust, but the emotional experience of the workplace that makes the metaphor—and certain recurrent others—plausible and, for many, emotionally apt and "right." '[2] Stein offers much evidence of a symbolic equation between 'corporate cleansing' and 'ethnic cleansing', both of which view the survival of the whole (the organization, the society) as depending on 'the expulsion of unwanted parts' (p. 69). He also offers evidence of survivors' guilt coupled with the **anxiety** lest they should be next in the line of cleansing. Dismissed colleagues are experienced as dead people while those to be sacked are viewed as walking corpses. The undue haste of the dismissals and the absence of any proper farewell or any acknowledgement of pain and grief compound the trauma.

Proximity to death, actual or symbolic, leaves strong marks. Psychologists Erich Lindemann and Elisabeth Kübler-Ross wrote influential studies on how communities deal with disasters that suddenly bring death in their midst by going through several stages of grieving, from denial to idealization of the lost ones, anger, guilt, and eventual acceptance.[3] In a seminal study conducted in a British hospital in the 1950s, Isabel Menzies investigated nurses working with terminally sick people.[4] She documented the extremely high levels of anxiety experienced by these nurses and, equally importantly, various ways of handling these anxieties that involved depersonalization, distancing, and self-deskilling. Menzies argued that these amounted to social **defence mechanisms** similar to individual defence mechanisms aimed at keeping anxiety at bay. She termed them 'social defenses' (against anxiety) and argued that they become embedded in the hospital **structure** and the **culture** and are part of professional training of nurses. She observed that many of these defences backfire, exactly as in the case of neurotic defences, causing more anxiety, guilt, and suffering than what they were intended to mitigate. Her research was influential in changing the assumptions about the containment of anxiety—acknowledgement, recognition, and support are now seen as essential needs of those working in close proximity with death. Thus, mourning and grieving rites are vital in helping us cope with death, actual or symbolic. Even the successful termination of a project can be experienced as a symbolic death unless properly acknowledged and marked in order to enable us to move on.

Building on the theories of Mary Douglas and Arnold van Gennep,[5] classicist Robert Parker has argued that contact with corpses (and in a different way with 'murderers') represents dangerous moments of **boundary** crossings that call for elaborate grieving measures which enable the dead to move on to the world of the dead and the mourning relatives to return to the world of the living.[6] Without these rituals, a condition that the Greeks referred to as 'miasma' occurs, a condition that stands at the centre of most tragedies. Miasma is a state of profound uncleanliness and pollution that affects and corrupts everyone in a state or a family. Miasma,

---

[1] Stein, 1997; 1998; 2001.   [2] Stein, 2001, p. 15.   [3] Lindemann, 1944; Kübler-Ross, 1969.   [4] Menzies, 1960.   [5] Douglas, 1966/2002; Gennep, 1960.   [6] Parker, 1983.

once it has taken grip, is exceptionally difficult to eradicate, resulting in profound depression, paralysing self-criticism, constant expectation of punishment, and a collapse of any desire to resist. Miasma can sometimes take hold of an organization, notably one that has undergone very rapid change, for example, through a shift from a public service ethos to a market-driven one or from product-based to customer-based values. The crucial factor for miasma, however, is the unseemly dismissals of visible members of staff and the perception of the leadership as having blood on its hands. In the absence of proper mourning, a generalized climate of depression, self-reproach, scapegoating, and mistrust sets in that becomes extremely difficult to alter.[1]

Decision and decision making

Decision making is generally regarded as a major aspect of organizations and human life in general. We make decisions, we act on them; some decisions prove sound, some less good, and some even disastrous. But this view of decision making often conceals something more multi-faceted and untidy. Scholars have developed numerous 'stage' models and theories of decision making, showing how it might be done as a sequence of rational steps. This rarely fits with how human beings *actually* reach decisions, especially in organizations. Many successful decisions are reached through highly idiosyncratic reasoning, while many unsuccessful ones are the products of careful and systematic reasoning. And many decisions that appear to have been successful turn out to have adverse long-term implications, while, alternatively, decisions that seemed to cause trouble at the time turn out to be 'blessings in disguise'.

Research on decision can be divided into two broad approaches. *Behavioural decision making* relies mostly on experimental work to examine how decisions are made under laboratory conditions. Particular decision games like the 'prisoner's dilemma' may be used in this connection, to reveal how decisions are reached in situations of uncertainty and risk, whether for example individuals opt to collaborate or fight under different circumstances. Game theory has largely evolved on the back of such research involving highly abstract mathematical models that simulate the behaviour and interaction of different actors engaged in collective games, where the **strategy** adopted by each one of them depends on assumptions about the strategies of the others. *Organizational decision making*, on the other hand, sacrifices mathematical precision in exchange for attempting to study decision making in the more messy, unpredictable, and politically charged circumstances which prevail in most organizations.[2] How do people make decisions under conditions of stress, denial, or panic? How do group decisions differ from individual ones? How does **power** influence the making of decisions? And how do **emotions**, including group loyalty, shame, pride, and so forth, affect decision making?

Rational choice models of decision making have long dominated economics. Individuals are then treated as rational actors; when faced with a decision, they carefully list the available alternatives, evaluate the advantages and costs of each one, and opt for the one that optimizes their gains and minimizes their losses. It is not surprising that such models of decision making have come to be viewed as inadequate in accounting for people's actions in organizations and indeed the strategic choices of organizations themselves. There are innumerable examples where the wrong choices were made and almost as many where the right options were selected for the wrong reasons. These include accidents and disasters, successes and failures in the launching of new products, mergers, acquisitions, career choices, relocations, restructurings, appointments, sackings, and so forth. All the same, **rationality** continues to feature in studies of organizational decision making.

---

[1] Gabriel, 2008b.   [2] Shapira, 1997.

One attempt to rescue a rational approach to decision making was through the concept of bounded rationality,[1] according to which a rational decision maker limits the range of options available and then chooses the first one to satisfy certain core criteria. Another attempt was the 'incremental' approach.[2] This suggested that decisions are often less monumental than generally assumed and that the process of decision making often consists of many small decisions which end up looking like one big one.

A particularly brilliant and influential account of decision making was offered by political scientist George T. Allison in his book *The Essence of Decision*.[3] Allison analysed closely the Cuban missile crisis (1962) which brought the United States and the Soviet Union to the edge of nuclear war, precipitated by the placing of Soviet nuclear missiles in Cuba. Trying to account for the crisis and its resolution, Allison proposes three alternative models of decision making. The rational actor approach treats each government as a single actor that acts in ways that deliver maximum pay-off. The **bureaucratic** process approach looks at decisions as outcomes of fixed procedures and mechanisms over which individuals have relatively little influence or control. Finally, the government process approach looks at decisions as the results of political bargaining within different blocs—individual decisions may appear to reflect a particular interest, but in reality they may be compromise formations resulting from different preferences. Allison argued convincingly that each approach has several strengths and weaknesses, but was most concerned to show that reliance on the 'rational actor' model led to disastrous consequences—decisions, in other words, may be especially irrational (and damaging) if each party assumes others to act rationally. This may apply equally to two organizations about to enter a price war, two partners suing each other for divorce, or two

governments about to inflict on their citizens the horrors of war.

A relatively recent approach to decision making places individual decisions within narrative patterns embedded in individual experiences.[4] According to this view, we make decisions consistent with the **stories** we write about ourselves, stories through which we sustain our **identities**. Thus a decision to quit one's job or to turn whistle-blower becomes part of a life story whose meaning resides in the way it fits in a plot—for instance, as the price to pay in order to maintain one's dignity and integrity or as the result of vicious bullying or discrimination.[5] A decision in this sense serves a narrative rather than a material purpose—contributing towards a plausible and even admirable story even if the material outcome is to the disadvantage of the person making the decision. This approach to decision making can be extended to many types of decisions, including our choices as consumers (we 'decide' to purchase products and services that enhance our life stories), our political choices (we vote for politicians whose message is consistent with the political stories we tell about ourselves), and even our moral choices (we make them in line with our self-image as moral agents). Approaching decisions from this angle suggests that researchers should explore much more closely the ways decisions 'fit' within life **narratives** and identity stories.

• See also *choice*

Deconstruction

A popular term of **postmodern** theory proposed by Jacques Derrida.[6] Derrida criticized Western philosophy for being preoccupied with discovering the essence behind appearances; instead he advocated a close study of language and texts, in which words are not seen as fixed to specific

---

[1] Simon, 1957.   [2] Mintzberg, Raisinghani, and Theoret, 1976.   [3] Allison, 1971.   [4] O'Connor, 1997.   [5] Sims, 2003; 2005.
[6] Derrida, 1976.

objects and activities, but rather acquire their meaning in their juxtaposition to other words, an idea that he inherited from Swiss linguist Ferdinand de Saussure.[1] Derrida argued that it is in the text itself rather than different linguistic and historical contexts that **meaning** resides. Deconstruction is a process which brings to the surface the tensions, contradictions, absences, and silences in the text, or as Barbara Johnson has put it 'a careful teasing out of warring forces of signification within a text'.[2] In this sense then deconstruction is different from **interpretation**— it does not look at the author's intentions, the social and historical contexts at the time a text was written, or anything at all outside the text in order to reveal the text's inner significance. This is not, however, always observed by numerous authors who routinely use the term to indicate interpretation or even analysis of a text, indulging in what Linstead terms 'vulgar deconstruction'.[3]

In organizational studies, the use of deconstruction has been the result of an increasing tendency to view organizations as texts, in other words not as concrete entities in a world 'out there', but as entities that come into being through references to them in **discourse**. Deconstruction of organization then starts with the observation that the very term 'organization' excludes elements of disorder and untidiness, which are, therefore, 'silenced' or marginalized. Organization then is seen as the dominant pole of an axis of meaning or signification whose other pole becomes invisible, along with the axis itself. Deconstruction often discovers similar dualities or dichotomies (male–female, white–black, heterosexual–homosexual), where the dominant term silences the subordinate one, without ever being able to obliterate it. In a similar way, 'management' can be deconstructed as the dominant pole of a duality of control and usage. Managers **control** resources, processes, and information; non-managers are controlled

as resources, therefore informed, used, and processed.

While deconstruction is most fruitful when applied to relatively small pieces of text, such as stories, euphemisms, labels, and 'spin', it has been used with some success in exploring the hidden assumptions of academic texts and theories.[4] Its greatest success has been in demonstrating how seemingly innocent texts are full of assumptions about what is normal and abnormal, right and wrong, good and bad, and in this way supports different **power** relations. For example, by deconstructing the term 'single parent' we can uncover assumptions of abnormality, failure, irresponsibility, but also the assumption that 'normal parents' are married. These power relations include many researchers themselves who take it upon themselves to classify, describe, and represent others. Instead, as Linstead has advocated deconstructive research emphasizes 'multiple realities, fragmentation, plurality, subjectivity, and a concern with the means by which social life is represented in accounts that create rather than transmit meaning'.[5]

• See also **discourse, postmodernism, reflexivity**

Defence mechanisms

Defence mechanisms are a group of psychological processes aimed at reducing painful and troubling feelings (notably **anxiety**) or at eliminating forces that are experienced as threatening the integrity or mental survival of an individual. These forces may include highly painful memories of real or imagined traumas. Freudian theory recognizes numerous defences, including regression, reaction formation, projection, introjection, isolation, reversal, and identification with the aggressor, though it treats repression as the archetypal defence. Repression is the fundamental defence mechanism, through

---

[1] Saussure, 1960.   [2] Cited in Culler, 1981/2001, p. viii.   [3] Linstead, 1993.   [4] Czarniawska, 1999; Kilduff, 1993.   [5] Linstead, 1993, p. 98.

which painful or threatening desires, ideas, and emotions are prevented from reaching consciousness, being restricted to the **unconscious**. 'The theory of repression is the cornerstone on which the whole structure of psycho-analysis rests,' wrote Freud.[1]

Much of the unconscious contains ideas and desires repressed in early childhood, but repressions continue throughout life, whenever something too painful threatens to reach consciousness. Repressed ideas and desires do not generally decay with the passage of time; they may surface in different guises, such as slips of the tongue ('Freudian slips'), neurotic symptoms, dreams, **fantasies**, and works of art. A distinction can be made between primary repression and secondary repression—the latter attempts to repress the symptoms which result from the former. Effective repressions tend to silence repressed ideas totally or allow them socially permissible ways to reach consciousness. Unsuccessful repressions lie at the heart of the causation of neurosis—they either fail to suppress an idea totally, or the symptoms which result are themselves debilitating or anxiety provoking. The relationship between repression and anxiety is a complex one. Anxiety is usually a trigger for repression; however, unsuccessful repressions may cause anxiety.

Since Freud's work, theorists have placed greater emphasis on two defences singled out by Melanie Klein,[2] splitting and denial. Splitting divides a mental structure or image into two, usually antithetical elements, of which one is seen as all-good and the other as all-evil. Splitting is of considerable interest in the study of organizations, where it usually takes a collective form: a group of individuals or even the majority of organizational members may collectively split the organization or its leadership into highly idealized good parts and highly vilified bad parts. Invariably, good parts are invested with love and introjected while bad parts become legitimate targets of hate and are scapegoated. Denial is a process whereby a painful aspect of the world or an aspect of the ego is denied, without, however, being excluded from consciousness as in repression. Denial may be confirmed on occasion through negation, the persistent and repeated rejection of a particular idea which does not call for such an overt disavowal. Alternatively, denial may be indicated through the dismissal of potential threats or dangers through constant joking and bantering.

In organizations, defence mechanisms are sometimes collectively deployed, as if all organizational members have agreed to repress a certain threatening idea or to idealize (or vilify) the organization itself. For example, it has been argued that some major accidents, such as the *Challenger* disaster, were due to the fact that organizational participants collectively repressed the possibility of such accidents happening rather than examining how they might have been avoided.[3] In addition to these defences, however, organizations offer individuals a number of 'social defences' against anxiety.[4] Organizational **hierarchies** and organizational **rituals** act in such a way, protecting individuals from feelings of anxiety and guilt when they have to make hard or painful decisions.[5] Some writers have argued that many managerial practices, such as forecasting, planning, monitoring, report writing, etc. are of limited usefulness for the organization, but act as mechanisms of self-protection and defence.[6] Furthermore, some organizations may be suffused by defensive mechanisms which reflect the personality of their chief executive; they may, for example, develop paranoid suspiciousness, megalomaniac delusions, or depressive denial, mirroring the leader's personal defence mechanisms.[7] Defence mechanisms undoubtedly seek to protect individuals, groups, and organizations from pain and anxiety. However, the result can be precisely the opposite, since they may immerse them in

---

[1] Freud, 1915/1984a. [2] Klein, 1987. [3] Schwartz, 1988. [4] Gabriel, 1999. [5] Hirschhorn, 1988; Jaques, 1955; Menzies, 1960.
[6] Cleverley, 1971; MacIntyre, 1981; Watson, 2001. [7] Kets de Vries and Miller, 1984.

individual or collective delusions, whose result is to exacerbate organizational problems and failings.

• See also *death, desire, unconscious*

Desire

Desire is a term used to explain human **motivation.** Unlike the concept of **need,** desire has a social and a psycho-sexual dimension. One may need shoes for warmth and comfort, but one desires a pair of designer running shoes because of what it stands for. Unlike the concept of want, desire also involves a transgressive aspect—one may desire sexually somebody who is out of bounds or may desire to hurt or be hurt by somebody. **Learning** may be driven by desire, especially when the object of knowledge, like the apple from the tree of knowledge, is viewed as alluring, dangerous, and forbidden.[1] Thus, whether directed towards a physical object, a human being, an activity, or a state of being, desire is driven not merely by instinct or need, but by the **meanings** we attribute to something. A toy may remain idle for a long time, until a child's attention focuses on it. And just then, the toy becomes an object of desire for every other child in the room. Desires may be fulfilled either in practice (for example, by buying the desired pair of running shoes) or in **fantasy,** by imagining that the wished for object or state has been achieved. Alternatively, desires may by frustrated. They may then be repressed into the **unconscious** or they may mutate into desires for different objects, which may be easier to fulfil.

Desire is studied by many different approaches in the human sciences. Sociologists have argued that desires are culturally constituted, as individuals learn to desire objects and states of being valued by their **cultures.** Consumer societies, for example, are said to place enormous value on material commodities and identify happiness with escalating material possessions.[2] In sociological studies, the word desire is often used interchangeably with 'wants'.

Depth psychologists, for their part, have emphasized the connection between desire (also referred to as 'wish') and pleasure. They view most desires as modified residues of earlier desires, mainly stemming from early childhood experiences; these early desires are originally frustrated or repressed and later seek fulfilment in new incarnations.[3] For example, belief in God is traced back to the child's desire to be protected by a loving father. The Oedipus Complex is a complex of desires and fantasies that dominate every child's experiences between the ages of 3 and 5. These desires whose target is the mother and in which the father features as the child's rival and foe are generally repressed, but can assume a variety of manifestations in later life, including desires for recognition, for power, for affection, and for **achievement.** Desire is at the forefront of the psychoanalytic theory of Jacques Lacan,[4] who was influenced by philosopher Georg Wilhelm Friedrich Hegel's view that desire *for* the other is the desire to be recognized *by* the other, the desire to be desired. Lacan argues that desire *for* the **Other** is always the desire *of* the Other, starting with the infant's early desire to be the exclusive object of the mother's desire. Desire for Lacan is decentred—it does not emanate from the subject but from his or her relations to others—it is essentially unfulfillable, 'eternally stretching forth towards *the desire for something else'.*[5]

More recently, **discourse** theorists have argued that desire is an element of the discourse on sexuality, in other words the complex and interconnected ways of thinking and talking about things sexual as against things unisexual.[6] The very **language** and words which dominate the discourse on sexuality **(gender, sex,** sexual **identity,** orgasm, body, and even desire

---

[1] Gherardi, 2004.   [2] Bourdieu, 1984.   [3] Freud, 1905/1977.   [4] Lacan, 1966/1977.   [5] Lacan, 1966/1977, p. 167.   [6] Foucault, 1978.

itself) are historically constituted as interconnected elements, in constant interaction with other discourses, like the discourse of power and the discourse of political economy.

• See also *sexuality, Other and othering*

Deskilling

In *Labor and Monopoly Capital*,[1] Harry Braverman argued that throughout the twentieth century, workers have been stripped of traditional **skills** and **competencies** by the onslaught of **Taylorism** and automation. Traditional skills of artisans, like printers, potters, engineers, machinists, cooks, and clerks, have been eliminated, either by being absorbed into the production process itself or by being overtaken by new technological processes. The deskilled worker loses not only much of his or her bargaining **power**, but also **control** over his or her work, and pride and dignity in his or her work. Braverman's theory sparked off a long-standing controversy. Especially vital has been the question of whether computerization of work processes and clerical work leads to further deskilling. Empirical studies have documented strong deskilling tendencies in numerous industries from fast food[2] to call-centre work.[3] The work of many professionals, including academics, may also be liable to deskilling under the influence of mass-produced textbooks, standardized PowerPoint slides, and increasing uniformity of teaching curricula. Nevertheless, there is also evidence of the emergence of a new range of skills, in response to the demands of new **technology**. It is argued, for example, that contemporary information technologies make demands on those who use them for regular retraining, a flexible attitude, and an ability to multi-task. It is also argued that technical deskilling may be partly compensated for by the increasing demand for emotional and aesthetic labour, which restores some autonomy and independence to the employees.

The issue of deskilling has been at the centre of **Labour Process Theory**, an approach which looks in detail into workplace control, politics, and **conflicts**. Labour process theorists have long been interested in the phenomenon of resistance: how, in other words, workers may seek to restore some control and meaning to their work. A long and rich tradition of studying resistance has uncovered the different forms that it can take, from strikes and sabotage to whistle-blowing and cynical withdrawal.[4] Such authors emphasize workplaces as 'contested terrains' where a constant war of attrition is acted out between the competing interests of managers and workers.

One particular type of deskilling that is worth noting is narrative deskilling. This involves the loss of ability to tell meaningful **stories** with individualized characters and plots that grip the imagination and generate emotion.[5] In a world dominated by the **narratives** created by the **mass media** and increasingly centred on **spectacle**, stories are transcended by mass-produced images, some of which assume iconic standing. Such images possess considerable emotional and rhetorical power and may even claim to 'tell a story' without anyone actually having to narrate it. Narrative deskilling can be viewed as part of a wider range of deskillings brought about by high modernity, which include deskilling at work, but also deskilling in a wide range of domestic, social, and political contexts. Why learn to cook and risk many disappointments when our local supermarket will reliably provide high-quality meals with which to impress our friends? Why learn to weave when machines produce high-quality woven materials? Why learn to tell stories, weaving plots, when stories are available in every type of medium? And more importantly, when stories are far outshone and outsped in their ability to stimulate

---

[1] Braverman, 1974.   [2] Leidner, 1993; Levitt, 1972; Ritzer, 1998.   [3] Korczynski, 2001; Sturdy and Fleming, 2003.   [4] Ackroyd and Thompson, 1999; Jermier, Knights, and Nord, 1994; Thompson and Ackroyd, 1995.   [5] Gabriel, 2000.

emotion, trigger symbolism, and change minds by photographs, **images**, and movies.

Many traditional skills involved patient application, concentration, and slow **learning**. By contrast, it can be argued that a new range of skills has emerged in our times that involve speed, multi-tasking, short bursts of concentration, and quick gratification. These are most clearly in evidence in children who are able to send text messages to their friends, play games on computer screens, *and* do their homework; their spelling may be erratic, but their ability to programme a DVD player or a mobile phone far exceeds that of their parents. Thus, we could argue that while destroying many traditional skills, late modernity is generating remarkable new skills. These include

- learning to filter out much that is irrelevant noise and focusing on what creates a memorable emotional experience;
- learning to tolerate uncertainty and absence of closure;
- learning to cope with pluri-vocality, with ill-defined and ambiguous moral messages;
- learning to juxtapose, compare, and criticize;
- learning to live experiences with ambiguous or opaque meanings, without closure;
- learning to enjoy puzzles without permanent solutions.

Discourse

The term discourse initially described a linguistic unit longer than a sentence. Philosophers such as Descartes used it to indicate a body of closely argued philosophical arguments. Currently, discourse stands at the centre of what is known as the 'linguistic turn' in the human sciences, a trend which views language not as a passive medium reflecting or describing the world, but as an active entity through which the world becomes meaningful to us. The study of **language** then assumes major importance for

the study of human phenomena. The way we talk about the world becomes constitutive of the world. Facts do not just exist, waiting to be described through language. Instead, they become products or outcomes rather than the instigators of discourse. Thus the opinion that smoking damages one's health becomes a 'fact' when it is recognized as self-evident. Saying that 'the crime rate has risen again', we are not simply referring to a fact called 'crime' and its increasing incidence, but we become part of a discourse which 'naturalizes' crime as an inevitable, uniform, and clearly identifiable phenomenon, and innumerable assumptions, such as the inevitable presence of (a minority of) criminals in every society, the requirement for a police force to control them, the social obligation of governments to bring the crime rate down and their perennial failure to do so, the experience of vulnerability of decent 'non-criminal' people to the activities of criminals, and so forth. As Foucault observed very well, discourse then entails different assumptions and silences, which reproduce relations of **power**.[1]

As a very popular term in the social sciences, discourse has assumed many distinct meanings. At the simplest level, it is used to indicate any body of knowledge that claims some coherence and value for itself. In this sense, it is almost interchangeable with 'doctrine', 'theory', or even '**paradigm**'. More specifically, it can be used to indicate any spoken or written text, story, conversation, or narrative which is then submitted to some form of discourse analysis. However, discourse is also sometimes used to indicate what may in the past have been referred to as 'organizational ideologies', in other words, thick tissues of self-reinforcing and consistent opinions, stories, assumptions, words, etc. which inform different practices. In this way, we can view a hospital as a terrain where a discourse of patient care and public service clashes with a discourse of financial performance and efficiency. In some organizations, several

[1] Foucault, 1977.

different discourses may compete for supremacy, or, alternatively, may coexist while taking little notice of each other.[1]

The use of 'discourse' in connection with organizations raises numerous issues. Least contentious is the view of organizations as terrains of discourse where conversations take place, documents are written, jokes are told, e-mails are sent, all of which may be analysed, interpreted, or deconstructed through discourse analysis. This view, however, presupposes that organizations exist independently of discourse, something that has been contested. Mumby and Clair,[2] for instance, argue that 'when we speak of discourse, we do not simply mean discourse that occurs in organizations. Rather, we suggest that organizations exist only in so far as their members create them through discourse. This is not to claim that organizations are "nothing but" discourse, but rather that discourse is the principal means by which organization members create a coherent social reality that frames their sense of who they are.' From this perspective, organizations share the fate of other effects of **modernity**, the sovereign self, the body, sexuality, and indeed 'facts': they are all viewed as discursive constructions. They are thus denaturalized—having been things, they become ways of looking at things. Other theorists, however, have looked at discourse as constitutive of organizations but not as fully constituting them. From this perspective, 'buildings are built, products are manufactured, services are rendered beyond (and because of) all this organizational talk. Thus discourse and talk are central to organization and organizing … but so is non-discursive action.'[3] Discursive formations may appear in many forms, some of which are privileged in organizations over others, yet they do not exhaust the domain of organization. Important as it is to study discourse, it is not enough for an understanding of organizational or social practices.[4]

One feature of discourse that has become increasingly recognized is the extent to which power relations become embedded in it. The use of particular ways of talking privileges certain views and certain interests, while silencing or marginalizing others. Hegemonic discourses are those discourses which tend to privilege and sustain those already in power; minority or counter-discourses, on the other hand, seek to voice experiences of disenfranchisement, marginalization, and oppression. On the whole, discourses are not as coherent or consistent as first thought. They entail numerous internal tensions and contradictions, which may be teased out through **deconstruction**. Furthermore, they have a tendency to fragment and disintegrate or mutate into other discourses. Finally, they are engaged in a constant interaction with other discourses. With some of them, they develop self-reinforcing or parasitic relations, with others they lapse into indifferent accommodation, with yet others they may engage in overt or covert struggle.[5]

In organizations, one often encounters official or hegemonic discourses which present the organization as a successful team or family, at the cutting edge of innovation, keen to meet the needs of its diverse **stakeholders**, and conscious of the importance of conducting business in an ethical and responsible manner. These discourses are often disseminated through a company's brochures, advertisements, and websites. Oppositional discourses may revolve around the inconsistencies, inefficiencies, and failings of the organization, being disseminated through stories, jokes, clandestine e-mails, or graffiti.

• See also *deconstruction, language, narrative*

Discrimination

Discrimination is the differential treatment of people on the basis of religion, gender, race,

---

[1] See e.g. O'Leary, 2003.   [2] Mumby and Clair, 1997, p. 181.   [3] Hardy, Lawrence, and Phillips, 1998, p. 63.   [4] See Fairclough, 1992; 1995.   [5] Fairclough, 1992; Grant, Keenoy, and Oswick, 1998; Heracleous and Hendry, 2000; Mumby and Clair, 1997; Potter and Wetherell, 1987; Van Dijk, 1997.

or some other characteristic. Nearly everyone would agree that such discrimination is a bad thing, standing as it does against the values of equality and justice. All the same, discrimination exists in many direct and indirect forms in organizations as well as in societies at large. Direct discrimination is the result of prejudice. It often operates unconsciously, not as a result of deliberate practice but because in numerous judgements, big and small, people often favour others like themselves, those who look like themselves, dress like themselves, and talk like themselves. The management of organizational **diversity** aims to reduce such discrimination, through a variety of regulations and provisions that allow for transparency and accountability in making judgements on appointments, promotions, and so forth. Indirect discrimination operates where an organization's regulations and procedures are themselves fashioned in such a way that they work in favour of certain groups and against others. Here it is not a case that the referee is biased against some players but that the rules of the game are themselves written in such a way that certain players receive an advantage at the expense of others. The expression 'institutional **racism**' is sometimes used to indicate that the institutions of an organization or of society at large operate to the disadvantage of a racial group, without anyone having to actually act in a prejudiced manner. In a similar way the structure of the job market can act as an obstacle to equality, with childbearing and child-rearing impeding the career chances of many women. The location of jobs and educational prerequisites can inhibit the chances of ethnic minority groups while the requirement for job experience can disadvantage young people.

Is it possible to have **institutions** that do not discriminate in any way? Consider, for example, the game of basketball. Is it not the case that the game, by its very nature, discriminates against all but the tallest players? Of course, what is acceptable in a game is not necessarily acceptable in society at large. Most democratic societies claim to treat their citizens equally. Each one of them

has a single vote in elections, the same rights and obligations. But as the French writer Anatole France once said, 'The law, in its majestic equality, forbids rich and poor alike to sleep under bridges, to beg in the streets, and to steal their bread.' Formal equality can mean very different treatment for different groups of citizens, since not all citizens have the same power or resources. The management of diversity then cannot be content with treating everyone equally, but must recognize that different groups of citizens start from different positions. Equal opportunity provisions may then seek to compensate for actual inequalities by offering certain concessions or advantages to underprivileged groups. Reconciling the demands of formal equality of all citizens and equality of opportunity which requires extra benefits for the disadvantaged is not easy. Different organizations and different societies deal with this dilemma in different ways, one such way being affirmative action programmes.

Affirmative action programmes developed following the American Civil Rights Movement in the 1960s. They aimed at improving the chances of young people from underprivileged backgrounds by enhancing their chances to enter higher education. In this way, they tried to counter the cumulative effects of social exclusion, discrimination, and injustice, by enhancing the chances of members of deprived social groups to reach positions of influence or power. Reverse discrimination was one of the measures used to this end—the adoption of lower 'objective measures' of **achievement** to compensate for deprivation. Additionally, quotas have been used in various organizations, stipulating that a certain proportion of recruits should represent different types of underprivileged or deprived groups in society. Affirmative action programmes prospered in academic environments (mostly in the United States) and, to a much lesser extent, state and commercial organizations in the 1970s and 1980s. Since then, however, they have been under pressure from groups defending meritocratic principles of recruitment. Such groups argue that affirmative action violates formal equality and lowers overall standards of **performance**.

There is another meaning to discrimination, one that links it to tastes and style. This is especially important in connection with discussions of **consumption**, where discriminating consumers are meant to be able to identify differences and make choices between very similar objects. A discriminating consumer can choose between innumerable types of wine, clothes, music, and so forth. This use of the word discrimination would seem to be less toxic than when the term is applied to people or groups. One is after all entitled to like one particular type of cheese and dislike another, without having to offer explanations and excuses. In purchasing her preferred type of cheese, the consumer does not have to offer any explanations to the producers whose cheeses she has spurned. She can discriminate at will. Pierre Bourdieu has argued that such discrimination can also be oppressive and cruel.[1] Dismissing a person's tastes in music, wine, or, indeed, cheese may be a way of 'keeping them in their place'. In the **status** stakes, people judge each other on their tastes and there are times where a bad taste in dress may incur more serious social disapproval than dishonest or corrupt practices. This is a phenomenon that starts at a very early age; schoolchildren, for example, are known to become objects of vicious baiting and bullying on account of the clothes or the shoes that they wear. Discriminating tastes then are not as innocent as they may seem.

Discrimination at work and discriminating tastes in the marketplace are not as far apart as it may appear. While most people would view arbitrary discrimination on the basis of specific characteristics as objectionable, this is precisely what consumer freedom boils down to—the ability to opt for specific commodities and discriminate against others without having to offer explanations or justifications.

• See also *diversity, race and racism, Other and othering*

Disney and Disneyization

The Disney phenomenon has attracted a large amount of research by social scientists. For many, Disneyland represents the ultimate manifestation of consumer capitalism, a place where children and adults expect their **fantasies** to come true and **experience** thrilling, memorable sensations. Disneyland is the apotheosis of **spectacle**, a spectacle that is entirely simulated but nonetheless exhilarating for it. Why risk going to the tropics to see 'real' crocodiles, unpredictable beasts that they are, when you can be guaranteed to get a great sight of them, take brilliant pictures of them, and even place your head inside the mouth of one in Disneyland? Disneyland appears to capture equally well the experience of the consumer and the predicament of the employee, the worker, who becomes part of a 'cast' of thousands, perfectly groomed, always smiling, always happy to make customers happy.[2]

Disney has attracted a great deal of criticism for what it does to its customers, what it does to its workers, and what it does to **culture** as a whole.[3] Many have seen Disneyland as the ultimate cathedral of consumption, the space where people today go to have profound emotional and even **spiritual** experiences, emerging rejuvenated and inspired. Thus Ritzer argues that late modernity reintroduces the magical, the bewildering, and the enchanted that had been extracted from public life by the **rational** procedures and forms of high modernity.[4] Spectacle has led to a partial re-enchantment of the world in late modernity's shopping malls, glass buildings, tourist resorts, sports venues and theme parks, all minutely planned and orchestrated. Bryman has argued that Disneyization is the extension of the organizing principles of Disney, like theming, ceaseless merchandising,

---

[1] Bourdieu, 1984.   [2] Van Maanen, 1991; 1992.   [3] Byrne and McQuillan, 1999; Giroux, 1999; Holbrook, 2001.   [4] Ritzer, 1999.

and emotional labour, to other fields of the economy, such as sport, entertainment, movies, and music.[1] Disneyization can be viewed as the other side of the coin of **McDonaldization**: while the experience of the consumer is ever drawn towards the magical, the production of the spectacles themselves is constantly designed, rationalized, and planned to every minuscule detail to enhance the spectator's experience. The consumer's bewitchment is gained at the cost of workers being constantly deskilled and emotionally drained.

There is another way in which Disneyland has been invoked—as emblematic of contemporary **narcissism**, the excessive contemporary preoccupation with **image** and presentation at the expense of rationality, hard science, and substance. Thus, Schwartz attributed the *Challenger* space shuttle disaster to the transformation of NASA from a technological pioneer to 'Disneyland in space'—in other words, an expression of America's unconscious fantasies about itself—fantasies that included technological omnipotence, showmanship, and the triumph of **diversity** in all its forms. Image ended up dominating the hard science necessary for launching spacecrafts, the engineers were silenced by the salespeople of collective dreams, and the result was the technical lapses that led to the disaster.[2]

Diversity

In statistics, 'diversity' has the same meaning as 'variance'. It is a population characteristic that refers to the level of difference among a group of elements. When used in connection with organizations, however, diversity generally carries some strong ideological resonances. These have two sources. The first is **globalization**. The interconnectedness of the world's economies has increased dramatically over the last fifty years and this has brought people from almost every area of the world into relationships

of cooperation and competition with each other. It has also created the need for larger and more powerful economic units. This, in turn, has resulted in people who are very different needing to identify with and understand one another, or at least to negotiate and understand the rules within which they would operate. This is a circumstance that becomes fraught with difficulties. In Europe, for example, economic integration has led to political integration among people with very different ideas about politics, history, culture, and much besides. Some common **identity** needed to be forged over and above national identities that had been derived largely from their difference from, and even antagonism toward, other national identities. Where, in a post-Christian era, could such a common identity be found? The term 'diversity' came to be viewed as a way of working toward such an identity, as something that different groups within the European Union had in common. Within this context, the advantages of diversity, most notably in the form of combining different points of view to stimulate innovation, could be mobilized. Diversity represented an attempt to manage a problematic situation; to make a virtue of necessity.

The second ideological context that moulded diversity is **postmodernism**. From this perspective, many current social and economic arrangements are the result of domination by a specific group, namely, white, heterosexual males, who have kept other groups in subjugation. The term 'diversity', in this connection, refers to the resurgence of previously oppressed groups. This resurgence has a moral and an emotional dimension that demand love for the oppressed groups and hate for the oppressors. These emotional requirements are codified and enforced by *political correctness*.[3] Postmodern diversity draws much of its intellectual backing from the intellectual pluralism that would result from demographic diversity. But this is at best dubious and at worst spurious, since the gain to

---

[1] Bryman, 1999.   [2] Schwartz, 1988.   [3] Schwartz, 2001.

intellectual diversity from postmodern diversity is limited. It consists primarily in the importation of stories of how the oppressed groups have been oppressed and adds little to contemporary problem solving. The attempt to clarify the differences between two forms of diversity and the extent to which they reinforce or impede each other is often seen as challenging the claims of postmodern diversity; it then falls under the taboo of political correctness and cannot be accomplished. The result has been that the term has assumed contradictory meanings at its core and may obscure more than it clarifies.

Claims that postmodern diversity generates advantages for business have not been supported. Although a large industry has arisen to advance the cause of diversity, no empirical research has demonstrated its value. Relatively little research has been attempted, and what has been done has come up empty-handed. MIT Professor Thomas Kochan, one of the few scholars who has conducted research on this question over five years, stated: 'The diversity industry is built on sand. The business case rhetoric for diversity is simply naïve and overdone. There are no strong positive or negative effects of gender or racial diversity on business performance.'[1] What is left to support postmodern diversity is the moralistic case, based on a specific social analysis that many find questionable or tendentious. Their resistance is often met, in organizations, by 'diversity training', which is designed to bring them around to the approved view. It is ironic that, in actual practice, 'diversity' may result in an intellectual monoculture, in the form of approved and politically correct attitudes, that detracts from intellectual diversity, rather than adding to it.

• See also *discrimination, ethnic groups and ethnicity, gender, homosexuality, multiculturalism, Other and othering, race and racism, voice*

HOWARD S. SCHWARTZ, UNIVERSITY OF OAKLAND

Downsizing

Lay-offs, discharging people from jobs, temporarily or permanently, have always been a feature of capitalist society. They are, for instance, a management solution to economic downturn or to increased product inventories due to poor sales. What distinguishes downsizing from all its predecessors is the relentlessness, fanaticism, automaticity, and finality (that is, the permanence and irreversibility) with which lay-offs are carried out. In downsizing, rampant since the early 1980s, termination—firing—is employed as a first and repeated strategy to solve different organizational problems, be they corporate, governmental, or public sector. Organizational leaders and boards hope to 'save' the company through one or more ritualized, symbolic 'sacrifices' of employees who are no longer seen as loyal, productive people, but are now seen as 'dead wood' or 'fat' to be trimmed from the corporate body. It is as if to say: employees or workers are the problem, and downsizing is often the only reasonable and dramatic management solution. Managers rarely acknowledge that poor planning on their part may have led to an organization's dire predicament, at least until they become themselves victims of downsizing.[2]

Executives frequently employ downsizing as a magical solution aimed at turning organizations around. Most often, the short-term economic bottom line has become the only measure of organizational success, and maximization of shareholder value in the quarterly report is the core **value**. After a mass firing, stock values artificially and briefly inflate, not because the organization is more productive and profitable, but because of an enormous cut in payroll. Long-term planning suffers, because management engages in a succession of temporary quick fixes that create the illusion of great profitability by dramatically cutting costs. It usually turns out that, contrary to management's heady wishes and expectations, downsizing is

---

[1] Hansen, 2003.   [2] Ehrenreich, 2005; Uchitelle, 2006.

mostly counter-productive. It leads to a demor-alized, fragmented, anxious, insecure workforce who often have to perform the job of two, if not three, people. The earlier **psychological contract** between employer and employee, based on mutual obligations and loyalty, is replaced by the ultimate disposability of everyone. Those who do the firing regularly become the next ones to be fired.[1]

'Downsizing' is part of a constellation of terms, which together constitute the core of an increasingly widespread cultural ethos that has governed much organizational life since the 1980s. These terms include: downsizing, reduction in force (further euphemized by the acronym 'RIF'), rightsizing, redundancy, restructuring, re-engineering, outsourcing, **deskilling**, and managed healthcare. Downsizing and its cognate terms are euphemisms, the largely **unconscious** purpose of which is to divert the user and recipient of these terms from the reality of brutality and emotional pain.[2] The user directs attention to supposedly rational-economic processes. This leads to such phrases as calling downsizing 'nothing personal, just business'.[3] Yet downsizing leads to despair, chronic grief, frenzied work to prove one's usefulness, survivor guilt, and the dread that one might be the next one to be fired.[4] Yiannis Gabriel has invoked the term 'miasma' to characterize the stage of chronic organizational emotional pollution that follows in the wake of downsizing and the enormous loss it creates. This involves a highly acute state of anxiety and depression, constant destructive criticism, and a paralysis of resistance.

• See also *death, unemployment, violence, work*

HOWARD F. STEIN, UNIVERSITY OF OKLAHOMA

[1] Stein, 2007.　[2] Stein, 1998.　[3] Stein, 2001.　[4] Faludi, 1999; Stein, 2007.

Economy

What is the economy? This simple enough question is surprisingly neglected by the mainstream ('neoclassical') economic tradition (alongside a parallel absence of any close analysis of the closely related concept of the **market**). If you consult the glossary or index of any undergraduate economics textbook, you are unlikely to find any entry under 'economy'. The idea that there is a realm of social interaction which is distinct from others in law and that this realm **institutionalizes** a specific set of rules and practices that we know as **economic** is today part of our taken-for-granted view of our world.

If we look for a universal definition applicable across the social sciences, then our starting point (following Polanyi and other economic sociologists) must be the recognition that the term *economic* is a compound of two distinct meanings with independent roots, the substantive and the formal. The substantive meaning of the concept is based on the empirical economy (or rather economies, for there are different types). 'It can be briefly...defined as an *instituted process* of interaction between man and his (or her) natural, social and cultural environment, which results in a continuous supply of want satisfying material means.'[1] On the other hand,

> the formal meaning of economic derives from the logical character of the means–ends relationship, as apparent in such words as 'economical' or 'economizing.' It refers to a definite situation of choice, namely, that between the different uses of means induced by an insufficiency of those means. If we call the

rules governing choice of means the logic of rational action, then we may denote this variant of logic, with an improvised term, as formal economics.[2]

The crucial limitation of the formal definition is that it assumes a market-dominated economy (and the accompanying rationalizing or economizing behaviour of actors that corresponds to that type of economy). The substantive approach takes as its starting point the need to specify the social, political, and cultural conditions which support a market or other type of economy along with their associated behaviours. In this view, market exchange is only one type of the general process of social interaction and, as such, is shaped not only by utilitarian interests but also by **norms** and **values** as well as **power**, **class**, and **status** relations, kinship **institutions**, etc.

Polanyi proposed three main analytic types of economic exchange: *reciprocity, redistribution,* and *market* (with household or self-provisioning making up a fourth type).[3] Reciprocal exchange occurs when the relevant norms and values and related cultural and political institutions prescribe that persons have reciprocal obligations by virtue of their statuses, typically involving *gift* relations. While reciprocal relations are most prominent in societies where kinship remains a dominant principle of social organization, they remain evident in modern society in family relations and areas of society where gift giving is sustained as the central orientation.[4] *Redistributive exchange* exists when norms and values prescribe and a centralized agency (or state) has the capacity to enforce contributions (in taxes, goods, or services) and redistribute them to other uses.

---

[1] Polanyi, 1957, p. 248, emphasis added.   [2] Ibid. 242.   [3] Polanyi, 1944; 1957.   [4] Hyde, 1983; Titmuss, 1971.

While common in historical societies, even in our own, the development of the modern welfare state is a typical redistributive agency which also produces and supplies key economically relevant resources (education, health, and law to name a few). *Market exchange* also depends on behaviour prescribed by certain norms and values and these must be instituted both informally and formally (in law). Thus, sociologists from Durkheim onward have stressed that the market depends on the institution of contract and what Durkheim called 'the non-contractual element in contract'. 'Market exchange only works if honesty is institutionalized and if deviations from it are sanctioned, either informally or in the courts through the whole law of contract.'[1] Thus, even if we accept that modern **capitalism** denotes a market-dominated economy, it still depends critically on other social and political institutions to enable, support, and enforce that set of economic relations.

Others have attempted to specify these social institutions with greater analytic precision. Thus, Fligstein delineates the following *institutions*, referring to shared rules which can be laws or collective understandings (formal or informal), held in place by custom, explicit agreement, or tacit agreement, but ultimately involving states in their creation and enforcement:

1. Property rights—institutions that define who has claims on the profits of firms. The constitution of property rights is a continuous and contestable political process, not the outcome of an efficient process, involving organized groups from business, labour, government agencies, and political parties.
2. **Governance** structures—formal (legal) or informal practices that determine relations of competition, cooperation, and how firms should be organized.
3. Conceptions of **control**—understandings that frame perceptions of how markets work and

can reflect agreements between actors in firms on principles of internal organization (i.e. forms of **hierarchy**), tactics for competition or cooperation, and the hierarchy or status ordering of firms in a given market.
4. Rules of exchange—regulations governing who can transact with whom and under what conditions, e.g. the enforcement of contracts.[2]

What can this institutional perspective tell us about our contemporary economy? First, the very **boundaries** and rules of what we call the economy constitute it as a 'field of struggles'.[3] That is, they are matters of political and social contestation and, as such, are part of the driving dynamic that shapes the development of the economy over time. At present, the predominant 'neoliberal' **ideology** invokes a strong preference for market exchange over other types of economic relations and includes specific recommendations regarding property rights, governance structures, conceptions of control, and rules of exchange, much of it implied by the slogan of 'shareholder value'. Second, the process by which this prevailing orthodoxy came to dominate is both relatively recent (over the last twenty-five years) and continuously marked by active state intervention in support of this conception as well as promotion by powerful groups (in particular institutional investors and CEOs of multinational corporations) in conflict with others.[4] Whether it proves successful or durable is another matter.

FRANK LONGSTRETH, UNIVERSITY OF BATH

Emotion

It is not so long ago since Fineman described organizations as 'emotionally anorexic'.[5] This was exactly how they were viewed by much academic scholarship. People at work were viewed as leaving their feelings at home, in the long

---

[1] Barber, 1995, p. 399.   [2] Fligstein, 1996.   [3] Bourdieu, 2005.   [4] Gourevitch and Shinn, 2005; O'Sullivan, 2000.   [5] Fineman, 1993b, p. 2.

Weberian tradition of working 'sine ira et studio'—with no wrath or bias.[1] To the extent that feelings were ever displayed in organizations they were seen as troublesome, interfering with **rationality** and efficiency. In the last fifteen years this has changed, not least due to the efforts of Fineman himself. A rich literature has developed on emotions in organizations which can justify Fineman's label of 'emotional arenas'. A wide range of emotions, including greed, enthusiasm, envy, trust, nostalgia, gratitude, love, friendship, hope, anger, anxiety, and disappointment, have come into focus and a rich understanding of their effects is gradually emerging.

Academic interest in emotions is itself related to wider social and cultural patterns that have brought emotion to the forefront of social life. Campbell,[2] for example, has argued that the suppression and denial of emotion were cardinal virtues of Puritanism, the Protestant **ethic**, and even the Enlightenment project that saw everything as subordinate to the Commonwealth of Reason, Progress, and Science. Today, by contrast, argues Campbell, under the influence of consumerism, Puritanism has given way to a *Romantic ethic*. This castigates the choking of emotions, raising their free expression near the summit of **values**. All emotions, including fright, anger, and jealousy, argues Campbell, can be vehicles for pleasure provided that we know how to express and contain them. 'Emoting' becomes a highly popular activity, whether it takes place in theatres and television shows, mass public festivals, or intimate encounters. Thus, the stiff upper lip ethic has given way to the mass demonstration of near-hysterical feeling, exemplified by the events following the death of Princess Diana. In this context, the heightened interest in emotion among academics is not surprising.

There are many different perspectives on emotions. For example, biologists and evolutionary psychologists have been examining how human emotions were 'hard wired' into the evolution of our bodies over millions of years of adaptation to our natural and social environment. Neurologists have explored the relations between the functioning of the brain, emotions, and cognitive processes. By contrast, **social constructionists** have focused on the subtle ways that different national and organizational **cultures** shape the ways emotions are experienced and expressed. Psychoanalysts, for their parts, have examined how early life experiences influence our later emotional life and our experiences of emotions like guilt, envy, and **anxiety**. Many experimental and other psychologists have pursued the long tradition of seeking to measure emotions, and economists have, more recently, sought to link emotions (like happiness and depression) to economic indicators like income per capita and unemployment rates.

One of the few things about which all of these approaches agree is that most emotions are not fully willed; we do not choose freely whether and when to have them (although many actors become very skilled at experiencing emotions commensurate with their parts). Emotions often seem to overpower us and to influence our judgements in profound ways. Our decisions and our **actions** when we feel angry or frightened or enthusiastic appear not to agree with the dictates of reason and prudence. Emotion is often experienced as something standing in opposition to **rationality**—a theme that has been pursued by philosophers since Plato and Descartes. Yet one of the most consistent and interesting findings of contemporary emotion research is that emotion and **cognition** cannot be separated. Research by Damasio,[3] Sacks,[4] and others suggests that both thought and emotion reside in the **body** rather than in an entity called 'the mind'; also, that emotion is an indispensable ingredient of rational action and rational decisions (though not a guarantee that a decision or an action will be rational). An emotional response to a situation always precedes a rational appreciation and almost invariably guides it. For example, the experience of a person who has

---

[1] Weber, 1946, pp. 215–16.   [2] Campbell, 1989.   [3] Damasio, 1994; 1999.   [4] Sacks, 1995.

been wronged produces in us responses such as anger and compassion that, in turn, inform our explanation of who wronged them and why they were wronged.

Organizational studies draw on all of the above approaches in their current attempt to study what, if anything, is different or unique about people's emotional experiences as employees and customers of organizations. Early interest in emotions in organizations centred around the concepts of job satisfaction and **stress**. These two categories generated large and inconclusive literatures. They proved too broad, transient, and tame to do justice to the sheer variety and turbulence of organizational emotions. Although research in these two topics has continued unabated (in quantity, if not in quality), the interest of many has shifted in other directions. Some of the dominant discourses concern (1) the concept of **emotional labour** and its relation to customer service and employee identity, (2) the emotions involved in **leader–followers** relations, especially in relation to the leaders' emotional intelligence and their capacity to manage emotions, and (3) the dynamics of emotions in **groups** and organizations, notably in relation to the quality of collective **decision making**.

One particular contribution of organizational theory to the study of emotions is to highlight the extent to which they are acquired or learned. Emotions themselves can be viewed as experiences whose meanings emerge through **culture**, communicated through culture, and even generated by culture. Specific cultural events, such as a funeral, a job interview, a downsizing announcement, or a business deal, call for appropriate emotional performances of those participating. Inspired by the work of Goffman,[1] different theorists have argued that emotions can be socially constructed just like other social phenomena. Emotions are then learned, they are not natural states that take possession of us. Indeed,

theorists like Heller,[2] Fineman,[3] Mangham,[4] and Flam[5] argue that emotions are learned, just as theatrical **roles** are learned. And just as theatrical actors learn to experience anger, sorrow, joy, or fear when their roles call for them, so too social actors learn to experience feelings appropriate to specific social settings.

Different social situations are governed by different emotional **rules** which dictate emotional performances and organize how emotion 'flows'. In this way, emotion can be seen as constructed, communicated, and disseminated from each individual to his or her audience. Thus when we find ourselves surrounded by sad people at a funeral, we feel sad, even if we do not have a great reason to feel sad; likewise when we find ourselves surrounded by a cheering, laughing, or jeering crowd we may become affected by these emotions, even if we have no personal reason for experiencing them. Emotions can change as they flow in different social settings. Despair can turn into anger, disgust into anxiety, envy into pride, joy into hate. An individual's display of a specific emotion may generate the same emotion in his or her audience or it may lead to a different emotional response. A leader, for example, may discover that her attempts to share her enthusiasm or pride with her subordinates lead to indifference or suspicion on their part. This is the point of entry for a **Critical Management Studies** approach to emotion where **power** relations enter the formation and enforcement of emotion rules.[6]

• See also *feelings, emotional labour and emotional work*

Emotional intelligence

Emotional intelligence was a term introduced in the late 1980s which became very popular through the works of Salovey and Mayer and, especially, Daniel Goleman.[7] It is interesting

---

[1] Goffman, 1959.   [2] Heller, 1979.   [3] Fineman, 1993a; 1996.   [4] Mangham, 1998.   [5] Flam, 1990a; 1990b.   [6] Fineman, 2007.
[7] Salovey and Mayer, 1990; Goleman, 1995.

that as 'intelligence' has become an increasingly problematic concept, difficult to operationalize and always politically suspect, 'emotional intelligence' has gained ever-greater popularity, claiming some of the ground previously occupied by intelligence. **Career** success, sound **decision making**, effective **leadership**, and numerous other accomplishments once assigned to intelligence are now routinely attributed to emotional intelligence.[1]

Emotional intelligence is a nice term—it refers to the ways emotion can be used 'intelligently' in different situations and the relative advantage this gives to people in their social interactions and to organizational performance as a whole. The emotionally intelligent, it is argued, know how to use their emotions effectively in different situations. They understand their emotions, they manage their emotions, and they recognize emotions in others. Advocates of emotional intelligence argue that cognitive intelligence—problem solving, thinking, abilities—works together with **emotion**. When confronted with thorny social issues emotion can shape and steer thinking and **cognition**. To do so we need the skills or competences to be able to perceive and evaluate emotional information.

One of the features that makes emotional intelligence a more politically acceptable quality than cognitive intelligence lies in the claim that it can be learnt through special training although, of course, some people are better endowed with it than others. As a result a small cottage industry of coaches and trainers is thriving purporting to boost the emotional intelligence of their clients. Extravagant claims have been made for emotional intelligence as a recipe for business success, especially by management consultants in what became something of a management **fad and fashion**. Academics have been more cautious, questioning its validity and measurements.[2] They have also questioned the **values** that it represents. Could it not be said that

emotional intelligence can turn into emotional manipulation and effective deception of other people?

Two things should be noted in connection with this term. First, its emergence appears to be a natural consequence of the term **emotional labour**. If we accept emotional labour on a par with intellectual and manual labours, it stands to reason that people's capacity to perform this type of labour differs and emotional intelligence captures this difference. Second, it does not take much reflection to realize that most aspects of emotional intelligence are what might have been viewed as traditionally **gendered** (feminine) social skills. Reading the moods of your children, husband, and parents, treading delicately and finding the right moment to raise particular issues of conversation, defusing potentially disruptive situations, and being able to talk about feelings in an intelligent way have long been associated with skills women exercised in the domestic sphere. Parenting is certainly an area of social life where these skills are very handy. Yet, for all this, women's success in leadership positions has been slow. It may well be then that emotional intelligence is not quite the trump card that it is made out to be.

Emotional labour and emotional work

The highly original concept of 'emotional labor' was developed by sociologist Arlie Hochschild in recognition of the fact that a great deal of people's work goes well beyond manual or intellectual labour.[3] Thus, a display of friendliness, involving direct eye contact and a smile, is not merely a bonus for sales or catering staff but an integral part of their job. Different occupations require different emotional displays or 'performances'—nurses must show care and affection, sports coaches enthusiasm and drive, funeral directors dignified respect, and

---

[1] See e.g. Goleman, 2001; Goleman, Boyatzis, and McKee, 2002.   [2] See e.g. Fineman, 2000b.   [3] Hochschild, 1983.

professional wrestlers anger and hate. Emotional labour describes those aspects of people's work which involve adopting an emotional attitude appropriate to their role. Since Hochschild's early work, emotional labour has been recognized as a core feature of a wide range of occupations (from secretaries to car mechanics, from computer analysts to Disneyland employees) especially in the service sector. Emotional labour also involves reading, assessing, and managing emotions, one's own as well as other people's.[1] A sales assistant must diagnose whether a customer's anger is real and serious and use his or her own techniques for defusing it or redirecting it.

The discourse on emotional labour has moved away from viewing emotions as disruptive elements in organizations; instead, they are viewed as vital resources to be marshalled and **controlled**, in a manner not dissimilar to other resources such as money, information, or materials. Putnam and Mumby noted that 'through recruitment, selection, socialization and performance evaluations, organizations develop a social reality in which feelings become a commodity for achieving instrumental goals'.[2] In this way, bureaucratic **rationality** expands to colonize affectivity and emotions. Mature **bureaucracy** need no longer be afraid of emotions—rather it may commandeer them, control them, and deploy them as it does other resources, like knowledge, money, or technology. Writers like Ferguson, Mumby and Putnam, and Hochschild herself have criticized the resulting self-estrangement, inauthenticity, and burn-out suffered by employees who, under pressure from management, adopt the emotions and even the feelings required by their **roles**.[3] They also recognize that at times employees may seek to **resist** management's attempts to manipulate their feelings, through acts of defiance, resistance, and escape, as in the following prototypical example:

A young businessman said to a flight attendant, 'Why aren't you smiling?' She put her tray back on the food cart, looked him in the eye, and said, 'I'll tell you what. You smile first, then I smile.' The businessman smiled at her. 'Good,' she replied. 'Now freeze, and hold that for fifteen hours.' Then she walked away.[4]

In line with this approach, several authors developed the notion of an 'aesthetic labour' (see **aesthetics**) to indicate that the employees' appearance is itself part of the work they deliver to their organizations. In many industries, employees may need to spend much time shopping and grooming themselves in order to meet the expectations of their managers and customers. The addition of aesthetic labour raises the obvious question of whether virtually any other type of labour could be added to the list. One could then have, for example, 'political labour' (involving the forging of alliances, cutting of deals, discrediting of opponents, and so forth), 'moral labour' (addressing moral dilemmas and ethical issues), 'identity labour' (the framing and sustaining of individual and group identities), and even '**spiritual** labour' (dealing with the spiritual well-being and growth of oneself and others). This may dilute or devalue the contribution of the 'emotional labour' just making it a label for anything involving emotions. At the same time, this approach would bring the term 'labour' close to what psychoanalysts describe as 'psychological work'—for example, 'dreamwork' (the work involved in turning day residues into dreams), 'mourning work' (the work involved in coming to terms with loss and separation), and 'story work' (the work necessary to turn everyday experiences into meaningful stories with characters and plots).

All in all, the concept of emotional labour seemed to unlock many doors behind which **emotion** lurked in organizations. Like many popular terms, it inspired several similar ones and

---

[1] Fineman, 1993a. [2] Putnam and Mumby, 1993, p. 27. [3] Ferguson, 1984; Mumby and Putnam, 1992; Hochschild, 1983. [4] Ibid. 127.

maybe it is currently being stretched in ways that limit its usefulness. Recent contributions to the emotional labour debate have noted that people at work often engage with others emotionally in ways that are not directly tied into the formal job requirements (most obviously, developing warm and supportive relationships with either co-workers or customers in the workplace out of personal choice).[1] Korczynski has referred to groups of employees forming warm and supportive emotional relationships as 'communities of coping'.[2]

In an important contribution, the late Ian Craib criticized emotional labour scholarship for focusing entirely on the public manifestations of emotions, the performance, the smile, the display, and the costs they exact. He argued that the term emotional work works better than emotional labour, because it suggests both an internal and an external dimension. 'Individuals, people—men and women—are by definition engaged in at least two interlocking forms of emotional work: The "internal" work of coping with contradiction, conflict and ambivalence and the "external" work of reconciling what goes on inside with what one is "supposed" or "allowed" to feel'.[3] Even unemotional behaviour may then involve emotional work, since suppressing one's emotions may require extremely hard psychological work. It may be time that emotion scholarship begins to examine the interrelations and interactions between internal and external psychological work.

Entrepreneurship

Today there is a great deal of public interest in entrepreneurship. Entrepreneurs have become stars. Their successes and personalities are extensively covered by the **mass media**. Executives and teenagers alike watch television shows on business creation and dream of striking out on their own. Equity investing has become celebrated. And governments try to spot, nurture, and attract future entrepreneurs to their region, in order to renew their economies and create new wealth and more jobs.

Despite the apparent importance of entrepreneurship for economic growth there is no agreed definition of the term. There is an old and continuing debate in the academic literature over what constitutes an entrepreneur or entrepreneurship. Some of the important issues central to this debate include: Is entrepreneurship the act of starting a new business or can we observe it also in established organizational settings? Are all new businesses entrepreneurial? Is entrepreneurship a *function*, a *personal characteristic*, or a set of *behaviours*?

This entry offers a historical overview of evolving conceptualizations of entrepreneurship followed by some more recent perspectives. Early discourses of entrepreneurship were dominated by 'functional' definitions—the entrepreneur is what the entrepreneur does. From the 1950s discussions of entrepreneurship moved on to 'indicative' definitions, seeking to establish the personality characteristics and traits by which entrepreneurs can be identified. In the last twenty or thirty years, the emphasis has shifted towards more 'behavioural' definitions—he or she who behaves like an entrepreneur can be considered to be entrepreneurial.

The entrepreneur in classical economic theory is the **decision maker** pursuing the ever-elusive equilibrium between supply and demand: elusive because supply and demand are always changing. In neoclassical economics the existence of the entrepreneur is almost irrelevant since the adjustment process between supply and demand is assumed to be instantaneous for the sake of analytical clarity. Thus, neoclassical economics has relegated entrepreneurship to a marginal activity; by contrast, other schools of economics have placed it at the heart of economic activity.

The term entrepreneur is French in origin and a literal meaning might translate as 'one who

---

[1] See e.g Bolton, 2005.   [2] Korczynski, 2003.   [3] Craib, 1998, p. 113.

takes between'. It was first used by Richard Cantillon (1680–1734) in his 'Essai sur la nature
de commerce en général' published in 1755
(twenty-one years after his death). Cantillon
distinguished between the wealth generated by
'entrepreneurs', arising out of **decision making**
and **risk** rather than the orthodox efforts of
'landowners' and 'hirelings'. Cantillon's entrepreneur is a *speculator*, a *trader*, a *dealer* with
an eye for opportunistic profit. Jean-Baptiste
Say (1767–1832) extended the thinking of the
'French school', adding that apart from market
maker (à la Cantillon) the entrepreneur had a
second role, to coordinate and combine *factors
of production*.

The 'Austrian school' of entrepreneurship
originated in the work of Carl Menger (1840–
1921) who suggested that the entrepreneur
directs and redirects resources in a state of perpetual equilibrium, bearing risk, under conditions of uncertainty. Israel Kirzner argued that
the entrepreneur is someone who is alert to profitable opportunities for exchange which exist
because of imperfect *knowledge*. The Kirznerian
entrepreneur is an intermediary who is alert and
spots opportunities to trade and rebalance the
economic equilibrium. An important deviation
from the general equilibrium model of neoclassical economics was provided by Joseph Schumpeter (1883–1950). Despite the fact that he is
often classified under the 'Austrian school', his
views on the entrepreneurial function are quite
different from those of Kirzner. Schumpeter saw
the entrepreneur as a special person, someone
who provides new products and processes via a
different and untried combination of inputs. He
is an *innovator*, who causes technological change
and disturbs the equilibrium state, rather than
responds to change to rebalance the equilibrium.

Hébert and Link collated this diverse theoretical background and identified twelve themes to
pinpoint what an entrepreneur is:[1] a risk taker,
a capitalist, an innovator, a decision maker, a

leader, a manager, an organizer and coordina-
tor, an enterprise owner, an employer of factors
of production, a contractor, an arbitrageur, and
a resource allocator. Following this overview of
some of the classic writers whose work underpins current theory of entrepreneurship, we now
turn to some contemporary perspectives:

1. Entrepreneurship as *new business creation*.
Low and MacMillan defined entrepreneurship as
strictly 'the creation of new enterprise'.[2] Therefore, entrepreneurship is the process by which
new organizations come into existence and it
ends when the creation stage of the organization
ends.

2. Entrepreneurship as *wealth creation*. Birley argued that entrepreneurship is about creating and growing wealth and that ownership
is a crucial aspect of this process.[3] As such, her
view of entrepreneurship is more inclusive than
the new business creation perspective. Entrepreneurship can include not just start-ups, but fran-
chising, corporate venturing, management buy-
outs, and inheriting a business. It can include
both private- and public-sector activities.

3. Entrepreneurship as an approach to management that begins with *opportunity*. Stevenson and his colleagues defined entrepreneurship
as the pursuit of opportunity without regard
for resources currently controlled.[4] In his view,
entrepreneurs commit themselves to the pursuit
of opportunities even without initial control of
all the required resources, in contrast to managers who strive to allocate optimally a given
amount of resources. Stevenson has argued that
entrepreneurial behaviour can be observed in a
variety of contexts including start-ups and large
enterprises. Shane and Venkataraman added
to this opportunity-based line of thought and
introduced a comprehensive and widely cited
contemporary definition of the term and of
the academic field.[5] We conclude with the latest version of their definition,[6] which positions

---

[1] Hébert and Link, 1988.   [2] Low and Macmillan, 1988, p. 141.   [3] See Wright, 2001, p. 129.   [4] Stevenson and Jarillo, 1990, p. 23.
[5] Shane and Venkataraman, 2000, p. 218.   [6] See Shane, 2003, p. 4.

entrepreneurship at the intersection of three elements, the opportunity, the individual(s), and
the required resources.

> Entrepreneurship is an activity that involves the
> discovery, evaluation and exploitation of
> opportunities to introduce new goods and
> services, ways of organising, markets, processes
> and raw materials through organising efforts
> that previously had not existed. Given this
> definition the academic field of
> entrepreneurship incorporates, in its domain,
> explanations for why, when and how
> entrepreneurial opportunities exist; the sources
> of those opportunities and the forms that they
> take; the processes of opportunity discovery
> and evaluation; the acquisition of resources for
> the exploitation of these opportunities; the act
> of opportunity exploitation; why, when and
> how some individuals and not others discover,
> evaluate, gather resources for and evaluate
> opportunities; the strategies used to pursue
> opportunities and the organizing efforts to
> exploit them.

VANGELIS SOUITARIS, CASS BUSINESS SCHOOL,
CITY UNIVERSITY

Environment

The environment is generally thought to include
all those aspects outside a **system** that can
influence its operations, by offering inputs and
receiving outputs, by presenting opportunities
and threats. In relation to organizations, it refers
to the social, economic, physical, political, and
cultural context in which organizations operate.
In a pioneering study of the influence of environment on organizations, Burns and Stalker
argued that firms operating in stable environments tend to adopt *mechanistic* **structures**, with
rigid hierarchies, rules, and regulations.[1] By
contrast, organizations operating in dynamic
environments tend to adopt *organic* structures

enabling them to respond flexibly and rapidly to
environmental threats and opportunities. This
was an early example of the use of **contingency**
theories.

The concept of organizational environment
has since assumed pride of place in management literature. Some organizations, such as
Microsoft or Vodafone, grow quickly in environments hungry for their products. Others,
like Polaroid, disappear just as fast when their
products become obsolete and find themselves
unable to renew themselves. Yet others, like
Nokia or General Electric, accomplish remarkable transformations in order to discover new
environments in which to survive and prosper
when the old environments have ceased to provide enough opportunities for success. As the
pace of technological innovation quickens, as
new countries emerge as serious competitors in
world markets, as political instability continues
to afflict many parts of the world (some rich in
energy resources), as natural resources become
scarcer, and as the natural environment becomes
more precarious, theorists of management have
looked closely at the relations between organizations and their environment.

These relations involve adaptation and alloplasis. Adaptation is a vital process for organizations. Failure to adapt to changing conditions
guarantees organizational decline and eventual
failure. But adaptation can be a slow process
for organizations. Developing new products to
compete with those of their rivals, reorganiz-
ing their structure to streamline their operations, relocating their factories to countries
with lower costs—these are all time-consuming
and risky operations that can easily backfire.
Even more time-consuming are attempts to
change their values or their **culture**. A different way that organizations can relate to their
environments is by seeking to anticipate them
and **control** them. This is sometimes known as
alloplasis—lobbying, advertising, mergers and

---

[1] Burns and Stalker, 1961.

acquisitions, partnerships and strategic alliance, charities and donations are some of the ways in which organizations seek to exercise a measure of control over their environment.

A large part of the literature on organizational environment is marred by a somewhat mechanistic approach to systems and their **boundaries**—organizations are ultimately viewed as analogous to mechanical or biological systems having fixed boundaries and relatively regular throughputs. More recently, **complexity** and **autopoiesis** theories have challenged this conceptualization, leading to more nuanced approaches. The environment may not be an 'objective reality' out there, but a **social construct**. In the first place, the perception of what constitutes the organization's environment may differ across different individuals and different groups. A chemical company's environment looks very different to different people in the organization. For instance, a public relations officer seeks to allay public fears about the company's record on protecting the natural environment; a production worker threatened with redundancy is concerned about the employment environment; a financial expert is concerned with the company's standing in the securities environment; and a retired employee may look at it as a pension provider.

Equally, in a collective way, the environment cannot be defined unless there is a shared sense of what the organization is all about. Is Chrysler to be seen as a car-making company (in which case the competitors' cars are a central feature of its environment) or is it a money-making organization (in which case the competitors' cars are less important as long as Chrysler can find new ways of making money, e.g. by trading in the currency markets)? This has led to the concept of the 'enacted environment'.[1] Instead of a 'given' environment 'out there', enacted environment is based on **sensemaking**, the continuous trading and juxtaposing of meanings and interpretations about the organization, its purpose, and the situations it faces.

It is curious that the study of the effects of the natural environment on organizations has lagged behind that of the social, technological, and cultural environments. In recent years, however, in the face of increasing global pollution, depletion of natural resources, and potentially catastrophic climate change, industry has been cast in a new role: as custodian of the natural environment. The natural environment, in this sense, is not an infinite resource to be exploited, but one to be protected and conserved. This has stimulated an array of 'green' management schemes, buttressed by national and international legislation.[2] The success, or otherwise, of these efforts has hinged upon how key leaders of organizations perceive their social responsibilities. The more enterprising have taken a 'triple bottom-line' perspective, weighting equally different facets of their working environment: financial, social, and natural.

There is now considerable evidence of the fragility of the earth's natural environment and the serious **risks** of the collapse of human civilization resulting from its degradation. In the past, many civilizations became extinct because they over-exploited their natural resources. In a powerful book called *Collapse: How Societies Choose to Fail or Succeed*,[3] Jared Diamond examined several societies that committed environmental suicide by ignoring the signs warning them of imminent catastrophe. Chief among them is the Easter Island society, which prospered for over 600 years until all trees were cut down for fuel and canoes, and all birds and animals were killed. Without trees, they could make no canoes for fishing, no fire, and no tools. They quickly ended up killing each other and destroying whatever was left of their island. When Europeans first landed on the island in the seventeenth century, they discovered just a

---

[1] Weick, 1995.   [2] See e.g. Fineman, 2000a.   [3] Diamond, 2005.

few survivors and several hundred enormous stone statues. As a last-ditch effort to appease their gods, the islanders had built these statues which, once they had lost hope, they toppled over. These statues have now been made to stand up again for tourists (whose flights to and from Easter Island cause considerable greenhouse effects)—they offer a lasting warning of what happens to societies that enter a vicious circle of environmental degradation, material exhaustion, and tribal warfare.

In the 1960s, the distinguished physicist James Lovelock developed the Gaia hypothesis that looks at the earth as a living biosphere, a superorganism, of less than 200 miles thickness in which all earthly life is suspended.[1] For this biosphere to function, many delicate equilibria have to be maintained. What makes the earth behave like a living organism is that as long as the changes that happen are not too wide, it can recover its equilibrium. Over centuries, continents have met and parted, ice has been formed and melted, temperatures have risen and fallen. Lovelock believes that for the first time in its history Gaia is facing a potential collapse, a calamity from which it may not recover. Even if some bacterial and other forms of life survive, human life is in serious jeopardy as a result of climate change, in the first place, and material depletion in the second. When he first proposed this theory in the 1970s, many scientists saw it as 'unscientific', mistaking an inspired metaphor for a literal argument. The earth did not procreate, like animals do, the most literal-minded critics argued. Today, however, Lovelock's view of the planet as a **system** that is subject to similar dangers and threats to a living organism has been embraced by many in and out of the scientific community. There can be very little doubt that as the social sciences concentrate increasingly on the effects of humans on their environment many of today's fierce arguments and debates will in a few years appear to be hopelessly blinkered.

Epistemology

Epistemology is a branch of philosophy that deals with **knowledge** and belief. It comes from the Greek ἐπιστήμη (episteme), one of the five intellectual virtues defined by Aristotle, the scientific knowledge of discoverable facts.[2] The key questions addressed by epistemology include 'What is knowledge?', 'How can we acquire it?', 'What are the different types of knowledge?', and 'How can we be absolutely sure about that which we know?' There are many different schools of epistemology. Some of them privilege particular types of knowledge over others. For instance, mathematical knowledge or scientific knowledge may be regarded as superior to knowledge that comes from tradition, intuition, divination, or revelation. Conversely, revelation may be viewed as superior knowledge to that which arises from our fallible intellects and easily deceivable senses. There are also schools of epistemology that minimize the differences between the truth claims of different types of knowledge, viewing such truth claims as emerging out of different **discourses**. Thus, a religious idea is judged according to different criteria from a management idea or a mathematical one.

Epistemology is often contrasted to *ontology* (from the Greek ὄν= being, deriving from εἶναι = to be), the branch of philosophy that deals with the nature of being. Certain philosophical traditions view ontology and epistemology as quite distinct. Others would argue that the nature of knowledge depends on that which is known and, equally, that what can be known to exist depends on assumptions we make about how we know. Hence ontology and epistemology are conceptually linked. Thus, for example, a realist ontology (an ontology that claims an independent and objective existence for things) is often coupled with a positivistic epistemology (that seeks to explain the behaviour of objects through immutable laws and formulas). By contrast, a hermeneutic epistemology looks at knowledge

---

[1] Lovelock, 1979; 2006.   [2] Aristotle, 1953.

as coming from *interpretation* of different texts and phenomena, seeking to discover their deeper significance and meaning. Reality is then viewed as, at least in part, **socially constructed**. This approach blurs the distinction between ontology and epistemology since interpretation becomes itself part of reality. It would be fair to say that many people use the terms ontology and epistemology in ill-informed manners, making extravagant and spurious claims. Dictionaries of social sciences should have a warning for students to tread carefully when using these terms.

• See also *knowledge, methodology*

Ethic

Ethic comes from the Greek word that means 'habit' and 'character'—'ethology' (the scientific study of the habitual behaviours and characters of animals) comes from the same origin. The Greeks believed that **ethics**, the study of the good and virtuous life, is intimately connected with the 'habits' which are to be found in the 'character' of different animals. Thus, the good life for a tiger is different from the good life for an eagle or a sheep. The same principle applies to humans— the good life for a man is not the same as the good life for a woman, since the two genders have different habits; nor is the good life for a king the same as the good life for a citizen. For this reason, 'ethic' is closer to the link with habit and character than ethics.

Ethic has come to mean a set of deeply held **values** and beliefs that become second nature to people—i.e. they are incorporated in their habits of thinking, feeling, and acting. Max Weber identified the *Protestant ethic* as a set of values that included hard work, cleanliness, frugality, community spirit, and a deep mistrust of physical pleasures. More recently, other ethics have been identified, often by analogy to Weber's Protestant ethic, such as the Confucian ethic, with its strong emphasis on hard work but also human relationships, loyalty, and learning. In moral philosophy, the ethic of justice, based on individual responsibility and equality of treatment, is juxtaposed to the ethic of care, which stresses respect, community, and caring about one's relationships with those close to one.

• See also *achievement, success*

Ethics

Ethics has been a major area of philosophy for centuries, addressing fundamental questions, like 'What is the good or virtuous life?', 'How should one live?', and 'How can we reliably distinguish between right and wrong, just and unjust, fair and unfair?' Moral **emotions**, like guilt, shame, compassion, and embarrassment, are elementary characteristics of human beings and are linked to the psychological agency of conscience. Yet ethics has proven to be one of the most difficult and inconclusive areas of philosophy, where several different schools and principles are competing, finding it hard to reach agreement even in the most elementary questions. Thus, for example, if the good life is to be found in happiness and happiness involves deceiving one's best friend, what should one do? Or, if it is right to tell the truth, should one tell the truth that harms or possibly destroys another human being? On a larger scale, ethical questions draw even more ambiguous answers. Is there a rightful war? Is capital punishment moral? Are there any circumstances under which torture is justified?

While philosophers have debated such issues for centuries, most people have relied on religion for moral guidance. Different religions have differed dramatically in the ways they approach virtue, justice, pleasure, truth, the relations between people, attitudes towards work, and so forth. **Modernity**, with its twin emphases on science and progress, sought to supplant religious ethics with truly scientific ethics. It spawned numerous traditions, from Kantian deontology to utilitarianism, none of which managed to resolve decisively the centuries-old questions on the nature of the good life. In fact, philosopher Alasdair MacIntyre was moved to argue that we live in an age of unprecedented moral confusion. We have lost faith in our ability to make rational arguments about moral matters and base our judgements on emotional hunches and whims. A picture of an animal in pain will persuade us that animal experimentation is a bad thing; later, a picture of a child whose life depends on a drug tested on animals will persuade us to change our mind. This is what he refers to as 'emotivism', 'the doctrine that all evaluative judgments and more specifically all moral arguments are nothing but expressions of preference, expressions of attitude or feeling, insofar as they are moral or evaluative in character'.[1]

One of the reasons for the current loss of faith in rational discussion about moral matters has been the systematic criticism to which morality, and in particular Christian morality, has been subjected by some major figures of modernity. Karl Marx argued that what pass as transcendental laws of right and wrong, like the sanctity of private property, are in fact expressions of **class** interest. Freud, for his part, pointed out that distinctions of right and wrong are products of early life experiences. In patriarchal societies, these are tied to an unquestioned **authority** of the father, who observes, judges, and punishes. Most damagingly perhaps, it was Nietzsche whose systematic assault on Christian morality sought to demonstrate that it was a quiescent, defeatist morality protecting mediocrity and suppressing excellence. All three of these great thinkers argued that morality offers various consolations for the sufferings of life in the form of wish-fulfilling illusions, whose consequence is the accentuation of such sufferings.[2]

Criticisms of morality have opened up the way for a widespread *moral relativism*—the belief that there are no absolute or universal principles and standards of moral behaviour. Actions can be judged from many different moral angles, in line with **values** that are specific to different cultures, historical periods, and even individual personalities. What is right for one person, in one set of circumstances, can easily be wrong for another person in a different set of circumstances. As Martin Parker has described the situation, it depends on the angle from which one is observing: 'one observer's emancipation is another observer's oppression.'[3]

The pervasiveness of moral relativism can explain the exceptional interest among scholars in the Nazi **genocide** of Jews, Gypsies, and others, an event which nearly everybody agrees represents evil. The Holocaust may then be seen as a barbaric regression to an immoral state, where all moral judgements have been extinguished. By contrast, theorists of organization, like Zygmunt Bauman and John Gray,[4] have argued that the Holocaust, far from being an aberration, represents a logical outcome of modernity, with its emphasis on universal truths, rational administration, and technical efficiency. Bauman thus argues that bureaucracy allows cruel things to be done by non-cruel people.

> Modernity was prominent for the tendency to shift moral responsibilities away from the moral self either towards socially constructed and managed supra-individual agencies, or through floating responsibility inside a bureaucratic 'rule of nobody'. The overall result was, on the one hand, the tendency to substitute ethics, that is a law-like code of rules and conventions, for moral sentiments, intuitions, and urges of autonomous selves; and, on the other, the tendency towards 'adiaphorization' [moral indifference], that is exemption of a considerable part of human action from moral judgement and, indeed, moral significance. These processes are by no means a thing of the past—but it seems that their impact is somewhat less decisive than in times of 'classic' modernity.[5]

---

[1] MacIntyre, 1981, pp. 11–12.   [2] See e.g. Rieff, 1959; 1966.   [3] Parker, 1999, p. 39.   [4] Bauman, 1989; Gray, 2002.   [5] Bauman, 1989, pp. 32–3.

Bauman's argument takes us from normative ethics which address questions of right and wrong to the sociology and psychology of moral behaviour (or descriptive ethics), the ways in which morality and ethics enter people's actions and decisions. His argument is that **bureaucracy** takes a wide range of social practices out of the moral domain, turning them into matters of administration. The individual bureaucrat may feel moral qualms about appropriating company stationery or cheating on his or her expenses, but will casually submit a report whose outcome will be to make a thousand workers redundant, unaware that such an action may have an ethical dimension. Equally, we may criticize a politician for cheating on their partner, while accepting or endorsing decisions that may lead to widespread misery and suffering.

Many scholars have turned their attention to descriptive ethics, abandoning normative ethics as a vain and ultimately fruitless pursuit outside academic philosophy. All the same, there continues to be interest in different ways of conceptualizing issues of right and wrong. There is the work of Emmanuel Levinas who located the basis of ethical behaviour in the face-to-face encounter with the **Other**, in which the other person is experienced as someone incredibly close and yet very distant and separate.[1] The work of Carol Gilligan should also be mentioned; Gilligan has sought to juxtapose an 'ethic of care' to the patriarchal 'ethic of justice'.[2] While the latter firmly deals in rewards and punishments the former represents a containing, relating, and respecting attitude to the other person. The ethic of care views each person as part of an interdependent set of relations rather than as a sovereign moral agent with rights and responsibilities.[3] This is reminiscent of the Chinese **value** of 'guanxi', the ability to maintain and support relations in a considerate and sensitive manner. Unlike the ethic of justice, the ethic of care does not aim for total consistency or absolute universality and it has been criticized for this. At the same time, it is an ethic that is being embraced by environmental groups and advocates of sustainability as the only moral basis on which people may collaborate in saving the planet for future generations.

• See also **business ethics, morality**

Ethnic groups and ethnicity

Ethnicity is, along with race and nation, one of a group of words that indicate communities or collectivities of individuals based on a shared quality, a shared origin, a shared tradition, or a sense of a shared destiny. A fundamental difficulty with these concepts lies in two often conflicting ways in which they are defined or **socially constructed**. On the one hand, groups of people may **identify** themselves with each other as members of the same ethnicity, nationality, or race, bound to each other through strong communal ties, based on shared heritage and shared experiences. On the other hand, particular groups, often made up of heterogeneous and diverse elements, may be defined as ethnic groups by others, who for reasons of convenience, ignorance, or power choose to lump them together, often **stereotyping** them as possessing certain common characteristics and disregarding important factors that keep them apart. Thus, the term 'Asian' in the United Kingdom represents a homogenizing label employed by the majority population and only occasionally by people labelled so. Ethnicity is a highly contested terrain where different interests and identities compete for supremacy.

Most scholars today would agree that ethnicity is never fixed or static, even if members of ethnic groups strongly believe in the immutable continuity of their traditions and beliefs. Instead, ethnicity is seen as highly contextual and continuously evolving. Boundaries between ethnic groups can emerge, harden, and disappear. Distinct ethnic groups may merge

---

[1] Levinas, 1969.   [2] Gilligan, 1982.   [3] See also Baier, 1985; Larrabee, 1993.

and coherent ones may fragment. Ethnicity, unlike **race**, lacks any perceived biological basis; unlike **nation**, it lacks an ambition of independent statehood and political autonomy. We can thus refer to Scots as a nation within the United Kingdom, but as an ethnic group in the United States. It is then a feature of ethnic groups that they almost always represent minority interests and identities within a society; they are groups that for certain reasons are seen as separate and often as 'strangers' to the mainstream of a society, liable to either assimilation or **discrimination** and exclusion. In spite of this, the term 'ethnocentrism' continues to denote the tendency by any group (including dominant ones) to regard its own values, achievements, and qualities as superior to those of others.

Ethnicity, along with race, **gender**, and nationality, has assumed increasing importance in contemporary societies as a result of some interrelated trends. First, traditional **class** politics have in advanced industrial countries been gradually supplanted by what are referred to as 'identity politics'. This contentious term refers to the struggles of different groups (ethnic and religious groups, women, sexual and other minorities) to discover a common **voice** to promote their shared interests by having their distinctness recognized and respected.[1] Identity politics can be viewed positively as celebrating cultural diversity and difference, or conversely criticized as an abandonment of universal humanist values and the possibility of rational discourse between different groups. Related to this is the emergence of the management of **diversity** (i.e. a plurality of ethnic groups, races, nationalities, genders, and other strong social identifiers) as a major issue for societies which can no longer take for granted the existence of unquestioned norms and values shared by all. This has brought ethnicity into the centre of discourses of organizations and management.

Ethnicity has been the focus of numerous organizational studies dealing with prejudice, **discrimination**, and **stereotyping**, all of which act to disadvantage particular groups in their employment and career opportunities. A different strand of literature has examined the way that ethnicity affects the accomplishment of different tasks or, more generally, the performance of groups and organizations. Cox, Lobel, and McLeod found that the ethnic composition of teams influences the extent to which they cooperate or compete.[2] Teams composed of people from collectivist cultural traditions display more cooperative behaviour than teams composed of people from individualistic cultural traditions. The question of whether ethnically diverse groups provide organizations with competitive advantage is a highly contested one, with as yet inconsistent findings.[3] There is some evidence that, when diversity is properly managed and differences acknowledged and honoured, heterogeneous groups can display greater **creativity** and **innovation** than homogeneous ones, even if homogeneous groups provide a stronger basis for identification and bonding. The management of differences then is viewed as one of the fundamental tasks of **leadership**.

• See also *diversity, multiculturalism, nation and nationalism, Other and othering, postcolonialism and postcolonial theory, race and racism*

Ethnographic approaches

Ethnography is a method of studying human groups and societies whereby researchers immerse themselves in them, seeking to understand their traditions, practices, and beliefs through close contact, identification, and interaction with their members. The roots of ethnography lie in cultural anthropology and in particular in early studies of pre-literate societies

---

[1] Alcoff, 2006; Nicholson and Seidman, 1995; Schlesinger, 1998. 2006; McLeod, Lobel, and Cox, 1996; Williams and O'Reilly, 1998.   [2] Cox, Lobel, and McLeod, 1991.   [3] Christian, Porter, and Moffitt,

by Western scholars, who spent considerable amounts of time trying to describe and understand the beliefs, practices, and relations of 'natives'. Subsequently, the ethnographic approach was used by many of the social sciences, to study the **cultures**, practices, and beliefs of groups ranging from psychiatric communities to accountants. Ethnographic approaches are almost entirely qualitative and interpretative; they often treat whole societies or groups as **case studies**. A distinction is sometimes made between 'emic' and 'etic' ethnographic accounts. The former try to make sense of cultures in terms of their own belief and value systems, whereas the latter tend to superimpose the observer's own sensemaking schemes. It often proves impossible to sustain this distinction as the very words used by ethnographers, such as 'family', 'ritual', or 'myth', may have fundamentally different meanings in the cultures they observe or may be absent from them altogether.

There is a wealth of ethnographic studies of occupational groups and organizations. Thus Auster has collected some twenty-five ethnographic case studies, which include various celebrated classics like Graeme Salaman's study of British railway workers, Howard Becker and Blanche Geer's discussion of the demise of idealism among medical students, and Jack Haas's study of how skyscraper builders conquer their fear of heights.[1] The richness of such case studies can be striking, offering greater insights into the world of work and organizations than much survey-based research. Other case studies in this book give the reader access into the world of professional thieves, basketball players, dustmen, direct sales staff, law students, male strippers, policemen and policewomen, machine operators, Hollywood actors, taxi drivers, women farmers, and others. Such case studies employ a qualitative methodology, compassion, imagination, and theoretical and interpretative acu-

men in portraying and analysing working lives of different groups of people. In doing so, politics, gender, race, conflict, technology, bureaucracy, family life, and group processes are viewed from the perspectives of those being studied. Well-known ethnographic research in organizational studies includes Kunda's study of an engineering company,[2] Van Maanen's study of Disneyland,[3] Watson's study of a telecommunications firm,[4] Orr's study of Xerox engineers,[5] and Tangherlini's study of paramedical crews.[6]

In some ways, ethnographic research has prospered in recent years, gaining credibility and respect. Increasing emphasis on **language** as creating the world rather than merely describing it, an appreciation of the importance of local practices, and a realization of the wide diversity of cultural traditions have all enhanced its standing. As a result, many of the concepts and theories that have long been the stock in trade of anthropologists, such as myths, rituals, ceremonies, taboos, and so forth, are now regularly being used by different social scientists to describe numerous aspects of modern organizational societies. Ethnographic approaches, however, have come under criticism from **postmodernism** for privileging the voice of the all-knowing ethnographer and his or her conceptual schemes at the expense of the many and diverse voices that he or she hears.[7] Looking at most of the classic works of ethnography by authors like Malinowski or Mead now, one is struck by how much of their authors' own personalities they express and how much of the reported observational material simply reflects their own outlooks, preferences, and prejudices.[8] It is not without reason then that ethnography is sometimes accused of representing a new form of neo-colonialism, where the researchers project or even force their own interests, anxieties, concerns, and cognitive schemes onto their 'subjects', engaging in one-sided exploitative relations.[9]

[1] Auster, 1996. [2] Kunda, 1992. [3] Van Maanen, 1991; 1992. [4] Watson, 2001. [5] Orr, 1996. [6] Tangherlini, 1998. [7] Boje, 1995; Linstead, 1993. [8] Malinowski, 1922; Mead, 1928. [9] Banerjee and Linstead, 2004.

In recent years, carrying ethnographic research on oneself has been proposed as a research method. This is referred to as auto-ethnography.[1] In some ways, this is not very different from what inquisitive researchers in the human sciences have always done—i.e. questioned their own experiences and responses, using them as material for analysis. Sometimes, autoethnography can end up with the researcher becoming the central or even the sole focus of his or her own enquiry. Only exceptionally gifted and probing researchers can then avoid the charge of **narcissistic** navel gazing of limited interest to others.

Evolutionary psychology

Evolutionary psychology is a branch of psychology that seeks to explain many psychological and mental traits of human beings (and, to a lesser extent, other animals) using the Darwinian theory of natural selection. Thus, language, memory, perception, and so forth can be viewed as conferring evolutionary advantages on humans. This approach extends to many phenomena, such as **gender** differences, **sexuality**, parent–child relations (and especially attachment), but also to **cognitive** and **emotional** phenomena. Evolutionary thinking has periodically made inroads into the social sciences but, in the past, was resisted mostly on the grounds of being too deterministic and too biologically driven. Historically, theories of social evolution and 'survival of the fittest' in society became ideological trademarks of eugenicist, right-wing, and racist doctrines.

More recently, however, there have been some calls to employ evolutionary psychology in order to explain organizational and group phenomena. In what amounted to a manifesto for evolutionary psychology in organizational studies, Nigel Nicholson argued that many features of traditional organizations (such as impersonality,

hierarchy, emotional control, etc.) create a poor fit with inherited human characteristics but saw signs of a better fit in new emergent flexible organizational patterns.[2] Nicholson's call has not yet been taken up by many theorists of organizations and has generated some hostile reactions. Graham Sewell,[3] for example, has questioned whether evolutionary psychology can find anything other than highly speculative and ideologically laden applications in the world of organizations. It is too early to know whether evolutionary psychology will be able to make substantive contributions to such areas as leadership, decision making, gender relations, and so forth but it would be a pity if it were dismissed merely because it ran contrary to certain politically correct **ideologies**.

Experience

Experience is a very interesting word with a long career that has witnessed peaks and troughs. The French encyclopedists Diderot and Alembert provided a rich entry on the term which they defined as 'the **knowledge** acquired through a long life, combined with the reflections made on what one has seen, and on the good and bad that has happened to us. In this sense, reading history is a highly profitable way of gaining experience; it tells us of events, and shows us the good or bad repercussions and consequences of these events. We come into this world without any knowledge of cause and effect; it is solely experience that allows us to see what is cause and effect, and then our own reflection forces us to notice the link and the chain of cause and effect.'[4] In days before knowledge could be committed to the written text, old people were valuable resources for their communities as repositories of knowledge. People who had travelled widely were likewise seen as having accumulated knowledge through their contacts with other people. Raymond Williams noted this sense of

---

[1] Bochner and Ellis, 2002; Ellis, 2004; Rodriguez and Ryave, 2002.   [2] Nicholson, 1997.   [3] Sewell, 2004.   [4] Diderot and Alembert, 1965.

the term which he aptly summarized as 'lessons from the past'.[1] He juxtaposed this to a different meaning of the term, something distinctly personal and intense, something subjective and, we may add, directly linked to the here and now. As you read these lines you find yourselves experiencing certain thoughts but also, possibly, certain **emotions**. Laing noted that we experience the world from the moment we are born to the moment we die.[2] He also observed that we can only experience our own experiences. We can experience other people experiencing, but we cannot experience *their* experiences. And yet, experience can be a profoundly social and communal one; nothing brings a **group** of people closer together than going through a profound experience together.

Experience is clearly linked to the evidence of our senses; we constantly experience the world, filtering out many stimuli and registering or observing others. But we also experience our own **self**, our **bodies** (including various aches, pains, and excitations), our moods, and our **emotions**. Thus when the writer Romain Rolland describes an experience of an 'oceanic feeling' to Freud inviting him to comment whether this may be the root of all religious experience,[3] he notes, first, that he often has this feeling that he describes as being part of a 'sensation of eternity', and, second, that he has heard other people describe a similar experience to him. Freud politely notes that he has not had any such experiences himself but goes on to attribute it to a resurfacing of primary **narcissism**, the early experience of union with the mother, the experience of a child that finds itself in the centre of a loving and benevolent world without boundaries and discontinuities—an ocean.

The term 'experiential learning' is now widely used in relation to the **learning** required of managers and other practitioners.[4] Thus, Kolb has argued that this learning assumes the form of a cycle which builds on experience through reflection, abstract conceptualization, and testing.[5] Learning from books may offer help with conceptualizing and testing but it is not enough. Learning to be a manager (like learning to play tennis or to be a parent) requires direct experience (knowledge from the past), though experience is not enough. It also requires reflection, theory, and testing.

Emphasis on experience as a source of **knowledge** has long had to compete against knowledge from scientific discoveries. This is a common way in which the conflict between the old and the new, tradition and rationality, is enacted—experience against expertise. During the high noon of modernity, the voice of experience often found itself silenced by the voice of the expert whose uncontested **authority** rested on scientific evidence, the unassailable authority of medicine, physics, chemistry, and so forth. Where the voice of experience was not entirely silenced, it found itself relegated to the standing of 'mere opinion', used in a condescending way by the expert as the raw material upon which to base diagnoses, generalizations, and theories. The term 'anecdotal' was used to this end. French ethnographer Claude Lévi-Strauss expressed this scientific mistrust of experience well, arguing that 'to reach reality one has first to reject experience, and then subsequently to reintegrate it into an objective synthesis devoid of sentimentality'.[6] Yet, in our times, the voice of experience has assumed a new authority. Having lived through an event, having direct experience of a condition (including depression, childbirth, or corporate downsizing), gives one considerable authority to speak about it, authority that even experts must acknowledge and respect. Thus a cancer sufferer may seek the doctor's expect advice, but he or she will also seek the advice of fellow sufferers, whose personal experience of the disease, of different treatments and different ways of handling the symptoms, may be every bit as helpful.[7]

---

[1] Williams, 1983.   [2] Laing, 1969.   [3] Freud, 1930.   [4] Kelly, 1955.   [5] Kolb, 1985.   [6] Lévi-Strauss, 1955/1992, p. 58.   [7] Gabriel, 2004c.

The natural medium of communicating experience is the **story**. Stories, as Walter Benjamin recognized, present facts-as-experience as against facts-as-information. Stories delve in the subjective, the intimate, and sacrifice accuracy for effect. Learning from other people's stories is what we now call *narrative knowledge*.[1] One of the fascinating discoveries of the last twenty years is that the very professionals whose expertise rests on the authority of their scientific disciplines (the medic, the accountant, the lawyer, the technician) also make extensive use of narrative knowledge in their professional practices.[2] For example, the treatment of diabetes as a general condition may be determined by the up-to-date scientific knowledge available to a physician (based on randomized control trials and so forth), yet the treatment of one particular person's diabetes with specific complications and idiosyncrasies may well be informed by stories of how other physicians treated similar cases. Experience can then be seen not to struggle against expertise but to tame it, humanize it, and guide it.

[1] Czarniawska-Joerges, 1995; Tsoukas, 1998a; Weick, 2001c. [2] Morris, 2001; Orr, 1996.

Fads and fashions (in management)

Referring to a managerial technique, like *Business Process Re-engineering* or *Total Quality Management*, as a fad or a fashion is not meant to diminish its significance or to question its effectiveness. It is meant to describe the way that such practices become disseminated and adopted by different organizations, different sectors, and different countries. In this, they share many of the features of **fashions** in clothes, foods, or holiday destinations—a rapid rise in popularity, followed by a rapid decline as they get superseded by later fads. Occasionally a particular technique may get rediscovered or it may assume a safe if unspectacular positioning in the repertoire of management practices.

Describing such techniques as fads also reflects some of the extravagant claims often made on their behalf by management gurus and **consultants**. They are then presented as panaceas to virtually all management problems and difficulties, creating the sense among some managers that, unless they adopt them, they are doomed to failure. The same goes for consultancy firms, business schools, or individual academics who may be unwilling to embrace or advocate particular techniques, and risk being accused of lagging behind the times. Management fads and fashions are, therefore, linked to academic fads and fashions. The way that management ideas emerge, become adopted by early trend-setters, and are subsequently disseminated has been researched by several academics and is of considerable interest to **institutional theory.**[1]

It is almost impossible to provide a comprehensive list of managerial fads and fashions without risking ridicule by some advocate of a technique left out of the list—'Why, have you not heard of *x*?' can be a devastating put-down to a consultant, a manager, or even an academic. Such a list is also liable to generate the opposite criticism: 'How could you include *x* as a management *fad*? Do you not realize that it is a serious and scholarly approach?' All the same, some of the most influential fads include:

☐ *Quality Circles*—pioneered in Japan, this approach involved groups of workers doing similar work who meet regularly and voluntarily to identify, analyse, and resolve work-related problems and to make innovative suggestions for improving product quality. This approach reached a zenith in the 1980s but has since gone into relative decline.

☐ *Corporate culture*—organizational culture came to be widely viewed as the key to organizational success in the 1980s, largely following the success of Peters and Waterman's *In search of excellence*;[2] managers were encouraged to use symbols, stories, and ceremonies to instil corporate values and enhance customer service, quality, and innovation.

☐ *Total Quality Management (TQM)*—one of the most popular sets of management ideas, TQM sought to reduce errors, waste, and wear-and-tear through a holistic approach to quality; the influence of this approach has ranged from narrow manufacturing operations to healthcare delivery systems and

---

[1] Abrahamson, 1991; 1996; Newell, Swan, and Robertson, 1998; Sturdy, 2004.   [2] Peters and Waterman, 1982.

financial services. Its ambition was both to deliver a higher quality of service to customers but also to create a richer and more empowering work experience for employees.

- ☐ *Lean production*—pioneered by Toyota (but traceable to Ford), this was a production system that encompassed many of the TQM principles but stretched them further; it emphasized high flexibility and responsiveness to consumer demands, the reduction or elimination of inventories, the achievement of zero product and service defects, and the systematic elimination of every type of waste (material, time, space, labour, etc.)
- ☐ *Re-engineering* (also known as *Business Process Re-engineering* or *BPR*)—initially proposed by former MIT professor Michael Hammer,[1] BPR has been one of the most influential management fads of the last twenty years. It has amounted to declaration of war on anything within organizations that fails to deliver value to the customer; in place of the humanistic rhetoric of TQM, it has aimed for radical rather than continuous improvements in organizational performance, disregarding the consequences in human suffering; it has been a significant **ideological** force behind **downsizing**.
- ☐ *Knowledge management* and the *learning organization*—unlike BPR, which approaches people as an expendable resource in the value chain, this approach has emphasized **learning** as the key resource accounting for **innovation** and organizational success. Many of its advocates have focused on industries at the cutting edge of technology to argue that learning may go beyond individuals working in organizations and become embedded in organizations themselves. The **management of knowledge**, according to this approach, must be viewed as an organization's primary concern.

As can be seen from this list, management fads can metamorphose into new ones, do battle against competing ones, and incorporate or merge with others. In addition to the above, other ideas that have assumed the character of management fads include emotional intelligence, complexity and chaos theories, and storytelling. Managerial practices such as **downsizing**, outsourcing, and diversification are also sometimes referred to as fads, although it would be more appropriate to describe them as movements. There are several good accounts of management fads and the gurus who have acted as their main advocates.[2]

• See also *fashion, knowledge*

Fantasy

Imagination is vital in our lives. For long parts of each day, we muse, we daydream, and fantasize. Fantasy can be the source of powerful experiences, at times more powerful than those prompted by our senses. Fantasies can influence our **actions**, at times propelling us to do things and at others stopping us from acting. They can be positive or negative, happy or sad; they may invade our thoughts suddenly or they may evolve over long periods of time. Some fantasies are intensely private, carefully sheltered from public scrutiny; others are public, shared with many, sometimes thousands or even millions of others. Fantasy is the birthplace of leaders' **visions**, of artists' masterpieces, and inventors' breakthroughs; it is also the birthplace of many crimes. Fantasy is one of the root causes of **emotions**: exhilaration, anger, love, disgust, awe, shock, nostalgia, hope, despair, and nearly every powerful emotion can be triggered by fantasy.

We can think of fantasy as a product of the imagination, which involves an idea, a **desire**, or a detailed scene or sequence of scenes. It may assume the form of conscious daydreaming or

---

[1] Hammer and Champy, 1993.   [2] See e.g. Clark and Fincham, 2002; Collins, 2000; Grint, 1997; Huczynski, 1993; Jackson, 2001.

rehearsal of different scenarios (e.g. imagining oneself vacationing on an island or exploring the implications of making a decision to follow a particular career path). In such instances, fantasy is a kind of experimental action—an action whose implications, side effects, and emotional yield are imagined before or in lieu of being realized. Alternatively, a fantasy may be **unconscious**, its contents partly or fully excluded from consciousness for one reason or other (e.g. the fantasy of being a princess or of killing a rival). 'Primal fantasies' are deeply unconscious fantasies which many individuals experience as they grow up (such as fantasies of castration and seduction, fantasies of being born of noble parents, etc.). Freud hypothesized that such fantasies are universal parts of the phylogenetic heritage of humanity, passed from generation to generation, whereas Jung viewed them as archetypes, emanating from humanity's deep and shared collective unconscious.

Some unconscious fantasies (which psychoanalysts spell 'phantasies') can be viewed as compromise formations between **desires** and the forces which oppose their realization. Such phantasies are the outcome of desire distorted to a greater or lesser extent by **defence mechanisms**. Within organizations such phantasies generally assume a clandestine existence, mostly censored by the forces of rationality, efficiency, and order. They do, however, occasionally surface in jokes and stories, office gossip, and lore and can provide a good way of understanding the deeper relations among individuals or between individuals and their work.

Most individuals are aware of the difference between fantasy and reality—between imagining being a victim of **bullying** and actually being one. Yet, many mental processes blur this distinction. This is one of the achievements of **stories**—narratives whose primary loyalty lies in expressing **experience** rather than staying truthful to factual truth. Stories give a legitimate vent to fantasy by privileging wish fulfilment

over verifiable fact. Psychologically, some of the most important stories we tell are the stories about ourselves—stories of victories and defeats, achievements and mistakes, good and bad luck, love, loss, and longing—which sustain those tangled webs of truths, half-truths, and wishful fantasies that make up our **identities**.

Fantasy should not be thought of as a purely psychological entity. Fantasy can raise armies and empires, business and otherwise. It fuels vast sectors of today's economies. Large areas of advertising, tourism, media, retail, fashion, entertainment, and the leisure and creative industries rest on the power of fantasy. Even solidly 'rational' industries, however, can be underpinned by fantasy. Where would the insurance industry be without the fantasy of disaster or the automobile industry without the fantasies of freedom and power?

Several social and cultural commentators have noted that today's **consumerism** is sustained by fantasy. Fantasy drives people to the 'cathedrals of consumption'—tourist destinations, theme parks, shopping malls, museums, movie theatres, cruise ships, casinos, and even fast food restaurants. There, many undergo quasi-spiritual experiences where 'dreams come true' and the world is purged of all that is dirty, ordinary, and depressing. Contrary to Weber's fears regarding **bureaucracy**, late modernity rediscovers enchantment and fantasy. Campbell argues that many objects we use in our lives are essentially props for different fantasies. Fantasy is 'the ability to treat sensory data "as if" it were "real" whilst knowing that it is indeed "false".... It is this "as if" response which is at the heart of modern hedonism.'[1] This hedonism is what Campbell call the 'Romantic **ethic**', the unending search for pleasure not in physical sensation but in exaggerated emotional excitations and the search for novel and stimulating **experiences**. A visit to Disneyworld may yield precisely such experiences, which are known to be fantastic but no less pleasurable for it. In Campbell's view,

---

[1] Campbell, 1989, p. 82.

the consumers' 'basic motivation is the desire to experience in reality the pleasurable dramas which they have already enjoyed in imagination, and each "new" product is seen as offering the possibility of realizing this ambition. However, since reality can never provide the perfected pleasures encountered in day-dreams (or, if at all, only in part, and very occasionally), each purchase leads to literal disillusionment.'[1] The power of fantasy in human affairs is such that it is surprising that it does not play a far larger part in the social sciences.

• See also *Consumers and consumption, desire, fantasy, sex, sexuality*

Fashion

Fashion is a crucial societal phenomenon, and no description of modern societies can be complete if it does not include it. However—most likely as the result of the US economist Thorsten Veblen's severe treatment of it in his *Theory of the leisure class*[2]—fashion is often portrayed as a marginal phenomenon, finding its expression in actions of women and frivolous men; no serious activity such as management or research can be claimed to follow fashion. Yet many puzzling events taking place within such serious activities might find a better explanation if the notion of fashion is explored more thoroughly.

The English language, choosing 'fashion' instead of 'mode' to denote a prevailing custom, usage, or style, has lost an insight preserved in many other languages, including Swedish and Italian. Especially in Swedish, it is impossible to say whether 'modern' is intended to mean 'modern' or 'fashionable'; indeed, the two are assumed to be one and the same. Although fashion was no doubt an important phenomenon in ancient Egypt and Rome, contemporary globalization movements paid fashion a service by helping it to spread; fashion reciprocated, helping **globalization** to choose what to globalize.

Indeed, fashion is that which gives the direction to *imitation*, another crucial phenomenon in need of more attention. The French sociologist Gabriel Tarde,[3] a contemporary of Veblen, was of the opinion that imitation is the central mechanism that explains how order is possible without knowledge. People invent new things all the time, and inventions and **innovations** become imitated; but as the imitation proceeds, the attractiveness of the original invention diminishes, and new inventions are searched for. Ideas, practices, or objects that are widely spread cease to be fashionable; an established fashion becomes its opposite—an **institution** or a custom. Fashion constantly renews itself, but it chooses among many inventions that are present at a certain time and place.

Which innovations are imitated? This question has been asked many times by scholars and fashion leaders alike, but answers can be only general, and formulated in hindsight. Those imitated are allegedly superior, on the grounds of their qualities (Tarde call these 'logical reasons'; pragmatic reasons may be a better term), or on the grounds of their provenence in time and place (Tarde's extra-logical reasons; at present one could call them power-symbolic). It is impossible to tell the difference between the two at any given time, as the power-symbolic superiority tends to masquerade as a superiority of quality. The third factor increasing the probability than an invention will be imitated is that it fits well (or at least does not threaten) the institutionalized thought structure of a given time and place.

After Tarde, few social scientists were interested in fashion. One of them was the German sociologist Georg Simmel,[4] yet another contemporary of Tarde and Veblen, who emphasized the paradoxical character of fashion: it expresses a **desire** to be different and to be identical, to conform and to deviate, to lead and to follow. Fashion creates **status** distinctions, which in turn may translate into power. Veblen's insights

---

[1] Ibid. pp. 89–90.   [2] Veblen, 1899/1925.   [3] Tarde, 1890/1903.   [4] Simmel, 1904/1971.

were taken up and developed in the 1960s by the US sociologist Herbert Blumer,[1] who postulated that fashion is a *selection mechanism*, which influences the **market** distorting the demand and supply curves, and which both uses and serves the economic competition. Its important element is a *collective choice* among competing tastes, things, and ideas; it is oriented toward finding but also toward creating what is typical of a given time.

Simmel and Blumer remained the sources of inspiration for culture scholars; students of management attempted to explain away the occurrence of **fads and fashions** in organizational practice. Fashion has been persistently depicted as irrational, while management and organizing were by definition rational activities. The undeniable fact of managers following fashions could be therefore explained either as a temporary deviation from the rational path, to be corrected; or as a more complex expression of **rationality**. The changing fashion could be framed either as an answer to supply and demand conditions; or at least as a striving for **legitimacy**, which is necessary and therefore rational in modern organizations. No attempts were spared to trace fashion setters in advance; after all, if they can be distinguished before a fashion spreads, fashion will prove manageable. These attempts remain frustrated. One possibility that remains open for organizational scholars is to follow the example of their colleagues in culture studies and to explore fashion as a cultural phenomenon, present in both management theory and practice. In both domains the urge to look for novelty and the fear of staying behind, the wish to become different and to be similar, to innovate and to imitate, are equally present. **Knowledge** is desirable; imitation is inevitable. Fashion directs both.

• See also *fads and fashion*

BARBARA CZARNIAWSKA, GÖTEBORG UNIVERSITY

Feelings

In recent years, the study of **emotion** has come to the forefront of social and organizational studies. Feelings, however, have lagged somewhat behind emotions. Disgust may be an emotion I learn to associate with filth or excrement, but why should I feel disgust about a meal of frogs' legs or about an amputation? Where do feelings come from?

It is fair to say that culture plays a big part in linking emotions to social occasions—grief to funerals, pride to graduation ceremonies, and so forth. Yet, it is also fair to say that *across* cultures, centuries, and continents people have shown a remarkable ability to understand each other's feelings and even to empathize with them. In fact, our ability to understand other people's beliefs and thoughts lags far behind our ability to relate to their feelings. And even within the same culture why should one person be overwhelmed by the death of a parent while their sibling is not, or one be paralysed by fear before an interview and another not?

Faced with this blind spot 'Where do emotions come from?', Fineman now juxtaposes emotion as the **socially constructed** and culturally displayed dimension of affect to 'feeling', its personal, private dimension.[2] One tradition that has always had an interest in personal feelings rather than public emotions has been **psychoanalysis**. Human beings are approached by psychoanalysis not merely as emotional but as desiring, passionate beings. Feelings are no simple side effects of mental life, no performances staged for the sake of audiences, no instruments of interpersonal manipulation (although they may under certain circumstances be all of these things). Instead, psychoanalysis approaches feelings as driving forces in human affairs.

For psychoanalysis, feeling lies at the heart of human **motivation**—emotion *is* motivation. It is not accidental that both words derive from the

---

[1] Blumer, 1969/1973.   [2] Fineman, 2000d; 2003.

Latin *emovere*, to move. The drive for money no less than the drive for power or the drive for work, they all derive from emotion and are liable to become passions. The drive for truth, that too is emotionally driven, rather than the expression of an abstract interest in **knowledge** and **learning**. Hence, too, illusion is no mere product of ignorance of error, but rather the product of fear, love, anxiety, desire, and passion. For psychoanalysis, feeling is what holds groups together ('necessity alone will not hold them together'[1]), and feeling too is what destroys them. Being in love and being under hypnosis are the two closest psychological states to being a member of a **group**, according to Freud (though Freud was wise enough to limit his formulations to groups 'without too much organization'[2]).

For this reason, the supposedly passion-free spaces of modern organizations (where precisely there is 'too much organization') were of relatively limited interest to psychoanalytic writers for many years. Groups, on the other hand, where feelings and **fantasies** can be dominant, were of much greater interest. The attempts of writers like Jaques,[3] Menzies,[4] Levinson,[5] and Zaleznik[6] to introduce a psychoanalytic dimension in the study of organizations were respectfully received, but until recently were not integrated in the mainstream of organizational studies (see **psychoanalysis and psychoanalytic approaches**).

Psychoanalysis views feeling as intimately linked to **desire**, its different manifestations, modifications, and frustrations. Feelings like nostalgia, hope, or greed represent different forms of desire oriented towards different states or objects. Desires and, therefore, feelings have a remarkable ability to mutate and transform themselves. A desire for revenge can turn into a desire for self-punishment ('to teach them a lesson') and then into a desire to starve oneself to death; feelings may correspondingly change from anger to guilt to resignation. In their many vicissitudes, feelings are the sources of perceptions and constructions that can be highly irrational and at variance with other people's constructions of reality. 'My parents never loved me', 'I have never wanted to harm anyone', and 'I am disgustingly fat' may all be wide of the mark, illusions that fly in the face of evidence.

A key psychoanalytic argument regarding affect rests on the concept of *transference*. Our feelings and emotions have histories that parallel our own histories as individual **subjects**. They are liable to return whenever we find ourselves in a situation that evokes an earlier one that left a powerful emotional mark on us. Many of these involved early relations with our parents. Emotions may, in this way, be transferred from a parent to a leader or to a coach—the same respect, awe, or love that we experienced as children may return subsequently.

Many feelings are ambivalent, involving both positive and negative aspects, love and hate, respect and fear. Ambivalent feelings, although very common, can be very confusing and disorienting—we like to organize our loves and our hates, our likes and dislikes, in a consistent manner. For this reason, we often repress those sides of feelings that we experience as dangerous or unacceptable. Jealousy towards a sibling may be repressed and replaced with excessive love and consideration. The fear of a parent may be replaced by excessive respect. The management and control of such feelings is not easy, nor are the outcomes certain. It can take a great deal of psychic work. Dealing with loss (or with disappointment, betrayal, or even falling in love) we may simply experience specific feelings, but these may conceal the great deal of work that we are undertaking in accepting loss, coming to terms with it, and reorienting our emotional life elsewhere (see **emotional labour and emotional work**).

• See also *emotion, fantasy*

[1] Freud, 1930, p. 122.   [2] Freud, 1921, p. 116.   [3] Jaques, 1952; 1955.   [4] Menzies, 1960; Menzies Lyth, 1970.   [5] Levinson, 1968/1981; 1972.   [6] Zaleznik, 1977; 1989.

Femininity

Femininity is a term used to describe equally the major features of female **sexuality** and the attributes of the female **gender**. Feminist theory in the 1970s and 1980s drew attention to distinct features of early childhood and socialization which mould the personality development of boys and girls and prepare them to assume different gender **roles**. The **social construction** of femininity explores how different 'agents' in society—men, magazines, story books, films, television, photographs, discourses—fashion images of femininity against which women (and men) measure themselves and shape their **identities**. The extent to which femininity is produced by such social factors as against biological and genetic ones is the object of extensive debates. Many theorists look at the emergence of femininity (and masculinity) as the product of interaction between genetic and social factors, thereby rejecting the more extreme views, either that women are 'by nature' different from men, or that women are made to be different and inferior from men through male discrimination and prejudice.[1]

Along with many other social sciences, organizational theory, in the last twenty years, has taken a great interest in femininity. Organizations are now seen by many scholars as 'gendered'. This means that they are not gender-neutral phenomena where some of the positions happen to be occupied by women and some by men. Instead, they are viewed as encompassing a gender dimension in their very constitution.[2] Thus, leadership is not a neutral phenomenon in which a male leader often happens to be assisted by a female aide; likewise, it is not accidental that a male physician is often assisted by a female nurse. Instead, these phenomena are gendered. They cast a woman as the subordinate, obedient, pliant, and caring partner in a relationship that casts the man as dominant, commanding, and

expert partner. Even when the roles are reversed, so that a female doctor is assisted by a male nurse or when a woman, like Margaret Thatcher becomes head of state, they are viewed as 'exceptional' situations calling for special types of explanations (e.g. 'unusual, masculine woman') which reinforce the accepted gender roles and do not undermine concepts of femininity or masculinity.

Discussions on the management of femininity within organizations centre on how different organizations deploy qualities like caring, supporting, tempting, and deferring, thereby reinforcing the view of these as essentially feminine qualities. This is most evident where employees act as an organization's 'front' to the customers, such as receptionists, sales assistants, holiday reps, and so forth. In certain organizations, relations between employees and customers become sexualized, part of a strategy to entrance and captivate the latter. In this way, femininity becomes an important organizational resource for jobs where **emotional** and **aesthetic** labour are essential.

Femininity in organizations is very widely discussed in connection with leadership, motivation, equal opportunities, sexual harassment at work, and occupational structures. Some of the key questions raised are:

- How is femininity constructed within different institutional settings (e.g. business, professional, government, etc.) and how does this affect women's chances of attaining full equality with men?
- How do organizations utilize femininity to lure and retain customers or, more generally, to carry out their operations?
- How do women perceive and construct their own femininity? To what extent are they influenced by representations from the media and other social agents?
- To what extent and how do women use their femininity in their work? In what ways do

---

[1] See e.g. Chodorow, 1978; Mitchell, 1975.   [2] Alvesson and Billing, 1997; Mills and Tancred, 1992.

such uses affect the representations of women in organizations?

Important contributions to the study of femininity in organizations have been made by Calas and Smircich,[1] Marshall,[2] Gherardi,[3] Wilson,[4] Simpson,[5] and many others.

• See also *discrimination, feminism, gender, sexual harassment, women's studies*

Feminism

Feminism is a social movement, a **discourse** seeking to articulate, demonstrate, explain, and contest women's subordinate position in society, and an **ideology** seeking to challenge and reverse this position. Militant pro-women statements and myths can be found deep in history but the origins of today's feminist movement are usually placed in the struggles for political equality of women and universal suffrage in the early twentieth century. Feminist activism and thinking grew in the 1960s and 1970s, primarily demanding equality for women in work and an end of **violence** against women in the domestic sphere. In addition to numerous great feminist statements from the literature of that period, many of the core ideas of feminism emerged from classic books like Betty Friedan's *Feminine mystique*, which challenged the view that women are by nature meant to reach fulfilment in domestic and child-rearing roles,[6] Germaine Greer's *The female eunuch*, which highlighted women's oppression at the hands of men and subsequently themselves,[7] and Kate Millett's *Sexual politics*, which linked sexuality with **power** inequalities in relationships between the genders.[8] More recently, feminist theorists like Naomi Wolf have highlighted how beauty acts as an oppressive and exploitative force on many women, creating and perpetuating deep insecurities and anxieties.[9] Authors influenced by the

work of Foucault, Lacan, and **post-structuralist** theorists have sought to highlight how structures of domination become embedded in discourses that systematically privilege the male, by casting the woman as the subordinate 'other'.

In spite of many disagreements and debates between different strands of feminism (sometimes identified as essentialist, liberal, socialist, radical, post-structuralist, postcolonialist, and so forth), there is considerable agreement that most contemporary societies are still a long way away from offering full equality to women. Women continue to occupy the lower positions in occupational structures, continue to encounter formidable difficulties when they reach top jobs, and are often the victims of male violence in the domestic sphere, in public spaces, and in war territories. In some ways, feminist ideas that were considered extreme in the 1960s and 1970s have now become part of the mainstream discourses and there is some evidence that women of a younger generation are less liable to form their **identities** around feminist principles than many of their predecessors. There has also been some backlash against what is referred to as 'victim feminism', feminism that thrives on preserving women's position as powerless and oppressed victims. The contentious term 'post-feminism' has been used, primarily by right-wing political commentators, to describe a situation where women have made enough progress in most spheres of social life so that they can supposedly celebrate their empowerment and success without a need for feminism.

Organizational theory has benefited greatly from the work of feminist theorists who have revealed how organizations use **femininity** as a way of sexualizing relations within organizations or between organizations and their customers and also the continuing obstacles that women face in fashioning successful **careers** in organizations. Many important theorists in the sphere of

---

[1] Calas and Smircich, 1992; 1996.   [2] Marshall, 1984; 1995.   [3] Gherardi, 1995.   [4] Wilson, 2003.   [5] Simpson, 1998.   [6] Friedan, 1965.   [7] Greer, 1970.   [8] Millett, 1970.   [9] Wolf, 1990.

organizations happily acknowledge the feminist label and have contributed to the development of a feminist critique of management.[1]

• See also *femininity, gender, women's studies*

Followership

Considering the huge amount of attention commanded by leaders and leadership, followers and followership seem to be neglected by scholars, practitioners, and most other commentators.[2] In one way, this is to be expected. Understanding **leadership** has long been seen as a worthwhile quest. It promises to deliver the key for identifying leaders and leadership qualities and the basis of effective leadership training and development programmes. What use is understanding followership? Who would wish to train people to be good followers? This is the rub. Who could hope to be a good leader *without* understanding his or her followers? Even if we assume that there is a single set of principles characterizing all forms of good leadership, such a set would undoubtedly include an intimate and sympathetic understanding of followers, their needs, aspirations, and capabilities. It would also include a sophisticated understanding of the nature of the bonds that tie followers to their leaders and the factors that can affect these bonds.

Among human relations few are as highly charged as those between leaders and followers. Whether we think of political leaders, business leaders, religious leaders, or even leaders of a school or a family, such people stir up strong **emotions** in their followers. The relations themselves are rarely static but constantly evolve— a bit like relations between parents and their children or husbands and wives. Like most powerful human relations, relations between leaders and followers are based on an understanding of obligations, responsibilities, and duties that different parties bring to the relationship. These understandings, mostly implicit, occasionally explicit (as when F. D. Roosevelt offered the American people 'a New Deal'), are referred to as **psychological contracts**.

Some of these psychological contracts tie citizens to their political leaders. Churchill promised the British 'blood, foil, tears, and sweat'. Most accepted this deal, seeing in him the leader capable of resisting the Nazis, even at an enormous cost. They placed their trust in the man capable of ensuring the survival of the nation, no matter what his demands were. What is interesting is that people are often bound up in psychological contracts with tyrants, leaders with scant respect for them and with a record of brutality, failure, and disappointment. This is sometimes referred to as a 'Faustian pact', a pact with the devil, whose consequences unravel much later. Such was the deal between Hitler and the majority of the German people who continued fighting to the bitter end, when the tragic consequences of his leadership were plain for all to see. While Hitler sought to muffle all dissent, forcing his followers into destructive consent, other leaders seem to empower and learn from followers, by accepting criticism and guidance from them. Keith Grint has likened leaders who recognize their own limitations and acknowledge the need to mobilize the talents of their followers and encourage constructive dissent to wheelwrights.[3] They hold an organization together by diffusing leadership and responsibility among the followers, allowing different followers to shine when circumstances demand it.

What then is it that followers offer their leaders and what do they ask in return? Most people expect to offer a degree of loyalty to their leaders. They are willing to subordinate their individual will to that of the leader. Many are prepared to work hard, endure hardships, and even make sacrifices. In return, most people expect their leaders to offer guidance and take

[1] Any such list is inevitably partial, but see e.g. Acker, 2006; Calas and Smircich, 1992; Ferguson, 1984; Kanter, 1977; Marshall, 1984; 1995; Martin, 1990; Martin, 2005; Thomas and Davies, 2005; Wallach Bologh, 1990.   [2] Collinson, 2005; 2006.   [3] Grint, 2005a.

responsibility for the success of their organization, their nation, or their group. They expect them to work tirelessly towards that goal. They expect their leaders to be honest and frank with their followers and they expect them to treat them with respect. They expect them to recognize their efforts and sacrifices. But above all, they expect their leaders to hold their organization, group, or nation together: to protect them from internal and external danger. *Protection* is something most people expect from their leaders. Think of a country in a state of lawless anarchy or an organization in which there is a power vacuum. In such situations, it is not surprising that people may yearn for a strong leader, 'a strong man', who will restore order, purpose, and direction. Even a tyrant may then appear better than chaos and disorder.

Followers then expect protection, personalized care, guidance, recognition, praise, but also inspiration and stimulation—a huge range of expectations by any measure. Much of the time, these needs are not conscious, yet they have a profound influence on the followers' outlooks and emotions. They are then liable to be expressed in different **fantasies**, in which leaders feature as larger than life characters, capable of performing extraordinary deeds, good and bad. They can be experienced as benevolent, father-like figures, as demonic schemers engaged in plotting and machination, as cunning wheeler-dealers who strike clever deals for the organization, as impostors who attained their position by deception, and so forth.[1]

Leaders often forget to their detriment how closely their status is aligned to their followers' fantasies—and how quickly they can switch from being revered to being vilified through no actions of their own. By appreciating the importance of fantasy in leader–follower relations, we can begin to understand the unreasonable expectations that many followers have of their leaders and the excessive standards against which they judge them. We can then temper our own expectations, qualify our hopes and judgements, and reach more balanced verdicts on the merits and weaknesses of individual leaders. And leaders themselves can learn to handle exaggerated expectations and stop them from acting in ways that are likely to end in frustration and failure.

Where do followers' fantasies about their leaders originate? Some of them are rooted in their **experiences**, good and bad, of previous leaders and in particular of the two important figures of **authority** that dominate most people's early lives, their mother and their father. To the eyes of the helpless and immature child, these figures appear immense and godlike, referred to as 'primal mother' and 'primal father'. The qualities and characteristics attributed to these figures through the child's fantasies form the basis of some subsequent fantasies about leaders. Psychologist Heinz Kohut has argued that some leaders are experienced by their followers as reincarnations of the fantasy of the primal mother, caring, giving, and loving.[2] Others are experienced as embodiments of the primal father, omnipotent, omniscient, but also strict and terrifying. Kohut referred to the former as *charismatic* and to the latter as *messianic*. In the presence of charismatic leaders, followers are liable to feel inspired and elated, whereas in the presence of messianic leaders, they are liable to feel submissive and overawed. Leaders may discover that their own actions have limited ability to modify the way their followers imagine them to be by projecting such powerful fantasies onto them. Leadership fantasies surface regularly in the mass media where high-profile leaders in politics, business, and sport are easily portrayed as having supernatural qualities, good and bad, thereby fuelling powerful public emotions towards such figures.

• See also *charisma, leadership*

---

[1] Gabriel, 1997.   [2] Kohut, 1971; 1976.

Fordism

Fordism is a system of manufacturing production pioneered by American industrialist Henry Ford in the early decades of the twentieth century. Ford made cars available to the masses by producing them in a highly rationalized and economical way that stretched many of the principles of **Scientific Management** to their logical conclusion. Cars were produced in continuously moving assembly lines that dictated the pace and quality of the work to the workers. Each worker carried out very simple assembly operations in a highly routinized and **controlled** manner. The work was stripped of all individuality and **skill** but the workers were paid substantially more than the average industrial wage at the time. Yet, such were the gains in productivity that Ford could sell his famous 'Model T' cars much more cheaply than those of his competitors. The cars themselves were highly standardized, summed up in Ford's phrase 'They can have it any colour they like, so long as it is black.' Standardization helped the efficiency of production and streamlining of distribution and generated considerable economies of scale.

While Ford is acknowledged as the father of mass production, he should also be seen as the father of mass consumption. Ford believed firmly that his cars would bring freedom and happiness to all, not merely to the elite. Thus the Model T, sold in millions, can be viewed as the herald of **consumerism**, the new phase in human history when consumption came to be seen not just as the means of survival but as the true path to the good and happy life. In the 'Roaring Twenties' an ever-widening range of consumer goods became available to the masses, including phonographs and records, radios, movies, and so forth. The success of Fordism did not come without a heavy price. In exchange for enjoying the fruits of consumerism, ever-increasing groups of workers were consigned to tedious and monotonous work that made little use of their qualities and talents as human beings. This *Fordist Deal*—ever-increasing standards of living in exchange for boring and repetitive work—became the foundation stone for the rise of modern consumerism.[1]

The latter part of the twentieth century saw a series of challenges to the rule of Fordism. Fordist production was seen as far too rigid and mechanical to meet the increasingly diverse and changeable demands of consumers in a global system of exchanges or to take advantage of new technological opportunities opened up by radical innovations in computing and telecommunications. Many scholars noted the coming of post-Fordism,[2] a concept that has still somewhat imprecise and competing meanings. Like **postmodernism** and **post-structuralism**, post-Fordism is defined by reference to what it is presumed to have superseded. Thus where Fordism was rigid, post-Fordism is flexible; where Fordism aimed for vertical integration, post-Fordism aims at outsourcing and lean production; where Fordism aimed at uniform products, post-Fordism supplies highly differentiated and tailored products; where Fordism sought to supply the masses with tangible material goods, post-Fordism seeks to create value through stimulating emotions and fantasies; where Fordism viewed price as the ultimate source of competitive advantage, post-Fordism aims at advantage through capturing the imagination of the consumers; where Fordism sought to **deskill** the worker, post-Fordism seeks to build on each worker's knowledge, tacit and explicit. As is the case of many other 'post-...isms', the excitement generated by post-Fordism should not obscure the obstinate endurance of many Fordist features in today's **capitalism**.

---

[1] Gabriel and Lang, 2006.   [2] Amin, 1994; Jessop, 1989; Lipietz, 1992; Piore and Sabel, 1984.

G

Gender

Gender refers to the socially constructed notions of what it means to be a man or a woman. It is helpful to distinguish it from **sex**, as the biologically based categories of men and women. This distinction was made in the 1960s by feminists who sought to separate sex as a biological 'given' from gender, seen as a product of social and cultural forces and therefore divorced from biologically determinist meanings.[1] This helped to challenge ideas, prevalent at the time, that hierarchical arrangements based on sex categories were somehow inevitable and 'natural' (i.e. men are dominant because they are men; women are subservient because they are women). Gender accordingly captures the normative conceptions of attitudes and behaviours that are deemed appropriate for one's sex category. Despite this distinction, sex as a biological category is still significant for different understandings of gender.

Modernist perspectives such as liberal and radical feminism promote an account of gender linked to sex. Both see gender as a stable or solid 'fact'—a role or trait that adheres to the individual and which has some relation to biology. Liberal feminism has a focus on the creation of a level playing field within what are seen as gender-neutral organizations while radical feminism highlights the problems for women of patriarchal organizational structures. Both perspectives foreground women's biology as an explanatory factor in gender disadvantage. For liberal feminists, women's childbearing and child-caring role is seen as another variable (such as the necessary level of education and skills) which has the potential to be problematic for organizations as well as for women's career progress—problems that must be 'solved' through equal opportunity initiatives. Radical feminists such as Ferguson also focus on biology but adopt a more critical stance.[2] Rather than accepting the implications of women's biology as 'given', they direct attention to patriarchal power and the ways in which men control women's bodies and their sexuality to their own ends—arguing that women need to 'reclaim' control.

Gender from these perspectives is seen as an unproblematic category that adheres to the individual and where **meanings** around gender are seen to be relatively stable and fixed. Poststructuralist accounts,[3] by contrast, see gender as contingent, fluid, and fragmentary and not tied in any determinist sense to biology. Gender has no solid, material reality but needs to be reproduced on an ongoing basis in different interactions and contexts. In this respect, **poststructuralists** conceptualize gender as ideologically and discursively produced. **Discourse** refers to signs, labels, expressions, rhetoric which form our thinking, attitudes, and behaviour and which, by creating meanings, constitute the norms of acceptable conduct. In other words, gender **identity** and how it is experienced at a subjective level (how it feels to be a man, how it feels to be a woman) will vary in different contexts and different **institutions**. Rather than seeking to understand the factors that make up gender difference, as in the above modernist accounts, this approach considers how discourse constructs difference and how difference is drawn upon in the performance and

---

[1] See e.g. Oakley, 1972.   [2] Ferguson, 1984.   [3] See e.g. Calas and Smircich, 1992; 1996; 1999; Gherardi, 1995.

display of gender. This moves away from seeing gender as 'problem' that attaches mainly to women to a deeper enquiry concerning how dominant discourses such as those of masculinity silence and suppress competing meanings. Gender is thus more easily opened up to include men.

From this more dynamic perspective, gender has been seen by some as an 'accomplishment' acted out or performed in day-to-day interactions according to prevailing norms and expectations.[1] Through these interactions and through their repetition, such **norms** and expectations take on the semblance of universality and are seen to constitute what counts as '**knowledge**' about gender, i.e. they are considered to be 'normal' or 'natural' ways of doing gender and so help to legitimize and maintain the gender hierarchy. Therefore, becoming a man or a woman is not something that is accomplished once and for all but has to be constantly reaffirmed and publicly displayed through repeated performances of gender, where these performances conform to (or sometimes actively resist) dominant definitions of masculinity and femininity.

For some post-structuralists,[2] these norms and expectations are then 'written on' the sexed **bodies** of men and women. Bodies therefore do matter but not in any determinist sense. Instead, the biologically fixed basis and essentialist understandings of the categories of sex are challenged. As with our accounts of gender, this highlights the social and cultural meanings attached to sexed bodies as well as their historic location and contingent nature. Thus gender has moved from a conceptualization based around traits, **roles**, and stable difference to a more dynamic and fragmented notion based on active performance in accordance with norms and expectations, i.e. as a product of discourse. Tied up in this development have been different meanings given to the category sex and the significance of sexed bodies.

• See also *body, femininity, feminism, sex, women's studies*

RUTH SIMPSON, BRUNEL UNIVERSITY

Genocide

The term genocide was conceived by the Polish-Jewish legal scholar Raphael Lemkin in 1943, drawing on the Greek *genos* (family, tribe, race) and the Latin *-cide* (to kill). It is perplexing that while genocidal acts have been a depressing and persistent aspect of human history, attempts to produce an agreed definition have remained elusive. The United Nations defined genocide as deeds 'committed with intent to destroy, in whole or in part, a national, ethical, racial or religious **group**'.[3] The destruction of **culture**, livelihood, or habitation are also viewed by many as acts of genocide. What is incontestable is that **images** and accounts of genocidal atrocities, particularly those associated with mass killings in the twentieth century, such as the Ottoman 'ethnic cleansing' in Armenia (1915–18), the Nazi Holocaust (1938–45), Pol Pot's Cambodia (1975–9), Serbian actions in Bosnia-Herzegovina (1992–5), and Hutu attacks on Tutsis in Rwanda (1994), have come to epitomize evil. Envisaging, planning, organizing, and executing genocide are all rightly considered among the most heinous and depraved acts within the scope of human conduct, so it is no surprise that the subject frequently invokes discussions of a moral and ethical nature. The definitional difficulties, therefore, result from the general agreement of the heinous nature of the phenomenon and the simultaneous attempt by certain groups to dissociate themselves from having done it and others insisting that they had it done to them. Defining genocide has thus become a highly political process.

The process of genocide is characterized by many facets. Stanton proposed an eight-stage

---

[1] West and Zimmerman, 1987.   [2] See e.g Butler, 1993.   [3] United Nations. Economic and Social Council, 1948, General Assembly resolution 260 A (III).

model incorporating *Classification* (categorization of the population(s)); *Symbolization* (assigning symbols evoking hate, for example, the Third Reich assignation of yellow stars for Jews); *Dehumanization* (rendering the targeted group as non-human in contrast to the humanness of the perpetrators); *Organization* (genocide needs to be planned and enacted by administrative and control structures—often state linked); *Polarization* (separation of the target group from the rest of the population); *Preparation* (identification and making ready of those to be killed); *Extermination* (the managed (mass-)killing of the now classified, symbolized, and dehumanized, isolated victims); *Denial* (lies and cover-up to avoid recriminations and justice).[1] Of particular importance within this process is the concept of marking and organizing *otherness* whereby identity of a group of individuals is negatively stereotyped in reaction, and in relation, to a perceived alternative group of people. Crucially, genocide also requires acts of *complicity* by individuals, agencies, and organizations away from the immediate act of killing. This distancing serves to obviate moral dilemmas and apparent implication.[2]

A range of derivations from genocide has been suggested, including autogenocide (the killing of a people by its own government), policide (the destruction of a given city), politicide (the murder of a political group or entity), gendercide (the killing of a particular sex in a population), femicide (the killing of female members of a population), ethnic cleansing (the elimination of people of particular ethnic origin from a geographical location), and eugenicide (the killing of people deemed not suitable to live within a given race, for example, the mentally ill, criminal, homosexual).

Concerns over genocide have generated a poignant series of literatures and commentaries in the fields of history, sociology, psychology, and other writings (for example, eyewitness and survivor accounts—see Levi[3]). This is supplemented by influential contributions in cinematic work including Claude Lanzmann's 1985 film *Shoah* ('chaos/annihilation' in Hebrew) and Steven Spielberg's *Schindler's List* (based on Thomas Keneally's 1982 book *Schindler's Ark*). Within the specific sphere of organization studies there exists awareness of the value of examining genocide in relation to organizational and management contexts.[4] Many of these commentaries make reference to Zygmunt Bauman's seminal work *Modernity and the Holocaust* (1989), which has been a most important influence on organization writing.[5] Nevertheless, the canon of work linking genocide to organization studies is embryonic. This is surprising given that planning, organizing, executing, and concealing genocide calls for extensive administrative, bureaucratic, and organizational skills. It might be anticipated that greater attention would have been dedicated to the phenomenon by the discipline. Although an extreme case, genocide offers many warnings for contemporary organizational life. The disaster of genocide is brought about as much by everyday-type incremental steps and **choices** as by major **decisions** on genocide and the 'banality of evil'. These seemingly small gestures—slips of integrity or moral courage, tacit collaborations, silences in place of speaking out during the course of daily life—may be viewed as an integral part of human experience, but a study of genocide illustrates starkly what the consequences might be given a slightly adjusted set of temporal and spatial circumstances.

PETER STOKES, UNIVERSITY OF CENTRAL
LANCASHIRE

Glass ceiling

Glass ceiling is a **metaphor** used to describe a situation where women in organizations can catch sight of the highest echelons but are stopped

---

[1] Stanton, 1998.   [2] For an analysis of the role in the Holocaust of the German population beyond activist Nazi Party members and SS units, see Goldhagen, 1996.   [3] Levi, 1979.   [4] See Clegg, Kornberger, and Pitsis, 2005.   [5] Bauman, 1989.

from reaching them mostly by invisible mechanisms of **discrimination** and prejudice.[1] The glass ceiling has proved a remarkably powerful and persistent metaphor, especially in the United States, where it was it was coined by Carol Hymowitz and Timothy Schellhardt in a *Wall Street Journal* article in 1986. It was subsequently used by many journalistic and research authors.[2] It captures some of the frustration experienced by those who can see their destination but are somehow prevented from reaching it. At the same time, it is interesting that since the early 1990s, the glass ceiling has often been seen as something that is capable of being 'smashed', circumvented, or avoided. The glass ceiling also raises issues about women who have successfully gone 'through it', but find that it is hard to operate effectively or to reconcile holding senior organizational positions with being a woman. It is therefore a metaphor that captures not only career issues, but also everyday enactment of **gender**.[3] Like many successful metaphors, the glass ceiling rendered vivid and palpable a widely held view and experience.

• See also *discrimination, femininity, gender*

Globalization

From the perspective of international trade the practice of globalization is not new, as evidenced by ancient trade along the Silk Road, cross-border trading by the European colonizers in the sixteenth century, as well as by the formation of the Dutch East India Company in the seventeenth century. It is only since the 1980s, however, that the phenomenon of globalization has become a prominent theme of conceptual debate in the social sciences and popular culture. Writers such as Kenichi Ohmae and Richard O'Brien have argued that increasing global integration and unhindered movements of **capital** facilitated by information and communication technologies render the world 'borderless', invalidate or severely challenge the influence of national boundaries and locales, and ultimately lead to the 'end of geography'.[4] This view builds on Theodore Levitt's influential statement on 'the globalization of **markets**' in the early 1980s, which helped to diffuse the concept of globalization in a business context, arguing that there was a worldwide convergence of **consumer** tastes and preferences that corporations should attend to.

Multinational corporations as actors are seen to accentuate this globalizing process and dominance over nation states and locales through being the principal actors of the cross-border transfer of people, capital, technologies, products, and services, and even cultural values associated with such products and services. From a strategic management perspective, prominent scholars Christopher Bartlett and the late Sumantra Ghoshal have analysed a variety of globalizing **strategies** and organization design configurations of multinational corporations.[5] They have proposed, as a fundamental strategic challenge for corporations, the simultaneous achievement of customization to local tastes and preferences, global integration of operations leading to high efficiency, as well as the transfer of **learning** across national frontiers—this ideal combination is rarely achieved in practice. International business scholars such as Alan Rugman have shown, however, that most multi-national corporations are in fact less global than commonly assumed, often having their senior management, headquarters, technological innovation activities, and revenues deriving from their home country.[6]

Several scholars such as the economic geographer Nigel Thrift and the sociologist Saskia Sassen have questioned the unhindered dominance of globalizing forces and 'end of geography' theses by highlighting the importance of local embeddedness and attendant social

---

[1] Auster, 1993; Greenglass and Marshall, 1993. [2] Bass and Avolio, 1994; Powell and Butterfield, 1994; Ridgeway, 2001. [3] Marshall, 1995. [4] Ohmae, 1990; O'Brien, 1992. [5] Bartlett and Ghoshal, 1989. [6] Rugman and Verbeke, 2004.

and organizational relations.[1] This is evident in locales such as Silicon Valley or the City of London that sustain their importance as spatial foci for a variety of industries. The sociologist Anthony Giddens has proposed the idea of 'time-space distanciation' to refer to the modes in which social systems are embedded in time and space, and in his writings such as 'the consequences of modernity' he has focused on the ways in which locales are influenced by distant events and vice versa.[2] Giddens and others such as Manuel Castells have addressed the interrelation of both homogenizing and differentiating forces,[3] or the interpenetration of the local and global in a form of dialectic interrelatedness, where neither globalizing nor locally embedded forces invalidate the other.

The ambiguity (or generative nature) of the globalization concept has led to various conceptualizations in different scholarly fields. In international business, for example, John Dunning and others have viewed globalization as a process of foreign direct investment by firms that is key to firms' sustained competitiveness.[4] It is suggested that the form and competitiveness of globalizing firms depends on whether they can take advantage of firm-specific or ownership-specific advantages such as transfer of proprietary know-how, country-specific or locational advantages such as those arising from regional clusters, or internalization advantages associated with different entry modes. The unit of analysis tends to be multinational enterprises (firm level) and their strategic **choices**. Key theoretical concerns here are how and why firms internationalize and what are the performance consequences of different choices.

In industrial organization economics, globalization is seen as a means of accessing efficient factors of production and relevant infrastructure through participation in locational clusters, as evidenced by the work of Michael Porter and others.[5] Understanding of the role of location in micro-economics has shifted over time from simply location as providing access to factor endowments, to providing the potential for productivity growth and innovation through effective networks and inter-organizational relationships. The units of analysis are mainly industries and clusters, and the main theoretical concerns revolve around the role and significance of location and industry clusters in the micro-economics of competition, and on the implications of findings for public policy and firm competitive strategy.

In economic geography, scholars such as Michael Storper and Nigel Thrift have viewed globalization as a force that interacts with states and locales that nevertheless persist in the face of globalizing forces such as **communication** and **information technologies** and actions of multinational corporations.[6] The unit of analysis tends to be processes of interaction among globalizing forces, locales, and states with often a focus on specific elements of globalization such as technology or financial markets. The theoretical concerns of economic geography revolve around such questions as how the activities of multinational corporations and their foreign direct investments influence locales; whether and how global inclusion engenders local exclusion and marginalization; and how globalization is related to potent forms of local attachment and differentiation.

Research in international business, industrial organization, and economic geography thus attributes much higher importance to states and locales than implied by the 'borderless world' or 'end of geography' theses consistent with relevant sociological perspectives on this issue. The activities of multinational corporations have not in fact led to an undifferentiated global factory or homogenized global tastes, nations are still key actors in global processes, and despite the significant cultural homogenization attendant on globalization, there is still robust regional

[1] Thrift, 1996; Sassen, 1998.   [2] Giddens, 1990.   [3] Castells, 1996b.   [4] Dunning, 2000.   [5] Porter, 1998.   [6] Storper, 1992; Thrift, 1996.

and national cultural differentiation around the globe.

• See also *information, networks, postmodernism*

LOIZOS HERACLEOUS, WARWICK UNIVERSITY

Goals

Goals are desired states of affairs that motivate our **actions**. They can be individual or collective—an individual goal may drive a person to travel, to study, or to get a particular type of job. A collective goal is one that requires several people to work together towards it, coordinating their actions and efforts. The difficulty with collective goals is that different people rarely see them in identical terms, even if they imagine themselves to be doing so. Thus a group of students collaborating on a project may each be working towards somewhat different goals—one may want to get the best possible mark, one may want to learn as much as possible, one may want to get a reasonable mark doing as little work as possible, and one may want to earn as much status and respect from his or her peers as possible, irrespective of the quality of the project itself.

Many authors regard goals as a defining feature of organizations. An emphasis on goals is seen as setting organizations apart from other groups or collectivities. A family, a crowd, or the audience of a movie do not have any shared goals. They find themselves together for shorter or longer periods of time. Organizations, on the other hand, not only have goals, but pursue them in a business-like, no-nonsense manner. At first, this appears unproblematic. The goal of a firm is to make profit, that of a university to educate people, that of a hospital to treat sick people. On closer inspection, however, the goals of an organization may differ in the view of different organization members.[1] A surgeon may see the goal of the hospital as operating successfully on many sick people to 'save

their lives'; the administrator, however, may be more concerned with minimizing waiting times and, maybe, reducing the number of necessary operations; and the public health professional may be more concerned with preventive health that minimizes the need for surgery due to bad health habits. Thus, the goals of an organization appear different from different angles. Even precise goals, like 'making profit', may mean different things to different people. Are we talking about long-term or short-term profit? Is profit to be maximized no matter what the cost to the welfare of employees, satisfaction of customers, or costs to the environment? Is profit more important than growth?

Organizational theory, following Max Weber's study of **bureaucracy**, has approached organizations as tools for the achievement of more or less fixed goals in a rational, systematic manner. However, Weber's own pupil Robert Michels pointed out in his Iron Law of **Oligarchy** that goals are *displaced* in accordance with changes in the organization's **environment**, to ensure organizational survival. Michels argued that political parties dedicated to particular causes regularly change their goals, if they turn out to be unrealistic or unpopular. Companies, likewise, change their portfolio of products, if there is no longer a market for them. And charities may change their goals if they no longer resonate with the sensitivities of potential donors. Thus, organizational goals have, over the years, moved from being seen as fixed and given features of organizations to being parts of a discourse that is continuously changing; they are themselves **socially constructed**. Sims and Lorenzi have argued that goal setting is in fact a task of **leadership**—leaders must work hard to ensure that there is a basic agreement among followers about what it is that they are striving towards.[2] According to this view, goals are far from evident to the members of an organization or to society at large. It is not surprising then that in recent years academic interest has shifted somewhat away

---

[1] Mohr, 1973.   [2] Sims and Lorenzi, 1992.

from organizational goals towards missions and **visions**. Both of these concepts suggest far more subjective, fantasy-rich, and political processes than the objective-sounding 'goals'.

Governance

In the study of organizations, the term 'governance' has come to refer to the ways in which the coordination of economic activity is achieved. It encompasses the sets of **rules** and **institutions** which provide the basis for the stability of economic interactions between and within organizations.

Its most common usage is in relation to the idea of 'corporate governance' referring to the rules which shape who should influence and monitor the activities of senior managers and how. Corporate governance describes the transformation of firms and organizations from being family owned and managed to being predominantly owned by outsiders, thus creating what is referred to as the principal–agent problem: how do the principals (the outside owners) get the agents (the inside managers) to pursue shareholder **goals** rather than goals of management self-aggrandizement? Rules about what should be revealed in company accounts are central here. How are senior managers to be held to account for their use of outsiders' funds? This concerns in particular the nature of the board of directors and ensuring that outside owners have board-level representatives who have the independence, competence, power, and resource to call senior managers to account for their stewardship of shareholder funds. Associated with this are the mechanisms available to shareholders to express dissatisfaction with the way in which the board is exercising its oversight **powers**.

National systems of corporate governance continue to differ significantly due to historical factors,[1] with the USA and the UK giving outsiders most powers to monitor and control insiders. These powers combine elements that are formal and public (embedded in legislation where infringement is subject to criminal law) and informal and private (based in voluntary codes and monitored through self-regulation where sanctioning is through loss of reputation and market position). Corporate governance systems also vary in the degree to which they provide a role for employees, the state, and other **stakeholders** (e.g. consumer groups).

At a more general level, the idea of governance as referring to the rules which 'govern' economic activity is associated initially with Williamson,[2] who defined three basic forms of governance— markets, hierarchies, and networks. In market forms of governance, coordination of actors is achieved through mechanisms of competition, supply and demand, and the setting of prices. Adam Smith described these mechanisms as the 'invisible hand' of the **market**, the outcome of the actions of large numbers of market participants pursuing their own preferences in a competitive context. Economic historians have sought to understand the conditions which make markets possible, focusing on issues such as the development of property rights and the rule of law and the decline of the arbitrary **authority** of monarchs.[3] Anthropologists and sociologists have in recent years looked at how specific markets emerge and the technological and social basis of their activities.[4]

Williamson contrasted the market form of governance to that of **bureaucratic hierarchy** as developed by Max Weber and theorists of bureaucracy. In hierarchies, coordination is organized according to strict rules and procedures and the principles of command and control. Governance is achieved more directly through a form of rule by position in the hierarchy and acting according to the rules as prescribed by the organization.

Network forms of governance describe contexts where relationships between organizations are long term and cooperative and yet also

[1] Morck, 2005.   [2] Williamson, 1975.   [3] North, 1990.   [4] Callon, 1998.

dependent on market **competition** within and outside the network. A network therefore can be described as a 'hybrid' form of governance between markets and hierarchies, combining advantages from both. Networks are increasingly seen as more flexible ways of governing economic activity than managerial hierarchies whilst avoiding the characteristics of short-termism and opportunism which can be identified in market contexts. Research suggests that network forms of governance are highly effective for particular sorts of innovations, where wide numbers of skills and resources need to be brought together.[1] Networks tend to be built on certain social features which can sustain them in this hybrid form, e.g. trust, reputation, family and friendship linkages, strong local and regional ties, and affiliations of associational characteristics, and contain network-like qualities.[2]

These models of governance can be restated in terms of three underlying principles that shape how organizations, singly and collectively, develop. Inside the single organization, we can identify elements of *market*, *hierarchy*, and *network*, a point originally developed by Ouchi in a classic article.[3] Market principles may be identified in particular types of salary and payment systems linked strongly to market performance; hierarchical principles in the definition of rules and roles; network principles in the development of **teams** in work organization. **Professional** services firms (lawyers, management consultants) may be characterized as most highly developed in terms of network characteristics; investment banking with its strong emphasis on the linkage between **performance** and rewards most highly develops market principles; public-sector organizations tend to be most bound by hierarchical principles as failure to follow rules and procedures can lead to unfairness and potential scandal. None of these organizations is, however, characterized by a single form of governance; they are more likely to be 'hybrids' with one dominant model of governance that may, more or less frequently, come into conflict with one of the other forms of governance.

These governance principles are also dominant in particular national contexts, shaping how organizations collectively develop. Thus the USA and the UK are frequently referred to as 'market societies' where even public-sector organizations are subject to 'market testing' (see **New Public Management**). Other societies are more dominated by hierarchical principles represented by a strong role for the state in economic life (e.g. in France or South Korea). Finally there are societies characterized as 'corporatist' because they involve high levels of cooperation between social partners (labour, capital, and the state) and are intensively networked. Again, most societies are characterized by hybrid forms of governance even if one principle is dominant.[4] These characterizations are however being modified in the light of **globalization** where debates about the nature of 'global governance' (i.e. how international political and economic relations should be organized) are increasingly common and engage with the respective roles of market, hierarchy, and networks in this process.[5]

GLENN MORGAN, WARWICK UNIVERSITY

Grand narratives

Grand narratives ('grands récits', also master-narratives or meta-narratives) refer to all-encompassing bodies of ideas which purport to offer sweeping explanations of history, nature, and every aspect of the human condition.[6] These bodies of knowledge were a chief feature of **modernity** though they also existed in earlier historical periods. They have a **narrative** character inasmuch as, like **stories** and myths, they unfold over time; but their chief characters are abstract

---

[1] Powell, 2001.   [2] For an overview of network debates, see Thompson, 2003.   [3] Ouchi, 1980.   [4] Campbell, Hollingsworth, and Lindberg, 1991.   [5] Slaughter, 2004.   [6] Lyotard, 1984/1991.

ideas rather than concrete people. Thus, Reason, with Science as its protagonist, can be seen as a powerful narrative promising to emancipate humanity from superstition, poverty, and suffering. Within this narrative, disease is caused by pathogenic agents (such as viruses and genetic factors) rather than inflicted on people as divine punishment. It can be overcome and even eliminated through scientific knowledge which has a universal validity and applicability, rather than prayer or traditional medicine. Socialism, communism, liberal democracy, fascism, but also Christianity and Islam all count as grand narratives. Within the human sciences, all-inclusive doctrines, such as Marxism, psychoanalysis, or positivism, are also seen as grand narratives.

Belief in progress coupled with a confidence that **knowledge**, in the form of science, will liberate humanity were the essential features of the Enlightenment project, upon which modernity was built.[1] Confidence in the Enlightenment project has declined in what many scholars view as postmodernity. It is argued by Lyotard and others that grand narratives fragment and disappear, being replaced by 'small stories', through which people seek to make sense of their **experiences** and communicate them to others. More particularly, it is argued that supposedly objective and eternal truths contain deeply enshrined **power** relations, including those related to colonial, **race**, **gender**, and **sexual** domination and subordination. Far from liberating humanity, grand narratives may represent the fiercest shackles.

Postmodernist theorists argue that a profusion of '**voices**' is now being heard where in the past there were sounds of choirs singing in unison. Where once everybody deferred to the power of the grand narrative, people are now seeking to discover their own voice, based on their own experiences and forging their own individual **identities**. Even science is being challenged, when the voice of the expert scientist, for instance the physician, is challenged and

contested by the voice of the patient, who is non-expert and non-objective, but has the authority of personal experience of an illness. Speaking with authority is no longer the exclusive privilege of the educated; it is the privilege of everybody who has an experience to narrate.

In the area of organizations, classical theories of **bureaucracy** by Weber and management, such as **Taylorism** and **Fordism**, are often described as grand narratives. These theories are now being challenged at two levels. First, it is argued that that grand narratives are no longer capable of explaining the phenomenon organization, and second, the phenomenon itself does not meet the criteria of a grand narrative any more. Parker draws a distinction between postmodern (no hyphen) theories of organization and post-modern (hyphenated) organizations.[2] At the level of knowledge, it is claimed that a grand theory of organizations, approaching them as objective realities in their own right, is fundamentally flawed and should be replaced by a multiplicity of narratives, describing the organizational realities of different participants. Organizations are not 'things' but **social constructions**, contested, challenged, and constantly recreated through talk and action. Managing people is not the application of scientific knowledge of immutable generalizations and universal principles. Instead it is now seen as more akin to the utilization of folk knowledge in ad hoc, opportunistic, and improvised ways, borrowing ideas, combining recipes, and adapting knowledge for new situations.[3]

Second, as we move from modernity to post-modernity, the nature of organizing and organizations changes. While modernity featured solid buildings, solid organizations, solid relations, solid selves, and solid signifiers, our times are characterized by flux, mutation, reinvention, and flexibility. Flexibility stands at the opposite end to rigidity, the chief quality of bureaucracy. The flexible organization (variously referred to as **network**, post-modern,

---

[1] Gray, 2003.   [2] Parker, 1992.   [3] Czarniawska, 1997; 1999; Gabriel, 2002; Tsoukas, 2002; Tsoukas and Hatch, 2001.

post-Fordist, post-bureaucratic, etc.) has emerged as the antidote to Weberian bureaucracy, a concept of organization which does away with rigid **hierarchies**, procedures, products, and boundaries, in favour of constant and continuous reinvention, redefinition, and mobility.[1]

While the case for the fragmentation of grand narratives is compelling, it has itself been contested. Defending the project of the Enlightenment and modernity, Jürgen Habermas has pointed out that the narrative of the collapse of grand narratives is itself a grand narrative.[2] More importantly, it would appear premature to argue that all grand narratives have disintegrated. In spite of challenges and contests, science maintains a high level of authority, claiming to provide solutions from environmental crises to economic growth and prosperity. Economic growth itself continues to be the core of a grand narrative, embraced not only by Western economists but increasingly by governments and people throughout the world as the key to happiness and the good life. The supremacy of a market-driven capitalism with unbridled **consumerism** as its cultural twin has emerged as a formidable hegemonic narrative, scarcely touched by attacks from post-modernists and their allies. In academia itself and especially in the human and social sciences, the dominance of the economic narrative, increasingly expressed in numbers and highly abstract modelling, is scarcely contested, at least in Anglo-Saxon countries.[3] In the light of such trends as well as the resurgence of religious fundamentalisms, Eastern and Western, it seems premature to consign grand narratives to the dustbin of history.

• See also *ideology, narratives and narrative knowledge*

Groups

A group is a small assembly of people who find themselves together for a period of time, and who generally have a sense of sharing a quality or a predicament. Many groups are set up for the purpose of accomplishing a joint task or meeting a challenge. They can be set up formally or informally, but relations among group members tend to be 'hot' and personal unlike the 'cold' and impersonal relations that prevail in organizations. In groups, people recognize each other's faces and **identities** and treat each other as individuals with histories and **emotions**, rather than merely as functionaries performing organizational roles. Most organizations contain different types of groups, big and small, permanent and temporary, that are called to carry out various tasks. These include teams, crews, project groups, panels, task forces, committees, working parties, and so forth. Groups are seen as vital for organizational **success**—so much so, that some scholars have proposed that the group rather than the individual is the fundamental building block of organizations.

Groups have been the focus of extensive studies from many different perspectives in the social sciences.[4] Early theories, inspired by observations of **crowds**, emphasized the loss of individuality that occurs in groups. The view that, when people find themselves in a group, the group 'mind' dislodges their own individual judgements, **values**, and **personalities** still surfaces in the work of social psychologists. *Group dynamics* is the academic discipline examining the formation and subsequent development of groups, the nature of interactions between their members, and their relations to other groups and organizations. The now classic 1920s and 1930s Hawthorne experiments in the USA (see **Human Relations**) first revealed the importance of group dynamics. The experiments showed how workers' informal allegiances, friendships, **norms**, and pressures to conform outweighed managerial attempts to manipulate productivity. The desire to be accepted by a group seemed more fundamental than the need to maximize earnings or enhance careers. The experiments also

[1] Gabriel, 2005.   [2] Habermas, 1981; 1984a.   [3] Mintzberg, 2004; Pfeffer, 1998; Pfeffer and Sutton, 2006.   [4] Brown, 2000.

highlighted that by being members of cohesive groups, members showed enhanced **motivation** and quality of work. Since then, it has been recognized that informal groupings meet the social, emotional, and security **needs** of individuals which cannot be addressed in the formal organization. Group dynamics developed subsequently through the work of Kurt Lewin and others in the United States,[1] Wilfred Bion and the Tavistock Institute in Great Britain.[2] Vital aspects of group dynamics concern the processes of group **leadership** and the ways groups handle **change**.

Most people have had some happy experiences in groups, when enthusiasm, commitment, and the cross-fertilization of ideas generated synergies. Such groups are capable of outstanding **achievement**. Most people also have experiences of being parts of groups overcome by bickering and conflict, suspicion and mistrust. Some of the most painful individual experiences can originate in being underappreciated, rejected, or bullied by groups. Each individual's concern about being accepted by the group ensures that groups act as powerful controlling mechanisms over the behaviours and even the thoughts and emotions of their members. This accounts for one of the major properties of groups, *conformity*—the strong tendency of individuals to adopt the views, emotions, and actions of a group, even if they individually disagree with them. Group pressures can have a dulling effect on individuals' intelligence and judgement. This is partly because groups have the effect of intensifying emotions and unleashing streams of positive and negative **fantasies.** These emotions include hope, enthusiasm, anger, solidarity, courage, and anxiety. The management of such emotions is a vital function of group leadership.

Psychoanalyst Wilfred Bion argued that failure to tame and contain potentially destructive emotions, especially anxiety, leads groups to lose sight of the tasks they seek to accomplish and

tips them into what he termed 'basic assumption' functioning.[3] By this, he meant that groups start to behave *as if* they held certain shared assumptions about each other, about the leader, and about the task they seek to accomplish. These assumptions are products of fantasy, collective delusions that severely distort their sense of proportion and reality. When groups lapse into basic assumption behaviour they are liable to experience overwhelming fears of annihilation from greatly exaggerated dangers or conversely excessive optimism and denial that they are under any real danger. They are liable to feel strong love and hate for particular objects and to misjudge seriously their capabilities and limitations. In this way, basic assumptions act as collective **defence mechanisms** that seek to alleviate groups' troubles, but end up by compounding them. The casual observer may have the impression that a group is working smoothly and even efficiently, yet in reality, the group may have lost its ability to interact with the outside world, to test its ideas against the evidence, and to act rationally.

Bion identified three types of basic assumptions—dependency, fight-flight, and pairing—each with a characteristic set of behaviours and emotions.

- In basic assumption *dependency* mode, group members act as if the leader, who is seen as a person of extraordinary qualities, will save them without them having to lift a finger. In this state, groups eventually become disappointed with their leader who cannot possibly live up to the members' exaggerated expectations.
- In basic assumption *fight-flight* mode, groups act as if there is a great danger that must be confronted, either by attacking it or by running away from it. This imaginary danger can be from inside or outside the group and typically acts as a scapegoat that obscures other, potentially serious dangers.

---

[1] Lewin and Lewin, 1948.   [2] Bion, 1961.   [3] Ibid.

☐ In basic assumption *pairing* mode, groups experience strong feelings of hopefulness, imagining that two members of the group will get together to generate an idea or give birth to a person who can solve all the group's problems. The focus of the group turns away from difficult issues of the present to an imagined future in which all such difficulties are overcome.

Bion's account is one of several theories of group *dysfunctions*, i.e. patterns of group functioning that are seen as counter-productive and damaging for both group members and organizations. Most people have some experiences of such groups, where overwhelming emotions and constant **conflict** effectively derailed every attempt to get a job done. Many have experienced the misery of being wrongly blamed for the group's shortcomings and the despair of being scapegoated for mistakes they patently did not make. Many have found themselves working hard to compensate for the inertia and irresponsibility of 'free-riders' or, conversely, have been accused of being free-riders when nobody seemed to treat them with respect or to be interested in their views.

There is an extensive literature on the characteristics of effective groups. These include a shared understanding and commitment to the group's **goals**, a high degree of mutual trust, effective leadership, and the means of resolving conflicts without avoiding them. Why it is so difficult for many groups to attain these characteristics is not so well established. While it is easy to blame poor leadership, inability to deal with conflict, or lack of mutual respect as causes of group troubles, these may very well represent the consequences rather than the causes of group dysfunctions.[1]

One of the most fundamental difficulties that many groups encounter is over different conceptions of 'the task' or group goals. In fact, talking about 'the task' may be misleading since it is more common for different people to envisage the task differently, especially in the early stages. A related difficulty is that of ensuring participation of all members in **decision making**, without spending excessive amounts of time before simple decisions are made. Problems of communication, divergent expectations, and competences compound these difficulties. The handling of every kind of difference, ethnic, religious, cultural, gender, age, political orientation, and so forth, is very important in determining whether a group will generate synergy and cross-fertilization or whether it will lapse into dysfunctional behaviours. Successful groups generally balance the needs of their members to maintain their individual voices while at the same time subordinating individual needs to collective purpose.

• See also *groupthink, teams and teamwork*

Groupthink

Groupthink is a term used by psychologist Irving Janis to describe a **group** dysfunction where members of a group facing an important decision lapse into a form of collective wishful thinking and **fantasy**.[2] They imagine themselves invulnerable, they dismiss opposing ideas, and take wild risks. There is a strong tendency to stereotype all opponents and to censor even the slightest dissenting voices. Conflict within the group is avoided, but at a serious cost to the quality of **decision making**. Groupthink can be seductive as each individual shares the group's sense of superiority and power. It can also have devastating results. Groupthink has been blamed for a number of major disasters at national and international levels, such as the Bay of Pigs military fiasco (the original case study in Janis's book), the space shuttle *Challenger* disaster, Britain's do-nothing policy towards Hitler prior to the Second World War, and the

---

[1] Anzieu, 1984.   [2] Janis, 1972.

unpreparedness of US forces on the eve of Pearl Harbor. More recently, in 2004, Lord Butler, in his commission's report on the Iraq War, used the term 'groupthink' to account for the total inability of the British government and intelligence services to countenance the possibility that Saddam Hussein did not possess weapons of mass destruction.

Groupthink has become a widely embraced theory describing risks faced by many groups, especially those in the highest echelons of organizations. A considerable body of literature has evolved on how to prevent it, which is then translated into practice by consultants and coaches. Various measures to pre-empt groupthink have been proposed. Group members should not interrupt each other, until trust and cooperation have been established. Individuals should not monopolize the discussion—this prevents particularly aggressive and 'loud' individuals from setting the agenda. At times, groups may pause and ask each member to explicitly state their view on a particular issue. One effective device is for each member of the group to write down their preferred course of action, before declaring it in public. In this way, people cannot simply change their minds because

a particular view has been advocated by one or two highly assertive individuals. Under certain circumstances (when agreement seems to be reached too easily), groups may appoint individuals to play devil's advocate before a particular decision is taken. Another important measure is for groups to agree on certain deadlines for making decisions or achieving some objectives. This reduces endless and often fruitless discussion. Finally, appointing an outside consultant may prevent a group from lapsing into groupthink and conformity. This outsider, however, may all too easily be sucked into a group's own dynamics.

There is evidence to indicate that groupthink, or suppressed disagreement, has played a part in many failures, accidents, and disasters. The belief that groupthink can explain all group dysfunctions can, however, itself assume the character of groupthink, with scholars, consultants, and policy makers all too readily agreeing that groupthink is to blame for everything. This overlooks the many diverse and complex difficulties that can lead groups astray, including scapegoating, free-riding, bickering, bullying, and every conceivable type of ineffective **leadership**.

H

Hawthorne experiments

The Hawthorne experiments take their name from the Hawthorne works of Western Electric, a company producing telephone equipment in the outskirts of Chicago. These experiments were carried out over a number of years in the 1920s and 1930s and left a strong legacy on the history of management and management thought, leading to the emergence of a tradition known as **Human Relations**. The most detailed exposition of the experiments themselves is offered by Roethlisberger and Dixon,[1] while a leading figure associated with them was psychologist Elton Mayo. The experiments themselves highlighted the importance of informal **groups** and group processes for the behaviour of people at work. In particular, they strongly suggested that people's **motivation** at work was fundamentally shaped by group **norms** of what a fair day's work represented. Such norms were distinct from management targets and ensured that each worker's output was roughly in line with that of the others, no one working too hard or too slackly. Deviant behaviour was discouraged, initially through hints and whispers, later on through ridicule and ostracism. In this way, groups **controlled** the behaviour of their members. Mayo concluded that productivity depends on motivation of the social unit, not on motivation of individual workers. People are social beings, not just individual economic ones.[2]

The experiments also indicated that when people find themselves the focus of attention as subjects of a scientific experiment, their behaviour changes as a result of being under observation. This has become known as the *Hawthorne effect*, and makes many generalizations from behaviours under experimental conditions problematic. The awareness of being part of an experiment has an impact on how most people behave. Finally, the experiments suggested that cohesive work groups whose work is appreciated and valued tend to raise their motivation and work effectively, irrespective of any financial incentives that may be attached to their output. In this way, the Hawthorne experiments provided the basis for an approach to worker motivation as 'social' rather than economic; they thus provided a counterweight to **Taylorism**.

• See also *groups, Human Relations*

Hermeneutics

Hermeneutics is an influential tradition in the human sciences which hinges on interpretation as the way of explaining. Its etymology derives from the Greek word ἑρμηνεία (interpretation), itself related to the god Hermes, known ambiguously for his ability to convey messages but also to extricate himself from difficult situations (hence the related word 'hermetic'). Hermeneutics emerged originally as the art of deciphering the deeper **meanings** of sacred texts, like the Bible, but eventually came to be seen as the search for deeper meanings in all texts and subsequently human actions, utterances, artefacts, and institutions. The hermeneutic tradition then emerged from a conviction that the human sciences operate from a fundamentally different premiss from the natural sciences. Instead of

---

[1] Roethlisberger, Dickson, and Wright, 1939.   [2] Mayo, 1949/1975; Roethlisberger, Dickson, and Wright, 1939.

seeking objective, lawlike generalizations about causes and effects, they strive to unmask what humans create but conceal from themselves. Thus, the meanings of a **story** (like 'Cinderella'), a work of art (like Michelangelo's *Moses*), an **institution** (like circumcision), or a neurotic symptom (like a young woman's anorexia) must be carefully extracted through the art of interpretation.

There are many hermeneutic approaches (though not all of them view themselves as branches of hermeneutics), including literary criticism, semiotics, **discourse** analysis, **deconstruction**, and **psychoanalysis**. What these approaches share is the treatment of particular phenomena (including texts, actions, artefacts, and institutions) as signs of deeper realities. These deeper realities can be revealed by piecing together an *interpretation* that reveals their deeper significance. Thus, a fundamental principle of interpretation is the *hermeneutic circle* which describes the process of moving from the parts to the whole and back to the parts as a way of building up compelling interpretations. A psychoanalyst, for example, may interpret a particular symptom as evidence of a deep-seated psychological process, such as repression, denial, and so forth. He or she will then seek to examine whether other symptoms, fantasies, dreams, and so forth, corroborate the interpretation or whether they call it into question. In the same way, the interpretation of a story tries to fit different elements of the story (plot, characters, moral message, etc.) within a plausible meta-story which leaves no loose ends or unanswered questions. This circular character of interpretation suggests that no interpretation is ever complete or total.

The task of hermeneutics has been likened to that of a detective who pieces together the evidence in order to reveal the underlying nature of a crime. Like a scientist, a detective may try to piece together an account of what happened from various observations. But unlike the natural scientist who seeks to unravel the mysteries of the universe unimpeded by any sentient opponent, the detective (and by implication the hermeneutic researcher) often finds him- or herself working against somebody who has deliberately tried to deceive or obstruct his or her task. Interpretation then is often a work that takes place against resistance. This is particularly so in the case of psychoanalysis, where **unconscious** resistances function to conceal and distort the meanings of particular phenomena.

As an art, hermeneutics can be practised with greater or lesser competence. A successful interpretation is capable of creating an experience of utter and sudden enlightenment, where in one moment what was dark and confused becomes clear and meaningful. However, clever or imaginative interpretations are not necessarily true. In some instances, 'wild' interpretations may appear truthful, only to disappoint later. A mother may be told and believe that her daughter's asthmatic attacks are a response to her husband's sudden explosions of temper but they may later turn out to be caused by a particularly dusty mattress. Wild interpretations can often hit home with vulnerable, sick, and gullible people. It is not accidental that some of the most skilful practitioners of interpretation can be found among astrologers, spiritualists, coffee-ground diviners, and fortune-tellers, all of whom seek to read large meanings about the past and the future in purportedly objective data.

In philosophy, it was Heidegger who established hermeneutics as a mainstream tradition. In the social sciences, hermeneutics is linked to the Weberian concept of 'verstehen', the attempt to understand human action through the meanings that it holds for the actors themselves. It has suffused nearly every tradition that has relied on qualitative research **methodology** and has been opposed by traditions such as behaviourism and positivism that sought to examine human phenomena using the same fundamental approaches as the natural sciences.

Hierarchy

Hierarchy is a system of ranking composed of several levels, in which higher levels enjoy more power, greater privileges, or more **status** than lower ones. Some hierarchies allow the movement of individuals or groups up or down, whereas others (such as the Indian caste system) prohibit or severely limit such movements. Hierarchies have long been features of armies and religious orders where, generally, the higher ranks controlled the lower ones. Hierarchy is a crucial feature of the **structure** of **bureaucracy**, where offices (or positions) are organized in such a way that higher offices control lower ones. In Weber's ideal-type bureaucracy, each office receives instructions from only one superior and there are no horizontal lines of communication or command. This type of hierarchy is very similar to the directory tree of a computer. Each branch starts in a root directory and the branches are not linked together.

Organizational hierarchies represent hierarchies of both **authority** and accountability. Within such hierarchies superiors hold certain rights over their subordinates, which include the rights to issue particular types of commands, to reward, and to discipline. At the same time, superiors are accountable both for their own actions and those of their subordinates to their own superiors. Subordinates, for their parts, are obligated to carry out the commands of their superiors, provided that they accord with the organization's impersonal system of **rules** and regulations. Thus, authority and accountability, from the organization's point of view, are not attached to individuals but invested in the positions within the hierarchy.

Organizational hierarchies can have a narrow 'span of control' whereby each official **controls** a small number (say six to ten) of subordinates or conversely a wide span of control where each official may control up to a hundred or more subordinates. The former lead to 'tall and thin' organizational hierarchies, the latter to 'short and fat' ones. Over the last thirty years, organizational hierarchies, especially in business organizations, have tended to become shorter and fatter, through the elimination of many middle management levels. Thus, companies like Ford were able to reduce the number of ranks in their hierarchies from more than twenty-five to six or seven over a few decades. This is due to a variety of factors, including new forms of computerized technologies that enabled managers to control an ever-larger number of subordinates and an ideological turn against bureaucracy that came to be viewed as rigid, uncompetitive, and wasteful. The reduction of levels of hierarchy limited **career** opportunities—shortening organizational ladders made the prospects of promotion by climbing up such ladders less propitious.

Hierarchies create rivalries, and rivalries create hierarchies. Thus, in addition to formal hierarchies, there are informal hierarchies that allow for comparisons to be made, victories to be won, and defeats to be endured. An organization may only have one rank of travelling salesperson but may reward its sales force with ten different models of automobile, from ostentatious to modest, depending on their sales performances. This creates distinctions of status and worth. Some of these informal hierarchies are known as 'pecking orders', following the practice of chickens to torment a bird of lower rank and submit to pecking from a bird of higher rank. This creates a 'top chicken' who enjoys all the privileges and a 'bottom chicken' that has none. Pecking order behaviours can be observed in some school playing yards, police academies, prisons, and other organizations where teasing, insulting, and **bullying** can be viewed as behaviour testing and establishing the individuals' positions in a pecking order. In politics, too, a leader may be surrounded by a number of followers who vie for positions of closeness to him or her. The great Polish journalist and political commentator, Ryszard Kapuściński offered the following insightful description of the way hierarchies functioned in the court of Ethiopian emperor Haile Selassie:

Those who were lower were determined to rise. Number forty-three wanted to be twenty-sixth. Seventy-eight had an eye on thirty-two's place. Fifty-seven climbed to twenty-nine, sixty-seven went straight to thirty four, forty-one pushed thirty out of the way, twenty-six was sure of being twenty-second, fifty-four gnawed at forty-six, sixty-three scratched his way to forty-nine, and always upward toward the top without end. . . . Our palace was a fabric of hierarchies and if you were slipping on one you could grab hold of another, and everyone found some satisfaction and reason to be proud of himself. Everyone spoke with admiration and jealousy of those who had made the list: 'Look who's going!'[1]

• See also *bureaucracy, governance*

Homosexuality

Homosexuality refers to a sexual preference for members of the same **sex**. While seen as a sin, a crime, or a disease by some **cultures**, it is condoned or even encouraged by others (like the ancient Greeks). Homosexuality is felt to be normal and natural for and by some men and women. It has been studied in numerous different cultures and societies, where it often merges with heterosexuality in a bisexual orientation. Psychologically, there is evidence of homosexual **desires** even among heterosexuals, even though such desires may remain repressed or may be sublimated into feelings of camaraderie and friendship. In spite of the decriminalization of homosexuality in the USA and Britain, it is still viewed with hostility by some, whose sexual **norms** it undermines or threatens. Within organizations, many gays and lesbians prefer to conceal their **sexuality** rather than face the intolerance and bigotry of their superiors, peers, and subordinates. Gay and lesbian liberation movements are fighting to eliminate prejudice and

discrimination and to ensure that people's opportunities and freedom are not restricted by their sexual orientation.

Research into the experiences of sexual minorities in the workplace is still in its early stages. Ward and Winstanley carried out an extensive piece of research in a UK government department using stories as part of their research methodologies.[2] They found that the experiences of gay and lesbian employees were mostly shrouded in silence. This silence was not a passive one but formed an integral part of the **identity** of these employees. At times, it assumed the character of self-censorship but, at times, it became a form of self-protection and resistance. The view of sexuality as a contested organizational terrain, which at times reinforces management controls and at times offers employees opportunities of empowerment, is supported by research conducted by Fleming and others.[3]

• See also *sexuality*

Human Relations

Human Relations is a movement in management practice and a school of management thinking that grew out of the work of Elton Mayo, Roethlisberger and Dixon, and the **Hawthorne experiments** in the 1920s and 1930s.[4] The Human Relations school emphasized the importance of social and group factors for understanding people's behaviour at work. It approached people as social beings with deep needs for belonging or affiliation, as well as for recognition and appreciation by others. In place of the selfish, utility-maximizing individual of neoclassical economics and **Scientific Management**, Human Relations looked at people's behaviour as driven by the **norms** and **values** of the groups to which they belong. People work hard, argued Elton Mayo, not for instrumental reasons (money,

---

[1] Kapuściński, 1983, pp. 61, 62.   [2] Ward and Winstanley, 2003.   [3] Fleming, 2007.   [4] Mayo, 1949/1975; Roethlisberger, Dickson, and Wright, 1939.

career, job security) but because they identify with cohesive work **groups** and do not want to let their comrades down. Mayo made it his life's ambition to counter the impersonality of **bureaucracy** of modern organizations with cohesive groups, in which people care for each other as people. He argued that management should promote informal group relations in order to increase output.

The School of Human Relations has been influential, among both managers and academics. Its emphasis on the informal aspects of organizations provided the inspiration for many subsequent management theories and ideas. Human Relations offered two enduring insights into the world of organizations and management.

- First, it underlined the importance of groups, teamwork, and informal ties. It showed the shortcomings of treating organizations merely as collections of individuals and highlighted the contribution made by groups working together. Groups came to be seen as doing wonders for motivation, pooling resources, generating cross-fertilization of ideas, and unleashing creativity. For many complex tasks and complex decisions the view that 'many heads are better than one' became self-recommending.
- Secondly, Human Relations suggested that the behaviour, **emotions**, and thoughts of individuals when they become members of cohesive strong groups are significantly altered. Within groups, people trade an important part of their **identity** and selfhood for the identity of the group, adopting the group's norms, the group's beliefs, and even the group's emotions as their own.

The legacy of Human Relations to business schools and universities was also considerable. Its emergence was instrumental in giving academic respectability to business as an area for scholarship, teaching, and research. In an interesting paper, O'Connor argued that the Harvard Business School was successful on the back of the success of the Human Relations School and that they both achieved legitimacy by presenting themselves as solutions to the social and economic problems of the inter-war period.[1] Undoubtedly, academic curricula in business and management were strongly influenced by the theories of Mayo and those who followed him. Large numbers of social scientists were drawn into the study of organizations and numerous academic publications, journals and books, emerged with analyses of work behaviour and topics of interest to managers, like leadership, motivation, group dynamics.

In spite of its far-reaching influence, it should be noted Human Relations never dislodged **Taylorism** and **Fordism** as the bedrocks on which much of twentieth-century production was founded. It would be fair to say that while many managers (especially those who attended management and business courses) thought along the humanistic lines of Human Relations (treat your workers with respect, encourage the formation of groups, show appreciation of their work, etc.), organizations continued to be dominated by the ideas and practices of Scientific Management—assembly lines, standardization, and **deskilling**. There were, however, some well-known and important exceptions. Chief among them is the example of the Volvo factories in Kalmar and Uddewalla which, in the 1970s and 1980s, manufactured cars by replacing assembly work with teamwork. These were successful for a time in reducing costs by lowering absenteeism and staff turnover and enhancing the quality of the finished products. The then Volvo Managing Director, P. G. Gyllenhammar, believed that these factories not only produced high-quality vehicles but highlighted the humane principles that appealed to Volvo's customers. Over the long term, however, such experiments did not offer the serious challenge to conventional assembly lines in the production of cars that was

---

[1] O'Connor, 1999.

to come later from Toyota and lean production systems.

Human Resource Management

The concept of Human Resource Management (HRM) has always been controversial. Its emergence in the management literature in the early 1980s aroused intense debate. The presumption that HRM represented a new and improved version of personnel management with a capacity to generate high employee commitment and transform the deeply rooted model of **industrial relations** was contested by many. Some critics pointed out that it was simply 'old wine in new bottles',[1] and others saw it as a version of 'the emperor's new clothes'.[2] Another key debate concerns whether one should conceptualize HRM in 'soft' or 'hard' terms.[3] The 'soft' approach, best represented by the developmental humanism model of the Harvard school,[4] places its emphasis on the value-added aspect of *human resource* management. It is closely associated with the resource-based view of the firm which regards the inimitable nature of tacit **skills** and **competences** of employees as a critical source of competitive advantage. By contrast, the 'hard' approach, reflecting what can be described as a utilitarian instrumentalism of the Michigan school,[5] stresses the importance of achieving a tight strategic fit between human resource policies and business objectives. The emphasis here is placed on managing employees as a headcount resource or factor of production in a way that supports business strategy. Thus, its focus is on human *resource management* for the maximization of economic return.

The distinction between the soft and hard models of HRM reflects the fundamental contradiction between attaining 'commitment' or 'control' in employee management. However, the two approaches are not necessarily mutually exclusive.[6] The so-called 'flexible firm' encapsulates both approaches in its distinction between the core and periphery workers. Guest's model of HRM identifies four underpinning policy goals: strategic integration, commitment, flexibility, and quality.[7] It argues that the 'hard' goal of achieving strategic integration between employment policies and the overall business objectives of the organization might be viable only through the adoption of 'soft', high-commitment and high-quality employment practices. Gratton et al.'s study of HRM practices in the so-called leading edge organizations suggests that the distinction between the two approaches may be meaningless in practice as the language of 'soft' HRM was often used by management to obscure the implementation of 'hard' HRM practices for the improvement of bottom-line performance.[8]

While the debate continues to expand and develop, HRM has emerged as a major contemporary influence on the management of employment relationships in a wide range of market economies. The increased uptake of HRM by firms in the USA and UK has been driven especially by the intensification of global product market competition, notably the challenge from Japan and other Far Eastern economies, and more recently, the growing importance of quality and innovation as sources of competitive advantage. In the UK, the rise of HRM during the 1980s also coincided with the desire of the then Conservative government to reform the old, adversarial model of industrial relations through privatization and anti-union legislation. The unitary and individualistic ethos of HRM was in accord with managerial attempts to introduce new labour practices and reorder collective bargaining arrangements. Throughout the 1990s and well into the present decade, the term HRM has come to be associated with the 'high-commitment' or 'high-performance' model of employee management that emphasizes the importance of motivation,

[1] Keenoy and Anthony, 1992.   [2] Legge, 1989.   [3] Storey, 1992.   [4] Beer, Spector, and Lawrence, 1984.   [5] Fombrun, Tichy, and Devanna, 1984.   [6] Legge, 2005.   [7] Guest, 1987.   [8] Gratton et al., 1999.

commitment, empowerment, teamworking, and TQM (Total Quality Management). The 'lean production' system pioneered by Japanese automobile manufacturers has been seen by many as an archetypal example of a high-performance work system building on commitment-inducing HRM practices, and cooperation of shop-floor workers. Researchers from a **labour process perspective**,[1] however, emphasize the work intensification and surveillance effects of lean production systems. They argue that work practices such as flexibility, teamworking, and quality control often result in high levels of stress and subordination among workers, questioning whether 'lean' production is in fact 'mean' production.

In recent years, the focus of attention on HRM has shifted away from searching for its meaning and defining features towards examining its impact on organizational performance. While there is some empirical evidence suggesting an association between HRM practices and positive organizational performance, there are doubts about the direction of causation, and little is known about the 'black box' of the process that links HRM with organizational performance.[2] Two unifying themes have emerged from the empirical studies. First, HRM practices are more widespread in sectors competing on quality and **innovation**, and exposed to international **competition**. And, second, the positive impact of HRM practices is likely to be more pronounced when they are implemented as 'bundles' in a mutually reinforcing fashion. The HRM–performance link remains an area of major interest among researchers and practitioners in the field of HRM.

Despite its early shaky career, HRM has continued to thrive both as a field of study and as an organizational practice. The scope of HRM has expanded and its growing focus on business performance means that it is now a critical component in the management of organizational change. The rise of HRM appears to have transformed personnel management, giving it a more powerful managerial role within organizations, although its increased fusion with business objectives has meant that many scholars in the field of industrial relations remain deeply critical of the HRM phenomenon.

• See also *industrial relations, trade unions*

ALICE LAM, ROYAL HOLLOWAY
UNIVERSITY OF LONDON

[1] See e.g. Delbridge, 1998.   [2] Godard, 2004.

Identification

Compared to the extreme interest in the concept of **identity** and its different dimensions (self, narrative, organizational, ethnic, gender, and so forth), the concept of identification has received slightly less attention. And yet in a curious way, identification was established as an important psychological concept before identity was introduced into the human sciences by philosopher George Herbert Mead,[1] psychologist Erik Erikson,[2] and others. Already in the 1920s Freud was using the concept of identification extensively to describe a process whereby an individual assimilates a quality of an object and incorporates it in his or her own constitution.[3] Thus, a child may identify with a parent or a follower may identify with a leader, imagining themselves to have some of the qualities of the person they identify with. What was important for Freud was that identification fundamentally transforms the **subject** who forges a new sense of identity by assimilating the perceived (and often idealized) attributes of the other person. Identification was seen by Freud as one of the two core processes of forming relations with others (the other being **love** for another person). He viewed the development of our mental personality as occurring through successive identifications with different people we admire. The view that identification with the parent of the same sex forms one of the commonest and firmest foundations of identity is also to be found in Erikson, who, however, argued that one must eventually 'disidentify' from such parent figures or risk lapsing into an identity crisis.[4]

A second very important way in which Freud used the word identification was to describe the relations among many people who share a quality or a predicament and, therefore, form parts of **groups**. Groups, argued Freud, are based on each follower identifying with the leader as an object of admiration (or in some cases contempt and hate) *and with each other*, by virtue of sharing the same relation to the leader. Identification is often combined with idealization. Thus members of an organization may identify with their organization, which is idealized and bolsters their sense of worth and self-esteem. In this way, members of an organization may identify not with the actual organization but with an idealized fantasy in which the organization features as all-powerful, all-moral, and possibly even as immortal. This is what Schwartz has referred to as the 'organizational ideal'.[5] The converse is also possible—a person who loses faith in somebody who once served as an object of identification and idealization turns against them. They then form what Erikson called a 'negative identity', 'often expressed in a scornful and snobbish hostility towards the roles offered as proper and desirable by one's family or immediate community'.[6] In organizations, this process often assumes the form of a cynical detachment (disidentification) from the company which comes to epitomize everything toxic and worthless. In opposition to such a negative fantasy of an organization, some individuals then forge their identities.[7]

More recently, the process of people's identification with their organizations has been studied through the **narratives** that they author, in their

---

[1] Mead, 1934. [2] Erikson, 1950/1978; 1959a. [3] Freud, 1921/1985. [4] Erikson, 1968. [5] Schwartz, 1987; 1990. [6] Erikson, 1959b, p. 141. [7] Fleming and Spicer, 2003.

attempts to make sense of their **experiences**, infuse their lives with meanings, and create plausible life **stories**. Humphreys and Brown have shown how identification works through a person interweaving his or her own life narrative with the narratives of their organization.[1] These authors have demonstrated that individuals may identify with certain parts of their organizations and disidentify with others. Attempts by managers to create ready identification with the organization through the dissemination of heroic stories often end up having the opposite effect. One particularly interesting form of identification is where an individual or group identifies with the organization of old, against which the organization of today is shown to be lacking. This creates a *nostalgia* for an organization's golden past which is viewed in glowing colours. For example, yesterday's organization may be viewed as family-like, full or interesting characters, caring relations, and high-quality work, whereas today's may be viewed as ruthless, bureaucratic, and shoddy.[2] Nostalgia can then sometimes complement cynicism as a system of identifications that derides the present and simultaneously glorifies the past.

• See also *identity*

Identity

Identity is an umbrella term understood and deployed in different ways in distinct social science disciplines. The word is also widely used in mathematics and philosophy. In general, social scientists use 'identity' to refer to that which putatively makes an entity definable or recognizable, most usually in terms of its possession of qualities or characteristics that distinguish it from other entities. One particular preoccupation of identity theorists is whether an entity can reasonably be described as being 'the same' (and if so, what 'same' really means) over time, and, if so, the criteria for deciding. Given the

huge array of meanings and uses associated with 'identity' this brief review is inevitably selective, focusing in particular on how the term has been appropriated to research individuals and collectives (groups and organizations).

At an individual level, identity refers to a person's comprehension of him- or herself as a discrete entity (a **self**). Theorists have made a number of important distinctions that structure quite different research traditions. The social philosopher Mead, for example, has distinguished between the processes by which a self-identity is formed (the 'I') and the specific content of a self-identity (the 'Me'). Mead argued that there is a conversation that occurs between the I and the me, identity emerging both as social and processual or dynamic. In cognitive psychology researchers tend to consider separately the personal idiosyncrasies which differentiate individuals (personal identities) and the various social roles that actors play (social identities). Sociologists and political scientists have focused specifically on individuals' social identities and how people come to label themselves as members of **nations**, social **classes**, **genders**, etc. Considerable work has been conducted by social psychologists under the broad labels 'social identity theory' (SIT) and 'self-categorization theory' (SCT) which suggest that individuals categorize themselves and others into in-groups and out-groups on the basis of the socio-cognitive processes categorization, self-enhancement, and uncertainty reduction.

One dominant conception of subjectively available identities represents them as reflexively organized **narratives** derived from participation in competing discourses. Such a perspective draws on the linguistic turn in the social sciences, and especially the idea that people are appropriately described as *homo narrans* or *homo fabulans*—the tellers and interpreters of narrative.[3] Within organization studies attention has often focused on the identity 'work' that individuals engage in as they form, repair,

---

[1] Humphreys and Brown, 2002; Brown, 2006.   [2] Gabriel, 1993.   [3] Fisher, 1985; Currie, 1998, p. 2.

maintain, strengthen, and revise the storied constructions that are productive of a sense of coherence and distinctiveness. Most often this has been accompanied by recognition that although identities may reasonably be conceived as projects of the self, these perpetual works-in-progress are also power effects that are shaped and constrained by local discursive practices.

Increasingly, scholars of organization and management have sought to apply the concept of 'identity' at collective levels, particularly to groups and organizations. In marketing, for example, the phrase 'corporate identity' is often used to describe the notional 'persona' of an organization as manifested in its designs (e.g. logos and uniforms), communications (e.g. public relations statements), behaviours, and values. In organization theory the phrase 'organizational identity' has been defined as that which is central, distinctive, and enduring about an organization,[1] how a collective understands itself as an entity,[2] the theory that members of an organization have about who they are,[3] and the totality of repetitive patterns of individual behaviour and interpersonal relationships.[4] As with individual-level conceptions of identity there is a discernible trend towards understanding organizational identities as linguistic constructs. Brown, for example, suggests that organizations' identities are constituted by the identity-relevant narratives that their participants author about them.[5]

Identity is a key term in the social sciences, with the potential to integrate research projects that span multiple disciplines and levels of analysis. It therefore seems likely to remain a significant word (domain of research activity) for the foreseeable future.

• See also *identification, Other and othering, self and selfhood, subject and subjectivity*

ANDREW BROWN, UNIVERSITY OF BATH

Ideology

Ideology refers to groups of interrelated ideas, doctrines, and values. A term coined by French philosopher Destutt de Tracy (1801), ideology was seen as the science of ideas that would eventually dispel prejudices and superstitions. The emancipatory power of ideas was a crucial feature of the European Enlightenment. In this context, ideas such as the ideals of the French Revolution, liberty, equality, and fraternity, and more generally ideas rooted in rational discourses, were viewed as driving away the obsolete ideas of the *ancien régime* as well as its economic, political, and social structures.

Karl Marx's intervention in the discussion of ideology was decisive. Marx created a fundamentally new concept for which he used the existing term ideology. Ideologies, he claimed, were part of the social superstructure: 'it is not the consciousness of men that determines their being, but, on the contrary, their social being that determines their consciousness.'[6] Far from initiating social **change** and transformation, ideas reflect the material conditions of production, and especially the interests of ruling classes. Ideas do not evolve by themselves, nor are they the product of some abstract **cognitive** processes. Still less are ideas manifestations of a sovereign reason or subjectivity. Instead they emerge, come into conflict with each other, prevail or decline, broadly in line with changing social, economic, and political conditions. Furthermore, ideologies (like the superstitions of old) are systematically distorted forms of consciousness, which allow for domination to go unnoticed or be regarded as 'natural'. Nowhere is this more evident than in Marx's well-known description of religion as 'the sigh of the oppressed creature, the sentiment of a heartless world, and the soul of soulless conditions. It is the *opium* of the people.'[7] Far from dismissing religion and other ideologies as

---

[1] Albert and Whetten, 1985.   [2] Pratt, 2003, p. 165.   [3] Stimpert, Gustafson, and Sarason, 1998, p. 87.   [4] Diamond, 1993, p. 77.
[5] Brown, 2006, p. 734.   [6] Marx, 1859/1972, p. 4.   [7] Marx, 1843/1972, p. 12.

irrelevant or redundant, Marx saw them as decisive weapons in **class conflict**.

With Marx, the concept of ideology acquires a deprecatory quality, as at best unscientific bundles of ideas and at worst false consciousness. Science, on the other hand, is seen as objective, yet unavailable to classes whose material interests it threatens. The distinction between science and ideology has been a constant focus of debate. The chronic difficulty in drawing a hard and fast line between the two made Marxism subject to its own critique, as the ideological expression of a particular class interest and a specific form of false consciousness.

Max Weber, in his *The Protestant Ethic and the Spirit of Capitalism*,[1] made a radical qualification to Marx's approach. While linked to material interests, Weber viewed ideas not merely as reflections of these interests, but as involving and even initiating social dynamics of their own. Thus, in the early phases of social or revolutionary movements, various groups and classes may espouse ideas of charismatic leaders, which are discordant with their material interests, at least in the short term. Gradually, with routinization setting in, followers tend to retain those elements of revolutionary ideas with which they continue to identify and which serve their interests, discarding those which are economically or psychologically disadvantageous. Thus Weber saw early capitalism as having a supporting 'affinity' with the ideas associated with the Protestant ethic, which included hard work, frugality, community orientation, and resistance to sensuous pleasures. These ideas encouraged instrumental **rationality**, calculation, and accumulation of capital; they consistently devalued what is present, sensuous, and material in the interest of the future, the **spiritual**, and the rational. Yet victorious capitalism, with its materialism and hedonism, no longer needed the Protestant ethic to sustain it and substantially discarded its ascetic heritage. Weber himself, as he became increasingly disenchanted with German politics,

tended to move more towards the Marxist position, where material interests swamp even the loftiest ideas. 'Not ideas, but material and ideal interests, directly govern men's conduct. Yet very frequently the "world images" that have been created by "ideas" have, like switchmen, determined the tracks along which action has been pushed along by the dynamic of interest'.[2]

In the second half of the twentieth century, an influential group of American social theorists who included Daniel Bell, Seymour Martin Lipset, and Philip Rieff saw ideology as a secular form of religion, an all-encompassing world view with a strong normative content. Ideologies not only divided the world into good and evil but also offered recipes of universal salvation from suffering. These thinkers argued that we were witnessing the *end of ideology*. Apocalyptic communal recipes of universal salvation through religion and politics were in terminal decline, replaced by an **ethic** of well-being, guided by enlightened self-interest and market values. Margaret Thatcher's claim that 'there is no such thing as society, only individuals and their families' summed up well this approach. Yet, in a curious way, it was ideological in its own right, representing a **consumerist** ethos that came to dominate both the public and the private sectors.

Since the 1970s, the concept of ideology has rather gone out of fashion, being reduced to its pejorative sense, used to denigrate 'everything that is doctrinaire, abstract, opinionated, rigid, and unrealistic'.[3] The discussion of ideas and their ability to influence social, economic, and political developments, however, has continued unabated, usually associated with the terms culture, discourse, or grand narratives, all of which seem to evade the strict requirement that truth claims should be substantiated by external criteria. Instead 'regimes of truth' are seen as residing within a culture, a discourse, or a body of knowledge itself. Following the work of Foucault,[4] numerous theorists

---

[1] Weber, 1958.   [2] Weber, 1946, p. 281.   [3] Burns, 1978, p. 249.   [4] Foucault, 1980.

(many of whom accept the labels '**postmodern**' or '**post-structuralist**') view these *regimes of truth* (according to which, for example, some ideas are viewed as common sense, others as aberrant, and others as 'politically incorrect') as inextricably linked to the operation of **power** in society and have adopted Foucault's term 'power/knowledge' to denote the impossibility of dissociating knowledge from power. Viewed this way, ideas are thoroughly entrenched in social and political practices. Practices do not follow ideas, but are coextensive with them. And ideas are most pervasive when invisible and unobtrusive. In the field of organizations, discussion of the dissemination of ideas across **institutions** has assumed major significance as a way of understanding how different types of management practices, ideas, and innovations spread and how they are resisted.

• See also *grand narrative*

Image

Image is something that we **experience** in the first instance through our eyes; it is a visual representation. One of the difficulties of the word 'image' is that some visual representations simply exist—for example the reflection of a mountain on a lake or of a person's face in a security camera—whereas others are put together in the form of pictures, photographs, paintings, movies, graphs, collages, and so forth for particular purposes. Image is thus both a natural phenomenon (studied by optics, a field of physics) and a cultural artefact invested with a variety of **meanings**. It is helpful to distinguish between *image*, the generic concept of a text that is appropriated visually without the help of an alphabet, and a *picture* that is a particular type of image, composed by an author, such as a painter or a photographer. A *spectacle* could then be seen as a complex association of images and pictures, often moving ones, produced by television or theatrical producers, architects, events organizers, museum curators, and so forth.

The proliferation of images, pictures, and spectacles has been one of the defining qualities of late **modernity**. Two hundred years ago, in order to experience a powerful image, such as a painting or a mountain peak, one had to visit the place where it could be found. Today, our daily universe has become saturated with images, jumping at us from our television sets, our magazines and newspapers, our computer screens and our digital cameras, our advertising billboards, our shop windows, and the packaging of nearly every object we purchase. Many of our experiences are visual experiences—we now routinely use expressions such as 'I saw it in slow-motion' or 'I went on fast forward' which indicate the extent to which we experience the world after the model of images. This is why in the 1960s Guy Debord described our society as a 'society of spectacle'.[1] This became the basis of his then fashionable 'situationist critique', when he argued that **spectacle** was replacing every form of social activity, including politics, sport, religion, and education, inducing stupefaction and passivity. Debord was ahead of his time in appreciating the power of the image but his assessment of its effect was rather too one-sided and polemical. Image creates victims—fashion victims, diet victims, shopaholics, and so forth. But image, it now seems, can also be a source of empowerment, an area where we can exercise **choice** and a vital part of our **identity**. This is where brands derive power, in helping us project images that give an expression to who we are.

Image is a remarkably fluid currency—by joining an organization, we absorb part of its image into our own self-image; by purchasing a particular brand, we appropriate part of its image for our own purposes; even, by choosing to go on holiday to a particular resort, to visit a particular museum, or to shop in a particular retail outlet, we absorb some of the image

[1] Debord, 1977.

associated with them. Notice that talking about image as 'currency', we have moved away from the original meaning of image as visual representation and started looking at it more as a set of meanings associated with particular visual representations. Thus the meanings we associate with the products of a particular brand become part of the brand image, which we may choose to buy into or not. Likewise the image of a particular company, like hi-fi manufacturer B&O, may be defined by the visual impact of its products which trigger off sets of meanings like 'stylish', 'exclusive', 'innovative', etc. The production of images is closely related to the production of self-images, the way that we wish to be perceived by others, as individuals, groups, organizations, or societies at large. We can then say that person *x* projects a stylish and aloof image, that organization *y* projects a 'cutting edge of innovation' image, or that country *z* projects an 'ideal tourist destination' image.

Meanings evoked by particular images are, as often as not, products of the imagination, **fantasies**, as much as objective attributes of objects, people, and organizations. This is what makes image not only a fluid but a powerful currency—through image we can reinvent ourselves, reconstitute our identities, and fashion our egos after what is desirable and alluring. We can neutralize our conventional job, by going on adventurous holidays; we can defuse our fear of powerlessness by purchasing powerful automobiles; we can defuse our fear of ageing by cosmetic surgery. Thus, as a set of fantasies, image occupies a very privileged position between reality and unreality—it is what Campbell described as an illusion known to be false, but felt to be true.[1] One particularly interesting feature on self-image is that it can be strongly affected by the image that others hold of us.

Given the importance of image in our culture, it is not surprising that companies spend substantial sums on it. A company's image is crucially affected by the appearance of its products,

the quality of its **advertisements**, its logo, the look of its corporate headquarters, its sponsorships, and virtually every visible sign associated with its name. The way that all of these are portrayed in the media is crucial. Companies employ many media advisers, communications experts, and every type of **consultant** to strengthen their brand equity. In order for a corporate image to be effective, it must be alluring, but also believable. This means that the different signs of a company must be consistent and self-reinforcing. Inconsistent messages risk contaminating the brand and destroying the image. This reveals one of the vulnerabilities of contemporary capitalism—a well-organized smear campaign, the activities of a few whistle-blowers or disenchanted employees, especially when backed with visual evidence or photographs, can have a disastrous effect on carefully produced and expensively maintained corporate images.

• See also *spectacle*

Industrial relations

Industrial relations is a set of 'activities and institutions associated with relationships between employers and groups of collectively organised individuals'.[2] It is also an academic discipline that flourished between the 1950s and 1970s, when, especially in the United Kingdom, it exercised a considerable influence on government **policy**. The origins of the field of industrial relations were threefold: first, the scholarship of Marx and Marxist scholars on **class** relations and especially workplace **conflict**; second, trade union historiography that documented (and to a lesser extent analysed) the struggles of working people to offset the disproportionate powers of their employers; and, third, a version of regulation theory that approached collective bargaining as a key **institution** for containing industrial conflict. In the United States, a **systems** approach to industrial relations was developed

---

[1] Campbell, 1989, p. 82.   [2] Watson, 2008b.

by Dunlop that sought to account, within a pluralistic perspective, for the **rules** governing relations between institutions, like firms, unions, and employers' associations.[1] This approach extended to international comparisons of industrial relations systems. A much-debated issue was the convergence thesis, according to which political and ideological differences between the industrial relations systems of different countries were fading away under the fundamental logic of industrialization.[2] Needless to say, following the collapse of communism in the East and the decline of trade unionism in the West, some of these debates now appear to have a museum-like character.

In Britain, an influential school of industrial relations thinking evolved with scholars like Allan Flanders, Alan Fox (in his early work), and Hugh Clegg having a degree of influence on politicians rarely seen in this country. In spite of internal disagreements, British industrial relations eschewed abstract or grand theorizing and tended to concentrate on close observation of collective bargaining, closed shops, and other workplace arrangements. They generally viewed such arrangements as preferable to direct government intervention in industrial relations, arguing that they encouraged greater independence and responsibility on the part of **trade unions** and employers. Many of their recommendations were embraced by the Donovan Report (1968) that urged government to encourage the institution of collective bargaining, rather than direct intervention through legislation, as a way of resolving industrial conflict. At the time, industrial disputes and other forms of industrial action (such as picketing, work-to-rule, and go-slows) in the UK were widespread; shop stewards, unofficial worker leaders, exercised a considerable degree of **power** by wielding the weapon of unofficial or wildcat strikes. Incomes policies had been repeatedly used to curb pay claims and inflation, but to rather limited effect. In fact, it was resistance to an

incomes policy that led to the defeat of the Callaghan government in 1977 and opened the way for Margaret Thatcher's Conservative government. On assuming power, Thatcher abandoned incomes policies and set out to diminish the power of unions through legislation and through direct industrial confrontation. This was a task for which she did not seek the advice of industrial relations academics (her own academic gurus originated in the economics of monetarism) and in which she turned out, after prolonged strife, to be remarkably successful.

Since that time, industrial relations, as an academic field, has gone into decline, broadly mirroring the decline of the trade union movement in most industrialized nations, the emergence of large non-union sectors in every economy, and the decline in traditional forms of worker militancy, industrial action, and overt **resistance**. Some parts of industrial relations were appropriated by the discourses of personnel management and subsequently **Human Resource Management**; other parts, notably the ones deriving from the Marxist tradition and the study of workplace conflict and resistance, were incorporated in **Labour Process Theory**. The field of industrial relations thus provides a fascinating example of how academic **discourses** rise and fall in relation to wider social and political developments.

• See also *trade unions*

Information

Information refers to the acquisition or exchange of new facts resulting from a variety of human activities, including observation, thinking, or **communication**. To inform means to mediate something new. Novelty is a defining attribute of information and so is its contingent and event-like character. A perception, utterance, or message can produce or convey information to the degree they are

---

[1] Dunlop, 1958.   [2] Kerr et al., 1960.

able to add something new, no matter how little, to what is already recorded or known. Novelty is regularly bound up with the illumination of particular details of social reality, i.e. a price change, a decision, a political shift, the disclosure of a secret, and so forth. Thus understood, information differs from data. The latter can be stored, the former not. It also differs from **knowledge** whose relevance is associated with the illumination of enduring aspects of reality. The usefulness of information is a function of its ability to unravel the novel, transient, and contingent. Framed in these terms, information is inextricably bound up with social agents and their dealings. Information generation takes place against a background of cultural and social practices and significations that shape both the meaning and value of information.[1]

Occasionally, the concept of information has been used (predominantly by natural scientists) in a wider sense to refer to patterns or relationships that are supposed to underlie natural and biological phenomena or the technologically produced structures of modern life such as buildings, bridges, or even databases. The structure of DNA, for instance, is said to contain a lot of information (it is interesting to ask for whom?). Particles, quarks, or genes may well be seen as interacting in lawful ways that involve the signalling of states that may be conceived as elementary units of information. But this stretches the concept of information substantially. It tends to equate the mapping of pattern or structure with information. The German-American philosopher of technology Albert Borgmann makes a distinction between this view of information that he refers to as *structural* and the one I gave in the preceding paragraph that he calls *cognitive*.[2] He claims that the structural view of information stretches the bounds of the concept to render it nearly meaningless.

The entrance of the term information to modern parlance owes very much to Shannon and Weaver, the founders of information theory, and their classic work on the mathematics of signal transmission.[3] According to Shannon and Weaver, semantics is irrelevant to the engineering of information and communication processes concerned with the mechanics of signal transmission. Much of cybernetics during the first two decades following the Second World War used the concept of information to refer both to mechanical, biological, and social (meaning-related) processes or phenomena. Later developments within cybernetics and the then emerging science of **cognition** led though to certain clarifications. In his imaginative essay 'Form, substance and difference', Bateson drew a distinction between *forces of energy* resulting in the causal patterns characteristic of the natural world and *differences* as cognitive states and relationships underlying information and communication processes.[4] Material impacts cannot fruitfully be used to understand and unravel the distinctive workings of information and communication. The letter you do not write, Bateson said, may have devastating implications. In his monumental definition, *information is but a difference that makes a difference*, Luhmann has since applied the concept of information as difference that makes a difference in understanding **mass media** in today's world.[5]

In social life, **meaning** is of course never disembodied. In order for humans to convey information they need the physical means through which they can encase the differences underlying information units and transmit them to others. In order to speak it is necessary to mould air to sounds known as phonemes; writing and other notations suggest that cognitive content needs marks to be conveyed. Sound, text, and image are widespread socially shaped physical devices for generating, transmitting, and recording information. In this respect the two levels, i.e. the level of meaning and the physical substratum by which meaning is supported, merge. It is thus far from accidental that theories of

---

[1] Brown and Duguid, 2000.   [2] Borgmann, 1999.   [3] Shannon and Weaver, 1949.   [4] Bateson, 1972.   [5] Luhmann, 2000.

information (and signification) have over the years quarrelled as regards the primacy of the one over the other. Indeed, following the lead of Lacan and Lévi-Strauss, **post-structuralists** often came close to the position of Shannon and Weaver, suggesting that the structure and play of signifiers (i.e. the physical aspect of signs) are the key mechanisms out of which the evanescent nature of meaning is captured and solidified.

Against the background of these observations it would seem relevant to distinguish between data and information. Such a distinction is important to uphold in the current world of technological information. Computer-generated information is sustained by a variety of electronically produced tokens or marks that are known as data. As already indicated, meaning itself cannot be stored, for it is produced in the encounters of agents with data items. While widespread, the distinction between data and information is frequently violated in everyday parlance and the terms are frequently used interchangeably. The automated rules by which software acts upon data items to produce new data and information have further blurred the distinction between them. Do the differences brought about by recourse to automated rules of data processing qualify as information? The answer is not straightforward but many widespread computer applications (e.g. search engines, profiling techniques) assume so.

Information should be distinguished from knowledge as well. The confusion runs deeper in this respect. A widespread understanding maintains that knowledge may result from forging information to a wider pattern of conceptual relationships or **cultural** meanings. Information obtains its value against the background of existing knowledge and cultural schemes, which it may itself help to enrich or illuminate. True as it may be, such an understanding conceals the fundamental fact that knowledge and information

are marked by widely different orientations. As already indicated, information obtains its informativeness (its value) from its capacity to add something new to what is already known. Reciting a statement that is already known does not qualify as information, no matter how important such a statement may be.[1] In order to be informative, information has to pick up a new fact or state and convey it. But novelty does not and cannot last. It dies at the very moment it is consumed. Information is thus perishable and for that reason easily disposable. Market information, for instance, that reaches stock exchanges all over the world in terms of price changes often lasts no more than few minutes. By contrast knowledge (and memory) is defined by its capacity to preserve a sets of facts or conceptual relationships across time. Even though knowledge changes periodically to accommodate new facts or experiences, it is not defined by its novelty but rather its capacity to resist easy depreciation.[2] Little wonder that T. S. Eliot decried already in 1934 the migration of knowledge to information so characteristic of modern life: 'Where is the wisdom we have lost in knowledge | where is the knowledge we have lost in information.'[3]

Information, as Luhmann suggests,[4] is no more than an event, a semantic flash created against the background of memory and knowledge to which it is assimilated. In so doing, however, the value of information is consumed. The pending evaporation of the value of information triggers a complex institutional game that seeks to maintain its value through a variety of mechanisms seeking to grasp and mediate the innumerable details underlying the fabric of social life. Key among them is the constant updatability of technological information.[5] The prevalence of information in modern life could thus be interpreted as the massive and technologically sustained introduction of the event and its ephemeral constitution (kept in abeyance by

---

[1] Borgmann, 1999.   [2] Kallinikos, 2006.   [3] Eliot, 1974.   [4] Luhmann, 2000.   [5] Kallinikos, 2006.

modernity's relatively stable structures) in social and institutional life.[1]

• See also *communication, information technology*

JANNIS KALLINIKOS, THE LONDON SCHOOL OF ECONOMICS

Information technology

Information technology (usually referred to as IT or ICT—information and communication technology) is often used to refer to electronic devices, including computers and telecommunications, that have revolutionized the handling of information over the past thirty years or so. In a wider sense, information technology includes all technologies concerned with creating, storing, processing, retrieving, and communicating **information**, including pen and paper, typewriters, and even writing and numbering systems. Yet the phrases 'IT' and 'ICT' have now come to denote exclusively electronic types of information and communication technologies. The emphasis on savings and **rationalization** accomplished through the use of IT has tended to obscure some of its indirect effects on styles and quality of **work**. Zuboff, for example, argued that information technology may be used in two distinct ways.[2] The first was termed 'automation'—a situation where the machine leaves the fundamental process unchanged but performs tasks previously carried out by humans or simpler machines. This generally leads to marginal gains in productivity, staff redundancies, and **deskilling** for the remaining workers. By contrast, Zuboff proposed a different mode of implementing new technology, for which she offered the term 'informate', whereby fundamental tasks are rethought and reconfigured in the light of new technology. By 'informating' rather than automating tasks, some of the negative consequences of new technologies are avoided; instead of deskilling and

alienating workers, new information technologies can lead to a reskilling and, in some cases, enhanced autonomy and control in the workplace.

At the same time, it was noted that with ever-increasing numbers of people spending their working times in front of computer screens, certain far-reaching and potentially damaging consequences ensued. Writing at the outset of what became known as the information revolution, Weick identified five types of deficiency resulting from working with computerized information **systems**: action deficiencies, because employees get less feedback (sounds, smells, etc.) from an information system than they do from any 'live' system; comparison deficiencies, because they cannot walk round and look at it from the other side, as they would with a physical object; affiliation deficiencies, because they are less likely to form opinions by talking through the output from an information system than by discussing with other people; deliberation deficiencies, as they struggle to see the wood for the trees, a particularly appropriate metaphor when thinking about the piles of printout that come out of computers; and consolidation deficiencies, as they easily assume that the hard work of thinking through the conclusions has been done as long as the computer is aware of it.[3] However, these deficiencies do not prevent us all from relying more and more on such technology and finding this an interesting and enjoyable experience.

Computerized information technologies have had far-reaching consequences for the nature of our societies and our economies. Whole sectors of business (including those represented by e-Bay, Amazon, Google, and so forth) have emerged and prospered. In hospitals, schools, and virtually every type of organization, the introduction of computerized information technologies does not merely lead to better and more efficient record keeping and **communication**, but alters in a fundamental way

---

[1] Lyotard, 1984/1991; Virilio, 2000.   [2] Zuboff, 1985; 1988.   [3] Weick, 1985.

the ways that services and goods are delivered and even the meaning of the words 'services' and 'goods'. The music industry, for example, has been totally reconfigured following the easy access to recorded music through the internet.

The effects of information technology on society have become so pronounced that some major sociologists, like Castells, refer to it as an *information age* or *informational capitalism*.[1] In such a society, the processing and management of information determines the competitiveness and productivity of economic units, be they firms, regions, or countries. Furthermore, because of the ease and speed with which information can be exchanged, many economic activities, such as the operation of markets, assume a **global** character. Finally, new information technologies allow for the emergence of new types of organizations, which assume qualities of virtuality or information **networks**.

What about organizations themselves in the information era? The introduction of new information technologies in organizations almost always encounters difficulties. There are numerous examples of organizations (from businesses to stock exchanges to health organizations) investing in expensive new information technologies that eventually had to be aborted because of massive implementation problems. Integrating information systems is one of the hardest parts in mergers and acquisitions, where departments and users find it difficult to adopt and accept new systems. The pages of journals for IT professionals are littered with crises and disasters surrounding the introduction of new IT—which of course have led to the emergence of a multi-billion consulting business aimed at helping organizations with their IT problems (and sometimes compounding them). In spite of all that, organizations from supermarkets to insurance companies can derive very extensive competitive advantages over their rivals through effective and imaginative use of the possibilities created by new IT.

Like major technological breakthroughs of earlier times, new information technologies have had a far-reaching impact on the nature and character of organizations themselves. They have enabled far-greater management **control** over information, resources, stock levels, outputs, and the deployment of people. The measurement of **performance** of individuals (from supermarket cashiers to hospital surgeons), departments, or organizations themselves has been vastly enhanced, hence the tendency to try and measure things in ever-greater detail. In a curious way, these developments have favoured some smaller economic units or networks of such units which have been able to compete effectively in different niches against larger units. This has encouraged practices like **outsourcing** and subcontracting and has led to a general **downsizing** of large commercial organizations. Many organizations have adopted flatter **hierarchies**, as individual managers are able to keep track of ever-increasing numbers of subordinates. Overall, theorists like Castells have argued that information technologies are driving economic units increasingly away from **bureaucracy** and toward network organizations.

• See also *information, technology*

Innovation

Innovation, along with the related concepts of **creativity** and **entrepreneurship**, is increasingly seen as a quality conferring competitive advantage on individuals, firms, or even nations. Innovation involves the channelling of creativity into the conceptualization of new products, new processes, new applications for existing things and new combinations

---

[1] Castells, 1996a.

of existing things. In his classic text *Capitalism, Socialism and Democracy* (1942), Joseph Schumpeter examined the technological forces underpinning economic growth. Schumpeter argued that entrepreneurs and industrialists are driven to develop new products and services by the 'carrot of spectacular reward' and the 'stick of destitution', resulting in 'gales of creative destruction' across society.[1] A rather more sober and contemporary definition of technological innovation commonly focuses on 'the successful commercial exploitation of new ideas'. In **voluntary** and **public-sector organizations**, innovation is usually defined as 'the successful implementation of new ideas', a definition that originated in the OECD's Oslo Manual,[2] the main guide used by economists collecting and using data on innovation in industry, now widely adopted by many governments.

In both private and public sectors economic success is determined by measuring the benefit conferred by a new idea and the extent to which this exceeds the cost and effort needed to bring it to **market** or to implement it over time. For the purposes of measurement and comparison of economic performance the definition of innovation is further refined to include ideas that are 'new to the world', 'new to an industry', or 'new to a particular firm'.

Technological innovation has two dimensions: type of **change** and extent of change. The type of change may involve a new product, a new service, or a new process. The extent of change may be incremental, resulting from efforts to continuously improve in well-understood areas, or radical, resulting from the development and deployment of new capabilities. Incremental innovation occurs frequently in many industries, involving exploitation of existing know-how, and is a major source of underlying profitability. Radical innovation involves a great deal of uncertainty and **risk**, occurs infrequently,

requires an organizational setting that promotes exploration (rather than exploitation), and may destroy existing **competencies**.[3] Occasionally, innovation results in the development of technologies that, over time, may have a profound impact on cost structures of whole industries, changing the underlying techno-economic system—such has been the case with the advent of microprocessors.

Technological innovation entails integration of scientific, engineering, and market opportunities. Invention, the creation of a new idea of potential practical application, is an important input to innovation, but not on its own sufficient to ensure commercial success. Invention is often closely linked to experimentation, problem solving, and trial and error. In order to progress, other inputs such as research, development, design, engineering, and commercialization strategies are required.[4] Different capabilities are needed at different stages in the innovation process. The high rates of failure in innovation show that this is a notoriously difficult process to manage. Failure is often caused by poor understanding of the risks of innovation, barriers and communication problems within and between organizations, and unreliable **information** about markets and technologies.

The pressures to innovate—market and/or technological opportunity, competition, regulatory pressures—and the innovation process itself have changed over the past four decades. Knowledge about how to manage the development of new ideas has become more sophisticated. Activities are now organized concurrently rather than sequentially, involving different **stakeholders**, such as customers, suppliers, and research collaborators. For these reasons, the management of innovation has become a strategic issue for many types of organizations. Innovation **strategy** and management have become main board issues and many firms

---

[1] Schumpeter, 1943. [2] OECD Oslo Manual, 1997. [3] March, 1991; Tushman and Anderson, 1986. [4] Dodgson, Gann, and Salter, 2008.

have appointed Chief Innovation Officers or Chief Technology Officers with responsibility for development and implementation.

In the past fifteen years, a range of information and communication technologies have converged with operations and production systems enabling firms to innovate more rapidly, efficiently, and accurately than ever before.[1] This 'Innovation Technology' (IvT), includes eScience, virtual reality, modelling, simulation techniques, and rapid prototyping.[2] Using this emerging technological infrastructure requires changes in the innovation process, with consequences for strategy and management. It offers the potential to overcome some of the barriers to innovation, making things that were previously costly and difficult to risk-assess more straightforward, providing better and more comprehensible information from researchers, customers, and other stakeholders. It can enable firms to develop new products and services more swiftly and efficiently than in the past, allowing people to create more adventurous innovations. It can also bring new risks and uncertainty about the quality of data and nature of decision making.[3]

Over time, it is possible that IvT will have as profound an impact on economic growth and social well-being in today's knowledge economy as the development of machine tools had on the industrial economy of the mid-nineteenth century. A number of contemporary issues, however, remain to be understood. For example, there is much debate about a shift from traditional 'closed' innovation processes, carried out within private R&D laboratories, and the opportunity to search for and use ideas in distributed networks of 'open' innovation. This presents an opportunity to span traditional boundaries between disciplines, within and between organizations, giving rise to new skills in innovation brokerage, and opportunities to innovate with lead users. The new innovation process may also provide lessons for managing other complex,

risky, and emerging fields such as in health, energy, and the environment.

DAVID GANN, IMPERIAL COLLEGE LONDON

Institution

Institution refers to a set of practices, a **system** of relations, or an **organization** which is infused with **value** and is widely recognized within a **culture** as part of the established way of doing things. The monarchy in Britain, a television soap opera, the Superbowl, Harvard University, Rolls Royce, and marriage are all institutions. In earlier eras, slavery, torture, and the burning of witches were institutions. Institutions sometimes acquire venerability with time as they become invested with special meaning and as they prove their staying power by becoming traditions. In *Leadership and administration*, Philip Selznick argued that the task of the **leader** is to infuse organizations with meaning, thus turning mechanical **bureaucracies** into institutions.[4] Institutions have a sense of permanence, consistency, and are seen as objects of **value** in their own right. Selznick's argument has resurfaced in more recent literature of organizational culture, in which a primary function of leaders is the management of an organization's values and **meanings**.

One key quality of institutions is that, in spite of being products of culture, they have the ability to appear inevitable, normal, and *natural*. It is for this reason that they derive three of their key features—first, they enjoy **legitimacy** and bestow legitimacy on many actions carried out as part of them; second, they exercise powerful **control** over the actions and thoughts of people; and third, attempts to change them tend to be resisted and take time. This does not mean that institutions do not change, but they do so when conditions for their continued existence become very problematic.

Throughout history, one of the chief qualities of most institutions is that they are **gendered**,

---

[1] Dodgson, Gann, and Salter, 2005.   [2] Gann and Dodgson, 2007.   [3] Dodgson, Gann, and Salter, 2007.   [4] Selznick, 1957.

i.e. they affect men and women in systematically different ways and they create different assumptions about what it means to be a woman or a man. Thus, marriage creates different sets of responsibilities and rights for men from those it creates for women; priesthood of many major religions is not open to women; many careers were not open to women and, conversely, many jobs were only available to women. Changes in gender relations, changes in fundamental beliefs regarding sexual preferences and sexual reproduction, as well as technological changes of all kinds have thus placed considerable pressure on institutions that relied on traditional gender assumptions. As a result some of these institutions are in the process of changing.

Approaching organizations as institutions downplays the extent to which organizations are products of human agency or the extent to which they are the result of rational design. Agency is downplayed along with individuals' ability to make rational **choices**. From an institutional perspective what constitutes agency, free choice, and rationality all derive from the logic of the institutions themselves. The emphasis is thus placed on culture and norms that shape organizational realities.[1] In general, talking about social practices and systems as institutions tends to obscure many tensions, **conflicts**, and contradictions that inhere in them. It is for this reason that **postmodern** theorists have looked at institutions as discursive phenomena, i.e. objects that come into being through **language** and are therefore capable of being **deconstructed** through language. This creates difficulties of its own. One may analyse the language of an institution like slavery as part of the mechanism that sustained and fed it; more importantly, however, one must come to grips with the economic, political, and moral conditions in order to account for the fact that such a grotesque abomination would come to be viewed as 'natural' and 'legitimate'.

• See also *Institutional theory*

Institutional theory

Institutional theory is a very popular approach to the study of organizations and one especially attuned to explorations of how **knowledge** and ideas are disseminated, how different management practices become **fads and fashions**, and, more generally, how organizations come to gain **legitimacy**. Institutional theory has its origins in work by Philip Selznick and functionalist sociologists of the post-war period.[2] These scholars emphasized that organizations 'become' institutions as they gain permanence, legitimacy, and prestige, becoming cultural features of their society. In this way, the BBC with its long traditions of impartial news coverage and its mission to educate was more than just an organization— it was part of Britain's cultural landscape and a valued 'institution'.

In more recent times, institutional theory was 'reinvented' as scholars started observing that many organizations are not preoccupied exclusively with economic efficiency and profitability, but try instead to strengthen their legitimacy. They often adopt practices and ideas that may actually inhibit or harm their efficiency—they do so, however, in the belief that they strengthen their authority within the wider society. This is sometimes referred to a 'New Institutionalism' of 'New Institutional Theory'.

Institutional theory emphasizes the institutional **environment** within which organizations function—the laws, norms, values, customs, recipes, ideas, beliefs, and conventions that are 'taken for granted', acquiring their sanctity from habit and repetition. In this sense, institutional theory argues that traditional **authority**, as defined by Weber, has not disappeared under the influence of **rationality**. On the contrary, rationality itself is often a justification of practices and ideas that acquire sanctity through repetition rather than through a careful consideration of ends and means. Thus a 'no smoking' rule in a lecture theatre appears rational today and

---

[1] Powell and Dimaggio, 1991.   [2] Selznick, 1957.

all kinds of justifications are offered to support it; in reality, however, banning smoking from public places accords with the spirit and norms of our times, rather than having been carefully considered and found to be the best means of ensuring health and safety in lecture theatres.[1] Rituals, in this manner, assume the appearance of being 'rational'. Institutions have both cognitive and normative consequences—they infuse **actions** with meaning and significance but they also discourage or proscribe particular types of behaviour. Thus, the 'no smoking' rule claims 'Smoking is a bad practice, especially when done in public places, because it is harmful to health, it is a fire risk etc.'; this is its cognitive aspect. Its normative aspect is to stop people from smoking in the classroom, and maybe encourage them to stop smoking altogether.

One consequence of institutional theory is the view that organizations operating in similar institutional environments develop similar **structures**, similar practices, and similar ideas. This is referred to as *isomorphism*.[2] Isomorphism can easily be understood by considerng cars across the decades—it is quite easy to tell a car of the 1940s from a car of the 1960s or 1990s. In spite of all their differences (in function, price range, market appeal, etc.), cars of different periods share certain shapes ('morphs') which reflect the priorities and values of their time.

In a similar way, organizations, irrespective of many differences, become similar to each other as they subscribe to the same management ideas and practices, to the same fads and fashions. If all organizations similar to yours have a Personnel Department, the odds are that yours will have one too. If their Personnel Departments are renamed 'Human Resource' Departments, the odds are that yours will be similarly renamed. If they adopt a system of production called 'Total Quality Management' it is likely that yours will also adopt it and when they drop it in favour of 'Business Process Re-engineering', it is likely that yours will do likewise. Imitation rather than rational choice decides many of the practices and patterns of today's organizations. Management ideas thus travel in a similar way to **fashion**,[3] not because they 'work' to boost efficiency but rather because they work to reassure people that they have not fallen behind the times.

Institutional theory has made considerable contributions to our understanding of organizations. Like most theories, there are features of organizations that are less well explained from that perspective, notably conflict, power, interests as well as those aspects of organizational behaviour covered by **strategy**.

Interpretation see hermeneutics

---

[1] Meyer and Rowan, 1977.   [2] Dimaggio and Powell, 1983.   [3] Abrahamson, 1991; 1996; Sturdy, 2004.

J

Jokes

Jokes are linguistic phenomena of considerable interest. They can offer a safety valve in moments of tension, provide a welcome diversion from hardships, create camaraderie and solidarity, and unleash powerful emotions. Two particularly important **emotions** associated with jokes are mirth (or amusement) and hostility—nearly all jokes, with the exception of puns, are directed against a certain target or butt who becomes the recipient of ridicule and mockery. The butt may be a competitor, a client, a department, an employee, or the storyteller him- or herself. Like myths, stories, and rituals, jokes are elements of organizational **culture**, which offer insights into the **feelings** and **desires** of organizational members.

Freud argued that jokes offer a partial amnesty, allowing repressed desires to surface and taboo ideas to be expressed.[1] More recently, it has been argued that jokes provide a symbolic route of escape out of the iron cage of **bureaucracy**, enabling the individual to poke fun at a system which is impersonal and inhuman.[2] At the same time, jokes may offer a safety valve that provides relief for boredom, stress, and unhappiness, blocking any real force for change.[3] There is thus an enduring tension as to whether jokes are an expression of **resistance** or whether they block more effective, 'real' resistance. What is certain, however, is that jokes enable individuals and groups to build a critical or cynical distance between themselves and their employer which allows them to build their **identities** in opposition to organizational values and norms.[4]

Some jokes, especially those reinforcing **stereotypes**, can be part of ritual humiliation or **bullying**, bolstering relations of domination and subordination. Other jokes (which may also rely on stereotypes) may be part of what are known as 'joking relations', where ritual horseplay and insults serve as the basis for trust and intimacy. Practical jokes too can build solidarity and function as rites of passage through which new recruits in organizations are tested before being subsequently accepted. Finally, humour is the basis for a distinct type of joke which is directed against the person who tells the joke. This is characteristic of Jewish jokes, but can also be found in organizations. Humour has a higher and finer quality—it is rebellious, defiant, and creative. Humorists tell jokes with themselves as the butt to show that they can survive adversities and that they do not take themselves too seriously. Black humour is especially common among people working in dangerous or macabre occupations, for example, in morgues and abattoirs—it provides a **defence mechanism** against dangerous emotions such as **anxiety**, guilt, and disgust, offering a certain degree of reassurance and superiority for those able to withstand the pressures of such occupations.

---

[1] Freud, 1905.   [2] Davies, 1988; Douglas, 1975b; Gabriel, 1995; Zijderveld, 1983.   [3] Collinson, 1988; Collinson, 2002.   [4] Fleming and Spicer, 2003.

K

Knowledge

Knowledge is the object of **learning** and the subject matter of **epistemology**. Knowledge is a fundamental characteristic of human beings and a distinctive feature of many of today's organizations and societies. A *knowledge organization* (such as a university, a consulting firm, a publisher, or an insurance company) is one much of whose essential business consists of generating, trading, and processing knowledge; a large part of the capital value of such an organization lies in its members' ability to exploit knowledge, turning it into competitive advantage. Where many organizations carry out this kind of work they are seen as a *knowledge economy*.

This use of the term knowledge creates two potentially misleading impressions—first, that knowledge is an object, a resource that can be bought, sold, and transferred at will, and, second, that knowledge is the same as **information**. The transfer of knowledge is an important subject partly related to the transfer of different professional and managerial practices (see **fads and fashions**). It is generally acknowledged but often forgotten that knowledge is not a fixed thing but one that changes as it moves from one person to another or from one organization to another. The transfer of knowledge involves both difficulties and possibilities—knowledge may be misunderstood, rejected, and ignored or conversely, it may be enriched, cross-fertilized, and developed as it gets communicated.

The confusion between information and knowledge is partly due to the use of the verb 'I know' to describe many different activities and states. 'I know the score' may refer to a simple piece of information, such as a football result; 'I know algebra/accounting/astrology' refers to specialist command of a discipline and how to use it in solving different problems; 'I know how to cook' refers to expertise in certain **competences** necessary to prepare food; 'I know how to handle crises' may refer to a range of intangible skills and experiences that enable me to deal with complex and unpredictable situations. One characteristic of knowledge organizations is their ability to use information in creative and original ways that generate value. Yet this should not obscure the fundamental difference between information and knowledge, the former being dependent on novelty, the latter being sustained over time.[1]

There are many different types of knowledge and many useful ways of classifying knowledge. It is helpful to distinguish between 'knowing how' (e.g. I know how to cycle) and 'knowing that' (e.g. I know that the square root of 8 is 2.828 . . .)'—the former suggests mastery of a craft, the latter mastery of a discipline.[2] Another important distinction is the one between explicit knowledge (things that I am aware that I know) and tacit knowledge (things that I know without being aware of doing so).[3] This is a distinction that has formed the basis of an influential theory of organizational knowledge creation, proposed by Nonaka and associates, according to which knowledge is created and turned into competitive advantage through its conversion from tacit forms to explicit forms and vice versa (see **socialization**).[4] This, in turn, has been challenged by scholars who argue that a great deal of organizational knowledge is not something 'owned' by anyone, but is situated in sets of ongoing

---

[1] Kallinikos, 2006.   [2] Russell, 1946.   [3] Polanyi, 1979.   [4] Nonaka, 1994; Nonaka and Takeuchi, 1995.

practices, hence it is always dynamic and provisional.[1]

The fundamental question of epistemology is how we can be sure about the truth value of knowledge. How can we tell true knowledge from false? One way of dealing with this question is to privilege certain types of knowledge, such as science and philosophy, over others, such as 'mere' **ideology** or belief. The former are products of certain strict **methodologies** and checks. Thus, *theories* are often seen as bodies of knowledge that go beyond opinion; they are characterized by

- a certain distancing from the subject matter; an ability to look at it with a certain detachment, practical, psychological, and conceptual;
- an attempt to be systematic rather than ad hoc—in this sense, theory must at some point seek to come up with some generalizations;
- a certain commitment to reason and rationality, where ideas and beliefs cannot be indefinitely held to be correct if they are in contradiction with each other.

In the case of *scientific* theories (rather than philosophical or pseudo-scientific like astrology) there is a certain commitment to empirical testing, which prevents the theory from being entirely inoculated against disconfirmation. Philosophers of science have long debated the nature of the relation between theory and empirical evidence as well as the relation between theory and **practice**. In general, scientific knowledge assumes the form of lawlike generalizations, such as 'water boils at 100 degrees Celsius' or 'groups make more risky decisions than individuals'. These may be true, untrue, or true in certain conditions (e.g. at sea level, normal atmospheric conditions, etc.).

This 'logico-scientific' knowledge is not the only knowledge with truth claims. For faithful believers, knowledge from revelation (such as that contained in the Bible and other holy books) bases its truth claims on the divine authority of its sources. Other types of knowledge are subject to different truth criteria. Relying extensively on Aristotle's theory of **narrative**, Jerome Bruner has argued that

> there are two modes [or paradigms] of cognitive functioning, two modes of thought, each providing distinctive ways of ordering experience, of constructing reality. The two (though complementary) are irreducible to one another. . . . Each of these ways of knowing, moreover, has operating principles of its own and its own criteria of well-formedness, they differ radically in their procedures for verification.[2]

Thus, to logico-scientific knowledge, Bruner juxtaposes *narrative knowledge*.[3] While the former relies on arguments, the latter relies on **stories**; the former bases its truth claims on proofs, the latter on the credibility or verisimilitude of stories.

Narrative knowledge includes myths, stories, anecdotes, and every type of recipe and narrative which helps people make sense of and deal with the situations they encounter. While this knowledge is sometimes associated with traditional or 'folk wisdom', it has become increasingly clear that it is of vital importance for managers, professionals, and even people working at the cutting edge of scientific discovery.[4]

Much of the knowledge traded in various **communities of practice** is precisely narrative knowledge. In this way, physicians at a conference may announce the latest scientific breakthrough in the treatment of diabetes, but in the informal discussions may swap stories about the effects of particular treatments on particular patients. Far from being the enemy of science, narrative knowledge may then emerge as its indispensable corollary—knowing the rules of the game is one

[1] Cook and Brown, 1999; Gherardi and Nicolini, 2001.   [2] Bruner, 1986, p. 21.   [3] Bruner, 1962; 1986; 1990.   [4] Chia, 1998; Czarniawska-Joerges, 1995; Orr, 1996.

thing, knowing how to play the game effectively is another.[1] **Experience** is a vital source of narrative knowledge.

Following the work of Foucault,[2] some theorists have come to view 'truth' as an attribute that does not describe the relation between knowledge and reality; instead, they view it as a result of certain social and political practices that privilege certain ideas over others. Knowledge and **power** form a self-reinforcing and indissoluble entity, power/knowledge, where the knowledge underpins power relations while the latter legitimize the knowledge. This approach has been applied to various theories/techniques extensively used by managers, such as performance appraisal, Total Quality Management, and Business Process Re-engineering.[3] This approach has, in turn, been criticized by Feldman as removing agency, criticism, and **resistance** from political and moral discourses.[4]

• See also *cognition, information, knowledge management, post-structuralism, science*

Knowledge management

The verb 'to manage' is increasingly applied to any object, resource, risk, or threat—we can speak of management of the oceans, management of emotion, and management of forest fires. It is not surprising then that knowledge can be the subject of management, most especially in organizations and economies that vitally depend on **knowledge** for their success. Knowledge management (sometimes labelled 'KM') is concerned with making sure that knowledge is effectively deployed in an organization, that people have the right knowledge to deal with the challenges they face, and that knowledge is used to generate value for an organization and its clients. In many organizations, people and departments solve problems that have already been solved elsewhere by someone else; they miss opportunities because they do not know that someone has the knowledge to take advantage of them; and they make costly mistakes, unaware that these same mistakes have been encountered by others who have already learnt how to avoid them.[5]

Knowledge management is sometimes confused with **information** management. Its task is then seen as building up complex databases of activities, solutions, ideas, and potential improvements so that different members of an organization can access them when needed. This has proved difficult or ineffective, partly because it results in information *overload*. When confronted with difficult situations, most people are deterred from using complex databases, preferring instead to ask somebody who has dealt with similar situations before. They seek advice rather than data, and advice comes in the shape of stories, recipes, and narrative knowledge rather than databases. Often, however, they do not know that there is someone who has the required knowledge to help them handle the situation or who may supply the key to such knowledge. This is where **networks** and **communities of practice** become very effective—a few contacts generally lead to the person who is able and willing to help. Recent work on knowledge management has emphasized more traditional, less formalized ways of sharing knowledge, such as trading experiences, stories, recipes, and informal know-how. It has also emphasized knowledge as a process rather than as an object to be traded. The concepts of **learning organization** and organizational **learning** have proved helpful in this regard, emphasizing the retention of knowledge in an organization, even if key individuals who possess knowledge leave.

Knowledge management, like many other uses of the word 'management', has a tendency to present rather too cosy a picture of the entity being managed.[6] It severely underplays the political dimension of organizational

---

[1] Tsoukas, 1998a; Tsoukas and Hatch, 2001.   [2] Foucault, 1980.   [3] Townley, 1993a; 1993b.   [4] Feldman, 1999.   [5] Scarbrough et al., 1999; Swan and Scarbrough, 2001.   [6] Alvesson and Karreman, 2001.

knowledge, the fact that a great deal of **power** rests on monopolizing certain domains of knowledge and preserving the exclusivity of handling certain types of problems. Far from 'sharing' knowledge happily after the image of a village square café, individuals, groups, and organizations that establish a certain privilege or advantage from knowledge will generally seek to protect and shield this from others.

Managing knowledge, like nearly every other form of management, is a set of activities that takes place against **resistance**. This is one of the reasons for the success of Foucault's concept of power/knowledge that treats knowledge as an entity that is inseparable from the workings of power in every society rather than a neutral resource to be effectively deployed and managed.[1]

[1] Foucault, 1980.

L

Labour

Labour is predominantly an economic category for **work**, the ability of human beings to generate value by using their creative capacities to mould nature to their **needs**. Marx argued that labour is what makes humans distinctly human, and that people's intellectual, spiritual, and technical capacities develop through labour.[1] Capitalist production impoverishes labour, **alienating** men and women from their products, from their creative activities, and from their fellow humans. Instead of marking the proud and joyful deployment of people's creative powers, labour comes to be equated with oppression, exploitation, and dehumanization. In such labour, man becomes like an animal, and only in **leisure** can he obtain a taste of freedom and fulfilment. Marx's uncompromising equation of labour with what makes man distinctly human has been criticized, or at least complemented by other uniquely human qualities, notably **symbolic** communication and **desire**. Nevertheless, Marx's contention that the social organization of labour has profound repercussions on every society's cultural, religious, legal, and family **institutions** has found substantial support in the work of anthropologists. In the last twenty years, many sociologists have been moving away from work towards leisure and consumption activities as the area of life where **identities** are shaped.

In addition to its economic meaning, however, the word labour has had a long-standing association with pain and hardship, evident in its application to childbirth. This meaning is also clear in the use of the word labour to describe the social **class** who rely on their ability to work for their livelihoods. In this sense, labour is always juxtaposed to **capital**, the class owning the means of production. As a political party in the United Kingdom, Labour has traditionally been associated with the interests of the working class, whose representatives, the trade unions, set it up.

Labour has traditionally been divided up into manual and intellectual, blue-collar and white-collar—the latter has traditionally enjoyed superior **status** to the former, even when wages and the actual conditions of work have not been superior. In one of the enduring paradoxes of the British class structure, white-collar employees consistently allied themselves with their employers and to a considerable extent viewed themselves as middle class.[2] Following the publication of Arlie Hochschild's *The Managed Heart: Commercialization of Human Feeling*,[3] it has become increasingly common to talk of other types of labour, such as **emotional labour**, **aesthetic** labour, or even narrative labour. Much of the work that people do today in industrialized countries relies on manipulation of symbols, the tapping of keys on computers, the display of appropriate emotional or physical attributes, or the striking of deals with others, activities that are not what are associated with traditional notions of labour.

• See also *work*

Labour Process Theory

Labour Process Theory is a tradition in industrial sociology focusing on the politics of production at the workplace that has sustained the Marxist argument regarding the antagonistic

---

[1] Marx, 1844/1972.　[2] Goldthorpe et al., 1969; Lockwood, 1958; Smith, Knights, and Willmott, 1991.　[3] Hochschild, 1983.

class position between **labour** and **capital**. This tradition is often seen as having been spawned by Harry Braverman's influential book *Labor and Monopoly Capital*, though many of its arguments are prefigured in earlier studies in the sociology of work, like those of Roy and Beynon.[1] Braverman's crucial argument was that **Scientific Management** represents monopoly capitalism's attempt to wrest **control** of production from the workers, through a systematic **deskilling**, a fragmentation of the labour process, and a divorce of conception of the productive process from its execution. Managers, argued Braverman, have used Taylorist (see **Scientific Management**) techniques to reduce the worker to a passive role where his or her only choice is whether to do the work or not. Control is thus incorporated within the process of production itself, notably in assembly lines and highly standardized work.

Subsequent contributions to the Labour Process Theory, such as those of Burawoy and Edwards,[2] emphasized that there is a wide range of strategies and tactics used by workers to reclaim a degree of control over the workplace. Other theorists have argued that the decline of traditional **skills** (such as those of machinists, bakers, tailors, etc.) has been partly compensated by new types of skills commensurate with a service economy that places a high premium on communication, appearance, and emotional displays. The concept of control itself has come under increasing scrutiny, following Friedman's distinction between two core types, direct control and responsible autonomy, a form of worker empowerment in return for a fundamental internalization of management **values** and aims.[3]

Labour Process Theory assumed an institutional basis through an annual conference that has been taking place in the UK since the 1980s, generating a very substantial amount of scholarship that has extended into many different industries (including white-collar ones, and the service sector including the professions) and has examined the effects of a wide range of factors in the labour process, including **globalization**, the emergence of new technologies, and new managerial techniques. The enduring feature of this scholarship has been a sharp interest in diverse forms of worker **resistance** even in times of declining working-class unionization and militancy. Different forms of resistance have been examined, including whistle-blowing, cynical withdrawal, and exit.[4]

Over the past fifteen years, Labour Process Theory has been forced to respond to the linguistic turn (see **language**) in social and management studies. A number of scholars have viewed **postmodernism** and its attendant preoccupation with discourse and the **social construction of reality** as 'fatal distractions' and have remained loyal to the traditional concerns of Labour Process Theory;[5] many others, however, have moved in the direction of **Critical Management Studies**, emphasizing the importance of **discourse** and seeking to denaturalize well-established entities like class, control, power, oppression, and exploitation.

Language

Wittgenstein's much-quoted 'the limits of my language mean the limits of my world' has become one of the emblematic statements of the twentieth century.[6] Throughout that century there was an increasing interest in language on the part of philosophy, the arts, and the human sciences, an interest that it would be fair to say turned into a preoccupation and even an obsession. Whether one looks at philosophy, psychology, economics, politics, anthropology, or sociology, one is struck by what is now referred to as 'the linguistic turn',[7] the view that

---

[1] Braverman, 1974; Roy, 1960; Beynon, 1973. [2] Burawoy, 1979; 1985; Edwards, 1979. [3] Friedman, 1977. [4] Friedman, 2004; Sewell and Wilkinson, 1992; Smith, 2006; Taylor and Bain, 2005; Tinker, 2002. [5] See, for example Ackroyd and Thompson, 1999; Thompson, 1993; Thompson and Ackroyd, 1995. [6] Wittgenstein, 1922/1961. [7] Alvesson and Karreman, 2000; Rorty, 1967; 1992.

knowledge and truth are created not just *through* language but *by* language; that language is not 'merely' a means of expression but a central faculty of the human mind, directly shaping the ways we think and feel. Far from describing an already existing world, language helps us construct a world, establishing new distinctions and constructing new realities. The contributions of Derrida and Foucault were decisive.[1]

Language is also seen as enabling us to contest particular views of the world and challenge particular **power** blocks. Language does not merely confer power on those who can use it skilfully, but it embodies and even perpetuates power relations, privileges, and social injustices. The use of particular words, like 'disabled', 'unemployed', 'homeless', and so forth, establishes categories of what is normal and what is abnormal that bolster social inequalities. This also reveals that language is not so different from **action**— indeed many uses of language *are* actions. 'I pronounce you man and wife' are words that, in the right circumstances, effect a marriage. They also perpetuate a power relation which defines the woman ('wife') in terms of her relation to the man ('man') rather than the other way round, leaving no doubt as to who is meant to be the dominant partner in this relation. Whether or not this is the case with most actual couples is a debatable point.

The linguistic turn has had a profound effect on our understanding of many social and psychological phenomena. It is notable how many cultural phenomena have come to be viewed through the prism of language, as *texts*— consider, for example, the shining surface of a motor car, a pair of running shoes, a photograph, a building, or a set of clothes, all of which can be viewed, analysed, and deconstructed as texts. The same linguistic turn has had a profound influence on our understanding of organizations.[2] Organizations can now hardly be viewed as objective realities independent of the discourses that construct them and negotiate them. At the most daring and extreme, some theorists have argued that organizations are themselves discursive effects, subnarratives within the **grand narrative** of **modernity**.[3] From this perspective, they share the fate of other effects of modernity, the sovereign self, the body, sexuality, and indeed 'facts', as discursive constructions. They are thus denaturalized—having been things, they become ways of looking at things. Organizations are then viewed as *texts*, which can be interpreted, analysed, and deconstructed as if they were plays, novels, narratives, or consumer objects.[4]

Other theorists have looked at **discourse** as constitutive of organizations but not as fully constituting them. From this perspective, 'buildings are built, products are manufactured, services are rendered beyond (and because of) all this organizational talk. Thus discourse and talk are central to organization and organizing . . . but so is non-discursive action.'[5] Discursive formations may appear in many forms, some of which are privileged in organizations over others, yet they do not exhaust the domain of organization. Important as it is to study discourse, it is not enough for an understanding of organizational or social practices.[6] In either case, theorists of organizations have increasingly turned their attention in the ways language is used in different written and spoken texts, including different formal and informal documents, stories, metaphors, and so forth. **Communication** is thus viewed not as one of many (and at times secondary) organizational processes but as a core process through which meanings are negotiated, 'facts' are established and challenged, and realities are constructed. 'Narratology' has emerged as a set of techniques for analysing organizational texts (rather than organizations as texts) which include conversations, stories,

---

[1] Derrida, 1973; Foucault, 1966/1970; 1969/1972.   [2] Grant et al., 2004; Westwood and Linstead, 2001.   [3] For a good discussion, see Czarniawska, 1997.   [4] For a powerful account of this approach, see Thatchenkery, 2001.   [5] Hardy et al., 1998, p. 63.   [6] See Fairclough, 1992; 1995.

pictures, metaphors, documents, websites, and so forth. Chief among these techniques has been **deconstruction** which has proved itself a powerful method for questioning different texts and especially for revealing assumptions that are embedded and hidden within particular discursive formations.

It would be fair to say that this present text is itself a product of the linguistic turn in the human sciences, one that offers a close scrutiny of the ways particular terms are used in different texts. Unlike conventional dictionaries that seek to offer authoritative definitions of words and encyclopedias that bring together many of the known facts about specific topics, the approach adopted here is one of trying to display how particular words are used in different social science texts and to reveal some of the problematic assumptions they embody.

So if we are to apply the same critical enquiry to 'language' itself, we must ask ourselves if there is a downside to today's preoccupation with this concept. Is there any harm in being sensitive to the way words are used and suspicious about the hidden assumptions they embody? Critics of deconstruction (or, more generally, critics of **postmodernism**) have pointed out that deconstruction can become a somewhat self-indulgent preoccupation with texts, disregarding all social contexts and the uses to which texts are put. One gets a very partial sense of the taste of food if one investigates it by reading recipe books (still less, by looking at the pictures) and watching cookery programmes on television without ever letting it cross one's lips. Preoccupation with language can 'reduce' all forms of oppression and exploitation to discursive practices, such as categorization, labelling, silencing, and a denial of **voice**. Denying a person or a group a voice can then become a more serious offence than exploiting them economically or oppressing them politically. This risks turning deconstruction along with other practices of discourse

analysis into a highly virtuosic and narcissistic exercise in powerless rhetoric.[1] Finally, it is often forgotten that large parts of the human and social sciences, most notably economics and a large part of psychology, have remained signally oblivious to the linguistic turn, as do substantial parts of organizational and management studies that remain wedded to a positivist approach.

• See also *deconstruction, discourse, modernism and modernity, narratives and narrative knowledge, postmodernism*

Leadership

The origins of the English word 'leadership' lie in its Old German and Old English roots *lidan* (to go) and *lithan* (to travel), and it has come to be defined as 'to set a direction', 'to go at the head', 'to initiate, to guide', or 'to cause to act'. Although leadership has always been an element of organization—and there are desperately few examples of non-hierarchical organizations—the nature of that leadership and our interest in it has changed across time and space. Plato and Sun Tzu are traditionally regarded as amongst the earliest systematic writers on leadership but perhaps it is with Machiavelli's *The Prince* that the contemporary western fascination with leadership really begins.[2] Written at a time of interminable civil war and invasion, *The Prince* sought to demonstrate two things: first, that successful leadership required the leader to do whatever was necessary for the public good; second, that the contemporary claims of various political and (Christian) religious leaders to morally principled leadership were disingenuous. Machiavelli's work was banned by the papacy and has since been associated with amoral or immoral leadership, despite his clear demonstration that respectable rhetoric covers nefarious actions. It is worth asking whether

---

[1] For accounts of the hidden dangers of the linguistic turn, see Craib, 1997; Feldman, 1998; 1999; Parker, 1995; 2002.   [2] Machiavelli, 1513/1961.

anything much has changed since Machiavelli's time.

For some authors the answer is—a lot. James McGregor Burns for example, suggested that we could distinguish between two aspects of leadership that Machiavelli, amongst others, conflated into one.[1] First, we could separate *transactional* from *transformational* leadership. The former relates to the normal exchange relationship that ensured the mundane aspects of work occurred every day: followers executed tasks as required because leaders paid them or rewarded them in some similar negotiated framework. Transformational leadership, however, implied that the leader could lift the mundane and self-regarding attitudes of followers to new and collective heights, not by paying people but by motivating them to want to go beyond the norm. For Burns, transformational leaders were always **charismatic** but not all charismatics were transformational because some charismatics were self-regarding or unethical in intent. This division between ethical and unethical leaders is an analytic quagmire since to the followers of Hitler or Osama bin Laden, their leaders probably appear very ethical—they just don't fit into conventional Christian norms of **ethics**. In other words, ethics probably are important to successful leadership—but it is the symmetry between the ethics of leaders and their followers that we need to understand, not whether enemies of the leader regard him or her as unethical according to their own standards.[2]

Beyond the question of **ethical** behaviour by leaders it is also worth questioning the extent to which leaders actually make much difference to their organizations or countries. For example, we conventionally attribute causality to leaders for all kinds of organizational outcomes with little if any proof. Indeed, scholars such as James Meindl, working in the Romance of Leadership area, suggested that if success or failure occurs we automatically assume that individual leaders are responsible—but if organizational performance is just 'average' we tend to ignore the leaders altogether.[3] That kind of scepticism about the utility of leaders is clearly not the framework for many of the so-called Heathrow Leadership books that claim to guarantee success if the reader follows the ten-point plan to world domination, but even the best of these books tend to be undermined by methodological problems. For instance, they tend to concentrate on success stories and assume that success is derived from 'visionary leadership' or 'strong **cultures**' and so on, but it is just as likely that the latter are manifestations of successful organizations rather than the causes of them. In short, the success of an organization—after it has become successful—is explained through the remarkable decisions of its CEO. But success is never predictable, nor is there usually a self-evident causal connection between the CEO and success; there is a correlation between the two, but that is a long way short of causality.

This 'halo' effect is compounded by refusing to compare successful with failed leaders and organizations, and by generating data on success on the basis of retrospective interviews with participants. This is the equivalent of the proverbial drunks looking for their keys under the lamplight, not because that is where the keys are but because that is where the light is. This halo effect is most conspicuous when former 'heroes' are portrayed as false gods. Take Rosenzweig's analysis of the response of the American public to President George W. Bush's apparent actions: his popularity rose with the beginning of the Iraq War, 9/11, and the discovery of Saddam Hussein, and it declined with the continuing war in Iraq and Hurricane Katrina.[4] We might expect that, but what we wouldn't expect—unless we accept that the halo effect is working—is that his handling of the economy is perceived to rise and fall in line with the popularity and unpopularity of the war in Iraq.

---

[1] Burns, 1978.   [2] Bratton, Grint, and Nelson, 2005.   [3] Meindl and Ehrlich, 1987; Meindl, Ehrlich, and Dukerich, 1985.
[4] Rosenzweig, 2007.

Even when we have comparative accounts of success and failure this correlational problem can still undermine robust analysis of leadership. Thus, for example, where men are defined as 'strong', the same behaviour exhibited by a woman is more likely to be considered 'aggressive'; and where women leaders demonstrate 'weakness' if they cry in public, men are more likely to be understood as demonstrating emotional intelligence or their 'positive feminine side'.

The romantic attachment to—and disparagement of—leaders reveals another aspect beyond the methodological poverty of many leadership writings, and that is the role leaders play in taking responsibility. Thus CEOs, generals, football managers, and political leaders are regularly fêted and blamed for all kinds of outcomes that may well have little to do with their actions or inactions. Durkheim suggested that this might well relate to the sacred nature of leadership, in the sense that leaders are treated both as gods and scapegoats for collective success and failure respectively, and this enables followers to remain non-responsible.[1] In sum, leadership is a Faustian pact that leaders make with their followers in which the rewards and privileges of current office are balanced by the probability that personal sacrifice will be required at some indefinite point in the future. It is precisely this exchange of reward for responsibility which prompts Heifetz to argue that leaders, since they cannot solve the collective problems of followers alone, must resist that very temptation and persuade followers that it is their collective duty to resolve collective problems.[2]

This shift from individual leader to collective leadership can also be tracked across time through the literature. Thus, if Carlyle's Victorian rant in favour of heroic 'men' as the sole movers of history is the high point of the Great Man theory we have now reached the opposite side of the circle to a point where Collaborative and Distributive Leadership are the words which prevail as normatively appropriate in contemporary circles.[3] But note that such a swing mirrors the same romantic problems associated with the heroic and charismatic model of former times—somehow, although it is never clear how precisely, the new collective approach to leadership will solve all the organizational problems left over by the vanity and hubris inherent in individual heroes. This schizophrenic attitude to leadership is also evident in the way many writers are rightly sceptical of the role of individual leaders, if not leadership more generally, but then persist in explaining all situations as the consequence of the actions of individual leaders. *Plus ça change.*

• See also *authority, charisma, followership, moral leadership*

KEITH GRINT, CRANFIELD UNIVERSITY

Learning

Learning is the capacity to doubt those things that seem unquestionable. The ability to learn is a fundamental human quality that allows us to engage with and to change our world. Learning implies an awareness of the limitations of existing **knowledge** as well as the ability to transform knowledge through new **information** or insight. In his book, *Steps to an Ecology of Mind*, Gregory Bateson defines learning at four different 'levels'.[4] Zero learning is based on predictable or specific responses that do not benefit from trial and error. This level of learning is simply about response, there is no reflection on **action**, and recognizing a wrong response would not contribute to a future skill. Learning 1 (L1) acknowledges **change** as a result of trial and error within a set of alternatives. Correction through trial and error has implications for future action. L1 signifies a shift from response to reinforcement, and therefore highlights a process of habituation. Learning 2 (L2) implies flexibility in the potential to act as opposed to reinforcement of

---

[1] Durkheim, 1973. [2] Heifetz, 1994. [3] Grint, 2005b. [4] Bateson, 1972.

action. It is therefore a change in the set of alternatives from which a **choice** is made. It signifies the capacity to 'learn how to learn', highlighting a shift in the frameworks from which choices are made. Learning 3 (L3) implies change in the underlying premises and belief systems that form frameworks. L3 signifies a capacity to examine and to transform the discursive regime within which action is based.

In organizations, learning is understood both as improvement in performance and as a continuous process of transformation. Learning is related to improvements in the ways in which a **role** or task is performed, individually or collectively. It is also a potential outcome of the relationship between reflection and action over time. Organizations need to be good at learning because of the importance of generating, appropriating, and exploiting knowledge for growth and renewal. A great deal has been written about the relationship between learning and organizing. Two particularly influential thinkers in this area are Donald Schön and Chris Argyris. Schön saw the need for societies to 'become adept at learning', to respond to changing situations and requirements; to invent and develop institutions as 'learning systems'—systems that are capable of bringing about their own continuing transformation.[1] Argyris and Schön developed the distinction between single-loop and double-loop learning, which illustrated the difference between transformational and non-transformational learning.[2] 'Single-loop learning occurs when errors are corrected without changing the underlying programme. Double-loop learning occurs when an error is corrected by first altering the underlying programme. For example, a thermostat is a single-loop learner. It is programmed to turn the heat up or down depending upon the temperature. A thermostat would be a double-loop learner if it questioned its existing programme that it should measure heat.'[3]

There are two particular ways in which the relationship between learning and organizing has been approached. The '**learning organization**' refers to an entity, an ideal type of organization which has the capacity to learn effectively and therefore to prosper. 'Organizational learning', on the other hand, refers to the study of learning processes of and within organizations, in order to understand and critique what is taking place.[4] The concept of 'the Learning Organization' was developed by Peter Senge in the USA and Mike Pedler and colleagues in the UK.[5] In his popular and influential book, *The Fifth Discipline: the Art and Practice of the Learning Organization*, Senge saw learning organizations as environments where 'people continually expand their capacity to create the results they truly desire, where new and expansive patterns of thinking are nurtured, where collective aspiration is set free, and where people are continually learning to see the whole together'. Similarly, the 'learning company' is 'an organization that facilitates the learning of all its members and continuously transforms itself'.[6] The term 'organizational learning' does not mean that an organization is itself learning, but learning and organizing are related. This connection has been captured to good effect by Gherardi and Nicolini when they talk about organizational learning as 'learning-in-organizing', recognizing that learning and organizing 'are not distinct activities within a practice'.[7] Efforts to understand organizational learning have been assisted in recent years by a general shift of interest towards understanding social processes of learning. An increasing focus on **emotion** and learning, collective learning, situated learning, **communities of practice**, and on politics, power relations, and learning, has helped to shift the academic study of organizational learning away from individuals' learning within organizations and towards social, political, and relational interpretations of learning and organizing.

---

[1] Schön, 1973.   [2] Argyris and Schön, 1978.   [3] Argyris, 2007.   [4] Easterby-Smith and Lyles, 2003.   [5] Senge, 1990; Pedler, Burgoyne, and Boydell, 1997.   [6] Ibid.   [7] Gherardi and Nicolini, 2001.

There have been various criticisms of 'learning' perspectives, particularly that it is not possible to transform bureaucratic organizations by learning initiatives alone and that the whole concept of organizational learning remains rather vague (this can be seen as an advantage as well as a criticism). Learning is likely to remain a particularly useful concept in relation to organizations because it is a lens through which researchers and practitioners can view the many and varied emotional and political dynamics from which our seemingly stable and rational organizations are made. One of the most interesting aspects of the relationship between learning and organizing is that learning is at the same time both desired and avoided in organizations. For example, leaders want to see a **structure** in place that supports improvements in individual practice and organizational **performance**. However, they also resist and avoid potential changes that derive from learning if these confront existing **power** relations and threaten 'the way we do things here'. Our attempts to define what should be learned (in order to police and to perpetuate 'the way we do things here') are double-edged. As soon as organizational members have identified a range of **competences** that indicate what should be known within particular roles, the limitations of that combination of competences become apparent. While it is often useful to prescribe a finite set of competences, skills, and behaviours to a role, it is equally important to realize that any prescriptive combination is as likely to inhibit as well as underpin knowledge, **innovation**, and further learning.

• See also **competences, knowledge, learning organization**

RUSS VINCE, UNIVERSITY OF BATH

(The) learning organization

The terms 'learning organization' and 'organizational learning' were probably used more interchangeably when the popularity of the term learning organization started to grow in the 1990s, but today most scholars draw a distinction between them. The most common way to differentiate between them is that organizational **learning** involves naturally occurring processes in organizations while the learning organization is a type of **organization** that demands special activities and efforts to realize. Another difference often mentioned is that organizational learning is the more academic concept, while learning organization is for consultants and the so-called practitioners. Such a distinction might be dangerous, though, since it may leave learning organization unnoticed and exempt from critical examination.

The idea of the 'learning organization' is often attributed to Peter Senge and his enormously successful book, *The Fifth Discipline*,[1] but several others used the term long before him both in educational science and in management studies. It is more difficult to say something definitive about the substance of the learning organization, which as many researchers and practitioners have recognized is extremely ambiguous and difficult to implement in practice. In my own work, I have sought to find out what authors who write about the learning organization, making use of it in their theories and practice, mean when they employ the concept as part of an inductive language game.[2]

My analysis revealed four different ways in which the learning organization is widely used. (i) *Learning at work*, i.e. learning takes place while work is being executed, instead of sending the employees on formal courses. (ii) *Learning climate* which encourages all employees to experiment and learn from their successes and failures, systematically reflecting upon them together with their workmates. (iii) *Learning structure* which is organic and decentralized, enabling employees to take necessary decisions fast; employees work in **teams** and, although

---

[1] Senge, 1990. [2] Örtenblad, 2002b.

they may be specialists, they learn to execute each other's tasks effectively (for example helping customers when the real expert is busy). Team members are supposed to help each other out if required; they are capable of doing so since they have a sound understanding of each other's work as well as an understanding of their organization's overall functioning. (iv) *Old organizational learning*, meaning that individuals in an organization learn as agents for their organization, either through single-loop or through double-loop learning (see **learning**).[1] But in order to call this learning *organizational* learning, it must be stored in the organizational memory, which consists of routines, **rules**, standards, procedures, manuals, etc. This enriched memory then becomes the starting point for the learning that follows, when individuals again learn as agents for their organization, but now with enhanced directions about what to learn. I have called this perspective *old* organizational learning, in contrast to the social or cultural perspective on organizational learning which refers to *new* organizational learning.[2] This perspective (which does not go under the heading of 'learning organization') argues that learning takes place at the level of a collective or a **community of practice** rather than those of the individual or the organization as such, and that all **knowledge** is highly contextual. This was not the case in any of the perspectives I identified in my own study. In fact, in none of these four perspectives did 'the learning organization' feature as something entirely new.

Much of what is written about the idea of the learning organization makes one think of paradise. The proponents praise the concept and promise that it will bring increased effectiveness and competitiveness, while threatening an early death for those organizations that choose not to implement it. There are, however, also those who have criticized the idea, either focusing on Senge's influential book or looking more broadly at the literature on the subject.

Opponents argue that the learning organization promises a humanistic workplace, but cannot live up to it.[3]

Critics argue that by offering managers **control** of informal networks, the learning organization enhances their power. Since employees are supposed to learn to execute each other's work tasks, the employer is less dependent on any single individual in the organization. Employees are supposed to reflect critically, but only superficially; they are not really allowed to question the learning organization **ideology**. Differences are marginalized and the learning organization does not value the unique **experience** or **needs** of each individual. Not everyone is comfortable in less structured organizations and participatory structures can be threatening to some people. People may feel unsafe and might defend themselves and their tacit knowledge from being translated into objective, collective knowledge.

The learning organization threatens the **boundaries** that most people place between their work and their private experiences. It assumes that everyone is interested in being part of something larger, that is the organization they work for, and that everyone is obsessed with learning—at least in order to keep their positions. But not everyone wants to learn constantly. Learning means uncertainty, insecurity, and the prospect of failure. Employees are also assumed to take more responsibility for corporate problems, at the expense of other commitments such as towards family and friends. Survival is supposed to be the ultimate **goal** for all organizations, but the question of whether it is good from the point of view of society as a whole that a particular organization survive is not raised. Perhaps organizational survival is not desirable in all cases.

Although the idea of the learning organization must continuously be critically examined there is something unhealthy about the debate

---

[1] Argyris and Schön, 1978.   [2] Cook and Yanow, 1993.   [3] For an overview, see Örtenblad, 2002a.

on the merits of the learning organization. This has now become extremely polarized and confused; it is often difficult to know exactly *what* the critics are criticizing or which of the four perspectives on the learning organization described above its proponents are advocating. More nuanced work on the learning organization, possibly using the starting point in the four perspectives, is needed, leading to a critical engagement or a synthesis of the optimistic view and the critical views.[1]

• See also *community and community of practice, knowledge, knowledge management, learning*

ANDERS ÖRTENBLAD, HALMSTAD UNIVERSITY, SWEDEN

Legitimacy

Legitimacy is an important term with social, political, legal, and psychological dimensions. Max Weber used the term to distinguish between coercion and legitimate **power**, or **authority**, where subordinates recognize the right of the superior to demand compliance.[2] He viewed charisma, tradition, and rational systems of law as alternative foundations of legitimacy. The issue of the legitimacy of organizations (including governments, companies, charities, political parties, mass media, trade unions, and so forth) themselves is of central concern to **institutional theory** which looks at the cultural environment in which organizations function. In this context, Suchman defines legitimacy as 'a generalized perception or assumption that the actions of an entity are desirable, proper, or appropriate within some socially constructed system of norms, values, beliefs and definitions'.[3] Legitimacy, according to this view, is achieved through three types of assessments, pragmatic, moral, and cognitive, according to which an audience or a public judge whether an organization is beneficial, worthy, and inevitable,

respectively. Cognitive legitimacy ensures that an organization will avoid questioning; in order, however, for it to mobilize positive commitments it must enjoy moral and pragmatic legitimacy.

Different organizations are judged by different standards; organizations like charities, religious groups, or companies that strongly proclaim their advocacy of environmental or other ideals invite stronger challenges on their **values** and **performance**.[4] To meet these challenges, organizations deploy different substantive and symbolic strategies aimed at enhancing their legitimacy and spreading the risk of sudden collapses of public trust. In doing so, they often appeal to different audiences, with different norms, values, and material interests, who are, therefore, likely to make different assessments of legitimacy. The result is that most organizations face periodic charges of hypocrisy from at least some quarters.

In his powerfully insightful book, *The Organization of Hypocrisy*, Nils Brunsson argues that, when faced with inconsistent or contradictory norms, organizations must adopt a policy where **conflicts** and problems are acknowledged and acted out in public. Far from seeking to eliminate problems, Brunsson argues that 'insoluble problems are a splendid vehicle for the reflection of many ideas and values. They can be endlessly discussed from all sorts of angles and without ever reaching a conclusion. Solutions that can reflect an equal variety of ideas are rare indeed.'[5] Charges of hypocrisy can then be defused by openly acknowledging contradictions and troubles rather than maintaining a profile of total rectitude and consistency. In this way, transparency emerges as the basis of organizational and even social legitimacy; hype, spin, dishonesty, manipulation, deception, fraud, ruses, trickery, scams, duplicity, cheating, lying, deceit, cons, corruption, and, above all, cover-ups are the cardinal sins of which

---

[1] For one such example, see Driver, 2002. [2] Weber, 1946. [3] Suchman, 1995, p. 572. [4] Ashford and Gibbs, 1990. [5] Brunsson, 2003, p. 23.

organizations can be found guilty in a culture emphasizing transparency—exposé by journalists, whistle-blowers, or saboteurs is the major risk.[1] This, in the view of some commentators, has led to a wider crisis of legitimization or legitimacy in many Western societies, where citizens mistrust virtually every economic, political, or social **institution**.[2]

Legitimacy is also an important concept in psychology, where it refers to the right of an individual to speak with authority, to be a leader, or to demand respect. This is related to various fantasies and anxieties that people experience early in life in relation to their parents and especially their father. These may include questions like 'Am I the legitimate child of my parents?', 'Is my "father" my real father?', and 'Does he have a right to judge me or to punish me?' Anxieties about legitimacy often resurface in later relations with leaders and various experts, such as legal advisers, physicians, or consultants, taking various forms: 'Does he know what he is talking about?', 'Has she tricked me?', 'Has he lied about his past or his qualifications?', 'Has she got an ulterior motive?'[3] Such anxieties sometimes affect people about their own legitimacy in what is known as the 'impostor syndrome'.[4] Such individuals may then worry (usually unnecessarily) that they are fakes, whose past success was not deserved. The classic symptoms of this impostor syndrome are fear of failure, fear of success, perfectionism, procrastination, and workaholism.

Love

Love is not generally seen as a core concept in the social sciences, though, with increasing emphasis on **emotions**, it has started to make some tentative appearances. Still, what would human life be without love? And what would poets do, if they did not create verses like these:

Love, invincible in battle,
Love, You who squanders the riches of the
   wealthy!
Who keeps vigil on the maiden's soft cheek,
Who roams the seas and pastures wild,
Who casts your magic on all you touch.
No god can escape your hold; nor any human
   whose life lasts but a day.

    (Sophocles, *Antigone* 781—translation Y.G.)

Love hardly roams the fields of social sciences. We do encounter it sometimes under strange guises of other, more scientific-sounding ideas, such as solidarity, affiliation or attachment. Sociology has always taken a keen interest in social bonds (from Marx's class solidarity to Durkheim's collective effervescence to Tönnies's distinction between community and society) but these bonds have rarely been put down to love.

One discipline that has long placed a strong emphasis on love is psychoanalysis. Freud saw love as the affective aspect of **sexuality**, capable of bringing people together in a wide range of social relationships, ranging from sexual passion to friendship, and from group solidarity to collective infatuation with a leader. Libido, the sexual energy behind love, is viewed as a force driving human beings towards pleasure,[5] but it also forges union with others; libido is a remarkably malleable entity capable of turning into sexual **desire**, creative urge, social bonds, romantic attachments, or even self-love through the phenomenon of **narcissism.** In his later work, Freud came to view love, now subsumed under the broader category of Eros, as the principle sustaining all life on earth by ever striving towards union as against the death instinct's unrelenting endeavour to return all life to inorganic inertia. In this view, Freud seemed to meet the pre-Socratic philosopher Empedocles of Acraga who had argued that life is the product of an eternal struggle between love and strife.

---

[1] Oliver, 2004; Tapscott and Ticoll, 2003; Vattimo, 1992.   [2] Glynn, 2000; Habermas, 1975; Kittrie, 1995.   [3] Chasseguet-Smirgel, 1976; Gabriel, 1997.   [4] Kets de Vries, 2005.   [5] Freud, 1905/1977.

While love has remained an important interest in psychoanalysis, many of Freud's heirs (starting with C. G. Jung) felt that he had overemphasized the importance of sexuality and turned their attention away from what they viewed as a biological essentialism of instincts towards different fantasies and relations. One of Freud's key concepts, *ambivalence*, the simultaneous combination of love with hate, attraction, and repulsion for the same object, has since acquired some currency.[1] Ambivalence is now widely used to describe many people's simultaneous attachment to and dislike of their jobs and their organizations, especially in our times when many feel that they have a choice as to the work they do.[2]

One sociologist who has explored love as a **social construction** has been Stevi Jackson.[3] Jackson developed a theory of love as part of a romantic discourse which juxtaposes 'being in love' to longer-term affection, arguing that this contrast is a feature of an **ideology** sustaining women's subordination in contemporary societies. According to this view, the mass media and other institutions have promoted a way of talking about love as a uniquely personal and mysterious force that seduces women and inhibits their participation as equals in social relations. Jackson's approach has been strongly critiqued from a psychoanalytic perspective by Ian Craib who argued that 'the social constructionist conception of emotions proffered by Jackson gives priority to **cognition**. However, if we think of emotions as having a life of their own, which might be in contradiction to, or expressed fully or partially through our cognition to different degrees in different times, we can think through all sorts of situations with which most people must be familiar: experiencing **feelings** we cannot express to our satisfaction; having feelings that we can express but that others find difficult to understand; and

most important perhaps, the regular **experience** of contradictions between our thoughts and our feelings.'[4]

In the area of organizations, love has featured primarily in three contexts. First, there has been some scholarship in romantic attachments at work. Much of this has been less interested in love itself and more concerned with the consequences of such attachments for organizational performance and their likelihood of degenerating into **sexual harassment**.[5] A few theorists have been more interested in the way people experience romantic relations in the workplace and how they convert them into stories.[6] Second, there has been an increasing interest in the love that binds **leaders** to their followers, which sometimes approaches erotic infatuation.[7] Third, there has been a muted attempt to link love to customer service,[8] usually subsumed under the label of **emotional labour**, the experience and display of emotions appropriate to different social situations.

There is yet another way in which organizations and love come together—organizations as objects of love and affection. Cynics may reject such a position out of hand; **institutional** theorists may seek to accommodate it in the view of organizations as institutions, i.e. objects of **value**. But certain theorists view organizations as quite literally objects of love. Schwartz argued that we love organizations inasmuch as they make us feel good about ourselves by rewarding our **narcissistic** desires.[9] We feel good about an organization that makes us feel good about ourselves. Sims goes a step further.[10] Starting with the story of the velveteen rabbit, a children's toy that comes alive whenever a child loves it, Sims asks why the same may not be true of organizations, some of which generate extraordinary amounts of affection and loyalty among their participants, while others languish as mere objects of

---

[1] Smelser, 1998b.   [2] Casey, 1999; Hoggett, 2006; Höpfl, 1995; Sturdy, 1998.   [3] Jackson, 1993.   [4] Craib, 1998, p. 110.   [5] See e.g. Mainiero, 1986; Pierce, 1998; Powell and Foley, 1998.   [6] Mano and Gabriel, 2006.   [7] Gabriel, 1997; Lindholm, 1988.   [8] Harrison, 1987.   [9] Schwartz, 1987.   [10] Sims, 2004.

instrumental usefulness and emotional indifference. People may then love organizations every bit as passionately as they love their pets, their toys, their children, and their work. In Sims's argument, there is the germ of the idea that organizations are not merely **socially constructed** entities but also emotionally constructed ones.

Love, and one would have to add hate, turn them into living objects.

All in all, in contrast to myth, literature, art, and religion where love is a vital force, often in competition with **power**, bringing bliss, despair, and madness to humans, it has still to gain its rightful position in the social sciences.

McDonaldization

McDonaldization is a term used by George Ritzer to describe a more advanced stage of Taylorism that extends the principles of **Scientific Management** (especially standardization and divorce of conception from execution) and **Fordism** to service industries and seeks to **control** not only behaviour but also the **emotional** displays of employees at the workplace.[1] McDonaldization represents a culmination of the **rationalization** of production and consumption that has unfolded throughout the twentieth century. It involves (a) the careful planning of standardized products and work routines, (b) escalating **deskilling** and, correspondingly, greater reliance on **emotional labour**, and (c) the homogenization of consumption and simultaneous proliferation of market niches and consumer **choice**.

Under the regime of McDonaldization, the role of the managers shifts. Whereas Fordist managers had their eyes firmly set on their workers, seeking to eliminate waste, increase efficiency, and intensify production, under McDonaldization, managers keep their eyes firmly on the customers, their desires, fantasies, and dreams. What the management of many organizations does is to furnish, in a highly rationalized manner, an endless stream of consumable **fantasies**. Whether offering motor cars, tourist destinations, fashion items, or movies, managers invite consumers to pick and choose how different products can enable them to turn their dreams into reality. Thus McDonaldization is the flip-side of **Disneyization**. If Henry Ford was the model manager for the early twentieth century, Walt Disney has belatedly emerged as the model manager for the twenty-first. The core qualities expected of managers today, argues Ritzer, are imagination, flair, and the ability to make their customers feel happy, by offering them opportunities to realize their fantasies. Ritzer offers many illustrations of the ways in which consumption is constantly promoted, enhanced, and controlled in these new settings, which he describes as cathedrals of consumption, which include shopping malls, supermarkets, tourist resorts, casinos, theme parks, sports venues, fast food outlets, theatres, and cinemas.

Management

Few words can compete with 'management' in its spread and ubiquity. Its meteoric rise mirrors the parallel rise of English as the international language of global business, politics, and academic research. 'Management' is one of the most successful exports of the English language, now fully assimilated in many different languages.

As a word, management provides excellent value. This is evident by the ease with which it has spread its remit within the English language. Management is linked to areas as diverse and grandiose as the management of the environment, the management of the economy, the management of the African elephant, the management of emotion, or still more ambitiously the management of the planet. It seems that nothing lies beyond the embrace of management—'Managing x' is the title of countless books, where x is virtually anything. The power of the word management is, in the view of

---

[1] Ritzer, 1993; 1993/1996.

some, attributed to the rise of management and managers as major forces in social and economic affairs. Thus, Peter Drucker argued that 'rarely in human history has any **institution** emerged as fast as management or had as great an impact as quickly. In less than 150 years, management has transformed the social and economic fabric of the world's developed countries. It has created a global economy and a new set of rules for countries that would participate in that economy as equals. And it has itself been transformed'.[1]

What then is management, what is its origin, and what are the reasons for its spectacular rise? The etymology of 'management' can be traced to the French *manège* and the Italian *maneggiare* which signified training a horse or putting a horse through its paces. The French *manège* gave rise to *ménage* meaning household and household management, hence *ménage à trois*. Management then originates in taming and domesticating a wild force of nature and turning it into a useful resource for humans. One of its affinities lies in *control*—controlling a horse is a necessary part of training it. But there are other affinities. To manage also means to treat with respect, to handle as well as to control. It also means to unleash a hidden potential—just as the potential of each horse is developed through its training, management aims at developing the potentials of ideas, resources, and, of course, people.

The rise of managers and management since the early twentieth century coincides with the high noon of modernity—the period of large corporations, big government, urban expansion, mass production, and mass **consumption**. It brought with it the development of management theory as an academic discipline and the emergence of business schools. Classical theories of management dating from this period include **Taylorism**, **Human Relations**, and, mainly by its setting the agenda for what became organization theory, Weber's writing on **bureaucracy**. Control, efficiency, and employee **motivation** were the key concerns of these approaches. Subsequently, management grew as a set of interrelated disciplines drawing their inspiration and most of their key concepts from economics, sociology, and psychology and spawning a large number of disciplines of its own, including organizational behaviour, marketing, information systems, human resources, and, of course, **strategy**. Henry Mintzberg criticized many of the traditional approaches for focusing on what managers *should* be doing rather than on what they actually do.[2] Based on intensive observation of actual managers, he found that much of their work involves **language** and **communication** and that it is conducted in short bursts of activity. Handling crises and emergencies takes a substantial part of their time; they have little time for systematic thought or planning and make most **decisions** on the basis of ad hoc information.

Since the 1980s, and partly as a result of focusing on what managers actually do, the **symbolic** dimension of management has acquired prominence in the literature. Management has come to be viewed increasingly as 'the ability to define reality for others' (see **management of meaning** and **management of emotion**). Instead of looking at managers as individuals who can run organizations smoothly, the emphasis now is on managers as agents of **change**, renewal, and **learning**. This brings the concept of management very close to that of **leadership**, and a substantial debate is going on as to whether managers and leaders are the same. There are many enduring academic discussions on managers, management, and the nature of managerial work which include:

1. the relationship between management and leadership;
2. the moral and ethical aspects and responsibilities of managerial work;
3. the extent to which management 'colonizes' other aspects of social, political, and even

---

[1] Drucker, 1988, p. 65.   [2] Mintzberg, 1973; 2004.

personal life (e.g. the **New Public Management** movement in public administration);

4. the nature of managerial knowledge and learning and their acquisition and development;
5. the limits of management and the extent to which some aspects of organizations (or life in general) are unmanaged and unmanageable;
6. the increasing preoccupation of managers with the **consumer** and the possible redefinition of their role from efficient deliverers of goods and services to orchestrators of consumer fantasies and experiences.

In the last twenty years or so, the study of management has been influenced by postmodern scholarship and critical theory.[1] This has led to the emergence of **Critical Management Studies** which has systematically questioned some of the assumptions concealed within the terms manager and management. MacIntyre, for example, argued that the manager represents one of the three chief character archetypes of **modernity**, epitomizing the moral assumptions of our times. The manager, he argued, 'represents in his *character* the obliteration of the distinction between manipulative and nonmanipulative social relations...The manager treats ends as given, as outside his scope; his concern is with effectiveness in transforming raw materials into final products, unskilled labour into skilled labour, investment into profits.'[2] Management, according to this view, treats people as *resources* to be deployed to the end of efficient administration, free of any political or moral considerations; it makes moral and political issues invisible, turning them into issues of technical efficiency. Practising managers seek to control people, information, and other resources in the face of continuous change and uncertainty. To this end virtually any concept or technique may be marshalled, including concepts such as

autonomy and empowerment, which are often assimilated into a rhetoric in which self-policing seeks to camouflage management control.

We can see then why management has proved such a useful term. Beyond neutralizing political issues and making moral issues invisible, management suggests that everything can be predicted, planned for, and controlled through the use of technical **knowledge**. Failing organizations, collapsing economies, decaying environment, misbehaving employees, disenchanted citizens, unruly children can all be 'managed', thus relieving many **anxieties** generated by the prospect of disorder and chaos. Management is a word whose mere presence is meant to reassure that life can be free of surprises and shocks, it is a necessary myth for our times of insecurity and fear, prompted by the awareness that there are large *unmanaged* **and** *unmanageable* aspects in groups, organizations, societies, but also individuals themselves. The belief that everything can be managed may then be viewed as a kind of hubris which inevitably brings about its own nemesis in the shape of crises, accidents, and disasters.[3]

Management of emotion

This term is often used in connection with **management of meaning**. Like the management of meaning, the management of emotion may seem to imply a measure of dissimulation and manipulation, though this need not be so. We routinely manage our emotions and intervene in the emotions of others to reassure them, entertain them, or frighten them. In fact, the management of emotion is sometimes seen as a way of differentiating between **leadership** and **management**. Managers, it is argued, operate at the level of cold rationality and careful planning whereas leaders are more liable to operate at the level of emotions and intuitions.[4] In relating to their followers, managers (and transactional

---

[1] See e.g. Alvesson and Willmott, 1992; Knights, 1992; Willmott, 1993.   [2] MacIntyre, 1981, p. 30.   [3] Gabriel, 1998a.   [4] Bennis and Nanus, 1985; Zaleznik, 1977.

leaders) will offer compelling deals, through which followers may achieve their aspirations. Leaders (or those whom Burns and Bass would consider 'transforming leaders'[1]), on the other hand, are more liable to form deep emotional bonds with their followers, working on their feelings. Such leaders may offer **psychological contracts** whose essence is not calculation, but loyalty, faith, and love. It is easy to exaggerate the distance between leadership and management as regards emotions; even the coldest administrator after all may stimulate emotions in others even if he or she does not display them. There can be little doubt that many leaders have a profound influence on the emotional lives of their followers, stirring up feelings of inspiration, dedication, and hope, conversely, disappointment, anger, and betrayal.

We get a glimpse of the overpowering emotions that leaders can generate in the following account from Tolstoy's *War and Peace*, when young Nikolai Rostov, who has fantasized countless times the moment when he might meet his Emperor, finally gets his chance on the morrow of a military defeat:

> But as a youth in love trembles and turns faint and dares not utter what he has spent nights in dreaming of, and looks around in terror, seeking aid or a chance of delay and flight, when the longed-for moment arrives and he is alone with her, so Rostov, now that he had attained what he had longed for beyond everything in the world, did not know how to approach the Emperor, and a thousand reasons occurred to him why it would be untimely, improper and impossible to do so.[2]

Leaders may evoke such powerful emotions. One only has to look at the newspaper headlines to realize this. But leaders also *work with* emotions, their own and those of their followers. This involves different aspects of emotional work:

☐ Leaders read the emotions of their followers and appreciate their consequences. Leaders communicate with their followers in different ways but effective ones have their finger on the followers' emotional pulse, being able to detect frustration, anger, hope, boredom, and other emotions.

☐ They are then able to intensify some emotions, especially by managing meaning in such ways that emotions become magnified. The word 'insult' will intensify anger just as the word 'challenge' will intensify commitment.

☐ Leaders may then be able to channel emotions to particular targets and objectives. Anger is then not dissipated in different directions and towards different targets, but gets focused on a particular object who becomes 'the enemy'. Hope is focused on a collective task which assumes the quality of a 'mission', and so forth.

☐ Leaders may then use the emotion to drive **action**, motivating and inspiring their followers to do things that might otherwise have appeared futile, excessive, immoral, or irrational. It is in this sense that leaders can be said to 'drive' their followers.

☐ While intensifying and channelling some useful emotions, leaders may also contain or neutralize some potentially dangerous emotions—in some cases leaders can be said to act as 'toxic sponges' absorbing negative emotions and preventing them from affecting their followers.

☐ Leaders may also offer safety valves that can find legitimate ways to express emotions. One such way is through acknowledging them and accepting them, for example acknowledging fear or apprehension; another is by offering stories or jokes (including self-disparaging ones) that defuse dangerous emotions.

The means by which leaders manage emotions revolve around the use of words and visible actions. Leaders may influence emotions by using symbolic **language**, including **stories** and

metaphors. Christ's use of the parables is an example of stories having powerful emotional effects. Churchill's use of metaphors, such as 'iron curtain' and 'cold war', set the emotional tone of post-Second World War politics. The use of emotional language with powerful words, such as 'betrayal', 'war', 'victory', 'rebirth', 'downsizing', 'challenge', and so forth, is capable of stimulating strong emotions, as are less emotive words like 'change', 'modernization', and 'merger' when used in particular contexts. In general, leaders manage emotions by offering explanations and interpretations that resonate with the **experiences** of their followers.

It is sometimes said that actions speak louder than words. There is little doubt that the leader's actions are scrutinized by the followers in ways that can have a profound influence on emotions. Whom did the leader reward and whom did she punish? Whom did he smile to? Did he smile at all? Where are the organization's resources going? What important decisions have been taken? Whom is the leader meeting? How attentively is she listening? What car is he driving? It will be noted that big and small actions can be invested with strong meanings and evoke strong emotions.

The management of emotions, like the management of meaning, is a particularly dangerous part of the leader's work. It can easily backfire. Words and actions regularly come back to haunt leaders. Once a genie is out of the bottle, it becomes impossible to put it back in. A word or an action that undermines the followers' trust in the leader will be difficult to reverse. What is especially damaging in this context is a visible discrepancy between what leaders say and what they do. This can easily give rise to cynicism and unleash strong negative emotions towards the leader or the organization as a whole. Among the many emotions that leaders manage, a particularly important one is **anxiety**. Failure to manage anxiety effectively can lead to serious failures. Excessive anxiety leads to panic or fatalism while excessively low anxiety leads to complacency and decay. The containment of anxiety is then seen as an important leadership function by many authors.[1]

When does management of emotion become emotional manipulation? This is a notoriously difficult question to answer. One can read Burns's great book *Leadership* as an attempt to answer it.[2] Burns would argue that a 'real' leader, as opposed to a tyrant, offers alternatives to his or her followers, places the shared aspirations above his or her own narrow self-interests, and eschews deception, sham, and manipulation. This line of argument often fails at what is known as the Hitler problem.[3] Was Hitler a conviction politician who made his intentions plain and drove his nation first to victory and then to ruin, or a cynical schemer and opportunist who deceived and manipulated his followers for his own aggrandizement?[4] Whatever the answer, few would disagree that Hitler was very adept at working with the emotions of his followers.

• See also *emotion, feelings*

Management of meaning

Defining 'management of meaning' usually begins with a definition of 'management' and a definition of 'meaning' in order to proceed with the explanation of those two terms linked by 'of'. 'Management' is then defined as leading (see **leadership**), directing, supervising, and controlling organized individuals clustered and related in organizations or their parts. The word comes from Italian *maneggiare* which derives from Latin and refers to an equestrian's handling of a horse. To manage means to plan, organize, lead, coordinate, and control. 'Meaning' is much harder to define because it is the underlying concept of a dictionary, which is constructed in order to explain the meaning of concepts communicated by words. Meaning can then be

---

[1] See e.g. French, 1997; Hirschhorn, 1988; Menzies Lyth, 1988; Obholzer, 1999.   [2] Burns, 1978.   [3] Tourish and Pinnington, 2002.
[4] For an excellent discussion of this issue, see Rosenbaum, 1999.

seen as the relation between a word and an entry in a dictionary which explains it. The meanings of concepts change over time, because they depend on relations between signs and on the context in which they are communicated. Meanings emerge out of past games that people played but are subsequently reconstructed according to some **values**, derived from evolving **cultural** systems. To understand the meaning of a word, an interaction, or an event, we use *definitions*, *interpretations*, or *negotiations*. We can *define* 'manager' as someone who can give orders, we can *interpret* a bride's 'yes' at the altar as consent to marriage, and we can *negotiate* whether 55 per cent of correct answers in a multiple choice test already means 'pass' or whether it means 'fail'. All three—definition, interpretation, and negotiation—require making sense of actors, networks, interactions, situations, contexts, and flows of events. They require **sensemaking** within a culturally relevant framework,[1] and they are part of the **social construction of reality**.[2]

Patterns of sensemaking vary across time and space. Let us begin with the most general, abstract, and universalist ones. Most historians agree that three major patterns of universal sensemaking have dominated the management of meaning over the centuries. In the Western academic tradition, these are *the religious* (embodied in the history of the Christian doctrine and religious **institutions**), *the rational* (represented by the Enlightenment and the rise of science), and an emergent one, which still does not have a name, but is often labelled ***postmodern*** in order to contrast it with the **modernity** of the Enlightenment and premodernity of the metaphysical, religious pattern of sensemaking. According to the Christian pattern, making sense of the world is guided by divine revelation. Men and women follow God's commandments, desire a just society and a personal salvation. Hence theology is the core of a university—the place for the systematic

study of the most fundamental meanings of the world and ourselves. God is the ultimate guarantee of all other, non-divine meanings reconstructed by men and women in all walks of life. This pattern had been subjected to a growing critique from the sixteenth to the nineteenth century. According to the thinkers of the Enlightenment, men and women do not need the hypothesis that God exists in order to discover the nature of the world and to forge their destinies. Human **reason**, embodied in science, should guide individuals as well as societies towards welfare and progress. Liberty, equality, and fraternity were viewed as rational principles invented and implemented in order to secure the greatest happiness for the largest numbers of individuals in pursuit of happiness. Personal happiness and fulfilment became socially desirable aims, the creative development of individuals replacing salvation as the ultimate ideal.

This pattern of sensemaking had been subjected to a growing critique in the course of the twentieth century. Critics pointed out that scientific **rationality** did not prevent industrialized societies from managing two world wars, from organizing genocide in Soviet and Nazi concentration camps, and from excluding most of the world's populations from the benefits of affluent democracies long after a formal dismantling of the colonial domination. The postmodern pattern of management of meaning emerged from five key modifications in sensemaking processes. *First*, from the phenomenological critique of universal Reason described as an abstract stage for logical thinking populated by categories, not phenomena.[3] Phenomenology led to the development of an existentialist philosophy which questioned abstract 'essence' of history and rooted knowledge in an analysis of individual experience.[4] It also questioned the universal validity of scientific discovery.[5] *Second*, from the **critical theory** of the Frankfurt School, whose representatives pointed out that belief in the universal logic of history led to industrialized

---

[1] Weick, 2001b.   [2] Berger and Luckmann, 1967.   [3] Husserl, 2006.   [4] Camus, 1956; Sartre, 1956.   [5] Kuhn, 1962/1996; Popper, 1959.

genocide and totalitarian designs for global domination.[1] *Third*, from the development of **psychoanalysis** by Freud and his followers and its influence upon the humanities and critical social theory.[2] Psychoanalytic insights into human personality allowed humanists to interpret the meaning of words and actions in terms of a dialectical struggle between social conformity and an expression of repressed **desires**. *Fourth*, from an increasing pressure on mainstream Western academic and media networks to account for 'people without history', 'forgotten people', and 'silent majorities', whose voices had been silenced or ignored.[3] *Fifth*, from the critical analysis of an increasingly 'seductive' **consumerism** and an excess of managerial **control** in the late capitalist societies.[4]

The postmodern pattern of management of meaning, like the previous two, has its own ideal, that of a transparent flow of social communications, in an open, **multicultural** society, built around the constant negotiation of meanings within complex social flows and transformations. For individuals, the ideal focuses on a creative and participative socialization which enables them to make a contribution to a **sustainable development**. It is based on the management of inclusion and access, preventing systematic **discrimination** and exclusion from real and virtual communities. Thus, communications, interactions, and feedbacks compose fluid and evolving clusters of social worlds (in the plural) of participating and changing actors (individual, organizational, social). Metaphorically speaking, Marx claimed to detect the hidden plot of human history as a symphony of progress played by struggling **classes**. Freud claimed to discover the hidden plot in the history of individuals liberating themselves from repression.[5] Sensemaking processes are then detected and analysed at an organizational level, or an intermediate level of explanation between those

of individuals and entire societies. Will their reconstruction contribute to the ongoing 'conversation of mankind'? Will it guide the evolution and development of human societies as gradual enlargement of individual, organizational, and social freedom successfully overcoming democratic deficits as they emerge?

• See also *communication, mass media, meaning, spirituality*

SLAWEK MAGALA, ERASMUS UNIVERSITY,
ROTTERDAM

Market

We encounter the market every day. Most of us produce *for* the market and all of us consume *in* the market. While different markets and different forms of trading can be traced far back in human history, it can be argued that the market has emerged as the distinctive feature of most national and post-national societies in the twenty-first century. We live in 'market societies',[6] where the market appears to dominate, directly or indirectly, nearly every aspect of contemporary social life—relationships, institutions, discourses. Yet, as Swedberg argued, 'neither economists not sociologists currently have a satisfactory theory of the markets'.[7] This should come as no surprise when one considers what is at stake. Fundamental categories of social and politico-economic thought, including the boundaries between the political, the economic, and the social domains, are supported, challenged, and contested by different conceptualizations of the market. To paraphrase Weber, who spoke about 'the battle of man against man [sic] in the market',[8] in social theory there is a battle of theorist against theorist to explain the market and its role in society.

The Austrian economist Friedrich Hayek saw the market as the perfect **communication** system,

---

[1] Arendt, 1958; Marcuse, 1964; Sloterdijk, 1988.   [2] Freud, 1933/1988; Rieff, 1966; Fromm, 1941/1966; Reich, 1970.   [3] A. G. Frank, 1998; Wallerstein, 1983.   [4] Debord, 1977; Foucault, 1977; Ritzer, 1993.   [5] Boje, 2001; Czarniawska, 1997.   [6] Slater and Tonkiss, 2001.   [7] Swedberg, 2005, p. 249.   [8] Weber, 1978, p. 108.

'not an **organization** but a spontaneous order', a 'catallaxy', the ancient Greek word meaning 'not only to exchange but also to receive into the community and to turn from enemy into friend' (pp. 28–9).[1] Markets bring people together in mutually beneficial exchanges, stimulate growth, and bring about a reconciliation of resources and human needs. By contrast, Lindblom saw the market as a prison,[2] 'an extraordinary system of repressing change' (p. 326), and Chomsky as 'socialism for the rich. The public pays the costs and the rich get the benefit—markets for the poor and plenty of state protection for the rich.'[3]

The economic and social historian Karl Polanyi wrote extensively on the market as a socially instituted process and regarded the attempt to establish it as *the* dominant **institution** in society as a 'stark utopia'. For Polanyi, the economic domain is inseparable from the socio-political domain, the latter regulating the rules of conduct between actors in the former (see **economy**). In his magnum opus, *The Great Transformation*, he argued that, traditionally, markets were embedded in a rich web of social relations that did not allow the 'market rationale' to dominate society. The market had to compete against other institutions of social exchange. In early capitalism, however, the fiction of a self-adjusting market became politically hegemonic, in spite of the fact that strong state action was required to establish and consolidate its supremacy. Market societies, in Polanyi's terminology, are societies where market exchange became the dominant rationale behind all social institutions and transactions. The market appeared to be simultaneously disembedded from the rest of society and its hegemonic principle.

While the market is never divorced from other social institutions, it appears to be guided by laws and principles beyond the control of any single agent or political party, Adam Smith's 'invisible hand'. As a result, the market has emerged as a formidable disciplinary

mechanism in contemporary societies. There are no consolations or leniency for failing in the marketplace.

> Ultimately...the **control** of the economic system by the market is of overwhelming consequence to the whole organisation of society: it means no less than running of society as an adjunct to the market. Instead of the economy being embedded in social relations, social relations are embedded in the economy.[4]

The advance of the market **ideology** is closely related to the rise of contemporary **consumerism**, which relies on markets to supply what are viewed as glamorous, stylish, and innovative goods and services, contrasted to the shabby, run-down offerings provided by the state. For political neoliberals and their academic allies, the market economy, driven by consumer **choice** and the free movement of goods, is the engine of **innovation** and the individual well-being. Critics (including Polanyi), on the other hand, have argued that untrammelled markets erode social solidarity, widen social inequalities, and create constant psychological insecurities and anxieties. Such critics observe that markets cannot restore services following natural and other disasters, nor can they restore confidence and morale. Indeed being blind to environmental, ethical, and political issues, markets are often directly or indirectly responsible for such disasters. It is the duty or governments and international bodies to control and restrain markets and also to offset some of their worst consequences. In spite of the dominance of the market ideology, then, its limitations should not be obscured. Whenever people are confronted with dramatic economic downturns, bank collapses, natural disasters, and military threats, they turn to governments for support, action, and leadership. It is then that they seek to act as citizens rather than as consumers.

Studies of organizations and management have taken a keen interest in the market over

---

[1] Hayek, 1968.   [2] Lindblom, 1982.   [3] Chomsky, 1997.   [4] Polanyi, 1944, p. 60.

the past thirty years. In an influential article, William Ouchi argued that the market is one of three fundamental mechanisms of organizational and social **control**, the others being bureaucratic **rules** and strong social **norms** ('clan controls').[1] Since the publication of Ouchi's article, many organizations have moved away from bureaucratic controls towards 'internal markets' and strong **cultures** as a means of disciplining different sub-units. Subcontracting and **outsourcing** have emerged as major instruments of enforcing market disciplines within organizations—inefficient or uneconomic activities are simply outsourced to other organizations that, ostensibly, can offer better value for money.

In the public sector, one of the pillars of the of **New Public Management** has been the growth of 'quasi-markets', structural enclaves designed to promote consumer choice and efficiency ostensibly without loss of quality.[2] Behind the rhetoric of quasi-markets, some scholars detected an attempt to curb the power of professionals (especially physicians), in favour of managers. Fitzgerald and Ferlie have argued that the main beneficiaries of quasi-markets in the hospital sector have been neither the patients nor the managers but professionals who have gained power by assuming 'hybrid roles', which require not only professional knowledge but also mastery of other control mechanisms, like peer reviews and medical audits.[3]

• See also *choice, consumerism, New Public Management*

THEODOR PAPADOPOULOS, UNIVERSITY OF BATH

Masculinity

Masculinity is a term used to describe equally the major components of male **sexuality** and the **role** attributes of the male gender. The study of masculinity has lagged behind that of

femininity but current interest in the gendering of organizations and other social institutions has brought it into focus. In the 1990s certain **stereotypes** of masculine behaviour were questioned, mostly in the United States. Books like Robert Bly's *Iron John: A Book about Men* and Sam Keen's *Fire in the Belly: On Being a Man* argued that the attainment of real manhood (and a male **identity**) is problematic for men, as are **stereotypes** of macho masculinity.[4] Such books sought to promote a new vision of masculinity at once caring and heroic, founded not on hate or contempt for women but on strong male bonding and a reappraisal of the relation between fathers and sons. The question of how boys should develop new mature male identities in the light of the fundamental reorientation of women's roles and identities has started to interest writers, some of whom have argued that boys risk becoming the 'second sex' as educational theories and practices have now introduced systematic biases that disadvantage the psychological development and academic success of boys.[5] Some have argued that there is now a crisis in masculinity—no doubt linked to what are referred to as the gender wars in America and the moral panic created by feminist ideas and the backlash to them.[6]

For a long time, masculinity in organizations was seen as generally unproblematic—the male was the **norm**, it was taken for granted. The stereotypical traits associated with the male **gender**, **rationality**, assertiveness, competitiveness, winning, exclusiveness, and so forth, were seen as serving organizations well. By the same token, hard physical work and attendant **class** solidarity were seen as a sound basis for the formation of strongly gendered proletarian identities, casting men as breadwinners, survivors of bruising battles with the employers, relying on their physical and moral strength to support their families.[7] Both of these assumptions are now being questioned in the light of the changing nature of organizations. Hard physical

---

[1] Ouchi, 1980.   [2] Ferlie et al., 1996.   [3] Fitzgerald and Ferlie, 2000.   [4] Bly, 1990; Keen, 1991.   [5] Sommers, 2000.   [6] Faludi, 1992; 1999.   [7] Collinson, 1982; 1988.

labour and bruising battles with employers are no longer key ingredients for large parts of advanced economies (although exceptions remain in industries such as mining, construction, and so forth). Nor is aggressive masculinity with its predilections for **authoritarianism**, rigidity, and **bullying** in tune with the demands of many of today's organizations for imagination, flexibility, creativity, and the ability to create networks and relations of trust. Finally, the increasing emphasis on organizational **diversity**, including the recognition and acceptance of **homosexuality**, has made displays of aggressive masculinity (with its hard-hitting homophobia) far less acceptable.

It would be fair, therefore, to acknowledge that while talk of a crisis of masculinity may be exaggerated, male identities over the coming decades will have to be reforged in the light of changing conditions. These are bound to include enduring social and economic changes as well as demographic (with gender and age imbalances in large parts of the globe) and technological changes (including fertility treatments, sex change operations, and genetic engineering) that will continue to influence the complex and fascinating relations between the genders.

Mass media

The term mass media (or simply 'the media') refers to all the different forms of communication **technology** that reach mass audiences. These include newspapers and journals, radio and television, film and records, the internet and cellular telephones. The media are viewed as one of the defining **institutions** of advanced capitalist societies and are the topic of constant fascination. They are the subject of numerous university courses, films, television programmes, books, newspaper articles in short the media have become a favourite subject for the media themselves. The word media comes from the Latin *medium* or means, and suggests a *means* of communicating messages. A manufacturer may communicate the excellence of the soap powder they produce by using different means of **advertising**, including press, television, radio, and so forth.

Yet, in an important sense the term media is a misnomer: the media do not simply communicate pre-existing reality but they *create* reality. An event watched on television or photographed for a newspaper comes to represent something different from one that has taken place quietly, anonymously, and unrecorded. Marshall McLuhan's statement 'the medium is the message' is probably the most famous sentence that anyone has uttered about the ways the media define, shape, and control our sense of reality and the way we engage with them and interact with each other. We now routinely use expressions like 'I saw it in slow motion' or 'It was just like a movie'. Events are hailed as 'media events' and individuals as 'media phenomena'. The lives of 'media celebrities' sometimes appear to be of greater significance for many people than those of their friends or acquaintances. The photo-opportunity and the sound-bite, two unique weapons in the arsenals of today's politicians, are themselves products of the age of the media.

At one level, the view that communication technologies create reality is not surprising. The speed and ease with which ideas and **information** are communicated have a direct impact on the ideas and information themselves. Thus, as Elizabeth Eisenstein has shown,[1] Gutenberg's invention of printing enabled many people to access the new ideas of the Protestant Reformation, enhanced the appeal of these ideas, encouraged the use of the vernacular (instead of Latin), promoted free thinking, and established the principle of authorship. At a deeper level, different communication technologies influence our perceptual and cognitive apparatuses, radically shaping the way that we view and experience the world. Thus, the advent of writing,

[1] Eisenstein, 1979.

according to Ong, marked a fundamental shift in human **cognition** from the world of sound to the world of sight, from orality to literacy.[1] The invention of typography itself further accelerated the cultural predominance of the visual over the oral and the aural.[2]

The rise of the mass media has brought about a domination of the speaker/writer leaving relatively little space for the listener/reader to respond and interpret. It seems entirely appropriate to link the mass media with the development of totalitarian states in the twentieth century—Hitler famously remarked that the Nazis could not have succeeded without the loudspeaker. One of the sharpest early commentators, C. Wright Mills, described the mass media as having two key characteristics—first, very few people can communicate to a great number, and, second, the audience has no effective way of answering back.[3]

The world created by contemporary media is one in which **image** and **spectacle** reign supreme. In *The image: or, what happened to the American dream*, Daniel Boorstin argued that people have become so addicted to what they experience through newspapers, television shows, films, photography, art, and sound recordings that they have ended up preferring image to 'reality'.[4] Thus the media are in the business of staging a continuous sequence of 'pseudo-events', events devoid of any **meaning** or significance but capable of holding the attention, becoming topics of conversation, and generating spurious controversies. For Baudrillard, this pseudo-reality created by the media becomes 'more real' than everyday reality, it becomes 'hyper-real';[5] theorists like Edelman and Postman have lamented what they see as the trivialization of politics, science, art, and every aspect of culture as soon as they are touched by the hand of the media.[6] In all of these areas, serious discussion becomes replaced by simplification, personalization, and the celebrity cult.

The captured image, the 'story', the 'row' replace information, conversation, and argument as the core elements of cultural life.

But the effects of the mass media reach deeper still, in shaping the actions of governments, corporations, other organizations, and groups. Organizations (including corporations, governments, **voluntary organizations**, political parties, and so forth) are keenly aware of how their policies and actions will 'play' in front of the media and plan, organize, and package their activities in ways that will generate the best possible publicity. But so too are environmental campaigners, like Greenpeace, who are particularly adept at capturing the limelight of the world media. And so too are **terrorists**, whose actions are driven by what Margaret Thatcher described aptly as 'the oxygen of publicity', something that she unsuccessfully sought to deny them. The conduct of warfare itself has been dramatically affected by the related battles to control the access of reporters to the scenes of conflict.

Over the last fifty years, the media have attracted many criticisms linking them to nearly every social ill from teenage pregnancies, to street violence, to mindless greedy **consumerism**, to terrorism, to the dumbing down of political debate. Some of these criticisms are based on the view that people are passive recipients of media messages, a view that is currently being challenged. Thus, John Thompson has argued that 'media messages are commonly discussed by individuals in the course of reception and subsequent to it ... [They] are transformed through an ongoing process of telling and retelling, interpretation and reinterpretation, commentary, laughter and criticism ... By taking hold of messages and routinely incorporating them into our lives ... we are constantly shaping and reshaping our skills and stocks of knowledge, testing our feelings and tastes, and expanding the horizons of our experience.'[7] In a way similar to that in which tragedy and myth

---

[1] Ong, 2002.   [2] McLuhan, 1962.   [3] Mills, 1956.   [4] Boorstin, 1962.   [5] Baudrillard, 1983.   [6] Edelman, 1988; Postman, 1986.
[7] Thompson, 1995, p. 42.

offered earlier generations a means of emotional expression and catharsis, today's media can be viewed as providing the material that enables people to engage with and discuss the burning issues of their lives, such as crime, discrimination, violence, and so forth.

A very large part of media theorizing has dealt with their effects on culture, on politics, and on people's emotions and attitudes; it has also dealt with the media as a homogeneous single block. Less attention has been paid to the media as organizations in their own right, organizations which operate in market economies, under varying degrees of competition, producing different products and finding themselves in conflict with each other or under pressures from social and technological forces. Thus the power of television may be currently challenged by the internet, the power of the music industry by technological developments that facilitate music piracy. More generally, the increasing ability to copy, plagiarize, paraphrase, borrow, distort, appropriate, and possibly to subvert the outputs of the media may allow for a wider variety of voices to be heard and a less uniform influence on the part of the media. If this happens, referring to the media in the now commonly accepted singular may become increasingly inappropriate.

• See also *advertising, communication, image, postmodernism, spectacle, technology*

Meaning

The meaning of a word, a text, an object, an action, or an event is what these vastly different entities stand for, it is the sense that we make of them. The quest for meaning is a fundamental aspect of human **experience**. Human beings can live through many troubles and sufferings but find the absence of meaning very hard to bear. Suffering itself becomes endurable if it seen to have a meaning—as punishment, as test of character, as the result of moral failure.

But senseless suffering can drive most people to despair. It is for this reason that we assiduously look for meanings, trying to *make sense* of the world around us. Aristotle noted that we look for meaning in everything, including accidental events like the collapse of a statue.[1]

We look for meaning in small things, like the tiniest spot on our body, and the largest—the meaning of our lives. This is what makes us symbolic animals. This is also what sets the human sciences, dealing with humans, their meaningful actions, and their quest for meaning, on a different course from the natural sciences, which address a universe that makes sense but is ultimately without meaning. Understanding the phenomenon of a solar eclipse as a natural phenomenon requires a different type of explanation from understanding the different meanings people may read into it. Medicine may offer many explanations of death, but its deeper meaning is to be found elsewhere. Religion has long sought to answer humans' deepest thirst for meaning and continues to do so for many. Others, in their search for deeper meanings, have turned to philosophy, **spirituality**, or mysticism.

An intriguing ambiguity surrounds meaning. We act as if meaning resides in the objects, symbols, signs, and events we experience, yet it is we who construct meanings for these entities. Meanings are *created, tested, traded, contested*, and *destroyed* through our thought and feeling processes and through our social relations. All of these crucially rely on **language** and other forms of **communication**, like gestures, expressions, and actions. Discovering the meaning of anything, like a joke, a poem, or an action, requires a process of *interpretation*. Sociologists, especially those known as symbolic interactionists, argue that meaning is the product of human interaction, with people trading interpretations and inferring contrasting meanings. Depth psychologists, on the other hand, emphasize that the meanings of mental phenomena, like dreams, accidents, obsessive acts,

---

[1] Aristotle, 1963, p. 19, 1452a.

slips of tongue or pen (the famous 'Freudian slips'), etc., are linked to repressed **desires**. Existential psychologists argue that men and women strive to create meaning through decisive acts of will, because without it life is unbearable. These views are not incompatible but illustrate some of the diversity of **discourses** surrounding the concept. As far as work is concerned, all three approaches have a significant contribution to make. Sociologists have argued that the meaning of work differs across different cultures, each of which has a distinct **work ethic**. Depth psychology emphasizes that many incidents of organizational life are invested with meanings which derive from unconscious desires and wishes. Existential psychology stresses that meaningless work is unbearable work, and engages in a critique of production techniques, like **Taylorism** which deny work its meaning and purpose.

How then are meanings created and sustained? Humans have created a large universe of **symbols**—**culture**—through which meaning is infused in every aspect of their lives. Some of these symbols are linguistic—using the word 'disaster' to describe a situation attributes different meaning from using the words 'crisis', 'reversal', or 'disappointment'. **Metaphors** too accomplish an instant infusion of meaning by transferring attributes of a well-understood entity to another. 'Our organization is a dinosaur' does not presuppose that we are more familiar with dinosaurs than with the organization in question since none of us (not even palaeontologists) is likely to be so. It does, however, transfer certain widely presumed characteristics of dinosaurs (large, slow, rigid, and, above all, doomed to extinction) onto an entity that we know intimately. **Stories** accomplish a similar end by different means. They infuse an event, such as a suicide, with meaning through the magic of plot, by interweaving it into a sequence of interrelated events. 'His business empire grew rapidly on the back of borrowed money, cheap labour, and many unscrupulous

deals. It came crashing down when he was discovered to have defrauded his company's pension fund, whereupon he drowned himself.' Stories travel—nearly every event or sequence of events acquires meaning by placing it in a familiar plot. As Karl Weick has argued, 'perhaps there is no more common sensemaking gambit than, "that reminds me of a story". This innocent phrase represents a unit of meaning. Something in the present reminds the listener of something that resembles it in the past.'[1]

Language is not the only symbolic system creating and sustaining meanings. Most material objects we consume, food, jewellery, cars, and clothes, make statements about ourselves. A wedding ring indicates a married person, a rich meal with turkey and all the trimmings indicates Christmas, and a fashionable set of clothes with matching accessories indicates a person of wealth, discriminating tastes, and social success. Some anthropologists have likened the system of objects we consume to a language, one through which we continuously communicate meanings both to ourselves and to others.[2] Goods, argues Grant McCracken, are 'bulletin boards for internal messages and billboards for external ones'.[3] Without the help of material objects, the meaning of situations and events begins to drift and collapse. Would Christmas be a special day if there were no material evidence to corroborate its arrival? In the last hundred years **advertising** has emerged as a formidable machine generating meanings, by attaching particular meanings to products stories, images, music, and other techniques. By constantly shifting signifiers ('safe', 'innovative', 'fresh', 'youthful', etc.) from one product to another, advertising also destroys meaning—the meaning of these words becomes unstable, fleeting, and banal. A perpetual noise of **information** and pseudo-symbols swallows meanings. As a result, authors like Baudrillard have argued that the world of contemporary consumption has become a black hole into which meaning disappears.[4]

---

[1] Weick, 1995, p. 131.   [2] Douglas and Isherwood, 1978.   [3] McCracken, 1988, p. 136.   [4] Baudrillard, 1988.

The **management of meaning** is viewed as an important aspect of **leadership**. This is especially so when a group, an organization, or even a nation face a situation that cannot easily fit into an existing plot or story or is too threatening and anxiety provoking. The words and visible actions of leaders then acquire vital significance in revealing the meaning of events. Many a military defeat (from Thermopylae, to Borodino, to Dunkerque) has been recast as a glorious moment, a tipping point auguring victories to come, through effective use of words. In moments of confusion and anxiety like those that followed the atrocities of 11 September 2001, people turn to their leaders to reveal the true significance of events. It is at such moments that the real worth of leaders shows. Will their reading of events 'resonate' with their followers? Will they 'buy' the leaders' accounts? Will they dismiss the leaders' explanations as spin and deception? Management of meaning often comes under the heading of '**communication**'. Business, political, and other leaders currently employ communications experts ('spin doctors') to help them cast each event in the best possible light, in order to maximize political advantage. This, is turn, sensitizes followers to what may amount to crude attempts at manipulation. Meaning is then contested, either by arguing for different interpretations of events or by casting doubt at the motives, reputation, and integrity of the 'spin doctors'. The management of meaning can be quite a difficult task of **management**. It can easily backfire or lead to contestation, cynicism, and ridicule.

• See also *communication, hermeneutics, management of meaning, symbols and symbolism*

Metaphors

'Truth', said Nietzsche famously, 'is a woman.' Metaphors (like Nietszche's) too, some may be tempted to think, are women—seductive, fascinating, dangerous. They are also omnipresent. Since the publication in 1986 of Morgan's *Images of organization*, metaphors have become a major preoccupation of organizational theorists, colonizing many areas of research and stimulating many debates.[1] Metaphors have long been viewed as powerful instruments for transferring **meaning** from one entity to another. Aristotle viewed them as one of the key ingredients of rhetoric, the art of persuasion, but also as a vital means of creating knowledge. 'When the poet calls old age a reed, he produces understanding and recognition through the generic similarity; for both have lost their flower.'[2] In a major contribution, Lakoff and Johnson argued that metaphors are not mere rhetorical or poetic devices.[3] Instead, they argued, metaphors structure our thinking and guide our lives. Thus 'Time is money' and 'Life is a journey' are not 'mere' cosmetic or rhetorical devices that we employ from time to time; they are *root or core metaphors* that dominate Western approaches to the meaning of life. Such metaphors carry with them certain deep cultural assumptions and implications, along with a whole vocabulary of waste and gain, career paths and obstacles, missions and destinations, and so forth, all of which become part of our cultural DNA.

Gareth Morgan has emphasized the importance of metaphors in our thinking about organizations, establishing how most theories of organizations are underpinned by implicit or explicit metaphors of organizations as machines, biological organisms, psychic prisons, brains, and so on.[4] He has further argued that by moving across metaphors important assumptions regarding organizations can be questioned and new insights may be gained. Through his concept of 'imaginization', he has advocated the use of metaphors as thought experiments aimed at stimulating new insights into the functioning of

---

[1] See e.g. Grant and Oswick, 1996; Lakoff, 1993; Ortony, 1993.   [2] Aristotle, 1991, p. 235.   [3] Lakoff and Johnson, 1980.   [4] Morgan, 1986; 2006.

organizations but also the way our minds operate when confronted by organizations. To this end, Morgan has employed various unorthodox metaphors, such as organizations as spider plants or as yogurts.

Some have criticized Morgan for confusing core, deeply entrenched metaphors, which express vital shared cultural **experiences**, with everyday conceptual metaphors which are heuristically contrived and emotionally dead.[1] Others like Robert Chia have developed Morgan's approach, extolling the virtue of constantly moving across metaphors (metaphor *is* movement) and underlining the danger of ossification which follows the widespread acceptance of a specific metaphor.[2] For Chia, metaphors easily become part of a linguistic arsenal which produces static images of reality, obscuring what is transient, precarious, and multivalent. Refusing to join those, like Mangham, who call for greater rigour in the use of metaphors, Chia advocates metaphorization as a sensual, emotional, and intuitive process, largely outside the realms of the intellect, leading to a continuous reinterpretation and re-evaluation of endlessly moving organizational realities. 'To retain their metaphorical potency, metaphors must not be allowed to solidify into literal structures. Metaphors must be constantly metaphorized in order that they retain their power to remind us of the precarious and artificially constructed nature of everyday experiences'.[3]

An attempt to synthesize different ways of thinking about metaphors was offered by Tsoukas, who first distinguished between three perspectives on metaphors: metaphors as ways of thinking embedded in our cognitive processes; metaphors as dispensable literary devices which add colour and flavour to an argument; and metaphors as political and ideological distortions that can function as instruments of domination ('cutting down the dead wood').[4] He proposes that although there is a gap between metaphorical and scientific languages, thinking and arguing 'analogically' (after the manner of metaphors) can function as a sound basis for developing scientific theories and models. In this way, Rutherford (1871–1937) developed a workable 'planetary' model of the atom in which electrons orbited a central nucleus. The uses and abuses of metaphors will continue to preoccupy social scientists, communications practitioners, literary theorists, psychologists, and narratologists for a considerable time in the future. One thing is certain—it is hard not to be seduced by metaphors or by the concept of metaphor itself.

Methodology

A standard feature of nearly every empirically based dissertation and research publication, methodology refers to the different methods employed in generating valid and reliable **knowledge**. This may refer to procedures of data collection, such as observations, experiments, questionnaires, and interviews, and also to techniques for identifying and measuring variables as well as for drawing inferences and generalizations. Methodology also includes statistical techniques for handling populations and samples but also addresses more fundamental assumptions about the nature of reality and the nature of knowledge. In this way, it strays into the realms of ontology and **epistemology**.

Method derives from the Greek word $\mu\acute{\epsilon}\theta o\delta o\varsigma$, signifying the following of a particular path or road. Method then can be seen as the generation of scientific knowledge by following strict rules and procedures for doing so. The assumption that by following certain reliable methods the quality of the knowledge could be guaranteed to be 'scientific' was challenged by several schools in the philosophy of science, starting with Popper and subsequently by Kuhn, Feyerabend, and others.[5] Many theories derived with what their authors thought was strict adherence to scientific method were shown to be spurious,

---

[1] Mangham, 1996.   [2] Chia, 1996.   [3] Ibid. 139.   [4] Tsoukas, 1993.   [5] Popper, 1959; Kuhn, 1962/1996; Feyerabend, 1975.

naive, and false; by contrast, many of the scientific breakthroughs were shown to have been the result of throwing accepted methodology books out of the window. In this way, major discoveries require serendipity, **creativity**, and the courage to move away from the beaten path, i.e. to work against at least some of the currently dominant methodologies. New discoveries generate new methodologies or legitimize and strengthen older ones. What this suggests is that methodology is not a pre-given that research invariably follows, but that methodology evolves along with actual research.

It is now increasingly argued that whether or not a particular theory acquires the label of 'scientific' has less to do with the strictness of the procedures under which it emerged. Instead, it is more likely to refer to the social and political practices that sustain it and legitimize it. No breakthrough in astrology is ever likely to be viewed as scientific whereas even minor advances in medicine are.

In the social sciences, there has been a prolonged and, at times, acrimonious split between quantitative and qualitative methodologies. The former aspire at establishing the social sciences on a 'proper' scientific footing like the presumed one of the natural sciences. The latter look at human behaviour as calling for a different type of explanation and analysis from that of other objects. Quantitative methodologies generally view scientific knowledge as the result of testing hypotheses with clearly defined variables, while qualitative methodologies generally seek to establish the **meanings** of different forms of human **action**. Thus, a quantitative study of anorexia nervosa may seek to establish variables, such as gender, personality, social class, and so forth, that are linked to the condition. By contrast, a qualitative study would seek to understand why a particular individual may be tempted to starve him- or herself and what he or she is seeking to achieve in this way. It is for this reason that quantitative research is often said to aim at nomothetic knowledge, i.e. lawlike generalizations for large-scale phenomena; qualitative

research, by contrast, is idiographic, i.e. it aims at plausible and enlightening **interpretations** and explanations of individual events and actions. Many scholars have advocated a reconciliation of the two approaches, but in most social sciences the split persists.

Modernism and modernity

Modernity is usually seen as a historical epoch that started with the European Enlightenment and the French Revolution in the eighteenth century and reached its culmination but not its conclusion in the first part of the twentieth century. The arrival of modernity coincides with the collapse of feudalism, industrialization, and the vast migration of people from the countryside to the emerging cities, the growth of business enterprises, the explosion of technological innovation, and the rise of the modern state. While the industrial revolution provided the fuel for modernity, modernity is the child of the Enlightenment, the great intellectual movement which sought to promote *reason* and *science* as the basis of human affairs. Enlightenment theorists believed that reason would blow away the cobwebs of tradition, superstition, and religion, bringing with it *progress* in every domain of human life. The project of the Enlightenment was to liberate human beings from self-inflicted slavery, slavery born out of ignorance, complacency, and fear. Belief in *managed* social **change** was a key feature of this project—the rise of **management** is itself part and parcel of modernity.

Modernism is a current that engulfed every cultural form including poetry, music, art, fiction, and maybe above all architecture in the early part of the twentieth century and continues to affect them today—it has many diverse manifestations, but it can be seen as an attempt to test and subvert all existing limits and **boundaries**. Thus, surrealist art, atonal music, non-representational painting, symbolic fiction, and the theatre of the absurd all endeavour to discover whether traditional cultural forms can survive such a systematic subversion.

In social, economic, and political terms, *modernization* is seen as a process in which traditional forms of production, exchange, and governance are overtaken and replaced by more 'rational' and efficient variants.[1] Modernization encompasses universal education, increased social mobility, urbanization, technological advances, universal suffrage, and the emergence of a welfare state. It is not surprising, therefore, that 'modernization' easily becomes a political slogan of renewal and regeneration—being modern becomes a core political **value** which is opposed by tradition and mindless convention. To be modern means being in line with **fashion** in an unambiguously positive way.

Whether the project of the Enlightenment has stalled or not is a widely discussed question among scholars. Undoubtedly, a strong current of opinion is no longer optimistic about the liberating powers of reason and science. Some theorists have argued that the worst disasters of the twentieth century, including world wars, Soviet gulags, and the Nazi concentration camps, were the direct results of the belief that progress would come out of imposing a blueprint for a better future on all and eliminating those that stood in its way.[2] The belief in absolute, objective, and scientific truths has also been shaken, as we have become more aware how 'truth' is itself created through **discourse** and **language**, that truth is not the source of power and emancipation, but very often the outcome of **power** and domination.

Our unqualified faith in progress, a world free of poverty, oppression, and ignorance, has also been shaken; trust in science and the other **grand narratives** of the past has weakened or collapsed. Authority is questioned everywhere. As a result, for the past thirty years or so, many theorists have argued that we have moved beyond modernity, into a new and as yet ill-defined era, **postmodernity**, the great unknown that comes after modernity. Whether postmodernity involves some structural transformation of society and social institutions or different ways of looking at them (or merely a different 'mood') is part of this debate. Some have argued that the nature of society has changed in some irreversible structural way—we have moved from a society of massive, concrete structures to a society of flexible and fragile networks and arrangements, from a society driven by mechanism and production to a society preoccupied with **spectacle**, **image**, and **consumption**. Others view the arrival of postmodernity more as a change of 'attitude'. In postmodernity, everything that appeared solid and authoritative turns out to be a mirage, a **social construction**, or, indeed, a 'story'. Thus, postmodernism invites us to mistrust many revered concepts of the social sciences, such as society, organization, nation, race, family, class, self, body, and so forth, arguing that they are products of discourse, assuming their significance in their shifting relations to each other rather than to some fixed points of reference in the world.

A curious feature of postmodernity is that attempts to establish it as something different from modernity draw it ever closer to it—every single feature of postmodern thought, culture, architecture, business, and so forth can be found to have its origins in the world of modernity or to be a reaction to modernity that reinforces that against which it reacts. The statement that there are no more grand narratives becomes a grand narrative in its own right. A large part of the natural and social sciences continue to follow scientific methodology with scant concern about the finer points of postmodern epistemology. It is as if the different paths that are meant to take us beyond modernity into postmodernity stubbornly end up by returning us to our point of departure. But then, modernity has proven such a powerful concept that attempts to escape from its orbit or to declare it finished continue to prove difficult. Postmodernity is that moment,

---

[1] Eisenstadt, 1966; 1968.   [2] Bauman, 1989; Gray, 2002; 2003.

constantly shifting, when modernity reflects on its own practices.

Morality

Although the terms 'moral' and 'immoral' are frequently used to describe particular people, actions, or practices, the term morality is less frequently used. When used by itself, it is frequently accompanied by a qualifier, such as 'Christian morality' or 'morality of the jungle'. In general, morality refers to a large sphere of human **experience** and **action** that is governed by considerations of good and bad, right and wrong, just and unjust.

Morality is the subject matter of **ethics**. It is then common to approach morality from two perspectives. One is *normative*—what are the fundamental distinctions between good and bad? How can we be sure about these distinctions? How should we live our lives? Why do we *not* live our lives in this manner? The other perspective is *descriptive*—how do people approach issues of morality? What situations are viewed as calling for moral judgements? What actions are viewed as moral or immoral? How do different societies, cultures, or groups draw distinctions between good and bad? This distinction is useful, in that it allows us to analyse different actions and practices (from female circumcision to genocide, from corporate restructuring to bribing) without having to pass judgement on them; it is enough to understand the extent to which participants in such practices construct them as moral or otherwise. The distinction can, however, become something of a moral blind spot in its own right—analysing genocide requires different moral resources from analysing a garden party.

Morality is often seen in connection with moral *codes*—sets of instructions on how to act. Attempts to establish universal codes of human behaviour by religion, philosophy, or political leadership have not been universally convincing. People may agree about what constitute violations of a highway driving code, of etiquette, or even of most laws. When it comes to moral codes, however, we often find profound disagreements—an action or a practice that appears to some as the pinnacle of virtue may shock others as deeply repugnant. While such moral disagreements are very common across cultures they are also regular within cultures. Consider the sixth biblical commandment that says unambiguously 'Thou shalt not kill'. Behind its seeming simplicity, it raises an infinity of questions. Does the commandment apply even when someone is acting in self-defence? Even when someone is acting as a soldier in a war situation? Even if someone is acting on behalf of the state as executioner? Does it apply equally to commission and omission—in other words, if death is the outcome of someone *not* acting? Does it apply to 'metaphorical killing', such as destroying a person's reputation, dignity, or livelihood? Does it apply to states, expressly declaring capital punishment to be immoral? And what about animals? The commandment does not specify killing 'other people'—it appears to forbid all killing. And how should those who violate this commandment be treated? Such are the disagreements on how to interpret even a fundamental moral principle.

Beyond acknowledging the wide variation of moral codes and their interpretations, what else can we conclusively say about morality? Undoubtedly, the vast majority of human beings have a moral sense, a sense that there *is* a difference between right and wrong. Most people experience guilt and shame when they knowingly do the wrong thing and are found out. And most people have large areas of action and experience that they exempt from moral scrutiny—they simply do not feature as moral decisions. Eating meat may be a matter of profound moral concern for some people and it may be entirely devoid of moral content for others—needless to say that one may find vegetarians as well as meat eaters in both groups.

We also all suffer from what David Sims terms 'moral blind spots'—areas that fall outside our moral vision, even when the consequences of our actions in these areas are profoundly moral. Such moral blind spots are especially pronounced when we act in some professional capacity or other. Thus, a manager may have a moral blind spot about firing subordinates, a teacher about failing students, a general about sending soldiers into battle. Moral blind spots are also liable to occur when we can hold someone else, especially a figure of **authority**, responsible for the consequences of our actions. Milgram's famous experiments offer powerful evidence that ordinary people are capable of inflicting much pain on others, if they see themselves following orders of a person in position of authority.[1]

Moral blind spots in organizations are often institutionalized and perpetuated by **professional** *codes of conduct*, whose aim is to lessen the moral burden of individuals by establishing rules and procedures according to which different cases should be handled. Such codes have been criticized from several perspectives. Bauman views them as responsible for diluting individuals' sense of moral responsibility and dulling their moral impulse. Bureaucratic **ethics**, argues Bauman, instil a sense of indifference to the suffering and experience of other people and provide a moral amnesty for highly dubious practices.[2] Along similar lines, Jackall who investigated the morality of managers concluded that most managers operate in a morality-free zone of their own creation where morality is reduced to compliance with legal and professional regulations and to public relations.[3] 'The most salient aspect of morality as the managers themselves see it [is] how their values and ethics appear in the public eye';[4] this appears consistent with MacIntyre's view of managers as essentially amoral agents whose very function in society is to convert moral issues into technical ones.[5]

This view has been challenged by other theorists, such as Watson and Fineman whose ethnographic studies present a compelling picture of (at least some) managers neither as moral illiterates nor as immoral robots, but as fallible and at times confused agents seeking to accommodate diverse demands, including ethical demands, made upon them.[6] In a very thought-provoking contribution, ten Bos and Willmott challenge the rationalist assumptions of **business ethics** that promote and legitimize a privileging of reason over **emotion** as a source of moral action.[7] Instead of inverting the dualism by privileging sentiment and intuition in the manner of Bauman, these authors advocate a rapprochement of reason and emotions as the basis of moral judgements. In philosophy itself, there is now some resurgence of the view that emotions do not necessarily lead us astray in moral matters but can be the basis of ethical living, a view represented by 'ethics of care' theorists and others.[8]

Researchers themselves are increasingly regulated by research ethics codes. A section on the ethical responsibilities of research is now required in many grant applications, research reports, and Ph.D. dissertations. Medical research is especially tightly regulated to prevent physical damage to subjects, but social and psychological research have also come under close regulation. It is very unlikely that Milgram would have been able to conduct his experiments today, given the distress they caused to many of the subjects. Yet, filling in elaborate forms ostensibly to protect research subjects often has the consequence of creating blind spots of its own about the moral responsibilities of researchers. Elaborate precautions often have dysfunctional consequences. As a distinguished Professor of Medicine and Public Health in Great Britain eloquently put it, 'were we to be honest about our research to the Research Ethics Committees, they would place restrictions on our practice that would make our work as researchers less ethical'.

[1] Milgram, 1963; 1974.   [2] Bauman, 1989.   [3] Jackall, 1988.   [4] Ibid. 15.   [5] MacIntyre, 1981.   [6] Watson, 1998; 2001; 2003; Fineman, 1998.   [7] ten Bos and Willmott, 2001.   [8] Baier, 1985; Held, 2006; Noddings, 1986; Rorty, 1993.

• See also *business ethics, conscience, ethics, moral leadership*

Moral leadership

The relationship between **morality** and **leadership** has been widely discussed. One question that has preoccupied scholars is whether morality is an intrinsic part of leadership (as opposed to tyranny or dictatorship) or whether successful and effective leaders can, in fact, be immoral. The former position is taken by Burns who draws a hard and fast line between leaders and tyrants, thus reinventing a Platonic tradition of philosopher-kings who act in wise and principled ways. According to this view, all true leadership is moral leadership:

> By … moral leadership … I mean, first, that leaders and led have a relationship not only of power but of mutual needs, aspirations and values; second, that in responding to leaders, followers have adequate knowledge of alternative leaders and programs and the capacity to choose among those alternatives; and, third, that leaders take responsibility for their commitments. … Moral leadership emerges from, and always returns to, the fundamental wants and needs, aspirations, and values of the followers.[1]

The opposite of this view, that all leaders have to act in ways that most would recognize as immoral, has long been adopted by many political scientists and theorists. Machiavelli, the great advocate of this view, argued that a leader's overwhelming responsibility is to maintain the unity and order of the state; to this end, any means, however brutal and even corrupt, are justified.[2] Lies, blackmail, threats, and even torture can all be justified when the security of the state is in danger. In the area of business leadership, Joanne Ciulla has argued strongly for the former position and Barbara Kellerman for the latter.[3]

Whether we view good leaders as necessarily moral or not, there are certain leaders, like Christ, Confucius, Muhammad, the Buddha, and Gandhi, whom we regard as 'moral leaders'. Some of them may have had legitimate claims to **power**, but many did not. No one, for example, elected or appointed Mother Theresa or Martin Luther King to any office. Such leaders have a moral vision and offer their own lives and actions as examples of how their vision may be lived out. In some cases, moral leaders do not actually lead anyone, do not seek to establish any social movement, and do not urge anyone to follow them but view themselves more as teachers than as leaders.

Moral leadership invites very close scrutiny which makes a division between public and private lives hard to defend. Are the leader's actions consistent with their message? Are his or her private actions consistent with his or her public proclamations? Moral leaders also run the risk of their teachings being severely misinterpreted and skewed by overenthusiastic supporters who then act in ways that compromise not only the leader's message but also his or her moral integrity.

More recently, it has been argued that companies, governments, and other organizations can offer moral leadership by being the first to embrace particular ethical practices and principles that resonate with their **stakeholders** and, in some cases, subsequently come into the mainstream.[4] In a similar way to moral leadership by individuals, companies that explicitly and loudly proclaim certain principles (e.g. no animal experimentation, no sweatshops, etc.) invite close examination; this can easily lead to charges of hypocrisy, if any discrepancy can be shown to exist between principles and actions. Needless to say, such discrepancies are often matters of interpretation and spin rather than absolute facts. The charge of hypocrisy easily tars all those who assume or are cast into the role of moral leaders. Politicians who openly proclaim their commitment to 'family values' can make themselves hostages to fortune if shown to have violated these values in their own personal lives. Thus, moral leadership is a heavy mantle to bear.

---

[1] Burns, 1978, p. 4.   [2] Machiavelli, 1513/1961; 1531/1983.   [3] Ciulla, 1998/2004; Kellerman, 2004.   [4] Windsor, 2004.

Motivation and motivation theories

Motivation usually refers to the forces that drive people to act in particular ways; understanding human **action** involves an understanding of its motives, especially if this action is unusual or non-routine. We are more likely to seek the motivation of a person who starves themself to death or commits a robbery than of one who takes a shower in the morning. Motivational theories try to explain the source, strength, and form of the forces that drive action. Many of these theories distinguish between intrinsic motivation, when the motive is to be found in the psychology of the actor, and extrinsic motivation that takes the form of different external sanctions and rewards that prompt specific actions. A person who is driven by the love of art, science, or justice to act in certain ways is said to be *intrinsically* motivated, whereas someone who responds to the promise of a reward or to a threat is said to be *extrinsically* (or *instrumentally*) motivated. In reality, the two types of motivation often merge—an athlete who trains hard in order to win a great prize may be both intrinsically motivated (her love of the sport and ambition) and extrinsically (the rewards and recognition that the prize will bring).

Theories of motivation are the stock in trade of almost every management and organizational behaviour textbook. Some of these theories have proved remarkably persistent in spite of their dubious theoretical robustness and practical usefulness. Chief among them are *need-deficiency* theories which examine how **needs** drive us towards the objects that satisfy them—hunger, for instance, will drive us towards food. Other commonly discussed needs include safety, self-esteem, achievement, affiliation (being part of socially cohesive **groups**), and self-actualization (developing our own creative potential). These needs are sometimes seen as constituting a hierarchy, ranging from more basic (physiological, safety) ones to higher ones (relatedness, self-esteem, and growth).[1] *Expectancy theories* attempt systematically to model and measure the attractiveness or otherwise of different actions, and predict the motivational effort that will ensue.[2] They are closely related to *equity theories*, which examine motivation in relation to how fairly people feel they are being treated and rewarded, compared with others.[3] Most of these theories tend to offer too 'rational' accounts of motivation—people act in sensible, no-nonsense ways to achieve what they need. They offer relatively few explanations for irrational, destructive and capricious actions.

A different approach to motivation is taken by **psychoanalysis** which has argued that many of our actions are driven by **unconscious** motives, motives of which we are unaware or which we systematically conceal from ourselves. Freud argued that actions can be compromise formations between unconscious **desires** and the demands placed on people by **morality** and society.[4] Many of the unconscious desires are shaped during our early relationships with different family members, figures of authority, and objects of **love** and **identification**. We may attribute rational reasons to different actions and remain convinced that they serve specific purposes, but often these are only **rationalizations**—convenient and conventional explanations that conceal our deeper motives. Looking for the ultimate sources of desire, Freud was driven to the twin theory of drives, sexuality and the death (or destructive) drive, which can assume many different forms and manifest themselves in different ways. While many psychoanalytic theories have been questioned, the view that a large part of our motivation is unconscious has now become part of common sense. It is also one of the theories of motivation that has proved itself of use to a wide range of practitioners, from therapists to **advertisers**.

---

[1] Maslow, 1943; 1954.   [2] Vroom, 1964.   [3] Adams, Berkowitz, and Hatfield, 1976.   [4] Freud, 1915/1984b; 1933/1988; 1940/1986.

The usefulness and overall effect of motivation theories is a hotly debated subject. Are the motivation theories that fill textbook pages effective, and, if so, are they means of manipulating workers, customers, and other people, by offering the secret of what makes them tick? In a trenchant critique of American motivation theories from the 1950s and 1960s, Sievers has argued that they were built on a number of assumptions, whose interest lies not in the fact that they are invalid, but in the fact that they reveal the deeper rationale of the theories themselves.[1] These theories approached human beings essentially as mechanical entities to be driven by pushing a simple button or two. People were seen in static, non-developmental terms, as though they had neither personal histories and **identities** nor social attachments. Such theories have no real interest in learning and development. The question of what drives human action is of concern only inasmuch as it may be applied by managers as a substitute for **power** and coercion. Organizations themselves are seen in narrow instrumental terms, where rational means are deployed to maximize output. Finally, despite their concern for supposed universal truths, these motivation theories are surprisingly naive about **culture** and politics—in fact, they are hardly theories at all, but rather 'an expression of the extreme individualism, self-interest and masculinity that are characteristics of American culture'.[2] Motivation, concludes Sievers, is a pseudo-concept; it 'only became an issue—for management and organization theories as well as for the organization of work itself—when **meaning** disappeared or was lost from work; that loss of meaning of work is immediately connected with the increasing amount of fragmentation and splitting in the way work has been and is still organized in the majority of our western enterprises. In consequence, motivation theories have become surrogates for the search for meaning'.[3]

A related critique of motivation theories has been offered by Watson.[4] In the wittily titled article 'Motivation: that's Maslow, isn't it?', he reports on a piece of research of management students who mostly approached motivation theories with cynicism and saw them as useful for passing examinations rather than enhancing their effectiveness as managers. Motivation theories, argues Watson, have little to do with explaining the motives of human action and are of hardly any use in actually controlling employees at work. They do, however, form part of a discourse of management control rooted in quasi-scientific knowledge. Instead of directly serving as tools of **control**, motivation theories are part of a vocabulary of control that pathologizes certain types of behaviour (laziness, recalcitrance, boredom, depression) and lionizes others (teamwork, hard work, passion for excellence).

• See also *desire, meaning, needs*

Multiculturalism

The 7 July London bombings, fears about increased migration, and British National Party successes in the UK, plus the Danish cartoons and headscarves controversies in continental Europe, have all conspired to keep multiculturalism high on the political agenda. In its broadest sense the term itself refers to a society sympathetic towards the diverse **cultures**, religions, and **ethnic groups** that comprise it.[5] The pragmatics of today's political climate force the issue of accommodation upon us. And the realities of globalization, mass migration, the war on terror, and the clash of civilizations mean that issues of respect and recognition are hardly likely to go away. It would be wrong to see multiculturalism as driven exclusively by these international realities, however. Culture—the thing which multicultural societies are said to have many of—can refer not just to ethnic or religious groups but to any form of life or set of people with distinct values,

---

[1] Sievers, 1986; 1994.   [2] Sievers, 1994, p. 7.   [3] Ibid. 9.   [4] Watson, 1996.   [5] See e.g. Modood, 2007; Parekh, 2006.

attitudes, and lifestyles. Thus the multicultural debate intersects with the **feminist** one, and on many issues—affirmative action, workplace discrimination, and under-representation in decision-making bodies—feminists and ethnic multiculturalists advance a common agenda. Demands that states recognize the validity of same-sex relationships also come under this wider multicultural banner.

It is useful to distinguish two senses in which **society** can be multicultural. One concerns the **norms** and **values** embedded in society's public culture. At stake here are the ideals that citizens take as their point of orientation and which are embedded in its major **institutions**. The other sense is more narrow, its object being those laws and policies which advance cultures' interests or aid their social reproduction.[1] These senses are related because ideally multicultural laws should enjoy wider public support, often implying a shift in citizens' attitudes; where they do not, resentment at special treatment often follows. A multicultural society in the first sense is one in which different groups enjoy rough parity in their public standing, and no individual is denigrated on account of her lifestyle or group affiliation. The alternatives to this are assimilation (sometimes coercively achieved) or toleration where a group difference from the common culture is respected—but only a multicultural society publicly affirms a group's identities. Demands for affirmation appeal to the idea that individuals internalize others' attitudes which are thus crucial in shaping their identities.[2] A person demeaned by others will not be able to realize his or her own **identity**. In practice, this has supported controversial measures such as banning campus 'hate speech' and including African-American and other minority writers in the literary canon taught to students. Both such measures appeal to the thesis that positive recognition by others is necessary to foster a secure identity. Critics of the 'politics of recognition' argue that it is impossible for *every* culture to

have special value, and that the need for recognition is overstated. At worst, this sort of approach can become a 'boutique multiculturalism' where we marvel at the strange, the unfamiliar, and the exotic. However, the notion that people require recognition is plausible enough, and societies that harass some of their members arguably do not give them due recognition *as persons* (if not as members of minority cultures).

Special cultural rights come in a variety of shapes and sizes.[3] Some are strictly speaking individual rights such as the right to positive discrimination, the right not to work on one's holy day, or the right to be educated in one's own **language** (Spanish in the United States, for example). Others are rights held by groups as groups, for example the rights of indigenous peoples such as the Canadian Inuit to hunt and fish in ways normally illegal or the right of religious minorities to educate their children as their faith demands. Reserved seats in state or federal legislatures and the devolution of **power** to ethnic and religious minorities are further examples of special group rights. The political structures of Canada and Australia (the first societies to declare themselves multicultural) and many other societies reflect a desire to give minorities a formal role in decision making. Critics of cultural rights argue that they impede the fight against poverty and **racism**; erode civic toleration and a common identity; falsely essentialize groups and ignore the fact that people have multiple, competing identities; are merely a partial special pleading; and are often impractical to realize—the claim of black Americans for reparations for slavery being a case in point. At the global level, cultural **diversity** is pitted against the powerful cosmopolitan idea that we are all at base human beings whose common needs and interests outweigh whatever accidental features divide us (one of the most powerful thoughts anyone has ever had).

Though the term multiculturalism is straightforward enough, its local meanings in different

---

[1] Seglow, 2003.   [2] Taylor, 1994.   [3] Kymlicka, 1995.

societies reflect their own ethno-cultural mix and political culture. In the UK, recent debates have focused much on the needs of immigrants from the former empire; in much of South America, it is indigenous groups who demand political recognition and a fair share of their societies' wealth; in North America, lifestyle multiculturalism mixes with powerful immigrant (e.g. black and Hispanic) and indigenous (native American) lobbies. Yet the notion that cultural affiliation should be taken seriously as a critical part of human social identity underlies all multiculturalism's various modes and accents.

• See also *diversity, nation and nationalism, Other and othering, postcolonialism and postcolonial theory*

JONATHAN SEGLOW, ROYAL HOLLOWAY, UNIVERSITY OF LONDON

Myth

Myths are **narratives** that carry a powerful symbolism, are capable of generating strong emotions, and have a profound effect on our thoughts and actions. The word myth derives from the ancient Greek μῦθος originally meaning 'plot' and subsequently denoting any text possessing a plot, but especially those sacral narratives involving gods, heroes, and larger-than-life characters. Today a very specific sense in which myth is used is to denote a popular untruth, as in 'ten myths about slimming'. Far from being trivial, this widespread use of the word suggests two important qualities of myths—their tenuous link with 'reality' and their powerful grip over our thinking and emotions.

Myths are vital ingredients of **culture**, containing coded messages about issues that have long preoccupied humans—the meaning of life and death, good and evil, obligations and freedom,

success and failure, justice and suffering, chance and fate. They are one of the most powerful carriers of a culture's **values** and **norms**, which they can transmit across generations. They also carry and sustain many of a culture's religious beliefs. It is for this reason that mythology has long been one of the key concerns of anthropologists and ethnographers who have made extensive and at times conflicting contributions in analysing and interpreting them.

Many social scientists view humans as myth-creating animals and argue that all societies are characterized by their particular myths.[1] An interesting question concerns whether mythology represents a type of thought that is gradually replaced by **rational** thought,[2] or whether it entails a rationality of its own.[3] Whether science displaces myth or whether it spawns myths of its own is another fascinating question, with some scholars proposing that **modernity**, far from dispelling mythical beliefs by science, has sparked some of the most destructive myths in history, including the myth of genetic purity and the myth of the perfectibility of humanity through the imposition of scientific systems of government.[4] Of great interest is C. G. Jung's view of myths as carriers of *archetypes* which reside in the collective **unconscious** of humanity and express timeless desires and anxieties.[5] Myths are the vital ingredient of the great stream of unconscious ideas and images that flows through the soul of every human being.

The content of myths, their narrative structure, their plots and characters have been submitted to extensive analyses from many different angles. Joseph Campbell approached them from a broadly Jungian perspective, arguing that 'the **symbols** of mythology are not manufactured; they cannot be ordered, invented, or permanently suppressed. They are spontaneous productions of the psyche, and each bears within it, undamaged, the germ power of its source.'[6]

---

[1] Armstrong, 2005.   [2] Lévy-Bruhl, 1923/1978.   [3] Lévi-Strauss, 1963; 1978.   [4] Gray, 2002.   [5] Jung, 1968.   [6] Campbell, 1949/1988, p. 4.

Campbell argued that at the heart of every myth lies a 'quest' by a protagonist, in the course of which he or she discovers themselves. Myths are thus seen as life-supporting narratives, affording spiritual solace, answering troublesome questions, building solidarity, and offering each individual a means of finding their own place in the world.

Campbell's romantic approach to myth stands at the opposite end from the structuralist analysis of Claude Lévi-Strauss, who approached myths as possessing a logic no less rigorous than that of science. The difference between myth and science, he argued,

> lies not in the quality of the intellectual process, but in the nature of the things to which it is applied. . . . What makes a steel ax superior to a stone ax is not that the first one is better made than the second. They are equally well made, but steel is a different thing than stone. In the same way we may be able to show that the same logical processes are put to use in myth as in science, and that man has always been thinking equally well; the improvement lies, not in the alleged progress of man's mind, but in the discovery of new areas to which it may apply its unchanged and unchanging powers.[1]

It is notable that, in spite of their fundamental difference, Campbell and Lévi-Strauss agree that there is something constant and unchanging about myths.

The theory of myth has found numerous applications in the area of organizations, especially in the last twenty-five years when their cultural dimension has come into prominence. Bowles has shown how various cultural elements within organizations can function as myths in Campbell's sense, elevating leaders to the standing of heroes, resisting falsification, and acting as life-sustaining illusions.[2] Moxnes has applied Jungian archetype analysis on organizational set-ups discovering consistently the same archetypes (king, queen, crown prince, princess, servant, hero, etc.) being acted out in organizational dramas.[3] Some authors, like Schwartz and Zaleznik,[4] have drawn attention to some negative aspects of organizational myths, as potentially destructive **fantasies** that resist correction by reality, cloud rational judgement, and are responsible for a variety of disasters and accidents.

A different approach to myths in organizations was taken by Meyer and Rowan in an influential article which argued that many organizational **structures** and practices (including highly technical ones) are themselves the enactments of institutionalized myths rather than responses to the objective demands of organizing work activities.[5] **Rationality** itself is seen as the product of institutionalized myths—thus, for example, the myth of 'best practice' offers the reassurance that behaviours consistent with current views on best practice are rational.[6] This is a premiss that has had considerable impact on **institutional theories** of organization.

The vocabulary of mythology (including heroes, victims, rituals, sacrifices, triumphs, quests, visions, ordeals, betrayals, dilemmas, and even miracles, monsters, and divine interventions) has now firmly penetrated the study of organizations in relation to structure, narrative, cognition, leadership, change, and so forth. Some authors, however, have cautioned that this may be corrupting and devaluing the concept of myth, stripping it of its cosmic, sacral, and overpowering symbolism. Nor can myth (unlike stories and other narratives) be produced on demand by consultants, spin doctors, and publicists. Most serious scholars would view myths as inevitable but largely **unmanageable** elements of culture.

• See also *narratives, story and storytelling*

---

[1] Lévi-Strauss, 1963, p. 194.   [2] Bowles, 1989; 1997.   [3] Moxnes, 1998; 1999.   [4] Schwartz, 1985; Zaleznik, 1989.   [5] Meyer and Rowan, 1977.   [6] Brown, 2004.

N

Narcissism

Narcissism is a term coined by Sigmund Freud that has proven remarkably useful in discussions of individual and clinical psychology as well as in cultural and organizational studies.[1] Inspired by Narcissus, the beautiful adolescent of Greek mythology who fell in love with his own image reflected in the clear waters of a lake, narcissism involves a range of phenomena in which **love** is directed towards a person's own ego. This 'self-love' can assume many different forms ranging from excessive preoccupation with self-image and beauty to burning ambition to a need to be constantly the centre of attention.

Freud distinguished between *primary narcissism* which occurs in the earliest part of human life, when there is no **boundary** between a child's ego and the rest of the world, and *secondary narcissism* which occurs later when we adopt our ego as an object of love, as though it were an external object. Narcissism is normal—everyone's sexuality is partly oriented towards themselves. However, very high levels of narcissism can become pathological and lead to both individual neuroses and social and **organizational pathologies**. Another important distinction is between *achievement narcissism* when a person wants to distinguish herself through **achievement** in any sphere of social activity, including business, sport, the arts, politics, or science, and *image narcissism* when a person wants to be admired for who she is (or what she looks like) rather than for what she has achieved. **Image** narcissism is inevitably a central feature of the culture of celebrity whereas achievement narcissism is often seen as an important

source of **career** motivation. In general, people who were only children and enjoyed the unalloyed love and admiration of their parents along with few disciplines and boundaries in early life are liable to develop strong narcissistic **desires** which influence their later lives.

Membership of different social groups, organizations, and societies is a mixed blessing to our narcissism. On the one hand, we identify with the great heroes, achievements, and ideals of our **culture** thus obtaining a measure of narcissistic satisfaction. Being a member of a prestigious organization or an alumnus of a famous college likewise boosts our narcissism. However, **modernity** and organizations inflict considerable damage to our narcissism too. Living in large cities, surrounded by millions of unfamiliar faces, people in the twentieth century had to learn to live as unknowns in the midst of unknowns. Impersonality is a fundamental affront to our narcissism. From being unique members of a family, a clan, or a group, organizations and urban life in general consign us to the status of cogs, dispensable and replaceable. In compensation, we seek to develop **identities** of our own, to distinguish ourselves from the crowd, to establish our own individuality and uniqueness. Freud proposed the term *narcissism of minor differences* to describe the pride of groups or communities along with the intense dislike of their neighbour as they seek to differentiate themselves from their closest neighbours, such as the petty antagonism of football supporters towards supporters of a club from an adjacent territory (see **Other and othering**).[2]

Narcissism is particularly important in connection with **leadership** and organizational

---

[1] Freud, 1914/1984.   [2] Freud, 1921/1985.

culture. Narcissistic leaders tend to be creative people who like to hog the limelight and be the centre of attention. Like all strongly narcissistic people, they have many childlike qualities, including creativity, imagination, moodiness, charm, and an inability to abide by most **boundaries**; they are generally good communicators and use their imagination to develop **visions** that are compelling for their followers. Many of their qualities make them ideal for leading organizations in an era of spectacle, image, and **fantasy**.[1] It would be impossible to think of anyone leading an organization like Disneyland without strong narcissistic qualities. Unfortunately, narcissistic leaders can lapse into excessive preoccupation with image at the expense of the organization's substance. They may neglect important details and become obsessed with countering every criticism of their organization. Their narcissism can infuse an organization's entire culture.

The tell-tale signs of a narcissistic culture include grandiose statements regarding the company's excellence, lavish functions, exhibitionism, a constant preoccupation with what others say about it, and a simultaneous disregard for the social, economic, and technological processes that would ensure the organization's continuing success. The ensuing narcissistic decay is, according to Schwartz,[2] the commonest cause of corporate failure. Numerous such failures from the *Challenger* disaster to the collapse of Barings Bank have been laid squarely at the door of leadership narcissism.[3]

In the last thirty years narcissism has been seen as a wider cultural phenomenon that defines Western culture. In *The culture of narcissism*, the American cultural historian and critic Christopher Lasch used narcissism to capture the spirit of an age obsessed with image, celebrity, and **consumption**, an age which has become disillusioned with politics, religion, and science as forces of social progress,

preoccupied with intimacy and approval, yet fearful of emotional commitments and responsibilities.[4] Unlike Narcissus, contemporary narcissists are not lost in self-love but depend on an admiring audience which they are unable to find. The result is a truly desperate, addictive, and mostly vain attempt to enhance their image through consumption of various beautifying accoutrements. Failing to find permanent solace and satisfaction in the world of consumption, narcissists develop a self-hatred, which is the result of their own disturbing inability to love themselves the way they believe they should be loved. To the narcissist, the world of objects, material and human, appears to hold the promise of delivery, yet they ultimately intensify his or her frustration and dissatisfaction. Other theorists do not share Lasch's highly pessimistic conclusions, but acknowledge that there are very pronounced narcissistic features in most cultures revolving around **consumerism**.[5]

Narratives and narrative knowledge

Most people understand narratives to be texts, spoken or written, that usually involve a plot of interconnected events binding different characters together. The definition of narrative, especially in relation to related concepts like text and story, has been highly problematic and many authors have stopped making any distinction between them. Others argue that not every text is a narrative and not every narrative is a story. Narratives are then viewed as particular types of text. Unlike other texts, (such as definitions, labels, lists, recipes, logos, proverbs, hypotheses, theories, and even buildings, clothes, musical scores, and so forth, all of which can be 'read' as texts), narratives involve temporal *chains* of interrelated events or **actions**, undertaken by characters. Narratives are no simple signs, icons, or images, still less are narratives material

---

[1] Maccoby, 2000.   [2] Schwartz, 1990.   [3] Schwartz, 1988; Stein, 2000.   [4] Lasch, 1980.   [5] Bauman, 1992; McCracken, 1988; Nixon, 1992.

objects—narratives require verbs denoting what characters did or what happened to them. They are not mere snapshot photographic images, but require *sequencing*, something noted by most systematic commentators on narratives.[1]

Whether a straight chronology of events is enough to constitute a narrative is another debatable point. Some theorists take the view that a *chronicle* is precisely a narrative involving a chronological record of events that simply happened, without any attempt to establish the meaning of these events, treating facts simply as **information**.[2] Others follow Forster, who famously argued that 'the king died, then the queen died' *is not* a narrative, but 'the king died, then the queen died of grief' *is* a narrative.[3] In either case, what is important is that as we move from narrative to story we are forced to recognize the importance of *plot* (Aristotle's '*mythos*'): 'The plot functions to transform a chronicle or listing of events into a schematic whole by highlighting and recognizing the contribution that certain events make to the development and outcome of the story....A plot is able to weave together a complex of events to make a single story.'[4] Thus the plot 'knits events together', allowing us to recognize the deeper significance of an event in the light of other events.[5] It can be seen immediately that in order to be considered a narrative, it is not enough that an event happened; it must reveal something about the significance of other events which cannot be grasped without it. Without knowing that the king dies, we cannot account for the queen's grief.

Since Aristotle's *Poetics*, narratives (including stories, novels, epic poems, myths, ballads, movies, drama, and so forth) have been studied by the discipline of literary criticism. As a result of the linguistic turn in philosophy and the social sciences, however, they have now become central to many other disciplines. Current interest in organizational narratives is part of a broader tendency of narrativization of organizational theory, an emphasis on language, scripts, metaphors, talk, stories, and narratives not as parts of a superstructure erected on top of the material realities of organizations but rather as parts of the very essence of organization. This has challenged standard views of organizations built around the themes of bureaucracy, hierarchy, and authority, and emphasizes, if not the primacy, at least the relative autonomy of the **symbolic** dimension. There are different approaches in the study of organizational narratives, ranging from looking at organizations as containing a variety of narratives to seeing them as narratives in their own right (see **language**).

Narratives are currently exercising immense fascination on social scientists and are the focus of a large amount of research. Following Lyotard,[6] many scholars share the view that while **modernity** was dominated by **grand narratives** ('grands récits') of science, religion, politics, and art, ours is the time of the everyday narrative ('petit récit'), the time when we constantly invent narratives to make sense of our experiences, share them, modify them, and discard them. Memories of grand narratives still exist (the grand theory, the ideology, the national myth, the religious faith), but these tend to fragment into many diverse and endlessly mutating variants. One reason behind the rise of narrative research (referred to inelegantly by some as 'narratology') is the recognition that a great deal of **knowledge** assumes narrative forms, such as stories, anecdotes, and tales. In contrast to scientific knowledge that guides engineers, physicists, and chemists, professionals and managers are often informed by narrative knowledge or experiential knowledge, the kind of knowledge that comes from experience of dealing with real-life problems, successfully or unsuccessfully.[7] Narrative knowledge is especially important for **communities of practice** that share knowledge

[1] Bruner, 1990; Culler, 1981/2001; Czarniawska, 1997; 1999; Labov, 1972; MacIntyre, 1981; Polkinghorne, 1988; Ricœur, 1984; Van Dijk, 1975; Weick, 1995.   [2] Benjamin, 1968; Gabriel, 2000.   [3] Forster, 1962, p. 93.   [4] Polkinghorne, 1988, pp. 18–19.   [5] Czarniawska, 1999, pp. 64 f.   [6] Lyotard, 1984/1991.   [7] Tsoukas, 1998a; Tsoukas and Hatch, 2001.

in informal and creative ways, borrowing ideas from each other and adapting them to situations at hand (see **bricolage).** There are numerous **ethnographic** studies showing how different groups of employees share knowledge (both of a technical and social knowledge) by swapping stories of critical cases; these include Orr's study of Xerox maintenance staff and Patriotta's study of Fiat workers.[1]

Narrative knowledge is not generalizable in the same way that scientific knowledge seeks to be. The statement 'water boils at 100 degrees Celsius' may be true, false, or true under particular conditions (e.g. at sea level and normal atmospheric conditions). By contrast, 'the king died and then the queen died of grief' is not generalizable. It is not the case that every time a king dies, his queen will die even if she loves him. Yet it is a statement whose truth is a narrative one, it 'makes sense' to us. It is for this reason that Jerome Bruner argued that 'logico-scientific' and 'narrative' knowing 'are two modes [or paradigms] of cognitive functioning, two modes of thought, each providing distinctive ways of ordering experience, of constructing reality. The two (though complementary) are irreducible to one another. . . . Each of these ways of knowing, moreover, has operating principles of its own and its own criteria of well-formedness, they differ radically in their procedures for verification'.[2] Bruner makes a strong argument that narrative truth is fundamentally different from factual truth—an element of a narrative is 'true' if it helps us make sense of the rest of the plot in a compelling and gripping way.

A second reason for the current popularity of narratives in social science lies in the recognition of their powerful persuasive effect in organizational **communication**. 'Having a narrative' has come to be viewed as vital in all communications, whether personal, organizational, or mass. A political party seeking re-election; a physician explaining to a patient the nature of her condition; an organization recalling one of its products alleged to be a health risk or announcing the closure of some factories; a parent disciplining a child; a leader or a government announcing the launch of a new initiative—they all rely on narrative. Narratives may be contested, subverted, or ridiculed, but, at least, they offer us a platform from which we make sense of situations. Without narrative, we risk 'losing the plot'.

A third reason for the popularity of narrative is its importance for the construction of individual, group, organizational, and even national **identities**. Identities are widely viewed as 'narrative', forged through the stories that we construct about ourselves, about our pasts and our futures. In making sense of our lives, we create many and different narratives. In some of them, we are in charge of events, confidently making decisions, overcoming difficulties, and shaping our destinies. In others, we are shaped by events, carrying the scars of different experiences, enduring and surviving, bending and suffering. In some, we are the protagonists, whether as heroes, victims, or survivors. In others, we focus our sight on the predicaments of others, friends, relatives, people with whom we work, helping them create their own narratives or at times undermining narratives that they have carefully created for themselves.

Just as we sometimes create the narratives of others, there are times when we allow others, doctors, parents, employers, to create our own narratives, and there are times when we contest and reject the narratives that they have created for us. In this way, scholars like Sims, Brown and Humphreys, and many others have theorized that identities are fluid, precarious, and subject to constant revisions.[3] They are also **reflexive**. Like the Escher etching showing two hands each drawing the other, the narrator and the narrative's central character co-create each other. At every moment the narrator creates a protagonist, whose actions and predicaments redefine the narrator. In telling the story of my life, I make

[1] Orr, 1996; Patriotta, 2003a; 2003b.   [2] Bruner, 1986, p. 21.   [3] Sims, 2003; Brown and Humphreys, 2002; 2006.

sense of past events and create a person living in the present as a continuation of that story. It is in this way that our **experience** becomes digested, meaningful, and the basis of our identities.

In spite of the current popularity of narrative in different areas of social and human sciences, some authors have cautioned against viewing every aspect of human experience as narrative. Strawson, for example, has argued strongly that not all people live their lives through a construction of a narrative, and not for everybody is narrative the preferred form of **communication**.[1] In my own work, I have emphasized the very different abilities and interests that people have in constructing narratives and the challenged posed to narratives by other forms of communication, most especially pictures and images.[2]

• See also *grand narratives, knowledge, language, story and storytelling*

Nation and nationalism

A nation, declared Ernest Renan in a lecture given in 1882, is 'a group of people united by a mistaken view about the past and a hatred of their neighbours'.[3] Instead of looking for the essence of nation in some shared racial or political characteristic, Renan was in fact identifying a nation by its people's sense of having 'achieved great things in the past and of wishing to do more of the same in the future'. At the same time, he was noting that a nation engages in collective amnesia, deleting from its past those less than glorious pages, such as military defeats and the massacres of others. The term **genocide** had not yet entered the vocabulary, but, had it done so, Renan would have insisted that a nation that perpetrated it must forget it in order to remain a nation, whereas one that suffered it and survived it must remember it.

Nation is an easy term to use and a hard one to define—in particular, it is difficult to define which groups constitute nations. Nationalism can be viewed as an **ideology** that binds people together in the belief that their destiny is profoundly shared. Although rudiments of nationalism existed in earlier periods, it became a major social force in the national liberation movements that led to the establishment of many European states in the nineteenth century and equally it was the force that fuelled anti-colonial struggles in the twentieth century. It was during the last two centuries that nation came to signify an idea and an ideal in the name of which millions of people died. Yet, neither nation nor nationalism has attained a core position in the social sciences, the way that class, religion, or the state did. Instead, they feature predominantly in discussions of ideology, **identity**, and, increasingly, **multiculturalism**—the relations between different ethnic groups in a single state.

Some authors have approached nation and nationalism as objective phenomena of **modernity** resulting from the rise of the modern state (and relatedly of mass education, universal suffrage, etc.) and impersonal conditions of work in bureaucratic organizations that require shared cultural assumptions.[4]

Others have looked at nations as **social constructs** that require considerable work to establish and sustain. In a highly influential book, Benedict Anderson developed a theory of nation around the concept of 'imagined communities'—communities that imagine themselves to be sovereign, united, and limited.[5] In Anderson's view, the rise of capitalism and the decline of religion were instrumental in bringing about new forms of imagined communities focusing on nation. This was amplified by the decline of Latin as the language of scholarly communication and its replacement by a number of national vernaculars brought about by the rise of the printing press. Along similar lines, and going beyond Renan's definition, the eminent British historian Eric Hobsbawm

---

[1] Strawson, 2004.   [2] Gabriel, 2004a.   [3] Renan, 1882/1996.   [4] Gellner, 1983; Smith, 1998; 2001.   [5] Anderson, 1983.

argued that many 'traditions' around which national **identity** consolidated were, in fact, relatively recent inventions.[1] Hobsbawm comments that inventing traditions is essentially a process of formalization and ritualization, characterized by reference to an imagined past, if only by imposing repetition. Vital elements of traditions sustaining national identities are **myths**, especially epics, and other heavily symbolic artefacts, such as shrines, birthplaces of heroes, costumes, songs, and so forth. It is telling that nationalist poets, composers, and artists play as important a part in the making of nations as the heroes who are celebrated through their work.[2] Whether nation and even nationalism can ever shed their chauvinistic connotations and find expressions that acknowledge, tolerate, or even engage creatively with other nations and other nationalisms is an unanswered question.

In the area of organizations, nations enter predominantly through the study of national **cultures** and the problems created for businesses by the need to operate across national frontiers. The much-quoted works of Hofstede and Hampden-Turner and Trompenaars are routinely relied upon to provide clues on national differences and their impact on the work of managers and the tastes of consumers.[3] These works come close to resurrecting the concept of 'national character'—a concept about which Max Weber had warned that it represented 'a mere confession of ignorance'[4]—and have attracted a number of substantive and methodological criticisms. National character studies have been criticized by scholars for attributing a false uniformity and homogeneity to people inhabiting particular countries, thus stereotyping different national cultures. In a multicultural, hybrid world, the notion of there being a national character becomes extremely hard to hold, as the citizens, constituents, and employees of organizations may themselves come from a great plurality of cultures. In this respect, national culture is very much a modernist conception, which appears outdated today.

• See also *globalization*

Needs

A need indicates a deficiency, a lack, an absence. It suggests a state of incompleteness. Needs have long been seen as the key to **motivation**, and, in particular, as a way of understanding what drives people's actions, among other things as workers and as consumers. The attractiveness of the concept of a need lies in its simplicity—if we can understand what needs people have, we can understand why they behave the way they do. And if we happen to be their employer, if we are seeking to sell them our products, if we are trying to teach them algebra or even to keep them in a prison, we can do a better job of it.

In a loftier way, philosophers, welfare reformers, human rights advocates, social democrats, and others have argued that all people have some fundamental needs for food, shelter, safety, education, health, and **voice** which constitute their human rights, and that it is the state's responsibility to ensure that these needs are satisfied at least to a degree referred to as a 'social minimum'.[5]

Hunger is seen as the prototypical need and food as the prototypical way of satisfying a need. At once we realize that this is unsatisfactory—people rarely eat just to satisfy hunger. The food we eat is usually prepared carefully to give more than satisfaction, for example, to give pleasure. Increasing numbers of people in industrial countries eat to the point of obesity while others starve themselves. Many people eat things that they know to be bad for their health and others carefully select what they eat, how they eat, where and when they eat, to meet other 'needs', such as the need to be with other people, the need to impress others, or to mark special

[1] Hobsbawm, 1983.   [2] See e.g. Ash, 1990.   [3] Hofstede, 1980; 2001; Hampden-Turner and Trompenaars, 1997; 2000.   [4] Weber, 1958.   [5] Doyal and Gough, 1991.

occasions. The same applies to other things that we consume, including clothes, cars, and so forth. Needs then go beyond the needs of our bodies to include needs for self-esteem, social acceptance, and so forth. The difficulty then is that a need can be speculated after the event for any kind of **action**. Does the teenager have a 'need' for an iPod, or is her desire for one the result of her 'need' to be like her friends who already have them, or the 'need' to enjoy her favourite music, or the 'need' to isolate herself from the shouting between her parents?

One way out of this difficulty is to distinguish between 'fundamental' human needs and others that derive from our cultural and social environments. A theorist who took this position was Marxist philosopher Herbert Marcuse. In his once influential critique of capitalism in *One Dimensional Man*,[1] Marcuse argued that throughout human history new needs are created—pre-literate people did not have a need for education, not did the ancient Romans have needs for cars. Furthermore, Marcuse notes that whether a requirement or a possibility is 'seized as a *need* depends on whether or not it can be seen as desirable and necessary for the prevailing societal institutions and interests'.[2] Notice Marcuse's sophisticated postulation of needs as **socially constructed** rather than as natural entities, long before the rise of **postmodernism**. Where Marcuse differed from postmodern thinkers is in viewing some needs as *true* and others as *false*:

> We may distinguish both true and false needs. 'False' are those which are superimposed upon the individual by particular social interests in his repression: the needs which perpetuate toil, aggressiveness, misery, and injustice. Their satisfaction might be most gratifying to the individual, but this happiness is not a condition which has to be maintained and protected if it serves to arrest the development of the ability (his own and others) to recognize the disease of the whole and grasp the chances of curing the

disease. The result then is euphoria in unhappiness. Most of the prevailing needs to relax, to have fun, to behave and consume in accordance with the advertisements, to love and hate what others love and hate, belong to this category of false needs.

> Such needs have a societal content and function which are determined by external powers over which the individual has no control; the development and satisfaction of these needs is heteronomous. No matter how much such needs may have become the individual's own, reproduced and fortified by the conditions of his existence; no matter how much he identifies himself with them and finds himself in their satisfaction, they continue to be what they were from the beginning—products of a society whose dominant interest demands repression.[3]

Marcuse's 'one-dimensional man' is the individual locked in an vicious circle of false needs for different consumer products and experiences for which he or she sacrifices an ever-increasing part of his life in **alienated** work. Such is the grip of false needs that people will forfeit the satisfaction of real needs (healthy food, decent clothes, a sound education, the love of others) in order to buy spurious goods that will provide short-lived euphoria and long-term disappointment. **Advertising** as well as other social institutions of capitalism were seen as manufacturing false needs.

This argument that once stirred students on the campuses of Berkeley and UCLA has now fallen out of favour. The concept of 'false needs', along with its Marxist progenitor 'false consciousness', is seen as indefensible. Who is to decide what needs are false and what are true? In contrast to the passive **consumer** addicted to different products and services envisaged by Marcuse, it has become now normal to talk of sophisticated and discriminating consumers who can see through the wiles of advertisers, merchandisers, and other 'hidden persuaders',[4]

---

[1] Marcuse, 1964.   [2] Ibid. 4.   [3] Ibid. 4–5.   [4] Packard, 1957.

and please themselves by selecting different products and experiences, creatively assimilating them in their lives. Campbell has thus argued that **desire** rather than need provides the motivation for contemporary consumption.[1] Needs require satisfaction, desire seeks pleasure—and pleasure today is predominantly provided not by physical sensation but by **fantasy**. 'Whilst only reality can provide satisfaction, both illusions and delusions can supply pleasure', argues Campbell.[2] The consumers' 'basic motivation is the desire to experience in reality the pleasurable dramas which they have already enjoyed in imagination, and each "new" product is seen as offering the possibility of realizing this ambition. However, since reality can never provide the perfected pleasures encountered in day-dreams (or, if at all, only in part, and very occasionally), each purchase leads to literal disillusionment'.[3]

The concept of needs continues to find uses in social policy studies; it remains a staple of motivation theories in management textbooks; but its heyday appears to have passed, as it gets overtaken by terms like desires, aspirations, and fantasies which seem more in tune with the spirit of our times.

Negative capability

Negative capability is an idea that first occurs in a famous and strange letter of the poet John Keats to his brothers George and Thomas Keats, dated 21 December 1817. In it, he refers to 'Negative Capability, that is when man is capable of being in uncertainties, Mysteries, doubts without any irritable reaching after fact and reason.' The idea was picked up by Keats's biographer Walter Bate,[4] and has recently exercised a considerable influence on studies of **leadership** and the creative process. A leader who displays negative capability is one who does not seek to **control** or fix everything, but can live with uncertainty and tension. Such a leader knows that at times

inaction is preferable to **action** and is able to contain the **anxieties** and fears created by uncertainty.[5]

Chia goes further in arguing that negative capability 'is a capability which entails an insistent refusal to be seduced by the dominant signifying systems characterizing contemporary modes of thought'.[6] A **creative** person, likewise, can live with uncertainty, avoiding premature closures of arguments, thoughts, and ideas. Instead of seeking solace in the certainty of definitions, proofs, and facts, such a person is able to sustain conflicting and contradictory views, allowing them to mature and gradually engage with each other.

Negative capability has some points of similarity to the core Taoism principle of *wu wei*, which requires knowing when to act and when not to act. In today's organizations and societies, when leaders are constantly expected to 'do something' about every problem and trouble, negative capability is a rare quality indeed. Yet it is one that comes from the wisdom of realizing that many human tragedies arise not when people fail to act but when they act prematurely, impetuously, and impulsively,

Networks

Among the many concepts and ideas that have sought to define society today as having moved beyond **modernity**, few have been as influential as network.[7] Networks are epitomized by the inter*net*, and themselves epitomize the mobile, global, fluid, non-authoritarian, information-dependent qualities of our times. If bureaucratic organizations dominated social and economic activity during modernity, networks, it is argued by many scholars, have become the defining social **institution** of our times. Networks, like organizations, can be viewed as social collectivities or associations—within networks, however, there is no **hierarchy**; instead networks comprise

---

[1] Campbell, 1989. [2] Ibid. 61. [3] Ibid. 61, 89–90. [4] Bate, 1976. [5] Bennis, 1998; Simpson, French, and Harvey, 2002. [6] Chia and Morgan, 1996, p. 40. [7] See e.g. Castells, 1996a; Piore and Sabel, 1984.

many independent units or 'nodes', which may be individuals, groups, organizations, or other networks, linked together for strength, size, and flexibility. Within networks, actors (or 'actants' if we follow **actor network theory)** interact, cut deals, exchange information, and tell stories—they do not generally give and receive orders. Networks are thus seen as supplanting **bureaucracies** and forcing organizations to reinvent themselves.

In accordance with the fractal qualities of complex systems (see **complexity and chaos theories**), one can discover networks across scales, at the highest and lowest levels, from the interpersonal, to the organizational, to the national and international. A 'network enterprise' includes autonomous segments or project teams interfacing simultaneously with other autonomous segments to provide each other with their particular resources and expertise. Unlike a literal net, the links between segments can be uncoupled, to find new partners at different times. For example, where an organization would once have been in charge of all its different functions—raw materials supply, production, research and development, human resources, sales, and marketing—now all these functions can be outsourced as required. Such inter-organizational networks can also apply to intra-organizational relations, where project teams and departments are loosely coupled to draw upon each other's expertise as and when required.

The prevalence of network arrangements within and across organizations has given rise to the view that we are witnessing the growth of a 'network society'. **Information technology** is seen as the essential driving force behind this; the nodes of the net can now spread globally and communicate with each other instantaneously. Thus, Castells has argued that industrial capitalism has evolved into 'informational capitalism'.[1] This has three fundamental features. First, economic activity is dominated by the production, exchange, and sharing of **information** rather than

material goods. Second, the new economy is global—financial markets, science and technology, international trade of goods and services, advanced business services, multinational production firms and their ancillary networks, communication media, and highly skilled **labour** are all mobile and not restricted by organizational or national boundaries. Third, economic activity is organized in networks which include firms of different sizes. These mobilize themselves on specific business projects, and dissolve into new networks when particular projects are finished.

Major corporations work through constantly shifting alliances and partnerships, specific to different products, processes, time, and space. Groups of organizations or departments of organizations thus become parts of networks. Such organizations are ill suited to traditional methods of management, calling instead for closer collaboration, trust, and sharing of information. They may have fuzzy **boundaries** with individuals belonging to two or more organizations at the same time. In this way, the term 'network' has come to suggest an association based on sharing, cooperation, and trust, rather than **competition** and **conflict**—it is for this reason that **communities of practice** are sometimes thought of as networks, sharing information and knowledge. This sharing is especially important in respect of **knowledge** and **information** which are traded either freely or in quasi-gift relations.

One consequence of all this is that 'networking' has emerged as a very important type of **work**, taking place in different forums including conferences, fairs, golf courses, and 'workshops' of every conceivable type. Networking involves the creation and cultivation of connections, most especially with people or groups who can prove useful now or in the future. This alerts us to some meanings of the word network that have been obscured by the emphasis on voluntary, non-authoritarian, and sharing relationships. These meanings can be found, for

---

[1] Castells, 1996a; 1996b.

instance, in the expression 'old-boy networks', i.e. highly exclusive and even secret societies of individuals who share more than a school tie or a golf course membership—they share political and economic interests which they assiduously cultivate, usually to the detriment of others. These kinds of networks have long been features of elite theories of the state and society.[1] They are also central to current discussions of social **capital**, i.e. the advantages that individuals may derive from their social connections.

Another concealed dimension to networks is revealed by the common use of the term 'sharing', most especially sharing knowledge and sharing information. Sharing relations undoubtedly suggest a degree of generosity and reciprocity in trading knowledge. This may seriously underestimate the realities of **power** hidden by the use of the term 'sharing'. As scholars of gifts have long known, gifts are parts of elaborate power relations, relying on **norms** of reciprocation and establishing pecking orders of power and status.[2] The view of networks as power-neutral associations then would appear to be seriously blinkered. Furthermore, many arrangements referred to as networks (such as between firms and their suppliers or their 'partners') frequently reveal themselves to be nothing but precarious **market** relations in which flexibility disguises an absence of loyalty or true partnership. In conclusion then, we might observe that emphasis on networks is justified by various developments in the nature of social relations, prompted by new information technologies. However, it should be remembered that 'network' is itself an ideologically laden term, a discursive effect, a way of talking about different phenomena that carries powerful and potentially misleading connotations.

New Public Management

The New Public Management (NPM) 'reform' wave is an internationally significant movement in public services management which started in the 1980s but which continues to be of significance today. It represents a successor form to the old 'public administration' and brought ideas, doctrines, and techniques from organizational economics, management, and accounting into those public-sector organizations that survived the concurrent privatization wave. It was both an ideological challenge and a practical reform project. As a result, conventional public administrative forms influenced by ideas from political science and law became less important. The NPM was part of the political project to 'downsize' the large public sectors characteristic of social democratic states following the taxpayers' revolts of the 1980s. It was often sponsored by finance ministries in their attempt to rein in high-spending departments.

Core NPM ideas include (i) the introduction of **market**-like mechanisms in core public services such as healthcare and education (quasi-markets; contracting out, market testing) to replace planning-based resource allocation; (ii) more assertive and powerful general management, especially in challenging traditional interest groups such as public-sector **trade unions** and public service **professionals**; public service managers are now paid more but set stretching **performance** targets and their tenure is riskier; (iii) more elaborate measurement and audit systems, including performance management regimes to monitor producers within a lower-trust public policy environment; these systems enabled **policy** makers to identify and put pressure on low-performing service providers; and (iv) a move to management through contract rather than old-style **hierarchies**. This led to so-called agentification in central government (the UK 'Next Steps' Agencies), where large operational agencies were decoupled from ministries and given more operational autonomy which empowered management. Central ministries downsized into a strategic core, ostensibly removed

[1] Mills, 1999; Parry, 1969; Paxman, 1990.   [2] See e.g. Belk, 1982; Mauss, 1925/1974; Yang, 1995.

from operational matters. However, the politics/administration line proved difficult to draw in sensitive policy arenas (e.g. was the escape of prisoners from jail an operational or a political/policy matter?) Within the delivery of core public services such as healthcare, there was a similar commissioner/provider split.

Key features of the NPM, including its broad international reach, were analysed by Hood.[1] NPM ideas were widely and rapidly diffused through international agencies such as OECD, the World Bank, and consulting firms. As NPM matured, sub-types became apparent with some internal contradictions between them, for example, between a desire for empowered management and intensified audit systems.[2] In the UK, audit-based NPM proved to be dominant and placed new forms of *ex post* restrictions on public managers.[3]

As well as system-level effects, the NPM had effects on individual **roles**, **careers**, and even work **identity**: it created New Public Managers. While there was 'managerialization', this process could be more subtle than sometimes assumed. Some public service professionals were drawn into professional/manager 'hybrid' roles including doctors who became Clinical Directors or senior academics who became University Vice Chancellors.[4]

NPM has sometimes been seen as an Anglo-Saxon managerial construct. While the UK and New Zealand are NPM index cases, in the USA, NPM ideas proved less influential than reforms (led by the Vice-President Al Gore in the 1990s) inspired by different ideas of empowerment and liberation management. NPM has had low impact on European jurisdictions such as Germany and France, influenced more by traditional neo-Weberian ideas of the strong positive state or *Rechtsstaat*.[5] The question of international divergence/convergence on the NPM is an important one, with strong signs of continuing local **path dependency** in some jurisdictions.

The NPM attracted strong supporters and critics, in terms of both its managerial implications and its academic foundations. Managerial supporters point to its emphasis on transparency (e.g. contracts, performance management), efficiency, and better value for money for taxpayers. Managerial critics argue that contract-based modes of **control** create a cat's cradle of contracts and subcontracts with weak governmental power to steer. Secondly, the NPM leads to highly vertical reporting and performance management lines and an erosion of the lateral flows of communication needed to tackle 'wicked problems' which span different ministries (e.g. social deprivation).

Within the academic domain, different disciplines see the NPM differently. For mainstream management, the NPM usefully imports ideas of the firm into sluggish public agencies (although the sub-discipline of public management argues there are important contextual differences). For economists, incentivization through contracts and performance-related pay is likely to increase effort levels and, if designed correctly, helps align principals and agents. Critics from political science draw attention to the NPM's *democratic deficit* and possible loss of legitimacy in public policy making (there was an important shift from elected to appointed decision makers as part of NPM). **Feminist** critics point to the gendered nature of NPM. It marks a hardening of managerial style within the public services: it is viewed as a man's movement. For **postmodernists**, NPM is yet another late modernist rationalist narrative which neglects more organic and less controllable themes of citizen governance or co-evolution of government with the environment.

Does NPM still matter? Some argue that public management shifted to a post-NPM or '**governance**'-based form,[6] characterized by an emphasis on public value, network-based forms of management ('joined-up government'),

[1] Hood, 1991; 1995.   [2] Ferlie et al., 1996.   [3] Power, 1997.   [4] Ferlie et al., 1996.   [5] Pollitt and Bouckaert, 2004.   [6] Newman, 2001.

and organizational **learning**. The pathologies of the NPM form have become more widely recognized. The New Labour regimes in the UK are cited as exemplars of the governance-based mode. Yet the NPM has shown surprising resilience even in the UK, with a persistence of performance management and a recent shift from **networks** back to quasi-markets (e.g. healthcare).

The post-9/11 security agenda may challenge NPM doctrines. Can the early twenty-first-century security state take risks in terms of loss of steering capacity in such strategic areas as control over borders, transport (e.g. privatization of airports), defence procurement, and infectious disease control? Will we see a move away from NPM and the reassertion of conventional Weberian hierarchies within the new security state?

EWAN FERLIE, KING'S COLLEGE, UNIVERSITY OF
LONDON

Norms

Norms (or social norms) have long been one of the core concepts of sociology and a vital element of human **cultures**. Norms are generally accepted standards of behaviour that exercise a powerful influence over the ways we act, we think, and we feel. As such, norms, along with **institutions**, are viewed as part of the social structure that shapes and controls our actions. Different groups, organizations, and nations have different social norms, which they come to view as natural, righteous, and self-obvious. A person who violates such norms is liable to experience various sanctions such as ridicule, exclusion, ostracism, scapegoating, or even violence. Norms govern many aspects of our lives—from the seemingly insignificant (how far away we stand when we are talking to someone) to the momentous (what kind of person we marry or whether we marry at all). Even when we believe that we are making independent **choices**, we are often unwittingly acting out some norm or other. Thus, when we choose a particular item

of clothing, we may indeed be acting in accordance with the dictates of **fashion**, imitating the actions of those who set the trends. When we choose what newspaper to read or where to go on holiday (or, again, whether to go 'on holiday' at all) we are often acting out the norms of peer groups, of people 'like ourselves'.

Most norms govern our behaviour in an **unconscious** way—we eat with a knife and fork or with chopsticks because this is the *normal* thing to do in specific situations. Normal behaviour is behaviour that complies with social norms. Thus, social norms control our behaviour more subtly than the **rules** of a bureaucracy—not by being written down but by making us feel embarrassed or exposed whenever we violate them. 'Internalization' is the process whereby norms cease to be external forces controlling people and are adopted as the 'normal' way to act. Even when a behaviour is governed by a rule, the way the rule is enforced depends on norms. Drivers who drive in a foreign country for the first time often discover that the rules may be the same, but they are applied in very different ways. The way norms are disseminated and enforced is through visible actions but also through stories and **narratives** of the sort 'Let me tell you what happened when Misha criticized the CEO's pet project to his face'.

The importance of norms was highlighted by the **Hawthorne experiments** and the ensuing **Human Relations** school of management which argued that how hard people work depends on the social norms that govern perceptions of 'a fair day's work', rather than financial incentives. As social animals, people work as hard as those around them—working much harder or much less hard than them is likely to elicit exclusion and other forms of sanctions. In general, the more cohesive a **group**, the stronger its norms. At the same time, not all people **conform** to norms with the same sincerity or enthusiasm. Goffman, for example, explored and demonstrated the ingenuity with which individuals can give the appearance of complying with norms while, at the same time, subverting or ignoring them.[1] Schein argued that between conformity and rebellion there is 'creative individualism', whereby an individual accepts some core norms, rejects others, and moulds some to his or her own **identity** and personality.[2] The concept of norm frequently obscures the **resistances** that different norms (from the right way to dress whether one is a businessman or a Muslim woman, to norms of sexual behaviour and norms of reciprocity) generate at many different levels—individual, group, organizational, and social.

While the concept of norm has proved useful in describing social actions, its theoretical possibilities seem to be somewhat limited and, in recent years, the concept has lost some of its earlier popularity. It is still discussed in connection with **motivation**, **conformity**, **multiculturalism**, and **structuration** theory, but no major debates or controversies seem to surround it at the moment. Yet the concept's relation to 'normality' reveals some interesting ambiguities. What is a normal person? What is a normal organization? What is normal behaviour? These are fascinating questions that have led to some intriguing answers.

Two such arguments are particularly notable—Freud's view that normality is an 'ideal fiction' and, relatedly, Foucault's argument that normality is not merely **socially constructed**, but that it is a fundamental element of a technology of power. In his paper 'Analysis terminable and interminable', Freud argued that 'a normal ego is, like normality in general, an ideal fiction'.[3] No individual is perfectly normal—both in their actions and in their thoughts, people behave in strange, unpredictable, destructive, and even 'mad' ways. Scratch beneath the surface of any person and you will discover madness, neurosis, and 'abnormality'. Yet the distinction between normal and pathological is not merely a mistake that can be corrected through better knowledge and understanding.

Building on Canguilhem's studies of how medicine defines certain conditions as pathological,[4] Foucault argued that normality is an illusion on which **power** rests,[5] through a technology that 'measures in quantitative terms and hierarchizes in terms of value the abilities, the level, the "nature" of individuals...In short, it normalizes.'[6] *Normalization* does not, as earlier theorists might have argued, merely restrict freedom by forcing compliance with social norms; instead, it destroys freedom, inasmuch as people only register as subjects through being viewed as normal or abnormal. Thus, for example, in an organization that normalizes sadism, individuals only register inasmuch as they act as sadists or inasmuch as they refuse to do so. The normalization of pathological conditions in and out of organizations is an issue that has attracted considerable attention in recent years (see **organizational pathologies**).[7]

• See also *culture, groups, socialization*

---

[1] Goffman, 1959; 1961.   [2] Schein, 1968.   [3] Freud, 1937, p. 231.   [4] Canguilhem, 1989.   [5] Foucault, 1961/1965; 1977; 1980.
[6] Foucault, 1977, p. 183.   [7] See e.g. Kets de Vries and Miller, 1984; Sievers, 1999.

Oligarchy and Iron Law of Oligarchy

Oligarchy is the rule of the few over the many. Based on a study of the German Social Democratic Party in the early part of the century, Robert Michels (1876–1936) argued that all organizations are subject to an *Iron Law of Oligarchy*. Arguing against his mentor, Max Weber, Michels claimed that organizations are not rational instruments for the accomplishment of administrative goals; instead, he saw political systems through which small elites control the masses. 'It is organization which gives birth to the dominion of the elected over the electors, of the mandated over the mandators, of the delegated over the delegators. Who says organization, says oligarchy.'[1] Weberian rules and procedures are nothing but an elaborate smokescreen, behind which a ruthless power game unfolds, a game through which leaders seek to perpetuate themselves in positions of **power**. To this end, the organization's survival becomes essential; **goals** become regularly displaced, values and doctrines are constantly compromised, and organization becomes an end in itself.

Michels argued that leaders have formidable mechanisms for overcoming any internal opposition. They control finances, **information**, and appointments, they can reward those loyal to them and marginalize those against them. They can divide the opposition or accuse it of 'rocking the boat'. They know the rules and regulations intimately and can use them to attain their own objectives. If the rules and regulations do not suit them, they have the power to alter them. They develop political skills through which they can manipulate their subordinates. Finally, and most importantly, they build their strength on the *apathy* of the organizational members, who do not have the time, the expertise, or the inclination to challenge the leaders' decisions.

Michels's theory offers a sophisticated explanation for **corruption**. Even honest leaders come to view themselves as indispensable for the survival and success of their organization. His theory led him to view all democratic and formal procedures as a deception perpetrated by the leaders and he ended his life as a supporter of fascism, in the strange belief that only direct action could liberate the masses. His pessimistic conclusions have been disputed by certain authors. Gouldner, for example, argued that there is an 'Iron Law of Democracy' opposing the oligarchic tendencies identified by Michels: the more oppressive, the more corrupt a regime, argued Gouldner, the stronger the opposition it breeds.[2] Some tyrants may survive for long periods of time, but many are toppled, even when their power appeared unshakeable. The political system that can eliminate corruption and power abuses in organizations or in societies at large has yet to be discovered—in Churchill's famous aphorism, 'democracy is the worst form of government except for all those others that have been tried.'

Organizational pathologies

A pathology is an abnormal condition, usually associated with an illness, mental or physical. It stands at the opposite end from 'normality' (see **norms**). Whether a pathology can be identified in any 'objective' manner is highly dubious. Many

---

[1] Michels, 1949, p. 401. [2] Gouldner, 1955.

theorists now view both normality and pathology as **social constructs**, as features of **discourse** rather than statements of 'fact'. Freud described normality as an 'ideal fiction',[1] and argued that neurosis is itself normal—what distinguishes people categorized as normal from others is that they hide their neurosis, that they adopt socially acceptable forms of neurosis, or that they have a diluted mixture of neurotic symptoms rather than any one specific one. 'The expectation that every neurotic phenomenon can be cured may, I suspect, be derived from the layman's belief that the neuroses are something quite unnecessary which have no right to exist.'[2] Many theorists today not only question whether there is any objective difference between normality and pathology, but align themselves with Foucault's view that the ability to define what is normal and what is pathological is an effect of **power**.[3] If power rested with the asylum's inmates, they would define themselves as normal and those who control and care for them as pathological.[4]

In spite of such reservations, there is an extensive literature on organizational pathologies as well as a number of recommendations on how to treat organizations that lapse into them. Thus it has been argued that organizations can be afflicted by a variety of pathologies that inhibit their smooth functioning, cause excessive distress to their members, and wrap them up in collective delusions. This echoes Freud's distinction between 'everyday unhappiness' and 'neurotic misery'.[5] All organizations, it is argued, inflict a measure of unhappiness, anxiety, and distress on their members, but some of them sink into profoundly unsettling states of paralysis, terror, panic, and delusion from which they find it impossible to extricate themselves.[6] Just like acutely disturbed individuals, organizations, according to this view, can become neurotic or even psychotic.[7]

Organizational neurosis, according to Kets de Vries and Miller generally mirrors the neurosis of its **leader**—thus, an organization can become narcissistic, paranoid, depressive, compulsive, or schizoid.[8] 'Our experience with top executives and their organizations revealed that parallels could be drawn between individual pathology—excessive use of neurotic style—and organizational pathology, the latter resulting in poorly functioning organizations. In dysfunctional, centralized firms, the rigid neurotic styles of the top executives were strongly mirrored in the nature of the inappropriate strategies, structures, and organizational cultures of their firms.'[9] Even more damaging are psychotic organizations, which are lost in a world of delusional make-believe divorced from reality, whose sole function is allaying powerful anxieties.[10]

Most people recognize that there is a difference between an organization that is going through hard times or is merely causing its fair share of trouble and one that is systematically oppressing and exploiting its members, forcing them to depression, paranoia, rage, and associated symptoms ranging from alcoholism to suicide. However, it is very difficult to establish where organizational normality ends and pathological processes take over. When, for example, does healthy scepticism end and paranoid anxiety start? When does healthy pride become narcissistic self-delusion or megalomania? When does optimism for a future project become a delusion of invulnerability? Some would argue that criteria of organizational pathology, like those of individual pathology, are relatively objective, to be found in the ability to work and express **emotion** freely. Others may argue that organizational pathologies are distinct from individual ones, inasmuch as perfectly healthy and normal individuals may be parties to highly contorted organizational relationships. There are yet others who argue that individual neurosis, far from being the enemy of organizations, may quite often be its ally, i.e. that unhappy, neurotic individuals may be quite functional

---

[1] Freud, 1937.   [2] Freud, 1933/1988, p. 189.   [3] Foucault, 1977; 1980.   [4] Laing, 1960.   [5] Freud and Breuer, 1895, p. 393.   [6] See e.g. Diamond, 1993; Hirschhorn, 1988; Obholzer and Roberts, 1994.   [7] Kets de Vries and Miller, 1984; Sievers, 1999.   [8] Kets de Vries and Miller, 1984.   [9] Ibid. 17.   [10] Sievers, 2003.

and even prosper within organizational environments.[1] In general, labelling an organization neurotic or psychotic is even more difficult than labelling so an individual.

• See also *authoritarianism, bullying, downsizing, narcissism, psychoanalysis and psychoanalytic approaches, violence*

Organizational theories, paradigms, and perspectives

Organizations have generated many different theories in the last hundred years. This is hardly surprising since they are major **institutions** of modernity and raise many questions of concern to different disciplines. Many of these theories have, in fact, originated in other disciplines, including economics, sociology, political theory, psychology, ethnography, and cultural studies.

It is remarkable how one-sided the flow of concepts, theories, and ideas has been. Organizational scholars have consistently borrowed, translated, and 'imported' concepts, theories, and ideas from other disciplines, whereas hardly any ideas from organizational scholarship have filtered out to the exporting disciplines. It would be unthinkable for any scholar of organizations not to have heard of Max Weber, Michel Foucault, Herbert Simon, or Anthony Giddens; yet there are remarkably few psychologists, sociologists, or economists who have ever heard of the work of the likes of Henry Mintzberg, Karl Weick, or Gareth Morgan.

Overall, scholars of organizations have been remarkably cosmopolitan in visiting **discourses** from other human sciences and translating them into the language of organizations.[2] A second source of concepts, ideas, and theories in the field of organizations has been management studies, whose purpose has unashamedly been to enhance the task of practising managers and

to make organizations better-run and, in some instances, more humane places. Some of these approaches have been translated into the language of popular management science of the sort that fills the bookshops of the world's airports.

Most influential theories of organizations and most theoretical traditions that have contributed to the study of organizations have their own entries in this thesaurus. They include:

☐ **Actor network theory**
☐ **Autopoiesis**
☐ **Contingency theory**
☐ **Critical Management Studies**
☐ **Human Resource Management**
☐ **Industrial relations**
☐ **Institutional theory**
☐ **Labour Process Theory**
☐ **Path dependence theory**
☐ **Population ecology**
☐ **Postmodernism**
☐ **Post-structuralism**
☐ **Psychoanalysis**
☐ **Psychodynamics**
☐ **Resource-based theory of organization**
☐ **Social construction of reality theory**
☐ **Socio-technical systems theory**
☐ **Structuration theory**

The differences between these theories are extensive. In some cases, they may compete against each other, in others they complement each other, and, in most instances, they are resolutely oblivious of each other or 'incommensurable'.[3] One way of explaining this messy situation is to view it as being what Kuhn described as a pre-paradigmatic state of knowledge, i.e. the state of a discipline which has still not acquired a dominant **paradigm**, one whose concepts have not yet become sufficiently precise. In such a discipline, many ideas compete for ascendancy, without any agreed criteria for judging them, without any agreed assumptions that can serve as starting points. Much of the dialogue during such a

[1] Gabriel, 1999; Gabriel and Carr, 2002.   [2] Czarniawska, 1999; Czarniawska and Joerges, 1996.   [3] Feyerabend, 1975; Kuhn, 1962/1996.

phase is, in fact, an attempt to 'define schools rather than produce agreement',[1] with different scholars desperate to make themselves heard in a cacophony of opinion. A feature of this pre-paradigmatic situation is that the object of study is conceptualized by different approaches in fundamentally different ways.

Two authors who have long explored the coexistence of different paradigms in the sphere of organizations have been Gibson Burrell and Gareth Morgan,[2] who identified some of the different ontological and epistemological assumptions underpinning the chief paradigms in this sphere. In a subsequent work that has assumed the status of a classic, Morgan proposed that different paradigms of organizations are inspired by different core **metaphors** that throw different features of organizations into sharp relief.[3] Chief among these metaphors are the organizations as machine (which inspired Weber's view of **bureaucracy** and Taylor's **Scientific Management**), as organism, as brain, as culture, as flux and transformation, as a psychic prison, as a political system, and as an instrument of domination and oppression. Morgan has emphasized the importance of metaphors in our thinking about organizations, establishing how most theories of organizations are underpinned by implicit or explicit metaphors of organizations. He has further argued that by moving across metaphors important assumptions regarding organizations can be questioned and new insights may be gained. Through his concept of 'imaginization', he has advocated the use of metaphors as thought experiments aimed at stimulating new insights into the functioning of organizations but also the way our minds operate when confronted by organizations.[4] To this end, Morgan has employed various unorthodox metaphors, such as organizations as spider plants or as yogurts.

Morgan's account views the multiplicity of paradigms and perspectives in the sphere of organizations as a strength, as long as scholars have the mental flexibility to move across them from time to time—a view endorsed by theorists like Chia.[5] Others, however, like Jeffrey Pfeffer and Lex Donaldson,[6] have been strongly critical of paradigm proliferation, arguing that this is detrimental both for building theoretical robustness and for the standing of organizational theory and its influence on government and company **policies**.

At the moment, the influence of organizational theory on policy cannot begin to compete with that of economics and, to a lesser extent, other social sciences. Its position in academia is, for the time being, relatively secure as most business and management schools view it as a core part of the management curriculum. It is not inconceivable, however, that at some future stage organizational theory will be absorbed by some other growing and more ambitious discipline—a prime candidate for such a takeover could conceivably be '**leadership** studies' or **strategy**.

Organizations

While **organizing** has always been part of human life, organizations are relatively recent social phenomena. Some organizations, such as armies, the Catholic church, and certain universities, go way back in history, but most of the organizations that dominate today's economic, social, and political landscapes are creations of the last hundred and fifty years. The rise of organizations thus coincides with the arrival of **modernity**, the migration of people from the country to the emerging cities, the growth of business enterprises, and the rise of the modern state. Organizations are one of the great **institutions** of industrial civilization and **capitalism.** They have made an undoubted contribution to rises in living standards, the accelerated pace of social, technical, and economic change, and the emergence of new social classes, like managers

---

[1] Kuhn, 1962/1996, p. 48.   [2] Burrell and Morgan, 1979.   [3] Morgan, 1986.   [4] Morgan, 1993.   [5] Chia, 1996.   [6] Pfeffer, 1993; Donaldson, 1995.

and clerical workers. Whether they have brought about social progress, the ultimate aim of the Enlightenment project, is open to discussion.

Organizations are difficult entities to define. We know intuitively that a nuclear family, a football crowd, a small market stall, or a group of friends playing bridge are not organizations. But there are many **groups** or **networks** to which it is not clear whether the title of organization applies. Is the British royal family an organization? The Sicilian mafia? A legal firm of two partners and a few secretarial staff? A family-owned small restaurant or shop? Some of the difficulties in defining organizations are the result of the multiplicity of institutions claiming to be organizations as well as of the diversity of perspectives from which they are studied. Organizations include entities as diverse as schools and prisons, businesses and charities, government departments and hospitals, armies and symphony orchestras, international bodies and worker cooperatives. Are there any features that all of the above share, which at the same time are not features of other social groups? And if, as we argued, organizations are themselves a part of modernity, in what ways could their unique features be said to stem from this historical period?

Many scholars have offered definitions of organizations; dominant elements of most such definitions include the following:

1. Long-term continuity. Organizations may not last forever; they are born and they die. But organizations have a definite lifespan and aim at sustained performance, surviving changes in personnel.
2. Impersonality and formality. If organizations survive changes in personnel, this is in part due to the fact that they do not rely on a single individual for their existence. Individuals in organizations occupy different positions whose responsibilities and duties are partly defined by written **rules** and regulations. Hence, in organizations there are *vacancies*, when positions are unoccupied. Vacancies, which are a consequence of

impersonality and formality, set organizations apart from families, crowds, gangs, and many other **groups**.
3. Organizations purport to have **goals**. Organizations' goals define their *raison d'être* and make them legitimate entities in the eyes of the public. These goals are over and above the goals of individual members. Yet it is notoriously difficult to establish the goals of particular organizations in any objective and generally agreed way. Different stakeholders are liable to view an organization's goals differently.
4. No-nonsense approach. Not only do organizations purport to have goals; they also go about achieving them in a methodical, systematic, no-nonsense way. They recruit members, mobilize resources, research different possible courses of action, and initiate different policies and campaigns. Of course, between organizations' actions and their proclaimed goals there may be inconsistencies. However, organizations do not sit idly relying on good luck in pursuit of their aims. Instead, they engage in purposeful, planned, organized, and sometimes feverish activity to achieve them. This means that in organizations, people **work**.
5. Division of **labour**. One of the characteristics of most organizations is that work is organized in such a way that different people do different tasks in a coordinated way. Some organizations have a rigid division of labour, each individual having a strictly specified set of tasks to perform. Other organizations have a more flexible division of labour where individuals are expected to perform many different tasks, when and as the situation requires. All the same, division of labour is a characteristic of all organizations.
6. Cooperation rather than coercion. In most organizations people work and collaborate voluntarily, without being forced to do so. There are exceptions, such as prisons and armies. In other organizations, people

sometimes act against their will—yet, much of the time, people collaborate with each other willingly or at least grudgingly, but without need of coercion or force.

These characteristics more or less define most organizations. There are some exceptions but most organizations comply with them. Of the six, it is impersonality and formality that are most essential and set apart the large organizations that dominate our societies today. Before the advent of modernity, most people spent most of their time in relations with people they knew personally, people whose families and histories they knew well. This is no longer the case. In a world of large organizations, most of our time is spent doing business with people about whom we know little beyond their name and job title, if that.

The study of organizations emerged as a distinct field in the twentieth century, drawing insights from sociology, psychology, management science, and, increasingly, ethnography. A substantial part of this scholarship was 'performative' in character—aimed at enhancing the effectiveness and productivity of organizations. Much of the early work on organizations was also ahistorical; it approached organizations as fixed social or political phenomena which did not vary across time. This is no longer the case. There is now a great interest in the ways organizations have evolved and transformed themselves in the course of the last hundred years and especially in the last thirty years or so.

Many scholars now view modernity as an era that is about to be superseded or that has already been superseded; organizations themselves have, therefore, come to look different from the organizations that dominated society fifty years ago. Many of them are smaller (as far as numbers of employees go), flatter, looser, more international, more flexible, less centralized, more likely to be in partnerships with other organizations, less pyramid-like, and more network-like.

One of the earliest and keenest observers of the changing nature of organizations was Stewart Clegg. Writing when computers were only beginning to make an appearance on every desk top, and before the fall of Soviet communism or the establishment of the internet, Clegg argued:

> Where the modernist organization was rigid, postmodern organization is flexible. Where modernist consumption was premised on mass forms, postmodernist consumption is premised on niches. Where modernist organization was premised on technological determinism, postmodernist organization is premised on technological choices made possible through 'de-dedicated' micro-electronic equipment. Where modernist organization and jobs were highly differentiated, demarcated and de-skilled, postmodernist organization and jobs are highly de-differentiated, de-demarcated and multiskilled. Employment relations as a fundamental relation of organization upon which has been constructed a whole discourse of the determinism of size as a contingency variable increasingly give way to more complex and fragmentary relational forms, such as subcontracting and networking.[1]

Of course, modernist organizations did not get replaced overnight by postmodern ones, but Clegg was drawing attention to enduring transformation in the character of organizations and their environments. Changes in organizations were accompanied by new ways of looking at organizations, drawing attention to many irrational phenomena, the importance of **language** and **discourse**, their fragmented and episodic character, and their diffuse or fuzzy **boundaries**. It was thus that Martin Parker proposed an ingenious distinction between post-modern (with a hyphen) organizations and postmodern (no hyphen) theories of organizations—the existence of a hyphen signifying a time-historical aspect, its absence a discursive practice.[2] Of

---

[1] Clegg, 1990, p. 181.   [2] Parker, 1992.

course, the central premiss of the distinction dissolves the minute it is drawn—while modernity separated the phenomena under observation from the theories seeking to explain them, such a distinction does not obtain in postmodernism. It would be premature to argue that modernist organizational theories have vanished to be replaced by postmodern variants—on the contrary, modernist assumptions continue to dominate much of the scholarship of organizations. What, however, has changed is the assumption that organization is an invariant phenomenon or one whose essence can be captured through a single theoretical gesture, the way that Weber tried to do through his theory of **bureaucracy**.[1]

• See also *bureaucracy, oligarchy and iron law of oligarchy, organizing*

Organizing

Organizing involves a range of activities aimed at making our lives more comfortable, more manageable, more predictable, and more orderly. It involves planning, controlling, coordinating different actions, and ensuring that resources are available where and when we need them to ensure that we can act effectively. Organizing tries to ensure that different things are where we expect them to be. An organized library is one where we know where to find different books when we need them. An organized holiday is one where we follow a plan, equipped with suitable papers (tickets, maps, reservations, passports, etc.) and so forth. Where organizing fails, we find ourselves spending much time looking for things, waiting in the wrong places, uncertain as to what to do, and getting frustrated and anxious. Of course, different people have different thresholds of what they regard as organized and disorganized.

Engineers use the concept of 'entropy' to describe the tendency of things to lapse into

disorder, if no effort is made to keep them tidy. As disorder sets in, energy must be spent to restore order. Once our kitchen utensils have got all jumbled up, we must spend time and effort sorting them out once again. Unlike the engineering idea of entropy, many of our organizing efforts involve other people. Organizing a holiday involves consulting with your partners, obtaining information from travel agents, making bookings with hotel staff, and so forth. People, unlike kitchen utensils, do not always behave in a predictable way—organizing them requires considerably more effort and skill. Much organizing is a *social* activity requiring people to **communicate** with each other, describe and explain what they are doing. It also involves imagination—envisaging in advance different situations and seeking to steer them in beneficial and desirable directions. Organizing then is a constant **sensemaking** process, a constant effort to impose some order on our perceptions, experiences, and expectations without which life would be impossible.[2]

We are acutely aware when organizing fails. 'Failure of organizing' is itself a sensemaking device, a way of explaining our feelings of frustration, anger, and impatience when we find ourselves in situations where we lack the resources to function effectively. Where some people 'read' a situation as a failure, others see it as an opportunity to improvise, to make do with the resources at hand and come up with creative, innovative solutions, resorting to **bricolage** to get themselves and others out of trouble, Yet others may read the situation as one requiring patience and fortitude until appropriate action may be taken; they exercise **negative capability**, tolerating uncertainty and holding back from making definitive judgements or taking precipitous action until more propitious times.

Organizing requires different resources, including money, time, labour (our own and other people's), knowledge, information, routines, instruments, recipes, and **technologies**.

---

[1] Thoenig, 1998. [2] Weick, 2001d.

The scope of technology in helping us organize is limitless. We may use diaries, telephones, computers, spreadsheets, and so forth. One of the simplest and more useful technologies for organizing is *lists*, notably lists of things to do. Lists reassure us that we are on top of things, that we have a plan of action that will enable us to keep things under control.

Human beings have always organized. They have organized their thoughts, their feelings, their time, their activities, and their possessions. The product of organizing is **organization.** Yet when we speak of *organizations* in the plural what we have in mind are social **institutions** that have come to dominate our societies in the last hundred and fifty years or so. Thus, while organizing can be viewed as a range of activities that have been part of human experience since time immemorial, organization can be viewed as a very specific historical phenomenon, one that comes into its own with the arrival of **modernity**.

The Other and othering

Othering is the process of casting a group, an individual, or an object into the role of the 'other' and establishing one's own **identity** through opposition to and, frequently, vilification of this Other. The Greeks' use of the word 'barbarian' to describe non-Greeks is a typical example of othering and an instance of **nationalism** *avant la lettre*. The ease with which the adjective 'other' generated the verb 'to other' in the last twenty years or so is indicative of the usefulness, power, and currency of a term that now occupies an important position in **feminist**, **postcolonial**, civil rights, and sexual minority discourses.

Othering is a process that goes beyond 'mere' scapegoating and denigration—it denies the Other those defining characteristics of the 'Same', reason, dignity, love, pride, heroism, nobility, and ultimately any entitlement to human rights. Whether the Other is a racial or a religious group, a gender group, a sexual minority, or a nation, it is made ripe for exploitation, oppression, and indeed **genocide** by denying its essential humanity, because, as the philosopher Richard Rorty put it, 'everything turns on who counts as a fellow human being, as a rational agent in the only relevant sense—the sense in which rational agency is synonymous with membership of *our* moral community'.[1]

The process of othering may be initiated by an encounter between civilizations that have no previous tradition of contact or understanding. Within a few years of Columbus's landing in the New World, its indigenous inhabitants were enslaved, tortured, and killed, their immense civilizations despoiled, desecrated, and destroyed for ever. Their conquerors questioned whether native Americans belonged to the same species as themselves. But othering can also take place between groups that know each other well and have lived in close proximity for centuries, as the genocide of Rwanda and the ethnic cleansing of Bosnia remind us. In these situations, othering is prompted by what Freud referred to as 'narcissism of minor differences'—the person or group that is 'othered' is the one in closest physical and symbolic proximity, as it is seen to present a major threat to one's **identity** and pride—precisely what was to happened to Freud and hundred of thousands of Jews in Germany and Europe.[2] The consequences of this **narcissism** of minor differences can range from the petty but serious antagonism of supporters of neighbouring football clubs or neighbouring towns, to ethnic cleansing and genocide.[3]

Theorizing the Other has drawn extensively on the work of three theorists who influenced each other—psychoanalyst Jacques Lacan, ethnographer Claude Lévi-Strauss, and philosopher Emmanuel Levinas. Lacan examined how the ego is formed during the early stage of infancy as the child comes to contemplate its own face in a mirror.[4] The child first encounters him- or herself as an Other and misrecognizes

---

[1] Rorty, 1993, p. 124.   [2] Freud, 1921; 1930.   [3] Blok, 2001.   [4] Lacan, 1988b.

him- or herself as a **subject**, thereafter sustaining this recognition in the gaze of the Other. There is thus an interesting link between theory of the Other and **alienation**. Othering is a process that may be applied to oneself, whereby one experiences oneself as a stranger; indeed Lacanian theory views this 'self-othering' as the process whereby the symbolic order is established—the **unconscious** is the stranger within ourselves. A man, for example, has no choice but to silence or even kill the 'woman in him'.

Lévi-Strauss proposed that throughout human history, people have employed two strategies in dealing with the Other, the foreign, the deviant, or the stranger—one is to incorporate them, as in the case of cannibalism, eliminating any boundaries between the same and the Other; the second strategy is to expel them and exclude them ('spit them out') by erecting strong **boundaries** and special institutions in which they are kept in isolation.[1] These strategies can be observed in many contemporary situations. Finally, Levinas based his moral philosophy on the face-to-face encounter with another human being, viewing the moment of this encounter as the one irreducible and concrete way of establishing a relation with the Other, as against relying on abstract and impersonal rules of ethics to do so.[2]

Many current discourses on the Other are taking an extremely pessimistic and bleak view of relations among human beings, returning to the Hobbesian view of *homo homini lupus* ('a human is a wolf to a fellow human'). Some authors have argued that Western identity and culture are fundamentally forged by an othering logic, one that dehumanizes or devalues other people, such as primitives, uncivilized, orientals, blacks, non-believers, women and so forth.[3] An essential feature of othering is denying the Other his or her own **voice**, denying him or her the opportunity to speak for him- or herself and instead attributing qualities, opinions, and views that refer to one's own identity and culture.

Whether one can speak on behalf of another whose voice has been silenced has become a hotly debated issue. Another debated issue is whether it is possible to transcend 'othering' and establish a genuine understanding with the Other, through the use of reason (for example, by appealing to a common humanity, as Kant did) or through empathy (for example, by appealing to compassion and feeling for the sufferings of others, as Hume and Schopenhauer did). It is maybe time that, along with the many fragmentations brought about by postmodernist discourses, the Other should be recognized as a diverse and complex entity—an object of **love** and **desire**, a potential enemy and victim, a model for emulation and identification, an object of care and hospitality, a subject of his or her own destiny. We may still come to recognize that the Other, like the Self, has many faces.

• See also *multiculturalism, postcolonialism and postcolonial theory*

Outsourcing

Outsourcing is the current trend by many businesses to subcontract what are viewed as non-essential functions or tasks to other organizations. This stands in opposition to an earlier business philosophy epitomized by Henry Ford whose ambition was to expand, diversify, and integrate his company's operations, seeking to eliminate uncertainty arising from having to rely on independent suppliers and middlemen. Ford famously produced car upholsteries using wool from company-owned farms. By contrast, outsourcing represents a philosophy according to which businesses should focus on their core **competences**, subcontracting everything non-essential to other companies that are

---

[1] Lévi-Strauss, 1955/1992. [2] Levinas, 1969. [3] Notably Said, 1985; 1994.

able to deliver better value, more quickly and more reliably. Another motive behind outsourcing is dissociating a company's name from risky or potentially embarrassing operations, such as animal experimentation or transportation of hazardous substances.

Some outsourcing goes abroad to companies operating in countries with cheaper labour, laxer environmental and occupational health legislation, or which are closer to raw materials. Other outsourcing may go to companies that specialize in particular services and products. One result of outsourcing has been a general **downsizing** of companies. Another result has been the growth of company **networks** which develop close cooperative relations. A third result has been an acceleration of **globalization**. Finally, outsourcing has placed **trade unions** and local employee organizations at a disadvantage, since companies can use the threat of outsourcing to tighten **control** and discipline among their workforces. Outsourcing has undoubtedly made employment prospects in industrial nations more precarious and has been the cause of extensive job insecurity and anxiety.[1]

Outsourcing started with functions like cleaning and catering that could be viewed as peripheral to an organization's core operations but is now applied to virtually any non-core activity, including payroll, product testing, recruitment, and customer relations. In a way, the logic has now been reversed. Any activity that can be outsourced 'profitably' (i.e. reducing overall costs) can no longer be viewed as a core activity for an organization. The immense growth of India's call centre business typifies the logic of outsourcing, and offers interesting insights into some of its consequences.[2]

Outsourcing is practised not only by companies in search of profits but also by government and local government organizations in their search for savings and efficiency (see **New Public Management**). Thus, a wide range of operations and services from running prisons to enforcement of parking regulations are now routinely subcontracted to independent (i.e. profit-driven) operators. Whether outsourcing is a *rational* response to new opportunities in a global economy, made possible by new **information technology** and network-like organizations, is questionable. There are certainly examples where outsourcing has proved counter-productive or damaging for companies. However, as an instance of a far-reaching change in management thinking and practice outsourcing has offered a useful testing case for different theories of diffusion of **innovation** across organizations and nations.[3]

• See also *downsizing*

---

[1] Uchitelle, 2006.   [2] Taylor et al., 2005.   [3] See e.g. Ang and Cummings, 1997.

P

Paradigms

Paradigm is a term introduced by the philosopher Thomas S. Kuhn in his famous book *The Structure of Scientific Revolutions* to describe different coherent theoretical perspectives of looking at the world.[1] These perspectives are composed of theories, concepts, and assumptions that do not only shape fundamental beliefs about the world, but also prescribe how these beliefs may be tested and confirmed. Paradigms thus embody numerous ontological and **epistemological** assumptions which condition the way scientists look at the world, the things they observe, and the way they think about their observations—they are mindsets as well as bodies of **knowledge**, mindsets from which it is very difficult to escape. Paradigms have a degree of cohesion achieved as communities of scientists come to share particular ways of looking at the world. Most of the time, Kuhn argued, scientists work within the parameters and assumptions of specific paradigms in what he termed 'normal science'. From time to time, however, anomalies begin to emerge that cannot be accommodated within a paradigm and anomalies may build up to the point where a crisis occurs and alternative and competing paradigms may emerge. It is then that a scientific revolution takes place as increasing numbers of scientists abandon the old paradigm for the new. The Copernican and the Einsteinian revolutions are such instances where an old paradigm rife with anomalies came to be supplanted by a new one.

Few concepts have had such a meteoric rise as paradigm. Within a few years paradigm had become one of the most frequently used concepts in philosophy and almost a household term. It quickly crossed the boundaries between philosophy, science, social science, and wider culture and came to be used in many different contexts and situations. The Kuhnian term 'paradigm shift' is now regularly used by businesspeople, politicians, and others whenever they call for the replacement of one set of ideas and principles by another. Inevitably, the term paradigm became a victim of its own success, as it assumed many distinct meanings to suit different circumstances. Already by 1970, Margaret Masterman argued that Kuhn himself had used the term paradigm in at least twenty-one subtly different ways,[2] and the figure could be multiplied manifold to account for the ways the term has been used by others. This proliferation of uses is not necessarily a bad thing—it demonstrates how a single concept can open up all kinds of possibilities and make us look at reality with fresh eyes.

One particular term linked to paradigm is that of 'incommensurability', used by Kuhn and Feyerabend to describe the coexistence of two or more paradigms which may use the same words and concepts but construct the world in fundamentally different ways; they are then unable to engage with each other.[3] Thus, Kuhn and Feyerabend argued that Einsteinian physics did not offer a more comprehensive explanation of the physical world than Newtonian physics, but used concepts like mass, velocity, and time in fundamentally different ways from earlier ones—so Newtonian and Einsteinian physics are said to be incommensurable. This idea was subsequently embraced by many theorists to explain why in specific fields, like sociology, psychology,

---

[1] Kuhn, 1962/1996.   [2] Masterman, 1970.   [3] Kuhn, 1962/1996; Feyerabend, 1975; 1978.

or organizational theory, several different traditions coexist which fail to take notice of each other. In an important contribution, Burrell and Morgan identified four paradigms in social sciences founded on core assumptions regarding the nature of reality, the existence of free will, the nature of experience, and the scope of science.[1] These are:

1. The *functionalist paradigm* which views human **action** as predominantly rational and uses hypothesis testing to develop scientific knowledge after the model of the natural sciences;
2. The *interpretative paradigm* which approaches the social world as **socially constructed** and seeks to understand how **meaning** is created through social interactions;
3. The *radical humanist paradigm* whose main concern is human emancipation through a liberation from different oppressive social constraints;
4. The *radical structuralist paradigm* which is based on an analysis of conflicts and contradictions that generate social change.

Notably absent from this list are **post-structuralist** and **postmodernist** paradigms, where a great deal of recent debate has been conducted. In recent times, the term paradigm has lost some of its popularity and some of its uses have been subsumed in the concepts of **discourse** and **narrative**. One difficulty of paradigm is that it can be applied at many levels and across many scales, from the most general to the relatively specific. One then easily ends up with a plethora of paradigms, some competing, some incommensurable, some mutually reinforcing, and some nestling within others. There is no ultimate way of deciding where one paradigm ends and another one begins. Thus the boundaries of paradigms, their *blind spots*, become invisible, and the term loses the very quality that gave it its sharpness.

• See also *organizational theories, paradigms, and perspectives*

Path dependence

Path dependence (or path dependency) is an idea that originated in economics but has found applications in some other areas of the social sciences, particularly those interested in the study of **innovations** and their diffusion. Path dependence claims that small accidents of history (or seemingly minor decisions) lead to enduring consequences that cannot be controlled or altered, because they generate an unstoppable momentum of their own. The classic illustration of path dependence is the general adoption of the QWERTY keyboard since its introduction in 1867 by typewriter inventor Christopher Latham Sholes. Originally, the arrangement of keys on the keyboard was meant to slow down the speed of typists thus reducing the incidence of jamming. In spite of improvements in typewriter technology that made jamming unlikely, the QWERTY keyboard has persisted, migrating from typewriters to computer keyboards.[2] Another interesting example of path dependence is whether vehicles in a certain country drive on the right or on the left side of the road. Once a country commits itself to driving on one side of the road it becomes increasingly and eventually prohibitively expensive to change.

Path dependence shares with **complexity and chaos theories** the principle of a system's sensitive dependence to its initial conditions. This is used as an explanatory principle in many situations, especially when an inferior innovation appears to override and persist in spite of the existence of superior ones (as in the well-documented case of the VHS format for video tapes prevailing against the superior Beta format). Some management theorists have argued that the same principle can be observed when an organization commits itself to a certain management practice (such as

---

[1] Burrell and Morgan, 1979.   [2] Leibowitz and Margolis, 1995.

Total Quality Management or Business Process Re-engineering) and persists with it after it has been overtaken by others.

Path dependence can then be seen as generating an involuntary escalation of commitment (see **cognition**) to a certain course of action, even when this proves less than optimal—it emphasizes the importance of certain irreversible **decisions** summed up in expressions like 'burning our bridges' or 'crossing the Rubicon', only in many cases the decisions are taken without a full awareness of their implications. Path dependence has become central to many current explanations of institutionalized trajectories, particularly in national business systems or varieties of **capitalism**. It is also important to evolutionary theorists outside the immediate field of technological innovation.

Performance

Performance is an interesting word used to signify both a theatrical or other performance on stage but also the financial performance of an organization and the effectiveness of its individual employees. At the heart of the idea of performance is *quality*: any performance, personal or corporate, can range from the excellent to the execrable, from the sublime to the inept. And this instantly presents us with a paradox—that of quantifying quality. How good was the performance we have witnessed? By what standards is it to be judged?

Theatrical performances become a **paradigm** for what has become known as the 'dramaturgical approach' to the study of social life. 'All the world's a stage, | And all the men and women merely players. | They have their exits and their entrances|', wrote William Shakespeare in *As You Like It*—a statement whose intuitive power people have long grasped but whose implications were explored in consummate detail by Kenneth Burke and Erving Goffman, who offered remarkable insights into people's everyday lives.[1] By looking at everyday actions as 'performances', these authors emphasized the importance of the **roles** that people play, of the settings in which they perform, and of the audiences who witness and evaluate the performances. Thus, when a lecturer delivers a lecture, the actual words that she uses may be less important than the setting, the lighting, the authoritative demeanour, and even the PowerPoint slides which define the situation as 'a lecture'. Goffman uses the term 'front' to describe a person's social **identity**, 'that part of the individual's performance which regularly functions in a general and fixed fashion to define the situation for those who observe the performance'.[2] Social actors, in order to present a compelling front, must both perform the duties of their social roles and communicate the activities and characteristics of these roles to their audience in a persuasive manner.

The dramaturgical approach has found many applications in studies of organizations. Notable among them is the study of emotions by Hochschild, who distinguished between deep acting and surface acting.[3] In deep acting, the actor gets inside the role, experiencing and displaying the corresponding **emotions**, while in surface acting, actors keep a distance from the roles they enact, displaying different emotions but not feeling them. Iain Mangham used a dramaturgical approach to great effect in analysing the dynamics of decision making and the executive process.[4]

Organizational performances, like theatrical performances, invite judgements of quality. These are often attached to different performance indicators, which are meant to assess how well an organization is doing in comparison to its competitors and rivals. Efficiency and effectiveness have long been treated as key indicators, the former referring to how well an organization uses its resources, the latter to whether it chooses

---

[1] Burke, 1945/1969; 1966; Goffman, 1959; 1961.   [2] Goffman, 1959, p. 22.   [3] Hochschild, 1983.   [4] See e.g. Mangham, 1986; Mangham and Overington, 1987.

the right strategies and policies to pursue. Effectiveness often calls for sacrifices in efficiency and conversely efficiency may compromise effectiveness. Thus a company that produces very economically a product that is about to become obsolete may be efficient but not effective.

In the commercial sector, profitability is a major criterion of organizational performance, although others are often used, ranging from growth, innovativeness, and attractiveness to prospective employees. In the public sector, the performance of organizations (including hospitals, schools, and government departments) has come under increasing scrutiny under **New Public Management** and a number of performance indicators and targets are being set by different governments. As has long been recognized, such indicators are part of a political process, which creates winners and losers, rewards and sanctions. It is also part of **policy** making—since the existence of an indicator instantly focuses the mind on what it seeks to measure and diverts resources away from activities and projects that are not reflected in the indicators.

This creates a culture of measurement, where organizations can become preoccupied with meeting targets and beating their rivals rather than discharging their missions and achieving their **goals**.[1] Thus, a police force that is judged exclusively by its crime-clearance statistics will focus its efforts on small crimes, often committed by young people, that are relatively easy to clear and withdraw resources from serious crime where the chances of successful detection are smaller. The process of benchmarking has emerged as a popular management technique for making comparisons between organizations or departments and those that are meant to represent excellence in their field. In spite of its widespread use, benchmarking often creates misleading impressions by comparing apples with oranges or by disregarding non-quantifiable aspects of performance. Most public utilities at the turn of the century would have

found it hard to benchmark themselves effectively against Enron, a company that won many plaudits and awards both for its financial performance and its record of innovation (including the 2001 MIT Sloan Annual Award as 'eBusiness of the Year'). Most of these companies are still in business today, unlike the industry benchmark standard bearer.

But organizations do not only seek to measure the performance of large departments or aggregates of people. Individual performance is assessed through detailed performance appraisals which seek to evaluate their employees' work progress. Performance appraisals are used to make decisions on salary, promotions, performance-related pay, retention, or termination. They can also provide an opportunity for feedback to an employee to identify strengths, weaknesses, and training needs. The format of appraisal can vary from the highly structured, using rating scales, to an open-ended counselling session. The effectiveness of performance appraisal depends on how well prepared both parties are, how serious they are about the event (i.e. is it 'for real' or an empty ritual), the skills of the appraiser, the reliability and validity of the rating scales, its regularity, and the extent to which decisions or agreements from the appraisal are honoured. Using Foucault's concept of power/knowledge, Barbara Townley has argued that performance appraisals are part of a disciplinary machinery whose net effect is to ensure that employees feel constantly under scrutiny and prompting different types of **resistance**.[2]

The term 'performative' has been used to describe those speech acts that perform an **action**, e.g. 'I declare this conference closed'. In Judith Butler's theory of gender, **gender** is produced through a continuous ritualized repetition of performative statements that constitute a subject as a man or a woman.[3] Performativity is viewed by **Critical Management Studies** as the production of statements, arguments, and

[1] Boyle, 2000; Power, 1997.   [2] Townley, 1993a; 1993b.   [3] Butler, 1993.

theories whose purpose is to constitute and rein-force the rule of **management** and the ideolo-gies that legitimize it.[1] Many theories of orga-nizations and management have been criticized for being performative, i.e. for ultimately aiming to enhance organizational performance in nar-row managerial terms, while disregarding other dimensions of organizational and social life.

Personality

Personality is a term that indicates those qual-ities that make a person different from others, unique. Raymond Williams offers a compelling account of the development of the term from the Latin *persona*, meaning mask, to person and per-sonal, words that were meant to signal out some-thing as a human being and *not* a thing.[2] Today the term 'personality' can be applied equally to people and to things, most especially to adver-tising brands to indicate their uniqueness, their individuality. Thus the terms 'weak personality', 'strong personality', or 'no personality' express how strongly someone or something stands out from his or her peers.

Personality is conceptually related to both **identity** and character, words that are also used to indicate the uniqueness and individuality of single specimens (and can also be preceded by 'strong', 'weak', and 'no'). What sets personality apart from both of these two terms is that it is more directly visible to others, in other words how one appears to others. Thus, we can talk of a 'pleasant personality' but not a 'pleasant iden-tity'; this is what makes the term personality well suited to describing celebrities and other indi-viduals featuring on shows and especially tele-vision. A television personality is someone who engages viewers and leaves a longer imprint on their memory.

The other main reason that sets personality apart from identity and character is the psy-chologists' enduring attempts systematically to

analyse it, operationalize it, and measure it. There are many personality theories seeking to explain how our individuality forms, develops, changes, and is structured. These tend to follow one of two broad approaches, nomothetic and idiographic.

Nomothetic approaches look for lawlike gen-eralizations by identifying the main 'types' of human personality, discovering the funda-mental dimensions or 'traits' of personality and then developing scales along which dif-ferent individuals may be placed. Psychological tests are indispensable elements of nomothetic approaches, hence a great deal of effort is dedi-cated to developing reliable and valid measures for different traits. These traits usually come in opposites—such as friendly–unfriendly, warm–cold, and so forth. Some traits, notably intel-ligence, have attracted very large amounts of research, although the findings of this research have been rather inconclusive. Currently, one of the most popular approaches to the nomo-thetic study of personality is the 'Big Five' (or OCEAN) approach, which identifies five key fac-tors or dimensions of personality, each consist-ing of several more specific traits. The 'Big Five' are:

- Openness to experience—appreciation of new ideas, ability to learn from experience, curiosity;
- Conscientiousness—self-discipline, a sense of duty, and need for **achievement**; emphasis on deferred gratification and planning;
- Extroversion—a tendency to seek excitement in the company of others; positive emotions and energy in social exchanges;
- Agreeableness—a cooperative and empathetic attitude;
- Neuroticism—a tendency to be easily derailed by unpleasant moods and emotions, especially anxiety, depression, and fear, often accompanied by emotional and mental insecurity and instability.

---

[1] Fournier and Grey, 2000.   [2] Williams, 1976, pp. 232 f.

Idiographic approaches, on the other hand, focus on unique, ad hoc, and accidental factors that shape personality. Thus an individual's personality may be the product of the influence of an overbearing parent, an experience of racial or gender prejudice and stereotyping, or a physical accident. These approaches do not search for generalizations but for plausible explanations that often assume a **narrative** form.

Chief among such approaches is the **psychoanalytic** theory of Sigmund Freud and his successors. Freud himself did not much like the term 'personality', which does not acknowledge the unconscious dimensions of mental and emotional functioning. He did, however, use the term (especially as 'mental personality') and repeatedly talked of the 'dissection of mental personality', by which he sought to indicate that personality is composed of different parts (or 'mental agencies'), mostly unconscious and mostly in conflict with each other. Thus, the *id* represents the unconscious source of desires and impulses, the *ego* is the seat of consciousness (though it too contains unconscious parts) and represents the demands of external reality, and the *super-ego* stands for the claims of morality and the social order. Freud viewed the mental personality as emerging out of profound experiences, mostly in early life, that leave lasting marks and condition subsequent responses to different social situations.[1] The surface personality that we observe in other people is the result of different conflicts and compromises between mental agencies and the fronts they have learnt to assume as parts of different **performances**. Thus, the Freudian theory does not approach personality as an integrated, coherent, and permanent whole, but as one that can be full of contradictions—an evidently self-confident woman can lapse into profound self-doubts under certain circumstances and a thoroughly well-adjusted man can at times lapse into acutely neurotic behaviours. Personality, according to

this view, is protean, liable to fragment, mutate, and even split.

More recently, a narrative approach to personality has started to emerge, one that brings personality very close to identity. According to this view, our identities are constantly created and sustained by the narratives that we construct about our lives.[2] These narratives are reflexive, inasmuch as the storyteller and the story's protagonist co-create each other: by telling a **story** about oneself, one adopts personality characteristics commensurate with the characteristics of the protagonist of the story, whether he or she is a hero, a victim, a survivor, and so forth.

Narrative accounts of identity take the fragmentation of personality even further than psychoanalytic approaches—individuals may be scarcely able to sustain particular identities longer than it takes to tell the corresponding stories. The stories themselves become highly unstable, constantly shifting depending on circumstances and audiences. This approach appears well suited to our times, when many of the **grand narratives** that sustained people's identities in the past seem to be fragmenting and most people's life stories have to be constantly updated (almost like their CVs or résumés). As one of the characters in T. S. Eliot's *Cocktail Party* confides, 'I have ceased to believe in my own personality', to receive the physician's troubled reply, 'Oh, dear yes; this is very serious. A common malady. Very prevalent indeed.'[3]

• See also *identity, self and selfhood*

Policy

In most Indo-European languages there is a single word for both 'policy' and the process of its making, 'politics'. This linguistic unity suggests that policy is not only the product of political behaviour but an expression of politics itself, irrespective of whether it is found

---

[1] Freud, 1933/1988, 1940/1986.   [2] Humphreys and Brown, 2002; McAdams, Josselson, and Lieblich, 2006; Polkinghorne, 1996; Rappaport, 1993.   [3] Eliot, 1969, p. 402.

in corporations ('HR policy'), in nation states ('criminal justice policy'), or between governments ('European Union competition policy'). However, in contemporary English, policy is generally viewed as an output of a **decision**-making process, where what matter are the alternatives, which policy is chosen, and whether it is successful or effective. It is easily treated as a technocratic matter, rather removed from organizational or institutional **politics**, and in consequence, the content of policy may legitimately be evaluated separately from the conditions of its production. This is despite long-standing arguments that organizations produce messy and unexpected policies in messy and unexpected ways precisely because they are a product of organizational politics, routine, and accident.[1]

It was not always so: a now obsolete meaning of policy in English recalls its connection to politics in this broad sense; where policy is political because it is an object of politicking and a stake in organizational struggles. Policy could mean shrewdness, cunning, and carefulness, also a stratagem or trick: so that policy used to refer to both political guile and to a product of such guile. Policy in this sense is not a single output of a particular decision-making process, but it is rather *politics-in-practice*. It is a crystallization and representation of **norms**, **rules**, and relationships of **power** and an instance of the politics of, and within, an organization or society. Such a view illuminates and challenges two common distinctions which are made, between policy and politics on the one hand, and policy and practice on the other.

Treating policy as politics-in-practice means that it is always both a product and a producer of organizational systems of order, interests, and identities. Quite conventionally, we see that policy is a result of competitive power plays and conflicts among organization members, but more than this, also that particular individuals and groups and their interests are excluded

from making policy, thus creating and recreating institutional structures and relationships. More fundamentally, and moving beyond policy as mere **decision making**, it draws attention to the ways in which policy can disguise the interests of some organization members as disinterested, or as being in the interest of the organization as a whole. This is because policy engages the politics of creating **meaning** and **identity** for an organization, and how this is represented to its collective self as well as to its members. It involves choosing **rules** and **norms** which encourage and discourage particular behaviours, which facilitate ways of identifying with an organization and its **goals**, and which provide reference points for the creation of institutional order in an organization, legitimizing and giving preference to some interests above others.

Treating policy as politics-in-practice challenges another common distinction—that between 'what people *actually* do' (practice), as opposed to what policy says they *should* do. While we do not usually think of policy as something which is 'done', it must still be done (i.e. implemented) or it remains merely rhetoric and pretension. Only in policy implementation do we move beyond intent and goal setting, but policies also change their **meaning** and meet the limits of their application when put into practice. It is therefore in implementation, in the routine conformity to, or contravention of, policy, that its politics is made manifest.

While policy articulates settlements or compromises of interest and identity, **resistance** to such settlements is often expressed in everyday behaviour and talk. In addition, disputes of interest and identity are debated, settled, avoided, and changed through policy, but also by its deliberate absence, where, apparently paradoxically, policy exists *only* in practice. Consistent modes of behaviour can develop in an organization which amount to the creation and implementation of norms and rules, or politics-in-practice, yet these are so taken for granted

---

[1] Cohen, March, and Olsen, 1972; Kingdon, 1995.

that explicit policies are not warranted. Alternatively, these norms and rules can be so otherwise objectionable that explicit policies cannot be developed (e.g. 'institutional **racism**' in the Metropolitan Police). The absence of a conventional policy statement or documents should not delude us into thinking that there is no policy at all.

In sum, policy as politics-in-practice formalizes, legitimizes, and organizes group identities and interests, in organizations and social formations, and, in doing so, can also reveal the relationships of power, authority, and oppression which shape them.

• See also *New Public Management, politics, strategy*

EMMA CARMEL, UNIVERSITY OF BATH

Political correctness

Political correctness is a term that first appeared in the *New York Times* in 1991 to refer to a 'strain of postmarxist leftist thought in which the struggle between economic classes had been replaced, as a primary ontological framework, with the more differentiated set of oppositions based on such differences as sex, race, and sexual orientation'.[1]

The concept is highly contested. Its advocates view it as a political intervention that aims to stop the uses of politically and ideologically offensive **language** which perpetuates prejudice and discrimination. Its critics view it as an attempt to limit free speech and control free expression that seeks to turn any idea or theory that might possibly upset a minority group into a taboo. Political correctness is an especially potent issue in American academia where it was seen by critics as undermining academic freedom, compromising academic standards, and playing into a victim culture. Its advocates, on the other hand, charged critics of political correctness with being reactionary

bigots and defenders of a status quo that disadvantages particular groups and perpetuates social inequality.

Politics

'The human being is by nature a political animal,' claimed Aristotle, and 'those who are unable to live in society, or who have no need because they are sufficient for themselves, must be either beasts or gods: they are no part of a state [polis]. A social instinct is implanted in all humans by nature.'[2] Political and social were synonymous for Aristotle. Living together with other people within a state automatically generates relations of power and subordination, calls for decisions that have differential impact on different individuals and groups, and results in all different types of conflicts of interests. Politics then is the process through which different groups and individuals seek to promote or defend their interests in society through the use, direct or indirect, of **power**.

The term politics applies, in the first place, to the large arenas of government and international relations. However, it has now become normal to speak of organizational politics, environmental politics, family politics, sex politics, race politics, and so forth—suggesting that wherever there are relations of power, overt or covert, there are politics. The 'personal is political' was a powerful slogan that emerged from **feminist** discourses in the 1960s, proclaiming that there are no politics-free zones in human affairs, not even in the relations between two individuals or the way a single person lives his or her life.

Political philosophy and political science have long studied different political systems, generating a vast literature on different forms of government (such as democracy, oligarchy, and monarchy) and different political **institutions** (such as slavery, elections, and parliamentary representation). The study of politics is thus very close to the study of **ethics**, since certain forms of

---

[1] Schwartz, 2001, p. 4.   [2] Aristotle, 1981, 1253a.

government and political institutions are held to lead to greater justice, fairness, and prosperity than others. The link between politics and ethics is further indicated by the ease with which the word politics acquires negative resonances, as in expressions like 'playing politics' or 'dirty politics'. It then comes to indicate the ruthless, devious, and immoral pursuit of power and political gain at the expense of other people or groups. Yet it is politics that at least in part seeks to check abuses of power and make leaders accountable for their decisions.

The use of force is part of politics, but so too is the threat of the use of force. 'War is the continuation of politics by other means,' famously claimed Carl von Clausewitz,[1] in a statement that was used as a justification for war, as if he had said that war is *nothing but* a different type of politics. In some ways, politics and war deploy similar strategies and tactics—they aim to build alliances and to keep the opposition divided, to use the advantage of surprise, to exploit the opponent's weak point, and so forth. Yet what Clausewitz had in mind was that the use of force, military or otherwise, eventually has to be normalized through a political process and a political agreement. Even a spectacular military victory has to be consolidated through a political process, something that the USA and its allies ignored to their cost during their fateful intervention in Iraq.

Whether the same principles, moral and strategic, apply in politics and war is highly debatable. Sun Tzu,[2] author of the famous Chinese war manual dating from the sixth century BC, did not think so. 'Benevolence and righteousness may be used to govern a state but cannot be used to administer an army. Expedience and flexibility are used in administering an army, but cannot be used in governing a state.'[3] Deception, according to this view, is an indispensable element of military strategy but is unacceptable in civilian **governance**.

In organizations, power and influence, conflicts and compromises, control and resistances are part of a complex web of processes known as organizational politics.[4] Politics takes place in meetings, in corridor conversations, through e-mails, and so forth. Different members of an organization form alliances, do deals with each other, anticipate one another's partialities and preferences, plot the downfall or the promotion of colleagues, and continuously push issues in and out of agendas to promote their interests. They use power in many different forms, including persuasion, emotional pressures, promises, rewards, sanctions, appointments, withholding of information, defending territories, inclusion, and exclusion.

Political activity is sometimes seen as undesirable and destructive, undermining consensus and trust in an organization. But it is also true to say that it is a universal activity, and most people engage in organizational politics as way of dealing with the different conflicts of interests over the distribution of resources, power, and status. Organizations with proclaimed strong **ethical** systems, such as charities, hospitals, and churches, are notorious for the robustness of their organizational politics. Indeed it is sometimes argued that the more people believe that what they are doing is for the good of others, the dirtier the tricks they are prepared to resort to, to get their way. The pervasiveness of politics has led to the belief that **leaders** (especially those referred to as 'transactional') and managers are ultimately more effective if they possess political skills—the capacity to anticipate and analyse the political ramifications of their own and others' actions, and to be able to steer a pathway between the different people's interests and concerns. Creative problem solving is the art of discovering compromises that leave all sides believing that they have gained something from the political process.

Workplace politics is a particular dimension of organizational politics that arises from the

---

[1] Clausewitz, 1968.   [2] Sun Tzu, 1963.   [3] Ibid. 81.   [4] Bacharach and Lawler, 1980; Hardy and Clegg, 1999.

nature of labour power—unlike other resources, labour power is one which is constantly negotiated as it is being delivered. Managers want to use the productive qualities of their employees on their own terms as they see fit, whereas employees seek to defend a measure of autonomy and **control** over their labour and working conditions. The resulting political game of give-and-take, compromise, pressure, deception, and accommodation has been extensively studied both from empirical and theoretical perspectives by **labour process theorists**.

In recent decades the term 'identity politics' has assumed considerable currency, used to describe the political activities of groups that seek to assert their **identities** in public discourses, discover a communal voice to defend their interests and tell their stories. Identity politics is seen as supplanting **class** politics based on the large-scale political process dominated by economic relations under capitalism. 'The personal is political' summarizes the essence of identity politics—the view that a person's gender, race, sexual preference, and so forth are critical aspects of their identity and that politics must acknowledge and respect these, rather than treat all individuals as members of a uniform citizenry. Throughout the last thirty years, a great deal of political activity has been generated by disadvantaged, discriminated, and disenfranchised groups, as they seek to assert their rights and, in doing so, affirm their identities.

• See also *leadership, legitimacy, oligarchy and the iron law of oligarchy, power*

Population ecology theory of organizations

In the late 1970s some organization theorists began to wonder how organizations developed and changed, when even their own leaders and managers seemed to have a limited grasp of what was going on. It was then argued that organizations could be seen as not directed by an executive or a governing bloc but as having lives of their own. The population ecology perspective uses the Darwinian principle of natural selection to argue that over a period of time the selection processes favour certain organizational forms over others. Survival has little to do with **strategy** and **choice** and it is to a large extent a matter of luck and chance factors. Whether a new organizational idea or form succeeds depends on whether external circumstances happen to support it—more so than the efforts of the executive or managerial team. New organizations are always appearing in the population, and organization populations are continually undergoing change. Like humans and other species, organizations struggle for existence and compete over available resources. The struggle is intense among new organizations, some of which, by chance, are better equipped to face prevalent environmental conditions. These include local and national politics, transport, and other infrastructure, relations with trade unions, customers, and government agencies.[1]

The population ecology perspective places organizations in a reactive role: they sink or swim depending on the **environmental** conditions that prevail. It is a radical and somewhat overstated view which takes little notice of the influences of organizational actors, of their ability to make rational choices and influence the performance of their organizations. It approaches organizational **environments** as given and underestimates the extent to which they are **socially constructed**, moulded and shaped by powerful organizations and influential **leaders**. It has, however, the advantage of studying organizations over long periods of time and in large numbers; when seen this way, many processes that are invisible within the hustle and bustle of everyday operations begin to emerge.

---

[1] Carroll, 1985; Hannan and Freeman, 1977; 1989.

Postcolonialism and postcolonial theory

Postcolonialism and postcolonial theory refer to a contemporary current of thinking (based mostly in literature departments of American universities) that looks at colonial relations and their legacy as paradigmatic of the way in which **power** and domination operate in a societies founded on colonial expansion. (The term postcolonialism with the hyphen is used to denote a more temporal usage, i.e. the period after the formal end of colonialism.) In particular, postcolonialism looks at how dominant **identities** in the West were forged by **othering** the colonized people and their cultures, denying them a **voice**, and violating their histories and traditions. Edward Said's *Orientalism* is a foundational text of postcolonial theory.[1] In it, Said looks at the 'Orient' as a mythical creation of a European culture that inspired many artists and writers, but bears no relation to the cultures of the colonized people; instead, romanticized images of Asia and the Middle East served to legitimize, with the collusion of local colonial elites, European superiority and colonial expansion.

According to postcolonial theory, colonial relations represent a paradigm of total domination of one people by another, a domination that does not merely oppress the colonized people politically and exploit them economically but seeks to inscribe its own ways of thinking onto them, thus obliterating all independent self-identity, pride, and resistance among them. Europeans had no interest in understanding or entering into dialogue with the people of India, Africa, or the Middle East, over whom they assumed an unquestioned superiority; instead, they imposed their own institutions, labels, and discourses on them, viewing them through a set of distorting mirrors that reduced them to stereotypical forms, such as 'the African

mentality' or 'the Indian mind' or the 'Arab psychology.'

In some versions of postcolonial theory, much of the edifice of Western **ethnography** and anthropology which sought to study 'primitive' people through the categories of the West (e.g. religion, magic, ritual, etc.) was itself a feature of the colonial project, a charge to which these disciplines now frequently have to respond. Thus, when anthropologist David Stoll exposed inaccuracies and contradictions in Rigoberta Menchú's harrowing narrative of the sufferings of Guatemala's peasantry at the hands of government militia in the 1970s and 1980s, he was accused of violating her culture, by failing to understand the nature of her testimony or the fact that she was speaking with a collective voice on behalf of all her people.[2] 'Stoll's larger agenda is an assault, not only on a number of other anthropologists, but on accounts of Latin American history that honour grassroots strivings for rights and social justice, and on political arguments offered by cultural studies and postcolonial criticism. His book resonates with parallel attacks from other, and diverse, quarters, while also embodying a range of vices as an anthropological analysis.'[3]

One field of postcolonial theory is known as subaltern studies, pioneered by a group of Indian scholars founded by Ranajit Guha.[4] They were influenced by the theories of Italian Marxist philosopher Antonio Gramsci, who first used the term subaltern to denote any person or group who are economically dispossessed, marginalized, and excluded on account of their class, religion, or race. The subaltern scholars sought to give a voice to the subaltern, notably the urban poor and the peasantry, whose narratives had been silenced from history and whose struggles against imperialism had remained substantially invisible. In her famous article 'Can the subaltern speak?', Gayatri Chakravorty Spivak argued that it is impossible for others (including

---

[1] Said, 1985. [2] Stoll, 1999; Menchù, 1984. [3] Gledhill, 2001, p. 135. [4] Guha, 1997.

intellectuals) to speak on behalf of the dispossessed and marginalized, without reinforcing their dispossessed and marginalized identity and forcing a false unity among highly heterogeneous people.[1] The assumption of a coherent subaltern collectivity, argued Spivak, is akin to the colonizing impulses of Western culture that fails to register the heterogeneity of those it seeks to colonize. The question of whether it is possible or desirable for anyone else to talk on behalf of the subaltern remains a highly debated one.

Postcolonial theory has started to make an impact on the study of organizations (especially through **Critical Management Studies**), with the concept of the subaltern making occasional appearances to describe those who are nearly invisible to conventional organizational theory. In a challenging critique of attempts by well-meaning management scholars to import the concept of ecological embeddedness from the practices of indigenous people to those of managers, Banerjee and Linstead have argued that such attempts mirror the failings of Western anthropology in comprehending indigenous people in their own terms.[2] Trying to learn from the practices of primitive people, argue Banerjee and Linstead, approaches these practices through our eyes, our concerns, and our mindsets, rather than theirs, in a repetition of the colonial paradigm that 'caricatures' indigenous behaviours by forcing them into the language of management. Thus Banerjee and Linstead acknowledge the enduring contribution of postcolonial theory which has been to sensitize us to the dangers of forcing one's own ways of thinking and perceiving on those who inhabit different worlds of thinking and perceiving.

Postcolonial theory has not escaped from criticisms, not least that its preoccupation with **discourse** has blinded it to the economics and politics of colonial domination and that it approaches **othering** in relatively bleak terms, disregarding the possibility of creative engagement with the Other and mutual **learning** and even emancipation resulting from such engagements.

• See also *identity, Other and othering, voice*

Postmodernism

It is widely agreed that all postmodern strands lead to Nietzsche, who rejected the Enlightenment of **modernity**. Enlightenment modernity banished premodern spiritual ecology, the idea of humans in living dialogue with animals, mountains, rivers, trees, ancestors, and other entities. Modern **science** and **technology** were promising a new world order beyond the premodern. Dating the transition from premodern to modern is impossible. It is not one date, but recurs with the Reformation, the Renaissance, the French Revolution, the industrial revolution, mechanization, automation, the First and Second World Wars, etc. What is clear is that with the spread of modern **capitalism**, the human, natural, and spiritual ecologies of the Third World are ravaged, the world is still embroiled in war after war while experiencing overpopulation, global warming, and species extinction at alarming rates.

On the way to postmodern, the struggle to reform modern capitalism's dark side fragmented into a thousand strands. An era approach is rejected—dating the arrival of postmodernism is impossible as is the construction of a linear episodic narrative, moving from the premodern to the modern and then to the postmodern. Instead postmodern methods, theories, and world views proliferate, as do modern and premodern ones. There are numerous postmodern approaches ranging from naive postmodernism ('McPostmodernism') that hails the arrival of postindustrial and complex/adaptive **organizations**, Baudrillard's and Lyotard's versions of radical breaks from modernity, to others seeking greater integration with **critical**

---

[1] Spivak, 1988.   [2] Banerjee and Linstead, 2004.

theory. Some claim to have moved beyond postmodern to something called post-postmodern that would include hybrids (postmodern variants with modern and premodern), language 'heteroglossia' (the coexistence of many **voices** at the same time, in tension with each other), and various 'dark side postmodernisms' looking at global reterritorialization, postmodern war, **postcolonialism**, and the ills of capitalism.

Several strands of postmodernism grew out of the latest French revolution. During the 1968 revolt, when students joined by workers brought France to a standstill, several postmodernists claimed to see an end of modernity. Debord thought the 'Society of the Spectacle' had arrived, so that Marx's production economy needed to be reimagined as a **consumption** economy.[1] Baudrillard and Lyotard proposed radical postmodern projects.[2] Baudrillard pushed Debord's **spectacle** to its limit, claiming unilaterally that all of society had become a simulation (or simulacrum). Lyotard's radical project to reform education was to be incredulous of all modernist **grand narratives**, including **systems** theory, universal **ethics**, and essentialist psychologies. But, in the aftermath of 1968, when the French people went back to school and work, 'modern' capitalism reclaimed its grip on society.

Derrida and Foucault are often classed as or accused of being postmodernists but it would be more accurate to view them as **post-structuralists** (rejecting structuralism).[3] Postmodernists often adopt Derrida's **deconstruction** style and Foucault's archaeology of knowledge, or his genealogical method, to unravel grand narratives. Habermas decided to reject them all, debating each of them in his books or on TV. Habermas held out the possibility that modernity was an unfinished project, and that with the help of a communicative **rationality**, the process of consensus dialogue could revitalize the public sphere.[4] Latour, for his part, claimed

that instead of modern succeeded by postmodern, we need to recognize 'we have never been modern'.[5] Premodern, modern, and postmodern ways of Being and of Knowing coexist in different hybrid combinations. Jameson argued that capitalism was in its late modern manifestation.[6] Every time there is a postmodern move to succeed it, modernism appropriates the move, tames it, and turns it into yet another commodity. McDonald's appropriates the simulation, by serving simulated (highly artificial) food. Nike rejects universal ethics, spinning virtual stories of its athletes' successes, and **stories** of turning sweatshops into exemplary workplaces. Wal-Mart imports 85 per cent of its products from China, but waves the Made In America flag. Las Vegas specializes in spectacles of postmodern architecture to attract more families to gamble. McDonald's, Wal-Mart, and Las Vegas are both modern and postmodern. In short, the postmodern has some very dark sides.

One of these dark sides is what Best and Kellner call postmodern warfare.[7] Unlike the First World War, the Second World War, or even the Vietnam War, the two Gulf Wars launched by the two Bush presidents relied extensively on media simulations. Animations were presented instead of showing the blood of soldiers and civilians on battlefields. Bush even stopped the media from showing flag-draped coffins of fallen veterans; instead, his *Top Gun* landing on USS *Lincoln* became a sign of victory, irrespective of the realities on the ground.

There are many other postmodern strands. As early as 1957, Peter Drucker claimed management had become postmodern when it ceased to rely on Cartesian thinking.[8] Bergquist, ignoring social **power** differences, argued that one is on the way to the Valhalla of postmodernism when one engages in complexity, instead of old-fashioned system thinking.[9] Gergen asserted that everything is a **social construction**, without a

---

[1] Debord, 1977.   [2] Baudrillard, 1968/1988; 1970/1988; Lyotard, 1984/1991.   [3] Derrida, 1976; Foucault, 1966/1970; 1969/1972.
[4] Habermas, 1984b; 1990.   [5] Latour, 1990.   [6] Jameson, 1984.   [7] Best and Kellner, 1991.   [8] Drucker, 1959.   [9] Bergquist, 1993.

material connection.[1] New Age postmodernists argue that CEOs focusing on spirituality will take us beyond the ills of late modern capitalism. I must confess I once thought there was hope that some kind of postmodern organization would emerge shorn of its dark sides. My current view is that one needs to be highly sceptical of postmodern thinking. Baudrillard and Lyotard are too radical. Not everything is a simulacrum. Over half the world's population do not have a computer, cell phone, or iPod. *Some* grand narratives, such as distributive **ethics**, spiritual ecology, and world peace are worth pursuing. When power and hegemony are ignored in highly affirmative or naive postmodern strands, guard your wallet and your home.

In organization studies, there are many strands. Clegg argued that the survival of traditional French bread making indicated that modern organization was consistent with the survival of premodern forms of organizing.[2] Burrell, in *Pandemonium*,[3] argues that we can juxtapose modern organization narratives with premodern ones. Calas and Smircich think it is time for the postmodern to be surpassed, and propose **postcolonial** theory as the new post-postmodern contender.[4]

On their way towards the postmodern, postmodernists could not agree on what was wrong with the modern, or on how to go to about reinventing it. So the modern quickly appropriated every postmodern idea, turning one after another into **consumption spectacles**. 'Managerialism' appropriated the moves of the postmodern, distilling them into the darkest side of the postmodern and marrying them off to modernity's Frankenstein bride. It thus claimed language games and social construction and made false sightings of the liberation of workers and modernity from McDonaldization, WalMartization, Las Vegasation, and Empire. What have remained most valuable in postmodern strands are all the theory and methods used

to question modern and (post) postmodern moves.

• See also *deconstruction, discourse, modernism and modernity, post-structuralism, story and storytelling*

DAVID BOJE, NEW MEXICO STATE UNIVERSITY

Post-structuralism

Post-structuralism is a loose philosophical movement that emerged in France during the 1960s. It is often associated with thinkers such as Jacques Derrida, Michel Foucault, Gilles Deleuze, and Julia Kristeva. It emerged as a reaction against Sartre's existential Marxism and grew out of an increased disenchantment with the structuralist approaches of anthropologist Lévi-Strauss and others. It proved to be influential during the student uprising in Paris in 1968. It subsequently was picked up by intellectuals working in the humanities and social sciences in the Anglo-Saxon world during the 1970s and 1980s.

Post-structuralism (also spelt 'poststructuralism' without a hyphen) places particular emphasis on how **language** constructs **reality**. It seeks to show how reality is not just described by the words which we use. Rather it asserts that reality is actively constructed by and through our language. For instance, the language of economics allows us to see a reality where individuals are largely driven by self-interest and seek to maximize this self-interest by engaging in exchange. If we did not have this language, we would find it difficult to see, much less describe, this reality.

Post-structuralism seeks to show how different languages produce different realities.[5] For instance, if a sexual liaison in the workplace is talked about using the language of romantic poetry a reality of **desire**, longing, love, and seduction might emerge. However, if that same liaison is described using the language of **Human Resource Management**, the affair

---

[1] Gergen, 1994.   [2] Clegg, 1990.   [3] Burrell, 1997.   [4] Calas and Smircich, 1999.   [5] Linstead, 2004.

may be seen as a source of inefficiency, an infringement of **rules**, and maybe even **sexual harassment**.

Post-structuralism also sets out to questions truth claims. This is because any truth claim constructs the reality it claims to describe. For instance, to claim that people are largely motivated by money leads a manager to act in a way which reinforces this reality. The result is that truth claims actually construct the reality they hope to describe. For instance, early claims about the importance of **management** actually constructed the figure of the manager and justified their role in organizational life.

In addition, post-structuralism puts forward an important critique of **science**. If we accept that reality is constructed through language, then we might see science as only a form of language for describing reality. Thus instead of seeing science as the 'royal road to truth', post-structuralism understands science as one way of knowing the world. However, this one way of knowing the world has been privileged over many other ways. This has been particularly important in the social sciences where scientific forms of knowledge have dominated during the last century. The result is that social reality is only understood through the language of science. For instance, our knowledge about how **organizations** work is largely dominated by scientific descriptions using large data sets. The result is a very one-dimensional and somewhat lifeless account of organizational life.

In order to challenge the dominance of scientific truth claims, post-structuralism seeks to recover other forms of **knowledge** about organizational life. These forms of knowledge may come in the form of personal experience, folk knowledge, aesthetic experiences, feeling, and emotion, as well as fragmented and disorganized **narratives**. This often takes the form of giving **voice** to people whose experiences have

been marginalized in our scientific descriptions of organizations. They might include workers, women, peoples of colour, queer groups, the disabled, and people from the global South.[1]

Post-structuralism also seeks to recover the fragmented, disorganized, or unspeakable aspects of organizational life. Instead of seeking to present smooth, flowing narratives of organizational life, post-structuralism aims to capture the ambiguities, uncertainties, and irrationalities which often lurk in organizations. This has pushed many researchers to turn traditional organization theory on its head and investigate processes of disorganization, disorder, and disorientation. Furthermore, post-structuralism seeks to register the unspeakable aspects of organizing. This involves recognizing those aspects of organizational life which escape our language, which cannot be said, and are yet to come. Thus an adequate theory of organization must acknowledge and indeed care for these unspeakable aspects of organizational life.

Post-structuralism has not been without its critics. Functionalist scholars argue that post-structuralism makes it very difficult to generate generalizable and useful findings that can help to guide practitioners. Interpretative scholars point out that post-structuralism's interest in texts and philosophy can distract researchers from recording actors' own interpretations and processes of understanding the social world. Finally, realists argue that post-structuralism has led researchers to become obsessed with language and neglect the structural aspects of organizational reality such as bureaucracy, capitalism, and imperialism.

• See also *authority, Other and othering, postmodernism, social construction of reality, structure and structuralism, unmanaged and unmanageable*

ANDRE SPICER, WARWICK UNIVERSITY

---

[1] Calas and Smircich, 1999.

Power

Power is a foundational concept in political theory, one that forms the core of a tight nexus of ideas that include politics, control, leadership, and conflict. 'Power is the medium through which conflicts of interest are ultimately resolved. Power influences who gets what, when and how.'[1] But power is also an important concept in psychology where it is often linked to motivation. 'Power is the ultimate aphrodisiac,' American Secretary of State Henry Kissinger claimed, alluding to its alluring, addictive qualities. In Nietzsche's later philosophy, the will to power forms the cornerstone of his philosophical monism, the central principle from which all human actions and experiences ensue. Yet, in spite of its importance, power remains a difficult and even elusive concept to define.

Karl Marx had no doubts. He viewed all power as ultimately residing in the economic order of each society, and in particular **control** over the means of production. This control was vested in particular **classes**—the aristocracy during feudalism, the capitalist class under **capitalism**. *Political power* was 'merely the organised power of one class for oppressing another'.[2] In capitalist societies, no matter what strange forms power may assume, it ultimately rests with the capitalists' control over the means of production, the land, the factories, the technology, the raw materials, the information, and the know-how. Workers have but one power, labour *power*, the ability to create value through their work. The competing powers of capital and labour result in **conflict**, a conflict in which the odds are initially overwhelmingly stacked in favour of the capitalists. They can force workers to work on their terms since workers have no other means of supporting themselves and their families. For a wide variety of reasons, Marx believed that gradually power shifts in the direction of the workers who become more united, more resentful of being exploited, and ultimately more aware of their

own power that rests in solidarity and concerted action. Eventually, Marx envisaged a revolution that would topple the capitalist ruling class and replace it with the rule of the proletariat, the working class.

Max Weber recognized the importance of social classes; however, living at the time of the rise of bureaucratic organizations, he was also aware that power can result from the occupancy of bureaucratic positions vested with **authority**. He defined power as the ability of one person or a party to dictate its will to another despite opposition. He then identified authority as legitimate power and went on to propose three types of authority, charismatic, traditional, and rational-legal. In Weber's conceptualization, **knowledge** commensurate with position is the basis of rational-legal authority—thus, a qualified manager or administrator may possess independent power, even if he or she does not control the means of production. Power then becomes dispersed in a **hierarchy** where those in superior positions control those below them. Those in subordinate positions may recognize the power of their superiors but often they do not—instead, they test it, resist it, and contest it. The exercise of power may augment it (for example, when its results are so brutal as to quell further resistance) or alternatively may erode and destroy it. The exercise or the threat of exercising power in conflict situations is the essence of **politics**.

More recently, we have become more attuned to the way that power may be exercised in more subtle, invisible, and diverse ways. Thus, Bachrach and Baratz argued that, instead of being used to dictate decisions, power may shape agendas of what decisions are possible.[3] Knowledge, **information**, and cunning may offset other forms of power, by sidestepping key decisions and setting the agenda for winnable ones. In his highly influential theory of power, Lukes proposed a three-dimensional model of power.[4] The first dimension consists of the power to

---

[1] Morgan, 1986, p. 158.   [2] Marx and Engels, 1848/1972, p. 352.   [3] Bachrach and Baratz, 1970.   [4] Lukes, 1975.

force someone to do something which they would not otherwise do. The second dimension is the power of managing situations and setting agendas in ways that effectively forestall the possibility of damaging decisions being taken. The third dimension is the most far-reaching one—it is the power to influence someone's perception of where their real interests lie.

This third dimension of power is often embedded in **ideologies**, **institutions**, and linguistic conventions that come to be viewed as normal and inevitable; it is akin to what Gramsci described as 'hegemony',[1] a form of invisible power, a power that comes not from stopping anyone from making their voice heard, but from making them believe that they have nothing to say. Gramsci's view was that hegemony was exercised by the capitalist class to obtain the spontaneous consent of the masses. Lukes's third dimension of power and Gramsci's hegemony can be seen as functioning by defining reality for others. They are part of the more general **management of meaning** through which situations come to be viewed in particular ways. Thus an 'unprofitable company' may be seen through the prism of downsizing, getting rid of dead wood, and belt-tightening rather than as calling for the replacement of existing management structures with elected workers' representatives.

Postmodern discourses have been inspired by the work of Foucault and place much emphasis on the ways power is exercised through discursive practices, i.e. through ways of using **language**, which privilege certain views over others, creating oppositions of normal and abnormal, healthy and sick, desirable and undesirable.[2] Power/knowledge is the indissoluble entity of regimes of truth and regimes of control and has been very helpful in raising the profiles of groups that have been disenfranchised, silenced, or '**othered**' in invisible ways, often adopting the very views of themselves which perpetuate their oppression.

Postmodern discourses of power can at times assume a metaphysical gloom that denies all possibility of change, **resistance**, or emancipation.[3] This position is countered by theorists like de Certeau,[4] who sought to identify unmanaged and unmanageable spaces in society and organizations, as well as **labour process theorists** who have explored numerous forms of resistance against discursive controls.[5] In truth, numerous scholars influenced by Foucault's ideas have also made substantial contributions to theorizing resistance.[6]

• See also *authoritarianism, authority, corruption, legitimacy, oligarchy and the iron law of oligarchy*

Practice/Praxis

'There is nothing so practical as a good theory.' In the most general sense, Kurt Lewin's much-quoted aphorism suggests that a theory, whether it is a philosophical one, a political one, or a management one, will have some practical implications.[7] Even a theory in abstract mathematics or in astronomy can change the way we live. For example, a theory about the origin of the universe can have practical implications by refuting various religious beliefs about the creation of the world. In a more specific way, the quote suggests that **knowledge** is a practical resource that finds useful applications in life. Thus knowing how to cook a cake enables you to cook one and knowing how to handle people enables you to do so effectively.

Lewin's quote raises some questions. How exactly do we define a 'good' theory? Why is it that so often theories that were generally acknowledged to be 'good' prove ineffective? And why is it that some less good theories (for example, **Scientific Management**) find many and even successful practical applications? The link between theory and practice or human

---

[1] Gramsci, 1971.   [2] Foucault, 1977; 1978; 1980.   [3] Parker, 1995.   [4] Certeau, 1984.   [5] See e.g. Ackroyd and Thompson, 1999; Edwards, 1979; Thompson Ackroyd, 1995.   [6] See e.g. most contributions in Jermier, Knights, and Nord, 1994.   [7] Lewin, 1951, p. 169.

action is not straightforward; it has preoccupied many of the brightest intellects, generating one of the thickest discursive traditions in Western thought. Some theorists have looked at moral action, others at political action, yet others at technical or entrepreneurial action. Yet the link between theory and practice has remained problematic.

The concept of practice is multifaceted. It can indicate a set of actions, informed by **knowledge**, undertaken on a more or less routine basis (as in 'practising medicine, law, or management'); alternatively, it may indicate the systematic attempt to acquire a set of skills or competences (as in 'practising the violin'); finally, it may be used in a sense which entails its juxtaposition to belief (as in 'practising what one preaches'). What is constant about these meanings is the closeness of practice to the material world of **action** rather than to the contemplative world of ideas. In an attempt to distinguish and privilege certain types of action from others, many scholars from a **critical theory** perspective preferred to use the Greek word *praxis* in preference to practice (which is also of Greek origin). Praxis does not refer to all types of action. Habit (or Weber's traditional action) is not praxis. Praxis entails an element of agency, associated with purpose, **choice**, knowledge, and possibly **rationality**.

In the area of organizations, the relation between theory and practice is further complicated by the close alignment of organizational knowledge to the interests of practising managers, who often pay for its production and dissemination. Thus many theories in this area claim to be of practical use to managers and managers claim to make use of them. Practical and even spectacular successes are sometimes claimed for particular approaches that assume the character of **fads and fashions**. At the risk of some simplification, we can identify four main tendencies regarding the relations between organizational theory and management practice:

1. *The toolkit-power-control tendency*. This dominant tendency is in line with the positivist tradition pioneered in the social sciences by Auguste Comte who said, 'To know in order to foresee, to foresee in order to anticipate.' The aim of theory is to understand events in order to control them. **Control** has undoubtedly been a central reason for the perceived value of organizational theory in practice. In their different ways, the theories of Taylor, Weber, and Peters and Waterman have made their marks as instruments for more efficient control of organizations and what goes on inside them—people, information, resources. Much of what Burrell refers to as NATO (North American Theory of Organizations), ranging from positivist research to guru theory, seeks to make itself useful to practitioners, offering them ways of achieving competitive advantage.[1] Variants of vulgar Marxism ('Correct practice follows from correct theory') aspired at using theory in similar ways to different ends.

2. *The reflective practice tendency*. This tradition has sought to use theory as part of a humanist project—theory is a force towards progressive **learning**, enlightenment, and growth. Most theorizing on management learning and reflective practice falls broadly within this tradition,[2] as do contributions from humanistic psychology and **psychodynamics**.[3] Their aim is to develop new forms of management practice which are less damaging to human growth and fulfilment and generate less dysfunctional forms of organization. Practice and theory are linked here in a feedback loop of mutual reinforcement and correction. In its loftier forms, this tendency views action and reflection as indispensable elements in a project of social emancipation, neatly summed up by the great Brazilian humanist Paulo Freire: 'Human activity consists of action and reflection: it is praxis, it is transformation of the world. And as praxis, it requires theory to illuminate it. Human activity is theory and practice; it is reflection and action.'[4]

---

[1] Burrell, 1996.   [2] Argyris and Schön, 1974; 1978; Schön, 1983.   [3] Hirschhorn and Barnett, 1993.   [4] Freire, 1970/1996, p. 106.

3. *The illusion-ideology tendency.* A different tradition in organizational theory views most such theory as essentially non-practical. Of course, practitioners may act under the illusion of putting into effect the latest theoretical findings; in practice, however, they use theory as a *post facto* rationalization for action. This tendency views theory as part of a **legitimizing** process, one that enhances the position of managers and bolsters their **authority**.[1] From a psychological point of view, theory, far from guiding action, offers comfort and security to the perplexed and confused practitioner.[2] When seen from this perspective, organizational theory corresponds quite well to the Marxist term **ideology** and the Freudian term illusion.

4. *The critical tendency.* At times this tendency may be found merged with one of the previous two, but it does have some distinctive qualities of its own. Chief among them is a militant anti-performativity,[3] i.e. an aversion towards any type of theorizing which is driven by the practical concerns of managers. This is consistent with a postmodern twist, which seeks to denaturalize concepts and ideas and promote reflexivity, through a **deconstruction** of managerial buzzwords and practices. Some critical theorists would like to see this tendency develop into an platform for an emancipatory project, though apprehension is expressed about whether it may not disintegrate into a project where the few 'emancipate' the many. The majority of theorists in this tendency have opted for asserting the primacy of **discourse**, either viewing theory itself as practice (theoretical practice) or arguing for a total discontinuity between theory and action.[4]

In recent years, the application of knowledge to practice is viewed as requiring a process of *translation* from the general to the specific and from the global to the local.[5] This translation of knowledge from one context to another is reminiscent of **bricolage**, the skilful deployment of available resources to deal with immediate problems. The term *paragramme* has been used to describe the creative use of ideas and theories, in contrast to their 'programmatic' applications. Organizational theories and ideas can be seen, somewhat like proverbs or recipes—their value lies not in their claims to universal validity but as resources that, in the hands of skilful practitioners, can enable them to address the immediate challenges that confront them.[6]

Professions and professionals

The terms profession and professional are widely used in everyday discourse, to imply competence ('the builders did a really professional job'), paid employment (as contrasted with an amateur/dilettante), and even instrumentality (as per the professional foul). Perhaps partly because of this frequent and wide-ranging usage, the theoretical anchoring of the concept of profession has become increasingly precarious.

Summaries of theories of the professions conventionally refer to several models. An early and rather normative stream of work focused on ethical superiority. For example, professions claimed to operate with an underlying set of **values** that guide the work of their members in providing a 'disinterested' service to a client or superordinate authority (the state, the court, the public) and a higher calling (e.g. in medicine, to do no harm). Another normative body of theorizing was trait based, such that the distinctive aspects of certain occupations marked them out as professions and by definition others failed the test. Professions have also been defined in terms of their occupational strategies, being occupations that pursue closure, or exclusive **control** of a jurisdiction of work on the basis of expertise, to sustain labour market power.[7] While these theories are not incommensurate they have usually been associated with contestation; thus, sociologists of the social closure school are evidently

[1] MacIntyre, 1981; Thomas, 1993.   [2] Lawrence, 1999; Obholzer, 1999.   [3] Fournier and Grey, 2000.   [4] Burrell, 1990; Knights and Willmott, 1989; Parker, 1992; 1995.   [5] Czarniawska and Joerges, 1996.   [6] Gabriel, 2002.   [7] Abbott, 1988; Freidson, 1986.

more critical of the motives of professions and professionals than those who outlined ethical or trait models.[1] Each type of theory retains some validity but they collectively raise wider questions on the general usefulness of the terms profession and professional. Do they offer predictive or other insights, for example, on what is distinctive about the everyday work of those who claim professional status or what is the distinctive about professions vis-à-vis other occupations?

Certain conditions in late modernity render the concept of a profession increasingly problematic, even as, at the same time, the development of a so-called **knowledge**-based society and knowledge-intensive industries and technologies seem to be tailor made for the proliferation of professions. First, the anti-deferential **ideologies** of contemporary society and wider scepticism towards **status** claims present a challenge to occupational prestige. Second, while it may be argued that a number of occupations, notably medicine and law, have successfully sustained some recognition of professional status, public scrutiny of particular cases where shortcomings occurred support a rhetoric of self-interestedness and undermine general prestige and trust: few would buy the ethical superiority argument unreservedly today and it is no accident that professions are subject to external control by regulatory bodies and statutes in ways that did not occur even twenty years ago.

Third, certain technological innovations have facilitated the spread of 'expert' knowledge. Mechanisms such as internet search engines allow the rapid diagnosis of a range of problems from medical to legal to social that were previously the preserve of specialists. Any such democratization of knowledge is therefore broadly inimical to claims of professionalism based on exclusive expertise (or knowledge asymmetry between professional and client) even if, in practice, the diagnostic power of such technologies is limited to routine problems.

Fourth, in addition to external controls, professionals have become less autonomous (and therefore less distinctive) by virtue of their subjection to managerial controls in both public and private sectors. For example, even in the elite firms of the business professions, partners, that is the owners of the firms, no longer have permanent tenure, have imported the paraphernalia of performance monitoring, and work increasingly long hours at the beck and call of their clients for their rewards.[2] Notions of job **control** and a higher calling have become irrelevant to everyday work as professionals are caught up in satisfying client needs.

Fifth, as the ecology of work changes, new occupations emerge to challenge professions' jurisdictions. These occupations are rarely organized on formal credentials, deriving power from the market or the state. Examples are to be found in the proliferation of occupations in the areas of **risk** and regulation. They can exploit the availability of new (and sometimes unorthodox) forms of knowledge to create niches that progressively chip away at the domains of professionals' work, for instance, in areas of complementary medicine, social welfare, academia, law, and psychology.

For scholars, therefore, the challenge is to come to terms with these broader themes and issues in their research. For example, research on the extent to which external regulation influences and is influenced by professions, as they seek to build and sustain jurisdictions, is currently lacking but clearly important. Careful examination of the everyday work of professionals and how ethical considerations of any kind affect the deployment of their expertise would be another valuable area to theorize further. Research is needed on how **globalization** creates interconnections and tensions between professions and how these are negotiated. Finally, further work is needed on the rhetoric and strategies that occupations use to pursue professionalization: in knowledge-intensive

---

[1] Larson, 1977.   [2] Brock, Powell, and Hinings, 1999.

environments one would predict any would-be profession would have to lay stress on technical expertise, but is this sufficient? Or, is there any value in emphasizing ethical standards, and if so why? Such research questions link to the wider project of studying changes to occupational structures and institutional frameworks that define which groups can, or cannot, build and sustain status.

TIM MORRIS, UNIVERSITY OF OXFORD

Psychoanalysis and psychoanalytic approaches

Psychoanalysis is a branch of depth psychology founded by Sigmund Freud. It is both a clinical practice aimed at alleviating mental disorders and a theoretical body of knowledge about **unconscious** mental processes and their conscious manifestations. While emerging from studies of mental disturbances, psychoanalysis addresses a wide range of mental phenomena (including dreams, sexuality, desires, emotions, creativity, and mourning) and has had a profound effect on literature, film, social sciences, and the arts. Psychoanalysis once reached unprecedented levels of influence and fashion in Western culture, prompting poet W. H. Auden to write shortly after Freud's death, 'to us he is no more a person now but a whole climate of opinion'. Freud is no longer such a commanding presence in the human sciences, though many of his ideas have become incorporated in different discourses and not a few have become part of common sense. He bequeathed numerous terms that are now part of everyday life, including narcissism, denial, repression, and, of course, the 'Freudian slip'.

The distinguishing feature of psychoanalysis is the assumption of an unconscious dimension to social and individual life. The unconscious is the mental territory where dangerous and painful ideas and **desires** are consigned through repression and other defensive mechanisms, and also as a source of resistance to specific ideas and emotions which present threats to mental functioning. Unconscious ideas, desires, and emotions may be of a sexual nature but may also be related to ambition, envy, fear (of death, of failure, of rejection, etc.), and so forth. These often reach consciousness in highly distorted or abstruse ways, requiring interpretation. One of the commonest manifestations of the unconscious are **fantasies**—mental representations which express unconscious wishes and desires as if they were already realized, yet often in a disguised and indirect manner. Fantasies are equally important in understanding the actions of people in and out of organizations: daydreaming consumers, ambitious leaders, bullied employees, budding entrepreneurs, disaffected voters, and so forth, are as liable to be guided and driven by their fantasies as by rational considerations of ends and means.

All people have an unconscious and all of us repress unpleasant and disturbing thoughts and emotions. All of us suffer from the consequences of these repressions. All of us experience mental **conflict**, ambivalence, anxiety, and behavioural symptoms which we sometimes find ourselves unable to tame or control. Some of us suffer from unusually severe and debilitating versions of these effects. A key task of psychoanalytic interventions is to restore to us some of the contents of our unconscious by undoing the effects of repressions and other defence mechanisms. This is especially the case if these mechanisms are dysfunctional; if, in other words, the **anxiety**, inhibition, and pain which they cause outweigh the comfort and protection which they afford. Psychoanalytic interpretation is the process whereby the hidden **meanings** of actions, desires, and emotions are gradually brought to light, by viewing conscious phenomena as the distorted expressions of unconscious ones. This is a difficult and time-consuming process, since the unconscious raises resistance against attempts to reveal its content.

Some of the other core theories of psychoanalysis concern the development of **sexuality** through a number of stages, the theory of **narcissism**, according to which all people address some of their sexual interest towards themselves, seeking to make themselves the centre of admiration, and the theory of transference, a process through which people transfer feelings and fantasies onto others, repeating earlier life experiences.

The world of organizations, impersonal, structured, and formalized, was for a long time thought of as being at the opposite end of the intimate, personal relations that formed the primary concerns of psychoanalysis. Gradually, however, the appreciation of irrational, emotional, and sexual aspects of organizations has opened up the possibility of using psychoanalytic insights in organizational analysis. Theorists who have adopted psychoanalytic insights in their engagement with organizations have done so from one of two directions.[1] One has been to study organizations as dominant features of Western society and culture, examining their demands on individuals, their influence on interpersonal relations in and out of work, their effects on people's emotional lives, the manner in which they feature in people's fantasies and dreams. A whole range of organizational phenomena can be approached in this manner, including leadership, group dynamics, insults and jokes, sexual harassment, psychological contracts and obedience, and so forth. This approach can be summed up as *studying organizations psychoanalytically*.[2]

A different approach that can be described as *psychoanalysing organizations* starts from a more pragmatic concern, seeking to psychoanalyse organizations as though they were ailing patients. If psychoanalysis can return a patient to normal functioning, can it not be used as *a* method of organizational intervention, enhancing organizational functioning? Organizational interventions seek to identify repressed forces, such as rivalries, fears of failure, anger over betrayals, disappointments, and frustrations, which systematically inhibit collaboration, creativity, harmony, and organizational

performance, and to redress them. Following important work on groups by Bion,[3] this approach was pioneered at the Tavistock Institute in London,[4] and in the United States, by scholars such as Levinson, Zaleznik, Hirschhorn, Diamond, Stein, Krantz, and theorists/consultants associated with the William Alanson White Institute.[5] This approach can go further still in 'psychoanalysing organizations' by diagnosing certain pathological processes in organizations, such as paranoia, megalomania, self-delusion, and anxiety, which directly mirror similar processes among individuals, so that, in a certain way, it can be said that the entire organization becomes afflicted by neurosis (see **organizational pathologies**). Such a neurotic organization, in turn, infects everyone who comes into contact with it, as an employee, as a stakeholder, or even as a leader. Organizations can then be seen as mirroring the individual psyche and, in particular, the psyche of their **leader**.[6]

The legacy of psychoanalysis is complex and diverse. Numerous powerful traditions emerged from scholars who fell out with Freud and struck out in their own directions. Chief among them was C. G. Jung, who founded analytical psychology and whose original ideas on archetypes and the collective unconscious continue to be of relevance to students of mythology, organizations, and wider culture today. Within psychoanalysis, numerous schisms followed the death of its founder, generating diverse traditions, including ego-psychology, which prospered in the United States, and object-relations theory, which dominated British psychoanalysis. Today, in both the United States and Great Britain, psychoanalysis is in relative decline. An important reason for this has been the questioning of the therapeutic efficacy of psychoanalytic treatments, something that would not have surprised Freud himself, who always acknowledged the limitations of his therapeutic technique. In continental Europe and elsewhere, however, there is

---

[1] Gabriel and Carr, 2002.   [2] See e.g. Carr, 1993; 1998; Gabriel, 1998b; 1999; Schwartz, 1987; 1990; Sievers, 1986; 1994.   [3] Bion, 1961.   [4] See e.g. Jaques, 1952; Menzies Lyth, 1988; Miller, 1976; Trist and Bamforth, 1951.   [5] See e.g. Diamond, 1993; Hirschhorn, 1988; Levinson, 1968/1981; Zaleznik, 1977.   [6] Kets de Vries and Miller, 1984.

continuing interest and scholarship in psycho-analysis. This has undoubtedly been prompted by the popularity of the work of French psycho-analyst Jacques Lacan,[1] whose works have had a considerable influence on feminist scholarship and postmodern studies.

Psychodynamics

Psychodynamics is a relatively loosely defined term that examines the actions and behaviours of individuals, groups, organizations, and even societies at large as the visible outcomes of con-flicting mental forces, many of which operate unconsciously. Freud viewed the 'dynamic point of view' as one of three levels of analysis from which psychoanalysis approached mental phe-nomena, the other two being the topographic (which looked at the movements of ideas and desires across boundaries dividing up the differ-ent parts of the mental **personality**) and the eco-nomic (which looked at how ideas and desires acquire potency by being charged with libido, or sexual energy). The dynamic point of view examined the conflicts between different forces, such as those of conscience, sexual desires, social obligations, and **norms**.

The term psychodynamics is currently used more widely than psychoanalysis in connection with organizations and encompasses many dif-ferent theories and concepts, but is mainly asso-ciated with the legacy of the Tavistock Insti-tute and the work of Melanie Klein, Wilfred Bion, and others (see **psychoanalysis and psy-choanalytic approaches**). The common feature of nearly all psychodynamic approaches is the view that in defending themselves against painful emotions (most especially **anxiety**) or danger-ous ideas, individuals and groups resort to cer-tain defensive psychological processes that very often result in accentuating rather than reduc-ing the pain and anxiety from which they stem. Another shared assumption of psychody-namic approaches is the view that such defensive

processes inhibit rational **decision making** and group work, sucking groups into highly disrup-tive processes where fantasy takes over from real-ity testing and ends up by dominating a group's mental life. Psychodynamics then informs the work of many consultants who seek to restore groups and organizations to healthy mental functioning that contains toxic fantasies and emotions.

Some of the core arguments in the psychody-namics of organizations include the following:

1. *People in and out of organizations are emo-tional and sexual beings, beings with personal and family histories.* Viewing people as emotional and sexual beings neither denies nor underesti-mates the importance of reason and rationality in human affairs. Even rational acts, however, are often underwritten by an emotional agenda, such as ambition, excitement, anger, fear, nos-talgia, and so forth. These emotions provide the fuel behind seemingly rational or reasonable acts. The key idea which links people's histories to their experiences in organizations is *transfer-ence*, a process whereby feelings (e.g. admiration, fear, resentment) and images (e.g. omnipotence, mystery, beauty) once attached to parental fig-ures become transferred onto figures who come to occupy similar unconscious locations in later life. Such figures may be idealized or vilified.

2. *Through work, people seek to fulfil deeper unconscious desires.* In contrast to **motivation** the-ories, psychodynamic approaches recognize the complexity and dynamic quality of human moti-vation. Motivation is not a question of finding the right button and pressing it, but recogniz-ing that, through work, people pursue many dif-ferent conscious and unconscious aims. Some people 'sublimate' or channel into work most of their physical and emotional energies. Yet oth-ers work hard to build their self-esteem, to earn the respect of others, or ostentatiously to display commitment to their organization. Some may work non-stop as workaholics to outperform

---

[1] Lacan, 1966/1977; 1988a.

their rivals (often acting like children seeking a special affection in the heart of a parent) or, equally, to dodge domestic obligations towards spouses, children, and other 'loved ones'. Some may even work as a means of overcoming their fear of death, seeking immortality in the legacy which they may leave.

3. *Organizations, as parts of society, become sites where broader social and cultural dynamics are enacted.* Psychoanalysis does not seek to 'reduce' organizations to the psychology of individuals. Social and cultural phenomena, such as religious ideas, political conflicts, and economic interests, become part of every individual's psyche through the influence of identification with role models and even through the different uses of **language**. In this connection, the term 'psychostructure' is used to describe the ways that language functions to 'embed' such social and cultural features into the individual psyche.[1] Organizations then become arenas where wider social dynamics, for instance those relating to class, race, gender, and forth, are acted out. Wider cultural trends, such as authoritarianism or narcissism, can also weave themselves into the psychostructures of organizations, affecting organizational phenomena, including leadership, communication, and group relations. Different organizations may have different psychostructures, for instance different configurations allow different displays of emotion, different manifestations of disagreement and conflict, different outlets for aggression and solidarity. These are expressed in different cultural and social artefacts that organizations use to express their identity, including buildings, logos, offices, language uses, communication devices, and so forth. All of these may then be interpreted to yield insights into shared conscious or unconscious fantasies among organizational members. In this way, a massive building may stand as a symbol of omnipotence, as a manifestation of arrogance and hubris, or as an indication of self-doubt and insecurity.

4. *Organizations offer certain defences against anxieties which they provoke.* Anxiety can be an incapacitating emotion which individuals seek to avoid through the mechanisms of **defence**. Organizations breed anxiety in many forms by making unyielding demands on individuals— that they should control their spontaneity and emotion; that they should work with people they do not necessarily like, doing tasks which they do not necessarily enjoy, often being treated in an impersonal and cold way; that they should display loyalty and commitment towards an entity that may casually dismiss 'redundant employees'; that they should do tasks for which they do not feel adequately prepared or clearly briefed, which are psychological demanding and, sometimes, physically dangerous. In addition, they exacerbate anxieties which individuals may carry with them, over their self-worth, their competence, and their ability to get on with others (including with leaders and followers). The containment of such anxieties within organizations has been the focus of numerous widely accepted theories developed by Elliott Jaques, Isabel Menzies Lyth, and others.[2] The downside of these organizational or social defences against anxiety is different dysfunctional routines which stunt **creativity**, block the expression of **emotion** or **conflict**, and, above all, undermine the organization's rational and effective functioning. If individual defences immerse the individual in a world of neurotic make-believe, organizational defences immerse their members in collective delusions, in which they pursue chimerical projects or run blindly away from non-existent threats, while disregarding real problems and opportunities.

5. *Organizations also open up possibilities of realizing collective visions and stimulating creativity.* While organizations make considerable demands on individuals' mental functioning, they also offer a variety of compensations and possibilities. They boost their members' sense of self-esteem by lending them their prowess and

---

[1] Carr, 1993; Maccoby, 1976.   [2] Jaques, 1952; Menzies Lyth, 1988.

glamour. To some, organizations offer creative outlets, to others opportunities to develop and exercise leadership qualities or other technical and social skills. The concept of organizational ideal is particularly useful—an idealized image of the organization which is endowed with desirable qualities, power, success, efficiency, and even immortality, which can then become part of the ego-ideal of many members, enhancing their sense of achievement and worth, enabling them to handle adversity, and drawing dedication, imagination, and even self-sacrifice out of them.[1]

• See also *psychoanalysis and psychoanalytic approaches*

Psychological contract

In contrast to a written contract of employment, the psychological contract refers to the more *implicit* or *inferred* understanding of *reciprocal* expectations that are to exist between employer and employee. The term was first used by Chris Argyris to describe the relationship between groups of employees and their foremen in two factories he studied.[2] Employees would undertake to be highly productive and in turn the foreman would ensure fair wages and conditions and that the **norms** of the employees' informal culture would be respected. This was what Argyris described as a 'psychological work contract'. Chester Barnard and Herbert Simon had previously championed theories of organizational equilibrium in which organizational survival was dependent upon employees' continued contributions in exchange for organizational inducements.[3] The notion of an 'inducement-contribution' balance (their terminology) was firmly linked to gaining and sustaining employees' compliance.

Whilst the term was coined by Argyris, and its antecedents are to be found in the work of Barnard and Simon, it is Edgar Schein with whom the term psychological contract is most commonly associated.[4] Schein refined the understanding of the idea of such a contract and gave it a presence in the **discourse** of organization studies such that the work of earlier contributors is often overlooked or goes uncited. Schein viewed the actual dynamics in establishing and maintaining the psychological contract as an unfolding interactive process of mutual influence and bargaining—a process that he notes Harry Levinson originally called *reciprocation*.[5] This process is envisaged to be one that involves an exchange where the organization provides the employee with a salary and a certain fairness in their working conditions and in return the employee reciprocates in working hard and generally showing a degree of concern for the quality of that work and the broader welfare of the enterprise. Schein argued that, from the organization's point of view, the inducement-contribution dynamic is aimed at gaining *compliance*. Schein conceived of **authority** as simultaneously a part of the psychological contract and an instrument to enforce the psychological contract. In this latter view Schein recognized the potential negative consequences, should contributions not meet organizational expectations. Organizational rights subsumed employees' rights. Organizations have the power to reward contributory behaviours and the authority to punish non-contributory behaviours.

Schein developed this theory, relying on the work of Amitai Etzioni.[6] Etzioni classified organizations in terms of the predominant **power** or authority they used, i.e. coercive (threat, physical sanctions, etc.); utilitarian (material and economic rewards); or normative (symbolic rewards, intrinsic value rewards). He then argued that subordinates may respond to this power or authority in a variety of ways in the form of particular types (or zones on a

---

[1] Schwartz, 1987.   [2] Argyris, 1960.   [3] Barnard, 1938; Simon, 1957.   [4] Schein, 1965; 1970.   [5] Levinson, 1963; Levinson et al., 1962.   [6] Etzioni, 1961; 1964.

continuum) of involvement, i.e. alienative (negative zone: psychologically detached from the organization); calculative (mild zone: involvement for fair return); or moral (positive zone: intrinsic value in contributing to the values and broader aims of the organization). Taking the three types of power and the three possible types of involvement, Etzioni produced a typology of nine types of compliance. Of those nine, three (coercive-alienative, utilitarian-calculative, and normative-moral) occurred more than the other six because, according to Schein,[1] they represented workable and 'just' psychological contracts.

Organization studies have not accepted Schein's rendering of the psychological contract in an uncritical manner. In particular, the notion has been criticized as an 'idealized' model that has an undeclared embrace of structural-functionalism and which almost anthropomorphizes and reifies the organization. At the same time, critics have argued that Schein's 'model' lacks detail, leaving unanswered fundamental questions, such as: What is the *psychology* part of the psychological contract? Or, expressed another way, what are the *psychological* processes at work here? How are we to comprehend the degree of 'mutualness' in the 'contract' or the 'choices' and 'fairness' in the inducement-contribution dynamic other than to accept them as some state of natural equilibrium? In recent times, these basic questions have led scholars to link the notion of the organization contract with the issue of the construction of **identity** in organizations and the manner in which particular traits might be stimulated and reinforced in organizations. Robinson, Rousseau, and colleagues have studied the strains under which the contract comes when perceived violations take place;[2] others have noted that, as a result of **downsizing** and lay-offs, psychological contracts have become precarious and violations endemic.[3] In a curious way, ascertaining the decline of the psychological contract in our times has accentuated its usefulness as a concept.

ADRIAN N. CARR, UNIVERSITY OF WESTERN SYDNEY

Public-sector organizations

The origins of the concept of organization lie in government and **governance**. Not so long ago, organization stood for *public* organization and was synonymous with administration, civil service, and officialdom. Max Weber's work on **bureaucracy**, for example, was written with the Prussian civil service in mind. Similarly, works by precursors of organization theory, such as Woodrow Wilson, Henri Fayol, Herbert Simon, Charles Lindblom, Michel Crozier, and many others, were concerned with various areas and aspects of *public administration*. The Western nation state extended its initial remit to enforce law and order and to secure defence into the provision of a wide range of services and benefits to its citizens, such as health, education, and housing, thereby providing a dominant model of administrative organization. Assuming this responsibility for an ever-increasing public **policy** sphere was an important source of the state's **legitimacy** in the eyes of its constituencies. Its rise has also spawned large numbers of specialized public-sector organizations, financed from public resources and tasked with the implementation of government policy.

Entitlement to comprehensive social protection is a European concept, born out of compulsory insurance schemes against occupational risk which were created in the aftermath of rapid industrialization and mass migration to the cities. However, only by the middle of the twentieth century was the principle of universal support unrelated to employment accepted and institutionalized via legislation. The creation of what would later become known as the European welfare state model rested on

---

[1] Schein, 1970.   [2] Robinson, Kraatz, and Rousseau, 1994; Robinson and Rousseau, 1994; Rousseau and Parks, 1992.   [3] Sennett, 1998; Uchitelle, 2006.

developmental and moral prerogatives rooted in wartime solidarity and the experience of lifting barriers among social classes, generating strong demands for citizenship and social justice.

Public intervention was therefore seen as necessary to counteract **market** failures by providing services that would be under-provided or not provided at all if they were left to the market alone. Classic examples are police and fire services but also arguably universal education and healthcare. The value of those services cannot be expressed in terms of economic efficiency, but they must be seen as *public goods* that can be used freely by all, in no competition to each other, which may be described as societal efficiency. Public service provision is therefore necessary whenever the market cannot put a price on them via demand-supply mechanism such as in the case of safe neighbourhoods, the availability of clean air, well-lit streets, an immunized population, and so on. There is no unanimity about the optimal level of the state's involvement and the corresponding size of the public sector, as these depend on the political traditions and institutional structure of different countries. However, on the whole there has been a steady growth of the public sector in the last twenty years, which now amounts to over 40 per cent of the GDP in OECD countries. This increase has occurred despite calls to 'roll back the state' and proclamations about 'the end of the big government' strongly voiced by conservative leaders in Anglo-Saxon countries since the 1980s.

In spite of the tendency of the public sector to grow, the provision of public services has been subject to vociferous and highly politicized academic debates, regarding the merits and demerits of state versus market provision. Neoliberal Austrian School economists (Friedrich Hayek, Ludwig von Mises, and Israel Kirzner) were the first to criticize the government's failure to allocate resources and services efficiently, attributing this to its inability to acquire the information needed. Among government's many vocal critics

were public choice economists James Buchanan and Gordon Tullock,[1] who studied spending by large bureaucracies, and applied the same analytic principles used to study people's actions in the marketplace, notably that their main motive, as voters, politicians, lobbyists, or bureaucrats, is *self-interest*. Despite the widespread influence of such economic theories on public policy it was not until the advent of the **New Public Management** (NPM) that public services were radically transformed. This was largely achieved by separating the role of government from that of providers of services, and by introducing the language of incentives, competition, and user **choice** into the public sector.

The reasons for these developments are variously attributed to the rejection of the postwar consensus about the primacy of equality and solidarity as policy objectives, the rise of **consumerism**, and users' desire to have more choice of where, how, and who provides public services. Ostensibly, the changes were driven by the search for greater efficiency in public services prompted by global economic trends and an increase in demand driven by an ageing population and advances in bio-medical technology which raised expectations. This has resulted in a profound congruence between the 'consumerist' user advocated by libertarian economists and the evolution of the passive recipient of services into a welfare **subject**.[2]

Offering *individual* choice to users of public services in many European countries is seen as a good in its own right and as a means of achieving diverse but potentially conflicting public policy objectives, including more efficient and equitable services. But choice is firmly rooted in neoclassical economics, deriving from a belief that it can best be served through the development of active, critical consumers even if they are not always acting as perfectly knowledgeable and rational agents. Choice was thus seen as the consumer's power of 'exit' from the system by the economist Albert Hirschman in his influential

---

[1] Buchanan and Tullock, 1962.   [2] Giddens, 1994.

treatise *Voice, exit and loyalty*,[1] and was opposed to 'voice' as a mechanism for citizen participation. According to Hirschman the opportunity to exercise '**voice**' diminished when users chose to opt out of public services. The pervasive interest in introducing choice and **competition** in public policy arguably represents an attempt to reconcile what is viewed as an 'artificial dichotomy' between exit and voice by many governments, in spite of the chronic failure of markets to deliver public services more effectively or less bureaucratically than public-sector organizations.

However, the choice discourse which was spawned by New Public Management values has rendered the meaning of public administration obsolete at both semantic and substantive levels. The focus on users' wants, which is the current flagship policy of many governments, signifies an increased reliance on the economic notion of demand denoting what users of services are prepared to pay for, rather than the **need** for services or goods that citizens think they may require at someone else's expense. This enhances individualism at the expense of altruism and solidarity as supreme social value. Another important consequence of the advent of New Public Management has been the increasing permeability of **boundaries** and interdependency between the private and public sectors and civil society with delivery of numerous services being devolved to the private and **voluntary sector organizations**.

• See also *New Public Management*

MARIANNA FOTAKI, UNIVERSITY OF MANCHESTER

---

[1] Hirschman, 1970.

Race and racism

Race is a difficult, dangerous, and contested concept. Unlike **nations** and **ethnic groups**, races are usually thought of as involving some inherited physical characteristics, most notably skin colour. Yet, physical differences between human groups tend to be far less significant in terms of biology than in terms of the political and symbolic **meanings** attached to them and particularly assumptions of supposed superiority and inferiority. Thus, the Nazis developed biological 'theories' of race and genetic purity, mainly as the basis for racist **ideology** and racist practices—genetic screening, genetic cleaning, and eventually **genocide**. Using race as a scientific concept has since been tainted as is evident from the furious controversies surrounding periodic attempts by psychologists to link it in some objective way to intelligence, another highly contested concept.[1]

Race has, of course, long before attempts by Nazis and others to give it scientific validity, figured as the basis and justification for slavery, conquest, dispossession, exploitation, and genocide. Race is by no means a uniquely Western idea; it is, however, Western conquerors and colonizers, slave traders and slave owners, who created a uniquely bleak legacy based on race, destroying entire **cultures**, denuding people of their living resources, and submitting them to treatments that were only imaginable inasmuch as victims could be seen as inferior to and less human than the perpetrators—as belonging to a different race. This legacy has had deepseated consequences for ensuing generations who find themselves locked in institutionalized

exploitative relations and whose lived experience is dominated by race. Thus, while race is a profoundly ideological concept, its economic, political, and psychological implications are very real and very far-reaching. Disadvantaged communities find it difficult to break out of a vicious circle of powerlessness, prejudice, discrimination, and **alienation**. Disadvantages in housing reinforce disadvantages in education, which, in turn, reinforce disadvantages in employment opportunities all contributing to marginalization, disenfranchisement, resentment, and disharmony.

The study of race and racism in organizations has been unjustly neglected.[2] The term *institutional racism* has been used to describe two deep-rooted aspects of racism in organizations. First, it describes entrenched attitudes in societies and organizations that systematically discriminate against people 'of colour'—it is in this connection that the inquiry headed by Sir William Macpherson into the murder of 18-year-old black boy Stephen Lawrence described the London police as being institutionally racist. Institutional racism of this type expresses itself in numerous assumptions, opinions, habits, and actions that lead to unequal and unfair treatment of citizens on the basis of race. A second meaning of the term refers to a rather more insipid set of institutional barriers that inhibit or stop different racial groups from reaching positions of **power** and **status**, without anyone ever having directly to discriminate against them, a kind of racism without racists. Institutional racism of this sort operates in an almost invisible way and yet its consequences can be even more far-reaching than those of direct discrimination and prejudice. Many organizations (including

---

[1] See e.g. Eysenck, 1971; Flynn, 1980; Fraser, 1995. [2] Nkomo, 1992.

the London Metropolitan Police) seek to counter institutional racism of both sorts through equal opportunities or **diversity** management policies and training. Although such measures are often criticized as inadequate, it would be a mistake to dismiss them.

Social theorizing on race has gone through several different phases, mostly dominated by American theorists. Neoclassical economists argued that race interfered with the operations of free markets and rather optimistically argued that in the long run discriminating employers would lose out to non-discriminating ones.[1] This view was strongly contested by radical economists who drew on an old Marxist argument that racism was a ruling-class strategy to divide the workers in order to better exploit them.[2] Theorists like Michael Reich argued that race **discrimination** created dual labour markets whose net effect was to lower the earnings of all employees, by undermining **trade unionism** and worker solidarity.[3]

A different view was taken by theorists of the so-called internal colonialism thesis who viewed African-American and other 'racialized' minorities as internal colonies, denied true citizenship rights, marginalized in social and economic affairs, and excluded from power.[4] African Americans themselves developed powerful traditions of theorizing race whose main point was not to describe the phenomenon but to combat it. There has been a long-standing tension in these traditions between integrationist and separatist tendencies, represented in the early part of the twentieth century by Booker T. Washington and W. E. B. du Bois respectively, and later by Martin Luther King and the Black Panther movement of the 1960s and 1970s. More recently, social theorizing on race has emanated from **postcolonial theory** and the politics of **voice** and diversity.

Following the terrorist attacks in New York, Washington, Madrid, and other European cities in the early part of the century, the term 'racialization' is used to describe the attribution of racial characteristics to members of particular national or ethnic groups, mostly Arabs and Pakistanis, in ways that draw them directly into the vicious circle of prejudice, discrimination, powerlessness, and alienation noted earlier. This process has been opposed both by members of the groups themselves and the majority of the populations in these countries. It is interesting, however, how useful the term 'racialization' can prove, mirroring similar conversion of nouns into verbs, like 'gendering' and 'othering'.[5]

• See also *Other and othering, postcolonialism and postcolonial theory, science*

Rationality

Rationality is, in the first instance, the power of reason to guide our **actions**. Rationality is thus a unique property of human beings to make **decisions** and act on the basis of careful assessment of information and evaluation of different courses of action. Economic theories make use of rationality as the core assumption regarding the **motivation** for people's actions, using a model sometimes referred to as *rational economic man*. According to this view, for example, consumers faced with a purchasing decision will try to get the best value for money. Of course, rationality is by no means the only driving force of human action. Many of our actions result from our emotional states, from accidental factors, or simply from habit and routine. Often, when we think we are acting very rationally, we may in fact be lapsing into the realm of the irrational and even the mad—'Though this be madness, yet there is method in 't', says Polonius about Hamlet.

Max Weber distinguished between two kinds of rationality. Rationality of means ('Zweckrationalität') implies that, given a certain set of **goals**, one adopts the optimum means for its achievement, on the basis of careful search,

---

[1] Becker, 1957.   [2] Cox, 1948.   [3] Reich, 1981.   [4] Blauner, 1972; 2001.   [5] Murji and Solomos, 2005.

calculation, and evaluation of the alternatives. The system of **rules** underpinning **bureaucracy** is rational inasmuch as it is carefully devised so as to enhance the achievement of organizational goals. This type of rationality is based on expert **knowledge** of the alternative courses of action available. It is the foundation of technical efficiency, even though it may be applied to entirely evil, insane, or arbitrary goals. For example, one can go about very rationally burning down one's own house. The rationality of the ends or rationality of values is the second type of rationality ('Wertrationalität') identified by Weber, though his view is that **science** is of little help here. The way of establishing this type of rationality is through systematic moral and political scrutiny and a careful examination of **values** rather than through scientific knowledge.

Some economists have argued that the classical criteria for rational action are too strict; people do not have perfect **information**, nor a perfect knowledge of all the risks associated with different choices. If we were to treat organizations (including firms, governments, and political parties) as rational actors, the same restrictions apply to them. Thus, economics Nobel Prize winner Herbert Simon suggested that decisions are not based on absolute rationality but on what he termed 'bounded rationality';[1] one makes a decision as soon as one has found a solution which is 'satisficing' or 'good enough'. Even bounded rationality, however, would seem to overestimate the importance of rationality in decision making. Rational models of human behaviour, like those favoured by economists and **Taylorist** management, tend to disregard or underestimate people's impulsive, **emotional**, **desiring**, and irrational qualities. These are of central importance to certain schools of thought in social psychology (like the **Human Relations** School) and depth psychology. Even supposedly rational actors, such as stockbrokers, can act under the impact of emotional forces, for example in panic buying and selling of stock.

As a medium of **communication** and persuasion, rational arguments are often less effective than appeals to fantasies and emotions, such as anxieties, ambitions, and hopes. It is for this reason that in the **management of meaning**, leaders routinely rely on **symbols** including **stories**, **visions**, and **metaphors** more extensively than on rational argumentation. In the view of some commentators, the belief in rationality is itself a **myth**, behind which other forces (including emotion, habit, and self-delusion often masquerading as 'common sense') are at work.[2]

Rationalization

This term is used to signify three different things: (1) Increasing the efficiency of an organization by eliminating supposedly redundant or non-profitable elements (including departments, operations, and people); (2) the provision of credible or plausible motives for one's **actions** which conceal the real motives; this includes the finding of convenient excuses; and (3) the tendency of organizations and societies to shed their traditional, emotional, supernatural, religious, aesthetic, and moral qualities in favour of ever-increasing concern with economic efficiency. **Fordism** and **McDonaldization** are parts of a process of rationalization of production and consumption in this third sense.

Starting with Max Weber,[3] many theorists argued that **modernity** is characterized by unprecedented degrees of rationalization in every sphere of human life, which result in a process of 'disenchantment', i.e. the elimination of charm, magic, and simple pleasure. Some theorists, however, are currently arguing that **postmodernity** brings about a partial re-enchantment of the world through the different mechanisms of **consumption**. Ritzer has suggested that spaces of consumption, such as shopping malls, theme parks, and the internet, have become 'cathedrals'.[4] This 'points up the quasi-religious, "enchanted" nature of these new settings. They

---

[1] Simon, 1957.   [2] Dimaggio and Powell, 1983; Putnam and Mumby, 1993.   [3] Weber, 1958.   [4] Ritzer, 1999, p. x.

have become locales to which we make "pilgrimages" in order to practice our consumer religion.' The thesis of the re-enchantment of the world must be accepted with caution—large spheres of social and economic activity are still governed by rationalization, breeding cynical detachment and disenchantment among employees, managers, and even consumers.[1]

• See also *rationality*

Reality

Reality has long been a problematic concept. Is reality something absolute, constant, 'out there', to be discovered through ever more sophisticated scientific enquiry? Or is what we call real but an illusion, as some Eastern religions believed, urging their followers to look inwards for what is truly real? A car may appear real enough, especially when it breaks down and leaves us stranded, but what makes it an object of desire, of status, and of display? In the opening scene of Stanley Kubrick's *2001: A Space Odyssey* two primitive tribesmen stand against each other ready to fight. Suddenly one of them notices a bleached thighbone lying nearby. He picks it up and uses it to beat his rival. The thighbone was real for both fighters, but what turned it into a weapon was human consciousness discovering a potential in it that had hitherto not been apparent. It is consciousness that turns inert nature into a piece of **technology**, primitive to be sure, but effective. *Phenomenology* argues that the world we inhabit is not an external one, but the product of human consciousness. *Realism*, on the other hand, argues that we live in a pre-given world, which we gradually learn to understand, to control, and to exploit with the help of science.

The nature of reality is the subject matter of ontology, whereas the way we can know and understand reality has been the domain of **epistemology**. Realism is an ontological

approach usually twinned with a positivist and empiricist epistemology; they regard reality as external to consciousness and strive for law-like generalizations based on careful observations and precise measurements—water boils at 100 degrees Celsius, independently of how much or how little water there is, who boils it, and what it is being boiled for. Such generalizations assume the status of 'truths' if they are regularly confirmed or at least if they robustly resist falsification. Critics of positivism argue that a large part of reality, maybe all of what we consider real including the concept of reality itself, is the product of human consciousness. Some argue that even physical reality, the reality of physics, chemistry, and astronomy, is symbolically constituted, whereas others argue that human reality, including economics, politics, culture, the arts, and so forth, is fundamentally different from physical reality and calls for a different form of **knowledge**. Some turn to **spirituality** or religion for enlightenment, others turn to phenomenological perspectives which seek to establish how **meanings** are created through human consciousness and interaction.

Positivist approaches retain a commanding position in the human sciences, most notably in economics and psychology, where measurement holds sway and highly mathematical and statistical models are employed to simulate different aspects of reality. Such approaches rely on *variables* that can be identified, isolated, measured, and linked to other variables in causal relationships of the sort 'a 1% rise in interest rates will slow down the economy by 0.27%, reduce inflation by 0.56%' or 'intelligence accounts for 50% of the variance in income distribution' or 'educational attainment has a correlation of 0.34 with the suicide rate'. In all of the above statements, entities like interest rates, inflation, intelligence, income, education, and suicide rate are treated as objective facts about the world that can be observed and measured.

---

[1] Fleming and Spicer, 2003; Kanter and Mirvis, 1989.

An increasing number of scholars in the social sciences are becoming disenchanted with positivism, most especially its inability to engage with sensemaking, meaning creation, and purposive action. Can a suicide be treated as 'a fact' with no regard as to its motives, the unique circumstances that prompted it, or its cultural significance? Such scholars have been turning to other philosophical traditions for an explanation of social, cultural, and psychological realities. Highly influential among them has been the view that reality is *socially constructed* (see **social construction of reality**); phenomena emerge as they acquire different meanings and significance through social interaction between people. Thus, an organization like Sony or Google is not an object or a thing but a social construction, the site of different conversations and the topic of many of them. Some social constructions are highly contested—what one person views as an accident another views as negligence and, as is well known, one person's terrorist is another person's freedom fighter. Thus, while a positivist epistemology aims for generalizations, an epistemology that approaches reality as socially constructed relies on **hermeneutics**, the systematic interpretation of the meanings of different phenomena.

There are many different philosophical approaches to the study of reality in addition to realism and social construction. One that has been quite influential in many spheres of knowledge is *pragmatism*, which looks at theory and practice as directly linked spheres of human **experience** and rejects any attempts to reduce reality to a single quality of all things. Instead of trying to represent reality, pragmatists approach knowledge as invariably linked to action and its truth value as depending on whether 'it works' in **practice** or not. *Postmodernism* has placed the emphasis on **discourse** as the basis on which things come to be viewed as real and has questioned the existence of any facts outside discourse. *Critical realism*, by contrast, has

sought to defend the existence of an objective reality and of facts (including suicides, wars, and accidents) while uncoupling the physical world from the natural world. It should be noted that many scientists, in both natural and social sciences, go about their research without being explicitly concerned about the nature of reality, often lapsing into different assumptions about what is real in different stages of their work, employing hybrid ontologies and epistemologies. Putting up with uncertainties and contradictions about the ultimate nature of reality and about the means of knowing it may be viewed as an instance of **negative capability**, part of the creative process, whereas forcing premature closure blocks further discovery.

• See also *epistemology*

Reflexivity

Reflexivity has now become quite a fashionable term, with the adjective 'reflexive' often used as a synonym for 'reflective', i.e. someone who is capable of taking a step back from a situation to reflect on it. Thus the 'reflective practitioner', as defined by Argyris and Schön,[1] is the manager or consultant who is capable of mentally withdrawing from the hurly-burly of **action** and **experience** to reflect and learn from them.

'Reflexive', however, is a term that can go beyond 'reflective'. A reflexive activity is one in which subject and object co-create each other. For instance, in telling the **story** of my life, I make sense of past events and create a person living in the present as a continuation of the story. In this way, I as the author of the story and the story's central character co-create each other. At every moment the storyteller creates a protagonist, whose predicaments redefine the storyteller.

Although this term was popularized by French **post-structuralist** philosophers, it was implicit in Marx's theory of labour, where the worker

---

[1] Argyris and Schön, 1978.

creates him- or herself as a worker in creating an object. Social research can be viewed as a reflexive practice, one in which the presence of the researcher and the act of research creates an object of study. Reflexivity emphasizes the ability of **language** to constitute social reality and has become a trademark of **Critical Management Studies** and approaches hostile to positivism. All the same, as Lynch has suggested,[1] it easily disintegrates into fashionable cliché through which the self-proclaimed reflexive individual seeks to elevate him- or herself above the supposedly non-reflexive others.

• See also *critical theory and Critical Management Studies*

Resistance

The concept of resistance is used in organization studies and the social sciences to describe how the establishment and/or the maintenance of organizational **control**, **power**, and domination might be subverted or refused by actors in positions of subordination. This simple definition, however, belies the multidimensional and notoriously ambiguous features of resistance. For example, resistance might be attempted by members inside the organization, via strike action and the go-slow, or by external stakeholders such as anti-globalization campaigners, student groups, consumer activists, etc. Resistance might involve acts of commission (actively thwarting the instruments of control) or omission (resisting by simply doing nothing such as failing to follow a new managerial protocol). The resistance may be largely behavioural, concrete acts that undermine power relations, or more subjective, such as cynically distancing oneself from a corporate commitment programme. The resistance might be overt and confrontational, or covert and hidden. It may be formal, organized, and planned or informal, individual, and opportunistic. It may be recognized as resistance

by the actors themselves, or consist of empirical phenomena labelled resistance only by an outside observer. To make matters more complex, an understanding of resistance must imply a theory of power as the object of resistance. Given the multiple theories of power available, then, the meaning and significance of resistance might look very different depending on the approach one takes.

The concept of resistance draws upon two interweaving connotations, one of which is 'hot' and political, and the other 'cold' and technical. The first evokes images of a subaltern (see **postcolonialism and postcolonial theory**) passionately striving for social justice against an unfair overlord—with the French Resistance Movement against the Nazis providing the indisputable template. This meaning of resistance identifies a clear agent of oppression (the manager, capitalism, etc.) and a subordinate group who resist in the name of justice, freedom, and liberty. The second connotation is more technical since the word resistance derives from Newtonian physics in which every primary action results in an equal and opposite reaction. This is the emotionless world of moving bodies where questions of justice, politics, and emancipation are secondary.

The 'hot' meaning of resistance was particularly important for the Marxian tradition of thought in organization studies during the 1970s and 1980s. The contradictions of **capitalism** enter political consciousness as resentment about the inherently exploitative and unjust nature of **work**. This stream of research is dominated by the figure of the factory worker whereby the power of capitalists and their managerial agents is met by organized opposition, strikes, sabotage, and pilfering. Given the absence of revolutionary **change**, however, more nuanced accounts of resistance followed, revealing how various acts of opposition might actually chain workers to their own subordination in a more profound manner. Investigations of

---

[1] Lynch, 2000.

resistance to boredom on the shop floor are poignant here, demonstrating how trivial acts of subversion actually make the production process run more smoothly. In this sense then, *effective* resistance involves political **action** driven by an idea of social justice that fundamentally undermines the structures of capitalist domination in progressive and emancipatory ways.

The cool Newtonian approach to resistance has generally predominated in the field of organization studies, which is perhaps indicative of the apolitical nature of **management** studies more generally. The most obvious figure here is Max Weber,[1] who described power as the ability for someone to impose their will despite resistance. Adaptations of Weber in organization theory and the social sciences reduced the problem to impersonal descriptions about A's power and **authority** over B.

Perhaps Michel Foucault offers the most famous 'cold' approach to resistance.[2] Initially, his theories of disciplinary power and subjectification were so popular in the early 1990s that the question of resistance was seen as largely redundant by many researchers. By the late 1990s, however, resistance was being rethought from a non-Marxist standpoint, with the Foucauldian themes of **identity**, **ethics**, and **self** at the forefront of the analysis. With the labour–capital divide displaced as the main site of struggle, resistance was viewed as a requisite feature of any 'technologies of power' relating to social control. These technologies are multidimensional and distributed in an uneven manner throughout the social body of the organization. The everyday and indeterminate nature of resistance is especially celebrated in this work, undercutting the Marxian bias for overt, confrontational, and organized antagonism. Resonating throughout this stream of research is Foucault's infamous Machiavellian amorality. With power and resistance relations thinned out into impersonal and calculative 'technologies of force', the reasons behind resistance become a normative black box. Like Machiavelli, Foucault was not concerned with questions of right or wrong, since the will-to-power is essentially prior to **moral** judgement. As a result, much organization studies research here becomes a descriptive butterfly-collecting exercise rather than an account of how claims for justice, dignity, and freedom are pursued and hotly contested.

At the present juncture, the concept of resistance remains troubled and conceptually fragmented in organization studies. Questions remain around what counts as effective resistance once we abandon the classic Marxian assumption that if subversion is not overthrowing capitalism then it must be reinforcing it. Does efficacy mean changing the source of power or simply its effects? Employee cynicism in the context of a culture management programme might challenge some of the aims of power (to create a biddable worker), but will hardly dismantle the HR department of the firm or the structures of **capitalism** consolidating the managerial prerogative. Indeed, following the work of Slovenian social theorist, Slavoj Žižek, cynical dis-identification could provide the very breathing space that allows capitalism to work even better, deflating more serious challenges to the system.[3]

This view is validated by the latest crop of managerial ideas about how knowledge-intensive firms ought to hire zanies, radicals, and anti-authoritarian workers in order to enhance innovation, creativity, and empowerment. Indeed, much of the 'dangerous' everyday resistance celebrated in organization studies is encouraged by some firms and is an important pillar for the new spirit of **capitalism**. Moreover, can we really hold on to the romantic idea that it is only the subaltern who resists? What about middle managers, shareholder activist groups, contractors, consultants, etc.? And what of taxpayers' rebellions? It is clear that the term resistance ought to be reserved for a certain type of social justice **politics**, but how do we draw

---

[1] Weber, 1946; 1947.   [2] Foucault, 1977; 1978; 1980.   [3] Žižek, 1989.

the lines? This question is especially pertinent now. The days when managers ran corporations have been partially superseded by shareholder capitalism, private equity funds, globalization, Third World outsourcing, and so forth. How do we understand 'worker' resistance in this context? These conceptual and empirical permutations will shape the future of the term resistance, which remains a powerful and yet frustratingly ambiguous analytical tool in organization studies.

PETER FLEMING, QUEEN MARY COLLEGE,
LONDON UNIVERSITY

Resource-based theory of organization

The resource-based view of the firm is a theory that examines closely the resources available to different organizations as the principal means of gaining competitive advantage against their rivals. **Strategy** aims at making the best use of resources which may include different physical assets (land, equipment), financial assets, know-how, routines, processes, products, reputational attributes (including brands), **information, knowledge**, and so forth. Many of these resources and capabilities reflect an organization's unique history, including relations it has built up with its stakeholders and the effects of various accidental factors.

The resource-based view can be traced back to economic theories of the firm dating from the 1950s, but the decisive contribution was made by Jay Barney in his much-quoted article 'Firm resources and sustained competitive advantage'.[1] In it, he proposed that there are four qualities that make organizational resources critical as sources of competitive advantage; such resources are valuable, rare, imperfectly imitable, and non-substitutable. One interesting feature of this approach is that firms sometimes are not aware of the true value of their resources,

most especially knowledge and information. Such tacit knowledge is a resource whose true value does not become plain until a competitor has matched it. An organization's *core competences* could then be viewed as critical resources of which it is unaware and which it fails to defend adequately.[2] Paradoxically, however, because the knowledge is tacit, it cannot be easily replicated.[3]

This approach has been quite influential in studies of strategy; in a more indirect way, it has prompted an appreciation of organizational **learning** and especially tacit learning as a valuable resource. It has, however, been criticized for being circular—a resource can always be viewed as conferring a competitive advantage on a firm *after the event*—thus an organization is successful because it possesses valuable resources and the resources are valuable because the organization is successful.

Risk

Fuelled by concerns about a variety of disasters—ranging from the collapse of financial markets to, the spread of AIDS, terrorist attacks, and climate change—a burgeoning interest in the field of risk developed during the latter part of the twentieth century. While there was some consensus that risk should be defined as the likelihood of the occurrence of adverse events, no such agreement has occurred around the broader understanding of the issues. On the contrary, the wider debate on risk constitutes a diverse set of disciplinary foci—the 'risk archipelago'[4]—where specialists from sociology, psychology, finance, economics, geography, health, and regulation studies hold widely differing views.

Quantitative approaches to risk go back a long way and are rooted in the 800-year-old Hindu-Arabic numbering system, the work of Renaissance mathematicians Pascal and Fermat,

---

[1] Barney, 1991.   [2] Prahalad and Hamel, 1990.   [3] Barney, 1986.   [4] Hood et al., 1992.

and Gauss in the nineteenth century. During the twentieth century, a succession of brilliant mathematicians—aided by unforeseen developments in new information technology—contributed to the growth of quantitative approaches to risk and risk management. In his history of quantitative approaches to risk, Bernstein names Markowitz, Black, Scholes, and Merton as key figures in the field.[1] These approaches have found application in areas as diverse as engineering, insurance, financial markets, and health. In engineering, risk is measured in terms of likelihood and impact. i.e. risk = (probability of an accident) × (losses per accident). In the finance sector, the Black–Scholes theorem—a method for measuring and pricing risk in options trading—is a key instrument that is championed globally by financial firms and regulators alike.

This contrasts sharply with developments elsewhere. For anthropologists Mary Douglas and Aaron Wildavsky,[2] risk is relative to **culture**: every culture chooses to avoid certain risks and to bear others, and, in doing so, each culture is quite different from others. Other social scientists have turned their attention to yet other aspects of risk. In coining the term 'risk society', Beck argued that modern **society** is no longer principally structured along **class**, race, or ethnic lines.[3] In his view a profound change has occurred: while industrial society was structured around the distribution of 'goods' (such as wealth, healthcare, education, etc.), contemporary 'risk society' is structured according to the distribution of 'bads' (such as environmental degradation, accidents, **terrorist** attacks, etc.). Accordingly, our 'social risk positions' or our exposure to social risks play a key role in shaping our lives and our positions in society.

Then there are those that examine the psychology and social psychology of risk in their study of *homo aleatorius* (or risk-taking man). Freudenburg, for example, has shown that we tend to have decreasing concern for risks in relation to which we have become familiar and over-confident over time.[4] This is known as 'the atrophy of vigilance' and leads to the conclusion that 'nothing recedes like success'. Starr shows that our inclination to expose ourselves to dangerous risks is greater when we believe we have voluntarily chosen to be so exposed, and thus believe that we have a greater sense of control.[5] There are also those that—applying ideas from **psychoanalysis** to problems of organization and risk—regard a variety of unconscious thought processes as having a limiting influence on our capacity to understand and manage risk. Thought processes such as unconscious defences against **anxiety**, as well as unconscious **narcissism**, are seen to have a particular impact on our capacities in this regard.[6]

Some authors have focused specifically on the link between risk and disaster. In their groundbreaking work, sociologist Barry Turner and psychologist Nick Pidgeon found that organizational disasters rarely emerge *ex nihilo*;[7] instead, they invariably occur after a substantial period of 'incubation' during which warning signs are—for a variety of reasons—not adequately recognized or heeded. A different, highly influential argument is provided by Perrow.[8] He holds that certain systems are so complex that organizational disasters are almost inevitable: especially in 'tightly coupled' systems—where processes happen very fast and cannot be turned off—problems in any one area are likely to have rapid, unpredictable, and often unintelligible impacts on other areas, leading to 'normal accidents'.

• See also *complexity and chaos theories, crisis management*

MARK STEIN, IMPERIAL COLLEGE LONDON

[1] Bernstein, 1996.   [2] Douglas and Wildavsky, 1982.   [3] Beck, 1992.   [4] Freudenburg, 1992.   [5] Starr, 1969.   [6] Stein, 2003.
[7] Turner and Pidgeon, 1997.   [8] Perrow, 1999.

Ritual

Ritual is one of the core terms of **ethnography** that has now infiltrated many of the social sciences including organizational theory. Ritual is a formal set of **actions**, normally repeated in a standardized way at particular times with great attention to detail. Rituals are a vital part of **culture**. Their essence lies in the **meaning** and **symbolism** they carry. Many rituals have a religious nature or a religious origin; this is especially true for rituals that accompany life's great transitions—birth, adolescence, marriage, death, the arrival of a new year or a new season. Some rituals, like exchanging gifts at Christmas or blowing out candles on a birthday cake, may lose their religious significance but continue to be observed. Others atrophy and may be referred to as 'empty' or 'hollow' rituals, having lost all connection to their symbolic significance. Eventually many rituals die out and may be replaced by others.

A large part of the literature on rituals looks at the *functions* that they perform in social life. Why do we need rituals? What is so important about them? One function of rituals is to maintain social bonds and shared **values**. Anthropologists Arnold van Gennep and Mary Douglas have emphasized the importance of rituals for sustaining systems of **meaning**, establishing **boundaries** (for example between married and unmarried, insider and outsider), and for dealing with the dangerous anxieties that are prompted by the 'betwixt and between' spaces when there is movement across boundaries.[1] Within organizations, knowing how to participate in rituals is a crucial part of becoming a fully-fledged, competent insider. Hence rituals are an important part of **socialization**.

Another important function of rituals is the containment of **anxiety**. This is linked to their compulsive, repetitive quality. As long as a proper ritual has been enacted down to all its minuscule details, participants feel that everything will be well. This is notable in large public rituals and celebrations that frame important occasions. It is also notable in private rituals that accompany dangerous or threatening situations, like the rituals of sportspeople before a vital game, soldiers before an engagement with the enemy, and students before an examination. Their exaggerated attention to detail, their highly repetitive quality, and their total disregard for **rationality**, argued Freud,[2] makes rituals a collective equivalent of neurotic symptoms. In exactly the same way that a neurotic finds solace in his or her symptoms (e.g. compulsive washing of hands), a ritual helps people cope with anxieties brought about by uncertainty and change, the more so when they involve many others.

Organizations, like other spheres of social life, generate their own rituals. Some of them, like the singing of a company anthem in Japanese corporations, are formal. Others, like gathering round the coffee machine for a chat at exactly 10.30 a.m. each day, emerge informally but acquire a formality of their own. Some are carefully planned and staged by management, marking significant moments in the year. Thus, Rosen examined the lavish breakfast event staged annually by an advertising agency, involving speeches, prize giving, elaborate seating arrangements, and so forth, and argued that the breakfast ritual 'reimpregnated bureaucratic consciousness with meaning' while also reinforcing the corporate **values** and reproducing the hegemonic **ideology**.[3] Other commentators have noted that organizational rituals are important for socializing new recruits, marking different rites of passage, and establishing continuity in the presence of constant change and uncertainty. Trice and Beyer have identified different types of rituals in organizations, including **rites of passage**, rites of degradation, and rites of renewal.[4] Organizations are also full of 'empty rituals', procedures that may once have served a useful purpose but persist long after this purpose has ceased to be important. Other procedures (such as fire drills)

---

[1] Gennep, 1960; Douglas, 1966/2002.   [2] Freud, 1907.   [3] Rosen, 1985.   [4] Trice and Beyer, 1984.

may ostensibly fulfil a purpose but assume a ritualistic quality as many people fail to connect with this purpose.

The endurance and even proliferation of ritual in spite of the **rationalizing** tendencies of **modernity** should not surprise us. In times when change is experienced as constant, turbulent, and threatening, ritual offers much-needed reassurance of continuity and order. Like many other symbols and meanings, however, rituals have tended to undergo fragmentation, proliferation, and secularization that has turned them into easy fodder for **consumerism**. Christmas, Mother's day, Valentine's day, weddings, bar mitzvahs, graduations, anniversaries, and so forth are now big spending occasions, marked by a riot of gifts, souvenirs, photographs, and other symbolic artefacts. And this maybe restores the element of sacrifice to contemporary rituals—having to pay often much more than we can 'afford' for a ritual marks it as a truly special occasion and allows it to function as a ritual.

Role

Role is a concept used widely across several human sciences to indicate a distinction between the duties, obligations, and expectations of particular positions and the individuals who occupy them. It is regularly found in expressions like **gender** roles, organizational roles, family and kinship roles, leadership roles, role models, and so forth. In a more general sense, the term role is used to signify the function or the purpose of a particular element within a **system** or of a system within a wider one. We can then speak of the role of the state or of the educational system in society, or of the role of the United Nations in international relations.

The concept of role is fundamental to several traditions of social theory that approach people as performing different types of roles throughout their lives. Some of these roles are temporary (dental patient) and others are permanent (Jewish). People are then seen as performing a multiplicity of roles, e.g. 'man', 'father', 'teacher', 'patient', 'consumer', 'protester', 'manager', 'club member', and so forth, drifting from one to the other as situations demand or performing several of them simultaneously. These different roles are sometimes unrelated (mother and pilot), sometimes overlapping (doctor and carer) or mutually reinforcing (man and manager), and sometimes at odds with each other (consumer and patient).

Role was a core concept in the structural-functionalist sociology of Talcott Parsons that was dominant in the USA in the 1950s and 1960s. Parsons viewed *role*, *collectivity*, *norm*, and *value* as the four central components of social structure, with role being the most particular and value being the most universal component.[1] At its simplest a structured social interaction involves two people enacting their social roles (doctor–patient, mother–child) which are governed by social **rules**, understood and shared by the role players. A collection of several roles constitutes a collectivity (for example, a school includes pupils, teachers, cleaners, governors, etc.) which are integrated through **norms**. **Values** represent the most universal patterns involving core beliefs about what is desirable in the social system. Roles represent the point of contact between **personality** and the social system—thus a father is father to his children but is also recognized as father in the role structure of wider society.

Of considerable significance in Parsons's conceptualization was the biological analogy—just as the heart or the liver perform vital functions for sustaining life, social structures require that specific social functions are fulfilled by different **institutions** and different roles. Thus doctors perform roles that fulfil the function of maintaining or restoring health necessary to maintain the social system. Parsons's theory went into decline in the 1970s partly because it tended to underestimate the importance of **conflict** in

---

[1] Parsons, 1951.

society. His view was based on a fundamental consensus of norms and values that sustain different social roles. This consensus is highly problematic, even with regard to basic roles and values. For example, is a woman's role to be determined primarily as a mother or as an employee? Is a worker's role to be defined as following passively instructions or as criticizing and resisting his or her superior?

These contradictions and tensions present in the concept of role were explored by a second major American sociologist, Erving Gofman,[1] whose conceptualization was as strongly influenced by the theatrical **metaphor** as Parsons's was by the biological one. Where Parsons emphasized roles as forms of standardized behaviour, Goffman emphasized the ability of different actors to perform their roles differently. He used the term 'role distance' to indicate the ability of individuals to negotiate a degree of freedom from their roles and then *improvise* beyond the social expectations linked to their roles. This view has had a lasting influence on organizational theory where roles are often viewed as negotiated and contested through social interaction rather than simply dictated by social structure. Goffman also made extensive use of the concept of *role conflict*, which involves conflicting sets of expectations that individuals are called to meet simultaneously. This is sometimes experienced by **professionals** working in organizations where their roles as doctors, lawyers, or academics may be at odds with their roles as members of profit-making and cost-cutting organizations. The continuing influence of Goffman on social sciences can be viewed in the extensive use of the theatrical metaphor and the language of **performances**, scripts, scenarios, and so forth.

An interesting contribution to an understanding of how roles are enacted in organizations was Gouldner's distinction between manifest and latent social roles.[2] Two individuals may occupy the same manifest roles in an organization (as managers, workers, professionals, etc.) but may perform them in radically different ways, because of the deeper or latent roles they enact. Gouldner described the two models of performing manifest roles as 'cosmopolitans' whose main allegiances lie outside their organization and 'locals' who are strongly attached to their organization. Cosmopolitans are more likely to move from company to company, seek recognition outside the company that employs them, and form their **identities** with relatively little concern for their direct employer. Locals, on the other hand, have a very strong **identification** with their employer, are thoroughly engrossed in the politics and procedures of their organization, and tend to have more direct influence due to their know-how and **networks** within their company.

The concept of role continues to offer a valuable service to social and organizational theory but it would be fair to say that it has lost its ability to offer sharp illumination into different facets of social life as it did during the early, heroic years of its own career.

• See also *performance*

Rules and regulations

Formal rules and regulations are not a new phenomenon. Medieval monasteries had rules banning different types of behaviour and specified detailed penalties for different offences. For instance, a monk guilty of sexual intercourse with an unmarried person was required to fast for one year on bread and water, a nun guilty of the same offence between three and seven years (depending on the circumstances), a bishop for twelve years.[3] However, the proliferation of rules at the workplace and in society at large coincides with the rise of the factory system and especially of large **bureaucratic** organizations where rules and regulations are a major form of social **control**.

---

[1] Goffman, 1969.   [2] Gouldner, 1957.   [3] Morgan, 1986, p. 208.

Unlike **norms**, rules are written down, often in minuscule detail; unlike laws, rules do not necessarily stand for deeply held moral **values**. What then is the justification for having rules? Some rules, argued Max Weber, are products of **rationality**; they permit organizations to achieve their objectives effectively and efficiently and enable individuals to know how to act in different social situations. A 'no smoking' rule unambiguously and simply stops people smoking, irrespective of who they are or how much they may wish to smoke. It does so not because smoking is immoral nor at the whim of a person who happens to dislike smoking, but rather because smoking is meant to bother non-smokers, be harmful to public health, and/or represent an unacceptable fire risk.

Notice that what is rational in one place at any one time is not necessarily seen as rational elsewhere—how genuine then is the rationality of different types of rules? For large sections of the British mass media, 'Brussels bureaucracy' has come to signify the supposedly mindless determination of EU officials to force redundant or ridiculous regulations on the unwilling citizens of European nations, eroding their freedoms and self-determination. Yet many rules that appear redundant or ridiculous when first introduced have a tendency eventually to assume the cloak of rationality. But not all. In a famous study at a gypsum-mining plant, American sociologist Alvin Gouldner observed that administrative rules and regulations were experienced in one of three ways—as disciplinary devices functioning in the interest of the owners ('punishment-centred bureaucracy'), as useful and rational devices of regulation ensuring the welfare of all at work ('representative democracy'), or as redundant measures dreamed up by out-of-touch administrators ('mock bureaucracy').[1] Some of the time, employees observed these rules in a ritualistic, resigned manner; at other times, they disregarded them, even with the collusion of management. In other

circumstances, they **resisted** them, tested them, or sought to redefine them.

In general, where there are rules, people will look for ways of getting more elbow room. Even in the strictest organizations they are likely to get some, with or without the collusion of their superiors. Studying the behaviour of people in organizations, therefore, must examine both the rules that guide behaviour and the ways in which the rules are interpreted and challenged. It would be short-sighted then to reduce all behaviour in organizations to a passive following of rules; yet it would also be short-sighted to disregard the profound and far-reaching implications of rules in our lives. Bureaucratic rules make very different psychological demands from **moral** laws. Individuals become dependent on rules to guide and justify their **actions**. They sometimes feel that any rule, *even a non-rational one*, is better than no rule. Rules save one the trouble of having to make awkward **decisions** and then having to explain and defend them. *Impersonality* means that each decision is unaffected by the specific circumstances of individuals. No amount of begging, pleading, or arguing will alter the decision. Some of the decisions people make in organizations are very unpleasant. Sacking an employee, putting a patient on a long waiting list, failing a student, are not easy or agreeable decisions. Impersonality cushions us from the suffering and misery of others. 'It was nothing personal, Mrs Jameson, but rules are rules!' Impersonality can also have advantages for those affected by decisions. If everyone is treated according to the rule, everyone is treated the same; there is no cause for complaint.

Rules then can become the opium of bureaucratic officials. Without the rules, they are lost, paralysed. With the support of the rules, they are persons with **authority**. Without rules, chaos. With rules, order and organization. Unlike the authority of the father or the mother in a family or of the founder of a movement, the officials'

---

[1] Gouldner, 1954.

authority is legal, it rests on the rules which define their rights and responsibilities. Their authority lies not in who they are but in the **roles** they play.

Management thinking about rules and procedures is changing. At one time the fine-tuning of rules and procedures was regarded as the secret of organizational success. Flexibility and initiative are the current fashion. In the past, the frictionless machine represented the managerial ideal of an organization. The lean, highly responsive organism lies closer to current thinking. It is increasingly argued that rules and procedures, however carefully designed, cannot cope with a highly complex and changing organizational **environment** or with massive **technological** changes.

In the past, some bureaucratic organizations prospered because of their predictability and order. Inflexibility and sluggishness were no problems in a stable, friendly environment. After all, dinosaurs ruled the earth for over two hundred million years, inflexible and sluggish though many of them were. No one knows for sure why dinosaurs died out, but we all assume that it had something to do with their inability to adapt to new environmental conditions, whether these were brought about by a colliding asteroid or some other cause. The same, argue modern management theorists, is the fate of rigid bureaucratic **structures**. They stifle innovation, discourage new ideas, fail to capitalize on advantages conferred by modern technologies, and are generally too slow and cumbersome to meet **competition**. It is for these reasons that they are already giving way to quicker, smaller, more adaptable, more enterprising organizations.

• See also *bureaucracy, emotion, rationality*

S

Science

Science is a particular type of **knowledge** that claims certain privileges against other forms of knowledge. Many disciplines may claim to be scientific, but not all are widely accepted as such. Most people regard as scientific, knowledge that has been carefully derived from empirical observations, rigorously tested, and assumes the form of lawlike generalizations like Newton's laws of motion. The belief that science represents some ultimate and unalterable truth is no longer sustainable, given that even Newton's laws of motion were subsequently shown not to be of universal validity. The demarcation between scientific and other knowledge is then a crucial issue. What is science and what is mere '**ideology**', conjecture, or rule of thumb? Should the term science be reserved for the natural sciences or can economics, sociology, and history claim to be scientific? What are the procedures through which scientific knowledge can be tested?

For a large part of the twentieth century, philosophy of science sought to establish a clear-cut boundary between science and non-science with inconclusive results. The logical positivists of the Vienna circle in the 1920s and, later, Karl Popper believed that they had discovered a means for establishing science in an objective way as qualitatively different from other types of doctrine and knowledge. Popper, for example, famously proposed that truly scientific theories are subject to one criterion—they should be *falsifiable* on the basis of empirical evidence.[1] He proceeded to dismiss Marxism and psychoanalysis as pseudo-scientific on the grounds that no evidence could ever be produced that would be capable of falsifying them.

Subsequent philosophers including Feyerabend, Kuhn, and Lakatos questioned falsifiability as the sovereign gold standard of what counts as science. They showed, for example, that the tests used to evaluate different theories are themselves not independent of the theories being tested, nor are facts and observations theory free. These philosophers were instrumental in moving the philosophy of science in the direction of sociology of science, i.e. approaching science as a web of different social **practices** involving different communities with their specific habits, conventions, and **values**. Much subsequent theorizing on science has adopted a sociologist's stance,[2] and, to a lesser extent, a psychologist's stance[3]—instead of asking whether sociology or psychology are 'really' scientific, the questions being asked concern the ways that science emerges and functions as a social **institution**, the ways in which it becomes enmeshed with power in society, and the ways the creative process generates scientific discovery.

The philosophers' inability to agree on fixed criteria about what constitutes science does not mean that any doctrine can lay claim to be scientific. On the contrary, different disciplines seek to safeguard the scientific standing of their theories through strictly enforced criteria of how research should be conducted, how theories should be tested, and how scientific findings must be reported. Thus, in medicine, randomized control trials have become accepted as the sovereign way of generating valid and reliable knowledge. Research publications

---

[1] Popper, 1959.   [2] See e.g. Latour, 1987.   [3] Feist, 2006.

go through a blind peer review process, and usually require several revisions, before eventual publication. Furthermore, research projects are submitted to quite exhaustive scrutiny by medical ethics committees at the planning stage to ensure that they comply with professional **ethics** and do not violate the rights of the subjects. Other disciplines may evolve different social conventions but they enforce them with equal vigilance. In spite of such self-regulation, many disciplines also come under external pressures, especially when they touch on controversial or politically sensitive issues. While the majority of stories about science in the **mass media** cast it in positive light, there are numerous 'rows' and pseudo-stories sparked by ostensibly flawed research or research on controversial and sensitive issues. These range from animal experimentation to research into intelligence, gender, and race, from genetic engineering to research into climate change or food scares, and from the safety of hormone replacement therapy and the MMR vaccine to the effectiveness of homeopathy.

Following the linguistic turn in philosophy and in many of the other human sciences,[1] some of the steam has been taken out of the debates on what should qualify as science and what should not. It is now widely accepted that many disciplines rely on **narrative** knowledge rather than on lawlike generalizations and that such knowledge can yield effective results. Even the sanctum of medicine has gradually registered the influence of the linguistic turn as increasing numbers of scholars and medical practitioners begin to recognize the value of **stories** and **narratives** told by patients and physicians themselves.[2] At the moment, it remains difficult for narrative knowledge to claim the label of science and it is maybe better to describe the practice of a healer (whether medically qualified or not) as an 'art' rather than as the application of science.

Faith in science was an important factor behind the growth of **management** as a distinct university discipline with entire departments dedicated to it. Nobody epitomized this faith to a greater extent than F. W. Taylor, the father of **Scientific Management**. Taylor's hope that management could be reduced to the application of 'rules, laws and formulae' has not materialized. Instead, there is an increasing recognition by many scholars that a large part of management is an art, based on a wide range of **competencies** and **skills** and involving much tacit knowledge. Far from being based on universal principles, management is now coming to be viewed increasingly as being able to translate experiences from one context into another and acting on the basis of limited information and uncertain outcomes.[3]

• See also *knowledge, methodology, paradigms, technology*

Scientific Management (or Taylorism)

Scientific Management is a highly influential school of management thought and practice developed by American engineer and manager F. W. Taylor (1865–1915)—hence it is also widely known as Taylorism. Taylor was a man obsessed with efficiency: his life's ambition was to place management on a scientific basis, using experiments, accurate measurements, and generalizable propositions to rationalize production. For too long, Taylor argued, managers had relied on the workers' traditional knowledge to get things done—it was now time to take the initiative and organize production in a scientific way. By replacing the idiosyncratic skill of the craft with the machine-like precision of standardized scientific production, Taylor believed that **conflict** between employers and employees would be overcome, as massive gains in productivity

---

[1] Rorty, 1967; Alvesson and Karreman, 2000.   [2] A. W. Frank, 1998; Hurwitz, Greenhalgh, and Skultans, 2004; Kleinman, 1988; Mattingly, 1998.   [3] Czarniawska-Joerges, 1995; Nonaka, Krogh, and Ichijo, 2000; Tsoukas, 1998a; Tsoukas and Hatch, 2001.

and profitability allowed standards of living to quickly rise.

Taylor proposed a number of principles of Scientific Management; these included:

- Divorce of conception from execution. Managers assume responsibility for planning, organizing, and controlling production; the workers merely execute instructions in minuscule detail. The worker becomes the 'hands' of the enterprise, while management assumes the role of the head.
- Fragmentation and standardization. Each task must be broken down to its simplest elements, so that the job of each worker becomes simple, repetitive, and reducible to the application of **rules**. The result is more efficient production but also a **deskilling** of the worker, whose task is narrowed down to a very simple repetitive operation.
- Financial Incentives. Taylor argued that workers are **rational** beings, who try to maximize their individual incomes—they are instrumentally motivated. Hence managers must offer them financial incentives tied to piece-work and productivity to enhance their motivation.
- Scientific selection of staff. Taylor viewed the selection procedure as a key area where scientific principles can be applied. Different types of task require different mental, physical, and emotional qualities. He was adamant that the skills and aptitudes required by each job can be quantified and standardized, enabling managers to match the individual to the task.
- Cooperation. Taylor was convinced that cooperation rather than coercion should be the basis of the relations between management and workforce. He argued that there was no ultimate difference in their interests and insisted that his techniques would benefit both sides. As rational beings, the workers realize that the application of scientific management in production will lead to higher productivity which, in turn,

will result in higher wages, at least for those willing to follow the instructions of management.

Taylorism is sometimes referred to, especially by its critics, as the science of the stopwatch. Taylor pioneered a number of techniques which relied on precise timing of workers' movements ('time study'), the precise design of tools and machines to minimize effort, and the measurement of outputs. He treated each worker as a rational individual who could be motivated by financial incentives. During his time at Bethlehem steel works, he conducted several experiments and reported dramatic increases in productivity as a result of the application of his methods.

Social scientists have always delighted in criticizing the naivety of Scientific Management, as a theory of human nature. Human beings are not simply motivated by the **need** to maximize their personal income; nor are their actions independent of their social **groups**; work means much more to people than just money (think of the problems associated with retirement or unemployment). Indeed, different people may be motivated by different considerations (e.g. career, status, social conscience, etc.). Nor are Taylor's arguments concerning cooperation convincing, as evidenced by the fact that few unionists were willing to accept his proposals.

Scientific Management drew worker **resistance** from the start. The introduction of Taylorism at the Watertown Federal Arsenal in 1911 led to a strike, resulting in a Congressional hearing in which Taylor was called to defend his doctrine. Taylor's performance at the hearing was not impressive, accusing his critics of misrepresenting his views and antagonizing the court. Eventually, Taylorism was ruled to be unscientific, biased, and inaccurate and was explicitly banned from government contracts. By the time of his death in 1915, Taylor was a deeply disappointed and bitter man. Yet the legacy of his management philosophy lived on, having had a dramatic influence in shaping the modern corporation.[1] The secret of its success lay in the strengthening of management **controls** resulting from worker deskilling. The principles of Taylorism were originally embraced by Henry Ford (see **Fordism**) who raised them to still greater heights and, more recently, they have provided the basis for **McDonaldization** which has extended Taylorism to service-sector industries. Subsequently, Taylorism was embraced by many political regimes (including fascist and communist) as the avenue towards rapid industrialization. Lenin famously declared that Taylorism and full electrification would bring about Soviet communism. Today, Taylorism continues to dominate large areas of production, both in manufacturing and in the service sectors. However, there is evidence that in knowledge-intensive and creative industries, the skills of the workforce are essential ingredients for competitive advantage.

• See also *deskilling, Fordism, McDonaldization*

Self and selfhood

Self is a term used extensively in philosophy and psychology; it also underpins a wide range of economic, social, and political theories. The self is generally used to refer to the uniqueness and separateness of each human being as a conscious, and sentient person; selfhood is each individual's awareness of being such a separate, unique, conscious, and sentient person. The self is what each one of us refers to through the use of the pronoun 'I'. There is a considerable overlap between self and **identity** which sometimes combine to create the term 'self-identity' as against 'social identity'. Social identity is linked to **identification** with different **ethnic**, religious, and other **groups** to which we belong, whereas self-identity is what we fashion through many and diverse identifications, **choices**, and actions throughout life.

The idea of a *sovereign* self as a moral agent making independent decisions and being responsible for his or her actions is a core tenet of philosophy, especially that propounded by the great German philosopher Immanuel Kant. For the past hundred years, this self-confident view of the self has been subjected to a prolonged interrogation and critique. In the first place, it approaches the self purely in mental terms, disregarding its physical dimension, the **body**. Even in mental terms, the self is seen as fully conscious, a view challenged by **psychoanalysis** as well as other schools of depth psychology. Freud argued that the conscious self, *the ego*, is only part of the self and a small and contingent part at that. We deceive ourselves in thinking that our actions follow from our thoughts—most of them are expressions of **unconscious** desires and impulses or responses to situations that we interpret in line with unconscious desires and impulses. In a paper called 'A difficulty in the path of psychoanalysis',[2] Freud argued that the psychoanalytic theory of the unconscious had inflicted a blow on our **narcissism** as human beings, on an even greater scale than two great earlier scientific discoveries. Copernicus's discovery shattered the view that the earth was the centre of the universe and Darwin's evolution theory destroyed the myth of man's uniqueness among animals; psychoanalysis adds a third blow which is probably 'the most wounding' for our narcissism because it showed that 'the ego is not master in its own house'.[3] Instead of a sovereign self, moving on to ever-higher achievements, psychoanalysis argues that the self is at odds with itself, fragmented, and systematically deluded—it

> is not a simple thing; on the contrary, it is a hierarchy of superordinated and subordinated agents, a labyrinth of impulses striving independently of one another towards action, corresponding with the multiplicity of instincts and of relations with the outer world, many of

---

[1] Braverman, 1974; Guillen, 1994.   [2] Freud, 1917a.   [3] Ibid. 189.

which are antagonistic to one another and incompatible.[1]

The coherent, fully conscious self, Freud argued, is an illusion, in the same way that 'God' or 'the nation' are illusions—they all fulfil unconscious wishes. The idea that we are coherent **personalities** with a sovereign reason that distinguishes us from other animals may be comforting but can hardly be defended on the evidence of our actions as a species—our propensity for violent inconsistencies, changes of heart, impulsive behaviours, and neurotic upheavals. Among psychoanalytic schools, the one that has been most critical of coherent representations of the self has been the one established by French psychoanalyst Jacques Lacan. Through a radical rereading of Freud and extensive use of structuralist linguistics, Lacan sought to shift the centre of attention in psychoanalysis away from the ego back to the **unconscious**.[2] Lacan argued that the subject, the self, and the ego are all fragmented and imaginary, traceable back to the 'mirror stage', when every child first encounters him- or herself as what appears an integrated entity in the mirror and 'misrecognizes' him- or herself as a **subject**. Subsequently, the subject is sustained by the recognition in the gaze of the **Other**.

Joining in the critique of unified, conscious, and sovereign self, John Gray has argued that 'selfhood in humans is not the expression of any essential unity. It is a pattern of organisation, not unlike that found in insect colonies.'[3] This critique of the sovereign self has been further developed by theorists, who argue that the self is constructed discursively and carefully managed to prevent it from splitting or fragmenting into separate pieces. Authors influenced by Foucault, like Nikolas Rose and Christopher Grey,[4] have argued that these discourses of selfhood, including therapeutic self-improvement, **career** improvement, self-realization, and so forth, constitute the self as a 'project' for individuals. Just as the body becomes a project to be accomplished through careful toning, pampering, and 'building', likewise the self becomes a project to be constructed, improved, developed, compared, and acclaimed. The project of the self is **reflexive**—the self is both producer and product, subject and object, storyteller and story-told. As Anthony Giddens writes, 'in the post-traditional order of modernity, against the backdrop of new forms of mediated experience, self-identity becomes a **reflexively** organised endeavour. The reflexive project of the self, which consists in the sustaining of coherent, yet continuously revised, biographical **narratives**, takes place in the context of multiple choice as filtered through abstract systems'.[5]

• See also *identity, personality, subject and subjectivity*

Sense and sensemaking

Since its appearance as a regular concept in social psychology in the late 1980s, sensemaking has emerged as an important category in the social sciences and the subject of numerous studies. Sensemaking is strongly associated with the work of Karl Weick and Dennis Gioia who have used it as the centrepiece of highly sophisticated theories of human behaviour in organizations. Sensemaking is seen as the product of the fundamental human quest for **meaning**. As Mary Douglas argued:

> whatever we perceive is organized into patterns for which we the perceivers are largely responsible . . . As perceivers we select from all the stimuli falling on our senses only those which interest us, and our interests are governed by a pattern-making tendency, sometimes called a schema. In a chaos of shifting impressions each of us constructs a stable world in which objects have recognisable shapes, are located in depth and have

---

[1] Freud, 1917a.   [2] Lacan, 1966/1977; 1988a; 1988b.   [3] Gray, 2002, p. 72.   [4] Rose, 1989; Grey, 1994.   [5] Giddens, 1991, p. 5.

permanence. . . . As time goes on and experience builds up, we make greater investment in our systems of labels. So a conservative bias is built in. It gives us confidence.[1]

When confronted with novel and unusual events or **experiences**, we try to make sense of them by fitting them into different cognitive schemata, linking them to earlier experiences, or placing them in plots that can be readily recognized, in short turning them into **stories**. 'Perhaps there is no more common sensemaking gambit than, "that reminds me of a story". This innocent phrase represents a unit of meaning. Something in the present reminds the listener of something that resembles it in the past.'[2] Weick argues that sensemaking is an ongoing process whereby events are read in the light of subsequent developments, being constantly reinterpreted and placed in new plotlines or schemata.

Sensemaking is grounded in people's constant struggles to construct their **identities**. Different people may make sense of an accident differently depending on whether they are victims, likely scapegoats, or emergency personnel seeking to minimize the damage. One person may 'read' an accident as evidence of managerial negligence, another as evidence of human fallibility, and a third as a freak occurrence—what all three have in common is that in their different ways they seek to make sense of it.[3]

Sensemaking like storytelling is driven by plausibility rather than accuracy; an event makes sense if it can be shown to resonate with people's experiences and accord with their **desires** and **emotions**. As Weick argues:

> If accuracy is nice but not necessary in sensemaking, then what is necessary? The answer is, something that preserves plausibility and coherence, something that is reasonable and something that embodies past experience and expectations, something that resonates with other people, something that can be

constructed retrospectively but also can be used prospectively, something that captures both feeling and thought, something that allows embellishment to fit current oddities, something that is fun to contrast. In short, what is necessary in sensemaking is a good story.[4]

Sensemaking is not a solitary pursuit but an ongoing social process, whereby people trade stories and interpretations, absorb, contest, or reject each other's stories, and frequently end up co-constructing or sharing them. In this connection Gioia and Chittipeddi have proposed the term *sense giving* as one's ability to influence others through one's reading of different social situations.[5] Sense giving is part of the wider process of **management of meaning** which is of vital importance in the study of leadership and entrepreneurship.

Both sensemaking and sense giving are then not just forms of contemplation but prompts for **action**—our actions emanate from the sense that we make of different situations. If we read a situation as an insult, we are likely to get angry and seek retaliation; if, on the other hand, we read it as a clumsy faux pas, an accident, or an insignificant trifle we are likely to react differently. Within an organization, we are likely to respond differently to a situation we collectively read as a crisis from one we read as a catastrophe, a difficulty, a problem, a blip, or 'business as usual'. Thus we 'enact' our **environments**.

Sensemaking and sense giving in our times can be seen to be affected by the general dislocation of meanings, the saturation of our mental apparatus by **information**, and the visual and audio bombardment of our sense by images, sounds, and noise. Sensemaking becomes episodic, ephemeral, and precarious. In a thought-provoking contribution, Peter Pelzer has used the old myth of the Flying Dutchman and his phantom ship cursed to sail the oceans as a parable for the discontents of **modernity**.[6]

---

[1] Douglas, 1966/2002, p. 45.   [2] Weick, 1995, p. 131.   [3] Gabriel, 1995.   [4] Weick, 1995, pp. 60–1.   [5] Gioia and Chittipeddi, 1991.
[6] Pelzer, 2004.

The Dutchman's eternal travels allow Pelzer to develop a highly original argument for humanity's loss of eternal meanings and absolute values. What Pelzer argues is that, when meaning loses its anchors, sensemaking becomes a surrogate. The journey without destination then becomes both the curse and the thrilling adventure of our time. At its worst, sensemaking disintegrates into spin, pseudo-stories, and meaningless verbiage; at its best, it offers the possibility to experiment with meaning creation free from the burdens of sacrosanct traditional meaning systems.

• See also *management of meaning, meaning, spirituality, story and storytelling*

Sex

Sex, observed Raymond Williams astutely, 'in one of its predominant contemporary senses—indeed at times the dominant everyday sense—has an interesting history, in that in this sense it refers to mainly physical *relations* between "the sexes", whereas in its early uses it is a description of the divisions between them'.[1] Sex is indeed both what distinguishes women from men and also a wide range of physical and sensuous actions and experiences driven by **desire** and pleasure. These may involve people of opposite sexes, people of the same sex, or single individuals. What distinguishes women from men may originate in biology, but it also has other dimensions, social, psychological, political, and cultural. It has now become customary to use sex to describe biological differences and **gender** to describe culturally specific **roles** and behaviours attached to the sexes.[2] But sex has far wider significance than to mark the anatomical differences between people.

Sex is ever present in Western cultures. It can reside in a poster, an image, a person, an item of clothing, a sound, a smell, or a word. Often mixed with **violence**, sex represents the regular output of a large part of the **mass media** and entertainment industries; it is the text, explicit or hidden, of numerous advertisements (where sex sells anything, from newspapers and clothes to cosmetics and food) and underpins a large part of contemporary **consumerism**. Sex is a regular part of many everyday conversations, TV chat shows, and jokes. It is the topic of innumerable books and manuals, offering to help people enhance and improve their sex lives. It is also a massive industry in its own right that includes prostitution, pornography, computer and video games, sex tourism, and so forth. For this reason Germaine Greer described it as the 'lubricant of consumer society', adding that 'in order to fulfil that function the very character of human **sexuality** itself must undergo special conditioning'.[3] Different historical periods and different **cultures** have very different ideas as to which things are meant to generate sexual feelings and which are not, appropriate and inappropriate sexual activities, as well as different ideals of physical attractiveness. Sexuality is then constructed, manifested, and experienced in very different ways across times and places.

Michel Foucault, in his unfinished but highly influential work *The History of Sexuality*,[4] argued that sex has been talked about continuously since the nineteenth century and has become an effect of **discourse**. This is itself a historical phenomenon that started several centuries earlier.

> This scheme for transforming sex into discourse had been devised long before in an ascetic and monastic setting. The seventeenth century made it into a rule for everyone. It would seem in actual fact that it could scarcely have applied to any but a tiny elite; the great majority of the faithful who only went to confession on rare occasions in the course of the year escaped such complex prescriptions. But the important point no doubt is that this obligation [to talk about sex] was decreed, as an

---

[1] Williams, 1983, p. 283.   [2] Oakley, 1972.   [3] Greer, 1984, p. 198.   [4] Foucault, 1978; 1984/1985; 1984/1986.

ideal at least, for every good Christian. An imperative was established. Not only will you confess to acts contravening the law, but you will seek to transform your desire, your every desire, into discourse.[1]

The result today is that a wide range of sexual desires, fantasies, and fears are constructed in different discourses including sexual manuals, advertising narratives and images, and endless discussions about child abuse, teenage pregnancies, abortion, sexually transmitted diseases including AIDS, prostitution, internet sex, sexual slavery, and so forth.

Pornography is a machine for constructing sex, generally depicting it as hard competitive work, frequently brutal and always gendered, mostly emotion free and humour free, aimed at the 'money shot' of the male orgasm. As a huge industry with a greater turnover than Hollywood, estimated at $60 billion in 2007, its main output is not the 200 films it churns out every week, but the way it portrays people as sexual beings and the **power** relations it sustains through these depictions. Sex, usually exploitative, brutish, nasty, and short, becomes a feature of all power relations— between men and women, but also between blacks and whites, young and old, homosexuals and heterosexuals, Christians and Muslims, teachers and pupils, and so forth. 'Sexuality is not the most intractable element in power relations, but rather one of those endowed with the greatest instrumentality: useful for the greatest number of manoeuvres and capable of serving as a point of support, as a linchpin, for the most varied strategies'[2]—in short, Foucault looked at sex as a feature of manoeuvres of domination as well as manoeuvres of opposition.

Interest in sex in organizations has been a relatively recent phenomenon. As we would expect from Foucault's perspective, much of the research has been prompted by concerns about **sexual harassment** and, to a lesser extent, a

fascination with office romances. Sex and love in organizations are regularly constructed as 'problems', disrupting and confusing power relations and undermining **performance**. Love in the workplace is a troublesome force to be contained, managed, and defused. What are less frequently discussed are non-exploitative, consensual, adult sexual relationships, the ways in which such relationships unfold, and their ramifications for the individuals and the organizations concerned.[3] In line with Foucauldian arguments, some recent work on the experiences of sexual minorities in the workplace has argued that sex in organizations is a contested terrain, at times forcing sexual 'deviants' into silence but at times enabling them to stage different forms of **resistance**.[4]

• See also *love, sexuality*

Sexual harassment

Sexual harassment is a concept dating from the early 1970s, describing the experience of physical or verbal **violence** of a sexual nature. Harassment can range from offensive language and sexist **jokes**, to exaggerated compliments, to sexual blackmail to extort favours. Sexual harassment can occur between superiors and subordinates in an organization (including between managers and workers, doctors and patients, teachers and pupils), between colleagues of a similar status, or between an organization's members and its customers or its suppliers.[5] Victims of sexual harassment feel anxious and oppressed and are reluctant to report it, feeling trapped and impotent.[6] Along with different forms of sexual abuse and violence including rape, sexual harassment is often experienced as bringing dishonour to the victim, as though it were their fault that landed them in trouble. This supports the view that such crimes are socially constructed by **discourses** that privilege men and cast women in

---

[1] Foucault, 1978, pp. 20–1.   [2] Ibid. 103.   [3] Hearn et al., 1989; Mano and Gabriel, 2006; Williams, Giuffre, and Dellinger, 1999.
[4] Ward and Winstanley, 2003.   [5] Guerrier and Adib, 2000.   [6] Pierce et al., 2004.

the **role** of seductresses using their **sexuality** to gain advantage.

Many, though not all, reported cases are of men harassing women. Some studies suggest that harassment is more commonly directed towards those women who are perceived by men as threats.[1] This further supports feminist arguments that sexual harassment is not exceptional, nor just an individual's problem, but a wider symptom of **power** relations between the **genders**. Some sexual harassment may also be directed against minority groups, including gays and lesbians, which reinforces institutional bias in favour of heterosexuals.

The response of many organizations to sexual harassment has been to establish policies and procedures, sometimes quite elaborate, for handling complaints. This has created a new form of harassment which involves the threat of making a complaint against an innocent party. In general, corporate attempts to manage the sexuality and love life of their employees underestimate the complexity and subtlety of these forces. While **policies** and procedures may offer some protection against the most blatant examples of sexual blackmail and abuse they cannot do justice to the various games of a sexual nature that people play with each other, or to most of the consequences when such games turn sour. The difference between an innocent compliment and oppressive attention is often a matter of interpretation, in the light of subsequent developments.

• See also *bullying*

Sexuality

Sexuality can be thought of as the complex of physical desires and their expressions in actions and fantasies. These expressions can be physical, emotional, verbal, or even artistic, but, in a direct or indirect way, sexuality is linked to *pleasure*. Human sexuality is strongly **gendered**— men and women act differently as sexual beings,

they construct their sexual **identities** differently. The sexuality of most individuals may seem consistent and stable, yet most social and psychological research indicates that sexuality is highly complex and variable. In contrast to animal sexuality which is mechanically linked to instinctual behaviour, human sexuality is mediated by **desires**, many of which are either learned or symbolically constituted. Sociologists and anthropologists have observed wide variations of sexual behaviours across different cultures and societies. For example, in the early part of the twentieth century, the anthropologist Bronislaw Malinowski studied the highly promiscuous sexual lives of the Trobriand islanders living off the eastern coast of New Guinea, which contrasted sharply with the rigidly controlled sexuality of some of their neighbours living on other islands in the region.[2] This suggested that there is no natural and unnatural sex, natural and unnatural desire; different cultures have different ways of establishing who and what is desirable, what gives pleasure and what pleasures, are forbidden.

Christianity, along with several other religions, has been intensely mistrustful of sexuality and has generally sought to contain it within marriage. Sexuality, linked to original sin and the expulsion of Adam and Eve from the garden of Eden, was viewed as disrupting people's struggles to achieve true **spiritual** virtue. Many famous authors from Immanuel Kant to Leo Tolstoy were deeply troubled by sexuality which they viewed as degrading and dehumanizing, reducing humans to 'mere' animals. Although Freud was not the first to draw attention to sexuality as a normal and 'natural' motivational principle, his theory was to have a far-reaching influence. In his 'Three essays on the theory of sexuality',[3] he proposed that human sexuality is polymorphously perverse, i.e. composed of numerous diverse desires, many of them at odds with each other, many of them **unconscious**, and many of them 'perverse' or 'abnormal', attached

---

[1] Di Tomaso, 1989; Gutek, 1989. [2] Malinowski, 1922. [3] Freud, 1905/1977.

to different part of the body. Some of these desires are aimed at people of the same sex and some are aimed towards people of the opposite sex. No hard and fast line between 'normal' and 'perverse' sexuality can be drawn, since many 'normal' people repress desires that could be classified as perverse. Sometimes such desires resurface unexpectedly, as perverse actions, as neurotic symptoms, as dreams, as jokes, as artistic creations, and so forth.

Freud also proposed that sexuality develops from early childhood; each adult's sexuality is substantially shaped by the way that they progressed through the early stages of sexual development, what frustrations and pleasure they encountered, and what sacrifices they made. The view that little children are sexual beings earned Freud a degree of notoriety. He proposed that in the first four or five years of life, infants go through four stages of sexual development: (1) The oral, in which most desires focus around the area of the mouth, (2) the anal, when most desires revolve around the control of the bowel movement, (3) the phallic, when the penis and the clitoris come into the centre of sexual feeling, and (4) the genital, which represents the usual terminus of sexual development, which incorporates features of the earlier stages.

Mature sexuality is a complex force, involving desires, fantasies, and emotions that originate in the early years of life. In his later works, Freud subsumed the sexual impulses in the concept of Eros, the core principle opposed by the death instinct. He argued that human **culture** is built on the basis of erotic bonds that join people together, but at the same time seeks to control and regulate desire at the cost of creating a great deal of sexual frustration, pain, and suffering. Freud's view of sexuality was complex and flexible. He viewed all people as being bisexual, even if most repress their homosexual desires. He also viewed sexuality as capable of being sublimated and redirected towards artistic, scientific, and cultural **achievements**. Yet

Freud remained convinced that systematically frustrated and repressed sexual desires generate consuming **anxieties** and readily act as nuclei for psycho-neuroses; hence, he advocated more progressive and tolerant sexual attitudes.

In the last hundred years, sexual attitudes have undergone extensive changes, at least in most Western societies, bringing about greater tolerance for different sexual preferences and greater freedom of sexual behaviours. In the 1960s a sexual revolution was said to have taken place, not least because of the discovery of oral contraception, allowing people unprecedented sexual freedom and pleasure. This is debatable—oral contraception introduced new complications, new sexual dynamics, and contributed to the spread of sexually transmitted diseases, old and new. What is not debatable is that **sex** suffuses contemporary culture and is widely talked about, generating new anxieties linked to sexual identity, potency, and enjoyment. The German philosopher Herbert Marcuse argued that the new permissive sexual **morality** and the lifting of traditional repressions, far from liberating Eros, constituted a new repressive regime which he termed 'repressive desublimation'.[1] The sexualization of every aspect of culture and the promise of pleasure in every offering of **consumerism** represent, according to Marcuse, a systematic manipulation of desire that enhances capitalist domination and the rule of commodities. Far from bringing sexual fulfilment, repressive desublimation awakens desire only to create addiction, dependency, and enduring **alienation**.

A different and very influential slant on sexuality was proposed by Michel Foucault, in his unfinished work *The History of Sexuality*,[2] where he argued that sex is a regular feature in most **power** relations:

Sexuality must not be described as a stubborn drive, by nature alien and of necessity disobedient to a power which exhausts itself trying to subdue it and often fails to control it

---

[1] Marcuse, 1955; 1964.   [2] Foucault, 1978; 1984/1985; 1984/1986.

entirely [contra Freud]. It appears rather as an especially dense transfer point for relations of power: between men and women, young people and old people, parents and their offspring, teachers and students, priests and laity, an administration and a population.[1]

Whether looking at sexuality as a biological force, as the origin of psychopathologies, as a core dimension of identity, or indeed as systematically repressed, sexuality, in Foucault's view, is constituted by the different ways in which it is talked about, in short by **discourse**. Foucault's discursive conceptualization of sexuality has influenced many subsequent discussions of the sexual constitution of **subjectivity** and wider power relations in society. It has also influenced many studies of the way sexuality is portrayed in the media, in film, in advertising, and so forth. In a curious way, it has become itself part of the discourse through which sexuality is socially constructed.

Skill

Skill describes the ability to carry out a competent or even virtuosic **performance** in virtually any kind of activity. Reading and writing, playing the violin, telling jokes, driving, swimming, speaking a language—all involve skills. Skills require **learning**, practice, and application. Yet there can be no doubt that people differ widely in their ability to develop different skills. Some people can play competent tennis or paint good paintings after few lessons while others have to struggle for a long time without ever 'mastering' an art. The word 'master' describes accurately a more than competent performer, someone who is a polished practitioner of an art.

A skilful practitioner is someone who can deal with many different situations not in a uniform or routine way, but in a way that is appropriate to each situation. A skill therefore involves the ability to 'read' different situations; it often requires

an ability to engage in **bricolage** as much as to provide highly polished performances under ideal conditions. A skilled cook knows when to use a particular recipe and when to vary a recipe in order to make the most of the ingredients at hand in the light of the demands of the meal or of those who will eat the food. Part of a cook's skill is the recognition that certain situations (e.g. a group of hungry children) call for quick and simple cooking rather than elaborate recipes.

Skills confer money, **power**, and **status** on those who have mastered them. In some cases, tiny advantages in the practice of a skill (e.g. playing golf) can make huge differences in earnings and prestige. But in order for skill to translate into privilege, it must not only be rare; it must be recognized and valued. Thus, domestic skills traditionally associated with women's work—the combined skills of looking after sick children, mending clothes, cooking several meals a day, keeping a clean household, getting the most out of the family budget, and maintaining a happy family atmosphere—may not translate into social power in most contemporary Western cultures. By contrast, certain skills that appear to have little social value (like kicking a football) may command enormous market capacity. In our times, the skill of staying in the public eye by various attention-grabbing gestures is one that can turn some people into media celebrities.

The nature of skill has preoccupied some philosophers, especially those interested in moral education, the theory of knowledge, and political philosophy. Plato devoted a considerable part of his work to the skills (*téchnai*) of **leadership**, while Aristotle in his methodical way distinguished between five different forms of knowing; these included *wisdom* (*sophia*), understanding from eternal abstract principles; *science* (*episteme*), knowledge of the general principles behind discoverable unalterable facts; *skill* or *art* (*techne*), competence in producing

[1] Foucault, 1978, p. 103.

things even if one is ignorant of the general principles; *practical wisdom* (*phronesis*), prudence, judgement, and ability to read and respond effectively to concrete situations; and *intuitive reason* or *intelligence* (*nous*). Among twentieth-century philosophers, the American pragmatist John Dewey explored extensively the concepts of skills and arts both as features of his educational philosophy which sought to develop the widest possible range of problem-solving skills among children and in his theory of art as experience and the arts of living.[1]

Skill is an important concept in organizational studies, yet there is no general agreement on the precise skills of organizing or managing. Some skills required by organizations are social and interpersonal, such as communication or team building. Other skills are of a more technical nature, for example computer programming or bookkeeping. Yet others may involve abstract reasoning and problem solving. One of the peculiarities of skill is that many people with highly developed skills (for instance at playing a musical instrument or at turning companies around) are not capable of articulating the precise nature of what they do. Perhaps this is not surprising; high levels of skill become part of oneself and one's **identity**; they are tacit rather than explicit. Other skilled practitioners (including good teachers, some managers, artists, and other highly skilled performers) are capable of describing and transferring their skills by placing themselves in the position of the novice; in addition to being skilled at their particular discipline, such people can be said to also possess the skill of communicating and sharing their skill with others.

Acquiring new skills is especially difficult for people who already possess highly developed skills. At the peak of his powers, when asked whether it was possible to play still better chess, Anatoly Karpov, then world champion, answered that he would first have to unlearn all the chess that he already knew. Old skills,

especially those that have served us well in the past (and maybe are the basis of our power and prestige) are difficult to sacrifice in the interest of acquiring new skills whose usefulness may be doubtful. Hence many of us cling strongly to the skills we have and defend them against attempts to reduce their relevance or value.

Deskilling is the process whereby skills that commanded considerable power are rendered valueless, mostly through technical or managerial **innovations**. In the early nineteenth century, hand-loom weavers in Great Britain constituted the aristocracy of labour, enjoying high wages and privileged conditions of work. The arrival of power looms forced them in a few short years into abject poverty.[2] Deskilling of the industrial workers was accelerated under the influence of **Scientific Management**, which sought to replace what it saw as 'the high-cost and erratic elegance of the artisan with the low-cost, predictable munificence of the manufacturer'.[3] Deskilling brought down the costs of labour and bolstered management **control** over the productive processes. Yet, in a talk to American businesspeople in the 1980s, Konosuke Matsushita, founder of Matsushita Corporation, offered the following warning:

> We are going to win and the industrial West is going to lose out; there is not much you can do about it because the reasons for your failures are within yourselves. Your firms are built on the Taylor idea—and even worse—so are your minds. Your bosses do the thinking; your workers wield the screwdrivers . . . we are beyond the Taylor model. The continued existence of business depends on the day to day mobilization of every ounce of intelligence.

In the years since Matsushita's warning much has changed in business strategy and deskilling is no longer viewed as the universal route to business success, notably in sectors where employee commitment, flexibility, and learning have assumed paramount importance. All the same, it is

---

[1] Dewey, 1925/1958; 1934/1959.   [2] Thompson, 1968, chapter IX.   [3] Levitt, 1972, p. 43.

probably true to say that large numbers of industrial workers throughout the globe rely on levels of skills for their jobs substantially lower than those required to use their mobile phones or play their video-games at home.

• See also *competences*

Social capital see capital

Social construction of reality

The social construction of reality is the process in societal and historical contexts whereby people give **meaning** to the world through cultural interaction. This 'world' is one that may well exist beyond language and processes of **interpretation**. But it is something which can only be known and related to by people through language-based processes of historical knowledge creation, cultural interpretation, and sense-making.

The 'social construction of reality' is a sociological-anthropological concept which deals with the fundamental questions of 'what is it to be human?' and 'what is the relationship between this humanness and the societies which the human species has created?' It is a notion which we can examine in its own right, without our being diverted by those projects which have taken up the term 'social construction' to create the 'isms' of social construct*ionism* and social construct*ivism*.

The book *The Social Construction of Reality* was a contribution to the sociology of knowledge by Berger and Luckmann originally published in 1966. The book was significant in the way it pushed the sociology of knowledge fully towards the centre of the discipline of sociology by defining **knowledge** in a very broad way. Knowledge is simply 'the certainty that phenomena are real and that they possess specific characteristics'.[1] This covers everything that is taken for granted

by any person, in any social situation—in everyday life as much as in philosophical debate—as the reality of the situation (with 'reality' being simply 'a quality appertaining to phenomena that we recognise as having a being independent of our own volition'). Anything that 'passes for knowledge' (regardless of how we might judge the validity of that knowledge), it was argued, is 'developed, transmitted and maintained in social situations', and the book set out to examine 'the processes by which this is done in such a way that a taken-for-granted "reality" congeals' for the person 'in the street'.[2] This, they said, is a matter of looking at 'the social construction of reality'. And the ensuing analysis identified three basic processes of externalization, objectification, and internalization. *Externalization* occurs when people act on the world by creating an object (some early cave dwellers inventing, say, a lasso for capturing animals) or devising a practice (working in a team with a lasso, say, to bring home the dinner). *Objectification* occurs as this way of acting becomes widely talked about, portrayed in cave paintings, and thus socially taken for granted as 'normal' or as 'what we do in this tribe'. Team hunting with a lasso is now an *objective* aspect of the world, a taken-for-granted element of the lives of these people. And all this is *internalized* as the new generation of tribe members learn about this practice as something which simply exists 'out there' in the social world, as opposed to something that some people, at some time, actually devised. It is simply an aspect of these people's reality.

The choice of an illustration of social construction from an imagined early stage in human history is quite deliberate. It was made to emphasize that the concept of social construction was devised to deal, in part, with the issue of the distinctiveness of the human species and how that species had to 'construct' its reality—unlike other animals which were much more 'complete' in that they come into the world equipped with an instinctual apparatus to guide

---

[1] Berger and Luckmann, 1967, p. 13.   [2] Ibid. 15.

their **actions**. There is 'no man-world in the sense that one may speak of a dog-world or a horse world'.[1] Human beings, it is being argued, have a given 'nature' to a fundamentally lesser extent than do other animals. They therefore have to construct their own nature. And in the process of this they create human cultures, institutions, and societies. Members of societies, not in an instant but over history, construct or make these 'things'. And in turn they are made by them.

Although this very significant contribution to sociology laid particular emphasis on the **cultural** aspect of human existence, it is not helpful to see it as representing a 'turn' in the social sciences: a marked turning away from established thinking. The authors are explicit about drawing on ideas from Marx, Plessner, Gehlen, Durkheim, Weber, and Mead. Their synthesis is nevertheless novel and, although subsequent thinking has moved beyond their original theorizing in a number of ways, Berger and Luckmann have provided the social sciences with a style of thinking which puts processes of *institutionalization* at the centre of how we theorize the relationship between human ingenuity, agency, and creativity and the pre-given world of **institutions**, **cultures**, **discourses**, and social **structures** into which we are all born. 'Structurational' and 'new institutionalist' thinking are just two examples of developments of this kind.[2] Unfortunately, however, the terms social construction*ism* and constructiv*ism* have been coined ('externalized') and taken on currency in much of the social science literature ('objectified' and 'internalized') to refer to a type of analysis which takes inspiration more from language-focused philosophy, post-structuralism, and postmodernism (note the 'isms' again!) than from Marx, Durkheim, Weber, or Mead. This new 'sensibility'—with its assumption that discourses and 'texts' *constitute* or 'bring into being' everything from **organizations** to human **identities**—is frequently connected with an alleged *linguistic turn* in the

social sciences. This is in spite of the fact that the 'linguistic turn' expression was created by Bergmann as part of a philosophical debate, as opposed to a social scientific one. And it is also in spite of the fact that Bergmann, in his last published work, argued that the 'linguistic turn' needed to be 'contained'.[3] He was worried that philosophy might be displaced by linguistics—a danger that social scientists too might contemplate.[4] That, however, is another story, as they say. The present entry is on *the social construction of reality*; a concept with a power of its own, whose continuing value should not be diminished by its being drawn into the maw of any kind of predatory 'ism'.

TONY J. WATSON, UNIVERSITY OF NOTTINGHAM

Socialization

Socialization is widely used in the social sciences to refer to the process by which people become part of a social unit. It is the taking on of the beliefs, norms, and values of the **culture** or organization of which they are members. Socialization starts in early life but continues throughout life. Key agents of socialization are parents, teachers, peers, leaders, elders, and different role models. Competing hard with these traditional sources are the **mass media** and entertainment—magazines, television, film, pop stars. From these various sources people learn their national cultural ways, including what is appropriate behaviour for their sex, social class, and status. Thus, socialization prepares individuals to perform **roles** consistent with their **identity**, including gender and sexual roles, family roles, and work roles. Socialization into gender roles is especially important because beliefs about the appropriate behaviours of men and women are among the most powerful ones within most cultures. Socialization is then a prolonged process of **learning** what to believe in and learning how to act in different social situations in line with social expectations. It is a concept

---

[1] Ibid. 65.   [2] Giddens, 1984; Scott, 2001.   [3] Bergmann and Heald, 1992.   [4] Watson, 2008a.

of interest to criminology and the sociology of deviance where delinquent behaviour may be viewed either as a failure of socialization, as the result of socialization into deviant norms and values, or as a drift between the two.[1]

The depth and uniformity of socialization differs across cultures. Thus, certain cultures permit a greater degree of variation in role **performances** and tolerate deviations from dominant patterns. Others enforce their values and norms with greater rigour and discipline, applying severe sanctions to deviants that may range from ostracism to imprisonment and death. Indoctrination and brainwashing are the most extreme forms of socialization, seeking to convert people into acolytes, uncritical followers of a regime. As vividly portrayed in George Orwell's *Nineteen Eighty Four*, such indoctrination seeks to destroy an individual's sense of **self** using a combination of fear and enticement to generate unthinking conformity and has long been used by authoritarian regimes. Brainwashing is also an attempt to eliminate all traces of earlier socialization and replace them with a totally new set of **values** and norms.

Individuals, for their part, are not uniform in their responses to socialization. Some fully conform, some resist and eventually conform, some rebel, and some find ways of evading cultural controls or appearing to conform while subverting them. Schein used the term 'creative individualism' to describe a middle position between conformity and rebellion—a position that involves the moulding of social norms and expectations around one's own needs, personality, and desires.[2] More extensively, in his discussion of social **roles**, Goffman noted a creative a difference between the actor and the performance, whereby different actors may perform the same role in different ways with different degrees of persuasiveness.[3] Hochschild developed a useful distinction between deep acting and surface acting—deep acting uses imagination, empathy, and deep identification with a role to produce performances in which the distance between role and performer disappears; surface acting relies on displaying, more or less convincingly, the behaviours and characteristics expected of a role without experiencing its emotions, creating, in other words, what Goffman describes as a 'front'.[4]

Organizational socialization is seen as a special case of socialization. Companies seek to mould employees into their way of thinking and doing things. They do this by stressing their values and expectations at the recruitment stage when **psychological contracts** are forged, by carefully selecting staff among those that are likely to be effectively socialized and screening out potential misfits. Socialization is subsequently reinforced by different **rituals** and rites of passage, training, criteria for promotion, and various forms of organizational communication, formal and informal. Assigning a *mentor* to a new employee to act as adviser and role model is a further attempt at strengthening socialization, ensuring that the employee absorbs visible and invisible elements of organizational culture. Some companies are known for the effort and expense they dedicate to socializing new employees. Certain merchant banks, for instance, may put potential recruits through dozens of interviews, role play simulations, personality assessments, and other forms of selection trials before engaging them, to be followed by prolonged and rigorous training and coaching, often away from home, which to some may seem as amounting to indoctrination.

Socialization is one of the four stages in the four-stage spiral model of organizational **learning** developed by Nonaka and Takeuchi,[5] based on Polanyi's distinction between tacit and explicit **knowledge**.[6] Tacit knowledge is context specific, subjective, and often comes in the form

---

[1] Matza, 1969; Sykes and Matza, 1957.   [2] Schein, 1968.   [3] Goffman, 1959.   [4] Hochschild, 1983.   [5] Nonaka and Takeuchi, 1995.
[6] Polanyi, 1964.

of stories. Explicit knowledge is systematic, formal, and codified. *Externalization* is the turning of tacit into explicit knowledge, by codifying it in manuals, routines, and procedures and incorporating it into products and processes. The reverse process whereby employees make the explicit knowledge of their organization their own is referred to as *internalization*. *Combination* refers to the dissemination of codified, explicit knowledge, whereas *socialization* represents the sharing of tacit knowledge through sharing of experiences, stories, and narratives. Nonaka and Takeuchi argue that socialization is part of an infinite spiral of organizational learning consisting of the constant sequence of socialization, externalization, combination, and internalization.

Still widely used in the social sciences, the concept of socialization is not without its critics. It is a concept that bears the strong imprimatur of functionalist theory that never really engaged with any critical or postmodernist scholarship. As a result, socialization conceals the immense **conflict** and struggle at the interface of the individual and the social. It assumes that these two entities are independent of each other and that somehow the social becomes constitutive of the individual, as if society was breathed into each one of its members through a uniform and smooth process, afflicted, at worst, by occasional hitches. Even where it appears to malfunction, as in the cases of deviant and delinquent behaviour, such behaviours can be viewed not as failures of socialization but as an internalization of or occasional drift into an alternative set of norms and values. Thus the concept of socialization remains oblivious to the **unmanaged and unmanageable** domains of the unconscious and of desire and the fascinating qualities of the forbidden and the foreign. Both individual and society are treated as coherent entities, free of their own contradictions, fragmentations, and inconsistencies. All in all, socialization has become a concept that is distinctly too 'comfortable'; this is the source of both its usefulness and its limitations.

Society

Society is the subject matter of the discipline of sociology and a word whose fortunes have waxed and waned. They reached a nadir in 1987 when Margaret Thatcher, then Conservative British Prime Minister, claimed that 'there is no such thing as society. There are individual men and women, and there are families.' What Thatcher was objecting to was people blaming society for their problems and expecting the state to resolve them. Paradoxically, Thatcher's bedfellows in denying the existence of society include Marxist philosophers Louis Althusser and Ernesto Laclau who viewed society as an ideological effect of **capitalism**, a term that systematically obscures its **class** and other political realities.

Society originates in the Latin *societas*, a 'friendly association with others' or 'company of others', a sense in which it is still occasionally encountered. The transition of society from a term describing something we seek to something we find ourselves in is well described by Williams.[1] Today, it is generally used to describe the totality of social relations, social organizations, and social **institutions** at the broadest level, which usually coincides with that of a **nation**. Society, however, acknowledges greater variation and change than nation; we can easily talk of French society in the inter-war years or Chinese society in the post-Mao years in a way we could not talk about the French or the Chinese nations. Society is also distinct from the state, which is used to refer to the institutions of government and **politics**. This distinction is further accentuated by the term 'civil society' which is used to include all non-governmental institutions, organizations, networks, and practices, including professional associations and trade unions, charities and faith-based organizations,

---

[1] Williams, 1976, pp. 292 ff.

advocacy and community groups, cooperatives and clubs.

A further influential distinction was proposed by German sociologist Ferdinand Tönnies between two forms of human association that he termed community and society, or *Gemeinschaft* and *Gesellschaft*.[1] Community involves a relative small association of individuals, held together by strong communal bonds, with shared **values** and beliefs, where individual self-interest is subordinated to maintaining good group relations. Society, on the other hand, tends to be a larger and more impersonal association of people, with diverse values and beliefs, whose actions tend to be driven by self-interest. If tradition is dominant in community, **rationality** assumes ever-increasing importance in society. Tönnies viewed the transition from traditional society to **modernity** as marking an irreversible shift from community to society, a view broadly in line with that of other contemporary sociologists, namely Weber, Durkheim, and Simmel.

The word society is very easy to use, especially when qualified by an adjective, for example, consumer society, class (or classless) society, multicultural society, free society, or network society. It is then helpful in drawing attention to some feature or quality that distinguishes one particular society from another. Part of the strength of the term lies in its ability to silence or keep in check all kinds of tensions and ambiguities. In talking about 'information society', for example, one does not have to specify what the boundaries of this society may be, whether it is national or international, whether it affects different groups or social classes differently, when it started or when it will finish. Furthermore, one does not have to explain whether an information society is consistent or compatible with a free society, a class society, or any other type of society one cares to speculate about.

Less comfortable is the use of society as an agent or as an actor. 'Society decided to abolish the death penalty' begs the question of who exactly made the decision, through what procedures, and with how much support. Jared Diamond's deliberately provocative title for his book *Collapse: how societies choose to fail or succeed* draws attention to this very point.[2] On the other hand, society is comfortably held responsible for needs and failures, for example, in sentences like 'societies seek to protect themselves from deviants' and 'society is to blame for the educational failure of children from poor homes' (the type of statement that Margaret Thatcher sought to rebut by denying that there is 'such thing as society').

What then is society? In what ways can it be said to exist or not to exist? The founders of sociology, including Comte who coined the term 'sociology', Marx, Durkheim, Simmel, Tönnies, and, more ambivalently, Weber, were in no doubt. Society exists as a distinct and sovereign entity over and above the individuals and the **institutions** that make it up. It has properties of its own, institutions of its own, and can be studied as having specific laws that govern it. Individuals draw most of their characteristics, beliefs, practices, and behaviours from the societies in which they live and the **roles** they play in these societies. Indeed, to the extent that they experience themselves as individuals, this is because of the individualistic **values** of the societies that they inhabit. This approach was embraced by most traditions in sociology, notably those that have approached society as a **system**, including structural-functionalism as well as neo-Marxist and neo-Weberian traditions. However, the tradition known as *methodological individualism* begins with individuals and views entities like society, organizations, and so forth as the sum of individual transactions. This approach is represented in modern sociology by Jon Elster,[3] who looked at societies as nothing more than the individuals that inhabit them, their actions, and their social interactions with each other. This is a view towards which some theories of organization have leaned, by denying that organizations

---

[1] Tönnies, 1887/1963.   [2] Diamond, 2005.   [3] Elster, 1989.

exist as wholes, over and above their constituent components.

The interface between the individual and society is one that is approached from both sociological and psychological angles. Sociologists generally approach it through the concept of **socialization**, the process whereby individuals become part of a wider social whole and learn to act different social roles. Psychology, for its part, tends to approach it through the concept of **learning**, the ongoing process of interaction between an individual and his or her social environment that leads to changes in behaviour and habits or to the acquisition of new **knowledge**, **skills**, and **competencies** for dealing with different social situations.

At a deeper level, the relation between individual and society has been a core problem of political philosophy. Some traditions dating back to Aristotle view human beings as essentially social animals who could not live outside society and whose societies reflect their naturally gregarious nature. Others traditions, most notably that associated with Thomas Hobbes, approach individuals as by nature selfish, antisocial, and disputatious; society, and in particular the state, then, is a supra-individual entity, the product of a social contract or covenant, that seeks to tame and control individuals, enabling them to live together. In his social theories, Freud sought to bring these conflicting traditions closer together by arguing that each individual is both social and antisocial, and that society and the individual form part of a complex relation that involves both conflict and continuity.[1] The different parts of the mental **personality** reflect this complex relationship. The id, according to this conception, is entirely blind to all cultural requirements, solely preoccupied with providing gratification for each and every one of an individual's desires. The super-ego, with its slavish and uncritical devotion to external law, is society's representative within each individual. Finally, the ego is the harassed and constantly overstretched agent, forever struggling to control externality and to reconcile conflicting demands made by society, the id, and the super-ego.

Socio-technical systems

Everyone has had an experience of a piece of technology which promises a lot and then fails to deliver—it is too stupid, too clever, too simple, too complicated, too fast, too slow. Managers often face a situation where a new technology, purchased at great cost, disappoints at the level of its implementation. In the 1950s, social scientists became aware that technology introduced with scant regard for the users' skills, abilities, habits, and social relations generates **resistance**, which may range from erratic handling to absenteeism to sabotage. In a seminal article, Trist and Bamford explored the implications of the long-wall mining techniques in the recently nationalized coal mines of Great Britain and discovered that, in spite of their technical advantages over earlier methods, they severely disrupted work relations and work patterns.[2] Many features of the study are fascinating, not least the collaboration of an academic and a worker (Bamford was a miner) in the belief that the workplace could become a more humane place.

Socio-technical systems grew as a major tradition in industrial sociology, mostly through the work of scholars from the Tavistock Institute, but also social theorists like Joan Woodward and Lisl Klein who were interested in the effects of **technology** at the workplace.[3] The key insight of this approach was that technology (machines, automation, methods of work, etc.) and social relations at the workplace were not two interacting **systems**, but a single system. Far from being separate, technology and social relations each incorporate assumptions from the other.

Technology is not just machines and recipes, but is mediated through social practices, habits, and conventions; and social relations are

---

[1] Freud, 1927; 1930.   [2] Trist and Bamforth, 1951.   [3] Woodward, 1958; 1965; Klein, 1976.

themselves constructed through different available technologies. Thus, a mobile phone is not just a more convenient type of telephone, nor is a car a faster means of transport than a horse and carriage; different technologies are assimilated according to different cultural practices and make new types of social relations and practices possible. Socio-technical systems theorists argued that far too often managers are seduced by technological possibilities of automation without regard for the social realities of the workplace—hence the implementation of new techniques often backfires. Their concern was to harmonize technical possibilities and human needs in order both to enhance production and make work a more rewarding and creative activity.

The influence of socio-technical systems theory has declined in recent decades. This is due in part to the severe questioning of the concept of system by **complexity and chaos theories**. It is also due to the increased importance given to **language** and the **social construction of reality** that have created the mistaken impression that socio-technical systems represent an outpost of old-fashioned positivist research. Finally, it may be that socio-technical systems underestimated the importance of **power** relations at the workplace—much of resistance to new technologies, after all, is generated by people, groups, and organizations striving to maintain privileges and patches of **control** that would be eroded by new technologies. Yet, even without acknowledgement, the concerns of socio-technical systems have resurfaced in trumps in the last twenty years when the placing of a computer on every desk, the internet, and new telecommunication technologies confronted practitioners with almost identical problems to the ones that preoccupied production, construction, and mining managers in the 1950s and 1960s. All too often, **information technology** is introduced with scant regard for the needs, interests, skills, and habits of users, customers, and other stakeholders with negative consequences. This is evident when merged companies find it hard to integrate the information systems or when inferior systems persist due to the loyalty of their users. The currently fashionable term 'technology-in-use' has developed the core socio-technical systems insight that there is a world of difference between the intentions of those who design technological **innovations** and those who use them.

Spectacle

A spectacle can be thought of as a sight, an event, or a process that is capable of generating strong emotional or even **spiritual** experiences, primarily through its visual impact. Spectacles involve complex associations of **images** and pictures, often moving ones, sometimes accompanied by other stimuli, including voices, sounds, tastes, and smells. Some spectacles (especially those referred to as 'shows') are created by producers, choreographers, or other agents, for the benefit of spectators or audiences who may themselves be part of the show. Such agents include playwrights, television and theatrical producers, architects, designers, town planners, events organizers, museum curators, and so forth. Spectacles can trigger off **fantasies** and leave long-lasting effects on the way people construct their **identities**. Some spectacles can be nothing short of life-changing experiences.

It is now commonplace to argue that we live in the era of the spectacle. Spectacle dominates our lives. Some spectacles, like television shows, movies, dance, drama, sporting events, and so forth, are explicitly constructed as shows. But many of today's public spaces have turned into spectacles in their own right—shopping malls, tourist resorts, theme parts, museums, fancy buildings. But so too have shops, restaurants and cafés, city squares, and even ordinary streets. On close reflection, a spectacle is as much an attitude of mind as a part of some objective reality out there. It is an attitude of mind restlessly on the lookout for something beyond the mundane, the ordinary, and the everyday; it is an attitude of mind looking for **experiences**.

Spectacle is as old as **ritual**, with which it shares many qualities. Torture and executions were public spectacles for a large part of European history. The Greeks invented drama and sporting competitions; the Romans famously ended up spending nearly half of the days of the year in the arenas, earning Juvenal's reproach: 'People, who once handled military command, high civil office, legions—everything, now restrain themselves and anxiously hope for just two things, bread and circuses.' This admonishment was echoed nearly twenty centuries later in Guy Debord's situationist manifesto, 'In societies where modern conditions of production prevail, all life presents itself as an immense accumulation of *spectacles*. Everything that was directly lived has moved away into representation.'[1] Allowing for the obvious hyperbole and the parody of Marx, Debord was arguing that mature **capitalism** was replacing 'real' experiences with spectacle—instead of playing sport, we watch sport on our television sets, instead of falling in love, we watch actors falling in love on the screen, and instead of taking control over our lives we watch politicians shadow-boxing about who can best represent our interests. Thus 'things that were once directly lived are now lived by proxy'.

Many scholars that followed Debord, including Bauman, Ritzer, and Baudrillard, concur—spectacle has become the dominant type of experience in late modernity, dominating almost every aspect of public and private lives. Many, if not most, of our experiences are visual experiences, on television screens and computer monitors, on posters, newspapers, and magazines, in our city streets and our homes. Spectacle offers 'the promise of new, overwhelming, mind-boggling or spine-chilling, but always exhilarating experience'.[2] What has changed since the situationist critique of the 1960s is that today most theorists offer a more equivocal evaluation. Image and spectacle are not seen as invariably inducing passivity and stupefaction. Appropri-

ating images is far from a passive experience. As consumers in a society of spectacle, we are frequently seduced by image. But we also learn to mistrust image, to question and probe it. We develop skills to read and decode, question and ignore, frame and unframe, combine, dismiss, and ignore images.[3] These are the skills we apply when we visit museums, walk in the streets, or watch television, using the spectacles on offer creatively to produce our own images and identities.

The emergence of a society of spectacle has been fuelled by galloping new technologies making possible a hitherto undreamt-of production and reproduction of images, sounds, and texts of all types. It is also inexorably linked to the rise of **consumerism** and its cathedrals of consumption (see **Disney and Disneyization**).

The effect of spectacle on the nature of organizations has been far-reaching. Vast areas of the economy (including media, advertising, sport, movies, music, entertainment, theatre, and so forth) are directly in the business of producing spectacles, dispatching fantasies, and 'making dreams come true'. But in a society of spectacle, as the old saying goes, every business becomes showbusiness. Hotels, restaurants, cafés, bars, and shops become foci of spectacle and sources of fantasy as much as dispensers of material objects. Employees become members of casts, whose image, appearance, and emotional displays are a vital part of the organization on show (see **aesthetics**). Few companies selling to the public today can rely on producing and selling functional, serviceable products, unless 'functional' and 'serviceable' can become attributes of a brand or corporate image that renders them desirable in their own way. In an era of spectacle, image suffuses the whole character of organizations.

In an era dominated by spectacle, organizations themselves assume the character of spectacle. During the high noon of modernity, when solid bureaucratic organizations

---

[1] Debord, 1977, paragraph 1.   [2] Bauman, 1997, p. 181.   [3] Gabriel and Lang, 2006.

produced solid material things, Max Weber provided the metaphor of the 'iron cage' as an abiding image of rigid, rational, and entrapping organizations.[1] In an era of spectacle, when preoccupation with efficient production and rational administration increasingly gives way to a fixation on collective fantasies and the venting of collective emotions through the power of image, the iron cage may have been replaced by a glass cage. As a material generating, distorting, and disseminating images, glass seems uniquely able to evoke both the glitter and the fragility of organizations in late modernity. Glass dominates today's architecture as safely as steel and concrete dominated the architectures of the past (see **buildings and architecture**). Glass creates an emphasis on display, making constraints invisible; it offers a powerful illusion of choice, a glamorization of image, and an ironic question mark as to whether freedom lies inside or outside the glass. Above all, there is an ambiguity as to whether the glass is a medium of entrapment or a beautifying frame. Glass also stimulates new forms of **resistance**, such as whistle-blowing and subvertizing (the spoiling of a company's advertisements and logos in material artefacts, like posters, but also on the internet), that are particularly aimed at besmirching an organization's image and spoiling its brand.[2] It is not accidental that the fragility of the glass cage of late modernity has been most cruelly exposed by **terrorism**, a phenomenon that many have characterized as the ultimate contemporary spectacle.

• See also *image*

Spirituality

Spirituality refers commonly to the quest for deeper **meaning** in life, which is different from and perhaps goes beyond what is offered by institutionalized religion. In organizational contexts, as the **management of meaning** becomes a central **leadership** activity and meaning gets reduced to **sensemaking**, a focus on spirituality shifts attention back to the fundamental quest for meaning as a core dimension of human **experience**. Consequently, spirituality has been advanced as an important aspect of **work** and as a response to the crisis of meaning in organizations.[3] Proponents of spirituality suggest that a more spiritual workplace can generate meaning in today's turbulent organizational environments and offer solace for the painful experiences of **downsizing**, re-engineering, and job insecurity. Spirituality can provide a context in which employees discover a transcendental purpose in creating meaningful **narratives** about their work and life experiences. This, it is argued, is crucial for employee and organizational well-being.

This raises questions about the meaning of well-being and the purposes served when organizations introduce spirituality in their **discourses**. Critics have suggested that the introduction of spirituality in the materialist context of organizational **performance** at best commodifies spirituality, as evidenced by the burgeoning sales of spiritually oriented consulting or management development services, and, at worst, sanctifies capitalist production so that profit making becomes a transcendental and even sacred accomplishment (something that is not so dissimilar to Weber's conception of the Protestant **ethic**). Spirituality then becomes a tool to extract more effort from employees while imbuing existing **power** structures with an **ideology** of higher meaning that undermines individual or collective **resistance**.[4]

Many proponents of spiritual management suggest that supporting individuals in finding higher meaning in and through work is good for organizational performance and advance this as an important reason for legitimizing a field that may easily be dismissed as unscientific or irrelevant. It is easy then to see why spirituality is often critiqued as yet another instrument for domination and exploitation. Indeed

---

[1] Weber, 1958.   [2] Gabriel, 2005.   [3] Gull and Doh, 2004.   [4] Bell and Taylor, 2003.

one of the enduring tensions of the spirituality discourse is the idea that spirituality as the idiosyncratic search for non-economic, non-material, and non-instrumental meaning can or should be a tool for instrumental gain, i.e. that organizations enhance profitability when their members find spiritual fulfilment at work. While some have argued that spirituality should be rejected wholesale, others suggest that the search for meaning that goes beyond mere **sensemaking** is entitled to a space in organizations today, representing an important dimension of how some individuals construct their subjectivities at work.[1]

One of the key arguments for organizational spirituality is that work and organizations have **value** beyond economic exchanges, as spheres where human beings interpret and create life meanings as part of the human quest for meaning in general. Work spirituality then becomes part of the important discourse of individual life narratives but can also reveal how the search for meaning amounts to a **myth** or **fantasy** that continues to fail. To the extent that spirituality promises a union with a higher power, the integration of multiple and often conflicting aspects of **identity**, and the fulfilment of profound **desire**, it reflects an imaginary construction of **subjectivity** or an illusion that work and organizations can fill the lack that marks lived experience. Some suggest that this illusion makes the discourse of spirituality a target for misappropriation. Organizations are economic entities and exist in a capitalist space that is dominated by instrumental **reason**. To the extent that organizational spirituality hides the contradictions of capitalism or suggests that the individual can take responsibility for resolving them through a determined personal quest, spirituality becomes an instrument for **control**.

Other scholars have suggested that spirituality can be the basis of a discourse capable of exposing some of the contradictions of capitalism. In particular, it may offer a way of explaining the crisis of meaning by examining what is meaningful but also meaningless for the individual and how the quest for spiritual meaning reveals a lack that work and organizations can never fill. As such, the discourse of spirituality may provide a space in which to engage with the organization as a **fantasy** that necessarily fails. The higher purpose we seek turns out merely to enhance the **ideology** of the bottom line while the harmony and growth we strive for is reduced to work **motivation**. The discourse of spirituality in organizations can therefore provide a space in which dominant discourses may be contested; this is a space in which subjectivity at work is constructed through a struggle of the simultaneous failure to obtain a deeper meaning and a continuing desire and thirst for such meaning.

• See also *meaning, myth, sense and sensemaking*

MICHAELA DRIVER, UNIVERSITY OF AARHUS

Stakeholder

A stakeholder is a group or an individual which is seen as having some special interest or *stake* in an organization and its activities and can influence them in some way or other. Most organizations have core stakeholders, such as owners and shareholders, employees, suppliers, and government. Other possible stakeholders are customers, local communities, financial institutions, environmental protection groups, and political parties. Stakeholders in organizations may be drawn more or less widely, and decisions about who a company regards as its stakeholders often reflect its **values** and priorities.

A stakeholder perspective was put forward as a way of recognizing that **strategy** is shaped by multiple interests and concerns rather than a single objective, such as maximizing shareholder value. Managers need to map their key

---

[1] Driver, 2005; 2007.

stakeholders, consider their expectations and demands, their interrelationships, and their power to influence the organization's outcomes and reputation.[1] Stakeholder theory sometimes assumes the form of old-fashioned pluralism, viewing organizations as political arenas in which different interest groups (or stakeholders) seek to influence the outcomes. The field on which the game is being played is rarely level and the **power** with which stakeholders enter the game is rarely evenly matched. In these circumstances, stickholder may be a better metaphor than stakeholder. The bigger stick prevails.

Status

Status, like **role**, indicates a social position. Yet status goes beyond **role** as it embodies an evaluation of merit, prestige, or honour. Age, gender, education, social connections, and lifestyles are all important sources of status, though their precise significance differs across **cultures**. A person's job or occupation, usually referred to as 'socio-economic status', is an important source of status in Western cultures. Within organizations, **professionals** and clerical workers traditionally enjoyed superior status to manual workers. Status **symbols** are visible signs establishing an individual's or a group's status. A BMW as well as a Smart car can be status symbols, as are the size of an executive's office, a fashionable pair of running shoes, a title such as Sir or Dr, an address in a fashionable part of town, or a badge on a piece of clothing.

Status is an important category in both sociology and ethnography. Following Max Weber, sociology has viewed status, along with **class** and **power**, as the major principles of social stratification. Status interacts with class and power, but has also an independent effect in determining an individual's position on different social ladders. **Ethnography** distinguishes between *ascribed status* that individuals acquire by virtue of their birth or social attributes (e.g. first born, woman, etc.) and *achieved status*, the status that individuals attain through their own efforts (e.g. successful entrepreneur, world-class athlete). The Indian caste system represents a system of ascribed status, while most forms of education aim at enhancing a person's achieved status. Ascribed and achieved status often interact and enhance each other. Status inconsistency occurs when an individual or group is differently ranked on different status scales—drug dealers, for example, may enjoy an ostentatious level of consumption that accords them status, though the source of their wealth is generally viewed with derision.

Status is no longer as widely used a concept in the social sciences as it used to be. Some aspects of status have been subsumed by other categories, such as **image**, **identity**, and cultural and educational **capital**. The declining interest in social status may reflect the collapse of deference to traditional status criteria associated with birth, lineage, and class. It would be wrong, however, to dismiss the concept as no longer relevant or useful. Consumer society prospers on competition for status and status distinctions brought about by different lifestyles and consumption patterns. Early theorists of **fashion** like Simmel and Veblen were in no doubt that fashion was driven by individuals' thirst for status—people sought to raise themselves above their peers by adopting the new fashion trends (differentiation from 'the masses') or tried to catch up in the status race by imitating the trend-setters.[2] Both of these theorists were keenly aware that fashion created anxiety and discontent; it created victims.

Some more recent commentators on fashion have taken a more optimistic view, arguing that today's proliferation of consumer goods, images, and symbols allows each and every individual to create their own unique identity, without antagonizing others. Thus, Bauman argues that status ceases to be a scarce resource in today's

---

[1] Freeman, 1984; Mitroff, 1984.   [2] Simmel, 1904/1971; Veblen, 1899/1925.

consumerist society. 'In the game of consumer freedom all customers may be winners at the same time. Identities are not scarce goods. If anything their supply tends to be excessive, as the overabundance of any image is bound to detract from its value as a symbol of individual uniqueness. Devaluation of an image is never a disaster, however, as discarded images are immediately followed by new ones, as yet not too common, so that self-construction may start again, hopeful as ever to attain its purpose: the creation of unique selfhood.'[1]

Others have not been so optimistic. In their provocative *Cool rules: anatomy of an attitude*, Pountain and Robins have described a 'Cool Ethic' emerging from the decomposition of the Protestant ethic which glorifies rebellious hedonism, ironic detachment, and nihilistic **narcissism**.[2] Cool, argue Pountain and Robins, is the dominant **ethic** of youth culture in Western societies, liquefying all other status hierarchies into the single pecking order of cool. 'Cool is an oppositional attitude adopted by individuals or small groups to express defiance to authority—whether that of the parent, the teacher, the police, the boss or the prison warden. Put more succinctly, we see Cool as a *permanent* state of *private* rebellion.'[3] Being cool emerges as the royal road to status, whether one is a musician, a drug dealer, or simply a smart dresser. Cool has its origins in earlier societies but reaches its apogee in hyper-individualistic, highly competitive, celebrity-obsessed, and consumerist Western cultures. Cool, even more than **sex**, becomes the fuel of consumer society, **advertising**, and branding. 'Cool is still in love with cigarettes, booze and drugs. It still loves the sharp clothes and haircuts, but has discovered a preference for winners over losers. It still loves the night, and flirts with living on the edge.'[4] Cool (like other status attributes) creates victims. In addition to losers in the status stakes, it all too often creates physical victims too—victims of nihilistic crime. If you cannot win, then refuse to play the game

by dismissing it as uncool or even by stopping others from playing it by knifing them in a street fight or by taking a firearm to the university campus.

Stereotypes and stereotyping

This term was introduced by the journalist Walter Lippman in 1922, who described stereotypes as 'pictures in our heads'. Stereotypes were seen by Wilson and Rosenfeld as 'clusters of preconceived notions'.[5] Stereotyping assumes that all the objects in some category share other characteristics. As crude negative generalizations about **groups** of people, stereotypes are part of the stock in trade of comics. They can then become the basis of prejudice and **discrimination**, acting as self-reinforcing vicious circles. The person who stereotypes tends to notice all confirming instances and discard all contradicting evidence; and the person or group who are stereotyped frequently find themselves entrapped—trying to break out of the stereotype frequently ends up reinforcing it in the eyes of the perpetrator. It is for this reason that stereotypes have been rightly criticized, most especially from advocates of **political correctness**. At times, to stereotype someone is viewed as a worse sin than exploiting them economically or oppressing them politically.[6]

Stereotyping has been linked to dysfunctional groups lapsing into **groupthink** and to **authoritarian** personalities. In these situations, negative stereotyping of the **Other** can function as a wish-fulfilling illusion, reinforcing belief in the superiority of one's own individual or group identity. Stereotyping one's rival as stupid, incompetent, or cowardly can then lead to disastrous decisions in business, politics, and other spheres of life. Yet it is doubtful whether anyone can escape altogether from the tendency to stereotype. Making judgements requires some generalized assumptions, explicit or implicit. Some stereotypes function in an **unconscious**

---

[1] Bauman, 1988, p. 63.   [2] Pountain and Robins, 2000.   [3] Ibid. 20.   [4] Ibid. 13.   [5] Wilson and Rosenfeld, 1990.   [6] Martinko, 1995.

way as cognitive shortcuts, enabling people to make sense of the complexities of the world and helping them make judgements and decisions quickly and even efficiently. Many qualities of intuition or 'gut feeling' displayed by leaders and others may be rooted in such unconscious stereotypes. Nor are all stereotypes negative—a decision to trust somebody or to go to someone's aid may be the result of positive evaluations that we draw on the basis of external characteristics. Ideally, one would try to replace stereotypes with more sound generalizations but this is not always possible. While it is difficult to escape from the hold of stereotypes, we can still maintain a critical and vigilant attitude over our generalizations, seeking to question and qualify them.

• See also *discrimination*

Story and storytelling

Storytelling has long been a feature of human societies, groups, and organizations. Stories are pithy **narratives** with plots, characters, and twists that can be full of **meaning**. While some stories may be pure fiction, others are inspired by actual events. Their relation to events, however, is tenuous—in stories, accuracy is often sacrificed for effect. Stories pass moral judgements on events, casting their protagonists in roles like hero, villain, fool, and victim. They are capable of stimulating strong **emotions** of sympathy, anger, fear, anxiety, and so forth.

Stories along with **myths** and other narratives have long been studied by ethnographers as vital ingredients of culture. In pre-literate cultures, stories represented the collective memory of communities, the legacy that passed from one generation to the next; they entertained, explained, informed, advised, warned, and educated. The rise of **modernity** seemed to sound the death knell of stories and storytelling for many theorists. The emergence of different forms of

entertainment, of electric light, and of different media of communication seemed to consign storytelling to the margins of society, the preserve of folklore. The simultaneous emphasis on **rationality**, factual accuracy, and verifiability, the rise of science and evidence-based knowledge, it was thought, would strike a further blow to stories as reservoirs of meaning and **knowledge**. Writing in the inter-war years, the great German scholar Walter Benjamin could view the storyteller as 'something remote from us and something that is getting ever more distant'.[1]

If modernity was composing requiems for stories and storytelling, **postmodernism** has rediscovered stories and storytelling in virtually every text, sign, and object. Journalists, politicians, scientists, consultants, managers, advertisers, impresarios, are all after 'stories'. Advertisements, material objects (including all commodities, branded and unbranded), images of all sorts, human bodies (especially as pierced, tattooed, and surgically modified), consultants' reports and performance appraisals, official documents and works of art, legal arguments and scientific 'theories' are viewed as stories. Of course, these stories are not like the stories told by the fireplace over long winter evenings, but they carry emotion, they carry meaning, and are richly symbolic. As Kearney has argued, 'old stories are giving way to new ones, more multiplotted, multi-vocal and multi-media. And these new stories are often, as we know, truncated or parodied to the point of being called micronarratives or post-narratives.'[2]

Industrial psychologists and sociologists were relatively slow in becoming interested in the stories told in and about organizations. Occasionally using stories as vignettes to support arguments, they shunned them as research material, in favour of other, more reliable forms of 'data', like questionnaires, interviews, and experiments. In a very early and visionary contribution, Mitroff and Kilmann drew attention to the importance of stories that managers tell

[1] Benjamin, 1968, p. 83.   [2] Kearney, 2002, p. 126.

which capture the unique qualities of an organization and serve as repositories of meaning.[1] *Even if not true*, stories can reveal people's deeper feelings about their organizations, their ambitions, disappointments, and grievances. Early contributions noted that stories in organizations (like their counterparts in folklore) revolve around a relatively small range of themes,[2] that they often act as cognitive maps assisting organizational **sensemaking**,[3] and that they can act as instruments of **control** encouraging compliance to an organization's norms and values.[4]

Research on organizational storytelling has accelerated considerably since the 1990s when stories started to make regular appearances as 'data' for organizational analysis, seeming to open windows into the cultural, political, and emotional lives of organizations. There are numerous uses to which storytelling has been put by theorists of organizations, including

1. stories as a part of an organization's sensemaking apparatus;
2. stories as crucial aspects of individual cognitive functioning and sensemaking;
3. stories as features of organizational **politics**, attempts at **control** and **resistance;**
4. stories as symbolic artefacts expressing deep mythological archetypes;
5. stories as rhetorical performances aimed at influencing hearts and minds;
6. stories as means of sharing, disseminating, and contesting knowledge and **learning;**
7. stories as vital ways of constructing individual and group **identities.**

Extensive contributions to the study of stories in organizations have been made by Boje, Czarniawska, Gabriel, Sims, Brown, and many more (for overviews, see Rhodes and Gabriel[5]). Boje has offered powerful accounts of organizations as storytelling systems, noting that stories in organizations tend to be multi-authored, terse,

fluid, polysemic (they contain multiple meanings), and are frequently unfinished.[6] His is a postmodern approach; in postmodern times stories become fragmented, disrupted, and even incoherent. For Boje, a story does not exist outside the moment that it is told; there is no fixed text, or plot, or characters; a story is 'an oral or written performance involving two or more people interpreting past or anticipated **experience**'.[7]

More recently, Boje has become concerned about attempts by large corporations to silence stories that they disapprove of and has proposed the concept of 'antenarrative'—a 'fragmented, non-linear, incoherent, collective, *unplotted*, and pre-narrative speculation, a bet, . . . a wager that a proper narrative can be constituted'.[8] Czarniawska and Gabriel, on the other hand, have tended to look at stories, *even organizational stories*, as having plots, characters, and relatively stable, if contested, meanings. In several of her works, Czarniawska has argued that even some most unstory-like texts, such as scientific theories and consultants' reports, can be seen as having underlying plot structures.[9]

In my own work, I have offered perhaps the most conservative (in the sense that it may be equally applied to folkloric and workplace narratives) definition of stories as 'narratives with plots and characters, generating emotion in narrator and audience, through a poetic elaboration of symbolic material. This material may be a product of fantasy or experience, including an experience of earlier narratives. Story plots entail conflicts, predicaments, trials and crises which call for choices, decisions, actions and interactions, whose actual outcomes are often at odds with the characters' intentions and purposes'.[10] Using this approach, I have sought to study a wide range of organizational phenomena, including leader–follower relations, group relations, insults and apologies, illness and suffering, and the user–technology interface.[11]

---

[1] Mitroff and Kilmann, 1975.   [2] Martin et al., 1983.   [3] Wilkins, 1984.   [4] Wilkins, 1983.   [5] Rhodes and Brown, 2005; Gabriel, 2004b.   [6] Boje, 1991; 1994; 1995.   [7] Boje, 1991, p. 111.   [8] Boje, 2001, p. 1, emphasis added.   [9] Czarniawska, 1997; 1999; 2004.   [10] Gabriel, 2000, p. 239.   [11] See e.g. Gabriel 1991; 1993; 1997.

Sims, Brown, and several others have studied stories in connection with the formation of individual and organizational identities. Sims has examined how individual identities are constructed, undermined, and contested as 'we create stories about ourselves and our situation, and then proceed to live out some of them. Some of the stories we create, however, are contested, denied or simply ignored by others. We are on the verge of living out a story which features a major victory, a pinnacle to our achievements, or a rescue of some deserving cause, when someone else shows total disdain for our narrative of our lives by walking roughshod over the story we are creating.'[1] Brown and his colleagues have carried out extensive researches on the interpenetration of individual and collective identities.[2] They look at identities as complex and precarious narrative accomplishments and instead of simplifying this complexity argue for a fluid and multiple conception of identity.

In recent years, numerous organizational **consultants** have turned to stories as vehicles for enhancing organizational communication, performance and learning, as well as the management of **change**. While the success of these approaches is qualified, there can be little doubt that, in the hands of imaginative leaders, educators, gurus, and prophets, stories are powerful devices for **managing meaning**. Among many authors who have offered practical advice to managers and leaders on how to best use stories to enhance their effectiveness, Armstrong's and Denning's work has been rightly influential.[3] A few authors, like Snowden,[4] have brought together the academic and practitioner perspectives by using sophisticated story-based research to enhance management systems and especially the machine–human interface.

The study of stories in organizational settings is still in its early stages. There is a possibility that interest in using stories as management tools may prove little more than a management **fad** **and fashion**, but the use of stories as research material is likely to accelerate as the recognition of their importance broadens.

Strategy

In organizational terms, strategy refers to a planned series of **actions** taken to achieve a predefined end or set of ends. Examples of strategic ends might include such things as maximizing the profitability of a given product/service in a given market, increasing the return on investment in a public service, or reducing poverty in a geographical region according to specifically defined criteria. Planned collective or individual actions taken in pursuit of general ends will also form part of a strategic response. With increased usage, the coinage of strategy has arguably become devalued. There is often confusion between what might properly be called competitive tactics and truly strategic thinking. For example, a marketing plan might now be referred to as a marketing strategy. The powerful connotations of the term strategy are often appropriated simply to lend routine organizational activities an air of importance.

As a discipline, strategic management exists at the intersection of theory and practice. There is considerable debate within both academic and practitioner communities over the applicability and efficacy of contrasting models of strategic planning. In establishing a strategic relationship between means and ends, however, executives typically engage in a range of activities that fall under a general rubric of strategy formulation. These include: evaluating the organization's capability through an audit of its relative strengths and weaknesses; scanning the competitive **environment** for perceived opportunities and threats; devising a specific set of objectives based on strategic analysis; establishing a plan for meeting these objectives;

---

[1] Sims, 2003, p. 1196.　　[2] See e.g. Brown, 2006; Brown and Humphreys, 2006; Brown, Humphreys, and Gurney, 2005.　　[3] Armstrong, 1992; Denning, 2000; 2005.　　[4] Snowden, 2001; 2002.

communicating that plan to organizational members; and implementing and monitoring adherence to the plan.[1]

Despite a growing body of critical theoretical and empirical dissent, mainstream models of strategic management are predominantly linear and rational in form. This linearity and rationality derive from strategy's complex historical heritage and are the outcome of a command and control mindset combined with assumptions drawn from neoclassical economics and game theory. Deriving from the Greek 'στρατός' = army, strategy refers historically to the office of a general. Devising corporate strategy has traditionally been the prerogative of senior executives and is thus linked closely to the concept of leadership.

There is general consensus that modern strategic management originated in mid-twentieth-century game theorization of decisions during the Cold War nuclear weapon stand-off between Western liberal democracies and the former Soviet bloc. Early management writers on strategy used a **rational** institutionalist framework to theorize and prescribe corporate practice. Foremost amongst these writers is Alfred Chandler, whose book *Strategy and Structure* paved the way for the development of a new field of strategic management.[2] Chandler's classic volume promoted the dictum of '**structure** follows strategy', based on a universal claim about the evolution of multidivisional organizational form and centralized control under growth conditions. *Business Policy: Text and Cases* introduced what became a widely employed pragmatic technique known as SWOT (Strengths, Weaknesses, Opportunities, and Threats) to assist in the development of strategic choice,[3] while Igor Ansoff's *Corporate Strategy* took as its focus a more mechanistic and systematic analysis of such factors as competitive advantage, synergy, growth, and product markets in order to help determine

future strategic choices.[4] The emphasis during this period of early development was on the relative 'fit' between the organization's capability (SW) and its environment (OT).

The 1970s and 1980s saw institutionalist-based strategic management supplanted by thinking rooted in industrial organization economics. One of the most influential contributions came from Michael Porter, whose *Competitive Strategy* (1980) advanced a 'five forces' model of the relationship between the firm and its competitive environment.[5] The forces analysed were suppliers, competitors, the availability of substitutes, potential entrants, and customers. Later in the decade Porter also introduced 'value chain analysis' to help organizations explore the revenue-generating potential of each link in the vertical line of business activities. This enabled firms better to discriminate between profitable activities that could be considered core and others which had the potential to be outsourced. More recently Hamel and Prahalad have popularized the case for organizational resources and capability, particularly '**knowledge**', being the foundation on which to generate strategy.[6] The emphasis has moved away from the determinism of the environment toward the volitional and innovative potentialities available *within* the organization.

Although arguably neoclassical economics is the discipline that has most dominated the mainstream of strategic management, scholars working within other disciplines, such as history, political science, sociology, and psychology, have also influenced debate. Over four decades, these various perspectives have helped the pendulum of debate swing between a series of oppositions: environmental determinism versus organizational agency, planned versus emergent strategy, structure versus process, 'fit' versus 'capability', a priori theory versus empirical case analysis. Critical voices from inside and outside the field have raised concerns about the

---

[1] Helms, 2000, p. 885.   [2] Chandler, 1962.   [3] Christensen et al., 1965/1973.   [4] Ansoff, 1965.   [5] Porter, 1980.   [6] Hamel and Prahalad, 1994.

determinism inherent in economic analysis of strategy and its uncritical **ideological** bias toward capitalist exploitation and unfettered global competition. Others have argued that the field is ethnocentric and lacks critical reflexivity. The privilege accorded to economic rationality and aggressive competitiveness within mainstream strategic management and the simultaneous downplaying of non-rational and softer sides of organizational process give it a predominantly masculine complexion.

Accusations of elitism, obsessive competitiveness, and ethnocentrism coupled with the inherently bellicose connotations of strategic language raise questions about the future efficacy and value of strategic management. In a world facing geopolitical crises caused by global warming, pollution, and overpopulation and needing desperately to discover forms of **political economy** that will promote peace and **sustainability**, might the very concept of strategy eventually find itself moribund? Might an alternative language emerge connoting and valorizing collaboration, partnership, networking, and non-rational systemic complexity? It seems unlikely. Insofar as political power resides with the West and liberal democratic capitalism acts as a global talisman to so-called developing nations, the prospects are not encouraging. Even were there to be a longer-term shift toward new hybrid forms of capitalism emerging from China and the Indian subcontinent, a **masculine** conception of competitive strategy looks almost certain to survive and prosper.

PETER CASE, UNIVERSITY OF WEST OF ENGLAND

Stress

Stress is a widely used term referring to unpleasant **feelings** and/or physical responses that people experience when they are working or living, for a prolonged period, beyond their capacities and levels of coping. The symptoms of stress include *psychological* ones, like **anxiety**, irritability, fear, depression, and panic attacks, *behav-*

ioural ones, like drugs and alcohol abuse, nervous twitches, and eating disorders, and *physiological* ones including skin ailments, high blood pressure, gastric complaints, heart disease, and a variety of psychosomatic disorders. There is a huge literature on stress, its measurement, its symptoms, its causes, its management and prevention. A considerable part of this literature comes from medical researchers who have explored the changes brought about by stress on the body's functioning, its effects on the nervous, endocrine, immune, and other systems. Other researchers have looked at the psychology of stress as well as its organizational and social manifestations.

Certain work situations are potentially more stressful than others. These may include high levels of noise, poorly designed equipment, conflicting **role** demands, very high work loads, poor support and supervision, and unpredictable **changes**. Responsibility for other people rather than 'things' (machines, equipment) can be particularly stressful. One approach to stress management, therefore, lies in improving the design and supervision of work. But the mechanisms of stress and coping with stress are also peculiar to the individual. One person's source of stress can be another's challenge. Stress, therefore, also, depends on a person's perception of how threatening a particular problem or situation is, physically, emotionally, or set against his or her capacities to cope. Long periods of unresolved stress can lead to burn-out and play a part in disabling or fatal diseases.

In recent years it has become acceptable and even fashionable to talk openly about stress problems, and stress has become something of an institutionalized problem in society. It is a cause of litigation for individuals who feel that their organization has put unreasonable demands on them. Consequently, company-based stress management programmes and counselling support have become more prevalent. This 'stress culture' has generated much debate and controversy, dividing commentators. Some regard it as recognition, at last, of the afflictions caused by modern organizations. Others take the view that stress has become fashionable, an excuse to view any organizational discontent as the fault of the employer.

In their conspectus of stress research, Cooper, Dewe, and Michael argue that many organizational initiatives to deal with stress tend to personalize the issue instead of dealing with it on a systematic level.[1] Their research suggests that this is of limited effectiveness; they advocate instead a holistic approach that looks at the totality of stressors within the working environment. Along with some other stress researchers,[2] they express serious concern about the way that the concept of stress itself imposes an outsider's definition with scant regard for the complexity of the employees' own **experiences** and their own definitions of stress. All in all, stress has emerged as an acceptable way whereby broadly positivist research deals with painful experiences, with emotions like anxiety, anger, and despair, without actually engaging with the experiences of individuals whose complex troubles are lumped under the concept of stress.

Structuration

Social scientists frequently introduce new words as fresh ways of conceptualizing different aspects of social reality. New words and old words with new meanings are especially common in management studies, where they can acquire cult status and offer themselves as panaceas for different organizational troubles. Consider, for instance, buzzwords like 're-engineering', 'blue ocean', or even the word 'buzzword' itself. Few of these neologisms have much staying power; they wax and wane as **fads and fashions** do. One term that has proved enduringly useful and influential has been structuration, proposed by British sociologist Anthony Giddens as an attempt to resolve a long-lasting tension in the social sciences between *structure* and *action*.[3] Theories

that emphasize **structure** tend to view individual actions as deriving from these structures (class relations, kinship systems, political and legal institutions, etc.), allowing little room for individual freedom and variation. Theories that emphasize **action**, on the other hand, show little recognition that these actions are constrained by social forces beyond the control of individuals. Giddens argued that social structures and human agency are locked in a relationship whereby structures are sustained and reproduced by individuals' routine actions. There is a similarity to the way **language** operates—its rules and grammar only exist when we use it, but we cannot use it in any way we please. Routines establish proper and improper uses and people react strongly when linguistic conventions are disregarded. In this way, structuration theory offers a plausible way of acknowledging human agency, **rationality**, **emotions**, and motives, while at the same time not overlooking the constraining influence of social structures.

The concept of structuration is currently finding an increasing range of applications in organizations. Two such applications involve organizational **technology** and organizational **discourse**. Yates and Orlikowski have advanced the view that organizational technologies involve two distinct dimensions, analogous to the duality of structure in Giddens's original theory.[4] 'Technology is *physically* constructed by actors working in a given social context, and technology is *socially* constructed by actors through the different meaning they attach to it and the various features they emphasize and use'.[5] Thus, while technologies (for instance, computers, mobile phones, security cameras, etc.) shape the actions of the people, they assume their meanings through the uses (and abuses) that people make of them, rather than through the proclamations of those who design and manufacture them. In a similar way, communication technologies generate new genres of communication

---

[1] Cooper, Dewe, and Michael, 2001.   [2] See e.g. Newton, Handy, and Fineman, 1995.   [3] Giddens, 1984.   [4] Orlikowski, 1992; Yates and Orlikowski, 1992.   [5] Orlikowski, 1992, p. 406, emphases added.

(e.g. the e-mail message, the PowerPoint presentation, etc.) that become institutionalized in new social practices but also assume their meaning through these practices. For example, PowerPoint does not merely replace blackboard and chalk or overhead transparencies in presentations and lectures, but redefines the nature of presentations and lectures and assumes its meaning through the actual uses to which it is put. Extending this approach, Heracleous and Hendry have argued that all forms of organizational discourse (including reports, presentations, conversations, and storytelling) can be viewed as a duality of communicative actions and structural properties, linked through the actors' interpretative schemes.[1]

Structure and structuralism

A structure is in the first place something that can support itself. A bridge or a building is a classic example of a structure. A structure can be *robust*, i.e. it can take a lot of weight without collapsing. It can also be *flexible*, inasmuch as the components can move relative to each other without breaking the structure's essential unity. By contrast, a structure can be *rigid*—strong as long as there is no movement. A structure can be *loose*—linked components but with each one enjoying a substantial degree of freedom.

The word structure applies to many different entities, including engineering structures, social structures, linguistic structures, musical structures, cell structures, and so forth. Many essays by students are criticized for lacking structure or losing sight of the larger structure, a failing that no doubt afflicts many of their teachers' lectures as well. An essay without structure is just a sequence of ideas and arguments with no interconnections and no sense of direction. Even if the ideas themselves are interesting or provocative, the absence of structure conspires against making sense of them.

The social sciences make extensive use of the concept of structure and an influential current in linguistics, narrative studies, ethnography, and sociology is referred to as *structuralism*. The common feature in different versions of structuralism is the view that relations between observable phenomena remain constant even when the phenomena themselves change. A simple but telling example of a structure can be observed on a plate of food. In typical Anglo-Saxon cultures, this may include a 'centrepiece' (meat, fish), a staple (rice, potatoes), and a lubricant (gravy, sauce).[2] This combination of ingredients may be observed in a wide range of foodstuffs. A sandwich, for example, is composed of bread (staple), butter (lubricant), and cheese (centrepiece). Different ingredients may change, by substituting ham for cheese or mayonnaise for butter, but the fundamental structure remains constant. If, however, one was presented with a plate that contained potatoes, bread, and pasta (three different staples) one would observe that the underlying structure had been violated.

Structures were used as a way of explaining many different phenomena in the human sciences, including kinship systems, linguistic forms, plot elements, social relations, and psychological agencies. While the origins of structuralism can be traced in the theories of Marx, Freud, and others, the widely recognized father of structuralism is the Swiss linguist Ferdinand de Saussure, whose ideas had a profound effect on numerous authors, including psychoanalyst Jacques Lacan, ethnographer Claude Lévi-Strauss, and others. Structuralism was dominant in the middle part of the twentieth century. It has since been criticized by and mutated into **poststructuralism**. One of the great strengths of structuralism was its ability to explain a bewildering variation of phenomena (including myths, kinship systems, linguistic and phonetic units, psychological and social phenomena) as permutations and variations of certain core and

---

[1] Heracleous and Hendry, 2000.   [2] Douglas, 1975a.

invariant patterns. Its enduring difficulty has been an inability to reconcile structure with the actual **actions** of classes, groups, and individuals that create, sustain, and sometimes overthrow existing structures. Hence, structuralism has been criticized for being *ahistorical* (i.e. disregarding the infinite variety of changing historical contexts that influence observable phenomena) and for favouring deterministic structural forces over the ability of individual people to act in mould-breaking ways.

Organizations have long been approached as structures. These approaches overlap with views of organizations as **systems**. A system is inconceivable without a structure that underlies the relations between its components. Organizations can then be seen as having a variety of structures, some formal, some informal. *Formal structures* refer to the way different parts and groups of the organizations relate to each other: some organizations are structured in geographical or product divisions, others in functional areas (such as marketing, finance, personnel, etc.). Matrix structures became popular in the 1980s and 1990s, involving two overlapping structural principles, for example, product and functional or product and geographical area. In addition to formal structures, organizations have long been seen as having *informal structures*, made up of networks, alliances, and informal groupings of different people as well as informal practices and habits that influence people's actions without being formally constituted or prescribed.

The optimal structure for different types of organizations is an issue that has long preoccupied management scholars and practitioners. **Contingency theories** sought to account for structural variations among different organizations, attributing such variations to different factors, such as size, **technology**, or organizational **environment**. By contrast, **strategy** scholars have approached structure as the result of deliberate strategic choices made by organizational

leaders guided by rationality. Finally, **institutional theorists** have looked at structure as subject to dynamics of imitation, differentiation, and experimentation. Along with many other management preferences, structures become the subject of **fads and fashions** with organizations undergoing constant bouts of restructuring as their leaders succumb to current views on the effectiveness of different types of structure.

Two widely debated issues in connection with organizational structures are, first, the move from rigid structures to more flexible ones, and, second, the effectiveness and costs of different 'restructurings'. The move to more flexible structures is frequently discussed in connection with what are viewed as increasingly competitive and unpredictable environments that make traditional **bureaucracies** less effective. Flexible organizational structures are often viewed as involving fuzzy inter-organizational boundaries, loosely defined roles and responsibilities, and a constant willingness to *restructure* as and when circumstances demand. Restructuring may involve **downsizing**, **outsourcing** different activities to other organizations, forming strategic alliances, as well as a constant cutting and pasting of organizational divisions, department, products, and sites, brought about by merger and acquisition activity. The human costs of restructurings in lost jobs, broken lives, and constant insecurity have generated a substantial academic literature of their own.[1]

• See also *bureaucracy, change, contingency theories, hierarchy, structuration, system*

Subject and subjectivity

Subject comes from the Latin *subjectum* which refers to something that lies underneath, an undercarriage. This origin of the term can still be discerned in the passive use of the term ('flights are subject to delays') and its traditional

---

[1] Ehrenreich, 2005; Sennett, 1998; Stein, 2001; Uchitelle, 2006.

appearance in politics ('the Queen's or British subjects'). It is also apparent in the use of the term as synonymous to 'topic' ('Let's change the subject'). In grammar, the subject of a sentence is the bearer of a property ('*Confucius* was wise'), the originator or undertaker of an action ('*Mother Theresa* helped the poor') or, when passive voice is used, the sufferer or target of an action ('*Poland* was conquered by Hitler'). What makes subject a rich, intriguing, and often confusing term is its juxtaposition to object and its more recent mutation into 'subjectivity'.

Raymond Williams offers a fascinating account of how the terms 'object' and 'subject' came to swap meanings at some point in the late seventeenth century shortly after the French philosopher René Descartes.[1] In its early use, the subject signified the physical substance of a dog, a ship, or a city 'out there' rather than its mental representation which was referred to as the object. This is exactly what we now refer to as the object, whereas the subject is used to denote the person, the mind, or the **self** that 'underlies' different perceptions and experiences. Thus we use the word 'objective' to indicate the qualities of an object irrespective of the attitudes, judgements, or tastes of the person who experiences it ('The table is square'); subjective, on the other hand, signifies the expression of a personal judgement ('This table is most attractive'). Objectivity becomes a desirable principle in judgements of culpability ('He was guilty of blackmail'), merit ('Her superlative performance won her first prize'), and values ('Tolerance is the basis of a multicultural society') as against subjective judgements which are based on personal attitudes, caprices, and prejudices. Countless arguments, mostly inconclusive, stem from the question of whether a judgement is objective or subjective. Students, for example, may feel that their work earned low marks not on its merits but because of the teacher's biases; artists may feel that the public rejected their work because they failed to appreciate its 'true' value.

If objectivity is a desirable quality in making judgements on issues of importance, subjectivity has assumed an entirely unconnected meaning—it has come to signify the quality of being a 'sovereign subject' or, in other words, a sentient and conscious **self**, capable of making judgements and **choices** and acting in a coherent, purposeful manner. In a curious way, the term subjectivity has become extremely popular because of the perceived difficulties and contradictions that people experience in constructing themselves as subjects and the sustained critique of the concept of sovereign subject. This is due in a large measure to the work of three very influential French theorists, Jacques Lacan, Louis Althusser, and Michel Foucault, who have in their different ways contributed to a 'decentring' of the subject. The subject, instead of being the centre of consciousness, **experience**, and **action**, emerges from their work as the *outcome* of discourse; instead of being the source of **meaning**, it becomes the product of meaning. Thus Lacan viewed the subject as an unconscious structure, being recognized in the gaze of the other, Althusser argued that subjects are constituted through different types of ideology, and Foucault proclaimed the death of 'man', a discursive construct that had more or less come to the end of its existence.

The decentring of the subject from sovereign self to discursive product has been fruitfully exploited by several scholars from the **Critical Management Studies** tradition.[2] The large literature that has emerged (much of it based on empirical research in numerous different workplaces) has demonstrated the different and discreet ways in which organizations colonize the subject, leading to the construction of **identities** that consolidate management controls and reduce **resistance**. Thus, a subjectivity built around the theme of **career** becomes a project

[1] Williams, 1976.   [2] See e.g. Collinson, 1982; 1994; Fleming and Spicer, 2003; Knights, 1990; Knights and Willmott, 1989; Willmott, 1990.

of self-management, that is to say a managerial colonization of the self.[1] At the same time, scholars have tried to demonstrate ways in which the subject discovers different forms of **resistance** to management colonization, creating **unmanaged and unmanageable** places where recalcitrant subjectivities can be fashioned.[2]

Success and failure

Success denotes in the first instance the favourable outcome of an individual or group effort. Failure, on the other hand, is a disappointing outcome, one that fails to fulfil our hopes and expectations. The difference between success and failure sometimes can be marginal: a hundredth of a second may make the difference between success and failure in breaking a world record. It can also be a matter of judgement or expectations. A silver medal at the Olympic Games can be viewed as a failure if one was confidently expecting a gold; and a military defeat (like that sustained by the British in Dunkerque or the Russians in Borodino) can be viewed as a success, inasmuch as it allows the loser to fight another day. Claiming something to be a success or a failure requires judgements which are part of the **management of meaning**, the process whereby particular events are charged with significance.

Success and failure are important judgements as part of any **learning** process. 'Failure is the mother of success,' claims a wise Chinese proverb. But failure can also become the mother and grandmother of failure, if we fail to learn from our mistakes. All learning involves feedback loops—a comparison between the intended consequences of our **actions** and the actual consequences. Argyris and Schön,[3] two influential American learning theorists, have distinguished between two types of learning: single-loop learning and double-loop learning.

Single-loop learning recognizes a mistake or a failure and avoids it in future. But avoidance closes possibility. Raw potatoes taste bad; had humans stayed away from them they would have missed out on a nutritious and tasty product whose introduction to Europe revolutionized Western tastes and diets.

Double-loop learning involves understanding how an error or a failure comes about and using it as the basis of something new and creative. Some of the greatest inventions of humanity were the result of errors. Double-loop learning is the source of innovation—it seeks to redefine a problem or a disappointment into an opportunity or a challenge. In so doing, it releases the creative possibilities of error, necessary to turn failure into success. Fear of failure is one of the most serious obstacles to learning. Early failures that brought with them disappointment, anger, and humiliation are often catalysts blocking double-loop learning and instilling avoidance. Organizations that seek to enhance **innovation** and experimentation must be prepared to tolerate and even sanction failure. Without failure there can be no success.

More generally, success is a **value** whose meaning may vary from one culture to another. Who is a successful person? What is a successful organization? What is a successful nation? What are the sources of success? How can success be measured? Are there any values that are more important than success, and if so what? These are questions that would be answered differently by different cultures that view the meaning of success differently.

The meaning of success in Western cultures has long been dominated by what sociologist Max Weber described as the *Protestant ethic*. The Protestant ethic is a set of values that include hard work, frugality, entrepreneurship, cleanliness, and community-mindedness that were central to Protestant Christianity. Success, from this perspective, comes in the form of

---

[1] Grey, 1994.   [2] Gabriel, 1995.   [3] Argyris and Schön, 1978.

material prosperity, fame, and honour as a sign of God's favour and a reward for hard **work**. Protestantism, according to Max Weber, encouraged a methodical and calculating attitude in the pursuit of wealth, which provided **capitalism** with the work ethic required for its early growth in the sixteenth century.

Nowadays, success has lost its religious and moral underpinning; it is no longer seen by everybody as the result of hard work, nor is it seen as generating a set of responsibilities and duties towards the community. Instead, some people would regard success as the result of opportunism, clever deals, or good luck. Sociologist Neil J. Smelser has argued that for many people today success is synonymous with 'the myth of California'.[1] California, Smelser argues, represented a land where people 'escaped', a land that stood for what is new, for gold, for plenty, and the good life. In 'California', success does not follow hard work, deprivation, and heroism as it did for the early Protestants; instead, *success comes easily* through the magic of 'being discovered'. Everyone is seeking to get discovered; inventors, actors, authors, politicians, and so forth. This requires perseverance, self-presentation, **image**, and finding oneself in the right place at the right time.

Different people may still see success differently. Some individuals may gauge success in terms of visible signs and **symbols**, especially material possessions, money, and celebrity, while others may tend to assess it in terms of more personal indicators, such as contentment, happiness, or **love**. Yet today's mass culture, with its obsessive interest in the private lives of the rich, the powerful, and the famous, may be seen as one that systematically creates failure rather than success. It is difficult for anyone who fails to capture the limelight of the world's media to claim success. And anyone who briefly captures the attention of the media and then drifts out of it becomes a 'has been'. The fleeting,

media-centred nature of our notions of success today is well captured in Andy Warhol's famous statement in 1968 that 'in the future, everyone will be world-famous for 15 minutes'.

• See also *achievement, narcissism*

Sustainable development

The conventional meaning and definition of the term 'Sustainable Development' (SD) is usually ascribed to that given by the 1987 Brundtland Commission. This defined sustainable development as 'meeting the needs of the present without compromising the ability of future generations to meet their own **needs**'.[2] In fact the term had already emerged in environmental circles over the preceding decade, championed from the 1970s by development economist Barbara Ward and ecologist turned accountant Richard Sandbrook, two early British 'green' thinkers and researchers.[3] The term had policy currency already by 1983, when the UN General Assembly gave the terms of reference to the World Commission on Environment and Development to be chaired by the Norwegian public health doctor and former Prime Minister Gro Harlem Brundtland. Dr Brundtland and her colleagues were asked to 'propose long-term environmental strategies for achieving sustainable development to the year 2000 and beyond'.[4]

Underlying much sustainable development thinking is the fear that societies can collapse if they destroy their **environments**. This is not a new theme. Opponents and commentators on industrialization have long noted that brutal efficiencies come at a cost: destruction of nature, consolidation of inequalities, pollution of air, water, and food, degradation of habitat, etc. This pessimistic account of 'progress' is as old as industrialization; and, indeed, there is evidence of earlier societies destroying themselves by consuming their environments.[5] No civilization can

---

[1] Smelser, 1984; 1998a.   [2] Brundtland, 1987.   [3] Ward and Dubos, 1972.   [4] United Nations General Assembly, 1983.   [5] Diamond, 2005.

expect to feed itself, for example, if it fails to look after its soil; or be healthy if it pollutes its nest; or take pride in its living space if it has wrecked it.

Sustainable development has become a core term within an alternative perspective to classical capitalist notions of economic and social development, which saw—and still can see—nature as an infinite resource to be mined and accept hierarchies as inevitable. That world view seeks to exploit natural resources (alongside capital and labour) in order to create goods and services and charges economics and management to help organize that process on a rational basis. This package was questioned by the modern environmental movement which emerged in the 1960s. This was a reactive movement; it reacted to the despoliation of the environment, and spawned numerous organizations worldwide committed to protect the environment. Whether confronting pollution of the seas and waterways, or profligate waste from packaging, or felling of ancient forests, or the encroachment of wildernesses, this ambitious environmental movement by the 1970s had to face the fact that it needed to engage seriously with the meaning of progress. Was environmentalism about turning the clock back? If so, economics and mass consumer behaviour were against them. As the United Nations and all development bodies knew, such a position would consign over half the world to poverty and indignity.

The term sustainable development thus emerged as part of the liberal response to this intellectual and ideological problem. Sustainable development promised a different pathway for development, one which promoted social justice alongside protection of the environment for future generations, which aspired to build environmental and social externalities into sustainable economics. Policy and politics, viewed from the perspective of sustainable development, are to accord equal emphasis to the environment, society, and economy, three foci always to be found in any use of the term. Sustainable development was the riposte to critics of environmentalism who said this lacked any notion of progress. The debates about what sustainable development means are about alternative visions of how **society**, economy, and the environment can sustain life for many generations. Before evidence mounted about climate change, its appeal remained at the fringe rather than the mainstream. But the urgency of climate change and other looming ecological crises—water, oil, food, population—has given sustainable development core respectability.

Important sections of commerce had begun to engage with sustainable development long before the serious politics began. Indeed, the thinking behind sustainable development owes much to environmentalists engaging with big businesses after the early years of seeing them as the source of all problems. Twenty years of mutual hostility began to shift during the uneasy dialogue by the 1992 UN Conference on Environment & Development at Rio de Janeiro. There big business leaders who started to take the long view—unlike most politicians whose horizons are limited by electoral cycles—engaged with environmentalists who claimed the same territory. The language of sustainable development became one version of that dialogue which continues. In a world where oil may be peaking, where water shortages are a global threat, where climate change reminds everyone of the enormity of what two centuries of industrialization have done, sustainable development has become an ideological totem pole around which all can dance.

The term sustainable development now sits at the centre of a web of terms which are about how to manage the future differently and better. Sustainable development is an intellectual perspective which sees the environment as the infrastructure of life; proposes ecology as the science to help unlock interconnectedness of existence; takes long time horizons when making present decisions; centres on the local but takes a global geographical framework for events; situates human activity within millennia of planetary development; is conservative about the use of energy; celebrates and supports bio- and social **diversity**; and, in theory, is mindful about international justice when allocating and using resources.

In some ways, sustainable development has become a victim of its own success. Conceived as an alternative mode of conducting human life and our relationship with Planet Earth, it is now too often translated as a 'bolt-on' approach: first one designs enterprises around conventional efficiencies (i.e. taking little account of the environment, social justice, or ecological economics) and then one bolts on a token piece of 'greenery'. The politics of sustainable development began with global bodies' member states trying to chart a shared vision for our relationship to the earth. Today, that vision is in danger of being reduced to a matter of individual lifestyle **choices**: whether to use long-life, low-energy light bulbs which cost more; whether to drive a car or a bike; whether to fund a notional tree to be planted to offset the carbon emissions from taking an aeroplane flight; whether to consume only organic food (with hidden food miles); and so on. Sustainable development is more than that.

• See also *business ethics, environment, globalization*

TIM LANG, CITY UNIVERSITY

Symbolic Interactionism

Symbolic Interactionism has been a persistent and fairly influential school of thinking in the social sciences that is traced to the works of American philosopher and psychologist George Herbert Mead and his follower sociologist Herbert Blumer who coined the term.[1] It is an approach that, although never as popular as the **social construction of reality** with which it shares many points, has continued to influence scholars, most especially through the highly original studies of Erving Goffman.[2]

For symbolic interactionists, human beings are above all meaning-seeking and meaning-creating animals. Human **actions** are driven by the **meanings** that people attribute to them, to the actions of others, and to objects they bring into their lives. But these meanings are not fixed; they are constantly traded, tested, and qualified through social interactions. People, therefore, constantly interpret their own actions and those of other individuals and are constantly looking for meanings in every aspect of their experience. As the name suggests, symbolic interactionists are interested in the interaction between people, often examining very carefully individual conversations and other social transactions.[3]

Language is crucial for symbolic interactionists. Naming something (e.g. declaring 'this situation is a crisis') assigns meaning to a state of affairs that may then be tested through social interaction ('This crisis could easily turn into a disaster'). Thought can be viewed as conversation that one may have with oneself, through which meanings are tested and new **interpretations** can be discovered ('Maybe this crisis is a blessing in disguise, if it gives us an excuse to abandon this fated project at last!').

Symbolic Interactionism has influenced some theorists of organizations, including Karl Weick's theories of **sensemaking** and Arlie Hochschild's theory of **emotion**. It is an approach that has been criticized on three grounds. First, it tends to underestimate the importance of social **structures** in guiding and influencing social interaction. When a patient and a doctor interact in the course of a medical examination, they do not merely test each other's interpretations and meaning systems; they also enact their **roles** within social structures including professional, organizational, and social ones. Second, symbolic interactionists have a rather too civilized view of human beings, tending to underestimate violent urges, destructive tendencies, and irrational cravings. Inner conflicts, dramas, and dilemmas tend to be airbrushed out of the

---

[1] Blumer, 1969.   [2] Goffman, 1959; 1961.   [3] Denzin, 1992.

picture. Third, they tend to underestimate some of the **power** dynamics in society, organizations, and groups, as if people are free to create their own interpretations unencumbered by political considerations.

These criticisms do not seem altogether fair when applied to sophisticated uses of symbolic interaction theory. One such was pioneered by organizational theorist Iain Mangham, who combined it with a dramaturgical approach, to generate insightful accounts of the executive process and of power dynamics in the high echelons of organizations.[1] Mangham argued that power, emotion, and interpretation are all dimensions of the ongoing social process whereby different social actors seek to pursue and enhance their interests by managing meaning in advantageous ways to themselves.

• See also *social construction of reality*

Symbols and symbolism

A symbol is something that 'stands for' something else. A wedding ring is a symbol of love and loyalty. A national flag is a symbol of the nation, its freedom and independence. A symbol is a token. 'Symbol' comes from the Greek σύμβολον—the union of two separate things 'thrown' together. It is said that when two friends parted, they would break a ceramic tablet into two, each of them taking one part. When meeting, years later, they would put their parts together as evidence of who they were. The tablet was the 'symbol' or token of their friendship.

Symbols are a fundamental part of human life. Some scholars view humans as symbolic animals.[2] While a dog may recognize the whistle of his master, people alone among animals have created a vast symbolic universe of **meanings** that shapes their experiences and drives their actions. A dog may understand when his master tells him 'Don't!', but it is humans that invented

the concept of the negative. 'To look for negatives in nature would be as absurd as though you were to go out hunting for the square root of minus one. The negative is a function peculiar to symbol systems, quite as the square root of minus one is an implication of a certain mathematical symbol system.'[3]

Symbols are present everywhere. A tree, a table, a crow, a black cat, can become charged with meaning, 'standing for' something else. The products of culture, the clothes we wear, the food we eat, the tools we use, all have a symbolic dimension. The branded goods of our consumer culture are designed for what they stand for as much as, if not more than, for what they actually do. To own a car of a particular make, colour, and shape can give others a clear sign of the sort of person that one is. Similarly, the clothes we wear indicate our social **status**, our lifestyles, and so forth.

Language, that uniquely human faculty, is a massive symbolic edifice, enabling us to employ words, like 'chair', 'happiness', or 'never', to denote objects, concepts, and ideas. **Culture** itself can be viewed as an immense coding machine, one that enables us to read the meaning of individual entities in creating large symbolic chains. The words 'turkey and all the trimmings' stands for a particular configuration of dishes at a table that themselves stand for Christmas, a special event that takes place every year. Christmas itself stands for certain ideals, for presents, for indulgence, or, in some cultures, for an orgy of **consumerism**.

The study of symbols and symbolism is an important aspect of many human sciences, most especially ethnography, which has long sought to understand the symbols of different cultures, literary criticism, which has investigated the deeper meanings of literary texts (like *Moby Dick* or *Hamlet*), semiotics, which explores the relations between signs, sociology (especially **symbolic interactionist** and **social construction of reality** approaches), and **psychoanalysis**, which

---

[1] Mangham, 1986; 1988.   [2] Burke, 1966; Cassirer, 1943/1992.   [3] Burke, 1966, p. 9.

looks at the deeper meaning of different powerful symbols.

Some important distinctions have been proposed in our study of symbols. One is the distinction between sign and symbol; a sign represents a relatively fixed relation between a signifier (e.g. red light) and a signified (e.g. 'Stop!'). According to the view of linguist Ferdinand de Saussure the relation between signifier and signified is arbitrary;[1] it acquires its significance in relation to other links between signifiers and signifieds. There is no reason why 'red' means 'stop'; it assumes its significance in relation to green which means 'Go!' In other systems, green and red may have different meanings. In sailing, for instance, green indicates the starboard (right) side of the vessel and red the port side. A symbol, on the other hand, can have many different meanings, some of them motivated and others not. It is also more likely to generate **emotion** than a sign. The *Titanic* was the name (i.e. sign) of a ship, but it was also a symbol of its size and prowess. Following its demise during its maiden voyage, it assumed many other meanings, ranging from technological hubris to a society about to be destroyed by the onslaught of war.

A second important distinction is that between public and private symbols.[2] Public symbols are those shared by a wide **community** while private ones may be shared by very few individuals or even by a single person. Public symbols are usually attached to distinctions of status and power—they make visible statements about the person who wields them. Private symbols, on the other hand, have a meaning, often a powerful one, for one person that may not be shared by anyone else. Between public and private symbols, there is a broad area of translation—a particular novel may contain many different symbols but may have a specific significance for me. Both public and private symbols represent forms of encoding

and decoding meanings and they both require *interpretation.*[3]

A third important distinction is that between conscious and **unconscious** symbols. The symbolism of flags, words, and badges is conscious—people are conscious of what they stand for. Psychoanalysts, however, argued that there are symbols, for example those we encounter in dreams, in myths, and in neurotic symptoms, which are the visible tips of wholly unconscious processes. These symbols are the products of intra-psychic **conflict** between the repressing tendencies and repressed desires and ideas.[4] A particularly important form of unconscious symbolism is that contained in Jungian archetypes. These archetypes are regularly encountered in myths, stories, and narratives (characters like the Hero, the Great Mother, or the Trickster); they are highly charged unconscious phantasies that represent the collective symbolic heritage of humanity flowing through each and every human being.[5]

The study of organizational symbolism emerged as a serious field in the early 1980s when numerous scholars became interested in organizational culture.[6] Since then, a wide range of symbolic phenomena in organizations have received extensive attention, including **stories** and **narratives**, **buildings**, products, brands, logos, and documents. Organizations themselves are now viewed as *trading* in symbols and even as *being* symbols. The core business of many enterprises lies in maintaining the symbolic value of their brands, their products, and their logos. Organizations can themselves become powerful symbols. Inasmuch as organizations become institutions, i.e. objects of value, they are symbols. Thus, the National Health Service in Great Britain has come to symbolize the equal claims of all citizens (irrespective of wealth, status, or merit) to receive free medical treatment at the point of delivery. At a more unconscious level, this

---

[1] Saussure, 1960.   [2] Firth, 1973.   [3] Devereux, 1979.   [4] Hook, 1979; Jones, 1938.   [5] Jung, 1968.   [6] Gagliardi, 1990; Gioia, 1986; Hatch, 1997; Pondy et al., 1983; Turner, 1986.

service may stand as the symbol of the struggle to avoid pain, suffering, and death. Another organization, NASA (the National Aeronautics and Space Administration), has stood as the symbol of the US technological primacy and its pioneering spirit.[1] It is these deeper symbolic dimensions that turn organizations into **institutions**. The prospect of changing, neglecting, or (perish the thought!) closing such an organization is then liable to generate extreme hostility and anger since it is viewed as part of the way of life of a group or even a nation.

• See also *interpretation, meaning, ritual, sense and sensemaking, status*

System

The word system is used very widely today. It is applied to a wide range of phenomena, including the solar system, the ecosystem, the education, transport and other systems that make up a **society**, the cardio-vascular system and other biological systems, and so forth. Organizations are often seen as having a variety of systems from information systems to fire-fighting systems. And many physical objects are often referred to as systems, ranging from missile systems to skin rejuvenation systems.

System comes from the Greek word σύστημα which means 'standing together'. This captures well one key property of systems—the ability of different components to stand together in some *orderly relation* to each other. A stomach, an oesophagus, and a length of intestine do not make a digestive system, unless they are all linked together in the proper fashion. The orderly arrangements between the system's different parts are commonly referred to as the **structure**, a word that is sometimes used to describe the system as a whole. Another fundamental quality of systems is the possession of a **boundary** that separates them from the **environment**. Inputs and outputs are crossings of the boundary line, some controlled, some clandestine.

Organizations are often studied as systems, made up of different components, such as departments, divisions, and so forth, which can themselves be treated as sub-systems. An organization's inputs from the environment may include raw materials, expertise, and money, while its outputs may include products, services and waste. Its environment includes many other organizations that are in a position to influence its actions, including suppliers, customers, governments, and so forth.

Not all systems behave in the same way and not all relate to their environments in the same way. A mechanical system, like a clock, may be influenced by heat and humidity but does not generally respond to its environment. Biological systems, on the other hand, seek to establish and maintain an equilibrium with their environments, adapting to changing conditions, avoiding dangers, and trying to take advantage of opportunities. Unlike mechanical systems, biological systems appear to have a built-in need for self-preservation. Depending on what kind of system an organization is seen as, different qualities are drawn out. A Weberian theory of bureaucracy highlights the mechanical qualities of organizations, the ready replaceability of parts, their efficient interaction, and their indifference to environmental change.[2] A functionalist approach that draws heavily on the biological analogy highlights an organization's responsiveness to external threats and opportunities, its progression through different stages of growth and maturation, and its adaptiveness to an environment.[3]

Is it possible to study organizations *not* as systems? It may be difficult to completely purge a theory of organizations of all references to system-like qualities, but there are approaches that de-emphasize these qualities.

[1] Schwartz, 1988.   [2] Weber, 1946.   [3] Katz and Kahn, 1978; Parsons, 1951.

These are approaches that study organizations as terrains of **action**, interaction, and **conflict**. Organizations are then viewed as spaces where people create **meanings**, face choices, and experience **emotions**; where they interact with others, sometimes willingly and sometimes unwillingly; where they form alliances, make deals, and seek to outsmart their rivals; and where they seek to influence others through the **management of meaning** and emotion. These are features which are generally underplayed by systems theory. Instead of looking at organizations as fixed aspects of reality to be studied in an objective way, non-systems approaches look at organization as something created through people's actions and interactions, discussions and differences. Organization is the outcome of organizing, an outcome that requires much effort and work and cannot be taken for granted.

Recently, the systems approach has been reinvigorated as a result of the introduction of new ideas, especially from chaos, complexity, **structuration**, **autopoiesis**, and evolutionary theories, which have questioned many of the assumptions of traditional systems theory, notably fixed boundaries, adaptive relations to a given environment, and integrated internal functioning. These theories have introduced concepts like 'fuzzy boundaries', strange attractors, sensitivity to initial conditions, and, above all, absence of overall **control** which are forcing a radical reconceptualization of the idea of a system and its applications to organizations.[1]

• See also *boundaries, complexity and chaos theories, environment, socio-technical systems, structure and structuralism*

---

[1] Stacey, 1992; Thietart and Forgues, 1995; Tsoukas, 1998b.

Taylorism see **Scientific Management**

Teams and teamwork

Teams are particular types of **group** in which the successful completion of a task depends as much on the interaction between the team members as on how well they each perform their individual tasks. A football team, like Real Madrid's 'galacticos', may include the most gifted footballers in the world and yet it may lose a match to a less brilliant but better-coordinated, better-balanced, and better-motivated team. Being a team player who values the **performance** of the team above individual excellence is often seen as a desirable characteristic when applying for a job. Teamwork has come to be viewed as one of the most desirable qualities for organizational **success**. This is particularly due to the synergy and **creativity** that successful teamwork can stimulate.

It would not be an exaggeration to say that teamwork is now recognized as the mother (and father) of **innovation** and invention. A lone genius may have discovered relativity but it took a team of highly gifted people intensively collaborating on the Manhattan Project at the Los Alamos secret laboratory under the leadership of Robert Oppenheimer to produce nuclear weapons. It is now argued that most important innovations emerge through group process, as people combine their skills, cross-fertilizing ideas off each other and collectively resolving problems. Whether the outcome is a new advertising logo, a breakthrough in medical research, a pioneering software design, or the conquest of a mountain peak, it is now recognized that it is important to pool the talents of many

compatible individuals to unleash the force of the team.

It is not surprising then that team building has emerged as a favourite management topic. Innumerable conferences, workshops, and outdoor training activities are organized aimed at building teams, enhancing synergy and cooperation, learning to solve problems and overcome interpersonal rivalries. These group training programmes continue the legacy of older traditions, such as t-group and encounter groups which were very popular in the 1960s and 1970s. The common feature behind them is the belief that by immersing themselves in a team, individuals can

- □ have powerful experiences that profoundly alter their self-image and **identity**,
- □ discover immense potentials that they did not know were there,
- □ overcome huge inhibitions that keep them from growing and developing, and
- □ contribute to group achievements that would have been beyond their wildest dreams.

The undoubted achievements of successful teams sometimes obscure the formidable difficulties that many groups face in operating effectively as teams. Some of these difficulties lead teams to lapse into dysfunctional behaviour, such as **groupthink**, constant squabbling, free-riding, victimization, **bullying**, and scapegoating.

• See also *groups*

Technology

It is always tempting to think of technology, in the first place, as tools and machines, which

le or complex tasks economical way. A ...d a car are exam- ...ings become imme- ...at a piece of 'raw' ...nology—a rock can help us crack a nut as well as a nutcracker. Second, unless one knows how to use these tools or machines, they are useless objects. In order to use machines, we need recipes, techniques, know-how, and what, in connection with **information technology**, is described as software. These are also, therefore, aspects of technology. Some of these 'ways of doing things' may involve ways of using human beings, for instance, by placing them on an assembly line or by devising a system for 'lean production'— these are sometimes known as social technologies. But technologies do not have to be elaborate or complex. A bump on the road is quite a simple piece of technology forcing drivers to slow down, an effect that may alternatively be accomplished by a security camera, linked to an automated computerized register of cars and a highly sophisticated ticketing system.

Life without technology is hard to imagine. The Greeks believed that there was a time when human beings lived in abject ignorance, darkness, and misery. This was the time before Prometheus the Titan gave them fire and the arts and crafts of taking advantage of it. From then onwards, humans were able to enjoy warmth, light, protection, as well all the numerous advances that enabled them to mould nature to their needs and create culture. Prometheus paid a heavy price for disobeying Zeus. Nailed on Mount Caucasus he was visited daily by an eagle which tore at his liver. Karl Marx saw in Prometheus the story of human self-emancipation, but also the costs of that emancipation.

Technology has given people unprecedented powers and may be credited with numerous achievements. With the aid of technology, human beings can travel rapidly and cheaply to any part of the globe and communicate instantly with whomsoever they wish; they have irrigated deserts and are able to produce food in unimaginable quantities and varieties; they have filled supermarkets and shopping malls with every conceivable gadget and have provided themselves with a dazzling variety of **spectacles** and sights to keep them from getting bored; they have reached to the moon and beyond and are capable of physically destroying the planet in any number of ways. As Freud observed, with the aid of technology people have acquired those godlike qualities that Zeus sought to deny them. 'Man has, as it were, become a kind of prosthetic God. When he puts on all his auxiliary organs he is truly magnificent; but those organs have grown onto him and they still give him much trouble at times.'[1] The irony of this statement by a man whose jaw was held in place with a medical prosthesis is self-evident.

Has technology made us happier? Has it offered solutions to poverty, ignorance, and violence? Has it provided answers to the questions of meaning and value? The myth that technology provides the answers to everything is one that we find difficult to give up. Yet we have become increasingly disenchanted with our Promethean universe, its inability to feed two billion people on the planet, to stop millions of our fellow humans dying of preventable diseases, or to raise the living standards of nearly half of the world's population who live on less that $2 per day. We are alarmed about technological surveillance eroding our civil liberties, about technology's ability to decimate jobs, destroy ways of life, and nail people of all nations and all classes to mind-numbing alienating jobs; we are distressed that technologies of **violence** spread fear and despair in urban centres; and, increasingly, we have become painfully aware of the prospect of an environmental cataclusm brought about by climate change, desertification, pollution, and depletion of vital materials that could return

[1] Freud, 1930, p. 280.

future generations of humans to the bleakness of a pre-Promethean universe. This is why the story of Frankenstein's monster, the human creation that acquires a life of its own that threatens its former masters, remains such a potent one in relation to the risks and dangers of technology.

One of the enduring debates on technology concerns whether technology itself is to blame for the troubles that it brings to our lives or whether these are the results of 'abuses' that may be prevented through a more enlightened approach. This debate is regularly rehearsed in connection with different technologies, from television to hand guns. Lewis Mumford, the great American historian of science and technology, was firmly in the latter camp. He argued that

> capitalism utilized the machine, not to further social welfare, but to increase profit: mechanical instruments were used for aggrandizement of the ruling classes. It was because of capitalism that the handicraft industries in both Europe and other parts of the world were recklessly destroyed by machine products, even when the latter were inferior to the thing they replaced: for the prestige of improvement and success and power was with the machine, even when it improved nothing, even when technically speaking it was a failure. It was because of the possibilities of profit that the place of the machine was overemphasized and the degree of regimentation pushed beyond what was necessary to harmony or efficiency. It was because of certain traits in private capitalism that the machine—which was a neutral agent—has often seemed, and in fact has sometimes been, a malicious element in society, careless of human life, indifferent to human interests. The machine has suffered for the sins of capitalism; contrariwise, capitalism has often taken credit for the virtues of the machine.[1]

Mumford's deeply ambivalent admiration for technology was shared by economist Fritz Schumacher whose book *Small is Beautiful* has rightly become an emblem for advocates of **sustainable development**.[2] In it, Schumacher advocated a new ethos for technology, an ethos that eschews the gargantuan proportions of contemporary technology in favour of technologies on a human scale, which support communities and their ways of life. He referred to such technologies as 'intermediate'; they are now more widely referred to as 'appropriate'. Thus, a solar-powered or winding transistor radio can bring information and entertainment to millions of people with no access to electricity; low-cost computers can bring the benefits of education and communication to those who have been disenfranchised through poverty.

Much more pessimistic towards technology was the approach of scholars from a **critical theory** perspective, notably Horkheimer and Adorno and Marcuse,[3] who argued that Western rationality is based on fusions of exploitation and manipulation of nature as well as human beings; as Marcuse argued, 'technology serves to institute new, more effective, and more pleasant forms of social **control** and social cohesion...Technology as such cannot be isolated from the use to which it is put; the technological society is a system of domination which operates already in *the concept* and construction of techniques.'[4] From this perspective, **Taylorism**, **Fordism**, and **McDonaldization** represent not distortions of technological rationality but its natural materialization within societies and economies driven by profit.

• See also *actor network theory, contingency theories, information technology, socio-technical systems*

Technology-in-use

The concept of technology-in-use represents an attempt to dissolve the distinction between technology as instruments, machines, and recipes on the one hand and the actual uses to which

---

[1] Mumford, 1934, p. 27.   [2] Schumacher, 1973.   [3] Horkheimer and Adorno, 1947/1997; Marcuse, 1964.   [4] Marcuse, 1964, pp. xv, xvi, emphasis added.

it is put on the other. It represents a similar effort to Foucault's fusion of power and knowledge in a single concept power/knowledge,[1] and even more to Giddens's fusion of **action** and **structure** through the concept of structuration.[2] Thus Orlikowski argues that 'technology is physically constructed by actors working in a given social context, and technology is socially constructed by actors through the different meaning they attach to it and the various features they emphasize and use'.[3] This approach rejects the view of technology as a neutral external force that 'impacts' on social and economic activities and looks at it as an integral dimension of these activities. This is an approach that has emerged from the works of Bruno Latour, Carlo Ciborra, as well as Orlikowski, Yates, and their co-workers.[4]

Approaching technology in this manner suggests that different inventions and **innovations** are constantly adapted, modified, and subverted in the course of different practices in and out of organizations. Consider the example of Power-Point, which has attracted much criticism as a technology that deskills presenters and 'dumbs down' audiences, tyrannically reducing knowledge to lists, pictures, and charts. Approaching PowerPoint as a technology-in-use suggests that different people enact it differently and with different results, often removed from the intentions of its designers and merchandisers. Power-Point may be used in an imaginative or dull way, to support or reinvent presentations. Creative users of PowerPoint can assimilate the technology in their own presentational styles, displaying many of the qualities of **bricolage** and improvisation that have long been associated with more primitive forms of technology. Used in this way, PowerPoint does not necessarily simplify, codify, and objectify knowledge but can become part of a multi-level engagement with organizational complexity.[5]

Terrorism

An acceptable, generic definition of terrorism has proved difficult to generate, for several reasons: (a) definitions change over time, as historically specific definitions, focusing on the most salient manifestation of the time, are superseded by new, also historically specific definitions; (b) as a result, its conceptual **boundaries** have been porous, including diverse forms such as state terrorism, genocide, ethnic cleansing, and guerrilla warfare as well as primarily individual forms such as school shootings, stalking, and mind games in addition to terrorism emanating from social movements; (c) the term has been used in a primarily emotive or labelling manner, stigmatizing rather than describing. The following definition appears to include terrorism's most unequivocal forms and to minimize the pejorative element: 'Terrorism consists of intended, irregular acts of violence or disruption (or the threat of them) carried out in secret with the effect of generating anxiety in a group, and with the further aim, via that effect, of exciting political response or political change.'[6] Terrorism has been described as a form of warfare, but most frequently it is not the conventional warlike activities of states deploying armies. It has been described as violence, but it includes disruption, mayhem, and psychological destabilization as well. It has been described as crime and it almost always involves criminal activities, but it is a broader, more collective category than crime.[7]

Scholars have traced terrorist actions as aspects of military, political, and religious conflict back to biblical times. In more recent history it was used self-consciously in the Reign of Terror during the French Revolutionary period. Visible eruptions since that time have included anarchist groups (employing mainly assassination) in late nineteenth- and

---

[1] Foucault, 1980. [2] Giddens, 1984. [3] Orlikowski, 1992, p. 406. Orlikowski, 1996; Yates and Orlikowski, 1992. [5] Gabriel, 2008a. [4] Latour, 1991; Ciborra, 2002; see e.g. Orlikowski, 1992; Tyre and [6] Smelser, 2007, p. 242. [7] For informative overviews, see Crenshaw, 1995; Hoffman, 1998.

early twentieth-century Russia, Europe, and the United States; the great **genocides** and ethnic cleansings of the twentieth century; anti-colonial violence (mainly guerrilla warfare), ethno-religious-nationalist conflict (often in postcolonial societies), ongoing right-wing radicalism, left-wing radicalism in the 1960s and 1970s in the United States and Europe, and single-cause (e.g. anti-abortion) terrorism. What we now understand as international terrorism began in the late 1960s after the Six-Day War in the Middle East, as dispirited Palestinian groups resorted to international kidnappings, killings, bombings, and skyjackings to gain attention for their cause.[1] In more recent decades international terrorism has been associated closely with fundamental religious groups (mainly emanating from the Middle East) and directed at the United States and Europe.

If we set state terrorism and its kindred forms aside, what can be said about the major determinants of terrorist activity? They are multiple and fall into the following categories:

□ A perceived sense of dispossession on the part of a group, best understood as a form of relative rather than absolute deprivation.
□ Articulation of this sense in the formulation of an extremist ideology, the appearance of radical leadership, recruitment of members (often through personal ties and networks), and cultivation of sympathetic audiences.
□ The availability of resources, specifically financing, weapons, and publicity, usually through the **mass media**.
□ A situation of both perceived lack of opportunity and perceived opportunity. The sense of 'lack of opportunity' is the unavailability or presumed futility of *alternative* strategies of **conflict**; the sense of 'opportunity' stems from real or perceived vulnerability of target groups, societies, or states, or, in the shorter run, evidence of recent successes of specific terrorist strategies.

As a political strategy, terrorism has seldom achieved its direct political aims. Its main political successes have been its role in establishing the state of Israel, the campaign of the Ethniki Organosis Kyprion Agoniston (EOKA) on behalf of the Greek Cypriots, and the Front de Libération Nationale (FLN) leading to Algerian independence. In all these cases, however, the colonial or controlling powers had their own motives for leaving the scene. The terrorism of the Irish Republican Army in Northern Ireland and the Basque nationalists in Spain could be described as partial though debatable successes. Other 'successes', such as the killing of Israeli athletes at the Munich Olympic Games in 1970 and the kidnapping of OPEC ministers in Vienna in 1975, were primarily media rather than political successes.

Despite this mixed record of attaining direct political results, terrorism, especially in its international guise, has established itself as a major world political phenomenon, and promises to remain so for decades to come. Why should this be? Specific spectacular events, notably the 2001 attacks on the Word Trade Center and the Pentagon, have imparted a long-lasting dramatic significance to it. Terrorism also carries with it the threat of moving from its traditional 'guns and bombs' mode to radioactive, nuclear, biological, and chemical forms. More generally, terrorism as a threat possesses the powerful combination of being rare, irregular in occurrence, and lethal—a combination calculated to keep the media in a state of attentiveness, the public anxious, and political leaders in a state of uncertainty, watchfulness, and fear of internal political criticism if a successful terrorist attack is carried out. Closely related, the threat of terrorism constitutes a continuous threat to civil liberties in a democracy—forever in tension with the exigencies of national security—and also sets the stage for prolonged seasons of the politics of fear, which can also constitute a basis for the erosion of democratic **institutions**.[2] Even

---

[1] Laqueur, 1977.   [2] Wilkinson, 2001.

more generally, terrorism promises to maintain its potency in the future because many of its generating factors—internal political divisions in states, international power arrangements, and primordial hatreds—are themselves long-term conditions with no ready solutions at hand.

• See also *spectacle, violence*

NEIL J. SMELSER, UNIVERSITY OF CALIFORNIA, BERKELEY

Trade unions

Trade unions are organizations formed by employees to promote their common interests. They emerged in the early part of the nineteenth century out of the powerlessness of the individual worker when confronted by the **power** of **capital**. They grew out of the gradual realization that by forming an association, workers could offer mutual protection, improve their conditions of work, and make more effective demands on the employers. Most early unions were craft associations, seeking to limit the supply of labour in skilled trades (like carpenters, engineers, plumbers, etc.) thus raising the market value of these **skills**—they were often referred to as 'friendly societies' and represented relatively privileged workers, offering their members different benefits, such as paying for sickness and funerals. Gradually, however, craft unionism was overtaken by industrial unionism, unions of largely unskilled or semi-skilled workers who sought to improve working conditions and rates of pay across the board through industrial action, like strikes, boycotts, and picketing. In this way, unions have sought to limit the powers of employers to hire and fire at will, unilaterally to impose conditions of work on a take-it-or-leave-it basis, and to offer only minimal standards of protection and welfare as part of the terms of employment.

In most industrial countries, following periods of acute conflict and confrontation, employers accepted unions as legitimate expressions of their employees' collective interests and recognized the **legitimacy** of collective bargaining as an **institution** for containing and settling industrial **conflicts**. This was enhanced as unions sought and gained a measure of political representation in most industrialized countries. In Great Britain, the trade unions provided the momentum behind the foundation of the Labour Party. In other countries, unions were closely tied to socialist and communist parties or extracted reformist concessions from centrist parties when in government. Political representation was important in creating legislation that enabled unions to gain recognition, without having to resort to industrial action. In countries like France and Italy, the main union blocs are tied to particular political parties.

In many sectors, trade unions were able to establish closed shops or union shops, sometimes with the help of appropriate legislation. A closed shop meant that only workers who were already members of a union could be hired, hence it is also known as 'pre-entry closed shop'. The last vestiges of closed shop could be found in sectors like print journalism and acting, though with a different name it remains a powerful institution for protecting the monopoly power of the **professions**. A union shop usually meant that workers had to join a trade union once they had been recruited, hence it is also known as post-entry closed shop. These enhanced the union's ability to act in a coordinated way and gave unions some extra leverage in their negotiations with employers. Some employers welcomed union shops as a way of regulating labour supply although many accepted them grudgingly following prolonged struggles.

A long-standing debate among socialists regarding unions is whether they represent 'schools of revolution' raising **class** consciousness and enhancing militance or whether they are reformist institutions that blunt the radical instincts of the masses by promising and sometimes delivering short-term benefits. Robert Michels, in his theory of **oligarchy**, firmly took the latter view, arguing that trade unions as well

as radical parties of the left end up being increasingly conservative and undemocratic, vehicles of
power for the leaders rather than emancipation
for the followers.[1]

In recent years, unions have been on the
defensive in Britain and the United States, as a
result of many different factors. These include:

□ New **technologies** which have wiped out
traditional strongholds of unions in the
skilled trades.

□ New **management** and political philosophies
which have placed heavy emphasis on the
individual employee as a bargaining agent or
as a member of a corporate **culture**.

□ The emergence of new sectors in the
economy, notably in services, where
unionization is difficult.

□ Globalization of production which allows
companies to shift productive operations

relatively easily to countries where costs are
low.

□ **Outsourcing** which enables companies
to close down entire departments (for
instance, those known for their
militancy or low productivity) and
subcontract their functions to other
organizations.

□ A more individualistic culture that
encourages employees to see themselves as
masters of their own choice who, if unhappy
with their job, have the option of leaving it.
and

□ Legislation that limited the effectiveness of
industrial action (including boycotts,
picketing, and strikes) and weakened or
abolished closed shop arrangements.

• See also *conflict, industrial relations, resistance*

---

[1] Michels, 1949.

U

Unconscious

The unconscious is the core concept of psychoanalysis, the theory established by Sigmund Freud, and an important term in other disciplines of depth psychology. Although sometimes the unconscious is seen as a mysterious entity, reminiscent of the Platonic depths where the world of pure forms seeks expression through language, the Freudian unconscious is normal, structured, and to a degree knowable. It is useful to distinguish between unconscious the adjective and unconscious the noun. As an adjective, unconscious describes the quality of an idea, a **desire**, or a mental process which is not accessible to consciousness. In the first instance, unconscious desires are desires which have undergone repression. Unconscious elements cannot be brought into consciousness at will, and may only be studied through their conscious manifestations, which include symptoms, symbols, dreams, fantasies, slips, jokes, emotional outbursts, cultural artefacts, and so on.

Unconscious ideas and processes behave in a different way from conscious ideas; they cannot be altered by appeal to reason or evidence, they are impervious to contradiction (in other words two conflicting ideas or desires can easily coexist), they often merge together through the process of *condensation* (for example, all negative qualities, like cowardice, duplicity, selfishness, etc. may merge in a single person who becomes a figure of hate) or meaning may be transferred from one unconscious idea onto another through the process of *displacement* (for example, fear of the father turns into a fear of horses).

As a noun, the unconscious was used by Freud to refer to the area of the mind which contains the unconscious ideas, desires, and processes. In addition to the repressed material, the unconscious also contains archetypal images and primal phantasies (see **fantasy**), which can be thought of as mental structures inscribed in the genetic make-up of human beings over millennia of evolution. In Freud's early theory, the unconscious featured as a mental system which included the representatives of the instincts (desires, wishes, phantasies) whose main purpose is to gain access to consciousness. In his later theory, the unconscious is no longer an agency—its agency-like properties are assimilated in what Freud called the id. In this later theory, the other two agencies, the ego and the super-ego, also contain unconscious elements and pursue many of their functions in ways which preclude access to consciousness. So, when the ego represses an idea, the process of repression itself is unconscious, i.e. the person is not aware of doing so. Most of the **defence mechanisms** operate unconsciously. In spite of surrendering its systemic qualities to the id, the quality of mental contents to be unconscious remained in Freud's view 'our one beacon-light in the darkness of depth psychology'.[1]

Carl Gustav Jung,[2] Freud's most controversial and creative disciple and, later, critic, argued that the individual unconscious is in part a manifestation of a deeper collective unconscious, through which all members of the human species are linked spiritually and psychically. This collective unconscious comprises the **spiritual** and mythical heritage of humanity,

---

[1] Freud, 1923/1984, p. 368.   [2] Jung, 1968.

symbols and archetypes—primordial images, fantasies and ideas, charged with **emotion**. Jung departed from the psychoanalytic tradition and developed a theory, analytic psychology, in which the individual psyche is part of a transcendental entity that defies time and space. His theory views the unconscious as a force of **creativity** as well as a force of destruction, but above all as a force of psychic union for humankind. Most psychoanalytic writers have shied away from this view, fearing the non-scientific or mystical implications of Jung's thought. Yet, in different ways, they have incorporated Jung's seminal idea of symbolic archetypes into their thinking.

While the unconscious is the central object of study of psychoanalysis, it is also a virtually indispensable assumption for most human sciences, including sociology, cultural studies, linguistics, art, and literary criticism. It is at once the psychic layer in which **culture** becomes embedded within the individual and also the source of fundamental needs and desires which cultural institutions seek alternately to express, modify, frustrate, tame, or gratify. It is for this reason that Foucault observed that 'the problem of the unconscious—its possibility, status, mode of existence, the means of knowing it and bringing it to light—is not simply a problem within the human sciences which they can be thought of as encountering by chance in their steps; it is a problem that is ultimately coextensive with their very existence ... an unveiling of the nonconscious is constitutive of all the sciences of man'.[1]

The unconscious has throughout the twentieth century pervaded our thinking about what makes us behave the way we do—it has virtually become common sense to view people as driven by desires and needs of which they are unconscious. The ideas that people have 'subconscious' motives, that they deny their desires, that they are gripped by powerful desires whose sources are hidden, that painful memories are obliterated from consciousness, are now commonplace. Yet, as Mitchell has rightly observed,[2] virtually all criticisms of psychoanalysis derive from an inability to accept the unconscious and its implications. It is all too easy for individuals (both in common and in academic discourses) to lapse into an assumption that others have unconscious minds, suffering from self-delusions, mysterious motives, and neurotic symptoms, whereas they themselves are entirely transparent, consistent, and rational. As Freud realized long ago, the existence of an unconscious part of our mind, a part of our mind which is beyond our direct knowledge and control, can be a highly disturbing one. The view that our ego (what we refer to as 'I') is not the master even in its own house may suggest that we all harbour a stranger (an 'Other') within ourselves. This can be a highly disconcerting thought, when we consider that this stranger has unpredictable, destructive, and self-destructive appetites (see **self and selfhood, subject and subjectivity**). Many contemporary schools of psychoanalysis have tended to give precedence to other concepts, notably the ego, object relations, **identity**, and so forth, over the unconscious.

One branch of psychoanalysis that has remained unerring in its focus on the unconscious has been that established by French psychoanalyst Jacques Lacan. Lacan developed the concept of the unconscious in a unique way, attributing views to Freud (or to a symptomatic reading of Freud's texts) which were quite novel and original and drawing extensively on the structuralist linguistics of Swiss pioneer Ferdinand de Saussure. Departing from the rather Freudian view of the unconscious as the censored chapter in each **subject's** individual history that must be extrapolated from the content of other chapters he reached his famous destination that 'the unconscious is structured like a language',[3] whose processes of condensation and displacement mirror

---

[1] Foucault, 1966/1970, p. 364.   [2] Mitchell, 1975.   [3] Lacan, 1966/1977, p. 58.

directly those of metaphor and metonymy. The originality in Lacan's position lay in linking language and speech, not to consciousness and the ego as Freud had done, but to the unconscious which he viewed as a structure that originates in the **Other**; hence his formulation that 'the subject's unconscious is the discourse of the Other'. Language and speech come, so to speak, from another place, outside the subject's consciousness. The ego, according to this view, is reduced to a mere artefact, an effect of the unconscious, a fictitious and precarious entity that is shaped early on in life but lacks any properties of agency and coherence. This view brought Lacan into conflict with the psychoanalytic establishment, though his theories became highly influential among philosophers, sociologists, and postmodern scholars.

• See also *defence mechanisms, psychoanalysis and psychoanalytic approaches*

Unemployment

Unemployment is both a statistical measure of the proportion of a population who, although willing, are unable to find paid work *and* the personal experience of a person who wants a job but does not have one. The measurement of unemployment is a particularly thorny issue and raises many questions. Should a person working part-time for one hour per week but wishing to work full-time be considered employed? Should a person who would like to work but has become discouraged by his or her failure to get a job be viewed as having dropped out of the workforce and, therefore, not counted as unemployed? The reason why such questions are important is that, in democratic countries, unemployment is one of the most politically charged of all statistical measures. The prospects of governments getting re-elected depend in some measure on their success or failure in handling unemployment. Not

only is high unemployment seen as an indication of economic failure, but it is also seen as the cause of innumerable social pathologies, including poverty, crime, ill health, and social dependency. Work, by contrast, is seen as the route towards independence, prosperity, and **success**.

Social attitudes towards unemployment reveal a core ambivalence; while governments (and to a lesser extent companies) are regularly blamed for the phenomenon of unemployment, unemployed people are also blamed for their inability to find work and stigmatized for this inability. Paid employment has long been a major feature of all industrialized societies, providing a source of **meaning** and **identity** for those who work—even in jobs which are dreary and alienating. The unemployed, many of whom have been victims of **downsizing**, often report a loss of time structure to the day, difficulties with their status and personal identity, a lack of 'place' at home, and more generally a sense of purposelessness and meaninglessness in their lives. **Stress** and illness are often greater amongst the unemployed.[1]

Poverty, or being less creditworthy, adds considerably to these difficulties. Unemployment seriously limits people's ability to make **choices** as consumers, having to rely instead on state benefits for their survival. The experience of deprivation can be especially painful for those who once enjoyed a high standard of living and were able to afford their own home, expensive goods, foreign holidays, and other benefits of consumer culture only to lose them due to unemployment. Even more painful is to find your children discriminated against or excluded from social activities at school by your penury. This is why Bauman has described the 'new poor' of advanced industrial societies as 'failed consumers'.[2]

Unemployment has been a feature of working-**class** experience since the rise of industrial capitalism. Many workers who had enjoyed

---

[1] Fineman, 1987.   [2] Bauman, 1998.

the status of a labour aristocracy (like hand-loom weavers in the early part of the nineteenth century) found themselves thrown into destitution by the arrival of new technologies that made their **skills** redundant.[1] Others found themselves unemployed due to the vagaries of the trade cycles. **Trade unions** generally did well in times of low unemployment, but were forced to retreat in times of high unemployment when militancy was thwarted by the ready availability of labour.

Unemployment today, however, has become a condition that afflicts people of different social classes and different levels of wealth. The onslaught of lay-offs, **downsizing**, **outsourcing**, mergers, and acquisitions in the last twenty years has made unemployment part of the experience of many who would describe themselves as 'middle-class', including managers, professionals, and workers in knowledge-intensive industries.[2] Many of those who do not experience unemployment directly, experience it indirectly through their colleagues, their friends, and their spouses. Many managerial and professional jobs come to be seen as precarious and uncertain. Thus unemployment can be said to act as a source of discipline for those in work, undermining **resistance** and bolstering the **power** of employers.

• See also *ethic, meaning*

Unmanaged and unmanageable

'No surprises' proclaimed the advertising logo of a well-known chain of international hotels. But life is full of surprises, some pleasant, many unpleasant. A treatise on the psychology or the sociology of surprises would make interesting reading, since surprises have been airbrushed out of the human sciences by the ubiquity of management discourses. Management offers reassurance that life can be ordered, organized, and controlled. In times of **change**,

stress, and uncertainty, it can be comforting to believe that international NGOs will manage the ecosystem, that the government will manage the economy, that doctors will manage our pain, and that we ourselves will manage our own lives. Management emerges as an idea with godlike qualities—caring, providing, protecting, and, above all, **controlling** the forces of chaos and disorder.

What are the forces that threaten order and predictability? In addition to natural catastrophes, floods, fires, earthquakes (themselves exacerbated by human activities), people are threatened by the slings and arrows of everyday life, by illness, accident, death, job losses, loss of loved ones, and so forth. They are also threatened by the activities of others, by wars, terrorist acts, discrimination and oppression, hatred, poverty, and much else besides. In the world of business, they are threatened by the vagaries of markets, the caprices of consumers, the surges of new technologies, the whims of CEOs and others. People are also threatened by inner disorder, by their own overwhelming cravings, irrational fears and anxieties, loss of self-esteem, fear of ageing and dying, rejection, guilt, and so on.

In addition to external forces, people in the course of their lives constantly create unmanageable areas for each other. Organizations, like other areas of social life, are full of unmanaged and unmanageable situations. Accidents, failures, and disasters strike with regularity and most people display a remarkable inability to learn from painful experiences. Mistakes are commonplace, and in spite of the best efforts of learning theorists to design them out, the same mistakes and the same accidents are repeated— on a small scale and on a large. Between the intentions of human **actions** and their outcomes, there are thick walls of unpredictability and unmanageability. If our actions consistently achieved their intended results there would be no space for **stories**. Nor would there be a space

---

[1] Thompson, 1968.   [2] Ehrenreich, 2005; Uchitelle, 2006.

for stories, if we lived in a perfectly ordered and rational world. But the world (both outer and inner) can be irrational, disorderly, puzzling, and threatening, our own actions and those of others often lead to unanticipated consequences; we regularly face situations which take us by surprise.

There are unmanaged terrains in every organization. Many of these terrains are crafted by people as they seek to evade organizational controls and the structures of power. People create niches which are not and cannot be managed, where they can individually and in groups engage in all kinds of uncontrolled, spontaneous activity. These activities occasionally engage with the practices of **power**, in unpredictable or indirect ways. I have referred to these terrains as the *unmanaged organization*, a kind of organizational dreamworld dominated by desires, fantasies, and emotions.[1] The unmanaged organization does not represent a direct challenge to the practices of power and management, but an attempt to sidestep or dodge them through spontaneous, uncontrolled activities which may involve clever ruses, privately coded texts, noise, silence, graffiti, cartoons, whispers, nods, smiles, secrets, gossip, subterfuge, stories, jokes, and laughter. Some of these take place around water coolers or the photocopying machines, others in corridors, over cups of coffee, or even using an organization's e-mailing system in clandestine and subversive ways. These spaces are at least temporarily unpoliced.

Of course, such spaces may be brought back under control, through fresh directives, commands, and regulations ('It has been brought to our attention that employees spend inordinate amounts of time around the water hydrant; henceforth . . .'). These may, in turn, be subverted or sidestepped by the creation of new unmanaged niches. At times, this cat and mouse game turns into guerrilla warfare or rebellion, where tactical strikes and retreats are

undertaken; victories and defeats are short-lived. At other times, however, engagement with the practices of power takes place through the medium of **fantasy**. Fantasy offers to individuals and groups a third way, one that amounts to neither conformity nor rebellion, but a symbolic refashioning of official organizational practices in the interest of pleasure, allowing a temporary supremacy of uncontrol over control and spontaneous emotion over the organization's emotional scripts. While such unmanaged spaces may be marginal much of the time, they are not unimportant as spaces where **identities** are fashioned, tested, and transformed. In these terrains a critical commentary on the official **symbols** of the an organization is maintained, chinks in their armour are discovered, and alternative, less docile, more recalcitrant identities can be fashioned.

The unmanaged terrains in organizations should not be thought of as synonymous with the informal or unofficial organization. For the greatest part, these are part of the managed organization, patrolled and policed in more or less subtle ways. Nor should all fantasies, individual or shared, be thought of as part of the unmanaged organization—such a view would fly in the face of the massive resources devoted to the creation and propagation of *corporate fantasies* for both internal and external consumption. Disneyland, the culture and heritage industries, public relations and advertising firms, a substantial part of the **mass media**, as well as companies' own PR departments and consultants, the various 'merchandisers of meaning',[2] are busily engaged in devising fantasies for consumption by customers or members of organizations. While many of these fantasies belong firmly to the realm of the managed organization as tools in the **management of meaning** and **culture**, they too can be subverted, altered, or embroidered in ways that draw them into the domain of the unmanaged organization.

---

[1] Gabriel, 1995; 2000.   [2] Sievers, 1986, p. 347.

An appreciation of the unmanaged and unmanageable qualities of life (in and out of organizations) dulls one's appetite for precipitous action, radical solutions, and ingenious schemes, all of which can easily backfire. Instead one learns to deal with uncertainty and insecurity, taking advantage of opportunities as and when they arise, as best as one can. **Negative capability**, the ability to accept uncertainty and insecurity without irritation, becomes a vital quality in dealing with these unmanaged and unmanageable situations.

V

Value and values

Value is a fundamental concept of economics where it is used to signify the worth of commodities. Marx distinguished between use values and exchange values;[1] use value refers to the value of a service or a product to a user, whereas exchange value represents its value relative to other services and products. According to the labour theory of value, the value of a commodity reflects the amount of **labour** involved in its production. This also applies to labour power itself when it is traded as a commodity—thus the labour power of a doctor has greater value than that of a labourer, inasmuch as it requires more time and other resources to train and sustain a doctor than a labourer. In neoclassical economics, this approach is dismissed in favour of a view that equates value to the *price* of a commodity in a free, open, and competitive market. Thus an object has value simply because people are prepared to pay a high price for it. Postmodern theory has added the concept of 'sign value'—an object may be wanted not because of its uses or the possibility of exchanging it but because of the **meanings** it carries. Brands are strong carriers of sign value—a branded product commands greater value than an identical unbranded one, because of the prestige and status that it brings to its owner.

Values are also important concepts in social and cultural studies as well as in moral philosophy, most especially that of Friedrich Nietzsche, whose lifelong project could be summed up in his phrase 'the revaluation of all values'.[2] Values are meant to represent core beliefs about what is important, right, good, and desirable. The expression 'a fool (or a cynic) is a person who knows the price of everything and the value of nothing' suggests that there are values superior to what money can buy. These values reside in the 'true' **meaning** of things, rather than in their superficial and faddish associations. By contrast the maxim 'every man has his price' suggests that all values can be corrupted by money. The tension between values and money is one that characterizes many discourses that approach money, markets, and economic relations as subverting and undermining values of a moral, social, and spiritual nature. Yet, materialism can itself be seen as a value, one that looks at happiness as coming from material well-being and, in some cases, the physical pleasures associated with it.

Values are widely viewed as major constituents of **culture**, reaching deeper than **norms**, and being less tangible than **symbols**. Each individual is seen as possessing a system of values, often in a hierarchy of importance, which may include equality, loyalty, freedom, harmony, honesty, hard work, respect for the natural environment and for others, and so forth. Values are products of **socialization** and the influences of parents, teachers, religious and other sources of authority. They are stable and stay with people over time. They are also seen as points of no compromise; they are issues on which people are prepared to make a stand, even if this involves pain and sacrifice. A cluster of reinforcing values is sometimes referred to as an **ethic**, such as the Protestant ethic, the Confucian ethic, and others. Actions that derive from particular values were described by Max Weber as 'value-rational' (see **rationality**).

---

[1] Marx, 1867/1967.   [2] Nietzsche, 1990.

The discussion of values in organizations and business is often subsumed in studies of organizational **culture**, business **ethics**, and **spirituality**. The values of most organizations are a curious amalgam of wider social values and their own particular ones, which in some instance are in **conflict**. Thus the social value of leadership by electoral mandate is at odds with the bureaucratic ethos of appointments. Interest in organizational values dates from the early 1980s, when culture assumed a major significance as an influence on productivity and success. It was then that many scholars, researchers, and management consultants observed the emphasis placed on values by Japanese corporations, at the time highly successful in their competition against American and European ones. The message was clear—organizations achieve excellence and competitive advantage through their commitment to strong values, such as quality, customer service, integrity, and so forth.[1]

Many companies rushed to proclaim their values, often with the help of consultants supplying them with 'values packages' and often with little regard as to whether visible policies and practices were consistent with the proclaimed values. Today, it has become clear that proclaiming values is one thing and acting in line with them is a different matter. Strongly associating a company's name with a particular value, like sustainable development, customer service, family values, and so forth, makes it liable to criticism and embarrassment should it appear to fail to live up to them. Strongly proclaimed corporate values can also generate inner conflicts in employees who believe that their organization is not acting in line with its values. This is epitomized by the *whistle-blower*, the individual who feels compelled to speak out publicly about what they regard as organizational acts of dishonesty, malevolence, or greed. Such individuals often have a very clear sense of ethical probity

on which they will not compromise or bargain, unlike others who move with the flow in an organization's **politics.**

One study that illustrated the power of organizational values when genuinely enacted was carried out by Swedish theorist of organizations Mats Alvesson.[2] The company, a computer consultancy, had experienced rapid growth, low turnover, and excellent financial performance, growing in size to 500 employees. The firm showed strong commitment to values such as openness, egalitarianism, friendship, fun, and informality, and made a conscious effort to recruit individuals who would share them. The company enacted these values regularly, for example through special functions like workshops and training sessions but also in the mountain walking, sailing, diving, and so forth that emphasized a family atmosphere. In this way, potentially conflicting values, like fun and profitability, were reconciled. The design of the corporate **building** itself sought to resemble a home rather than a sterile office environment, and included a sauna, kitchen, pool, piano bar, television sets, comfortable furniture, and so forth. In this company, Alvesson notes, organizational values acted like 'social glue', holding the organization together, keeping labour turnover low, and fostering an atmosphere of openness, **innovation**, and trust. Such a happy reconciliation of values is tested in periods of crisis when some of the values may unravel—when all is plain sailing, cultures can maintain their proud profiles of values, but it is in rough weather that the truly core values show themselves in sharp relief against their rhetorical shadows.

An important debate regarding the nature of **science** concerns the extent to which it is or should be 'value free' or 'value neutral'. The view that science is and must remain value free was put forward by Max Weber in a celebrated paper called 'Science as a vocation'.[3] In it he argued that science, in contrast to philosophy, religion,

---

[1] For classical statements of this position, see Ouchi, 1981; Pascale and Athos, 1981; Peters and Waterman, 1982.   [2] Alvesson, 2002.
[3] Weber, 1946.

or **ideology**, has nothing to say on Leo Tolstoy's fundamental question 'How should we live our lives?' Science represents objective knowledge whereas value judgements are essentially **subjective**. Scientists, in both natural and social sciences, should aim for value neutrality—the adoption of any specific value stance contaminates and invalidates **knowledge**. Of Weber's many theses, this has been one of the most furiously contested. Opponents of the thesis have argued, first, that scientists, like other human beings, have their own values (partly derived from the **ethics** of their disciplines) which they cannot keep out of their research. Second, even if scientists could pursue their vocation in a value-neutral manner, others will exploit and use their discoveries in line with different (and possibly disastrous) consequences; one only need reflect on the uses of science by the Nazis to realize that a scientist carrying out 'value-neutral' research on poison gas would be a fool. Third, value neutrality itself represents a value position, indeed one of moral and political cowardice that, when adopted, has had detrimental consequences on sciences as well as on humanity at large.

• See also *culture, ethics, meaning, norms*

Violence

Every human life encounters violence, in large or in smaller ways. Many lives start in violence (rape) and end in violence. Violence is an important part of society at large as well as of different social groupings, including families, crowds, and organizations. Violence is action that harms, hurts, or destroys another person or different objects and it can assume many different forms. **Genocide**, war, torture, enslavement, plunder, deracination, expropriation, imprisonment, forced transportation are forms of violence on a large scale. On a more personal scale, murder, rape, physical, sexual, or verbal abuse,

assault, harassment, and **bullying** are all direct forms of violence. Other forms of violence can include persistent and unjust criticism, humiliation, degradation, or denial of resources necessary for a person or a community to survive, grow, and flourish. Violence may be perpetrated by a person, a group, or a society on its members knowingly and explicitly or through ignorance and neglect. Although the most brutal forms of violence are easily recognized, there are many forms that are more ambiguous. This is especially the case when it is presented as retaliation for earlier injuries or when it is experienced by one party but not recognized by another.

Violence is a topic in many social sciences—politics usually discusses it in connection with political power and domination, psychology in relation to human destructiveness and aggression, sociology in relation to crime, deviant behaviour, and social disturbance. Given the aversion and even revulsion that most people express towards violence, it is remarkable what an endemic and far-reaching phenomenon it is, occurring on the largest scale as genocide and combat, and on the most intimate scale as war between two individuals. Although different animals are known to inflict suffering on each other, many scholars have argued that no species perpetrates the same extent of wanton intra-species aggression as humans—indeed, some of the main threats to human existence come from other human beings. Controlling violence through laws, rules, and values is one of the major functions of every society, prompting Max Weber's famous definition of the state as a political **organization** 'that (successfully) claims the monopoly of the legitimate use of force [violence] within a given territory'.[1] Violence or the threat of violence is then seen as the ultimate source of state **power**. Whether the use of force by the state (for example in the name of preserving democracy or combating **terrorism**) can ever be characterized as 'legitimate' has been strongly challenged.[2]

---

[1] Weber, 1946, p. 78.   [2] See e.g. Chomsky, 2006.

The link between violence and power is ambiguous. To be sure, few forms of power are as complete as brutal force or terror—it can destroy, at least temporarily, all opposition and resistance. Terror can destroy most human bonds and **values**, forcing blind obedience. Yet at least some theorists have argued that violence in the long run destroys power by breeding further violence and undermining any attempt to establish legitimate order.[1] Non-violent **resistance** has then been advocated and embraced by leaders like Gandhi and Martin Luther King as a way of assuming the superior moral ground from which to oppose violence and injustice.

Given how important and unsettling violence is, it is not surprising that it is a core ingredient of narrative, literature, drama (including tragedy and comedy), film, and the other arts. Often mixed with **sex**, violence is a core preoccupation of the culture and entertainment industries, including television, journalism, computer games, and so forth. Its depiction in most Hollywood movies (most especially as shootings, fights, explosions, crashes, and, increasingly, torture) and other cultural products raises perennial questions as to whether these encourage violent acts or, conversely, whether they act as a cathartic container for such acts. Much depends on how violence is portrayed, whether it glorifies the perpetrator and the act or whether it generates sympathy for the victim. But as the film *A Clockwork Orange* sought to demonstrate, the same violent acts that create revulsion in some people may inspire others to violence, either through imitation or through retaliation.

An extensive literature has emerged dealing with organizational violence, in its diverse forms including bullying, humiliation, sexual harassment, and even homicides.[2] Beyond gratuitous violence, however, several theorists have looked at the violence perpetrated against individuals

by organizations as a matter of routine, notably during the extensive business **downsizing** and dislocation undergone by many industrial societies but especially the United States since the 1990s.[3]

One theorist who has made a significant contribution to the psychological and social damage caused by these phenomena has been Howard F. Stein, a psychoanalytic anthropologist who has made extensive studies in organizations undergoing downsizing. Stein has argued that the very terms used to describe the destruction of jobs and livelihoods are euphemisms that represent not a **social construction of reality** but a systematic assault on **meaning**.[4] Terms such as 'downsizing', 'rightsizing', 'RIF' (or reduction in force), 'managed health', 're-engineering', and so forth are not merely attempts to conceal the bleak and brutal realities of many American workplaces, but violate the human spirit, by forcing on it a seemingly unanswerable logic of markets, economic necessity, and bottom lines. Stein argues that many workplaces have become places of darkness, where emotional brutality is commonplace and different forms of psychological violence, dehumanization, including degradation, humiliation, and intimidation, have become the norm.

A form of violence that has been attracting attention is that associated with denying a person or a group a **voice**. **Postcolonial** discourses have drawn attention to the colonial strategy of complementing military force and political domination with silencing the voices of colonized people. This argument is currently being rehearsed in relation to companies that deny their employees a voice, leaving them with a stark **choice** of accepting employment on the organization's terms or leaving.

The target of human violence is not always human and animal life. Advocates of environmental and spiritual values have critiqued what they view as the violence perpetrated against

[1] Arendt, 1970.　[2] Czarniawska, 2002; Diamond, 1997; Martin, 2000; Pearson, Andersson, and Wegner, 2001; Sims, 2003.
[3] Ehrenreich, 2005; Uchitelle, 2006.　[4] Stein, 1998; 2001.

the earth's natural environment, the reckless exploitation of its resources, and the slipshod dumping of toxic substances. A Schumpeterian 'creative destruction' may lie at the heart of capitalist **innovation** and economic development; its cost is the 'violation of Gaia', a hubris that may yet meet its nemesis in the shape of disastrous climate changes and overwhelming threats to the continuing existence of all life on the planet.[1]

• See also *aggression, conflict, power, terrorism*

Virtual organization

Virtual organization is often used to describe an organizational form that has assumed significance in late modernity and is distinct from the bureaucratic organizations associated with **modernity**. Along with everything else qualified by the adjective 'virtual', a virtual organization is one that is treated as if it were a real organization and has many of the attributes of real organizations, but relies extensively on **information** and **communication** technologies to sustain it. The term virtual organization has assumed several different and overlapping meanings. It can describe a real organization that **outsources** a large number of its core functions to other organizations often in distant locations, for example, a Canadian utility outsourcing its call-centre services to India. Alternatively, virtual organization can refer to an organization that does not have a centre in a specific geographic location but is widely dispersed; many or all of its employees may work from home or from virtual workplaces, but they deliver 'real work', like computer code or musical scores. Virtual organization may refer to still more loosely coupled **networks** of individuals or cells which collaborate without there being a central executive point for decision making. This is how some **terrorist** networks, such as al Qaeda, are viewed. Virtual **teams** are **groups** of people working together on particular projects, such as designing new products or delivering particular services, who rarely or never come into face-to-face contact with each other, but communicate through the internet, telephone, video-conferencing, and so forth.

Computerized information and communication technologies, especially the internet, are vital in sustaining virtual organizations, since their members rarely come into physical contact with each other. This accords virtual workplaces some advantages, notably allowing people to work during their preferred hours; it also reduces many costs. Virtual workplaces, however, have some limitations. The absence of physical contact may reduce the degree of trust people feel for each other and may amplify some of the deficiencies experienced by people who, cut off from human contact, work for very long hours staring at computer screens (see **information technology**). In a curious way, the emergence of virtual organizations and virtual teams has led to a greater appreciation of the advantages drawn by people and teams working in close geographic proximity, who can engage in casual conversations and quick exchanges of views when needed. Many innovative and creative ideas are sparked off by such conversations that would not be possible over the internet. Collocation, in spite of its costs, may then be a source of competitive advantage that cannot be regularized or codified into standard procedures. This is one of the reasons for the intense concentration of highly innovative industries in specific geographic locations, epitomized by Silicon Valley.

• See also *globalization, networks*

Vision

Vision is in the first place the ability to see (in this connection, see **image** and **spectacle**). In organizations, it has emerged as a concept

---

[1] Lovelock, 2006.

describing a fundamental quality of **leadership**, the ability to envision a situation in the future that grows out of the present and is attractive and inspiring. In pursuit of such a vision, people can work hard and endure hardships and privations. Visions are often attributed to single individuals. Martin Luther King's 'I have a dream...' speech articulated precisely such a vision. Many social movements, however, develop their visions gradually and collectively, as people share experiences with each other and discover their **voice**. Vision shares with terms like **strategy** and **career** the quality of serving as a retrospective **sensemaking** device. A leader is said to have had a particular vision *after* a successful or desirable outcome was achieved. In this way, it can lionize the leader, by obscuring the contributions of other people as well as those of accidental and random factors.

In organizations, vision is often complemented by 'mission'. Leaders share their visions with their followers in order to formulate their organization's mission, what it is that the organization is seeking to create. Along with many other management buzzwords, vision can be viewed as a noble term that has been trivialized and banalized to the point of becoming virtually meaningless.[1] It is now not uncommon for organizations to employ consultants, who, after cursory acquaintance, produce vision statements, mission statements, and value statements, many of which feature in corporate websites and literature, bearing little relation to what an organization actually stands for.

Yet vision remains a useful concept. It describes well the ability to read the present as a set of circumstances pregnant with opportunities for the future but also with threats. It also captures well the restless, imaginative, and inspirational qualities of leadership. A vision is not just a dream; it is a call for action, for commitment, for sacrifice. A vision is not content to leave well-enough alone, but strives for **change**. A vision cannot be a narrow, selfish,

and mean project; it must at least aspire to representing something of **value**, something noble. Yet a vision can also represent a very partial engagement with the present and the future, where contact is lost with reality or where one particular objective is elevated above all others, often at considerable human costs. It then becomes a kind of 'tunnel vision', a form of blindness.

• See also *image, spectacle, leadership*

Voice

Voice has emerged as an important category in the social sciences, denoting the ability of an individual, a group, or a nation to articulate and express their experiences, their demands, their grievances, their **identity**—or even, their mere existence. 'Finding a voice' describes well an artist honing his or her craft, an emerging social movement seeking to define its identity, and a disadvantaged group seeking to make its plight known to a wider public. If voice does not always represent the struggle for respect, it always represents the struggle for recognition. At a stretch, it can describe the young man riding his ear-splitting motorbike through a quiet town or the terrorist planting a bomb. Silencing somebody means denying them recognition, through systematic derision and dismissal, or mere indifference.

The term *voice* was first used by economist Albert O. Hirschman as one of three strategies in response to decline in firms, organizations, and states.[2] Voice represents citizen participation—the concerted attempt by members to influence government or organizational **policy** by voicing their interests and concerns. The other two responses are *loyalty*—a 'grin and bear it' attitude, whereby members of an organization put up with hardships—and *exit* or leaving the organization. The formal simplicity of Hirschman's scheme and the strength of

---

[1] Collins, 2000.   [2] Hirschman, 1970.

the concepts of voice and exit account for its extensive influence, in spite of reducing to a simple trichotomy a vast kaleidoscope of responses which can include active and passive **resistance**, grudging submission, qualified obedience, and cynical withdrawal.

The concept of voice is embedded in a **multicultural** society, where different groups struggle for recognition of their identity, interests, and views. It is also embedded in a highly individualistic culture where every individual is expected to fashion a unique and individual identity, communicate it to others through their actions, their experiences, and their narratives, and have it recognized. Finding a voice becomes a challenging project in a culture saturated by information, images, and noise which make it difficult to register individual or group voices.

The 'voice discourse' represents a position in sociology which seeks to vindicate the right of different individuals and groups to discover their voices, express their views, and have them recognized and legitimized.[1] Voice discourses generally argue that **modernity** privileged the voice of the expert over the voice of experience, **grand narratives** (predominantly white, male, universalistic, etc.) over personal stories. Thus the voice of the physician silenced the voice of the patient, the voice of the teacher silenced the voice of the pupil, and the voice of the scientist silenced most other voices. Voice discourses have sought to vindicate **experience**, long discarded as subjective, partial, and inadequate, as a source of genuine and valid **knowledge** and as a potential determinant of **policy**. If modernity privileged **science** as the voice of authority, in late modernity experience has recovered some of its authority. The person who has directly experienced a particular condition, the patient, the discriminated against, the crime victim, acquires an authority to speak about this condition that 'experts' cannot match through their mastery of scientific knowledge alone. The Internet has

been quite helpful in enabling people to at least search for and sometimes find their own voice, by discovering other people who have shared similar experiences to theirs and with whom they can identify. Thus, on being diagnosed with a serious disease, a patient will usually hear the advice of the physician but will also seek to contact other sufferers of this disease to find how they live with their disease and how they manage their condition.

One difficulty with voice discourses is a tendency of voice to fragment into highly specific and partial experiences. In its extreme form, the voice discourse asserts that *only* someone who has experienced something directly can speak authoritatively about it. Thus only a woman is authorized to speak on behalf of women's experiences, only a woman with children on behalf of mothers, and only a mother with children suffering from bulimia can speak on behalf of mothers with children suffering from bulimia. The result is the silencing of people who do not conform to the recognized identity signifiers—a man, for example, cannot speak against rape. 'Speaking as an *x*' (where *x* can be victim of crime, gay man, Muslim woman, recovered alcoholic, etc.) becomes an automatic entitlement to a voice denied to those who are not *x*.

This view has been criticized as denying any common humanity that enables people to empathize and understand others across different divides and also devaluing scientific knowledge that reaches beyond specific experiences to what is generalizable and universal.[2] A different criticism concerns the self-inoculating qualities of the voice of experience. 'Thou shalt not deny my experience, thou shalt not silence my voice' is a powerful slogan that can easily be exploited by impostors, fantasists, and other attention seekers. Numerous examples of abuses of audience trust can be named, instances where personal **stories** and testimonials were believed as genuine and sincere when they were at odds with

---

[1] Gabriel, 2004c.   [2] For the different positions on the voice discourse in the field of education, see Bernstein, 1999; Moore and Muller, 1999; Young, 2000.

material evidence. Ultimately, the voice of experience and the voice of expertise must discover a way of addressing each other and communicating together. Neither should claim unqualified authority and both should be open to critical and honest scrutiny.[1]

In discussions of **public-sector organizations**, voice is sometimes opposed to **choice**. The former represents citizen sovereignty in the running of organizations like schools, universities, and hospitals, whereas the latter relies on **market** forces to enhance efficiency and customer service (see **New Public Management**). Voice requires that public-sector organizations listen and respond to what their constituents demand, whereas choice privileges the better-off, since they have greater freedom to relocate where these provisions are of a higher standard or even opt out of the state provision altogether. This contrast between voice and choice may be more rhetorical than real, but it returns to Hirschman's core argument that sees voice as the hard-won prerogative of those inside and choice as the privilege of those who have the option of exit.

• See also *identity*

Voluntary organizations

Voluntary or non-profit organizations (abbreviated here as NPOs) represent collectively organized human efforts to deal with social issues that have been neglected or are only partially addressed by public bodies. NPOs are the baseline for aid in the expanding economic sector known as independent sector or Third Sector, expressing the ideals of civil society in promoting the education and involvement of citizens in the betterment of conditions for all social groups.

NPOs are not legal organizations according to international law (except for the International Committee of the Red Cross which was formed under the Geneva Convention). The status of NPOs depends on each country's legal and social welfare systems. Legally, NPOs must comply with national regulations regarding the establishment and management of non-profit organizations. With the exception of religious institutions, NPOs are similar to businesses, in that they have boards of directors or trustees and steering committees to ensure that they meet their fiduciary duties and maintain public trust.

The origin of many non-profit organizations can be found in actual or perceived violations of social justice. Different **cultures** bring different interpretations or dimensions to the concept of social justice. When these concepts become widely recognized and embraced, voluntary organizations, formal or informal, emerge as the vehicles for their achievement. However, many NPOs today pursue wider **goals** (e.g. professional, cultural, sports, etc.) that may not be directly related to social justice, reflecting 'optimal' rather than 'basic' **needs**. Generally, local or national NPOs are more likely to deal with social injustices, aiming to improve living conditions for the disadvantaged, whereas international NPOs tend to pursue global causes such as promoting **sustainable development** and protecting the natural environment. An important dimension of NPO work is to encourage self-help groups. The 'micro-credit' NPOs in India and developing areas of Asia and Africa seek to initiate and sustain economic activity on the basis of small-scale **entrepreneurship**, by empowering women in active economic **roles** and thereby reducing poverty.

NPOs grew in many countries and gained wider **legitimacy** in the post-Second World War period which placed greater emphasis on social welfare. There are now more than 1.6 million non-profit organizations worldwide, and 10,000 new such organizations are formed daily. In the past thirty years, 2 million NPOs have been established in the USA; Russia has an estimated 400,000 active NPOs, and there are 1–2 million

---

[1] Gabriel, 2004c.

such organizations, formal or informal, in India. Expansion of the formal voluntary sector is linked to the rise of the telecommunication industry and the funding potential of increasingly affluent middle and upper classes

Most voluntary organizations are funded by private and public donations, grants and fellowships, membership dues, and the sale of goods and services. Fund-raising activities constitute a major aspect of the their operations. The extent of support from the public, the corporate, and government sectors differs from country to country. Thus, in Japan, the Third Sector (known as 'Daisan') is a collaboration between the public and private sectors. By contrast, in the UK and the USA it is almost totally independent of business and government, while in developing countries it is often supported by public funds.

Early research approached NPOs either as a partner to government and business in the provision of social services or as an adversary that introduced new goals and **values**.[1] Subsequently Salamon reviewed the degree of autonomy of NPOs and distinguished between four types of relations between governments and the Third Sector, depending on the degree of cooperation, accommodation, competition, or symbiosis: government-dominant, dual, collaborative, and Third Sector dominant.[2] Accordingly, the amount of public support varies. The Nobel Prize-winning 'Doctors Without Frontiers' (MSF) receives 46 per cent of its funding from government sources, while the British government contributes only 25 per cent of funds for the UK's Oxfam Poverty and Famine Relief Organization.

Most national legislations encourage individuals and private organizations to donate in exchange for substantial tax benefits and almost all NPOs rely for their survival on exemptions from federal, state, and local taxes. Recent legislative efforts worldwide, however, have sought to limit (a) the level of NPO salaries, (b) the

proportion of salaried to voluntary employees, and (c) the maximum level of state-funding resources. Hence, the classification of an organization as a NPO or a charity becomes an important political issue. To be considered as non-profit, an organization must generally (a) have a legal charitable purpose and/or support an issue of private or public concern; (b) redirect its income to maintain and extend organizational processes and goals rather than enriching organization members, directors, or officers; and (c) include volunteers in the management and achievement of these goals.

Typically, the NPO **structure** comprises three basic functions: **governance**, central administration, and programmes. Governance concerns overall strategic planning and controls in regard to both long-term and short-term goals. Effective governance depends on the cooperation of a large number of stakeholders, service recipients, directorates, employees, management, and leaders of public opinion. Programmes are viewed in terms of inputs, processes, outputs, and outcomes. Inputs are the resources necessary to run them, such as money, facilities, and staff. Processes concern the implementation of each programme, for instance how battered women can receive protection and counselling or how welfare recipients can be represented to the authorities. Outputs are the units of actual service delivery, and are often debated along with outcomes by **stakeholders** as measures of organizational **success**. Central administration concerns the organizational structure and composition of staff, both salaried and voluntary. Non-profit organizations usually strive to keep administration costs low by increasing the proportion of volunteers.

'To volunteer is to choose to act in recognition of a need, with an attitude of social responsibility and without concern for monetary profit.'[3] The degree of commitment to volunteering depends on one's degree of involvement in a cause. A high degree of commitment

[1] Kramer, 1981; Knoke, 1990.   [2] Salamon, 1995.   [3] Ellis and Campbell, 1990, p. 4.

is associated with self-help groups and voluntary associations that offer immediate benefits to all members. Demographic profiles of volunteers suggest that older women are more likely to volunteer than other social groups, particularly in social welfare-related organizations. However, in many countries, there is now more volunteering among younger, male, and better-educated individuals, including student groups mobilizing for socio-political and environmental causes.

Voluntary organizations are now a universal phenomenon. They emerged as local expressions of care for people's welfare and social justice to become an international movement seeking to enable groups to make their **voices** heard, enhance the quality of their lives, and benefit future generations.

• See also *legitimacy, public-sector organizations*

RITA MANO, UNIVERSITY OF HAIFA

Women's studies

Women's studies grew rapidly as an interdisciplinary academic field in the 1970s and 1980s, exploring the position of women in society, often in a historical perspective. While there is some overlap with **gender** studies, women's studies concentrates on women's history, women's art and literature, women's sexuality and health, women's representation in politics and business, and so forth. A substantial part of women's studies has addressed women and work, both domestic and public, and women's experiences in organizations. Strongly influenced by **feminism**, women's studies is now a popular course in many British and American colleges and universities, driven by the conviction that women have, for a very long time, been invisible to many traditional academic disciplines and discourses which have been indifferent to gender and have treated the male as the normal subject of their enquiries.

Women's studies has criticized extensively disciplines like history, economics, sociology, psychology, politics, and anthropology for disregarding women or treating them as the permanent **Other**. In the 1950s, French philosopher and author Simone de Beauvoir argued that women were 'the second sex',[1] an assumption that most women accepted themselves, with very serious consequences. It was held, in other words, that male attitudes, male desires, and male behaviours represented normality, while women's attitudes, desires, and behaviours were in some ways aberrations. Unpredictable, capricious, and emotional, women were seen as fundamentally different from rational, orderly, and purposeful

men. This widely held assumption was a part not only of popular discourses but also of scholarly arguments. In a view that stretches from Aristotle to Freud, women were cast as the unreliable, mysterious, and anomalous half of humanity. This assumption was sustained in many languages by the habit of using the male pronouns (he, his, him) and the generic 'Man' and 'mankind' when referring to humans in general. One of the core discoveries of women's studies was that **language** is profoundly 'gendered', embodying systematic assumptions about the positions and standings of the genders. **Feminism**, both as a discourse and as a political movement, has challenged some of these assumptions. Women's studies has then emerged as a systematic attempt to give women a voice, enabling them to speak as subjects rather than to be spoken about as objects.

While women's studies represents a highly diverse field that encompasses a wide range of perspectives and interests, it is brought together by its critique of patriarchy. Patriarchy represents the common ground, and for some the common enemy. It is a term that originally meant the rule of the father but is more widely used to refer to male dominance in society. One of the early critics of patriarchy was American feminist Kate Millett,[2] who focused on male dominance and **violence** within marriage and the family. An important threat of patriarchy is a fear of female **sexuality** and a systematic attempt to suppress it, often through brutal humiliation, something Millett demonstrates with reference to the works of Normal Mailer, D. H. Lawrence, and Henry Miller. Millett, along with other American critics of

---

[1] Beauvoir, 1953.   [2] Millett, 1970.

patriarchy Betty Friedan and Shulamith Fire-
stone, is highly critical of Freud and his theory of female sexuality revolving around penis
envy. Some subsequent commentators on patriarchy have viewed penis envy itself as an effect
of patriarchy, one that expresses women's resentment at being subordinated and disempow-
ered.[1] Women's studies have turned increasingly
to French **post-structuralist** thinkers, especially
Michel Foucault, Jacques Lacan, Julia Kristeva,
Hélène Cixous, and Luce Irigaray, to analyse
patriarchy as a symbolic order embedded in **language** to which every child submits when she or
he renounces desire for the mother in what she
or he perceives as an act of submission to pater-
nal authority. Language has therefore remained
at the centre of attention for women's studies,
whether they look at women's representations in
film, the construction of women's **bodies** by contemporary medicine, or discrimination against
women in places of work.

The study of women at work has been an
expanding field in the past thirty years or so.
This encompasses research on women's participation in the economy, the nature of the
jobs that they do, the difficulties that they
encounter at work, as well as barriers to advanc-
ing their careers, the effects of measures to alleviate these difficulties, and the challenges in
achieving a work–life balance. In most organizational settings, gender continues to act as
a formidable divide, often invisible, that consigns women to lower echelons of organizations, in generally low-pay, low-status industries. Even in high-pay, high-status industries,
women are concentrated disproportionately in
low-skill grades. Gender also results in women
being over-represented in 'caring' roles within
organizations. Some of these inequalities are due
to old structures of prejudice and **discrimination**, which inhibit women's progress and career
opportunities. More subtly, gender **stereotypes**
presenting men as rational, tough, aggressive,
and task oriented and women as emotional,

soft, caring, and process oriented have further
disadvantaged women. Skills associated with
service occupations where there is a great concentration of female employees, notably in clerical, sales, and catering jobs, are often taken
for granted and lead to neither material nor
symbolic rewards. Nevertheless, it is becoming
increasingly accepted that **femininity**, often tied
to a sexual undercurrent, is made to work for
organizations to promote their sales, enhance
their image, and lure customers.[2]

Women have started to make some inroads
into **leadership** and senior management positions though their representation at the highest echelons of business remains limited. Only
a handful of Fortune 500 companies are led by
women CEOs (ten in 2006), though the number
of women CEOs is slowly growing, including
some high-publicity appointments (and in some
instances ousters) like Carly Fiorina at Hewlett
Packard, Anne Mulcahy at Xerox, Margaret C.
(Meg) Whitman at eBay, and Marjorie Scardino
at Pearson. Inroads into leadership positions
in other spheres, including public and voluntary sectors, academic institutions, publishing,
media, and entertainment, have been more pronounced. The advance of women in politics
has been highly uneven across different countries, but the trend has been consistently for a
higher representation of women in senior political posts. Eighteen of 192 heads of state in 2006
were women.

The gradual appearance of women in senior
positions raises many issues. One concerns the
continuing presence of a '**glass ceiling**' that
inhibits women's advancement to the top, the
forces that keep it in place, and also the forces
that make women's exercise of leadership at top
level more problematic.[3] Another concerns the
differences in leadership approaches or 'styles'
between men and women, whether, for example,
women leaders are more likely to favour empathetic, participative, democratic, and transforming leadership than men. Research findings in

---

[1] Mitchell, 1975.   [2] For a comprehensive and informative textbook on women at work, see Wilson, 2003.   [3] Marshall, 1984; 1995.

this area have been inconsistent, failing to establish conclusively whether it is the leadership exercised by women that is different or whether it is perceived as being different *because* it is exercised by women.[1] Given the gendered nature of organizational discourses, it is unlikely that these two factors can ever be separated.

• See also *discrimination, femininity, feminism, gender, sexuality*

Work

Unlike **labour**, which is a concept drawn from political economy, work is in the main a sociological and a psychological concept. It incorporates a wide range of cultural assumptions regarding what constitutes work, what is the purpose and **meaning** of work, and what its values and rewards are. 'What work do you do?', for example, is a question which cannot be answered without understanding the meaning which a **culture** attributes to work, the expectation of receiving payment or the **status** and prestige of different kinds of work. Different cultures have assigned widely diverging meanings to work and its corollary, leisure. Some have approached it as a primeval curse afflicting humanity, some as the true road to holiness and **success**, and some, like the ancient Greeks, as a lower form of occupation, unworthy of free individuals. Clusters of meanings around work, especially those regarding the relations between work and the good life, are often said to constitute work **ethics**.

The sociology of work has been an important field of sociology, drawing its core concepts from some of the founders of the discipline, notably Marx's theory of work **alienation**, Durkheim's work on the division of labour in society, and Weber's theory on the Protestant work **ethic** and the spirit of capitalism.[2] In the last twenty or thirty years, however, the sociology of work has tended to fragment into several fields, including

organizational theory, the sociology of **professions** and occupations, **Human Resource Management**, **Labour Process Theory**, gender relations, and even cultural studies. Psychology never approached work in the same single-minded way that sociology did and much of the psychology that addresses work situations has been absorbed into what is now known as *Organization Behaviour*, a discipline that examines all aspects of psychology in organizations large and small, including employee motivation, personality, groups, leadership, attitudes, and so forth.

Two of the reasons why studies of work have tended to fragment into different disciplinary areas are, first, the growing differentiation of work itself into many diverse activities, and, secondly, the ever-increasing importance of **consumption** (as opposed to production) as the terrain where new cultural, political, and social trends appear. In the past, sociology (and to a lesser extent psychology) could address the industrial proletariat as a fairly uniform social **class** of workers, who earned their livelihood and supported their families through the sweat of their brow, whether as unskilled labourers, skilled craftsmen, or white-collar staff. Work today assumes a wide variety of forms, full-time and part-time, free-lance and on contract, voluntary and unpaid, and so forth. Different areas of work, such as service work, information-processing work, media work, and professional work, make very different demands on those who carry them out. It becomes difficult then to generalize about 'work' as an activity across all these different sectors, each of which has its own patterns. As a result, class as the dominant principle of social stratification, the category that used to define a person's social allegiances as well as his or her social attitudes, has been supplanted by other categories, especially **gender** and ethnicity, but also ownership of cultural and educational **capital**.

---

[1] Eagly and Johnson, 1990; Eagly, Makhijani, and Klonsky, 1992; van Engen and Willemsen, 2004.   [2] For an informative conspectus of the discipline, see Grint, 1998.

Possibly even more important than the fragmentation of work itself is the emergence of consumption as a sphere of social activity where social **identities** are fashioned. While industrial workers during the early days of sociology were forced to spend all their earnings in supporting themselves and their families, throughout the twentieth century, consumption has emerged as a vibrant field of activity for ever-increasing sections of the population of industrial nations. Consumption is not just a means of fulfilling needs but permeates social relations, identities, perceptions, and images; it provides a vital source of **meanings** in people's everyday lives.

Consumption itself is intimately linked with production—at the level of economic exchange, the same goods and services that are consumed are also produced through work. They are also linked at the level of cultural, social, and psychological experiences—people's expectations and outlooks towards their work are shaped by their experiences and aspirations as consumers. Already from the early part of the twentieth century, the Fordist Deal—ever-increasing standards of living in exchange for boring and repetitive work—had become the critical bridge linking production and consumption (see **Fordism**). Finally, for many people work *is*, at least in part, consumption and consumption *is* work. In the course of their work today, many people consume services and goods in hotels, restaurants, golf courses, airport lounges, and so forth. They consume books, magazines, information technology, and so forth. Thus, the growing importance of consumption and its interrelation with the world of work has made it more difficult to generalize about the meanings and nature of work in isolation.

In spite of difficulties in making generalizations about the nature of work in contemporary societies, certain issues surface regularly in work discourses. These include:

- The work–life balance, the increasing difficulty in establishing boundaries between what is work and what is leisure, and the attendant phenomena of workaholism and work burn out.
- The increasingly precarious nature of work in many industries and many occupations, in consequence of **downsizing**, **outsourcing**, and other contemporary management trends.
- The changing nature of demands made by workers working in a 'virtual' work environment, devoid of direct face-to-face contact with others.
- The call for greater worker flexibility and the emergence of the chameleon employee, the employee who can fit in many different work situations and adapt effectively to different work challenges.
- The importance of lifelong **learning** and acquisition of new skills in order to keep up with the changing demands of work and work-related technologies.
- The changing and expanding forms of workplace **controls** and new forms of employee resistance, including whistle-blowing, sabotage, and subvertizing.
- The enduring inequalities and discriminatory practices that create insurmountable barriers for many social groups, most especially women and members of certain ethnic minorities.
- The changing nature of **careers** in the light of new patterns of work and new patterns of consumption.

• See also *emotional labour and emotional work, labour*

REFERENCES

Abbott, Andrew Delano. 1988. *The system of professions: an essay on the division of expert labor*. Chicago: University of Chicago Press.

Abrahamson, Eric. 1991. Managerial fads and fashions: the diffusion and rejection of innovations. *Academy of Management Review*, 16(3): 586–612.

——— 1996. Management fashion. *Academy of Management Review*, 21(1): 254–85.

Acker, Joan. 2006. *Class questions: feminist answers*. Lanham, Md.: Rowman & Littlefield Publishers.

Ackroyd, Stephen and Thompson, Paul. 1999. *Organizational misbehaviour*. London: Sage.

Adams, J. Stacy, Berkowitz, Leonard, and Hatfield, Elaine. 1976. *Equity theory: toward a general theory of social interaction*. New York: Academic Press.

Adorno, T. W., Frenkel-Brunswik, E., Levinson, D., and Sanford, N. 1950. *The authoritarian personality*. New York: Harper and Row.

Albert, S. and Whetten, D. A. 1985. Organizational identity. In L. L. Cummings and B. M. Staw (eds.), *Research in organizational behavior*: vii. 263–95. Greenwich, Conn.: JAI Press.

Alcoff, Linda. 2006. *Identity politics reconsidered* (1st edn.). New York: Palgrave Macmillan.

Allison, G. T. 1971. *Essence of decision: explaining the Cuban missile crisis*. Waltham, Mass.: Little Brown.

Alvesson, Mats. 2002. *Understanding organizational culture*. London: Sage.

——— and Billing, Yvonne Due. 1997. *Understanding gender and organizations*. London: Sage.

——— and Karreman, Dan. 2000. Taking the linguistic turn in organizational research: challenges, responses, consequences. *Journal of Applied Behavioral Science*, 36: 136–58.

——— ——— 2001. Odd couple: making sense of the curious concept of knowledge management. *Journal of Management Studies*, 38(7): 995–1018.

——— and Willmott, Hugh (eds.). 1992. *Critical management studies*. London: Sage.

Amin, Ash. 1994. *Post-Fordism: a reader*. Oxford: Blackwell.

Anderson, Benedict. 1983. *Imagined communities*. London: Verso.

Ang, S. and Cummings, L. L. 1997. Strategic response to institutional influences on information systems outsourcing. *Organization Science*, 8(3): 235–56.

Ansoff, H. Igor. 1965. *Corporate strategy; an analytic approach to business policy for growth and expansion*. New York: McGraw-Hill.

Antonacopoulou, Elena P. and Gabriel, Yiannis. 2001. Emotion, learning and organizational change: towards an integration of psychoanalytic and other perspectives. *Journal of Organizational Change Management*, 14(5): 435–51.

Anzieu, Didier. 1984. *The group and the unconscious*. London: Routledge and Kegan Paul.

Arendt, Hannah. 1958. *The origins of totalitarianism*. Cleveland: Meridian Books.

——— 1970. *On violence*. New York: Harcourt.

Argyris, Chris. 1960. *Understanding organizational behavior*. London: Tavistock.

——— 2007. Double-loop learning in a classroom setting. In M. Reynolds and R. Vince (eds.), *The handbook of experiential learning and management education*. Oxford: Oxford University Press.

——— and Schön, Donald A. 1974. *Theory in practice*. San Francisco: Jossey-Bass.

——— ——— 1978. *Organizational learning: a theory in action perspective*. Reading, Mass.: Addison-Wesley.

——— ——— 1996. *Organizational learning II: theory, method, and practice*. Reading, Mass.: Addison-Wesley.

Aristotle. 1953. *The Nicomachean ethics*. Harmondsworth: Penguin.

——— 1963. *The poetics*. London: Dent.

——— 1981. *The politics*. Harmondsworth: Penguin.

——— 1991. *The rhetoric*. Harmondsworth: Penguin.

Armstrong, D. A. 1992. *Managing by storying around: a new method of leadership*. New York: Doubleday.

Armstrong, Karen. 2005. *A short history of myth*. Edinburgh: Canongate.

Ash, Marinell. 1990. William Wallace and Robert the Bruce: the life and death of a national myth. In R. Samuel and P. Thompson (eds.), *The myths we live by*. London: Routledge.

Ashford, B. E. and Gibbs, B. W. 1990. The double-edge of organizational legitimation. *Organization Science*, 1: 177–94.

Auster, Carol Jean. 1996. *The sociology of work: concepts and cases*. Thousand Oaks, Calif.: Pine Forge Press.

Auster, Ellen. 1993. Demystifying the glass ceiling: organizational and interpersonal dynamics of gender bias. *Business and the Contemporary World*, 5(Summer): 47–68.

Axley, S. R. 1984. Managerial and organizational communication in terms of the conduit metaphor. *Academy of Management Review*, 9: 428–37.

Bacharach, Samuel B. and Lawler, Edward J. 1980. *Power and politics in organizations*. San Francisco: Jossey-Bass.

Bachrach, Peter and Baratz, Morton Sachs. 1970. *Power and poverty: theory and practice*. Oxford: Oxford University Press

Baier, Annette C. 1985. What do women want in a moral theory? *Nous*, 19(1): 53–63.

Banerjee, Subhabrata Bobby and Linstead, Stephen. 2004. Masking subversion: neocolonial embeddedness in anthropological accounts of indigenous management. *Human Relations*, 57(2): 221–47.

Barber, B. 1995. All economies are embedded: the career of a concept, and beyond. *Social Research*, 62(2): 387–413.

Barnard, Chester I. 1938. *The functions of the executive*. Cambridge, Mass.: Harvard University Press.

Barney, Jay B. 1986. Organizational culture: can it be a source of sustained competitive advantage? *Academy of Management Review*, 11: 656–65.

—— 1991. Firm resources and sustained competitive advantage. *Journal of Management*, 17(1): 99–120.

Bartlett, Christopher A. and Ghoshal, Sumantra. 1989. *Managing across borders: the transnational solution*. Boston: Harvard Business School Press.

Bass, B. M. 1999. Two decades of research and development in transformational leadership. *European Journal of Work and Organizational Psychology*, 8(1): 9–32.

—— and Avolio, B. J. 1994. Shatter the glass ceiling: women may make better managers. *Human Resource Management*, 33(4): 549–60.

—— and Seltzer, J. 1990. Transformational leadership: beyond initiation and consideration. *Journal of Management*, 16(4): 693–703.

Bate, Walter Jackson. 1976. *Negative capability: the intuitive approach in Keats*. New York: AMS Press.

Bateson, Gregory. 1972. *Steps to an ecology of mind*. London: Intertext Books.

Baudrillard, Jean. 1968/1988. The system of objects. In M. Poster (ed.), *Jean Baudrillard: Selected Writings*. Cambridge: Polity Press.

—— 1970/1988. Consumer society. In M. Poster (ed.), *Jean Baudrillard: Selected Writings*. Cambridge: Polity Press.

—— 1983. *In the shadow of the silent majorities*. New York: Semiotext(e).

—— 1988. Simulacra and simulations. In M. Poster (ed.), *Jean Baudrillard: Selected Writings*: 166–84. Cambridge: Polity Press.

Bauman, Zygmunt. 1988. *Freedom*. Milton Keynes: Open University Press.

—— 1989. *Modernity and the holocaust*. Cambridge: Polity Press.

—— 1992. *Intimations of postmodernity*. London: Routledge.

—— 1993. *Postmodern ethics*. Oxford: Basil Blackwell.

—— 1997. *Postmodernity and its discontents*. Cambridge: Polity Press.

—— 1998. *Work, consumerism and the new poor*. Buckingham: Open University Press.

Beauvoir, Simone de. 1953. *The second sex*. London: Jonathan Cape.

Beck, Ulrich. 1992. *Risk society: towards a new modernity*. London: Sage.

Becker, Gary Stanley. 1957. *The economics of discrimination*. Chicago: University of Chicago Press.

Becker, Howard Saul. 1964. *The other side; perspectives on deviance*. New York: Free Press of Glencoe.

Beer, M. and Nohria, N. (eds.). 2000. *Breaking the code of change*. Boston: Harvard Business School Press.

—— Spector, B., and Lawrence, P. R. 1984. *Managing human assets*. Boston: Harvard Business School Press.

Belk, Russell W. 1982. Gift giving behavior. *Research in Marketing*, 2: 95–126.

Bell, Emma and Taylor, Stephen. 2003. The elevation of work: pastoral power and the new age work ethic. *Organization*, 10(2): 329–49.

Benjamin, Jessica. 1988. *The bonds of love*. New York: Pantheon.

Benjamin, Walter. 1968. The storyteller: reflections on the works of Nikolai Leskov. In H. Arendt (ed.), *Walter Benjamin: Illuminations*. London: Jonathan Cape.

Bennis, Warren G. 1998. *On becoming a leader*. London: Arrow.

—— and Nanus, Burt. 1985. *Leaders: the strategies for taking charge*. New York: Harper and Row.

Berger, Peter and Luckmann, Thomas. 1967. *The social construction of reality*. Garden City, NY: Anchor.

Bergmann, Gustav and Heald, William Smith. 1992. *New foundations of ontology*. Madison: University of Wisconsin Press.

Bergquist, William. 1993. *The postmodern organization: mastering the art of irreversible change*. San Francisco: Jossey-Bass.

Berle, Adolf Augustus and Means, Gardiner Coit. 1933. *The modern corporation and private property*. New York: Macmillan Co.

Bernstein, Basil. 1999. Vertical and horizontal discourse: an essay. *British Journal of Sociology of Education*, 20(2): 157–74.

Bernstein, Peter L. 1996. *Against the gods: the remarkable story of risk*. New York: John Wiley and Sons.

Best, Steven and Kellner, Douglas. 1991. *Postmodern theory: critical interrogations*. New York: Guilford Press.

Beynon, Huw. 1973. *Working for Ford*. London: Allen Lane.

Bion, Wilfred R. 1961. *Experiences in groups*. London: Tavistock.

Blauner, Robert. 1964. *Alienation and freedom*. Chicago: University of Chicago Press.

—— 1972. *Racial oppression in America*. New York: Harper and Row.

—— 2001. *Still the big news: racial oppression in America* (rev. and expanded edn.). Philadelphia: Temple University Press.

Blok, Anton. 2001. *Honour and violence*. Cambridge: Polity.

Blumer, Herbert G. 1969. *Symbolic Interactionism: perspective and method*. Berkeley and Los Angeles: University of California Press.

—— 1969/1973. Fashion: from class differentiation to collective selection. In G. Wills and D. Midgley (eds.), *Fashion Marketing*, 327–40. London: Allen & Unwin.

Bly, Robert. 1990. *Iron John: a book about men*. New York: Addison Wesley.

Bochner, Arthur P. and Ellis, Carolyn. 2002. *Ethnographically speaking: autoethnography, literature, and aesthetics*. Walnut Creek, Calif.: AltaMira Press.

Boje, David M. 1991. The storytelling organization: a study of story performance in an office-supply firm. *Administrative Science Quarterly*, 36: 106–26.

—— 1994. Organizational storytelling: the struggles of pre-modern, modern and postmodern organizational learning discourses. *Management Learning*, 25(3): 433–61.

—— 1995. Stories of the storytelling organization: a postmodern analysis of Disney as 'Tamara Land'. *Academy of Management Review*, 38(4): 997–1035.

—— 2001. *Narrative methods for organizational and communication research*. London: Sage.

Bolton, Sharon. 2005. *Emotion management in the workplace*. Houndmills: Palgrave.

Boorstin, Daniel J. 1962. *The image or what happened to the American dream*. New York: Atheneum.

Borgmann, Albert. 1999. *Holding on to reality: the nature of information at the turn of the millennium*. Chicago: University of Chicago Press.

Bourdieu, Pierre. 1984. *Distinction: a social critique of the judgement of taste*. London: Routledge.

—— 1993. *The field of cultural production: essays on art and literature*, ed. Randal Johnson. New York: Columbia University Press.

—— 2005. Principles of an economic anthropology. In N. J. Smelser and R. Swedberg (eds.), *The handbook of economic sociology*: 75–89. Princeton: Princeton University Press.

Bowles, Martin L. 1989. Myth, meaning and work organization. *Organization Studies*, 10(3): 405–21.

—— 1997. The myth of management: direction and failure in contemporary organizations. *Human Relations*, 50: 779–803.

Boyatzis, Richard E. 1982. *The competent manager: a model for effective performance*. New York: Wiley.

Boyle, David. 2000. *The tyranny of numbers: why counting can't make us happy*. London: HarperCollins.

Bratton, John, Grint, Keith, and Nelson, Debra L. 2005. *Organizational leadership*. Mason, Oh.: Thomson/South-Western.

Braverman, Harry. 1974. *Labor and monopoly capital*. New York: Monthly Review Press.

Broadbent, Donald Eric. 1958. *Perception and communication*. London: Pergamon Press.

Brock, David, Powell, Michael J., and Hinings, C. R. 1999. *Restructuring the professional organization: accounting, healthcare, and law*. London: Routledge.

Brockner, J. 1992. The escalation of commitment to a failing course of action: toward theoretical process. *Academy of Management Review*, 17(1): 39–61.

Brown, Andrew D. 2004. Authoritative sensemaking in a public inquiry report. *Organization Studies*, 25(1): 95–112.

—— 2006. A narrative approach to collective identities. *Journal of Management Studies*, 43(4): 731–53.

—— and Humphreys, Michael. 2002. Nostalgia and narrativization of identity: a Turkish case study. *British Journal of Management*, 13: 141–59.

—— —— 2006. Organizational identity and place: a discursive exploration of hegemony and resistance. *Journal of Management Studies*, 43(2): 231–57.

—— —— and Gurney, Paul M. 2005. Narrative, identity and change: a case study of Laskarina Holidays. *Journal of Organizational Change Management*, 18(4): 312–26.

Brown, J. S. and Duguid, P. 1991. Organizational learning and communities of practice: toward a unified view of working, learning and innovation. *Organization Science*, 2(1): 40–57.

—— —— 2000. *The social life of information*. Boston: Harvard Business School Press.

Brown, Rupert. 2000. *Group processes: dynamics within and between groups* (2nd edn.). Oxford: Blackwell Publishers.

Brundtland, Gro Harlem. 1987. *Our common future: report of the World Commission on Environment and Development (WCED) chaired by Gro Harlem Brundtland*. Oxford: Oxford University Press.

Bruner, Jerome S. 1962. *On knowing; essays for the left hand*. Cambridge, Mass.: Belknap Press of Harvard University Press.

—— 1986. *Actual minds, possible worlds*. Cambridge, Mass.: Harvard University Press.

—— 1990. *Acts of meaning*. Cambridge, Mass.: Harvard University Press.

—— 1991. The narrative construction of reality. *Critical Inquiry*, 18: 1–21.

Brunsson, Nils. 2003. *The organization of hypocrisy: talk, decisions, and actions in organizations*. Copenhagen: Wiley.

Bryman, Alan. 1999. The Disneyization of society. *Sociological Review*, 47(1): 25–47.

Buchanan, James M. and Tullock, Gordon. 1962. *The calculus of consent: logical foundations of constitutional democracy*. Ann Arbor: University of Michigan Press.

Burawoy, Michael. 1979. *Manufacturing consent*. Chicago: Chicago University Press.

—— 1985. *The politics of production*. London: Verso.

Burke, Kenneth. 1945/1969. *A grammar of motives*. Berkeley and Los Angles: University of California Press.

—— 1966. *Language as symbolic action: essays on life, literature, and method*. Berkeley and Los Angles: University of California Press.

Burnham, James. 1945. *The managerial revolution*. Harmondsworth: Penguin.

Burns, James McGregor. 1978. *Leadership*. New York: Harper and Row.

Burns, Tom and Stalker, George M. 1961. *The management of innovation*. London: Tavistock.

Burrell, Gibson. 1990. Fragmented labours. In D. Knights and H. Willmott (eds.), *Labour process theory*: 274–96. London: Macmillan.

—— 1996. Normal science, paradigms, metaphors, discourses and genealogies of analysis. In S. Clegg, C. Hardy, and W. Nord (eds.), *Handbook of organization studies*: 642–58. London: Sage.

—— 1997. *Pandemonium: towards a retro-organization theory*. London: Sage.

—— and Morgan, Gareth. 1979. *Sociological paradigms and organizational analysis: elements of the sociology of corporate life*. London: Heinemann.

Butler, J. 1993. *Bodies that matter: on the discursive limits of 'sex'*. New York: Routledge.

Byrne, Eleanor and McQuillan, Martin. 1999. *Deconstructing Disney*. London: Pluto.

Calas, Marta B. and Smircich, Linda. 1992. Using the 'F' word: feminist theories and the social consequences of organizational research. In A. J. Mills and P. Tancred (eds.), *Gendering Organizational Theory*: 222–34. Newbury Park, Calif.: Sage.

—— 1996. From the woman's point of view: feminist approaches to organization studies. In S. Clegg, C. Hardy, and W. Nord (eds.), *Handbook of organization studies*. London: Sage.

—— 1999. Past postmodernism? Reflections and tentative directions. *Academy of Management Review*, 24(4): 649–71.

Callon, Michel. 1998. *The laws of the markets*. Oxford: Blackwell.

—— and Latour, Bruno. 1981. Unscrewing the big Leviathan: how actors macro-structure reality and how sociologists help them to do so. In K. Knorr-Cetina and A. V. Cicourel (eds.), *Advances in social theory and methodology: toward an integration of micro- and macro-sociologies*: 277–303. Boston: Routledge and Kegan Paul.

Campbell, Colin. 1989. *The romantic ethic and the spirit of modern consumerism*. Oxford: Macmillan.

Campbell, John L., Hollingsworth, J. Rogers, and Lindberg, Leon N. 1991. *Governance of the American economy*. Cambridge: Cambridge University Press.

Campbell, Joseph. 1949/1988. *The hero with a thousand faces*. London: Palladin Books.

Camus, Albert. 1956. *The rebel; an essay on man in revolt* (1st Vintage edn.). New York: Vintage Books.

Canguilhem, Georges. 1989. *The normal and the pathological*. New York: Zone Books.

Carlzon, Jan. 1989. *Moments of truth*. New York: Harper and Row.

Carr, Adrian. 1993. The psychostructure of work: bend me, shape me, anyway you want me, as long as you love me it's alright. *Journal of Managerial Psychology*, 8(6): 2–6.

—— 1998. Identity, compliance and dissent in organisations: a psychoanalytic perspective. *Organization*, 5(1): 81–9.

—— and Lapp, Cheryl A. 2006. *Leadership is a matter of life and death: the psychodynamics of Eros and Thanatos working in organisations*. New York: Palgrave Macmillan.

Carroll, G. R. 1985. Concentration and specialization: dynamics of niche width in populations of organizations. *American Journal of Sociology*, 90: 1262–83.

Casey, Caherine. 1999. 'Come join the family': discipline and integration in corporate and organizational culture. *Human Relations*, 52(2): 155–78.

Cassirer, Ernst. 1943/1992. *An essay on man: an introduction to a philosophy of human culture*. New Haven: Yale University Press.

Castells, Manuel. 1996a. *The information age: economy, society and culture*, i: *The rise of the network society*. Oxford: Blackwell.

—— 1996b. *The rise of the network society*. Malden, Mass.: Blackwell Publishers.

Certeau, Michel de. 1984. *The practice of everyday life*. Berkeley and Los Angles: University of California Press.

Chandler, Alfred Dupont. 1962. *Strategy and structure: chapters in the history of the industrial enterprise*. Cambridge, Mass.: MIT Press.

Chasseguet-Smirgel, Janine. 1976. Some thoughts on the ego-Ideal: a contribution to the study of the 'illness of ideality'. *Psychoanalytic Quarterly*, 45: 345–73.

Chia, Robert. 1996. Metaphors and metaphorization in organizational analysis: thinking beyond the thinkable. In D. Grant and C. Oswick (eds.),

Metaphor and organizations: 127–45. London: Sage.

—— 1998. From complexity science to complex thinking: organization as simple location. *Organization*, 5(3): 341–69.

—— and Morgan, Stuart. 1996. Educating the philosopher-manager: de-signing the times. *Management Learning*, 27(1): 40–55.

Chodorow, Nancy. 1978. *The reproduction of mothering: psychoanalysis and the sociology of gender*. Berkeley and Los Angles: University of California Press.

Chomsky, Noam. 1997. How free is the market?, *Lip Magazine* <http://www.lipmagazine.org/articles/featchomsky_63.htm>.

—— 2006. *Failed states: the abuse of power and the assault on democracy* (1st edn.). New York: Metropolitan Books/Henry Holt.

Christensen, C. Roland, Andrews, Kenneth Richmond, Bower, Joseph L., and Learned, Edmund Philip. 1965/1973. *Business policy: text and cases* (3rd edn.). Homewood, Ill.: R. D. Irwin.

Christian, J., Porter, L. W., and Moffitt, G. 2006. Workplace diversity and group relations: an overview. *Group Processes & Intergroup Relations*, 9(4): 459–66.

Ciborra, C. 2002. *The labyrinths of information: challenging the wisdom of systems*. Oxford: Oxford University Press.

Cilliers, P. 1998. *Complexity and postmodernism: understanding complex systems*. London: Routledge.

Ciulla, Joanne (ed.). 1998/2004. *Ethics, the heart of leadership*. Westport, Cann.: Praeger.

Clark, Timothy and Fincham, Robin. 2002. *Critical consulting: new perspectives on the management advice industry*. Malden, Mass.: Blackwell Publishers.

Clausewitz, Carl von. 1968. *On war*, trans. J. J. Graham (new and rev. edn.). Harmondsworth: Penguin.

Clegg, Stewart. 1990. *Modern organizations: organization studies in the postmodern world*. London: Sage.

—— Kornberger, Martin, and Pitsis, Tyrone. 2005. *Managing and organizations: an introduction to theory and practice*. London: Sage.

Cleverley, G. 1971. *Managers and magic*. London: Longman.

Cohen, M. D., March, J. G., and Olsen, J. P. 1972. A garbage can model of organizational choice. *Administrative Science Quarterly*, 17: 1–25.

Coleman, J. S. 1988. Social capital in the creation of human-capital. *American Journal of Sociology*, 94: S95–S120.

Collins, David. 2000. *Management fads and buzzwords: critical-practical perspectives*. London: Routledge.

Collinson, David. 1982. *Managing the shopfloor: subjectivity, masculinity and workplace culture*. Berlin: Walter de Gruyter.

—— 1988. 'Engineering humour': masculinity, joking and conflict in shop-floor relations. *Organization Studies*, 9(2): 181–99.

—— 1994. Strategies of resistance: power, knowledge and subjectivity in the workplace. In J. Jermier, W. Nord, and D. Knights (eds.), *Resistance and power in organizations*: 25–68. London: Routledge.

—— 2002. Managing humour. *Journal of Management Studies*, 39(3): 269–88.

—— 2005. Dialectics of leadership. *Human Relations*, 58(11): 1419–42.

—— 2006. Rethinking followership: a post-structuralist analysis of follower identities. *Leadership Quarterly*, 17(2): 179–89.

Cook, S. D. N. and Brown, J. S. 1999. Bridging epistemologies: the generative dance between organizational knowledge and organizational knowing. *Organization Science*, 10(4): 381–400.

—— and Yanow, D. 1993. Culture and organizational learning. *Journal of Management Inquiry*, 2(4): 373–90.

Cooper, C. L., Dewe, P., and Michael, P. O. D. 2001. *Organizational stress: a review and critique of theory, research, and applications*. Thousand Oaks, Calif.: Sage.

Cox, Oliver Cromwell. 1948. *Caste, class, & race: a study in social dynamics* (1st edn.). Garden City, NY: Doubleday.

Cox, T. H., Lobel, S. A., and McLeod, P. L. 1991. Effects of ethnic-group cultural-differences on cooperative and competitive behavior on a group task. *Academy of Management Journal*, 34(4): 827–47.

Craib, Ian. 1997. Social constructionism as a social psychosis. *Sociology*, 31(1): 1–15.

—— 1998. *Experiencing identity*. London: Sage.

Craig, R. 1999. Communication theory as a field. *Communication Theory*, 9: 119–61.

Crenshaw, Martha. 1995. *Terrorism in context*. University Park, Pa.: Pennsylvania State University Press.

Culler, Jonathan. 1981/2001. *The pursuit of signs: semiotics, literature, deconstruction* (Routledge Classics edn.). London: Routledge.

Currie, Mark. 1998. *Postmodern narrative theory*. New York: St Martin's Press.

Cutler, Ian. 2000. The cynical manager. *Management Learning*, 31(3): 295–313.

—— 2005. *Cynicism from Diogenes to Dilbert*. Jefferson, NC: McFarland & Company.

Czarniawska, Barbara. 1997. *Narrating the organization: dramas of institutional identity*. Chicago: University of Chicago Press.

—— 1999. *Writing management: organization theory as a literary genre*. Oxford: Oxford University Press.

—— 2001. Is it possible to be a constructionist consultant? *Management Learning*, 32(2): 253–66.

—— 2002. *Humiliation: a standard organizational product*. Paper presented at the Subaltern Storytelling Seminar, University College Cork, 28–9 June.

—— 2004. *Narratives in social science research*. London: Sage.

—— and Joerges, Bernard. 1996. *Travel of ideas*. Berlin: de Gruyter.

Czarniawska-Joerges, Barbara. 1995. Narration or science: collapsing the division in organization studies. *Organization*, 2(1): 11–33.

—— and Joerges, Bernard. 1990. Linguistic artifacts at service of organizational control. In P. Gagliardi (ed.), *Symbols and artifacts: views of the corporate landscape*. Berlin: Walter de Gruyter.

Damasio, Antonio R. 1994. *Descartes' error: emotion, reason, and the human brain*. New York: Putnam.

—— 1999. *The feeling of what happens: body and emotion in the making of consciousness* (1st edn.). New York: Harcourt Brace.

Davies, C. 1988. Stupidity and rationality: jokes from the iron cage. In C. Powell and G. E. C. Paton (eds.), *Humour in society*: 1–32. London: Macmillan.

Dean, J. W., Brandes, P., and Dharwadkar, R. 1998. Organizational cynicism. *Academy of Management Review*, 23(2): 341–52.

Debord, Guy. 1977. *Society of the spectacle*. Detroit: Black and Red.

Delbridge, Rick. 1998. *Life on the line in contemporary manufacturing: the workplace experience of lean production and the 'Japanese' model*. New York: Oxford University Press.

Denning, Stephen. 2000. *The springboard: how storytelling ignites action in knowledge-era organizations*. Oxford: Butterworth-Heinemann.

—— 2005. *The leader's guide to storytelling: mastering the art and discipline of business narrative*. San Francisco: Jossey-Bass.

Denzin, Norman K. 1992. *Symbolic interactionism and cultural studies: the politics of interpretation*. Cambridge, Mass.: Blackwell.

Derrida, Jacques. 1973. *Speech and phenomena*. Evanston, Ill.: Northwestern University Press.

—— 1976. *Of grammatology*. Baltimore: Johns Hopkins University Press.

Devereux, George. 1979. Fantasy and symbol as dimensions of reality. In R. H. Hook (ed.), *Fantasy and symbol*: 19–31. London: Academic Press.

Dewey, John. 1925/1958. *Experience and nature (the 1925 Paul Carus lectures)*. New York: Dover Publications.

—— 1934/1959. *Art as experience*. New York: Capricorn Books.

Diamond, Jared M. 2005. *Collapse: how societies choose to fail or succeed*. Harmondsworth: Penguin.

Diamond, Michael A. 1993. *The unconscious life of organizations: interpreting organizational identity*. London: Quorum Books.

—— 1997. Administrative assault: a contemporary psychoanalytic view of violence and aggression in the workplace. *American Review of Public Administration*, 27(3): 228–47.

Diderot, Denis and Alembert, Jean Le Rond d. 1965. *Encyclopedia; selections [by] Diderot, d'Alembert and a society of men of letters*, ed. and trans, Nelly S. Hoyt and Thomas Cassirer. Indianapolis: Bobbs-Merrill.

Dimaggio, P. J. and Powell, W. W. 1983. The iron cage revisited: institutional isomorphism and collective rationality in organizational fields. *American Sociological Review*, 48(2): 147–60.

Di Tomaso, Nancy. 1989. Sexuality in the workplace: discrimination and harassment. In J. Hearn, D. L. Sheppard, P. Tancred-Sheriff, and G. Burrell (eds.), *The sexuality of organization*: 71–89. London: Sage.

Dixon, Norman. 1976. *On the psychology of military incompetence*. Harmondsworth: Penguin.

Dodgson, M., Gann, D. M., and Salter, A. 2005. *Think play do: technology, organization and innovation*. Oxford: Oxford University Press.

—————— 2007. 'In case of fire, please use the elevator': simulation technology and organization in fire engineering. *Organization Science*, 18(5): 849–64.

—————— 2008. *The management of technological innovation: strategy and practice*. Oxford: Oxford University Press.

Donaldson, Lex. 1995. *American anti-management theories of organization: a critique of paradigm proliferation*. Cambridge: Cambridge University Press.

Douglas, Mary. 1966/2002. *Purity and danger* (Routledge Classics edn.). London: Routledge.

—— 1975a. Deciphering a meal. In M. Douglas (ed.), *Implicit meanings: essays in anthropology*: 179–92. London: Routledge.

—— 1975b. Jokes. In M. Douglas (ed.), *Implicit meanings: essays in anthropology*: 179–92. London: Routledge.

—— and Isherwood, Baron. 1978. *The world of goods: towards an anthropology of consumption*. London: Allen Lane.

—— and Wildavsky, Aaron B. 1982. *Risk and culture: an essay on the selection of technical and environmental dangers*. Berkeley and Los Angeles: University of California Press.

Doyal, Len and Gough, Ian. 1991. *A theory of human need*. New York: Guilford Press.

Driver, Michaela. 2002. The learning organization: Foucauldian gloom or Utopian sunshine? *Human Relations*, 55(1): 33–53.

—— 2005. From empty speech to full speech? Reconceptualizing spirituality in organizations based on a psychoanalytically-grounded understanding of the self. *Human Relations*, 58(9): 1091–110.

—— 2007. A spiritual turn in organization studies: meaning making or meaningless? *Journal of Management, Spirituality and Religion*, 4(1): 56–86.

Drucker, Peter F. 1959. *Landmarks of tomorrow* (1st edn.). New York: Harper.

—— 1988. Management and the world's work. *Harvard Business Review*, 66(September–October): 65–76.

du Gay, Paul. 1996. *Consumption and identity at work*. London: Sage.

—— 2000. *In praise of bureaucracy*. London: Sage.

—— and Salaman, Graeme. 1992. The cult(ure) of the customer. *Journal of Management Studies*, 29(5): 615–33.

Dunlop, John Thomas. 1958. *Industrial relations systems*. New York: Holt.

Dunning, John H. 2000. *Regions, globalization, and the knowledge-based economy*. Oxford: Oxford University Press.

Durkheim, Emile. 1951. *Suicide*. New York: Free Press.

—— 1973. *On morality and society: selected writings*. Chicago: University of Chicago Press.

Eagly, A. H. and Johnson, B. T. 1990. Gender and leadership-style: a metaanalysis. *Psychological Bulletin*, 108(2): 233–56.

—— Makhijani, M. G., and Klonsky, B. G. 1992. Gender and the evaluation of leaders: a Metaanalysis. *Psychological Bulletin*, 111(1): 3–22.

Easterby-Smith, Mark and Lyles, M. A. (eds.). 2003. *Handbook of organizational learning and knowledge management*. Oxford: Blackwell.

Edelman, Murray. 1988. *Constructing the political spectacle*. Chicago University of Chicago Press.

Edwards, Richard. 1979. *Contested terrain: the transformation of the workplace in the twentieth century*. London: Heinemann.

Ehrenreich, Barbara. 2005. *Bait and switch: the (futile) pursuit of the American dream* (1st edn.). New York: Metropolitan Books.

Einarsen, S. 2000. Harassment and bullying at work: a review of the Scandinavian approach. *Aggression and Violent Behavior*, 5(4): 379–401.

Eisenstadt, S. N. 1966. *Modernization: protest and change*. Englewood Cliffs, NJ: Prentice-Hall.

—— 1968. *The Protestant ethic and modernization: a comparative view*. New York: Basic Books.

Eisenstein, Elizabeth L. 1979. *The printing press as an agent of change: communications and cultural transformations in early modern Europe*. Cambridge: Cambridge University Press.

Elias, Norbert. 1994. *The civilising process* (one-volume edn.). Oxford: Blackwell.

Eliot, T. S. 1969. *Collected works*. London: Faber.

—— 1974. *Collected poems, 1909–1962*. London: Faber.

Ellis, Carolyn. 2004. *The ethnographic I: a methodological novel about autoethnography*. Walnut Creek, Calif.: AltaMira Press.

Ellis, Susan J. and Campbell, Katherine Noyes. 1990. *By the people: a history of Americans as volunteers* (rev. edn.). San Francisco: Jossey-Bass Publishers.

Elster, Jon. 1989. *Nuts and bolts for the social sciences*. Cambridge: Cambridge University Press.

Engen, M. L. van and Willemsen, T. M. 2004. Sex and leadership styles: a meta-analysis of research published in the 1990s. *Psychological Reports*, 94(1): 3–18.

Erikson, Erik H. 1950/1978. *Childhood and society* (2nd edn.). New York: Norton.

—— 1959a. *Identity and the life cycle*. New York: Norton.

—— 1959b. The problem of ego identity. In E. H. Erikson (ed.), *Identity and the life cycle*: 108–76. New York: Norton.

—— 1968. *Identity: youth and crisis*. London: Faber and Faber.

Etzioni, Amitai. 1961. *A comparative analysis of complex organizations*. New York: The Free Press.

—— 1964. *Modern organisations*. Englewood Cliffs, NJ: Prentice-Hall.

—— (ed.). 1998. *The essential communitarian reader*. Lanham, Md.: Rowman and Littlefield.

Eysenck, H. J. 1971. *Race, intelligence and education*. London: Temple Smith, Ltd. [for] 'New Society'.

Fairclough, Norman. 1992. *Discourse and social change*. Cambridge: Polity.

—— 1995. *Critical discourse analysis: papers in the critical study of language*. London: Longman.

Fairhurst, Gail T. and Putnam, Linda L. 2004. Organizations as discursive constructions. *Communication Theory*, 14(1): 5–26.

Faludi, S. 1992. *Backlash: the undeclared war against women*. London: Chatto and Windus.

—— 1999. *Stiffed: the betrayal of the American man* (1st edn.). New York: W. Morrow and Co.

Featherstone, M. 1991. *Consumer culture and postmodernism*. London: Sage.

Feist, Gregory J. 2006. *The psychology of science and the origins of the scientific mind*. New Haven: Yale University Press.

Feldman, Stephen P. 1998. Playing with the pieces: deconstruction and the loss of moral culture. *Journal of Management Studies*, 35(1): 59–79.

—— 1999. The levelling of organizational culture: egalitarianism in critical postmodern organization theory. *Journal of Applied Behavioral Science*, 35(2): 228–44.

Ferguson, K. 1984. *The feminist case against bureaucracy*. Philadelphia: Temple University Press.

Ferlie, E., Ashburner, L., Fitzgerald, L., and Pettigrew, A. 1996. *The new public management*. Oxford: Oxford University Press.

Festinger, Leon. 1962. *A theory of cognitive dissonance*. London: Tavistock Publications.

Feyerabend, Paul. 1975. *Against method*. London: New Left Books.

—— 1978. *Science in a free society*. London: New Left Books.

Fiedler, Fred Edward. 1967. *A theory of leadership effectiveness*. New York: McGraw-Hill.

—— and Chemers, Martin M. 1974. *Leadership and effective management*. Glenview, Ill.: Scott.

Fine, Ben. 2001. *Social capital versus social theory: political economy and social science at the turn of the millennium*. London: Routledge.

Fineman, Stephen. 1987. *Unemployment: personal and social consequences*. London: Tavistock.

—— 1993a. *Emotion in organizations*. London: Sage.

—— 1993b. Organizations as emotional arenas. In S. Fineman (ed.), *Emotion in organizations*. London: Sage.

—— 1996. Emotion and organizing. In S. Clegg, C. Hardy, and W. R. Nord (eds.), *Handbook of organization studies*. London: Sage.

—— 1998. The natural environment, organization and ethics. In M. Parker (ed.), *Ethics and organizations*: 238–53. London: Sage.

—— (ed.). 2000a. *The business of greening*. London: Routledge.

—— 2000b. Commodifying the emotionally intelligent. In S. Fineman (ed.), *Emotion in organizations* (2nd edn.): 101–15. London: Sage.

—— (ed.). 2000c. *Emotion in organizations* (2nd edn.). London: Sage.

—— 2000d. Emotional arenas revisited. In S. Fineman (ed.), *Emotion in organizations* (2nd edn.): 1–24. London: Sage.

—— (ed.). 2003. *Understanding emotion at work*. London: Sage.

—— (ed.). 2007. *The emotional organization: critical voices*. Oxford: Blackwell.

—— and Sturdy, Andrew. 1999. The emotions of control: a qualitative exploration of environmental regulation. *Human Relations*, 52(5): 631–63.

Firth, Raymond. 1973. *Symbols, public and private*. London: Allen and Unwin.

Fisher, W. R. 1985. The narrative paradigm: an elaboration. *Communication Monographs*, 52: 347–67.

Fitzgerald, Louise and Ferlie, Ewan. 2000. Professionals: back to the future. *Human Relations*, 53(7): 713–39.

Flam, Helena. 1990a. Emotional 'man' I: the emotional 'man' and the problem of collective action. *International Sociology*, 5(1): 39–56.

—— 1990b. Emotional 'man' II: corporate actors as emotion-motivated emotion managers. *International Sociology*, 5(2): 225–34.

Fleming, Peter. 2007. Sexuality, power and resistance in the workplace. *Organization Studies*, 28(2): 239–56.

—— and Spicer, André. 2003. Working at a cynical distance: implications for power, subjectivity and resistance. *Organization*, 10(1): 157–79.

Fligstein, N. 1996. Markets as politics: a political-cultural approach to market institutions. *American Sociological Review*, 61(4): 656–73.

Flynn, James Robert. 1980. *Race, IQ, and Jensen*. London: Routledge and Kegan Paul.

Fombrun, Charles J., Tichy, Noel M., and Devanna, Mary Anne. 1984. *Strategic human resource management*. New York: Wiley.

Forster, E. M. 1962. *Aspects of the novel*. Harmondsworth: Penguin.

Foucault, Michel. 1961/1965. *Madness and civilization: a history of insanity in the age of reason*. New York: Vintage Books.

—— 1966/1970. *The order of things: an archaeology of the human sciences*. New York: Vintage Books.

—— 1969/1972. *The archaeology of knowledge*. New York: Harper and Row.

—— 1977. *Discipline and punish*. London: Allen Unwin.

—— 1978. *The history of sexuality: an introduction*, vol. i, trans. R. Hurley. Harmondsworth: Penguin.

—— 1980. *Power/knowledge: selected interviews and other writings 1972–1977*. Brighton: Harvester Books.

—— 1984/1985. *The history of sexuality*, ii: *The use of pleasure*. New York: Vintage Books.

—— 1984/1986. *The history of sexuality*, iii: *The care of the self*. New York: Vintage Books.

Fournier, Valerie. 1997. Graduates' construction systems and career development. *Human Relations*, 50(4): 363–91.

—— 1998. Stories of development and exploitation: militant voices in an enterprise culture. *Organization*, 5(1): 55–80.

—— and Grey, Chris. 2000. At the critical moment: conditions and prospects for critical management studies. *Human Relations*, 53(1): 7–32.

Fox, Stephen R. 1984. *The mirror makers: a history of American advertising and its creators* (1st edn.). New York: Morrow.

Frank, Andre Gunder. 1998. *ReOrient: global economy in the Asian Age*. Berkeley and Los Angeles: University of California Press.

Frank, Arthur W. 1998. Just listening: narrative and deep illness. *Families, Systems and Health*, 16: 197–216.

Fraser, Steve. 1995. *The bell curve wars: race, intelligence, and the future of America*. New York: Basic Books.

Freeman, R. Edward. 1984. *Strategic management: a stakeholder approach*. Boston: Pitman.

Freidson, Eliot. 1986. *Professional powers: a study of the institutionalization of formal knowledge*. Chicago: University of Chicago Press.

Freire, Paulo. 1970/1996. *Pedagogy of the oppressed*, trans. M. B. Harmondsworth: Penguin.

French, J. R. P., Jr. and Raven, B. H. 1959. The bases of social power. In D. Cartwright (ed.), *Studies in social power*. Ann Arbor: University of Michigan Press.

French, Robert. 1997. The teacher as container of anxiety: psychoanalysis and the role of the teacher. *Journal of Management Education*, 21(4): 483–95.

Frenkel, Stephen J., Korczynski, Marek, Shire, Karen, A., and Tam, May. 1999. *On the front line: organization of work in the information economy*. Ithaca, NY: Cornell University Press.

Freud, Sigmund. 1905. *Jokes and their relation to the unconscious*. London: Hogarth Press.

—— 1905/1977. Three essays on the theory of sexuality. In S. Freud (ed.), *On sexuality*: vii. 33–169. Harmondsworth: Pelican Freud Library.

—— 1907. *Obsessive actions and religious practice* (Standard edn.). London: Hogarth Press.

—— 1914/1984. On narcissism: an introduction. In S. Freud (ed.), *On metapsychology: the theory of psychoanalysis*: xi: 59–97. Harmondsworth: Pelican Freud Library.

—— 1915/1984a. Repression. In S. Freud (ed.), *On metapsychology: the theory of psychoanalysis*: xi: 139–58. Harmondsworth: Pelican Freud Library.

—— 1915/1984b. The unconscious. In S. Freud (ed.), *On metapsychology: the theory of psychoanalysis*: xi: 159–222. Harmondsworth: Pelican Freud Library.

—— 1917. *A difficulty in the path of psycho-analysis* (Standard edn.). London: Hogarth Press.

—— 1921/1985. Group psychology and the analysis of the ego. In S. Freud (ed.), *Civilization, society and religion*: xii. 91–178. Harmondsworth: Pelican Freud Library.

—— 1921. *Group psychology and the analysis of the ego* (Standard edn.). London: Hogarth Press.

—— 1923/1984. The ego and the id. In S. Freud (ed.), *On metapsychology: the theory of psychoanalysis*: xi. 341–406. Harmondsworth: Pelican Freud Library.

—— 1927. The future of an illusion. In S. Freud (ed.), *Freud: civilization, society and religion*, vol. xii. Harmondsworth: Penguin.

—— 1930. Civilization and its discontents. In S. Freud (ed.), *Freud: civilization, society and religion*, vol. xii. Harmondsworth: Penguin.

—— 1933/1988. *New introductory lectures on psychoanalysis*. Harmondsworth: Pelican Freud Library.

—— 1937. *Analysis terminable and interminable* (Standard edn.). London: Hogarth Press.

—— 1940/1986. An outline of psychoanalysis. In *Historical and expository works on psycho-analysis*: xv. 371–443. Harmondsworth: Pelican Freud Library.

—— and Breuer, Josef. 1895. *Studies in hysteria* (Standard edn.). London: Hogarth Press.

Freudenburg, W. R. 1992. Nothing recedes like success? Risk analysis and the organizational amplification of risks. *Risk: Issues in Health and Safety*, 3(1): 3–35.

Friedan, Betty. 1965. *The feminine mystique*. Harmondsworth: Penguin.

Friedman, Andrew. 1977. *Industry and labour*. London: Macmillan.

—— 2004. Strawmanning and labour process analysis. *Sociology: The Journal of the British Sociological Association*, 38(3): 573–91.

Friedman, M. 1970. The social responsibility of business is to increase its profits. *New York Times Magazine*, 13 September: 32–3.

Fromm, Erich. 1941/1966. *Escape from freedom*. New York: Avon Library.

Frost, P. J., Moore, L. F., Lundberg, C. C., and Martin, J. (eds.). 1991. *Reframing organizational culture*. London: Sage.

Furnham, Adrian. 1992. *The Protestant work ethic: the psychology of work-related beliefs and behaviours*. London: Routledge.

Gabriel, Yiannis. 1984. A psychoanalytic contribution to the sociology of suffering. *International Review of Psychoanalysis*, 11: 467–80.

—— 1991. On organizational stories and myths: why it is easier to slay a dragon than to kill a myth. *International Sociology*, 6(4): 427–42.

—— 1993. Organizational nostalgia: reflections on the golden age. In S. Fineman (ed.), *Emotion in organizations*: 118–41. London: Sage.

—— 1995. The unmanaged organization: stories, fantasies and subjectivity. *Organization Studies*, 16(3): 477–501.

—— 1997. Meeting God: when organizational members come face to face with the supreme leader. *Human Relations*, 50(4): 315–42.

—— 1998a. The hubris of management. *Administrative Theory and Praxis*, 20(3): 257–73.

—— 1998b. Psychoanalytic contributions to the study of the emotional life of organizations. *Administration and Society*, 30(3): 291–314.

—— 1999. *Organizations in depth: the psychoanalysis of organizations*. London: Sage.

—— 2000. *Storytelling in organizations: facts, fictions, fantasies*. Oxford: Oxford University Press.

—— 2002. *Essai*: on paragrammatic uses of organizational theory: a provocation. *Organization Studies*, 23(1): 133–51.

—— 2004a. Every picture tells a story: losing the plot in the era of the image, *Tanaka Business School Discussion Papers <https://www3.imperial.ac. uk/pls/portallive/docs/1/40406.PDF>*. London.

—— 2004b. Narratives, stories, texts. In D. Grant, C. Hardy, C. Oswick, and L. L. Putnam (eds.), *The Sage handbook of organizational discourse*: 61–79. London: Sage.

—— 2004c. The voice of experience and the voice of the expert: can they speak to each other? In B. Hurwitz, T. Greenhalgh, and V. Skultans (eds.), *Narrative research in health and illness*: 168–86. Oxford: Blackwell.

—— 2005. Glass cages and glass palaces: images of organizations in image-conscious times. *Organization*, 12(1): 9–27.

—— 2008a. *Essai*: against the tyranny of PowerPoint: technology-in-use and technology abuse. *Organization Studies*, 1.

—— 2008b. Oedipus in the land of organizational darkness: preliminary considerations on organizational miasma. In M. Kostera (ed.). *Organizational epics and sagas: tales of organizations*: 39–52. Basingstoke: Palgrave.

—— and Carr, Adrian. 2002. Organizations, management and psychoanalysis: an overview. *Journal of Managerial Psychology*, 17(5): 348–65.

—— and Lang, Tim. 1995. *The unmanageable consumer: contemporary consumption and its fragmentation*. London: Sage.

—— —— 2006. *The unmanageable consumer*: London: Sage Publications.

Gagliardi, Pasquale. 1990. *Symbols and artifacts: views of the corporate landscape*. Berlin: W. de Gruyter.

Galbraith, John Kenneth. 1967. *The new industrial state*. New York: Signet.

Gann, D. M. and Dodgson, M. 2007. *Innovation technology: how new technologies are changing the way we innovate*. London: NESTA.

Gellner, Ernest. 1983. *Nations and nationalism*. Oxford: Blackwell.

Gennep, Arnold van. 1960. *The rites of passage*, trans. M. B. Vizedom and G. L. Caffee. London: Routledge & Kegan Paul.

Gergen, Kenneth J. 1994. *Realities and relationships: soundings in social construction*. Cambridge, Mass.: Harvard University Press.

Gherardi, Silvia. 1995. *Gender, symbolism and organizational cultures*. London: Sage.

—— 2004. Knowing as desire: Dante's Ulysses at the end of the known world. In Y. Gabriel (ed.), *Myths, stories and organizations: premodern narratives for our times*: 32–48. Oxford: Oxford University Press.

—— and Nicolini, Davide. 2001. The sociological foundations of organizational learning. In M. Dierkes (ed.), *The handbook of organizational learning and knowledge*. London: Sage.

Giddens, Anthony. 1984. *The constitution of society: outline of a theory of structuration*. Cambridge: Polity Press.

—— 1990. *The consequences of modernity*. Stanford, Calif.: Stanford University Press.

—— 1991. *Modernity and self-identity: self and society in the late modern age*. Stanford, Calif.: Stanford University Press.

—— 1994. Living in a post-traditional society. In U. Beck, A. Giddens, and S. Lash (eds.), *Reflexive modernisation: politics, traditions and aesthetics in the modern social order*: 56–109. Cambridge: Polity.

Gilligan, Carol. 1982. *In a different voice: psychological theory and women's development*. Cambridge, Mass.: Harvard University Press.

Gioia, Dennis A. 1986. Symbols, scripts and sensemaking: creating meaning in the organizing experience. In H. P. Sims and D. A. Gioia (eds.), *The thinking organization*: 49–74. San Francisco: Jossey-Bass.

—— and Chittipeddi, Kumar. 1991. Sensemaking and sensegiving in strategic change initiation. *Strategic Management Journal*, 12(6): 433–48.

Giroux, H. A. 1999. *The mouse that roared: Disney and the end of innocence*. Lanham, Md.: Rowman and Littlefield.

Gledhill, J. 2001. Deromanticizing subalterns or recolonializing anthropology? Denial of indigenous agency and reproduction of northern hegemony in the work of David Stoll. *Identities: Global Studies in Culture and Power*, 8(1): 135–61.

Gleick, James. 1987. *Chaos*. Harmondsworth: Penguin.

Glynn, M. A. 2000. When cymbals become symbols: conflict over organizational identity within a symphony orchestra. *Organization Science*, 11(3): 285–98.

Godard, J. 2004. A critical assessment of the high performance paradigm. *British Journal of Industrial Relations*, 42(2): 349–78.

Goffman, Erving. 1959. *The presentation of self in everyday life*. Garden City, NY: Anchor.

—— 1961. *Asylums*. Garden City, NY: Doubleday.

—— 1963. *Stigma: notes on the management of spoiled identity*. Englewood Cliffs, NJ: Prentice-Hall.

—— 1969. *The presentation of self in everyday life*. London: Allen Lane.

Goldhagen, Daniel Jonah. 1996. *Hitler's willing executioners: ordinary Germans and the Holocaust* (1st edn.). New York: Knopf.

Goldthorpe, J. H., Lockwood, D., Bechhofer, F., and Pratt, J. 1969. *The affluent worker in the class structure*. Cambridge: Cambridge University Press.

Goleman, Daniel. 1995. *Emotional intelligence*. New York: Bantam Books.

—— 2001. What makes a leader? In J. Henry (ed.), *Creative management*: 125–39. London: Sage.

—— Boyatzis, Richard, and McKee, Annie. 2002. *Primal leadership: realizing the power of emotional intelligence*. Cambridge, Mass.: Harvard Business School Press.

Gouldner, Alvin W. 1954. *Patterns of industrial bureaucracy*. Glencoe, Ill.: Free Press.

—— 1955. Metaphysical pathos and the theory of bureaucracy. *American Political Review*, 49: 469–505.

—— 1957. Cosmopolitans and locals: toward an analysis of latent social roles. *Administrative Science Quarterly*, 2(3): 281–306.

Gourevitch, Peter Alexis and Shinn, James. 2005. *Political power and corporate control: the new global politics of corporate governance*. Princeton: Princeton University Press.

Gramsci, Antonio. 1971. *Selections from the prison notebooks of Antonio Gramsci (1929–35)*, ed. G. Nowell-Smith, introd. Q. Hoare. London: Lawrence and Wishart.

Grant, David, Hardy, Cynthia, Oswick, Cliff, and Putnam, Linda L. (eds.). 2004. *The Sage handbook of organizational discourse*. London: Sage.

—— Keenoy, Tom, and Oswick, Cliff (eds.). 1998. *Discourse and organizations*. London: Sage.

—— and Oswick, Cliff (eds.). 1996. *Metaphor and organizations*. London: Sage.

Gratton, Lynda, Hope-Hailey, V., Stiles, P., and Truss, C. 1999. *Strategic human resource management:*

corporate rhetoric and human reality. Oxford: Oxford University Press.

Gray, John. 2002. *Straw dogs: thoughts on humans and other animals*. London: Granta.

—— 2003. *Al Qaeda and what it means to be modern*. London: Faber.

Greenglass, E. and Marshall, J. 1993. Special issue: women in management. *Applied Psychology: An International Review/Psychologie appliquée: Revue internationale*, 42(4): 285–8.

Greer, Germaine. 1970. *The female eunuch*. London: Granada.

—— 1984. *Sex and destiny: the politics of human fertility*. London: Secker and Warburg.

Grey, Christopher. 1994. Career as a project of the self and labour process discipline. *Sociology*, 28(2): 479–97.

Griffin, Douglas, Shaw, Patricia, and Stacey, Ralph. 1998. Speaking complexity in management theory and practice. *Organization*, 5(3): 315–39.

Grint, Keith. 1997. TQM, BPR, JIT, BSCs and TLAs: managerial waves or drownings. *Management Decision*, 35(10): 731–8.

—— 1998. *The sociology of work: an introduction* (2nd edn.). Oxford: Polity Press.

—— 2005a. Leadership Ltd: white elephant to wheelwright: <http://www.iveybusinessjournal.com/view_article.asp?intArticle_ID=537>, *Ivey Business Journal*.

—— 2005b. *Leadership: limits and possibilities*. Basingstoke: Palgrave Macmillan.

Guerrier, Yvonne and Adib, Amel S. 2000. 'No, we don't provide that service': the harassment of hotel employees by customers. *Work Employment and Society*, 14(4): 689–705.

Guest, David. 1987. Human resource management and industrial relations. *Journal of Management Studies*, 24(5): 503–21.

Guha, Ranajit. 1997. *A subaltern studies reader, 1986–1995*. Minneapolis: University of Minnesota Press.

Guillen, Mauro F. 1994. *Models of management: work, authority, and organization in a comparative perspective*. Chicago: University of Chicago Press.

—— 1998. Scientific management's lost aesthetic: architecture, organization and the Taylorized beauty of the mechanical. *Administrative Science Quarterly*, 42(4): 682–715.

Gull, G. A. and Doh, J. 2004. The 'transmutation' of the organization: toward a more spiritual workplace. *Journal of Management Inquiry*, 13(2): 128–39.

Gutek, Barbara A. 1989. Sexuality in the workplace: key issues in social research and organizational practice. In J. Hearn, D. L. Sheppard, P. Tancred-Sheriff, and G. Burrell (eds.), *The sexuality of organization*. London: Sage.

Habermas, Jürgen. 1975. *Legitimation crisis*, trans. T. McCarthy. Boston: Beacon Press.

—— 1981. *The theory of communicative action: reason and the rationalization of society*. London: Beacon Press.

—— 1984a. *The philosophical discourse of modernity*. Cambridge: Polity Press.

—— 1984b. *The theory of communicative action, i: Reason and the rationalization of society*. Boston: Beacon Press.

—— 1990. *Moral consciousness and communicative action*. Cambridge: Polity.

Hackley, Christopher E. 2005. *Advertising and promotion: communicating brands*. London: Sage.

—— and Kover, A. J. 2007. The trouble with creatives: negotiating creative identity in advertising agencies. *International Journal of Advertising*, 26(1): 63–78.

—— and Tiwsakul, R. 2006. Entertainment marketing and experiential consumption. *Journal of Marketing Communications*, 12(1): 63–75.

Haley, Alex. 1976. *Roots* (1st edn.). Garden City, NY: Doubleday.

Hamel, Gary and Prahalad, C. K. 1994. *Competing for the future*. Boston: Harvard Business School Press.

Hammer, Michale and Champy, James. 1993. *Reengineering the corporation: a manifesto for business revolution*. London: Nicholas Brealy.

Hampden-Turner, Charles and Trompenaars, Alfons. 1997. *Mastering the infinite game: how Asian values are transforming business practices*. Oxford: Capstone.

—— —— 2000. *Building cross-cultural competence: how to create wealth from conflicting values*. New Haven: Yale University Press.

Hancock, Philip and Tyler, Melissa. 2000. 'The look of love': gender and the organization of aesthetics. In J. Hassard, R. Holliday, and H. Willmott (eds.), *Body and organization*. London: Sage.

Handley, Karen, Sturdy, Andrew, Fincham, Robin, and Clark, Timothy. 2006. Within and beyond communities of practice: making sense of learning through participation, identity and practice. *Journal of Management Studies*, 43(3): 641–53.

Handy, Charles B. 1991. *The Age of unreason* (new edn.). London: Business Books (Random Century Group).

—— 1994. *The empty raincoat: making sense of the future*. London: Hutchinson.

Hannan, M. and Freeman, J. 1977. The population ecology of organizations. *American Journal of Sociology*, 83: 929–84.

—— 1989. Organizations and social structure. In *Organizational Ecology*: 3–27. Cambridge, Mass.: Harvard University Press.

Hansen, Fay. 2003. Diversity's business case doesn't add up. *Workforce Management*, April: 28–32, <http://www.workforce.com/section/11/feature/23/42/49/index.html>.

Hardy, Cynthia and Clegg, Stewart S. 1999. Some dare call it power. In S. S. Clegg and C. Hardy (eds.), *Studying organizations: theory and methods*: 368–88. London: Sage.

—— Lawrence, Thomas B., and Phillips, Nelson. 1998. Talk and action: conversations and narrative in interorganizational collaboration. In D. Grant, T. Keenoy, and C. Oswick (eds.), *Discourse and organization*: 65–83. London: Sage.

Harrison, R. 1987. *Organization culture and quality of service: a strategy for releasing love in the workplace*. London: Association of Management Education and Development.

Hassard, John, Hogan, John, and Rowlinson, Michael. 2001. From labour process theory to critical management studies. *Administrative Theory and Praxis*, 23(3): 339–62.

Hatch, Mary Jo. 1990. The symbolics of office design: an empirical exploration. In P. Gagliardi (ed.), *Symbols and artifacts: views of the corporate landscape*: 129–35. Berlin: Walter de Gruyter.

—— 1997. *Organization theory: modern, symbolic and postmodern perspectives*. Oxford: Oxford University Press.

Hayek, Friedrich A. von. 1968. *The confusion of language in political thought, with some suggestions for remedying it*. London: Institute of Economic Affairs.

Hearn, Jeff, Sheppard, Deborah L., Tancred-Sheriff, Petra, and Burrell, Gibson (eds.). 1989. *The sexuality of organization*. London: Sage.

Hébert, Robert F. and Link, Albert N. 1988. *The entrepreneur: mainstream views & radical critiques* (2nd edn.). New York: Praeger.

Heifetz, Ronald A. 1994. *Leadership without easy answers*. Cambridge, Mass.: Harvard University Press.

Held, Virginia. 2006. *The ethics of care: personal, political, and global*. Oxford: Oxford University Press.

Heller, Agnes. 1979. *A theory of feelings*. Amsterdam: Van Gorkum Assen.

Helms, Marilyn M. (ed.). 2000. *Encyclopedia of management* (4th edn.). London: Gale Group.

Heracleous, Loizos and Hendry, John. 2000. Discourse and the study of organization: toward a structurational perspective. *Human Relations*, 53(10): 1251–86.

Hernes, T. 2004. Studying composite boundaries: a framework of analysis. *Human Relations*, 57(1): 9–29.

Heyning, Charles. 1999. Autonomy vs. solidarity: liberal, totalitarian and communitarian traditions. *Administrative Theory and Praxis*, 21(1): 39–50.

Hirschhorn, Larry. 1988. *The workplace within*. Cambridge, Mass.: MIT Press.

—— and Barnett, Carol K. 1993. *The psychodynamics of organizations*. Philadelphia: Temple University Press.

Hirschman, Albert O. 1970. *Exit, voice, and loyalty: responses to decline in firms, organizations, and states*. Cambridge, Mass.: Harvard University Press.

Hirshberg, Jerry. 1998. *The creative priority: driving innovative business in the real world* (1st edn.). New York: HarperBusiness.

Hobsbawn, Eric. 1983. Inventing traditions. In E. Hobsbawn (ed.), *The invention of tradition*. Cambridge: Cambridge University Press.

Hochschild, Arlie R. 1983. *The managed heart: commercialization of human feeling*. Berkeley and Los Angeles: University of California Press.

Hoel, H. and Beale, D. 2006. Workplace bullying, psychological perspectives and industrial relations: towards a contextualized and interdisciplinary approach. *British Journal of Industrial Relations*, 44(2): 239–62.

Hoffman, Bruce. 1998. *Inside terrorism*. New York: Columbia University Press.

Hofstede, Geert. 1980. *Culture's consequences*. London: Sage.

—— 1991. *Cultures and organizations: software of the mind*. London: McGraw-Hill.

—— 2001. *Culture's consequences: comparing values, behaviors, institutions,* and *organizations across nations* (2nd edn.). Thousand Oaks, Calif.: Sage Publications.

Hoggett, Paul. 2006. Conflict, ambivalence, and the contested purpose of public organizations. *Human Relations*, 59(2): 175–94.

Holbrook, Morris B. 2001. Times Square, Disneyphobia, HegeMickey, the Ricky principle, and the downside of the entertainment economy:

it's fun-dumb-mental. *Marketing Theory*, 1(2): 139–63.

Hood, C. 1991. A public management for all seasons. *Public Administration*, 69(1): 3–19.

—— 1995. The New Public Management in the 1980s: variations on a theme. *Accounting Organizations and Society*, 20(2–3): 93–109.

—— Jones, D. K. C., Pidgeon, N. F., Turner, B. A., and Gibson, R. 1992. Risk management. In Royal. Society (ed.), *Risk: analysis, perception and management*: 135–92. London: Royal Society.

Hook, R. H. 1979. Phantasy and symbol. In R. H. Hook (ed.), *Fantasy and symbol: a psychoanalytic point of view*: 267–91. London: Academic Press.

Höpfl, Heather. 1995. Organizational rhetoric and the threat of ambivalence. *Studies in Culture, Organizations and Society*, 1(2): 175–88.

Horkheimer, Max and Adorno, Theodor. 1947/1997. *Dialectic of enlightenment*, trans. J. Cummings. New York: Herder and Herder.

Huczynski, Andrzej. 1993. *Management gurus: what makes them and how to become one*. London: Routledge.

Humphreys, Michael and Brown, Andrew D. 2002. Narratives of organizational identity and identification: a case study of hegemony and resistance. *Organization Studies*, 23(3): 421–47.

Hurwitz, Brian, Greenhalgh, Trisha, and Skultans, Vieda (eds.). 2004. *Narrative research in health and illness*. Oxford: Blackwell.

Husserl, Edmund. 2006. *The basic problems of phenomenology: from the lectures, winter semester, 1910–1911*, trans Ingo Farix and James G. Hart. Dordrecht: Springer.

Hyde, Lewis. 1983. *The gift: imagination and the erotic life of property*. New York: Random House.

Jackall, Robert. 1988. *Moral mazes: the world of corporate managers*. Oxford: Oxford University Press.

Jackson, Brad. 2001. *Management gurus and management fashions*. New York: Routledge.

Jackson, Stevi. 1993. Even sociologists fall in love: an exploration in the sociology of emotions. *Sociology*, 27(1): 201–20.

Jameson, Fredric. 1984. Postmodernism, or the cultural logic of late capitalism. *New Left Review*, 146: 53–92.

Janis, Irving L. 1972. *Victims of groupthink*. Boston: Houghton Mifflin.

Jaques, Elliott. 1952. *The changing culture of the factory*. London: Tavistock.

—— 1955. Social systems as a defence against persecutory and depressive anxiety. In M. Klein, P. Heimann, and R. E. Money-Kyrle (eds.), *New directions in psychoanalysis*. London: Tavistock.

Jermier, John, Knights, David, and Nord, Walter R. 1994. *Resistance and power in organizations*. London: Routledge.

Jessop, Bob. 1989. *Thatcherism: the British road to post-Fordism?* Essex papers in politics and government 68. Colchester: Department of Government, University of Essex.

Jones, E. 1938. The theory of symbolism. In E. Jones (ed.), *Papers on psychoanalysis*. London: Bailliere, Tindall and Cox.

Jung, C. G. 1968. *The archetypes and the collective unconscious*. London: Routledge.

Kallinikos, Jannis. 2006. *The consequences of information: institutional implications of technological change*. Northampton, Mass.: Edward Elgar.

Kanter, D. and Mirvis, P. 1989. *The cynical Americans: living and working in an age of discontent and disillusion*. San Francisco: Jossey-Bass.

Kanter, Rosabeth M. 1977. *Men and women of the corporation*. New York: Basic Books.

—— 1983. *The change masters*. New York: Simon and Schuster.

Kaplan, R. S. and Norton, D. P. 1992. The balanced scorecard: measures that drive performance. *Harvard Business Review*, 70(1): 71–9.

—— —— 1993. Putting the balanced scorecard to work. *Harvard Business Review*, 71(5): 134–42.

Kapuściński, Ryszard. 1983. *The emperor*. London: Picador.

Katz, D. and Kahn, R. L. 1978. *The social psychology of organizations* (2nd edn.). New York: Wiley.

Kaufmann, Walter Arnold. 1968. *Nietzsche: philosopher, psychologist, antichrist* (3rd edn.). New York: Vintage Books.

Kearney, Richard. 2002. *On stories*. London: Routledge.

Keen, Sam. 1991. *Fire in the belly: on being a man*. New York: Bantam Books.

Keenoy, Tom and Anthony, Peter. 1992. Human resource management: metaphor, meaning and morality. In P. Blyton and P. Turnbull (eds.), *Reassessing human resource management*: 233–55. London: Sage.

Kellerman, Barbara. 2004. Leadership warts and all. *Harvard Business Review*, 82(1): 40–5.

Kelly, G. A. 1955. *The psychology of personal constructs*, i: *A theory of personality*. New York: Norton.

Kerr, Clark, Harbison, F., Dunlop, J. T., and Myers, C. 1960. *Industrialism and industrial man: the problems of labor and management in economic growth*. Cambridge, Mass.: Harvard University Press.

Kets de Vries, M. F. R. 2005. The dangers of feeling like a fake. *Harvard Business Review*, 83(9): 108–16.

—— and Miller, Danny. 1984. *The neurotic organization*. San Francisco: Jossey-Bass.

Kilduff, Martin. 1993. Deconstructing organizations. *Academy of Management Review*, 18: 13–31.

Kingdon, John W. 1995. *Agendas, alternatives, and public policies* (2nd edn.). New York: HarperCollins College Publishers.

Kittrie, Nicholas N. 1995. *The war against authority: from the crisis of legitimacy to a new social contract*. Baltimore: Johns Hopkins University Press.

Klein, Lisl. 1976. *A social scientist in industry*. London: Tavistock.

Klein, Melanie. 1987. *The selected Melanie Klein*, ed. Juliet Mitchell (1st American edn.). New York: Free Press.

Klein, Naomi. 2000. *No logo: taking aim at the brand bullies*. London: Flamingo.

Kleinman, Arthur. 1988. *The illness narratives: suffering, healing, and the human condition*. New York: Basic Books.

Knights, David. 1990. Subjectivity, power and the labour process. In D. Knights and H. Willmott (eds.), *Labour process theory*. Basingstoke: Macmillan.

—— 1992. Changing spaces: the disruptive impact of a new epistemological location for the study of management. *Academy of Management Review*, 17(3): 518–45.

—— and Morgan, Glenn. 1993. Organization theory and consumption in a post-modern era. *Organization Studies*, 14(2): 211–34.

—— and Willmott, Hugh. 1989. Power and subjectivity at work: from degradation to subjugation. *Sociology*, 23(4): 535–58.

Knoke, David. 1990. *Organizing for collective action: the political economies of associations*. New York: A. de Gruyter.

Knorr Cetina, Karin D. 1981. *The manufacture of knowledge: an essay on the constructivist and contextual nature of science*. Oxford: Pergamon.

Kohut, Heinz. 1971. *The analysis of the self*. New York: International Universities Press.

Kohut, Heinz. 1976. Creativity, charisma and group psychology. In J. E. Gedo and G. H. Pollock (eds.), *Freud: the fusion of science and humanism*. New York: International Universities Press.

Kolb, David A. 1985. *experiential learning: experience as the source of learning and development*. Englewood Cliffs, NJ: Prentice Hall.

Korczynski, Marek. 2001. The contradictions of service work: call centre as customer-oriented bureaucracy. In A. Sturdy, I. Grugulis, and H. Willmott (eds.), *Customer service: empowerment and entrapment*: 79–101. Basingstoke: Palgrave.

—— 2003. Communities of coping: collective emotional labour in service work. *Organization*, 10(1): 55–79.

Kramer, Ralph M. 1981. *Voluntary agencies in the welfare state*. Berkeley and Los Angeles: University of California Press.

Kubie, Lawrence S. and Schlesinger, Herbert J. 1978. *Symbol and neurosis: selected papers of Lawrence S. Kubie*. New York: International Universities Press.

Kübler-Ross, Elisabeth. 1969. *On death and dying*. Toronto: Macmillan.

Kuhn, Thomas S. 1962/1996. *The structure of scientific revolutions* (3rd edn.). Chicago: Chicago University Press.

Kunda, Gideon. 1992. *Engineering culture: control and commitment in a high-tech corporation*. Philadelphia: Temple University Press.

Kymlicka, Will. 1995. *Multicultural citizenship: a liberal theory of minority rights*. Oxford: Oxford University Press.

Labov, William. 1972. *Language in the inner city*. Philadelphia: University of Pennsylvania Press.

—— and Waletzky, Joshua. 1967. Narrative analysis: oral versions of personal experience. In J. Helm (ed.), *Essays on the visual and verbal arts: proceedings of the American Ethnological Society*: 12–44. Seattle: University of Washington Press.

Lacan, Jacques. 1966/1977. *Écrits*, trans. A. Sheridan. London: Routledge.

—— 1988a. *The seminar of Jacques Lacan, Book 1: Freud's papers on technique 1953–1954*. New York: W. W. Norton.

—— 1988b. *The seminar of Jacques Lacan, Book 2: the ego in Freud's theory and in the technique of psychoanalysis, 1954–1955*. New York: W. W. Norton.

Laing, R. D. 1960. *The divided self: a study of sanity and madness*. London: Tavistock Publications.

—— 1969. *Self and others* (2nd edn.). London: Tavistock Publications.

Lakoff, George. 1993. The contemporary theory of metaphor. In A. Ortony (ed.), *Metaphor and thought* (2nd edn.). Cambridge: Cambridge University Press.

—— and Johnson, Mark. 1980. *Metaphors we live by*. Chicago: Chicago University Press.

Lamont, Michele and Molnar, Virag. 2002. The study of bourndaries in the social sciences. *Annual Review of Sociology*, 28: 167–95.

Lang, Tim and Heasman, Michael. 2004. *Food wars: the global battle for mouths, minds and markets*. London: Earthscan.

Laqueur, Walter. 1977. *Terrorism*. London: Weidenfeld and Nicolson.

Larrabee, M. J. 1993. *An ethic of care: feminist and interdisciplinary perspectives*. London: Routledge.

Larson, Magali Sarfatti. 1977. *The rise of professionalism: a sociological analysis*. Berkeley and Los Angeles: University of California Press.

Lasch, Christopher. 1980. *The culture of narcissism*. London: Abacus.

Latour, Bruno. 1987. *Science in action*. Cambridge, Mass.: Harvard University Press.

—— 1990. Postmodern? No, simply amodern! Steps towards an anthropology of science. *Studies in History and Philosophy of Science*, 21(1): 145–71.

—— 1991. Technology is society made durable. In J. Law (ed.), *A sociology of monsters: essays on power, technology and domination*: 103–32. London: Routledge.

Lave, Jean and Wenger, Étienne. 1991. *Situated learning: legitimate peripheral participation*. Cambridge: Cambridge University Press.

Lawrence, W. Gordon. 1999. A mind for business. In R. French and R. Vince (eds.), *Group relations, management, and organization*: 40–53. Oxford: Oxford University Press.

Layard, Richard. 2005. *Happiness: lessons from a new science*. London: Allen Lane.

Lebergott, Stanley. 1993. *Pursuing happiness: American consumers in the twentieth century*. Princeton: Princeton University Press.

Le Bon, Gustave. 1885/1960. *The crowd: a study of the popular mind*. New York: The Viking Press.

Legge, Karen. 1989. Human resource management: a critical analysis. In J. Storey (ed.), *New perspectives in human resource management*: 19–40. London: Routledge.

—— 2005. Human resource management. In S. Ackroyd, R. Batt, and P. Tolbert (eds.), *The Oxford handbook of work and organization*: 220–41. Oxford: Oxford University Press.

Leibowitz, Stan and Margolis, Stephen E. 1995. Policy and path dependence: from QWERTY to Windows 95, <http://www.cato.org/pubs/regulation/reg18n3d.html>, *Regulation*, 18.

Leidner, Robin. 1991. Serving hamburgers and selling insurance: gender, work and identity in interactive service jobs. *Gender and Society*, 5(2): 154–77.

—— 1993. *Fast food, fast talk: service work and the routinization of everyday life*. Berkeley and Los Angeles: University of California Press.

Leiss, William, Kline, Stephen, Jhally, Sut, and Botterill, J. 2005. *Social communication in advertising: persons, products & images of well-being* (3rd edn.). London: Routledge.

Levi, Primo. 1979. *If this is a man; and The truce*. Harmondsworth: Penguin.

Levinas, Emmanuel. 1969. *Totality and infinity: an essay on exteriority*. Pittsburgh: Duquesne University Press.

Levine, David P. 2005. The corrupt organization. *Human Relations*, 58(6): 723–40.

Levinson, Harry. 1963. *Reciprocation: the relationship between man and organization*. Paper presented at the American Psychological Association, New York.

—— 1968/1981. *Executive*. Cambridge, Mass.: Harvard University Press.

—— 1972. *Organizational diagnosis*. Cambridge, Mass.: Harvard University Press.

—— Price, C., Munden, K., Mandl, H., and Solley, C. 1962. *Men, management, and mental health*. Cambridge, Mass.: Harvard University Press.

Lévi-Strauss, Claude. 1955/1992. *Tristes Tropiques*. Harmondsworth: Penguin.

—— 1963. The structural study of myth. In C. Lévi-Strauss (ed.), *Structural anthropology*: i. 206–31. Harmondsworth: Penguin.

—— 1966. *The savage mind*. Oxford: Oxford University Press.

—— 1978. *Myth and meaning: the 1977 Massey Lectures*. London: Routledge.

Levitt, T. 1972. Production-line approach to service. *Harvard Business Review*, 50(September): 41–52.

Lévy-Bruhl, Lucien. 1923/1978. *Primitive mentality*. New York: AMS Press.

Lewin, Kurt (ed.). 1951. *Field theory in social science: selected theoretical papers*. New York: Harper and Row.

—— and Lewin, Gertrud Weiss. 1948. *Resolving social conflicts: selected papers on group dynamics*. New York: Harper & Row.

Lindblom, Charles E. 1982. The market as prison. *Journal of Politics*, 44(2): 324–36.

Lindemann, Erich. 1944. Symptomatology and the management of acute grief. *American Journal of Psychiatry*, 101: 141–8.

Lindholm, Charles. 1988. Lovers and leaders: a comparison of social and psychological models of romance and charisma. *Social Science Information*, 27(1): 3–45.

Linstead, Stephen. 1993. From postmodern anthropology to deconstructive ethnography. *Human Relations*, 46(1): 97–120.

—— (ed.). 2004. *Organization theory and postmodern thought*. London: Sage.

—— and Grafton-Small, Robert. 1990. Organizational bricolage. In B. A. Turner (ed.), *Organizational symbolism*: 291–309. Berlin: De Gruyter.

Lipietz, Alain. 1992. *Towards a new economic order: postfordism, ecology, and democracy*. Oxford: Oxford University Press.

Lockwood, David. 1958. *The blackcoated worker: a study in class consciousness*. London: Allen and Unwin.

Lorenz, Konrad. 1966. *On aggression*. London: Methuen.

Lovelock, James. 1979. *Gaia: a new look at life on earth*. Oxford: Oxford University Press.

—— 2006. *The revenge of Gaia: why the earth is fighting back - and how we can still save humanity*. London: Allen Lane.

Low, M. B. and Macmillan, I. C. 1988. Entrepreneurship: past research and future challenges. *Journal of Management*, 14(2): 139–61.

Luhmann, Niklas. 1990. *Essays on self reference*. New York: Columbia University Press.

—— 2000. *The reality of the mass media*. Cambridge: Polity Press.

Lukes, S. 1975. *Power: a radical view*. London: Macmillan.

Lynch, M. 2000. Against reflexivity as an academic virtue and source of privileged knowledge. *Theory, Culture and Society*, 17(3): 26–54.

Lyotard, Jean-François. 1984/1991. *The postmodern condition: a report on knowledge*. Manchester: Manchester University Press.

McAdams, Dan P., Josselson, Ruthellen, and Lieblich, Amia. 2006. *Identity and story: creating self in narrative* (1st edn.). Washington, DC: American Psychological Association.

McClelland, David C. 1961. *The achieving society*. New York: Van Nostrand.

Maccoby, Michael. 1976. *The gamesman: new corporate leaders*. New York: Simon and Schuster.

—— 2000. Narcissistic leaders: the incredible pros, the inevitable cons. *Harvard Business Review*, 78(1): 69–77.

McCracken, Grant. 1988. *Culture and consumpton: new approaches to the symbolic character of consumer goods and activities*. Bloomington, Ind.: Indiana University Press.

McDougall, William. 1908/1932. *An introduction to social psychology* (22nd edn.). London: Methuen.

Machiavelli, N. 1513/1961. *The prince*. Harmondsworth: Penguin.

—— 1531/1983. *The discourses*. Harmondsworth: Penguin.

MacIntyre, Alasdair. 1981. *After virtue*. London: Duckworth.

McLeod, P. L., Lobel, S. A., and Cox, T. H. 1996. Ethnic diversity and creativity in small groups. *Small Group Research*, 27(2): 248–64.

McLuhan, Marshall. 1962. *The Gutenberg galaxy: the making of typographic man*. London: Routledge and Kegan Paul.

McPhee, R. D. and Zaug, P. 2000. The communicative constitution of organizations: a framework for explanation. *Electronic Journal of Communication*, 10: 1–16.

Maffesoli, Michel. 1995. *The time of tribes: the decline of individualism in mass society*. London: Sage.

Mainiero, Lisa A. 1986. A review and analysis of power dynamics in organizational romances. *Academy of Management Review*, 11: 750–62.

Malinowski, Bronislaw. 1922. *Argonauts of the western Pacific*. London: Routledge.

Mandelbrot, Benoit. 1982. *The fractal geometry of nature*. San Francisco: Freeman.

Mangham, Iain L. 1986. *Power and performance in organizations: an exploration of executive process*. Oxford: Blackwell.

—— 1988. *Effecting organizational change: further explorations of the executive process*. Oxford: Blackwell.

—— 1996. Some consequences of taking Gareth Morgan seriously. In D. Grant and C. Oswick (eds.), *Metaphor and organizations*: 21–36. London: Sage.

—— 1998. Emotional discourse in organizations. In D. Grant, T. Keenoy, and C. Oswick (eds.), *Discourse and organization*: 51–64. London: Sage.

—— and Overington, Michael A. 1987. *Organizations as theatre: a social psychology of dramatic appearances*. Chichester: John Wiley.

Mano, Rita and Gabriel, Yiannis. 2006. Workplace romances in cold and hot organizational climates: the experience of Israel and Taiwan. *Human Relations*, 59(1): 7–37.

March, James G. 1991. Exploitation and exploration in organizational learning. *Organization Science*, 2(1): 71–87.

Marchand, Roland. 1985. *Advertising the American dream: making way for modernity, 1920–1940*. Berkeley and Los Angeles: University of California Press.

—— 1998. *Creating the corporate soul: the rise of public relations and corporate imagery in American big business*. Berkeley and Los Angeles: University of California Press.

Marcuse, Herbert. 1955. *Eros and civilization: a philosophical inquiry into Freud*. Boston: Beacon.

—— 1964. *One-dimensional man: studies in the ideology of advanced industrial society*. Boston: Beacon Press.

Marshall, Judi. 1984. *Women managers: travellers in a male world*. Chichester: Wiley.

—— 1995. *Women managers moving on: exploring career and life choices*. London: Routledge.

Martin, B. 2000. Mobbing: emotional abuse in the workplace. *Journal of Organizational Change Management*, 13(4): 401–6.

Martin, Joanne. 1990. Deconstructing organizational taboos: the suppression of gender conflict in organizations. *Organization Science*, 1: 1–22.

—— 1992. *Cultures in organizations: three perspectives*. Oxford: Oxford University Press.

—— Feldman, Martha S., Hatch, Mary Jo, and Sitkin, Sim B. 1983. The uniqueness paradox in organizational stories. *Administrative Science Quarterly*, 28: 438–53.

Martin, Patricia Yancey. 2005. *Rape work: victims, gender, and emotions in organization and community context*. New York: Routledge.

Martinko, Mark J. 1995. Stereotyping. In N. Nicholson (ed.), *Encyclopedic dictionary of organizational behaviour*. Oxford: Blackwell.

Marx, Gary T. 1995. The engineering of social control: the search for the silver bullet. In J. Hagan and R. Peterson (eds.), *Crime and inequality*: 225–46. Stanford, Calif.: Stanford University Press.

—— 1999. Measuring everything that moves: the new surveillance at work. In I. Simpson and R. Simpson (eds.), *The workplace and deviance*. Greenwich, Conn.: JAI Press.

Marx, Karl. 1843/1972. Contribution to the critique of Hegel's Philosophy of Right. In R. C. Tucker (ed.), *Marx-Engels reader*: 11–23. New York: Norton.

—— 1844/1972. Economic and philosophic manuscripts of 1844. In R. C. Tucker (ed.), *Marx–Engels reader*. New York: Norton.

—— 1859/1972. A contribution to the critique of politial economy. In R. C. Tucker (ed.), *Marx–Engels reader*: 3–6. New York: Norton.

—— 1867/1967. *Capital*. New York: International Publishers.

—— and Engels, Friedrich. 1848/1972. The Communist Manifesto. In R. C. Tucker (ed.), *Marx–Engels reader*. New York: Norton.

Maslow, Abraham H. 1943. A theory of human motivation. *Psychological Review*, 50: 654–61.

—— 1954. *Motivation and personality* (1st edn.). New York: Harper.

Masterman, Margaret. 1970. The nature of a paradigm. In I. Lakatos and A. Musgrave (eds.), *Criticism and the growth of knowledge*: 59–89. Cambridge: Cambridge University Press.

Maton, K. 1998. *Recovering pedagogic discourse: Basil Bernstein and the rise of taught academic subjects in higher education*. Paper presented at Knowledge, Identity and Pedagogy, University of Southampton.

Mattingly, Cheryl. 1998. *Healing dramas and clinical plots: the narrative structure of experience*. New York: Cambridge University Press.

Maturana, Humberto and Varela, Francisco. 1980. *Autopoiesis and cognition: the realization of the living*. London: Reidel.

Matza, David. 1969. *Becoming deviant*. Englewood Cliffs, NJ: Prentice-Hall.

Mauss, Marcel. 1925/1974. *The gift: forms and functions of exchange in archaic societies*. London: Routledge.

Mayer, J. P. 1956. *Max Weber and German politics*. London: Faber.

Mayo, Elton. 1949/1975. *The social problems of an industrial civilization: with an appendix on the political problem* (1st edn.). London: Routledge and Kegan Paul.

Mead, George Herbert. 1934. *Mind, self and society*. Chicago: University of Chicago Press.

Mead, Margaret. 1928. *Coming of age in Samoa: a psychological study of primitive youth for western civilisation*. New York: W. Morrow & Company.

Meindl, James R. and Ehrlich, Sanford B. 1987. The romance of leadership and the evaluation of organizational performance. *Academy of Management Journal*, 30(1): 91–109.

—— —— and Dukerich, Janet M. 1985. The romance of leadership. *Administrative Science Quarterly*, 30(1): 78–108.

Menchú, Rigoberta. 1984. *I, Rigoberta Menchú: an Indian woman in Guatemala*, trans. E. Burgos-Debray. London: Verso.

Menzies, Isabel. 1960. A case study in functioning of social systems as a defence against anxiety. *Human Relations*, 13: 95–121.

Menzies Lyth, Isabel. 1970. *The functioning of social systems as a defence against anxiety*. London: Tavistock Institute.

—— 1988. *Containing anxiety in institutions: selected essays*. London: Free Association Books.

Meyer, J. W. and Rowan, B. 1977. Institutionalized organizations: formal structure as myth and ceremony. *American Journal of Sociology*, 83(2): 340–63.

Michels, Robert. 1949. *Political parties*. New York: Free Press.

Milgram, Stanley. 1963. Behavioural study of obedience. *Journal of Abnormal and Social Psychology*, 67(4): 371–8.

—— 1974. *Obedience to authority*. New York: Harper and Row.

Millennium Ecosystem Assessment (Program). 2005. *Ecosystems and human well-being: synthesis*. Washington, DC: Island Press.

Miller, Eric J. 1976. *Task and organization*. New York: Wiley.

—— and Rice, A. K. 1967. *Systems of organizations: the control of task and sentient boundaries*. London: Tavistock Publications.

Millett, Kate. 1970. *Sexual politics* (1st edn.). Garden City, NY: Doubleday.

Mills, Albert J. and Tancred, Peta. 1992. *Gendering organizational analysis*. Newbury Park, Calif.: Sage Publications.

Mills, C. Wright. 1956. *The power elite*. Oxford: Oxford University Press.

—— 1999. *The power elite*. Oxford: Oxford University Press.

Mingers, John. 1995. *Self-reproducing systems: implications and applications of autopoiesis*. New York: Plenum Press.

Mintzberg, Henry. 1973. *The nature of managerial work*. New York: Harper and Row.

—— 2004. *Managers not MBAs: a hard look at the soft practice of managing and management development*. London: FT Prentice Hall.

Mintzberg, Henry, Raisinghani, D., and Theoret, A. 1976. Structure of unstructured decision-processes. *Administrative Science Quarterly*, 21(2): 246–75.

Mitchell, Juliet. 1975. *Psychoanalysis and feminism*. Harmondsworth: Penguin.

Mitroff, I. I. 1984. *Stakeholders of the corporate mind*. San Francisco: Jossey Bass.

—— 2004. *Crisis leadership: planning for the unthinkable* (international edn.). Hoboken, NJ: Wiley.

—— and Kilmann, Ralph H. 1975. Stories managers tell: a new tool for organizational problem solving. *Management Review*, 67(7): 18–28.

Modood, Tariq. 2007. *Multiculturalism: a civic idea*. Cambridge: Polity.

Mohr, L. B. 1973. The concept of organizational goal. *American Political Science Review*, 67(2): 470–81.

Moore, Rob and Muller, Johan. 1999. The discourse of 'voice' and the problem of knowledge and identity in the sociology of education. *British Journal of Sociology of Education*, 20(2): 189–206.

Morck, Randall. 2005. *A history of corporate governance around the world: family business groups to professional managers*. Chicago: University of Chicago Press.

Morgan, Gareth. 1986. *Images of organization*. Beverly Hills, Calif.: Sage.

—— 1993. *Imaginization: the art of creative management*. Thousand Oaks, Calif.: Sage.

—— 2006. *Images of organization* (updated edn.). Thousand Oaks, Califf.: Sage.

Morris, Timothy. 2001. Asserting property rights: knowledge codification in the professional service firm. *Human Relations*, 54(7): 819–38.

Moxnes, Paul. 1998. Fantasies and fairy tales in groups and organizations: Bion's basic assumptions and the deep roles. *European Journal of Work and Organizational Psychology*, 7(3): 283–98.

—— 1999. Deep roles: twelve primordial roles of mind and organization. *Human Relations*, 52(11): 1427–44.

Mumby, Dennis K. 2007. Organizational communication. In G. Ritzer (ed.), *The encyclopedia of sociology*: 3290–9. London: Blackwell.

—— and Clair, R. 1997. Organizational discourse. In T. A. van Dijk (ed.), *Discourse as structure and process*, vol. ii. London: Sage.

—— and Putnam, Linda L. 1992. The politics of emotion. *Academy of Management Review*, 17: 465–86.

Mumford, Lewis. 1934. *Technics and civilization*. New York: Harcourt, Brace and World.

Murji, Karim and Solomos, John. 2005. *Racialization: studies in theory and practice*. Oxford: Oxford University Press.

Nahapiet, J. and Ghoshal, S. 1998. Social capital, intellectual capital, and the organizational advantage. *Academy of Management Review*, 23(2): 242–66.

Neisser, Ulric. 1967. *Cognitive psychology*. Englewood Cliffs, NJ: Prentice-Hall.

Newell, Sue, Swan, Jacky, and Robertson, Maxine. 1998. A cross-national comparison of the adoption of business process reengineering: fashion-setting networks? *Journal of Strategic Information Systems*, 7(4): 299–317.

Newman, Janet. 2001. *Modernising governance: New Labour, policy and society*. London: Sage.

Newton, Tim, Handy, Jocelyn, and Fineman, Stephen. 1995. *Managing stress: emotion and power at work*. London: Sage Publications.

Nicholson, Linda J. and Seidman, Steven. 1995. *Social postmodernism: beyond identity politics*. Cambridge: Cambridge University Press.

Nicholson, Nigel. 1997. Evolutionary psychology: toward a new view of human nature and organizational society. *Human Relations*, 50(9): 1053–78.

Nietzsche, Friedrich Wilhelm. 1990. *Twilight of the idols; and The Anti-Christ*, trans. R. J. Hollingdale. Harmondsworth: Penguin Books.

Nixon, Sean. 1992. Have you got the look? Masculinities and shopping spectacle. In R. Shields (ed.), *Lifestyle shopping: the subject of consumption*. London: Routledge.

Nkomo, Stella M. 1992. The emperor has no clothes: rewriting 'race in organizations'. *Academy of Management Review*, 17(3): 487–513.

Noddings, Nel. 1986. *Caring: a feminine approach to ethics & moral education*. Berkeley and Los Angeles: University of California Press.

Nonaka, I. 1994. A dynamic theory of organizational knowledge creation. *Organization Science*, 5(1): 14–37.

—— Krogh, G. v., and Ichijo, K. 2000. *Enabling knowledge creation: how to unlock the mystery of tacit knowledge and release the power of innovation*. Oxford: Oxford University Press.

—— and Takeuchi, H. 1995. *The knowledge creating company: how Japanese companies create the dynamics of innovation*. Oxford: Oxford University Press.

North, Douglass Cecil. 1990. *Institutions, institutional change, and economic performance.* Cambridge: Cambridge University Press.

Oakley, Ann. 1972. *Sex, gender and society.* London: Temple Smith.

Obholzer, Anton. 1999. Managing the unconscious at work. In R. French and R. Vince (eds.), *Group relations, management, and organization*: 87–97. Oxford: Oxford University Press.

—— and Roberts, Vega Zagier (eds.). 1994. *The unconscious at work: individual and organizational stress in the human services.* London: Routledge.

O'Brien, Richard. 1992. *Global financial integration: the end of geography.* New York: Council on Foreign Relations Press.

O'Connor, Ellen S. 1997. Telling decisions: the role of narrative in organizational decision making. In Z. Shapira (ed.), *Organizational decision making*: 306–23. Cambridge: Cambridge University Press.

—— 1999. The politics of management thought: a case study of the Harvard Business School and the Human Relations School. *Academy of Management Review*, 24(1): 117–31.

OECD Oslo Manual. 1997. The measurement of scientific and technological activities: proposed guidelines for collecting and interpreting technological innovation data. Paris: OECD/Statistical Office of the European Communities.

Ogbonna, E. and Harris, L. C. 2002. Organizational culture: a ten year, two-phase study of change in the UK food retailing sector. *Journal of Management Studies*, 39(5): 673–706.

Ohmae, Kenichi. 1990. *The borderless world: power and strategy in the interlinked economy.* New York: HarperBusiness.

O'Leary, Majella. 2003. From paternalism to cynicism: narratives of a newspaper company. *Human Relations*, 56(6): 685–704.

Oliver, Richard W. 2004. *What is transparency?* (1st edn.). New York: McGraw-Hill.

Ong, W. J. 2002. *Orality and literacy: the technologizing of the word.* London: Routledge.

Orlikowski, Wanda J. 1992. The duality of technology: rethinking the concept of technology in organizations. *Organization Science*, 3(3): 398–427.

Orr, Julian E. 1996. *Talking about machines: an ethnography of a modern job.* Ithaca, NY: ILR Press/Cornell.

Örtenblad, Anders. 2002a. Organizational learning: a radical perspective. *International Journal of Management Reviews*, 4(1): 87–100.

—— 2002b. A typology of the idea of learning organization. *Management Learning*, 33(2): 213–30.

Ortony, Andrew. 1993. *Metaphor and thought* (2nd edn.). Cambridge: Cambridge University Press.

O'Sullivan, Mary. 2000. *Contests for corporate control: corporate governance and economic performance in the United States and Germany.* Oxford: Oxford University Press.

Ouchi, William G. 1980. Markets, bureaucracies, and clans. *Administrative Science Quarterly*, 25(1): 129–41.

—— 1981. *Theory Z: how American business can meet the Japanese challenge.* Reading, Mass.: Addison-Wesley.

Packard, Vance. 1957. *The hidden persuaders.* Harmondsworth: Penguin.

Parekh, Bhikhu C. 2006. *Rethinking multiculturalism: cultural diversity and political theory* (2nd edn.). Basingstoke: Palgrave Macmillan.

Parker, Martin. 1992. Post-modern organizations or postmodern theory? *Organization Studies*, 13/1: 1–17.

—— 1995. Critique in the name of what? Postmodernism and critical approaches to organization. *Organization Studies*, 16(4): 553–64.

—— 1999. Capitalism, subjectivity and ethics: debating labour process analysis. *Organization Studies*, 20(1): 25–45.

—— 2002. *Against management.* Cambridge: Polity.

Parker, Robert. 1983. *Miasma: pollution and purification in early Greek religion.* Oxford: Clarendon Press.

Parry, Geraint. 1969. *Political elites.* London: Allen & Unwin.

Parsons, Talcott. 1951. *The social system.* New York: Free Press.

Pascale, R. and Athos, A. 1981. *The art of Japanese management.* Harmondsworth: Penguin.

Patriotta, G. 2003a. *Organizational knowledge in the making: how firms create, use, and institutionalize knowledge.* Oxford: Oxford University Press.

—— 2003b. Sensemaking on the shop floor: narratives of knowledge in organizations. *Journal of Management Studies*, 40(2): 349–75.

Paxman, Jeremy. 1990. *Friends in high places: who runs Britain?* London: Michael Joseph.

Pearson, C. M., Andersson, L. M., and Wegner, J. W. 2001. When workers flout convention: a study of workplace incivility. *Human Relations*, 54(11): 1387–419.

Pedler, M., Burgoyne, J., and Boydell, T. 1997. *The learning company: a strategy for sustainable development* (2nd edn.). Maidenhead: McGraw-Hill.

Pelzer, Peter. 2004. The Flying Dutchman and the discontents of modernity. In Y. Gabriel (ed.), *Myths, stories and organizations: premodern narratives for our times*: 137–50. Oxford: Oxford University Press.

Perrow, Charles. 1999. *Normal accidents: living with high-risk technologies*. Princeton: Princeton University Press.

Peters, Tom S. and Waterman, Robert H. 1982. *In search of excellence*. New York: Harper and Row.

Pettigrew, Andrew. 1985. *The awakening giant: continuity and change in Imperial Chemical Industries*. Oxford: Blackwell.

—— Woodman, R. W. and Cameron, K. S. 2001. Studying organizational change and development: challenges for future research. *Academy of Management Journal*, 44(4): 697–713.

Pfeffer, Jeffrey. 1993. Barriers to the advance of organizational science: paradigm development as a dependent variable. *American Management Review*, 18(4): 599–620.

—— 1998. *The human equation: building profits by putting people first*. Boston: Harvard Business School Press.

—— and Sutton, Robert I. 2006. *Hard facts, dangerous half-truths, and total nonsense: profiting from evidence-based management*. Boston: Harvard Business School Press.

Pierce, C. A. 1998. Factors associated with participating in a romantic relationship in a work environment. *Journal of Applied Social Psychology*, 28(18): 1712–30.

—— Broberg, B. J., McClure, J. R., and Aguinis, H. 2004. Responding to sexual harassment complaints: effects of a dissolved workplace romance on decision-making standards. *Organizational Behavior and Human Decision Processes*, 95(1): 66–82.

Piore, Michael J. and Sabel, Charles F. 1984. *The second industrial divide: possibilities for prosperity*. New York: Basic Books.

Plato. 2004. *Cratylus*, trans. with an introduction by Benjamin Jowett, eBooks@Adelaide, University of Adelaide. <http://www.fullbooks.com/Cratylus3.html>: 113.

Polanyi, Karl. 1944. *The great transformation*. New York: Farrar and Rinehart.

—— 1957. The economy as instituted process. In K. Polanyi, C. M. Arensberg, and H. W. Pearson (eds.), *Trade and market in the early empires*: 243–70. Glencoe, Ill.: The Free Press.

Polanyi, Livia. 1979. So what's the point? *Semiotica*, 25: 207–41.

Polanyi, Michael. 1964. *Personal knowledge*. New York: Harper and Row.

Polkinghorne, Donald E. 1988. *Narrative knowing and the human sciences*. Albany, NY: State University of New York Press.

—— 1996. Explorations of narrative identity. *Psychological Inquiry*, 7: 363–7.

Pollitt, Christopher and Bouckaert, Geert. 2004. *Public management reform: a comparative analysis* (2nd edn.). Oxford: Oxford University Press.

Pondy, L. R., Frost, P. J., Morgan, G., and Dandridge, T. C. (eds.). 1983. *Organizational symbolism*. Greenwich, Conn.: JAI Press.

Popper, Karl. 1959. *The logic of scientific discovery*. New York: Basic Books.

Porter, Michael E. 1980. *Competitive strategy: techniques for analyzing industries and competitors*. New York: Free Press.

—— 1998. The Adam Smith address: location, clusters and the new microeconomics of competition. *Business Economics*, 33: 7–13.

Postman, Neil. 1986. *Amusing ourselves to death*. London: Heinemann.

Potter, J. and Wetherell, M. 1987. *Discourse and social psychology: beyond attitudes and behaviour*. London: Sage.

Pountain, Dick and Robins, David. 2000. *Cool rules: anatomy of an attitude*. London: Reaktion Books.

Powell, G. N. and Butterfield, D. A. 1994. Investigating the glass ceiling phenomenon: an empirical-study of actual promotions to top management. *Academy of Management Journal*, 37(1): 68–86.

—— and Foley, S. 1998. Something to talk about: romantic relationships in organizational settings. *Journal of Management*, 24(3): 421–48.

Powell, W. W. 2001. The capitalist firm in the twenty first century: emerging patterns in western enterprise. In P. J. Dimaggio (ed.), *The twenty first century firm*: 33–68. Princeton: Princeton University Press

—— and Dimaggio, P. J. (eds.). 1991. *The new institutionalism in organizational analysis*. Chicago: University of Chicago Press.

Power, Michael. 1997. *The audit society: rituals of verification*. Oxford: Oxford University Press.

Prahalad, C. K. and Hamel, G. 1990. The core competence of the corporation. *Harvard Business Review*, 68(May–June): 57–69.

Pratt, M. G. 2003. Disentangling collective identity. In J. Polzer, E. Mannix, and M. Neale (eds.), *Identity issues in groups: research in managing groups and teams:* vol. v. 161–88. Stamford, Conn.: Elsevier Science.

Putnam, Linda L. and Mumby, Dennis K. 1993. Organizations, emotion and the myth of rationality. In S. Fineman (ed.), *Emotion in organizations*. London: Sage.

Putnam, Robert D. 1995. Tuning in, tuning out: the strange disappearance of social capital in America. *PS: Political Science and Politics*, 28(4): 664–83.

—— 2000. *Bowling alone: the collapse and revival of American community*. New York: Simon and Schuster.

—— 2002. *Democracies in flux: the evolution of social capital in contemporary society*. Oxford: Oxford University Press.

Rappaport, J. 1993. Narrative studies, personal stories, and identity transformation in the help context. *Journal of Applied Behavioral Science*, 29: 239–56.

Rayner, C. 1997. The incidence of workplace bullying. *Journal of Community & Applied Social Psychology*, 7(3): 199–208.

—— and Hoel, H. 1997. A summary review of literature relating to workplace bullying. *Journal of Community & Applied Social Psychology*, 7(3): 181–91.

Redding, W. C. 1985. Stumbling toward identity: the emergence of organizational communication as a field of study. In R. D. McPhee and P. K. Tompkins (eds.), *Organizational communication: traditional themes and new directions*: 15–54. Beverly Hills, Calif.: Sage.

Reich, Michael. 1981. *Racial inequality: a political-economic analysis*. Princeton: Princeton University Press.

Reich, Wilhelm. 1970. *The mass psychology of fascism*. New York: Farrar, Straus and Giroux.

Renan, Ernest. 1882/1996. *Qu'est-ce qu'une nation? et autres écrits politiques*. Paris: Imprimerie Nationale.

Rhodes, C. and Brown, A. D. 2005. Narrative, organizations and research. *International Journal of Management Reviews*, 7(3): 167–88.

Ricœur, Paul. 1984. *Time and narrative*, volume i. Chicago: University of Chicago Press.

Ridgeway, C. L. 2001. Gender, status, and leadership. *Journal of Social Issues*, 57(4): 637–55.

Rieff, Philip. 1959. *Freud: the mind of a moralist*. New York: Doubleday.

—— 1966. *The triumph of the therapeutic*. New York: Harper and Row.

Ritzer, George. 1993. *The McDonaldization of society: an investigation into the changing character of contemporary social life*. London: Pine Forge Press.

—— 1993/1996. *The McDonaldization of society* (2nd edn.). London: Sage.

—— 1998. *The McDonaldization thesis*. London: Sage.

—— 1999. *Enchanting a disenchanted world: revolutionizing the means of consumption*. Thousand Oaks, Calif.: Pine Forge Press.

Roberts, J. 2006. Limits to communities of practice. *Journal of Management Studies*, 43(3): 623–39.

Robinson, S. L., Kraatz, M. S., and Rousseau, D. M. 1994. Changing obligations and the psychological contract: a longitudinal-study. *Academy of Management Journal*, 37(1): 137–52.

—— and Rousseau, D. M. 1994. Violating the psychological contract: not the exception but the norm. *Journal of Organizational Behavior*, 15(3): 245–59.

Rodriguez, Noelie and Ryave, Alan. 2002. *Systematic self-observation*. Thousand Oaks, Calif.: Sage.

Roethlisberger, Fritz Jules, Dickson, William J., and Wright, Harold A. 1939. *Management and the worker: an account of a research program conducted by the Western Electric Company, Hawthorne Works, Chicago*. Cambridge, Mass.: Harvard University Press.

Rorty, Richard. 1967. *The linguistic turn: recent essays in philosophical method*. Chicago: University of Chicago Press.

—— (ed.). 1992. *The linguistic turn: essays in philosophical method*. Chicago: University of Chicago Press.

—— 1993. Human rights, rationality and sentimentality. In S. Shute and S. Hurley (eds.), *On human rights*: 112–34. New York: Basic Books.

Rose, Nikolas S. 1989. *Governing the soul: the shaping of the private self*. London: Routledge.

Rosen, Michael. 1985. Breakfast at Spiro's: dramaturgy and dominance. *Journal of Management*, 11(2): 31–48.

Rosenbaum, Ron. 1999. *Explaining Hitler: the search for the origins of his evil*. London: Macmillan.

Rosenzweig, Philip M. 2007. *The halo effect: and the eight other business delusions that deceive managers*. New York: Free Press.

Rousseau, D. M. and Parks, J. M. 1992. The contracts of individuals and organizations. *Research in Organizational Behavior*, 15: 1–43.

Roy, Donald F. 1960. Banana time: job satisfaction and informal interaction. *Human Organization*, 18: 158–61.

Rudé, George. 1959. *The crowd in the French Revolution*. Oxford: Oxford University Press.

Rugman, A. M. and Verbeke, A. 2004. A perspective on regional and global strategies of multinational enterprises. *Journal of International Business Studies*, 35(1): 3–18.

Russell, Bertrand. 1946. *The philosophy of Bertrand Russell*. Evanston, Ill.: Library of Living Philosophers.

Sacks, Oliver. 1995. *An anthropologist on Mars*. Oxford: Blackwell.

Said, Edward W. 1985. *Orientalism*. Harmondsworth: Penguin.

—— 1994. *Culture and imperialism*. London: Chatto and Windus.

Salamon, Lester M. 1995. *Partners in public service: government–nonprofit relations in the modern welfare state*. Baltimore: Johns Hopkins University Press.

Salovey, P. and Mayer, J. D. 1990. Emotional intelligence. *Imagination, Cognition and Personality*, 9: 185–211.

Sandelands, Lloyd E. and Boudens, Connie J. 2000. Feeling at work. In S. Fineman (ed.), *Emotion in organizations* (2nd edn.): 46–63. London: Sage.

Sartre, Jean-Paul. 1956. *Being and nothingness: an essay on phenomenological ontology*. New York: Philosophical Library.

Sassen, Saskia. 1998. *Globalization and its discontents*. New York: New Press.

Saussure, Ferdinand de. 1960. *Course in general linguistics*. London: Peter Owen.

Scarbrough, Harry, Swan, Jacky, Preston, John, and Institute of Personnel and Development. 1999. *Knowledge management: a literature review*. London: Institute of Personnel and Development.

Schein, Edgar H. 1965. *Organizational psychology*. Englewood Cliffs, NJ: Prentice-Hall.

—— 1968. Organizational socialization and the profession of management. *Industrial Management Review*, 9: 1–15.

—— 1969. *Process consultation*. Reading, Mass.: Addison-Wesley Pub. Co.

—— 1970. *Organizational psychology* (2nd edn.). Englewood Cliffs, NJ: Prentice-Hall.

Schlesinger, Arthur M. 1998. *The disuniting of America: reflections on a multicultural society* (rev. and enlarged edn.). New York: W. W. Norton.

Schön, Donald A. 1973. *Beyond the stable state. public and private learning in a changing society*. Harmondsworth: Penguin.

—— 1983. *The reflective practitioner: how professionals think in action*. New York: Basic Books.

Schor, Juliet B. 1998. *The overspent American: upscaling, downshifting and the new consumer*. New York: HarperCollins.

Schumacher, E. Fritz. 1973. *Small is beautiful: a study of economics as if people mattered*. London: Abacus.

Schumpeter, Joseph Alois. 1943. *Capitalism, socialism, and democracy*. London: G. Allen & Unwin ltd.

Schwartz, Howard S. 1985. The usefulness of myth and the myth of usefulness: a dilemma for the applied organizational scientist. *Journal of Management*, 11(1): 31–42.

—— 1987. Anti-social actions of committed organizational participants: an existential psychoanalytic perspective. *Organization Studies*, 8(4): 327–40.

—— 1988. The symbol of the space shuttle and the degeneration of the American dream. *Journal of Organizational Change Management*, 1/2: 5–20.

—— 1990. *Narcissistic process and corporate decay*. New York: New York University Press.

—— 2001. *The revolt of the primitive: an inquiry into the roots of political correctness*. Westport, Conn.: Praeger.

Scott, W. R. 2001. *Institutions and organizations*, (2nd edn.). London: Sage.

Seglow, Jonathan. 2003. Theorising recognition. In B. Haddock and P. Sutch (eds.), *Multiculturalism, identity and rights*: 78–93. London: Routledge.

Selznick, Philip. 1957. *Leadership and administration*. New York: Harper and Row.

Sen, Amartya Kumar. 1987. *On ethics and economics*. Oxford: Basil Blackwell.

—— and Harvard Institute of Economic Research. 1991. *Markets and freedoms*. Cambridge, Mass.: Harvard Institute of Economic Research, Harvard University.

Senge, Peter. 1990. *The fifth discipline: the art and practice of the learning organization*. New York: Doubleday.

Sennett, Richard. 1998. *The corrosion of character: the personal consequences of work in the new capitalism.* New York: Norton.

Sewell, Graham. 2004. Yabba-dabba-doo! Evolutionary psychology and the rise of Flintstone psychological thinking in organization and management studies. *Human Relations*, 57(8): 923–55.

—— and Wilkinson, Barry. 1992. Someone to watch over me: surveillance, discipline and the just-in-time labour process. *Sociology*, 26(2): 271–89.

Shane, Scott Andrew. 2003. *A general theory of entrepreneurship: the individual-opportunity nexus.* Cheltenham: E. Elgar.

—— and Venkataraman, S. 2000. The promise of entrepreneurship as a field of research. *Academy of Management Review*, 25(1): 217–26.

Shannon, C. and Weaver, W. 1949. *The mathemetical theory of communication.* Urbana, Ill.: University of Illinois Press.

Shapira, Zur. 1997. *Organizational decision making.* Cambridge: Cambridge University Press.

Shilling, Chris. 1993. *The body and social theory.* London: Sage.

—— 2007. *Embodying sociology: retrospect, progress, and prospects* (1st edn.). Malden, Mass: Blackwell Pub.

Sievers, Burkard. 1986. Beyond the surrogate of motivation. *Organization Studies*, 7(4): 335–51.

—— 1994. *Work, death and life itself.* Berlin: Walter de Gruyter.

—— 1999. Psychotic organization as a metaphoric frame for the socioanalysis of organizational and interorganizational dynamics. *Administration and Society*, 31(5): 588–615.

—— 2003. Your money or your life? Psychotic implications of the pension fund system: towards a socio-analysis of the financial services revolution. *Human Relations*, 56(2): 187–210.

Simmel, Georg. 1904/1971. Fashion. In D. Levin and G. Simmel (eds.), *On individuality and social form.* Chicago: Chicago University Press.

Simon, Herbert A. 1957. *Administrative behavior.* New York: Macmillan.

Simpson, Peter, French, Robert, and Harvey, Charles. 2002. Leadership and negative capability. *Human Relations*, 55(10): 1209–26.

Simpson, Ruth. 1998. Presenteeism, power and organizational change: long hours as a career barrier and the impact on the working lives of women managers. *British Journal of Management*, 9(3): 37–51.

Sims, David. 2003. Between the millstones: a narrative account of the vulnerability of middle managers' storying. *Human Relations*, 56(10): 1195–211.

—— 2004. The velveteen rabbit and passionate feelings for organizations. In Y. Gabriel (ed.), *Myths, stories and organizations: premodern narratives for our times*: 209–22. Oxford: Oxford University Press.

—— 2005. You bastard: a narrative exploration of the experience of indignation within organizations. *Organization Studies*, 26(11): 1625–640.

Sims, H. P. and Lorenzi, P. 1992. *The new leadership paradigm: social learning and cognition in organizations.* Newbury Park, Calif.: Sage.

Slater, Don and Tonkiss, Fran. 2001. *Market society: markets and modern social theory.* Cambridge: Polity Press.

Slaughter, Anne-Marie. 2004. *A new world order.* Princeton: Princeton University Press.

Sloterdijk, Peter. 1988. *Critique of cynical reason.* London: Verso.

Smelser, Neil J. 1984. Collective myths and fantasies: the myth of the good life in California. In J. Rabow, G. M. Platt, and M. S. Goldman (eds.), *Advances in psychoanalytic sociology.* Malabar, Fla.: Krieger.

—— 1998a. Collective myths and fantasies: the myth of the good life in California. In N. J. Smelser (ed.), *The social edges of psychoanalysis*: 111–24. Berkeley and Los Angeles: University of California Press.

—— 1998b. The rational and the ambivalent in the social sciences. In N. J. Smelser (ed.), *The social edges of psychoanalysis*: 168–94. Berkeley and Los Angeles: University of California Press.

—— 1998c. Vicissitudes of work and love in Anglo-American Society. In N. J. Smelser (ed.), *The social edges of psychoanalysis*: 93–107. Berkeley and Los Angeles: University of California Press.

—— 2007. *The faces of terrorism: social and psychological dimensions.* Princeton: Princeton University Press.

Smith, Anthony D. 1998. *Nationalism and modernism: a critical survey of recent theories of nations and nationalism.* New York: Routledge.

—— 2001. *Nationalism: theory, ideology, history.* Cambridge: Polity Press.

Smith, Chris. 2006. The double indeterminacy of labour power: labour effort and labour mobility. *Work, Employment and Society*, 20(2): 389–402.

Smith, Chris, Knights, David, and Willmott, Hugh (eds.). 1991. *White-collar work: the non-manual labour process*. London: Macmillan.

Snowden, David J. 2001. Narrative patterns: the perils and possibilities of using story in organisations. *Knowledge Management*, 4(10): 1–14.

——2002. Complex acts of knowing: paradox and descriptive self-awareness: <http://www.kwork.org/Resources/snowden.pdf>.

Sommers, Christina Hoff. 2000. *The war against boys: how misguided feminism is harming our young men*. New York: Simon & Schuster.

Spivak, Gayatri Chakravorty. 1988. Can the subaltern speak? In Cary Nelson and Lawrence Grosberg (eds.), *Marxism and the interpretation of culture*: 271–313. Urbana, Ill.: University of Illinois Press.

Stacey, Ralph D. 1992. *Managing chaos: dynamic business strategies in an unpredictable world*. London: Kogan Page.

——1995. The science of complexity: an alternative perspective for strategic change processes. *Strategic Management Journal*, 16: 477–95.

Stanton, G. 1998. The eight stages of genocide, *Yale Genocide Series, GS01*. New Haven: Yale University Press.

Starr, C. 1969. Social benefit versus technological risk. 165(899): 1232–38.

Staw, B. M. and Ross, J. 1987. Understanding escalation situations: antecedents, prototypes and solutions. In B. M. Staw and L. L. Cummings (eds.), *Research in organizational behaviour*, vol. ix. Greenwich, Conn.: JAI Press.

Stein, Howard F. 1997. Death imagery and the experience of organizational downsizing: or, is your name on Schindler's list? *Administration and Society*, 29(2): 222–47.

——1998. *Euphemism, spin, and the crisis in organizational life*. Westport, Conn.: Quorum Books.

——2001. *Nothing personal, just business: a guided journey into organizational darkness*. Westport, Conn.: Quorum Books.

——2007. *Insight and imagination*. Lanham, Md.: University Press of America.

Stein, Mark. 2000. The risk-taker as shadow: a psychoanalytic view of the collapse of Barings Bank. *Journal of Management Studies*, 37(8): 1215–29.

——2003. Unbounded irrationality: risk and organizational narcissism at Long Term Capital Management. *Human Relations*, 56(5): 523–40.

Stevenson, H. H. and Jarillo, J. C. 1990. A paradigm of entrepreneurship: entrepreneurial management. *Strategic Management Journal*, 11: 17–27.

Stimpert, J. L. L., Gustafson, L. T., and Sarason, Y. 1998. Organizational identity within the strategic management conversation: contributions and assumptions. In D. A. Whetten and P. C. Godfrey (eds.), *Identity in organizations, building theory through conversations*: 83–98. Thousand Oaks, Calif.: Sage.

Stoll, David. 1999. *Rigoberta Menchu and the story of all poor Guatemalans*. Oxford: Westview Press.

Storey, John. 1992. *Developments in the management of human resources: an analytical review*. Oxford: Blackwell.

Storper, M. 1992. The limits to globalization: technology districts and international-trade. *Economic Geography*, 68(1): 60–93.

Stott, C. and Drury, J. 2000. Crowds, context and identity: dynamic categorization processes in the 'poll tax riot'. *Human Relations*, 53(2): 247–73.

Strati, Antonio. 1999. *Organization and aesthetics*. London: Sage.

Strawson, Galen. 2004. Against narrativity. *Ratio*, 17(4): 428–52.

Strong, Edward K. 1925. *The psychology of selling and advertising*. New York: MGraw-Hill.

Sturdy, Andrew. 1997. The consultancy process: an insecure business. *Journal of Management Studies*, 34(3): 389–413.

——1998. Customer care in a consumer society: smiling and sometimes meaning it? *Organization*, 5(1): 27–53.

——2004. The adoption of management ideas and practices: theoretical perspectives and possibilities. *Management Learning*, 35(2): 155–79.

—— and Fleming, Peter. 2003. Talk as technique: a critique of the words and deeds distinction in the diffusion of customer service cultures in call centres. *Journal of Management Studies*, 40(4): 753–73.

—— Grugulis, Irena, and Willmott, Hugh (eds.). 2001. *Customer service: Empowerment and entrapment*. Basingstoke: Palgrave.

—— Schwarz, M., and Spicer, André. 2006. Guess who's coming to dinner? Structures and uses of liminality in strategic management consultancy. *Human Relations*, 59(7): 929–60.

Styron, William. 1979. *Sophie's choice*. London: Cape.

Suchman, M. C. 1995. Managing legitimacy: strategic and institutional approaches. *Academy of Management Review*, 20: 571–610.

Suddaby, R. and Greenwood, R. 2001. Colonizing knowledge: commodification as a dynamic of jurisdictional expansion in professional service firms. *Human Relations*, 54(7): 933–53.

Sun Tzu. 1963. *The art of war*, trans. S. B. Griffith. Oxford: Oxford University Press.

Swan, Jacky and Scarbrough, Harry. 2001. *Knowledge management: concepts and controversies*. Oxford: Blackwell.

————— and Robertson, M. 2002. The construction of 'communities of practice' in the management of innovation. *Management Learning*, 33(4): 477–96.

Swedberg, Richard. 2005. Markets in society. In N. J. Smelser and R. Swedberg (eds.), *The handbook of economic sociology* (2nd edn.): 249–52. Princeton: Princeton University Press.

Sykes, Gresham M. and Matza, David. 1957. Techniques of neutralization: a theory of delinquency. *American Sociological Review*, 22: 664–70.

Tangherlini, T. 1998. *Talking trauma: paramedics and their stories*. Jackson, Miss.: University Press of Mississippi.

Tapscott, Don and Ticoll, David. 2003. *The naked corporation: how the age of transparency will revolutionize business*. New York: Free Press.

Tarde, Gabriel. 1890/1903. *The laws of imitation*. New York: Henry Holt.

Taylor, Charles. 1994. The politics of recognition. In A. Gutmann (ed.), *Multiculturalism: examining 'The politics of recognition'* (2nd edn.): 25–73. Princeton: Princeton University Press

Taylor, P. and Bain, P. 2005. 'India calling to the far away towns': the call centre labour process and globalization. *Work, Employment and Society*, 19(2): 261–82.

ten Bos, René and Willmott, Hugh. 2001. Towards a post-dualistic business ethics: interweaving reason and emotion in working life. *Journal of Management Studies*, 38(6): 769–93.

Terkel, Studs. 1985. *Working*. Harmondsworth: Penguin.

Thatchenkery, Tojo Joseph. 2001. Mining for meaning: reading organizations using hermeneutic philosophy. In R. Westwood and S. Linstead (eds.), *The language of organization*: 112–31. London: Sage.

Thietart, R. A. and Forgues, B. 1995. Chaos theory and organization. *Organization Science*, 6(1): 19–31.

Thoenig, Jean-Claude. 1998. How far is a sociology of organizations still needed? *Organization Studies*, 19(2): 307–20.

Thomas, Alan B. 1993. *Controversies in management*. London: Routledge.

Thomas, R. and Davies, A. 2005. What have the feminists done for us? Feminist theory and organizational resistance. *Organization*, 12(5): 711–40.

Thompson, E. P. 1968. *The making of the English working class* (new edn.). Harmondsworth: Penguin.

Thompson, Grahame. 2003. *Between hierarchies and markets: the logic and limits of network forms of organization*. Oxford: Oxford University Press.

Thompson, John B. 1995. *The media and modernity: a social theory of the media*. Cambridge: Polity Press.

Thompson, Paul. 1993. Postmodernism: fatal distraction. In J. Hassard and M. Parker (eds.), *Postmodernism and organizations*: 183–203. London: Sage.

—— and Ackroyd, Stephen. 1995. All quiet on the workplace front? A critique of recent trends in British industrial sociology. *Sociology*, 29(4): 615–33.

Thrift, N. J. 1996. *Spatial formations*. London: Sage.

Tichy, Noel M. and Devanna, Mary Anne. 1986. *The transformational leader*. New York: Wiley.

Tinker, T. 2002. Spectres of Marx and Braverman in the twilight of postmodernist labour process research. *Work, Employment and Society*, 16(2): 251–81.

Titmuss, Richard Morris. 1971. *The gift relationship: from human blood to social policy* (1st American edn.). New York: Pantheon Books.

Tolstoy, Leo. 1869/1982. *War and peace*, trans. R. Edmonds. Harmondsworth: Penguin.

Tönnies, Ferdinand. 1887/1963. *Community and society*. New York: Harper Torchbook.

Tourish, Dennis and Pinnington, Ashly. 2002. Transformational leadership, corporate cultism and the spirituality paradigm: an unholy trinity in the workplace? *Human Relations*, 55(2): 147–72.

Townley, Barbara. 1993a. Foucault, power/knowledge and its relevance for Human Resource Management. *Academy of Management Review*, 18(3): 518–45.

—— 1993b. Performance appraisal and the emergence of management. *Journal of Management Studies*, 30(2): 228–38.

Trice, H. M. and Beyer, J. M. 1984. Studying organizational cultures through rites and ceremonials. *American Management Review*, 9: 653–69.

Trist, E. L. and Bamforth, K. W. 1951. Some social and psychological consequences of the longwall method of coal getting. *Human Relations*, 4: 3–38.

Tsoukas, Haridimos. 1993. Analogical reasoning and knowledge generation in organization theory. *Organization Studies*, 14(3): 323–46.

—— 1998a. Forms of knowledge and forms of life in organized contexts. In R. C. H. Chia (ed.), *In the realm of organization: essays for robert cooper*. London: Routledge.

—— 1998b. Introduction: chaos, complexity and organization theory. *Organization*, 5(3): 291–313.

—— 2002. Knowledge-based perspectives on organizations: situated knowledge, novelty, and communities of practice—introduction. *Management Learning*, 33(4): 419–26.

—— 2005. *Complex knowledge: studies in organizational epistemology*. New York: Oxford University Press.

—— and Hatch, Mary Jo. 2001. Complex thinking, complex practice: the case for a narrative approach to organizational complexity. *Human Relations*, 54(8): 979–1013.

Turner, Barry A. 1986. Sociological aspects of organizational symbolism. *Organization Studies*, 7(2): 101–15.

—— and Pidgeon, Nick F. 1997. *Man-made disasters* (2nd edn.). Boston: Butterworth-Heinemann.

Turner, Bryan S. 1984. *The body and society: explorations in social theory*. Oxford: Blackwell.

—— 1996. *The body and society: explorations in social theory* (2nd edn.). London: Sage Publications.

Tushman, Michael L. and Anderson, P. 1986. Technological discontinuities and organizational environments. *Administrative Science Quarterly*, 31(3): 439–65.

Tyler, Melissa and Taylor, Stephen. 1998. The exchange of aesthetics: women's work and 'the gift'. *Gender, Work and Organization*, 5(3): 165–71.

Tyre, Marcie J. and Orlikowski, Wanda J. 1996. The episodic process of learning by using. *International Journal of Technology Management*, 11(7–8): 790–98.

Uchitelle, Louis. 2006. *The disposable American: layoffs and their consequences*. New York: Knopf.

United Nations. Economic and Social Council. 1948. Convention on the Prevention and Punishment of the Crime of Genocide. New York: United Nations.

United Nations General Assembly. 1983. Resolution A/38/161: Process of preparation of the Environmental Perspective to the Year 2000 and Beyond. New York: United Nations.

Van De Ven, A. H. and Poole, M. S. 1995. Explaining development and change in organizations. *Academy of Management Review*, 20(3): 510–40.

Van Dijk, Teun A. 1975. Action, action description, and narrative. *New Literary History*, 6: 275–94.

—— (ed.). 1997. *Discourse as structure and process*. London: Sage.

Van Maanen, John. 1991. The smile factory: work at Disneyland. In P. J. Frost, L. F. Moore, C. C. Lundberg, and J. Martin (eds.), *Reframing organizational culture*: 58–76. London: Sage.

—— 1992. Displacing Disney: some notes on the flow of culture. *Qualitative Sociology*, 15: 5–35.

Vattimo, Gianni. 1992. *The transparent society*. Baltimore: Johns Hopkins University Press.

Veblen, Thorstein. 1899/1925. *The theory of the leisure class*. London: George Allen and Unwin.

Virilio, Paul. 2000. *The information bomb*. New York, NY: Verso.

Vroom, Victor Harold. 1964. *Work and motivation*. New York: Wiley.

Wallach Bologh, Roslyn. 1990. *Love or greatness: Max Weber and masculine thinking—a feminist inquiry*. London: Unwin Hayman.

Wallemacq, Anne and Sims, David. 1998. The struggle with sense. In D. Grant, T. Keenoy, and O. Cliff (eds.), *Discourse and organization*: 119–33. London: Sage.

Wallerstein, Immanuel Maurice. 1983. *Historical capitalism*. London: Verso.

Ward, Barbara and Dubos, René J. 1972. *Only one Earth: the care and maintenance of a small planet: an unofficial report commissioned by the Secretary-General of the United Nations Conference on the Human Environment*. Harmondsworth: Penguin.

Ward, Jamie and Winstanley, Diana. 2003. The absent presence: negative space within discourse and the construction of minority sexual identity in the workplace. *Human Relations*, 56(10): 1255–80.

Warhurst, C., Nickson, D., Witz, A., and Cullen, A. M. 2000. Aesthetic labour in interactive service work: some case study evidence from the 'new' Glasgow. *Service Industries Journal*, 20(3): 1–18.

Watson, Tony J. 1994. *In search of management: culture, chaos and control in managerial work.* London: Routledge.

—— 1996. Motivation: that's Maslow, isn't it? *Management Learning*, 27(4): 447–64.

—— 1998. Ethical codes and moral communities: the Gunlaw temptation, the Simon solution and the David dilemma. In M. Parker (ed.), *Ethics and organizations*: 253–69. London: Sage.

—— 2001. *In search of management: culture, chaos and control in managerial work* (2nd edn.). London: Thomson Learning.

—— 2003. Ethical choice in managerial work: the scope for moral choices in an ethically irrational world. *Human Relations*, 56(2): 167–85.

—— 2008a. Business discourse, narratives and the sociological imagination'. In F. Bargiela-Chiappini (ed.), *The handbook of business discourse*. Edinburgh: Edinburgh University Press.

—— 2008b. *Sociology, work, and industry* (5th edn.). London: Routledge.

Weber, Max. 1946. *From Max Weber: essays in sociology*, trans. H. H. Gerth, and C. W. Mills. London: Routledge and Kegan Paul.

—— 1947. *The theory of social and economic organization*. New York: Free Press.

—— 1949. *Max Weber on the methodology of the social sciences*, trans. Edward Shils, (1st edn.). Glencoe, Ill.: Free Press.

—— 1958. *The protestant ethic and the spirit of capitalism*, trans. T. Parsons. New York: Charles Scribner and Sons.

—— 1978. *Economy and society*, ed. and trans. G. Roth and C. Wittich. Berkeley and Los Angeles: University of California Press.

Weick, Karl E. 1979. *The social psychology of organizing*. Reading, Mass.: Addison-Wesley.

—— 1985. Cosmos vs chaos: sense and nonsense in electronic contexts. *Organizational Dynamics*, Autumn: 50–64.

—— 1995. *Sensemaking in organizations*. London: Sage.

—— 2001a. Improvisation as a mindset for organizational analysis. In K. E. Weick (ed.), *Making sense of the organization*: 284–304. Oxford: Blackwell.

—— (ed.). 2001b. *Making sense of the organization*. Oxford: Blackwell.

—— 2001c. Organizational culture as a source of high reliability. In K. E. Weick (ed.), *Making sense of the organization*: 330–44. Oxford: Blackwell.

—— 2001d. Sources of order in underorganized systems. In K. E. Weick (ed.), *Making sense of the organization*. Oxford: Blackwell.

—— and Sutcliffe, Kathleen M. 2001. *Managing the unexpected: assuring high performance in an age of complexity* (1st edn.). San Francisco: Jossey-Bass.

Wells, William D. 1997. *Measuring advertising effectiveness*. Mahwah, NJ: L. Erlbaum Associates.

Wenger, Étienne. 1998. *Communities of practice: learning, meaning and identity*. Cambridge: Cambridge University Press.

Wernick, Andrew. 1991. *Promotional culture: advertising, ideology and symbolic expression*. London: Sage.

Werr, A. and Stjernberg, T. 2003. Exploring management consulting firms as knowledge systems. *Organization Studies*, 24(6): 881–908.

West, Candace and Zimmerman, Don H. 1987. Doing gender. *Gender and Society*, 1(2): 125–51.

Westwood, Robert and Linstead, Stephen (eds.). 2001. *The language of organization*. London: Sage.

Wilkins, A. L. 1983. Organizational stories as symbols which control the organization. In L. R. Pondy, P. J. Frost, G. Morgan, and T. C. Dandridge (eds.), *Organizational symbolism*. Greenwich, Conn.: JAI Press.

—— 1984. The creation of company cultures: the role of stories in human resource systems. *Human Resource Management*, 23: 41–60.

Wilkinson, Paul. 2001. *Terrorism versus democracy: the liberal state response*. Portland, Ore.: Frank Cass.

Williams, Christine L., Giuffre, Patti A., and Dellinger, Kirsten. 1999. Sexuality in the workplace: organizational control, sexual harassment, and the pursuit of pleasure. *Annual Review of Sociology*, 25(1): 73–93.

Williams, K. Y. and O'Reilly, C. A. 1998. Demography and diversity in organizations: a review of 40 years of research. *Research in Organizational Behavior*, 20: 77–140.

Williams, Raymond. 1976. *Keywords: a vocabulary of culture and society*. New York: Oxford University Press.

—— 1983. *Keywords: a vocabulary of culture and society* (Flamingo edn.). London: Fontana Paperbacks.

Williamson, Oliver E. 1975. *Markets and hierarchies, analysis and antitrust implications: a study in the economics of internal organization*. New York: Free Press.

Willmott, Hugh. 1990. Subjectivity and the dialectics of praxis: opening up the core of labour process analysis. In D. Knights and H. Willmott (eds.), *Labour process theory*: 336–78. Basingstoke: Macmillan.

—— 1993. Strength is ignorance; slavery is freedom: managing culture in modern organizations. *Journal of Management Studies*, 30: 515–52.

—— 2000. Death. So what? Sociology, sequestration and emancipation. *Sociological Review*, 48(4): 649–65.

Wilson, D. C. and Rosenfeld, R. H. 1990. *Managing Organizations*. London: McGraw Hill.

Wilson, Fiona M. 2003. *Organizational behaviour and gender* (2nd edn.). Aldershot: Ashgate.

Windsor, D. 2004. The development of international business norms. *Business Ethics Quarterly*, 14(4): 729–54.

Winnicott, Donald W., Winnicott, Clare, Shepherd, Ray, and Davis, Madeleine. 1986. *Home is where we start from: essays by a psychoanalyst* (1st American edn.). New York: Norton.

Wittgenstein, Ludwig. 1922/1961. *Tractatus logico-philosophicus*. London: Routledge.

Witz, A., Warhurst, C., and Nickson, D. 2003. The labour of aesthetics and the aesthetics of organization. *Organization*, 10(1): 33–54.

Wolf, Naomi. 1990. *The beauty myth*. London: Chatto and Windus.

Woodward, Joan. 1958. *Management and technology*. London: HMSO.

—— 1965. *Industrial organisation: theory and practice*. London: Oxford University Press.

Worsley, Peter. 1970. *Introducing sociology*. Harmondsworth: Penguin.

Wright, M. 2001. Entrepreneurship and wealth creation (an interview with Sue Birley). *European Management Journal*, 19(2): 128–40.

Yang, F. 1995. *Gifts, favors and banquets: the art of social relationships in China*. Ithaca, NY: Cornell University Press.

Yates, JoAnne and Orlikowski, Wanda J. 1992. Genres of organizational communication: a structurational approach to studying communication and media. *Academy of Management Review*, 17(2): 299–326.

Yin, Robert K. 2003. *Case study research: design and methods* (3rd edn.). Thousand Oaks, Calif.: Sage Publications.

Young, Michael F. D. 2000. Rescuing the sociology of educational knowledge from the extremes of voice discourse: towards a new theoretical basis for the sociology of the curriculum. *British Journal of Sociology of Education*, 21(4): 523–36.

Zaleznik, Abraham. 1977. Managers and leaders: are they different? *Harvard Business Review*, 55(May–June): 47–60.

—— 1989. The mythological structure of organizations and its impact. *Human Resource Management*, 28(2): 267–77.

Zijderveld, A. C. 1983. The sociology of humour and laughter. *Current Sociology*, 31(1): 1–100.

Zimbardo, P. G., Maslach, C., and Haney, C. 1999. Reflections on the Stanford prison experiment: genesis, transformations, consequences. In T. Blass (ed.), *Obedience to authority: current perspectives on the Milgram paradigm*: 193–237. Mahwah, NJ: Erlbaum.

Žižek, Slavoj. 1989. *Sublime object of ideology*. London: Verso.

Zuboff, Shoshana. 1985. Automate/informate: the two faces of intelligent technology. *Organizational Dynamics*, 14(2): 5–18.

—— 1988. *In the age of the smart machine*. Oxford: Heinemann.

INDEX

In the index, readers will find page references to a wide range of terms in the social and organizational theories. Terms that have their own entries in the thesaurus feature in **bold**. Likewise, the names of contributing authors as well as the pages of their contributions feature in **bold**. For the sake of economy and simplicity, references to authors do *not* include references to footnotes in the book's main text or to the concluding bibliographical references. The letter f following a page number indicates that the reference extends to the following page; the letters ff indicate extension to several following pages.